The International Rule of Law: Rise or Decline?

The International Rule of Law: Rise or Decline?

Foundational Challenges

Edited by

HEIKE KRIEGER
GEORG NOLTE
ANDREAS ZIMMERMANN

OXFORD
UNIVERSITY PRESS

Great Clarendon Street, Oxford, OX2 6DP,
United Kingdom

Oxford University Press is a department of the University of Oxford.
It furthers the University's objective of excellence in research, scholarship,
and education by publishing worldwide. Oxford is a registered trade mark of
Oxford University Press in the UK and in certain other countries

Published in the United States of America by Oxford University Press
198 Madison Avenue, New York, NY 10016, United States of America

British Library Cataloguing in Publication Data
Data available

Library of Congress Control Number: 2019937072

ISBN 978–0–19–884360–3

Printed and bound by
CPI Group (UK) Ltd, Croydon, CR0 4YY

Preface

It has become almost commonplace, in 2019, to claim that the international legal order is in crisis. During the last decade perceptions of the state, the role and the function of international law have changed dramatically from a self-confident assertion of a continuing legalization and increasing institutionalization of the international order to a more hesitant assessment of its future development and even its resilience. It is in light of these developments that we look at the current turbulences and ambivalences in the development of international law from structural perspectives and ask whether the international rule of law is on the rise or in decline. We have therefore invited a group of colleagues to address and evaluate, from multiple perspectives, some of the foundational challenges which we believe international law is currently facing. We hope that we can thereby provide a broader basis for understanding the long-term implications of on-going changes, as well as of indications for lingering shifts in the international legal order.

The book constitutes a building block for a larger research project on 'The International Rule of Law – Rise or Decline?'. We conduct this project within the framework of a Research Group (Kolleg-Forschungsgruppe) which is generously funded by the German Research Foundation (DFG). This Berlin Potsdam Research Group examines the role of international law in a changing global order. It brings together international lawyers and political scientists from five institutions in the Berlin-Brandenburg region, namely Freie Universität Berlin, Hertie School of Governance, Humboldt-Universität zu Berlin, Universität Potsdam, and the Social Science Research Center Berlin (Wissenschaftszentrum Berlin). The Research Group runs a fellow programme for visiting researchers who join the group for periods up to two years. The Group thereby benefits from an intense exchange among senior scholars, practitioners, postdoctoral fellows, and doctoral students from diverse academic backgrounds and from all over the world. We are grateful to all members of the Group—past and present—for the valuable input which they have provided for the project generally, as well as for this book more specifically.

As editors, we would like to express our gratitude to the authors who have enthusiastically engaged with our research question during the opening conference in April 2016 and during the ensuing process of putting this book together. Thanks are also due to Merel Alstein and Jack McNichol at Oxford University Press. Above all, we owe a great deal to members of our Research Group. The editorial process benefitted tremendously from the diligent work of our postdoctoral researchers Dana Burchardt and Felix Lange. We would also like to thank our student assistants

Frederika Haug, Gwinyai Machona, Lars Schlenkhoff, Ines Schroeder, Sophie Schuberth, and Beria Ulusoy for their support in the preparation of this book. Finally, our heartfelt thanks go to Kerstin Schuster who has, for four years, steadily, competently, and enthusiastically taken care of our Research Group and of all its projects, including this book.

Heike Krieger
Georg Nolte
Andreas Zimmermann

Contents

List of Contributors

Eyal Benvenisti, Whewell Professor of International Law, University of Cambridge; Director of the Lauterpacht Centre for International Law, University of Cambridge.

Tomer Broude, Associate Professor of Law, Hebrew University, Jerusalem.

Jutta Brunnée, Professor of Law and Metcalf Chair in Environmental Law, University of Toronto.

Dana Burchardt, Dr. iur., Post-doctoral researcher, Humboldt University Berlin.

Simon Chesterman, Dean and Professor at the National University of Singapore Faculty of Law.

Jean d'Aspremont, Professor of International Law, Science Po School of Law; Professor of International Law, University of Manchester.

Jeffrey L Dunoff, Laura H. Carnell Professor of Law, Temple University Beasley School of Law, Philadelphia.

Andrew Hurrell, Montague Burton Professor of International Relations, University of Oxford and Fellow of Balliol College, Oxford.

Markus Jachtenfuchs, Professor of European and Global Governance, Hertie School, Berlin; Director of the Jacques Delors Centre at the Hertie School.

Maurice Kamto, Professor of Law, University of Yaoundé II.

Heike Krieger, Professor of Public and International Law, Freie Universität Berlin.

Felix Lange, Dr. iur., Post-doctoral researcher, Humboldt University Berlin.

Andrea Liese, Professor of International Organizations and Policies, University of Potsdam.

Tiyanjana Maluwa, H. Laddie Montague Chair in Law and Professor of Law, School of Law; Professor of International Affairs, School of International Affairs, Pennsylvania State University.

Thilo Marauhn, Professor of Public and International Law, Justus Liebig University Gießen; Head of Research Group Public International Law, Peace Research Institute Frankfurt (PRIF).

Georg Nolte, Professor of Public, International and European Law, Humboldt University Berlin.

Professor Dr. Dr. h.c., Dr. h.c. **Angelika Nußberger**, MA, Vice-President of the European Court of Human Rights, Professor of Constitutional and International Law, Cologne University.

Anne Peters, Professor of Law at the University of Heidelberg, Freie Universität Berlin, University of Basel, and William W. Cook Global Law Professor at the University of Michigan; Director at the Max Planck Institute for Comparative Public Law and Public International Law, Heidelberg.

Aniruddha Rajput, Member of the United Nations International Law Commission.

Nina Reiners, Dr. rer. pol., Post-doctoral researcher, University of Potsdam.

Geir Ulfstein, Dr juris, Professor of Public and International Law, University of Oslo, Oslo, Norway.

Jochen von Bernstorff, Professor of Constitutional Law, Public International Law and Human Rights Law, Eberhard Karls University Tübingen.

Norman Weiß, Dr. iur. habil., extraordinary Professor at the Law Faculty and Permanent Senior Fellow at the Human Rights Centre of the University of Potsdam.

Jan Wouters, Full Professor of International Law and International Organizations, Jean Monnet Chair, Director, Leuven Centre for Global Governance Studies—Institute for International Law, KU Leuven; Adjunct Professor, Columbia University; Visiting Professor, College of Europe, Sciences Po, LUISS University, University of Ottawa and University of Trento; Of Counsel, Linklaters. Publications on international and EU law, global governance, corporate, financial law.

Andreas Zimmermann, Professor of Public, Public International and European Union Law, as well as European and Public International Business Law, University of Potsdam; Director of the Human Rights Centre of the University of Potsdam.

Michael Zürn, Professor of International Relations, Freie Universität Berlin; Director of Global Governance Unit, WZB Berlin Social Science Center.

PART I

INTRODUCTION

1

The International Rule of Law—Rise or Decline?—Approaching Current Foundational Challenges

Heike Krieger and Georg Nolte

I. Introduction

In 1950, Josef Kunz wrote about the 'swing of the pendulum'. He argued that a period of overestimating international law during the League of Nations years was followed by a period of underestimating it. Kunz described the 1920s Geneva spirit, where 'legal arguments were at the core of every debate' and 'literature on international law was greatly influenced by this general trend of optimism'—a development that later led to a wide discrepancy between the 1930s political facts and the approach of parts of academic writings:

> They had, as a first effect, the going to extremes, especially by a literature of wishful thinking. Fancy interpretations of the Kellogg Pact were put forward; the more 'collective security' was shown to be non-existent, the more the utopian writers emphasised it. The more the facts were in contradiction to their writings, the more lyrical they grew. The confusion between lex lata and lex ferenda, the mistaking of often contradictory trends and tendencies for new rules of international law already established ... grew worse.[1]

With the Charter, according to Kunz, the pendulum swung to underestimating international law, as shown by the Charter itself, but in particular by the contemporary diplomatic and political practice: 'The oratory contrasts strikingly with that of Geneva. If the most undiplomatic language, bitterness, invectives and political propaganda constitute realism, then there is plenty of realism.'[2]

We think that it is again time, due to signs of crisis in the development of international law and international relations, to ask whether we are overestimating or underestimating international law. Of course, the development of international law,

---

[1] Josef Kunz, 'Swing of the Pendulum: From Overestimation to Underestimation of International Law' (1950) 44 American Journal of International Law 135, 137ff.
[2] ibid 139.

and of international relations more generally, often takes place in the form of crises.[3] The assertion of a crisis may even be used by some to further their political causes. Thus, claims about a crisis must be treated with caution. But while we do not aim to 'revel in a good crisis'[4] we think that lawyers should not close their eyes in the face of present developments. We submit that we are currently witnessing a systemically relevant crisis of unusual proportions which requires a reassessment of the state and role of international law:[5]

Can we, under the current significantly changing conditions, still observe an increasing legalization of international relations based on a universal understanding of values, or are we, to the contrary, rather facing a tendency towards an informalization or a reformalization of international law, or an erosion of international legal norms? Would it be appropriate to revisit classical elements of international law in order to react to structural changes, which may result in a more polycentric or non-polar world order? Or are we simply observing a slump in the development towards an international rule of law based on a universal understanding of values?

In the following, we want to elaborate on these questions for two distinct purposes: The first is to introduce and to situate the challenge, as we see it, as a larger research project for which the present book is a building block.[6] The beginning of this project has prompted the exploratory character of this introduction. It reflects our personal approach to interpreting some of the foundational and current challenges which the international legal order faces. In order to test our assumptions and to draw a broader picture, we invited a group of scholars to offer their own 'approaches' to some of the questions we raise. The second purpose of this introduction is to provide a framework for the various chapters of this book.

II. 'The International Rule of Law' as the object of 'Rise or Decline'

The question whether international law is 'on the rise' or 'in decline' can only be answered within a larger historical context.

International law has evolved, more or less since the Peace of Westphalia, as a European-centred, primarily inter-state system of law with specific subjects, sources, and basic rules. In the course of the twentieth century, the system was further developed

---

[3] See, eg, Michael Scharf, *Customary International Law in Times of Fundamental Change: Recognizing Grotian Moments* (Cambridge University Press 2013) 8; Wilhelm Grewe, *Spiegel der Kräfte in der Weltpolitik: Theorie und Praxis der internationalen Beziehungen* (Econ 1970) 367–68.

[4] Hilary Charlesworth, 'International Law: A Discipline of Crisis' (2002) 65 Modern Law Review 377.

[5] It is, of course, always necessary not to fall into the trap of the contemporaries who often overestimate the significance of their own times and selves.

[6] See Kolleg-Forschergruppe 'The International Rule of Law—Rise or Decline?' <www.kfg-intlaw.de/index.php?ID=1> accessed 17 September 2018; an earlier version of the present text has been published as KFG Working Paper Series No 1, October 2016, at <https://papers.ssrn.com/sol3/papers.cfm?abstract_id=2866940> accessed 1 March 2019.

by the League of Nations, the United Nations Charter, and various other rules, principles, and institutions. Whereas states and other relevant actors, as well as academic authors, have conceived this legal system in different ways, widespread agreement about its basic features was reached among the relevant actors during the Cold War, despite important ideological differences.[7] By the end of this phase, international law had somewhat transcended its originally European, or northern, character as a result of the process of decolonization. Here, we call international law as it developed until about 1990, 'classical Charter-based international law'—although we are aware that the expression 'classical international law' is often used for the pre-Charter or the pre-League of Nations international law.

The roughly thirty years which have elapsed since the end of the Cold War have seen significant changes which, at a minimum, have added another layer to classical Charter-based international law.[8] Suffice it to mention the expansive practice of the Security Council (SC), the conclusion of certain key multilateral treaties (eg the United Nations Framework Convention on Climate Change (FCCC), or the Agreement Establishing the World Trade Organization (WTO)), the widening and deepening of the legal protection of individuals (increase in human rights adjudication, International Criminal Court (ICC)), an explosion of international adjudicatory bodies and adjudication more generally,[9] and a perception that many new actors, in addition to states and international organizations, have entered the scene. On a more general level, the added layer consisted primarily in a higher degree of institutionalization at the international level, a tighter network of rules in many areas, and a recognition of 'thicker' human rights standards, including in areas where the applicability of human rights had been contested, as in the field of economic and social rights or with certain aspects of the extra-territorial application of human rights.

Such developments have raised the question whether international law has even changed its character. As much has been suggested by different theoretical approaches, coming not only from international lawyers,[10] but also from political scientists,[11]

---

[7] Grigory I Tunkin, *Theory of International Law* (William E Butler ed/tr, Allen & Unwin 1974).

[8] The term 'classical international law' can have many meanings, just as the term 'rule of law' itself: Joseph Weiler, 'The Geology of International Law: Governance, Democracy and Legitimacy' (2004) 64 Zeitschrift für ausländisches öffentliches Recht und Völkerrecht 547; Susan Marks, 'The End of History? Reflection on Some International Legal Theses' (1997) 8 European Journal of International Law 449; also, *mutatis mutandis*, Robert Jennings, 'International Law Reform and Progressive Development' in Gerhard Hafner, Gerard Loibl, and Alfred Rest (eds), *Liber Amicorum: Professor Ignaz Seidl-Hohenveldern* (Kluwer 1998) 325–37; Wolfgang Friedman, *The Changing Structure of International Law* (Columbia University Press 1964).

[9] Exemplary: Karen Alter, *The New Terrain of International Law: Courts, Politics, Rights* (Princeton University Press 2014) especially ch 4.

[10] See, eg, the debates on the fragmentation of international law: Martti Koskenniemi and Päivi Leino, 'Fragmentation of International Law: Postmodern Anxieties?' (2002) 15 Leiden Journal of International Law 553; on constitutionalization, eg: Jan Klabbers, Anne Peters, and Geir Ulfstein (eds), *The Constitutionalization of International Law* (Oxford University Press 2009); on international legal pluralism: Alec Stone Sweet, 'Constitutionalism, Legal Pluralism, and International Regimes' (2009) 16 Indiana Journal of Global Legal Studies 621.

[11] For the neo-institutionalist approach, eg, Robert Keohane, *International Institutions and State Power* (Westview Press 1989); Joseph S Nye and John D Donahue, *Governance in a Globalizing World* (Brookings Institution Press 2000); for the liberal theory of international relations, eg, Anne-Marie Slaughter, 'International Law in a World of Liberal States' (1995) 6 European Journal of International Law 503.

philosophers,[12] and other social scientists. For our purposes and for the time being we merely assume that the classical Charter-based international law of the late Cold War has made what may be called an 'advance', or to put it more neutrally: a move, during the first two decades after the end of the Cold War.[13] We try to designate this advance over the classical Charter-based international law by using the term 'the international rule of law', instead of simply saying international law.

But is the choice of '1990' as the beginning of a new phase compelling, or does it simply represent a Germanocentric or a Eurocentric perspective hinging on the fall of the wall?[14] It is true that, from a historical point of view, many developments which came to fruition in the 1990s have earlier roots, such as the human rights revolution,[15] the proliferation of environmental law, or the rise of China. But we submit that '1990' is ultimately a good point of reference. After all, many developments which had started before 1990 significantly manifested themselves in the international legal sphere only after that date.

We use the term 'the international rule of law' in order to describe the kind and the characteristic elements of international law as they have manifested themselves after the end of the Cold War in the eyes of mainstream international lawyers. We are aware that the term 'the international rule of law' has been given many meanings, just as the term 'rule of law' itself.[16] Our definition therefore only claims to apply for the purposes of this chapter and the larger research project of which this book forms part. The way in which we use the term 'the international rule of law' is both open and restricted:

It is open as it invites the reader to look at modern developments without placing undue emphasis on any one of them. For example, we do not limit the term 'the

---

[12] See, eg, Ronald Dworkin, 'A New Philosophy for International Law' (2013) 41 Philosophy & Public Affairs 2; John Rawls, *The Law of Peoples: With the Idea of Public Reason Revisited* (first published 1997, rev edn Harvard University Press 2001).

[13] See the 'Declaration of the High-level meeting of the General Assembly on the Rule of Law at the National and International Levels' (19 September 2012) UN Doc A/67/L.1., recognizing several of these 'advances', such as the establishment of the WTO and the ICC.

[14] For an overview of alternative narratives: Dominic Sachsenmaier, *Global Perspective on Global History: Theories and Approaches in a Connected World* (Cambridge University Press 2011), especially the introduction on 'Neglected Diversities'.

[15] Kathryn Sikkink, *Evidence for Hope: Making Human Rights Work in the 21st Century* (Princeton University Press 2017) 25–31, 57; but see also: Samuel Moyn, *Human Rights and the Uses of History* (Verso 2014) xviii, 15–18.

[16] Arthur Watts, 'The International Rule of Law' (1993) 36 German Yearbook of International Law 34; James Crawford, 'International Law and the Rule of Law' (2003) 24 Adelaide Law Review 3; Simon Chesterman, 'An International Rule of Law?' (2008) 56 American Journal of Comparative Law 331; Speech by President of the International Court of Justice Rosalyn Higgins at the United Nations University, 'The ICJ and the Rule of Law' (11 April 2007) <archive.unu.edu/events/files/2007/20070411_Higgins_speech.pdf> accessed 17 September 2018; Mattias Kumm, 'International Law in National Courts: The International Rule of Law and the Limits of the Internationalist Model' (2003) 44 Virginia Journal of International Law 19; Hisashi Owada, 'Reconceptualization of the International Rule of Law in a Globalizing World' (2008) 51 Japanese Yearbook of International Law 3; Peter Tomka, 'The Rule of Law and the Role of the International Court of Justice in World Affairs' Inaugural Hilding Eeek Memorial Lecture at the Stockholm Centre for International Law and Justice (2 December 2013) <https://www.icj-cij.org/files/press-releases/8/17848.pdf> accessed 1 March 2019; Sienho Yee, *Towards an International Law of Co-Progressiveness* (Martinus Nijhoff Publishers 2004) ch 3; Brian Tamanaha, *On the Rule of Law: History, Politics, Theory* (Cambridge University Press 2004); Jeremy Waldron, 'The Rule of International Law' (2006) 30 Harvard Journal of Law & Public Policy 15; Robert McCorquodale, 'Defining the International Rule of Law: Defying Gravity?' (2016) 65 International & Comparative Law Quarterly 277; Robert McCorquodale, 'The Rule of Law Internationally' in Clemens Feinäugle (ed), *The Rule of Law and Its Application to the United Nations* (Hart/Nomos 2016) 51–74.

international rule of law' to referring to the question whether 'the law' is actually 'ruling' at the 'international level'.[17] Such a compliance-based understanding of the term focuses on adherence to the law and accountability.[18] Although compliance has gained a particular importance in the roughly past two decades as a means for assessing the state and direction of international law, it is only one of several aspects which may be relevant for such an undertaking. Another characteristic aspect is the 'domestic analogy' in the sense of viewing contemporary international law through the lens of domestic standards of the rule of law and to ask whether it reflects, or should reflect, a 'thick' or a 'thin' version of 'the rule of law'.[19] This understanding of the term 'international rule of law' permits to conceive international law as a system which conforms to a certain standard, but which does not go so far as to construct analogies with forms of state governance, as they are suggested by constitutionalist approaches.

The designation of international law which manifested itself and was conceived after the end of the Cold War as 'the international rule of law' is restricted insofar as we want to focus on the particular role of international *legal* norms (rules and principles), in their interconnectivity as a system, as well as on the intrinsic value which law offers (*Eigenwert des Rechts*) for international relations in comparison to other normative orders.

III. 'Rise or decline'—Why now?

The outcome of the referendum in the United Kingdom on membership in the European Union (EU) and the presidential elections in the United States, both in 2016, have finally provoked a broader debate whether international law is in crisis.[20] However, we do not think that even these important national decisions are necessarily symptoms of a crisis in international law of unusual proportions. In fact, the research project of which this book forms a part was conceived before these events took place. It may well turn out that the outcome of this particular UK referendum and of that particular US election are digressions from the point of view of long-term developments.

---

[17] See, eg, the debate at the UN General Assembly's Sixth Committee on 'The Rule of Law at the National and International Levels' 68th session; for a summary of the comments made by the states: <www.un.org/en/ga/sixth/68/RuleOfLaw.shtml> accessed 7 December 2017.

[18] See, eg, Report of the UN Secretary-General, 'The Rule of Law and Transitional Justice in Conflict and Post-conflict Societies' (23 August 2004) UN Doc S/2004/616.

[19] Chesterman (n 16) 340–43; McCorquodale, 'The Rule of Law Internationally' (n 16) 51–74, 52–55; Ian Hurd, 'The International Rule of Law: Law and the Limits of Politics' (2014) 28 Ethics and International Affairs 39.

[20] Philip Alston, 'The Populist Challenge to Human Rights' (2017) 9 Journal of Human Rights Practice 1; Karen Alter, 'The Future of International Law' in Diana Ayton-Shenker (ed), *The New Global Agenda: Priorities, Practices, and Pathways of the International Community* (Rowman & Littlefield 2018) 25; David Bosco, 'We Have Been Here Before: The Durability of Multilateralism' (2017) 70 Journal of International Affairs 9; Harlan Cohen, 'Multilateralism's Life Cycle' (2018) 112 American Journal of International Law 47; James Crawford, 'The Current Political Discourse Concerning International Law' (2018) 81 The Modern Law Review 1; Mikael Rask Madsen, Pola Cebulak, and Micha Wiebusch, 'Backlash against International Courts: Explaining the Forms and Patterns of Resistance to International Courts' (2018) 14 International Journal of Law in Context 197; Ximena Soley and Silvia Steiniger, 'Parting Ways or Lashing Back? Withdrawals, Backlash and the Inter-American Court of Human Rights' (2018) 14 International Journal of Law in Context 237; Eric Posner, 'Liberal Internationalism and the Populist Backlash' (2017) 49 Arizona State Law Journal 795.

On the other hand, even if such events ultimately turn out to have been short-term or medium-term interruptions of long-term advances, they may justifiably be conceived by contemporaries as ground-shaking and requiring at least a certain level of theoretical reconsideration. To use an extreme example: It may be said today that the Second World War was an interruption of a long-term development over two centuries towards an international rule of law, but this war certainly required a considerable amount of theoretical reflection by international lawyers, including a reconsideration of past premises.

We suspect that it is premature to speak, for example, of 'International Law in the Age of Trump'[21]—if the use of the term 'Age' is meant to attribute a longer-term significance to this particular election. We are rather interested in structural and systemic developments which go beyond specific events and electoral outcomes or cycles. We see numerous indications for such lingering shifts in the international legal order:

1. Political developments

Some indications lie beyond the strictly legal sphere, but they constitute the political background which influences the evolution of international law. Andrew Hurrell mentions three general developments: First, 'the return of geopolitics', which has been particularly visible in the case of the conflict in Syria (with its revival of the bipolar constellation, the involvement of regional powers, and ideological confrontation), but also in the cases of Crimea and the South China Sea.[22] Second, 'the changing problem of legitimacy', referring to challenges for the current distribution of decision-making power between the national and the international level. And third, 'the shift of power away from the core Western industrialized world'.[23]

Specific expressions of these general tendencies are changes in economic conditions (eg the rise of China, the world financial crisis, the evolution of a middle class in the Global South, a drop in oil prices), technological advances (eg cyber, clean energy, arms), political alliances (eg the group of Brazil, Russia, India, China, and South Africa (BRICS), or the rupture between the North Atlantic Treaty Organization (NATO) and Russia), domestic political conditions (eg the blockade of the US political system, or the disintegrative tendencies in the EU, and populist governments), and shifts in widespread beliefs (eg the loss of faith in liberal economic policies, reassertion of nationalism, demands for transitional justice, or public pressure to combat terrorism).

Some of those developments may be of the 'usual' kind, but it is certainly worth inquiring whether they have an unusual effect on the international rule of law.[24]

---

[21] Monica Hakimi, 'International Law in the Age of Trump' (EJIL Talk, 28 February 2017) <www.ejiltalk.org/international-law-in-the-age-of-trump/./> accessed 17 September 2018.
[22] Andrew Hurrell, 'International Relations and the Global Rule of Law: Some Reflections on the Long-run Picture' (unpublished manuscript) 6.
[23] ibid 6–8.
[24] Thomas Hale and David Held, *Beyond Gridlock* (Polity 2017) 252ff.

2. Systemically relevant disregard for international law

Violations of international legal rules may be important indicators for a challenge to, or a change of direction of, international law. We submit that certain typical contemporary violations are unusual in the sense that they call basic rules into question.

The rules on the use of force, which are the basic rules in any legal system, have been dealt with differently at the international level in recent years.[25] Whereas alleged violations of the prohibition on the use of force at least triggered significant legal debates among states during the Cold War, more recent tendencies suggest a disregard for a classical Charter-based understanding of international law which is systematically more relevant:[26]

Unilateral interventions and unilateral interpretations of UN Security Council resolutions, as in the cases of Kosovo, Iraq, and Libya, have contributed to undermining the credibility not only of the intervening states, but have more fundamentally called into question the working of the Charter system as a whole. The lack of a more forceful UN General Assembly reaction to the attempt by the Russian Federation to annex Crimea may be another indication for a loss of normative certainty.[27] The long paralysis of the Security Council in the face of the armed conflict in Syria and in disregard of the 'Responsibility to Protect' under the World Summit Outcome Document[28] questions the legitimacy of the Charter system. Prohibitions under customary international law have been weakened. The cases of Libya and Syria suggest that states have deviated and continue to deviate from established understandings of their obligations in relation to the prohibition of the use of force and the right of self-defence, for example in view of the delivery of arms to Libyan and Syrian rebels.[29] The Paris terror attacks 2015 have brought the old question to the fore whether the state-centred *ius ad bellum* is fit to

---

[25] Paulina Starski, 'Silence within the Process of Normative Change and Evolution of the Prohibition on the Use of Force: Normative Volatility and Legislative Responsibility' (2017) 4(1) Journal on the Use of Force and International Law 14, 30; François Alabrune, 'Fondements juridiques de l'intervention militaire française contre Daech en Irak et en Syrie' (2016) 120(1) Revue générale de droit international public 41; Dapo Akande and Marko Milanovich, 'The Constructive Ambiguity of the Security Council's ISIS Resolution' (EJIL Talk, 21 November 2015) <www.ejiltalk.org/the-constructive-ambiguity-of-the-security-councils-isis-resolution/> accessed 7 December 2017; Daniel Bethlehem, 'Self-Defense Against an Imminent or Actual Armed Attack By Nonstate Actors' (2013) 106 American Journal of International Law 770; Christian Marxsen, 'Self-defence in Times of Transition' (2017) 77 Zeitschrift für ausländisches öffentliches Recht und Völkerrecht 3.

[26] 'A Plea Against the Abusive Invocation of Self-defence as a Response to Terrorism' (29 June 2016) <cdi.ulb.ac.be/wp-content/uploads/2016/06/A-plea-against-the-abusive-invocation-of-self-defence.pdf> accessed 3 December 2017; for an alternative reading, however: Monica Hakimi and Jacob Katz Cogan, 'The Two Codes on the Use of Force' (2016) 27 European Journal of International Law 257; Christian Marxsen, 'Violation and Confirmation of the Law: The Intricate Effect of the Invocation of the Law in Armed Conflict' (2018) 5 Journal on the Use of Force and International Law 8.

[27] UN General Assembly (27 March 2013) UN Doc A/RES/68/262; Erika de Wet, 'The Modern Practice of Intervention by Invitation in Africa and Its Implications for the Prohibition of the Use of Force' (2016) 26 European Journal of International Law 979, 989; Andreas Zumach, *Globales Chaos–Machtlose Uno* (1st edn, Rotpunktverlag 2015) 109; Brazil, India, and South Africa have apparently abstained in the vote on the GA resolution on Crimea in reaction to perceived excesses of Western states during the Libyan intervention.

[28] UN General Assembly (24 October 2005) UN Doc A/RES/60/1, paras 138 and 139.

[29] Tom Ruys, 'Of Arms, Funding, and Non-Lethal Assistance: Issues Surrounding Third-State Intervention in the Syrian Civil War' (2014) 13 Chinese Journal of International Law 13; on the parallel case of Libya: Olivier Corten and Vaios Koutroulis, 'The Illegality of Military Support to Rebels in the Libyan War: Aspects of Jus Contra Bellum and Jus in Bello' (2013) 18 Journal Conflict and Security Law 84.

deal with challenges arising from violent non-state actors. The mix of a loss of credibility and legitimacy, occasional challenges for some of the most fundamental rules of
international law, as well as an apparent lack of capacity to reform the UN system of collective security, may be indications for a decline of the international rule of law, at least
when compared to the role which the Security Council played in the 1990s.

More importantly, it seems that—leaving the case of Kosovo 1999 aside—the
2003 invasion of Iraq was not simply the exceptional breaking of the rules by a big
power, but the beginning of a generally more liberal, or rather permissive, attitude
towards the rules regarding the use of force as an instrument of state power. The invasion and occupation of Crimea has been justified, in part, with reference to the
case of Kosovo, and the debates among international lawyers about the legality of
the different interventions in the civil wars in Iraq and Syria has not received much
attention in state practice or in the general public.[30] Indeed, Brazil has criticized that
the practice of states regarding the obligation to inform the Security Council about
their exercise of the right of self-defence, which 'might set dangerous precedents',
and the silence of other states regarding such uses is a reason for concern.[31] It is of
course necessary to bear in mind that the death of the rules on the use of force have
on previous occasions been announced prematurely, and that those rules should not
too easily be discarded.[32] At the same time certain structural developments, such
as the coming into existence of a cyberspace or the difficulty to characterize cyber
attacks and to attribute them to states, have added to the more fundamental challenge of those rules.[33]

3. Structural developments

Whereas relevant political developments and forms of disregard of international law
are often readily apparent, it is more difficult to determine whether and to what extent
the structure of international law, as it has evolved since the end of the Cold War, has
been affected. After all, the basic structures of international law are quite resilient, as
it became clear around the turn of the century when it was debated whether US hegemony threatened the foundations of international law.[34] Therefore, the existence of
challenges to the structure of international law would bear out the legitimacy of our
question more clearly.

---

[30] The Russian intervention in the Syrian civil war has not been challenged on legal grounds by any state
participating in the UN Security Council debate of 30 September 2015, UN Doc S/PV.7527.

[31] Statement of Brazil of 4 October 2017 in the Sixth Committee during the debate on Measures to eliminate
international terrorism <http://statements.unmeetings.org/media2/16152568/brazil.pdf> accessed 1 March 2019.

[32] Thomas M Franck, 'Who Killed Art. 2 (4)? Or: Changing Norms Governing the Use of Force by States' (1970)
64 American Journal of International Law 809; Michael J Glennon, 'Why the Security Council Failed' (2003) 82 (3)
Foreign Affairs 16, 22–24.

[33] Joel P Trachtman, *The Future of International Law* (Cambridge University Press 2013) 96; Lucas Kello, 'Cyber
Security—Gridlock and Innovation' in Hale and Held (n 24) 205–28, 205, and 215.

[34] See the contributions in: Michael Byers and Georg Nolte, *United States Hegemony and the Foundations of
International Law* (Cambridge University Press 2003).

One significant structural development concerns the calling into question, in certain areas, of the role of international law as a necessary or useful tool for international relations and cooperation. Some are observing a 'stagnation of international law' as states appear to be concluding fewer multilateral treaties than would be expected, and often prefer informal forms of cooperation which give them more flexibility.[35] This tendency may entail significant advantages in terms of flexibility, the possibility of involving non-state actors, and of leaving room for democratic decision-making at the national level. On the other hand, such a tendency also carries with it all the disadvantages of informalization, in particular the increase of hegemonic governance, decrease of legal accountability, and a lack of legitimation through democratic procedures.

The difficulties for concluding new multilateral treaties are compounded by the calling into question of certain existing treaties as not serving their purpose in our times.[36] Fortunately, the challenging of the Geneva Conventions after the terror attacks of 9/11 had led to an intense debate, in which national courts played an important role, and which resulted in a reappraisal and thus a re-legitimation of the Conventions.[37] However, it is unlikely that this example will repeat itself for most other treaties should they be challenged in a comparable way.

But the structural challenges go beyond political obstacles for the further codification and progressive development of international law. They also go to the sources of international law: For international lawyers, the expansion and diversification of international judicial dispute settlement since the end of the Cold War, and the ensuing wealth of decisions by international courts and tribunals, have created the possibly misleading impression that the sources of international law are constantly being re-affirmed and applied. On the other hand, it is precisely this expansion and diversification which has introduced considerable insecurity about how to interpret and identify rules from different sources of international law.[38] Should the practice of states parties have a decisive influence on the interpretation of a treaty, or should courts and tribunals be led more by what they perceive to be the object and purpose of a treaty, or by views of non-governmental organizations (NGOs)? Similar questions arise in the context of customary international law. Behind them stands the larger question about how we should conceive international law: more as a state-driven system, or rather as a system with many more legally relevant actors? It is perhaps symptomatic that the International Law Commission in its work on treaty interpretation and the identification of customary international law has recently emphasized the role of states in the

---

[35] Joost Pauwelyn, Ramses Wessel, and Jan Wouters, 'When Structures Become Shackles: Stagnation and Dynamics in International Lawmaking' (2014) 25 European Journal of International Law 733; Hale and Held (n 24) 3–9.

[36] Clint Peinhardt and Rachel L Wellhausen, 'Withdrawing from Investment Treaties but Protecting Investment' (2016) 7 Global Policy 571; Posner (n 20) 796.

[37] Georg Nolte, 'Persisting and Developing between Hope and Threat: International Law During the Past Two Decades and Beyond' in James Crawford and Sarah Nouwen (eds), *Select Proceedings of the European Society of International Law*, vol 3 (Bloomsbury Publishing 2012) 75–78.

[38] Jan Klabbers, 'International Legal Positivism and Constitutionalism' in Jörg Kammerhofer and Jean D'Aspremont (eds), *International Legal Positivism in a Post-Modern World* (Cambridge University Press 2014) 264, 286.

process of creating and interpreting international law.[39] This suggests that the 'rise' of classical Charter-based international law towards an international rule of law with more actors may be limited or reversed.

On a more specific level, customary international law, as a source of international law, seems to be significantly more contested, both at the international and at the national level. At the international level, the insecurity about the character and the interplay of its elements leaves its authority affected.[40] Moreover, it is questionable whether customary international law can accommodate certain rapidly changing international developments, for instance the impact which new technological advances might exert on international humanitarian law. At the national level, customary international law is sometimes called into question as a binding source of law and sometimes treated as being inferior to national legal concepts,[41] in particular because it might run counter to certain domestic legal standards of legality and legal security.

4. Contestations, rejections, or erosions of a value-based international law?

International law can be understood as a value-based system. Certain contestations, rejections, or erosions of its rules and principles may then be perceived as symptoms of a crisis of the international rule of law. Here, we proceed from the widely shared assumption that the process of legalization and judicialization which accelerated in the 1990s has transformed classical Charter-based international law with its emphasis on state-oriented principles and underdeveloped human rights obligations towards a more value-based order which is actually capable of protecting and serving individuals as well as other common goods. The World Summit Outcome Document demonstrates that, in 2005, not only legal theorists but also states have proclaimed a global legal order in which universal values and the rights of individual persons are reinforced and certain

[39] See Report of the International Law Commission on its 70th session, UN Doc A/73/10, Draft Conclusion 5 of the topic 'Subsequent agreements and subsequent practice in relation to the interpretation of treaties' 14; and Draft Conclusion 4 of the topic 'Identification of customary international law' 119.

[40] International Law Association, London Conference 2000, Committee on Formation of Customary (General) International Law, Final Report, 'Statement of the Principles Applicable to the Formation of General Customary International Law' 5–8; Noora Arajärvi, 'The Requisite Rigour in the Identification of Customary International Law' (2017) 19 International Community Law Review 9; Laurence Helfer and Ingrid Wuerth, 'Customary International Law: An Instrument Choice Perspective' (2016) 37 Michigan Journal of International Law 563; Niels Petersen, 'The International Court of Justice and the Judicial Politics of Identifying Customary International Law' (2017) 28 European Journal of International Law 357; Sienho Yee, 'Report on the ILC Project on "Identification of Customary International Law"' (2015) 14 Chinese Journal of International Law 375; Michael Wood, 'The Present Position within the ILC on the Topic Identification of Customary International Law: In Partial Response to Sienho Yee, Report on the ILC Project on Identification of Customary International Law' (2016) 15 Chinese Journal of International Law 3.

[41] J Patrick Kelly, 'The Twilight of Customary International Law' (2000) 40 Virginia Journal of International Law 449; European Court of Justice, Judgment of the Court of 16 June 1998, Case 162/96 *A Racke GmbH & Co v Hauptzollamt Mainz*, para 52 ('However, because of the complexity of the rules in question and the imprecision of some of its concepts to which they refer, judicial review must necessarily, and in particular in the context of a preliminary reference for an assessment of validity, be limited to the question whether, by adopting the suspending regulation, the Council made manifest errors of assessment concerning the conditions for applying those rules').

common goods are protected, whereas sovereignty-related discourses were moved to the background. Some authors have tried to describe this development by using notions such as 'cosmopolitan law',[42] 'humanity's law',[43] 'moralisation', or 'humanisation'[44] of international law[45] relying, in particular, on a liberal human rights vision. We try to capture this 'moralisation' of international law and international relations,[46] as far as it has manifested itself in legally relevant texts, by using the concept of legal values. This concept refers to normative conceptions of certain interests or goods which are protected by international law.

Indications for a decline of the international rule of law, thus understood, will accordingly lie in tendencies which call into question the recognition and established interpretation of universal value-based legal rules and principles. Here, it is important to distinguish between contestations and straightforward rejections. While contestations are part of any political or legal process, currently, we seem to witness more radical rejections of certain legal norms which, in turn, contribute to the perception of a significant crisis of international law. Of course, any diagnosis of decline depends on the normative position of the observer. The question of rise or decline of legal values therefore also concerns the prioritization of values. Some think that the most important value of the current international legal order lies in the recognition of classical individual human rights and of the right to self-determination; for others it is the sovereignty of states, peace, and security; still others emphasize duties of solidarity regarding collective goods, such as sustainable development or a healthy environment. It is true, but also too easy, to say that all these values are inherent in the international legal order and that they need to be pursued simultaneously. The answer to the question of priorities thus reflects whether international law, as it has evolved since the end of the Cold War, is now again turning into another type of law. For example, debates about exceptions to immunities before national courts in cases of international crimes[47] as well as the 'peace *versus* justice' debate raise questions as to whether certain forms of 'moralisation' and prioritization have really been generally accepted by states as relevant actors.

---

[42] Mary Kaldor, 'Cosmopolitanism and Organized Violence' in Steven Vertovec and Robin Cohen (eds), *Conceiving Cosmopolitanism: Theory, Context, and Practice* (Oxford University Press 2002) 268.

[43] Ruti Teitel, *Humanity's Law* (Oxford University Press 2011).

[44] Theodor Meron, 'The Humanization of International Law' (2006) 94 American Journal of International Law 239.

[45] Tilmann Altwicker and Oliver Diggelmann, 'How is "Progress" Constructed in International Legal Scholarship?' (2014) 25 European Journal of International Law 425.

[46] Kimberly Hutchins, 'The Possibility of Judgment: Moralizing and Theorizing in International Relations' (1992) 18 Review of International Studies 51; for a critical view: David Kennedy, *The Dark Side of Virtue: Reassessing International Humanitarianism* (Princeton University Press 2005).

[47] See the debate in the Sixth Committee, 72nd session (23 October to 1 November 2017) on Draft Art 7 which the International Law Commission adopted in the context of the project 'Immunity of State Officials from foreign criminal jurisdiction' <papersmart.unmeetings.org/ga/sixth/72nd-session/statements> accessed 24 September 2018; the debate is synthesized in Janina Barkholdt and Julian Kulaga, 'Analytical Presentation of the Comments and Observations by States on Draft Art 7, para 1, of the ILC Draft Articles on Immunity of State officials from foreign criminal jurisdiction, United Nations General Assembly, Sixth Committee, 2017' (April 2018) KFG Working Paper No 14, available at: <https://papers.ssrn.com/sol3/papers.cfm?abstract_id=3172104> accessed 1 March 2019; Heike Krieger, 'Between Evolution and Stagnation—Immunities in a Globalized World' (2014) 6 Goettingen Journal of International Law 2.

5. Institutional challenges[48]

The multiplication and expansive practices of international organizations and international courts has often been interpreted as proof for a maturation of international
law.[49] In particular, the judicial and quasi-judicial settlement of international disputes
is understood to be a symptom of the judicialization of the international order and an
important element of the international rule of law.[50] However, the reluctance of states
to accept the jurisdiction of international courts or to participate in their proceedings
questions the proposition of a 'rise' of international courts. Recent examples suggest
that many states are re-emphasizing their sovereignty and may then be less likely to
participate in judicial or arbitral proceedings.[51]

Even under the European Convention of Human Rights, sovereignty-based conceptions are merged with arguments based on democratic values in order to reject human
rights protection by an international court. Such arguments have most prominently
been raised in the United Kingdom[52] but can also be found, for example, in France,[53]
Hungary,[54] the Netherlands,[55] Russia,[56] and the Scandinavian countries.[57] Moreover,
there are indications that an increase of the number of cases does not necessarily entail
a strengthening of the role of international courts and therefore of the international rule
of law. Some disputes may even become more difficult to resolve if dealt with in international judicial or arbitral proceedings.[58] The development of the international rule
of law by international courts will probably be impeded by the fact that in some areas,
in particular in investment arbitration, ad hoc arbitral tribunals are unable to deliver a

---

[48] The text under this subheading has been written together with Andreas Zimmermann.

[49] For the impact of a judicialization of international law see, eg, Gernot Biehler, *Procedures in International Law*
(Springer 2008); for the role of international institutions in general see José E Alvarez, *International Institutions as
Law-makers* (Oxford University Press 2006).

[50] Alter (n 9).

[51] *The South China Sea Arbitration (The Republic of Philippines v The People's Republic of China)* PCA Case No
2013-19, Award (12 July 2016) para 61; *The Arctic Sunrise Case (Kingdom of the Netherlands v Russian Federation)*
Provisional Measures, International Tribunal for the Law of the Sea, No 22, Order (22 November 2013) para 9;
*Obligations concerning Negotiations relating to Cessation of the Nuclear Arms Race and to Nuclear Disarmament
(Marshall Islands v India)* Judgment (5 October 2016) ICJ Reports 2016, 255, para 4; Yuval Shany, *Assessing the
Effectiveness of International Courts* (Oxford University Press 2014) 31ff; Jonas Tallberg and James McCall Smith,
'Dispute Settlement in World Politics: States, Supranational Prosecutors, and Compliance' (2012) 20 European
Journal of International Relations 118.

[52] Björnstjern Baade, *Der Europäische Gerichtshof für Menschenrechte als Diskurswächter* (Springer 2017);
Julia Rackow, *Die Legitimität der EMRK in Europa* (Dr Kovač 2017).

[53] Patrick Wachsmann, 'Réflexions sur l'interprétation "globalisante" de la Convention européenne des droits
de l'homme' in Patrick Titiun (ed), *La conscience des droits. Mélanges en l'honneur de Jean-Paul Costa* (Dalloz
2011) 667.

[54] Kim L Scheppele, 'Hungary and the End of Politics' (The Nation, 6 May 2014) <www.thenation.com/article/
179710/hungary-and-end-politics> accessed 24 September 2018.

[55] Barbara Oomen, 'The Application of Socio-legal Theories of Legal Pluralism to Understanding the
Implementation and Integration of Human Rights Law' (2014) 4 European Journal of Human Rights 471.

[56] Matthias Hartwig, 'Vom Dialog zum Disput? Verfassungsrecht vs Europäische Menschenrechtskonvention—
Der Fall der Russländischen Föderation' (2017) 44 Europäische Grundrechte Zeitschrift 1.

[57] Juha Lavapuro, Tuomas Ojanen, and Martin Scheinin, 'Rights-based Constitutionalism in Finland and the
Development of Pluralist Constitutional Review' (2011) 9 International Journal of Constitutional Law 505.

[58] As examples for cases before the ICJ: *Application of the International Convention on the Elimination of all
Forms of Racial Discrimination (Georgia v Russian Federation)* Provisional Measures, Order (15 October 2008) ICJ
Reports 2008, 353; *Application of the Convention on the Prevention and Punishment of the Crime of Genocide
(Croatia v Serbia)* Judgment (3 February 2015) ICJ Reports 2015, 3.

coherent and foreseeable jurisprudence.[59] The debate in some European states, but also in states like India and South Africa, over the legitimacy of the current system of investment protection reflects such concerns. When—for various reasons—states withdraw from international organizations, courts, and tribunals, this will probably have repercussions on the character and authority of public international law as a whole and may contribute to a decline of the international rule of law.

IV. Generally held expectations and aspirations

The metaphorical question of 'rise or decline?' evokes Edward Gibbon's 'Decline and Fall of the Roman Empire'.[60] But we are neither historians nor do we want to be so pretentious as to try to predict the future. We do not, in particular, have a hidden agenda to see or to postulate a 'rise' or a 'decline' for any particular political purpose. We are rather interested in reassessing the state and the development of international law in our time from the perspective of international law's self-understanding. We are aware that there are thinkers who contest the possibility of identifying such a self-understanding. Our inquiry is, however, not narrow. It involves asking whether there is reason to question certain widely held assumptions about the general development of international law, be they (factual) *expectations* or (normative) *aspirations*.

Perhaps the most important *expectation* is the well-known image of an increasing inter-connectedness in a globalizing world 'rendering obsolete the old Westphalian world of Great Power rivalries'.[61] This expectation, or the reversal of this expectation, exerts some influence on the possibility or desirability of regulation in certain areas, in particular in economic relations or in cyberspace.[62] Today, we are seeing powerful political movements—domestic, transnational, and international—which question important forms of economic globalization, including its legal dimension (eg the WTO, or the projects of a Transatlantic Trade and Investment Partnership (TTIP), and a Trans-Pacific Partnership (TPP)). Such movements are having an effect on the actual working and further evolution of international legal regulation. The effects of such movements seem to go beyond their immediate political goals and affect the perception of what 'globalization' means and whether the determinism that is associated with it is justified.

The most significant *aspiration* is the notion of progress,[63] a notion which is enshrined in the Preamble of the UN Charter ('to promote social progress and better standards of life in larger progress') and in its Article 13 ('progressive development of international

---

[59] Stephan W Schill, 'System-Building in Investment Treaty Arbitration and Lawmaking' (2011) 12 German Law Journal 1083.

[60] Edward Gibbon, *The History of the Decline and Fall of the Roman Empire* (Penguin Classics 1993).

[61] Hurrell (n 22) 1; on such an expectation: Eyal Benvenisti, 'Sovereigns as Trustees of Humanity' (2013) 107 American Journal of International Law 295.

[62] On the interrelatedness between assumptions about a constantly evolving process of globalization and the structural development of international law: Benvenisti (n 61) 298f; Trachtman (n 33) 66–84, 288–98.

[63] See, eg, Altwicker and Diggelmann (n 45); Thomas Skouteris, *The Notion of Progress in International Law Discourse* (TMC Asser Press 2009); Francis Fukuyama, *The End of History and the Last Man* (first published 1992, Free Press 2006) 56–70.

law'), and which presupposes the existence of a shared common understanding of the direction international law will and should take. Whereas serious doubts about the notion of progress as such have not emerged at the official international level, the question of how to prioritize and distribute political and economic benefits (and thus 'progress') in certain areas and under present conditions has moved to the fore.[64]

Generally held expectations and aspirations inform theoretical approaches to international law. After the end of the Cold War, a liberal view on the direction history is taking became a generally held expectation, and even assumed a hegemonic role.[65] Some contemporary theories of international law are closely linked to such a background understanding of the processes of legalization and judicialization of international relations which accelerated in the 1990s. The evolving understanding of basic legal concepts, such as international community, sovereignty, right to democratic governance, universal human rights, and the role of NGOs in international law, have often relied on expectations regarding a continuing process of legalization and they tend to see international law as developing in a certain direction. Such concepts have also been fed by a 'global governance frame' which replaced a more anarchical view of international relations.[66] The lasting impact of such theories depends, at least partly, on the viability of the underlying background assumptions.

Generally held expectations and aspirations are not merely of academic relevance but also of immense practical importance since they have a direct impact on the legal practices of states and other pertinent actors. States usually negotiate treaties only when they expect that a legally binding agreement between them can be reached and will be implemented. International organizations and states consider whether formal legal regulation is more preferable than informal coordination, including with non-state actors. Courts will adopt particular interpretations on the assumption that certain expectations will be fulfilled. The assertion of a 'trend' often plays an important role in international legal argument- and decision-making when the emergence or the change of rules is alleged.[67] This is true, in particular, for assumptions about the emergence of community interests or values within the international legal order.[68] Non-state actors prioritize their activities on the basis of assumptions of future developments, as in the case of the envisaged conclusion of regional economic integration agreements.

---

[64]   Hurrell (n 22) 212.

[65]   Hurrell (n 22) 3; Bruno Simma and Andreas Paulus, 'The "International Community": Facing the Challenge of Globalization' (1998) 9 European Journal of International Law 266, 276 ('Globalization' seems to call for a 'neoliberal' theory of international law leading away from institution-building towards a belief in solutions reached without regulation by international authorities).

[66]   Hurrell (n 22) 213.

[67]   See, eg, the debate in the ILC on immunity of state officials from foreign criminal jurisdiction: Report of the International Law Commission on its 69th session, UN Doc A/72/10 (June–August 2017) 168–70.

[68]   *Case concerning the Arrest Warrant of 11 April 2000 (Democratic Republic of the Congo v Belgium)* Judgment (14 February 2014) ICJ Reports 2002, 3; Joint separate opinion of Judges Higgins, Kooijmans, and Buergenthal, 63, paras 47, 75; Eyal Benvenisti and Georg Nolte (eds), *Community Interests Across International Law* (Oxford University Press 2018); Santiago Villalpando, 'The Legal Dimension of the International Community: How Community Interests Are Protected in International Law' (2010) 21 European Journal of International Law 387, 394 and 407.

V. International law as a unified object of observation?

Asking about a rise or decline of 'international law' contains a contestable assertion regarding international law, which is whether it makes sense to raise the general question of the development of 'international law' *as such*, as if international law could be a unified object of observation. To ask this question runs counter to modern approaches which break international law down into various elements, or regimes. Theories of fragmentation tend to deconstruct the idea that there is a coherent system of international law[69] by focussing their attention on an analysis of specific regimes and the interaction of these regimes with one another and with their respective non-legal 'contexts'. In fact, simple common sense suggests that a 'rise' in one area, for example security cooperation against terrorism, may happen simultaneously with, or even go hand in hand with, a 'decline' in another area, for example human rights or world trade.

There is, however, also the reverse risk of not seeing the wood for the trees. A legal adviser who articulates the opposition of a state against a decision of the International Criminal Court may not think that she has something in common with the legal adviser who formulates the justification of a government for a purported annexation of a particular territory. The connecting element between the two could, however, be a general increase of self-assertiveness and a corresponding relative loss of belief in the long-term beneficial effects of regulation at the universal level.

Thus, while it may be easier to apply the 'rise or decline' metaphor to developments in specific areas of international law, more comprehensive assessments are also possible and desirable. Still, we must be careful with any kind of broad linear narrative. A linear progress narrative is as much an oversimplification as a linear decline narrative would be. International law may be temporarily in a slump which could be more easily overcome than it appears at any particular moment.

VI. How to assess 'Rise' or 'Decline'?

How can we assess whether international law is 'rising' or 'declining'? Against which standards do we assess the state of the law? How far can lawyers answer such questions on the basis of their methodological tools and how far is it advisable to turn to historians, political and other social scientists for help?

We think that classical legal methodology can contribute significantly to an analysis of the state and development of contemporary international law. Lawyers have always observed how legal rules are formed, they have identified contestations and violations, and they have determined whether and how the law is treated in comparison to other

---

[69] But see Martti Koskenniemi, 'Fragmentation of International Law: Difficulties arising from the Diversification and Expansion of International Law. Report of the Study Group of the International Law Commission' UN Doc A/CN.4/L.682 (13 April 2006) especially paras 481ff.

forms of social organization. And they have almost always felt responsible for giving overall assessments about the state of 'the law'[70] even if such assessments may appear to be empirically incomplete or theoretically deficient. There are certainly limitations to intra-legal analysis, but we believe that such analysis is useful and serves a purpose which is difficult to replace.

1. Symptoms and causes

Our hypothesis that we are faced with a significant crisis of the international legal system is based on the observation of symptoms: such as instances of systemically relevant disregard for international law, structural and institutional developments which challenge its integrity, as well as contestations or rejections of a value-based international law. The identification of such symptoms does not need to imply any strong assertion regarding the 'real causes' for developments in international law.

It is at this point where lawyers and political scientists often pursue different agendas. Political scientists are interested in determining mechanisms that drive normative change or in the conditions under which such changes occur. To take an historical example: the end of the bipolar international order of the Cold War may have resulted from the economic crisis of the Soviet Union, or the exhaustion of the belief in socialism, or some combination of the two. For operating lawyers, such causes may be relevant for their broader understanding of the international order, but they cannot directly integrate them into their analysis of the law. They rather tend to observe, in the first place, certain phenomena, or symptoms which challenge a particular rule, or system of rules or which lead to their different operation. They then try to deal with the changed mode of operation of the rules by applying certain secondary rules of that system ('sources'). Thus, for lawyers, the decline of the Cold War order may have manifested itself in the conclusion of certain agreements that had been impossible to conclude before (eg the Intermediate-Range Nuclear Forces (INF) Treaty), or the occasional use of certain institutions which had been blocked before (eg the SC in the late 1980s), or the acceptance of a certain new language.

Numerous political and social transformations may ultimately affect law today. These include changes in economic conditions, technological advances, political alliances, domestic political conditions, and shifts in widespread beliefs.[71] The effect of those developments is, however, not direct: It may simply be the product of a political process, like the conclusion of a treaty, which results in a legal act that is designed to resolve a new problem. It may be more complicated when factual phenomena do not translate into some sort of legal formalization, but when they are merely taken into

---

[70] See, eg, Hersch Lauterpacht, 'The Grotian Tradition in International Law' (1946) 23 British Yearbook of International Law 1; Hans Morgenthau, 'Positivism, Functionalism, and International Law' (1940) 34 American Journal of International Law 260; Friedman (n 8) 81ff; Bruno Simma, 'From Bilateralism to Community Interest' (1994) 250 Recueil des Cours de l'Academie de Droit International 229.

[71] See above at III. 1.

account in the interpretation or application of a given legal principle or rule. In any case, factual phenomena need to be translated somehow into the legal system, or they are not taken into account at all.

Thus, lawyers may, to a certain extent, be agnostic of political or social developments which affect the law. This does not mean that they can afford to ignore the political or social context. Lawyers are, however, in the first place supposed to determine the relevance of certain facts according to legal reasoning and legal standards. Such standards are not identical with the standards which are used in social sciences. For example, for lawyers it is not of primary importance whether the rule of customary international law which requires armed forces to distinguish between combatants and civilians came into existence for humanitarian reasons or in order to preserve military discipline. However, in order to understand the significance of this rule for political, moral, historical, or other purposes, including for the secondary legal purpose of the interpretation of the rule, this is essential to know.

The same is true for the assessment of contemporary international law more generally. It may be possible to identify certain changes of the law without knowing their political or other social causes for sure. Thus, when we concentrate on systemically relevant disregard for international law, structural and institutional developments which challenge its integrity, as well as contestations of a value-based international law, we do not want to conceal hidden assumptions about possible explanations for a 'rise or decline' of international law. As lawyers, we are methodologically not equipped to empirically determine, for example, whether a domestically induced blockade by a major state or a more antagonistic international environment contributes more to an observed stagnation in the conclusion of treaties. We are certainly aware that such phenomena are relevant for our findings regarding the development of the international legal order, but, as lawyers, we think that we can say something meaningful about them from a perspective of legal reasoning.

2. The standard and criteria

Ultimately, our assessments regarding the rise or decline depend on the standard we apply and its criteria. By relying on 'the international rule of law' in the sense of international law as it has evolved after the end of the Cold War, we apply a substantive normative standard as a point of reference. But what are the pertinent criteria for identifying whether this order is rising or declining? Are we talking about a qualitative or a quantitative understanding of 'rise or decline' of the international rule of law? Does 'rise' signify the idea that more international law necessarily constitutes more progress,[72] or do we rather look for certain substantive changes in the law?

---

[72] For such an understanding: Trachtman (n 33) 22ff, ch 4; on this ideal and its history: Jochen von Bernstorff, 'International Legal Scholarship as a Cooling Medium in International Politics' (2014) 25 European Journal of International Law 977; for a more critical perspective on this progress narrative: Jan Klabbers, 'International Institutions' in James Crawford and Martti Koskenniemi (eds), *Cambridge Companion to International Law* (Cambridge University Press 2012) 228.

From a comparative perspective the most obvious substantive standard is to ask whether the contemporary 'type'[73] of international law is being transformed into another type of international law. Should contemporary international law now best be characterized as moving towards some kind of global law, be it ordered or messy, or should it be conceived as returning towards a more classical type in which the primacy of states goes together with considerably more room for political pressure and developments? This inquiry is both agnostic and engaged. It is agnostic insofar as it recognizes that a possible 'decline' of the international rule of law (in the sense of contemporary international law) may well result in the 'rise' of a (better) system of global law. If they are thus understood, rise or decline are not synonymous with desirable or undesirable. On the other hand, the inquiry is engaged in the sense that we want to assess whether 'the international rule of law', as it stands, continues to represent an appropriate model for conceiving international law. Neither the agnostic nor the engaged approach implies, however, any inherent normative pre-understandings about whether international law as it stands is inherently good or deserves to be preserved.

Any substantive evaluation of the appropriateness of the 'type' of contemporary international law will need to identify its functions and characteristics and thus define the intrinsic value of international law (*Eigenwert des Rechts*), in comparison to other normative orders. Here we pursue a rather classical pragmatic approach based in positive law. For us, the international rule of law does not encompass what any particular theory or substantive perspective, such as constitutionalism, global administrative law, or critical legal studies, conceives as contemporary international law. We rather choose to focus on the self-description of this system of rules as the normative framework for the development of international law, or the more or less agreed self-understanding of the relevant actors for international law-making, which are primarily states. In terms of methodology, this approach means to focus on shifts in the wording, interpretation, and understanding of legally relevant texts and practices, such as treaties, declarations, speeches as well as decisions of national and international courts. Simultaneously, the analysis of mainstream theoretical discourses on the nature of international law in the period after the end of the Cold War may offer an additional clue to understanding processes of overestimation or underestimation of international law.[74]

The perceived role of law in the international order will impact on any assessment of whether law is rising in the sense of a progressive development or whether it 'produces the wrong results' and obstructs 'just' outcomes. The question whether contemporary international law is overestimated or underestimated is intrinsically related to

---

[73] Max Weber, *Economy and Society* (University of California Press 1978) 784–808, 212–301; Max Weber, *Wirtschaft und Gesellschaft* (JCB Mohr (Paul Siebeck) 1922) 455–66, 122–76.

[74] Heike Krieger, 'Verfassung im Völkerrecht—Konstitutionelle Elemente jenseits des Staates?' (2016) 75 Veröffentlichungen der Vereinigung der Deutschen Staatsrechtslehrer 439.

the question whether we hold more or less ambitious views about what international law can do.[75] Debates around global justice will at least partly depend on whether law is considered as a means for promoting or processing social change.[76] Defining characteristics of the international order, such as the international law's claim for universality and multilateralism, will also bear upon any evaluation. If universality is an intrinsic feature of 'the international rule of law', a shift to regional legal orders will imply significant changes. If multilateralism counts, the international rule of law is challenged when states increasingly act unilaterally. We also assume that the development of 'the international rule of law' should not be measured against the standards of national law,[77] as this would obscure perceptions of international law's particular functions and characteristics.

An assessment of the direction of international law also needs to take into account the specific features for 'law-reform' in the international system. Obviously, formal law-making processes are important indicators for progress or regression in international law. However, since the development of international law relies heavily on interpretative processes, discursive practices, and informal strategies, relevant transformations can also be identified on the basis of structural changes in the overall legal system or within its individual rules. For instance, a shift from regulating substance to regulating procedure, from providing for detailed rules to setting broader frameworks, may likewise reflect a decreasing ability of states to agree on common substantive legal rules.

Developments in international law can, of course, be assessed differently than through the lens of the dichotomy 'rise or decline'. Non-compliance and contestations, for example, may be regarded as symptoms of an ongoing dialectical process of legalization and politicization of international rules and institutional interventions.[78] A decrease in the conclusion of new treaties may simply indicate that international law has matured or that there are more refined ways to adapt treaties. Moreover, current developments in the international system may not so much reflect a crisis of the law but may rather signal a need for reconfiguring the role of the state more broadly or the crisis symptoms in international law may foreshadow more fundamental shifts in the function of law as a regulatory mechanism, including in national law. Alternative explanations must be kept in mind. But we think that the metaphorical question of 'rise or decline' is fruitful.

---

[75] cf Hurrell (n 22) 8.

[76] cf Georges Abi-Saab, 'Whither the International Community' (1998) 9 European Journal of International Law 248, 256.

[77] See, however: Hersch Lauterpacht, *The Function of Law in the International Community* (first published 1993, Oxford University Press 2011) 439ff; Dana Burchardt, 'The Functions of Law and Their Challenges: The Differentiated Functionality of International Law' German Law Journal (forthcoming).

[78] Michael Zürn, Martin Binder, and Matthias Ecker-Ehrhardt, 'International Authority and its Politicization' (2012) 4 International Theory 69; Armin von Bogdandy and Ingo Venzke (eds), *International Judicial Lawmaking: On Public Authority and Democratic Legitimation in Global Governance* (Springer 2012).

VII. Approaches for assessing the rise or decline of the international rule of law

We propose a multi-angle perspective for assessing the role of contemporary international law. Here, we distinguish between historical, actor-centred, system-oriented, and justice-focused approaches and we have invited the authors of our book to choose one of these approaches for painting their picture of the foundational and current challenges which the international legal order faces.

1. Historical approaches

Past transformations of the international legal order offer different standards for assessing present changes. Contemporary discourses are often rooted in earlier debates.[79] Contestations of the past offer alternative readings of legal developments.

One may doubt, for example, whether a paradigm shift actually took place around 1990, or whether there was just a blossoming of certain elements of the classical Charter-based international law. If, in contrast, one reads '1990' as representing a turn to Western hegemony in the process of creating international law, 'the international rule of law' as it has emerged during the last thirty years may appear much more as an exception in the overall development of international law than as representing the rule. Fruitful historical inquiries can go back further in time.

One possibility is to look at the era of the 'first globalisation' during the 'long' nineteenth century[80] and the time after the First World War which also gave rise to an initial conception by liberal international lawyers of a more demanding international rule of law. Looking at the present from the perspective of the idea(l) espoused by the International Committee of the Red Cross, the *Institut de Droit International*, Lassa Oppenheim, Hans Kelsen, and others, we may come to the conclusion that the development of international law since the end of the Cold War may have brought some progress, which nevertheless remained quite limited if compared to idea(l)s which were propagated as a real possibility before and after the First World War. Jochen von Bernstorff, in his chapter 'The Decay of the Rule of Law Project in International Relations (1990–2015)' indeed uses this historical approach as a yardstick for our epoch.

Another possible historical approach is to broaden the historical frame even further and take a fresh look at both the classical Eurocentric Westphalian narrative and its critiques, as they have emerged over the past half century or so. Perhaps it is time again to look at the development of international law from a long-term perspective over the centuries, bringing into the focus tectonic plates and shifts, such as the interaction over time of geopolitical regions and entities. Felix Lange, in his chapter 'Coercion,

---

[79] Hurrell (n 22) 1.
[80] Anthony Anghie, *Imperialism, Sovereignty and the Making of International Law* (Cambridge University Press 2004); Jürgen Osterhammel, *The Transformation of the World: A Global History of the Nineteenth Century* (Patrick Camiller tr, Princeton University Press 2014).

Internalization, Decolonisation: A Contextual Reading of the Rise of European International Law Since the Seventeenth Century' situates the current situation in a complex reading of the long-term evolution of international law and makes the universalization of international law a central yardstick for its rise. Andrew Hurrell, in his comment, agrees with Lange's narrative but emphasizes that power shifts and a more diverse range of actors participating in the international order require us to question how the rise and decline of the international rule of law is evaluated and by whom.

Here, and elsewhere, discussing historical analogies and prior experiences can be as useful as comparing more theoretical assessments of previous generations of scholars which may, at the same time, offer some insights for a self-reflective approach about the role scholars take in periods of transition and paradigmatic change. Anne Peters highlights this perspective in her comment 'The Rise and Decline of the International Rule of Law and the Job of Scholars'.

2. Actor-oriented approaches

Many political scientists and economists recommend adopting an actor-oriented perspective on the law. While international lawyers traditionally tend to treat the law as a 'system' from which rules and orders emanate, political scientists often emphasize that the law is formed by actors which pursue specific interests. This has in turn been criticized by some legal scholars as over-emphasizing specific power relationships at the expense of relatively stable structural features. Still, debates about the effect of the United States as a dominant or a declining power, for example, demonstrate that relevant legal developments can also be explained on the basis of an actor-centred approach.[81] Such actor-centred approaches can, *inter alia*, focus on the role of more or less powerful states, or on the role of non-state actors.

If we are indeed witnessing a shift from a 'unipolar' to a 'multipolar', or even a 'zeropolar' world, the position of recently empowered or relapsing states, or other actors, may well indicate international law's structural features and its general direction. Actor-centred approaches may thus generate reasons for structural changes in the international order. Therefore, we need to inquire whether the concept of 'rising powers' (or relapsing powers) can contribute to evaluating the current state and future development of international law. Are there indications that new power relationships affect basic rules, community values, and interests or do they simply render negotiations more difficult? Can we observe different priorities in terms of legal values, or greater indeterminacy in the structure of legal rules or stronger contestations or even rejections of universal institutions? Aniruddha Rajput aims to answer these questions by focussing on 'The BRICS as "Rising Powers" and the Development of International Law'. He subscribes to a reading of the current international order as developing from a unipolar to a multipolar order in which, in particular, the BRICS states (Brazil, Russia,

---

[81] Byers and Nolte (n 34).

India, China, and South Africa) play an influential role. He sketches their participation in shaping international law by focussing on the UN Security Council, trade and
investment law, climate change, and human rights. Thus, he delineates their role in the
current transformation of international law. He assumes that the BRICS states will attempt to shape international law in accordance with their priorities while continuously
participating in the existing structures. Therein he sees a chance for increasing the legitimacy of international law. Simon Chesterman, commenting on these assumptions,
predicts that a zeropolar world order will result in a messier period for international
law than any other period after the Second World War and will eventually challenge the
role of the state as such.

In this vein, an actor-oriented perspective also asks whether non-state actors contribute
to a rise or a decline of international law: are they strengthening or weakening the international legal system? For constitutionalist approaches NGOs play an important part in
legitimizing international law. They focus on democratic deficits which they perceive in
the international system and against which they call for the participation of individuals
and NGOs in global governance. NGOs are thus perceived as a means to introduce individual participation.[82] The importance of NGOs within international organizations, their
successful attempts to act as 'norm-entrepreneurs', and their role in furthering compliance
are thus part of a narrative on the rise of international law.

At closer inspection, however, this picture becomes blurred. NGOs must not conform to specific criteria. Even the far-advanced rules of the Council of Europe do not
require NGOs to have democratic structures themselves, a fact which throws their legitimizing role somewhat into doubt.[83] Most influential NGOs have their roots and
support in the Global North.[84] The role of NGOs as norm-entrepreneurs is ambiguous.
In the debate on food security, for example, some NGOs push for more sovereignty
rather than for more international rules.[85] In international humanitarian law, the debate on autonomous weapons, as it was influenced by NGOs, allegedly suffers from
serious misinterpretations of the law. The introduction of the concept of 'meaningful
human control' may dilute established international legal principles.[86] Finally, the political will to include NGOs or other non-state actors into law-making processes leads to
more informal rules or standards. Participation of NGOs is easier to realize in informal
regulatory processes since states and non-state actors (who lack international legal

---

[82] Anne Peters, 'Dual Democracy' in Klabbers, Peters, and Ulfstein (n 10) 263–341, 315ff.
[83] Heike Krieger, 'The Conference of International Non-Governmental Organisations of the Council of Europe'
in Marten Breuer and Stefanie Schmahl (eds), *The Council of Europe: Its Law and Policies* (Oxford University Press
2017) 314.
[84] Stephen Hopgood, 'Human Rights: Past their Sell-by Date' (18 June 2013) <www.opendemocracy.net/
openglobalrights/stephen-hopgood/human-rights-past-their-sell-by-date> accessed 24 September 2018.
[85] von Bernstorff (n 72) 989.
[86] For the debate: International Committee of the Red Cross, Expert Meeting, 'Autonomous Weapons
Systems: Technical, Military, Legal and Humanitarian Aspects' (26 to 28 March 2014) <reliefweb.int/sites/
reliefweb.int/files/resources/4221-002-autonomous-weapons-systems-full-report%20%281%29.pdf> accessed 24
September 2018; on the problem of weakening established protection standards: Rebecca Crootof, 'A Meaningful
Floor for "Meaningful Human Control"' (2016) 30 Temple International and Comparative Law Journal 53.

personality) can act on a more equal footing in such contexts.[87] Thus, transparency and participation comes with costs for the formal international legal order.

Violent non-state actors challenge the international legal order. Since the 1990s, we have witnessed particularly far-reaching changes of the application of the UN Charter in response to challenges by violent non-state actors. The international legal system has changed as a result, but it is hard to say whether this would be a rise or a decline. Maybe it is rather an instance of the endless recalibrations which take place in the process of adapting the law to new challenges. As far as compliance is concerned, violent non-state actors contribute more clearly to a decline of the international rule of law, as shown by efforts since the 1990s to apply international humanitarian law in non-international armed conflicts.

Such an approach may be viewed with scepticism. Thus, Jean d'Aspremont in his chapter criticizes that the question of rise or decline and the idea of its interrelatedness to the role of non-state actors springs from a liberal pre-understanding of the function and role of international law and serves the purpose of a self-fulfilling prophecy. Michael Zürn, in his comment, challenges this critique and stresses that an inquiry into which direction international law takes fulfils a hermeneutical purpose under diverging theoretical approaches.

International institutions, in particular international courts, are not only an object of contestations but are themselves actors that may have caused, may respond to, and may redirect rejectionist approaches by states. In her chapter 'From High Hopes to Disillusionment? Human Rights Protection in Europe in an ever more Hostile Environment', Angelika Nussberger discusses the interplay between the jurisprudence of the European Court of Human Rights and the challenges which the Court has been facing in recent years. She then asks whether and, if so, how the Court can deal with these challenges, in particular whether it is time to reconsider certain strands of its jurisprudence. Geir Ulfstein, in his comment, emphasizes that the Court should carefully apply an evolutive interpretation in its jurisprudence in order to address member states' concerns for their sovereign rights.

3. System-oriented approaches

In international relations theory, signs of crisis have prompted a shift in the focus from 'norm diffusion' to 'norm erosion'.[88] Such theories often consider that the existence

---

[87] cf Pauwelyn, Wessel, and Wouters (n 35) 742.

[88] Nicole Deitelhoff and Lisbeth Zimmermann, 'Things we lost in the fire: How different types of contestations affect the validity of international norms' (December 2013) PRIF Working Paper No 18; for constructivist approaches: Martha Finnemore and Kathryn Sikkink, 'International Norm Dynamics and Political Change' (1998) 52 International Organization 887; Thomas Risse, Stephen Ropp, and Kathryn Sikkink, *The Power of Human Rights: International Norms and Domestic Change* (Cambridge University Press 1999); Thomas Risse, Stephen Ropp, and Kathryn Sikkink, *The Persistent Power of Human Rights* (Cambridge University Press 2013); for a cycle theory of norm change: Wayne Sandholtz and Kendall Stiles, *International Norms and Cycles of Change* (Oxford University Press 2009); Wayne Sandholtz, *Prohibiting Plunder: How Norms Change* (Oxford University Press 2007); also: Abram Chayes and Antonia H Chayes, 'On Compliance' (1993) 47 International Organization 175; for approaches of legal scholars, *inter alia*: Myres McDougal and W Michael Reisman, 'The Prescribing

of a legal rule or a social norm depends on the degree of compliance with it.[89] When distinguishing the decline of a legal rule from its mere violation authors assess disputes/contestations in order to determine the relevance of normative arguments about the binding character of a rule and its content.[90] Parts of international law have always suffered from a lack of compliance. Violations of the law also happen in states under the rule of law without impairing the perception of the continued validity of the legal order.[91] There is a well-founded professional reluctance among lawyers to draw far-reaching normative conclusions from violations of the law or compliance deficits, even where these violations are accompanied by attempts to justify them. To what extent are these methods for determining the state of certain legal rules therefore relevant for identifying a 'rise or decline' of international law as a system? Is the lack of compliance with certain of its rules already symptomatic of transformations at a deeper level, or must we look for a systematic lack of compliance throughout the entire legal system?

In his chapter 'Is Compliance an Indicator for the State of International Law? Exploring the "Compliance Trilemma"', Jeffrey Dunoff examines whether compliance is a useful tool for assessing the state and direction of international law. He questions whether higher compliance rates are interlinked with a thicker international rule of law. Instead, he offers an explanation based on a 'compliance trilemma' according to which the international rule of law pursues three goals which cannot all be attained at the same time: widespread participation, ambitious legal norms, and high rates of compliance. He claims that such an approach offers a better yardstick for understanding ongoing processes because it explains trade-offs between pursuit of heightened compliance and other desirable outcomes, such as increased participation and increased depth of international legal norms. Markus Jachtenfuchs, in his comment, questions the alleged 'compliance trilemma' from a practical perspective, pointing at apparently contradicting cases from the EU context, as well as from a more theoretical point of view, advising us that 'the compliance trilemma should not lead us to a fatalist view on the limits of global governance under anarchy but rather to think about institutional design'.[92]

A system-oriented approach also throws light on other possible causes for structural changes of the international legal order. Scholars focussing on the protection of global public goods sometimes doubt the capacity of international law to constrain

---

Function in the World Constitutive Process: How International Law Is Made' in Myres McDougal and Michael Reisman (eds), *International Law Essays: A Supplement to International Law in Contemporary Perspective* (Foundation Press 1981) 355–80; Harold H Koh, 'Why Do Nations Obey International Law?' (1997) 106 Yale Law Journal 2599.

[89] See, eg, Michael Glennon, 'How International Rules Die' (2005) 93 Georgetown Law Journal 939.
[90] Sandholtz (n 88); on contestations also: Antje Wiener, *A Theory of Contestation* (Springer 2014); cf also: *Military and Paramilitary Activities in and against Nicaragua (Nicaragua v United States of America)* Merits, Judgment (27 June 1986) ICJ Reports 1986, 14, para 186.
[91] Doubting the value of this analogy: Gerry Simpson, 'On the Magic Mountain: Teaching Public International Law' (1999) 10 European Journal of International Law 70, 74.
[92] Below at Chapter 13.

or push states to act in the community interest. This doubt entails two aspects: some regulatory challenges, in particular in the environmental field, may be so complex ('wicked problems'[93]) that traditional forms of law may not be able to provide an effective regulatory mechanism. Does such an approach explain why environmental law is characterized by informal standard setting and soft law structures, such as important parts of the Paris Agreement on Climate Change? Jutta Brunnée assesses the capacity of international law to tackle complex problems in her chapter 'The Rule of International (Environmental) Law and Complex Problems'. She discusses how environmental treaty law has evolved to balance challenges of complexity with the demands of the rule of law on the basis of the example of the 2015 Paris Agreement. Tomer Broude in his comment doubts that complexity poses any specific current or foundational challenge for international law.

Moreover, views have been expressed according to which self-interested states are incapable or unwilling to act for the global good. There is a literature focussing on law-making alternatives to multilateral treaties on global public goods.[94] They postulate a turn to unilateralism ('unfriendly unilateralism'; EU climate protection measures) or hierarchical law-making (Security Council and climate change/ Security Council and Ebola crisis). Does such a shift to other fora and structures imply a rise or a decline, or just a 'simple' change? It will be significant, for example, whether the Paris Accord on Climate Change will lead to a reassessment of the debate about stagnation in treaty-making.[95] Against this backdrop Jan Wouters reasserts the importance of informal international law-making as both an alternative to, and an element of, traditional international law-making for mitigating the alleged inability of traditional public international law to adapt the challenges of globalization. In his view, the spread of populist movements and increased contestation by non-Western actors may promote such a process of adaptation. Alternatively, public international law may lock itself in and exist as one option amongst others for regulating international affairs, ultimately raising the question as to how these diverging regulatory options interrelate. Andreas Zimmermann and Norman Weiß, in their comment, question Wouters' assumptions. They doubt, in particular, that informal law-making is a panacea against populist contestations of international law.

---

[93]   Horst Rittel and Melvin Webber, 'Dilemmas in a General Theory of Planning' (1973) 4 Policy Sciences 155.

[94]   Anne van Aaken, 'Is International Law Conducive to Prevent Looming Disaster?' University of St Gallen Law & Economics Working Paper No 2015-09; Monica Hakimi, 'Unfriendly Unilateralism' (2014) 55 Harvard International Law Journal 105; Nico Krisch, 'The Decay of Consent: International Law in an Age of Global Public Goods' (2014) 108 American Journal of International Law 1.

[95]   For the debate on stagnation: Pauwelyn, Wessel, and Wouters (n 35); specifically on the Paris Accord: Joost Pauwelyn and Liliana Andonova, 'A Legally Binding Treaty or Not? The Wrong Question for Paris Climate Summit' (EJIL Talk, 4 December 2015) <www.ejiltalk.org/a-legally-binding-treaty-or-not-the-wrong-question-for-paris-climate-summit/> accessed 24 September 2018; but see Anne-Marie Slaughter, 'The Paris Approach to Global Governance' (28 December 2015) <www.project-syndicate.org/commentary/paris-agreement-model-for-global-governance-by-anne-marie-slaughter-2015-12> accessed 24 September 2018.

4. Legitimacy and justice

The rise or decline of the rule of international law may finally be viewed through the lens of legitimacy and justice. The search for legitimacy in international law may be a symptom of a normative crisis, but also of rising expectations and norm development. Modern legitimacy discourses date back to the 1990s[96] which suggests that they are not necessarily a symptom for 'decline': Indeed, legitimacy may be invoked to justify growing powers of international organizations and thus correspond to the 'rise' of international law and international institutions in the 1990s. But the legitimacy discourse has also turned into an instrument for criticizing the influence of international law and international institutions in general. Where the assessment and enforcement of legal claims is left to the states themselves and where it is not transferred to international organs with enforcement powers, arguments of legitimacy tend to dissolve binary legal categories (legal–illegal). A classic example is the conclusion of the Independent International Commission on Kosovo according to which the humanitarian intervention in Kosovo was 'illegal but legitimate'.[97] Such an approach gives room to break the law in order to reform it, but also to abuse legitimacy arguments for specific interests.[98] Such use of legitimacy discourses is not restricted to the rules on the use of force but can also be observed, for example, where states are unwilling to implement international law domestically.

Thilo Marauhn discusses the role of legitimacy considerations for a diagnosis of the state of international law, ultimately arriving at a sceptical conclusion. He insists on a clear distinction between (subjective) legitimacy claims and their (objective) factual underpinnings, as well as on a distinction between legally informed and other legitimacy claims. It would only be on the basis of such distinctions that lawyers could hope to arrive at satisfactory conclusions which would not inadvertently contribute to the undermining and ultimately the decline of legal norms by creating false expectations about what is possible. According to Marauhn, the blurring of the lines between legality and legitimacy, and the formulation of legitimacy claims beyond a solid legal analysis may eventually weaken the international rule of law, and thus contribute to its 'decline' rather than a 'rise'. Dana Burchardt, in her comment, disagrees from a norm-theoretical perspective by emphasizing the extent to which 'legal norms and legitimacy norms *compete* and *complement* each other'. She stresses that the double-edged relationship between legality and legitimacy can be used both for undercutting and for defending each category of norm.

---

[96] Thomas M Franck, *The Power of Legitimacy among Nations* (Oxford University Press 1990).

[97] The Independent International Commission on Kosovo, 'The Kosovo Report, Conflict, International Response, Lessons Learned' (Oxford University Press 2000) <reliefweb.int/sites/reliefweb.int/files/resources/6D26FF88119644CFC1256989005CD392-thekosovoreport.pdf> accessed 24 September 2018, 4 and 186.

[98] Christopher Daase, 'Die Legalisierung der Legitimität: Zur Kritik der Schutzverantwortung als emerging norm' (2013) 88 Friedens-Warte 41; Georg Nolte, 'Kosovo und Konstitutionalisierung: Zur humanitären Intervention der NATO-Staaten' (1999) 59 Zeitschrift für ausländisches öffentliches Recht und Völkerrecht 941.

Considerations of legitimacy often underpin value-oriented international human rights law.[99] In his contribution, 'The Contestation of Value-Based Norms: Confirmation or Erosion of International Law?', Tiya Maluwa focuses on contestations of international human rights law. Choosing the example of the fight against impunity for international crimes and its relation to heads of states' immunity, on the one hand, and the debates about humanitarian intervention and the responsibility to protect on the other, Maluwa argues that the contestations of the states of the African Union have promoted a rise of international law. In their comment, Andrea Liese and Nina Reiners question Maluwa's narrative as one which relies too heavily on the 'eyes of the beholder'-perspective and thereby misses opportunities to identify inter-subjectively valid values and norms.

Eventually, the question of global justice, distributive[100] and otherwise, is one of the greatest present-day challenges. A widely perceived inability of international law to provide for or sufficiently contribute to global justice can trigger a decline narrative insofar as international law does not meet the normative aspirations of parts of global public opinion.[101] But is it at all appropriate to expect that international law, as it stands, can play a major role in improving distributive justice?[102] Is overloading international law with expectations of justice an indication for political failure? Do attempts to claim global justice before international and national courts entail serious costs for other legal principles, such as legal security (eg retroactive application of the law)? The CARICOM claim for reparations for historical injustices linking reparations with development issues is a pertinent example.[103]

Eyal Benvenisti approaches the question of global justice from an institutional perspective. He questions the aim of many to identify or develop substantive standards of global justice, and to transform those standards into rules. He rather looks at the structural conditions which prevent weak states and disfavoured communities articulating their interests in a sufficiently effective way, and he sees the role of international law in providing 'hooks, not fish'. Under current conditions, rules on transparency, independent (judicial) review, and access to 'private' (big) data would provide such hooks which could lead to a 'rise' of global justice by indirect means. Maurice Kamto, in his comment, largely agrees with this approach but claims that certain more conventional institutional mechanisms should not be overlooked.

---

[99] Steven Ratner, *Thin Justice of International Law* (Oxford University Press 2015) 73–83; Allen Buchanan, *Justice, Legitimacy, and Self-Determination: Moral Foundations for International Law* (Oxford University Press 2004) ch 3, 118–90; but see also: Joseph Raz, 'Human Rights Without Foundations' in Samantha Besson and John Tasioulas (eds), *The Philosophy of International Law* (Oxford University Press 2010) 321, 336f.

[100] Thomas M Franck, *Fairness in International Law and Institutions* (Oxford University Press 1995) 413.

[101] See, eg, Thomas Pogge, 'The Role of International Law in Reproducing Massive Poverty' in Besson and Tasioulas (n 99) 417, 420; David Kennedy, *A World of Struggle—How Power, Law, and Expertise Shape Global Political Economy* (Princeton University Press 2016) 199f; but cf also: James Crawford, *Chance, Order, Change: The Course of International Law* (Martinus Nijhoff 2014) 506.

[102] Jochen von Bernstorff, 'International Law and Global Justice' (2015) 26 European Journal of International Law 279; Crawford (n 101) 468f.

[103] 'Address delivered by Professor Sir Hilary Beckles, Chairman of the CARICOM Reparations Commission, House of Commons, Parliament of Great Britain' (16 July 2014) <https://caricom.org/media-center/communications/speeches/address-delivered-by-professor-sir-hilary-beckles-chairman-of-the-caricom-r> accessed 24 September 2018.

VIII. Outlook

To ask about the rise or decline of the international rule of law implies that international law may at present not merely undergo a simple process of transformation but that its progress may be interrupted or even reversed. It assumes that certain current contestations are not necessarily beneficial for international law. By alluding to Gibbon's 'Decline and Fall of the Roman Empire', the question even gives room for the idea that 'Law's Empire', like other empires, may eventually fall. Thus, the question may arouse resistance among lawyers.

But, to ask about the rise or decline of the international rule of law is also a metaphor for a constructive approach. By choosing the 1990s as a point of reference we also propose to explore how a progressive development of international law can be made sustainable. We propose to evaluate this move with hindsight. Did the 1990s end of ideological confrontation lead international lawyers to overestimate international law's prospects for progressive development?[104] Is 'the end of ideologies' now substituted by 'the end of illusions'? Thus, the question about the rise or decline of the international rule of law throws some light on the mechanisms, challenges, and perplexities of norm evolution. It illuminates the balance which law needs to maintain between providing stability and allowing for change. It thereby refers to other foundational questions, such as regarding the relationship between law and politics, between law and social progress, and it asks about the awareness of the role of lawyers within such processes: When and how does law need to be changed? Which conditions are conducive for pushing advances in law and society, and which conditions require lawyers to preserve what has been achieved? These questions invite international lawyers—practitioners and academics alike—to reflect on how to respond in their work to the current challenges the international legal order faces. Can lawyers escape the trap of over- or underestimating international law which Josef Kunz has described in 1950?

Eventually, there may be no clear and definitive answer to the question of the rise or decline of the international rule of law. Yet, we need to pursue it. There are not only sufficient indications for being apprehensive. Most legal and political scientists did not consider the possibility of a Brexit before it happened. As much as a Brexit is not necessarily the end of European integration, certain challenges to the international rule of law will probably not lead to its demise. But it is also important to face the challenges, to reflect upon the resilience of the international legal order, and to identify the possibilities for its progressive development.

---

[104] Kim L Scheppele, 'Worst Practices and the Transnational Legal Order' (2016), 9; available at: https://www.law.utoronto.ca/utfl_file/count/documents/events/wright-scheppele2016.pdf.; last accessed 1 March 2019accessed 1 March 2019.

PART II
HISTORICAL PERSPECTIVES

2

The Decay of the International Rule of Law Project (1990–2015)

*Jochen von Bernstorff**

The 'international rule of law' is a mystical concept. It can be both a horizon of a more just international legal order and a vehicle of domination and exploitation. Being firmly anchored in the tradition of nineteenth-century Western liberalism, the 'rule of law' notion usually transports a positive image of law as a societal medium that limits and controls the exercise of otherwise arbitrary state power. As an issue of general juris-prudential debates, however, the 'rule of law' concept is an embattled concept. Since Aristotle, scholars agonize over the question of whether the 'rule of law' notion must be distinguished from mere 'legality' and about the central components of a more substantive understanding of the concept. Among the suggested components we find procedural requirements like clarity, publicity, generality, and predictability of the law, but also separation of powers, independence of the judiciary, and equality before the law are often squeezed into—or indignantly thrown out of—the contested container-term. With all its positive connotations, however, insisting on the 'rule of law' can also be a perfect vehicle of hegemony, or class rule as Marxian historians would have it, by concealing oppressive rule by those in power as the 'rule of law'.

In modern international legal discourse, the rule of law debate, beginning in the late nineteenth century, has always had a more existential tone than in domestic contexts. This is not surprising, given that the existence of legality in international relations as such kept being disputed and denied by many contemporaries. In the absence of centralized law-making and compulsory adjudication, the quest for an 'international rule of law' was often framed as a reformist or even utopian political project. It is closely connected to the 'move to institutions' (David Kennedy) in international law in the early twentieth century. The Preamble of the 1919 League Covenant promotes 'the firm establishment of the understandings of international law as the actual rule of conduct among Governments'. Even though all the components of more substantive notions of the rule of law referred to above also surfaced time and again in international legal debates and in ambitious institutional blueprints, the twentieth-century 'international rule of law' project arguably developed

* I wish to thank Christoph Wahlicht for research assistance and formatting.

its own distinct features. But what exactly are the main elements of this project, what are its twentieth-century emanations, and was the post-1990 period under review in this book in any way a notable phase for the international rule of law? The legal climate in the post-1989 era started with a reinvigoration of the rule of law discourse in international legal scholarship. The Cold War was over. The United Nations (UN) Security Council authorized the military intervention against Iraq with the goal to restore the territorial integrity of Kuwait.[1] From a Western perspective, a new phase of international institutionalization seemed to commence based on an allegedly emerging global consensus about the value of collective security, multilateralism, human rights, and effective international judicial controls. A number of new international institutions were created under the uncontested leadership of the United States and its European partners. Twenty-five years later, the atmosphere is much less optimistic as the editors to this book note and the notion of 'crisis' and of the 'return of the Cold War' is mushrooming in the literature.[2]

As I want to argue in this contribution, rise and decline narratives with the 1990s as the beginning of a golden era of the international rule of law and its demise today do arguably not withstand a critical re-appraisal. Instead, and perhaps counterintuitively from a Western perspective, the time since the 1980s is here portrayed as a time of decay of the rule of law project. Politically, this era was the climax of a phase of a US-dominated international institutional system, which began in the interwar period and which might gradually come to an end in the first half of the twenty-first century. It was a phase of relatively uncontested Western hegemony realized through transnational institutions often but not necessarily created by international law.[3] However, many institutional characteristics of this era conflicted or continued to conflict fundamentally with central elements of the original early twentieth-century rule of law project in international relations. It might at best have been an era of the 'rule by law' (Brian Z Tamanaha) but only to a limited extent a peak of the 'rule of law' in a more substantive and historically informed sense of this notion. The United States and its Western partners arguably missed out on the opportunity to use the 'unipolar' moment in modern world history, to eventually realize and entrench a fair rule of law system in international relations.

What we witness today, almost thirty years later, is the gradual demise of this era of Western hegemony in international politics, which came with a relatively low or at least a highly selective appreciation of institutionalized legality in international relations by leading Western elites. Like an ancient torso, the early twentieth-century international rule of law project nostalgically reminds us of the enormous potential international lawyers once accorded to the legal medium in international relations.

---

[1] UNSC Res 678 (29 November 1990) UN Doc S/RES/678.

[2] Heike Krieger and Georg Nolte, 'The International Rule of Law—Rise or Decline?—Approaching Current Foundational Challenges' in this book.

[3] On the United States and strategic instrumentalization of international law: Nico Krisch, 'More Equal than the Rest? Hierarchy, Equality and US Predominance in International Law' in Michael Byers and Georg Nolte (eds), *United States Hegemony and the Foundations of International Law* (Cambridge University Press 2003).

In order to corroborate my reading of the post-1990s era as a phase of accelerated decay, the remainder of this chapter will in a first step reconstruct original building blocks of the rule of law project in international relations, including its contemporary critics (I). As a second step, the chapter will discuss selected post-1990 developments against the backdrop of these reconstructed elements (II).

I. Elements and origins of the rule of law project in international law

Historically, the origins of the rule of law project in international relations can be located in the late nineteenth and early twentieth centuries. It has animated international legal scholars and civil society activists for at least 100 years; many of its core aspirations, however, have remained unfulfilled. As I will show in more detail below, an international rule of law movement during and after the First World War considered a rule-based international order as the only possibility to tame the detrimental forces of European nationalism and nineteenth-century-style imperialism. Key features of this project were a strong and centralized court system with compulsory adjudication, a law-based system of collective security, equal representation of all nations in both law-making and institutionalized implementation, as well as the codification of unwritten rules and unregulated areas of international cooperation. In form of an overview, the basic tenets of the international rule of law project thus were the following:

Compulsory jurisdiction: international legal scholars and activists campaigned for a centralized world court with compulsory jurisdiction; but neither the Hague Conventions from 1899 and 1907, nor the statute of the Permanent Court of International Justice (PCIJ) (1919), nor the largely identical statute of the International Court of Justice (1946) contain an obligation of state parties to recognize the jurisdiction of these judicial institutions for all legal inter-state disputes. Jurisdiction of these courts can be limited or excluded by the state parties to these instruments.

Rule-based collective security: the idea to have a strong and inclusive world institution endowed with a monopoly on the use of force, enforcing peace in international relations based on clear legal rules on the prohibition of the use of force, has only partially been accomplished in both the League Covenant and the United Nations Charter.

Sovereign equality of states: as an element of the rule of law project, smaller non-European states since the nineteenth century demanded not only to be recognized as independent states but also equal participation in general rule-making and in decision-making procedures in international institutions. It lasted until the end of the decolonization period in the 1970s before full formal recognition of all nations organized as states in the sense of classic European international law had been completed. Equal participation in law- and decision-making in international institutions, however, remained unfulfilled in various other areas of international cooperation.

Codification: a further essential element of the rule of law project was the struggle for formalized written international rules enshrined in general so-called 'law-making treaties'. The peak of formal codification lasted from the end of the nineteenth century until the 1980s.

1. The historical origins of the project

Already in the nineteenth century, public law scholars witnessed the emergence of highly formalized domestic legal systems encompassing codification, compulsory adjudication, and centralized law-creating institutions. By analogical reasoning, international lawyers perceived international law as 'primitive',[4] 'anarchic',[5] or 'incomplete'[6] law, which needed to be institutionally strengthened by introducing centralized organs of law creation and application. Modern Western centralized national legal systems with their great domestic codification projects became consciously or subconsciously the assumed yardstick for international law.[7] This explains the vigorous nineteenth-century German debates about the character and binding basis of international law in the absence of a general system of compulsory adjudication.

As a consequence, the ever more dominant 'positivist' trend in scholarship adopted an evolutionary perspective on international law. Even though it still was 'primitive' in its decentralized structure and in its reliance on non-formalized legal sources, it had the potential to expand and develop in order to overcome and solve concrete problems occurring through the separation of sovereign entities and jurisdictions.[8] During the 'long' nineteenth century, it was increasingly perceived as a medium to answer regulatory needs created by the first wave of economic globalization. Between 1860 and 1914, more than thirty international institutions based on multilateral treaty law were founded, most of which served purposes of technical and scientific cooperation between states. Moreover, during the same time international law was discovered as a medium to foster universalistic political projects. Western transnational civil society organizations began to project their humanitarian and pacifist causes on the progressive development of international law.[9] In order to serve these progressive purposes it had to create institutions for standard setting and progressive law-creation.

---

[4] As a 'primitive' legal system, international law in the 1930s was for Kelsen in a stage of evolutionary transition to a legal system where law creation and law application would be transferred to centralised organs: Hans Kelsen, 'The Law as a Specific Social Technique' (1941) 9 University of Chicago Law Review 97.

[5] Georg Jellinek, *Allgemeine Staatslehre* (2nd edn, Häring 1905) 368.

[6] Carl V Fricker, 'Noch einmal das Problem des Völkerrechts' (1878) 34 Zeitschrift für die gesamte Staatswissenschaft 399.

[7] On the myth of progress and the domestic law analogy in current international law scholarship: cf Paul W Kahn, *The Cultural Study of Law: Reconstructing Legal Scholarship* (Chicago University Press 1999) 109–10; on progress in international law generally: Thomas Skouteris, *The Notion of Progress in International Law Discourse* (Asser 2010).

[8] International law as 'primitive' law: Hans Kelsen, *Unrecht und Unrechtsfolge im Völkerrecht* (Springer 1932) 586; cf Lassa Oppenheim, *International Law—A Treatise*, vol 1, Peace (Longmans, Green and Co 1920) 11, 25 who calls it the weaker law as compared to municipal law.

[9] The international Red Cross movement, the international pacifist movement, as well as the international workers movement are cases in point, on late nineteenth century political internationalism: Jürgen Osterhammel, *Die Verwandlung der Welt—Eine Geschichte des 19. Jahrhunderts* (Beck 2013) 726–34.

Hence, in the first decades of the twentieth century, at the peak of European nationalism, this domestic law analogy began to merge with pacifist and humanitarian sensibilities in the revolutionary postulate for a world organization, capable to ensure peace in and outside of Europe through a system of compulsory judicial settlement of international disputes and collective peace enforcement. More and more international lawyers engaged in lobbying for compulsory jurisdiction in international law within the Hague movement and the cosmopolitan interwar struggle to reform and bolster the PCIJ and the vision of a judicially controlled rule of law in international relations.[10] For the cosmopolitan avant-garde, a strong international judiciary meant more peace and justice for the world. A significant group of European, US, and Latin-American interwar international lawyers were inspired by this ideal aiming to reduce the institutional gap between highly developed national legal systems and international law. Theoretically, the main obstacle for them was the principle of national sovereignty. Progressive development, codification, institutionalization, and compulsory adjudication in international relations became common ideals of the cosmopolitan 'Geneva-spirit'.[11]

Josef L Kunz, a disciple of Hans Kelsen and one of the most influential international lawyers of the interwar period, described the political atmosphere of the early 1920s as follows:

> Away with power politics! No more secret diplomacy, no more entangling alliances, no longer the forever discredited balance of power, no more war! Democracy and the rule of international law will change the world.... In all the dealings of the League, international law was at the heart of the discussion. Idealistic approach, optimism, emphasis on international law created the 'Geneva atmosphere'.[12]

The movement from 'Faustrecht'—'the law of the jungle', where might is right—to international rule of law is identified with breaking away from a primitive, sovereignty-obsessed international law to a more developed international legal system.[13] This 1920s international rule of law project was a visionary one, aiming at a pacifist revolution of international politics, a project that has animated the brightest international law scholars of the twentieth century, such as Hans Kelsen and Hersch Lauterpacht. The shared enthusiasm for a changed, more peaceful world order prompted legal scholars in various countries, coming from different methodological backgrounds, to try and prepare, scholarly, the road to what they called 'a new international law'. The autonomy

---

[10] See on the US movement for compulsory jurisdiction: Benjamin A Coates, *Legalist Empire: International Law and American Foreign Relations in the Early Twentieth Century* (Oxford University Press 2016).

[11] James W Garner in 1931 sought to provide an overview of the reform movement in the 1920s: James W Garner, 'Le development et les tendencies récentes du droit international' (1931) 35 Recueil des Cours de l'Académie de Droit International 605.

[12] Josef L Kunz, 'The Swing of the Pendulum: From Overestimation to Underestimation of International Law' (1950) 44 American Journal of International Law 135, 136; on Kunz and the reform movement: Jochen von Bernstorff, *The Public International Law Theory of Hans Kelsen* (Cambridge University Press 2010).

[13] The theoretical criticism focused above all on Jellinek's doctrine of self-obligation allegedly representing a sovereignty-obsessed nineteenth-century international law: James L Brierly, 'Le fondement du caractère obligatoire du droit international public' (1928) 23 Recueil des Cours 463, 482–84; Hersch Lauterpacht, *The Function of Law in the International Community* (first published 1933, Garland 1973) 409–12.

of international law vis-à-vis its 'other'—which was in their view unregulated violence and war—required compulsory jurisdiction, a strong global institution as a guardian of world peace regulated by international law, sovereign equality understood as egalitarian rule-making and as equality before the law, and codification—conceptionalized as a replacement of vague customary rules of European eighteenth- and nineteenth-century origin by new regional and universal treaty law. As part of this movement figured scholars like Lammasch, Nippold, and Krabbe, from the prewar generation, and for the younger generation Kelsen, Scelle, Lauterpacht, Kunz, Schücking, Politis, Alvarez, Guerrero, and Brierly.[14]

The quest for formal equality of states aimed to protect small states against great power dominance in a new and more egalitarian international law. For Hans Kelsen, the principle of formal equality of states, which had only been imperfectly realized in the League institutions, was the essence of a juridical notion of international justice.[15] Originally, the quest for a more egalitarian international legal order had been an emancipatory project of Latin-American states and international lawyers from other so-called 'semi-peripheral' states (Russia, Ottoman Empire, China).[16] By the admission of a number of new states to the League and the introduction of a unanimity rule in both the League Assembly and the great power-dominated League Council, those smaller nations that had acquired the recognized attributes of statehood were granted the possibility to block decisions by the League organs. Nonetheless, as Lenin had famously put it, the oppressed and non-independent (colonized) nations of the earth in 1919 still amounted to 70 per cent of the world's population,[17] without membership status in the League. A minimal form of League supervision had only been institutionalized for the former colonies of Germany and the Ottoman Empire, which had become so-called 'League Mandates' under British or French control.[18]

An important battlefield between big and small states during the interwar period was the recognition of fully independent statehood and the struggle against intervention by European Powers, the United States, and Japan. Ironically most of these great power-interventions were justified as unilateral enforcement measures to restore legality after alleged breaches of international law by states in the periphery.[19] Even though the Western pacifist movement regarded the universal Kellog-Briand Pact from

---

[14] James W Garner, in The Hague lectures in 1931, sought to provide an overview of the reform movement in the 1920s: James W Garner, 'Le development et les tendencies récentes du droit international' (1931) 35 Recueil des Cours 605; on the reform movement von Bernstorff (n 12) introduction.

[15] Hans Kelsen, 'The Principle of Sovereign Equality of States as a Basis for International Organization' (1944) 53 Yale Law Journal 207.

[16] Arnulf Becker Lorca, *Mestizo International Law* (Cambridge University Press 2014).

[17] Wladimir I Lenin, 'Rede in der Aktivversammlung der Moskauer Organisation der KPR (B) vom 06.12.1920' quoted after Reinhart Koselleck (ed), *Geschichtliche Grundbegriffe Band 3* (Klett-Cotta 2004) 225.

[18] On the practice of the mandate system Susan Pedersen, *The Guardians: The League of Nations and the Crisis of Empire* (Oxford University Press 2015).

[19] Joseph Weiler speaks of an 'initial stratum of horizontal, dyadic, self-help through mechanisms of counter-measures, reprisals and the like': Joseph H H Weiler, 'The Geology of International Law—Governance, Democracy and Legitimacy' (2004) 64 Zeitschrift für ausländisches öffentliches Recht und Völkerrecht 547, 550; on such 'order related' justifications for the use of force employed primarily in the semi-periphery of the great powers Jochen von Bernstorff, 'The Use of Force in International Law before WWI: On Imperial Ordering and the Ontology of the Nation State' (2018) 29 European Journal for International Law 233..

1928 at least as a symbolic breakthrough, the reform movement considered it much less important for the fight against great power-interventionism. In its focus on 'war', the Briand Kellog Pact had not outlawed the most frequent form of military intervention into smaller states, so called 'measures short of war' and the declarations of both the United States and the United Kingdom had made clear that it had no bearing on forcible interventions in their respective zones of influence.[20] It was thus predominantly through membership in the League that small states had hoped to achieve full recognition, participation in law-making, and institutionalized protection against interventions by great powers.[21] After a policy change of the new Roosevelt administration, the Pan-American movement in 1933 eventually was able to formalize the non-intervention principle in the Montevideo Convention at least on the regional level, without, however, ruling out unilateral enforcement after alleged violations of international legal rules.[22] During the Second World War, blueprints for a new world order based on the ideals of the rule of law project proliferated. A strong world court with compulsory jurisdiction, including over acts of aggression and individual violations of international humanitarian law was at the centre of these reform proposals.[23]

2. Early critics of the international rule of law project

One of the first and influential authors who criticized the rule of law project in international relations as an imperial project was Carl Schmitt during the interwar period. For Schmitt international law inevitably represented the prevailing power structures in a particular historical context. The assumed dichotomy between law and power was wrong to begin with. Legal institutions inevitably received their meaning and telos from the underlying hegemonic political structures and therefore could never effectively restrain them.

Carl Schmitt, from the early 1930s onwards, revealed entrenched discursive distinctions at the heart of modern Western imperialism and its law. For Schmitt, both the European distinction between Christian and non-Christian states in the sixteenth century and the distinction between civilized and non-civilized (half civilized) peoples in the nineteenth century constituted discursive strategies to justify hegemonic colonial intervention and exploitation outside of the Western hemisphere. The mandate system of the League of Nations and the League Covenant which defined the further development of the former German and Turkish colonies as the 'sacred trust of civilisation' for

---

[20] Josef L Kunz, 'Der Kellog-Pakt' (1927) 9 Mitteilungen der Deutschen Gesellschaft für Völkerrecht 75.

[21] And indeed after Italy had invaded the League Member Abyssinia, the League Assembly condemned the act and at least initiated economic sanctions against Italy. But due to a lack of political will among the great powers, both the Italian invasion of 1935 and Japan's annexation of Manchuria in 1931 remained without dire consequences imposed on the aggressors by the League.

[22] The history of interwar international lawyers from Latin America and their role in the formation of central principles of modern international law has recently been intriguingly explored by Lorca (n 16) ch 9.

[23] Memorandum submitted by the Secretary General, 'Historical Survey of the Question of International Jurisdiction' (1949) UN Doc A/CN.4/7/Rev.I, 2–3; on the reform movement and the quest for compulsory jurisdiction: von Bernstorff (n 12) ch 6.

him was the 'most concise example of the legitimising function of the dichotomy of civilised and non-civilised nations, which is used by the civilised nations to give themselves the right to "educate", that is to control, the less "civilised" nations in the form of mandates, protectorates and colonies'.[24]

Schmitt, as a staunch critic of Anglo-American early twentieth century international political dominance, had an unmatched sense for the power of conceptual representations of violence and economic interests in the language of international law. According to Schmitt, in the interwar period, a number of basic doctrinal structures, advanced as elements of a 'universal' law, fostered economic hegemony and exploitation through major Western powers by establishing global capitalist structures; his critical position not accidently was in line with the German interwar and later Nazi-revisionist cause. His own anti-Versailles and anti-American agenda, however, led him to unmask the economic dimensions of late nineteenth and early twentieth century economic imperialism,[25] which after 1919—as Schmitt sensed much earlier than others—could no longer openly maintain the civilized/non-civilized dichotomy. American economic imperialism had in his view for that very reason transformed this distinction into the less controversial dichotomy between borrower states and creditor states, and continued to deeply intervene in the states belonging to the former category.[26] His often ironically toned writings 'admire' and critically detect how US-American discursive interventions manage to portray particularistic economic interests as the pursuit of cosmopolitan or universal values.[27] He acutely analyses how the political aim of creating and penetrating new markets, as well as the robust protection of US banks and investors operating in foreign markets, are being advanced and legitimized as international legal concepts and claims:[28]

> One of the overall most significant phenomena in the legal and intellectual life of mankind is the fact that those who possess true power are themselves able to inherently determine words and concepts.... Imperialism creates its own concepts.[29]

These lucid critical examinations of what can be called economic imperialism in the language of the rule of international law usually end with a lamentation on how unjust and detrimental the Western-dominated discursive status quo was for Germany after the First World War. Only after the rise to power of Nazism did Schmitt, the fervent anti-Semite, start to provide himself discursive justifications for Germany's new claim to regional and ultimately universal hegemony and nascent German hegemonic

---

[24] Carl Schmitt, 'Völkerrechtliche Formen des modernen Imperialismus' in Carl Schmitt, *Positionen und Begriffe, im Kampf mit Weimar—Genf—Versailles 1923-1939* (first published Hanseatische Verlagsanstalt 1940, Duncker & Humblot 1988) 164.

[25] Martti Koskenniemi, 'International Law as Political Theology: How to Read "Der Nomos der Erde"?' (2004) 11 Constellations 492, 494.

[26] Schmitt (n 24) 164.

[27] ibid 178.

[28] ibid 172–79.

[29] ibid 179.

geopolitical claims (theory of the 'Grossraum').[30] But Carl Schmitt was not the only critical voice that pinpointed the gap between the rule of law ideal and its concrete realization in the interwar period. In 1939, the famous international relations scholar Edward Hallet Carr in his book *The 20 Years' Crisis*, found: 'The utopia of 1919 was hollow and without substance .... Like all utopias which are institutionalised, the post-War utopia became the tool of vested interests and was perverted into a bulwark of the status quo'.[31] Moreover, authors who advocated the introduction of compulsory jurisdiction in the interwar period faced criticism by sceptical voices, which held that international law at the time was much too rudimentary or too fragile as a normative structure to allow for compulsory jurisdiction of international courts[32] in vital matters of international concern.[33]

3. The UN Charter and the international rule of law project

After the collapse of the League of Nations in the late 1930s, many international legal scholars projected their hopes on a new world organization. However, in light of the expectations of the interwar rule of law movement, the result of the Dumbarton Oaks and San Francisco Conferences were a huge disappointment. Regarding the status of international law within the UN, Cold War-New York proved to be an altogether different place than the higher-minded cosmopolitan Geneva of the 1920s. Born in a realistic spirit, the UN organs and the P5 from the very beginning had a relatively low esteem for legal issues. In the words of a contemporary observer:

> The strong emphasis which was placed upon international law in the League of Nations has been replaced by a subordinate role given to international law in the United Nations. Both the assembly of the League and the General Assembly of the

---

[30] Now was the time for Schmitt to put his unmatched insights into discursive legal strategies of hegemonic forces to the service of the 'new' Germany. Without doubt these later texts like many other of his publications aim—often in a problem-solving mode—at solidifying specific political acts and institutions (Nazi rule in Germany): Carl Schmitt, 'Der Führer schützt das Recht' in Carl Schmitt (n 24).

[31] Edward H Carr, *The Twenty Years' Crisis 1919–1939* (Macmillan and Co 1939) 287–89.

[32] Sir Alfred Zimmern, in his famous monograph *The League of Nations and the Rule of Law 1918–1935*, already influenced by the beginning 'realism' within the international legal discourse, revealed a sceptical attitude towards international law:

> There is in fact, whatever the names used in the books, no system of international law—and still less, of course, a code. What is to be found in the treatises is simply a collection of rules which, when looked at closely, appear to have been thrown together, or to have been accumulated, almost at haphazard. Many of them would seem to be more appropriately described as materials for the etiquette book for the conduct of sovereigns and their representatives than as elements of a true legal system.

In Alfred Zimmern, *The League of Nations and the Rule of Law 1918–1935* (first published 1936, rev 2nd edn 1939, Russel & Russel 1969) 98.

[33] Hans J Morgenthau, *Die internationale Rechtspflege, ihr Wesen und ihre Grenzen* (Noske 1929); Martti Koskenniemi, 'Morgenthau's Books on International Law with Kelsen' in George O Mazur (ed), *Twenty-Five Year Memorial Commemoration to the Life of Hans Morgenthau (1904–2004)* (Semenko Foundation 2006) 152–58; later, in a similar vein, Carr, in his famous book *The Twenty Years' Crisis, 1919–1939* (n 31) 186, noted, with reference to Lauterpacht, that the view of international law as a legal system that was institutionally completed by compulsory jurisdiction was another 'distinguished international lawyer's dream of an international community whose centre of gravity is in the administration of international justice'.

United Nations had, or has, six main committees. It is, perhaps, symbolic that in the League the first committee dealt with constitutional and legal questions and the last one with political problems, whereas in the United Nations, exactly to the contrary, the first committee handles security and political and the last committee legal questions. But even so the Legal committee plays no particular role.[34]

This sense of degradation of international law within the UN was widely shared in the 1940s and 50s.

Five years after the adoption of the Charter, the British attorney-general in a speech before the sixth committee deplored:

> Where legal questions are dealt with in a haphazard or ad hoc manner, sometimes ignored entirely or overlooked, sometimes deliberately brushed aside, there must be a danger that the institution will be subordinated to considerations of expediency. Only upholding the rule of law fosters objectivity.[35]

Moreover and like its predecessor, the newly established International Court of Justice (ICJ) did not introduce a general system of compulsory jurisdiction. Unlike modern Western legal systems in international law, the jurisdiction of the ICJ remained dependent on the consent of the respective parties to a conflict. And instead of introducing a general jurisdiction of the ICJ for individual violations of international humanitarian law, the victorious allies only established ad hoc tribunals in order to try German and Japanese war criminals (Nuremberg/Tokyo trials).

Nor did the UN become a strong and impartial global institution capable of enforcing world peace and respect for international law. From the 'peace through law' perspective, the most important failure of the UN approach to peaceful settlement of conflicts between states was the fact that participation in a settlement procedure—let alone the involvement of judicial institutions—was at no point obligatory for the parties to a conflict.[36] Chapter VI of the UN Charter refrained from establishing a compulsory system of dispute settlement, which envisaged clear procedural obligations imposed on the respective state parties. Neither the Security Council nor other principal UN organs were obliged to refer disputes of a predominantly legal nature to the ICJ. The role of the Security Council in the dispute settlement phase under Chapter VI was phrased in rather vague terms and includes a right to investigation (Art 34 UN Charter) as well as a right to make recommendations at any stage of the settlement process (Art 38 UN Charter). This illustrates that the only reference to the ICJ in Chapter VI that was accepted by the Allies in San Francisco was phrased in extremely weak and evasive language. According to Article 36(3) UN Charter, the Security Council in its recommendations to the parties of a dispute merely 'should also take into consideration that

---

[34] Josef L Kunz, 'The United Nations and the Rule of Law' in Josef L Kunz (ed), *The Changing Law of Nations, Essays on International Law* (Ohio State University Press 1968) 594.
[35] Quoted in ibid 598.
[36] Unless they had expressed their respective consent to the court's jurisdiction.

legal disputes should as a general rule be referred by the parties to the International Court of Justice, in accordance with the provisions of the Statute'. Binding enforcement measures against states or individuals under Articles 41 and 42 according to the Charter could be decided upon and implemented outside of any constraining legal criteria and preconditions, except for the conditions set out in Article 39 UN Charter, which requires a 'threat to peace' as a minimum requirement for Council enforcement measures under Chapter VII. Whether or not one of the parties to a conflict was responsible for a breach of international legal rules—according to the Charter—was not supposed to influence, let alone determine, the Security Council's handling of the issue. A mechanism for effective judicial control of Security Council action is missing. From the rule of law perspective, the whole collective security system of the Charter is thus coined by the deliberate absence of legal regulations and controls to the benefit of a wide and uncontrolled political discretion of the P5-controlled Security Council.[37]

As to the idea of formal equality of states and a legal system effectively protecting small states against great power dominance, the UN Charter could also not be considered a decisive step forward. While the Charter explicitly de-legitimized racial discrimination, it did not abolish colonialism. Instead, through the Trusteeship Council[38] it perpetuated to a considerable extent the quasi-colonial structures established by the League's Mandate system.[39] Nonetheless, the nineteenth- and early twentieth-century emancipatory project of Latin-American states and international lawyers from other 'semi-peripheral' states (Russia, Ottoman Empire, China) became a Third World project in the 1950s. Through the General Assembly (UNGA) and its resolutions, the UN, fifteen years after its foundation, provided the formal decolonization process with international political legitimacy. As is well known, the Charter in Article 2(1) enshrines sovereign equality as a foundational principle of the UN once independent statehood has been acquired. Within the most powerful organ of the UN, the Security Council, however, the Charter introduced a system of 'institutionalised inequality'.[40] By granting the veto-right to permanent members only and combining it with majority voting, the UN Charter added a historically unprecedented hierarchy between member states, which went way beyond the concept of permanent membership in the League of Nations. In the League Council, which acted under the unanimity rule, permanent members had the same voting rights as the non-permanent members. As a result, small member states had to be included in decision-making processes within the body because of procedural (voting-) equality. By contrast, decision-making processes in the UN Security Council are clearly dominated by the five permanent members. Informally, the P5 attempt to find a consensus on important decisions first. For

---

[37] Kelsen convincingly made this point in his UN Charter Commentary: Hans Kelsen, *The Law of the United Nations: A Critical Analysis of its Fundamental Problems* (2nd edn, The Lawbook Exchange 1951).

[38] For an overview: Andriy Y Melnyk, 'United Nations Trusteeship System' in *Max Planck Encyclopedia of Public International Law* (Online Edition <www.mpepil.com> last update April 2013) paras 1–41.

[39] On the role of the League and the UN in colonialism: Tania Tuori, *From League of Nations Mandates to Decolonization: A History of the Language of Rights in International Law* (University of Helsinki 2016).

[40] Benedict Kingsbury, 'Sovereignty and Inequality' (1998) 9 European Journal of International Law 599; Gerry Simpson, *Great Powers and Outlaw States—Unequal Sovereigns in the International Legal Order* (Cambridge University Press 2004).

whenever the P5 can agree on a draft resolution, it is not particularly difficult for them to pass a resolution in the Council, since in these cases the P5 only need to convince less than half of the remaining non-permanent members (four members today) to support the respective motion. Given that great powers usually can rely on smaller 'client states' whose governments economically or militarily depend on them, sufficient support within the Council is—in the vast majority of cases—available once all permanent members promote a draft resolution.[41] Another example of institutionalized inequality was the establishment of the World Bank and the International Monetary Fund (IMF) at the end of the Second World War, which were created outside of the United Nations Charter. The World Bank for instance was from the very beginning controlled by a small great power-dominated Board of Directors with permanent representation of countries with the largest numbers of shares and an immensely powerful secretariat ('management'), which is directed since 1944 exclusively by former high-ranking US-officials.[42]

All in all, in the area of collective security as well as in some other areas of high politics the rule of law ideal could only be realized to a very limited extent in the early UN era. Institutionalized inequality and the absence of independent judicial controls with regard to both rule-making and (enforcement) measures prevailed in the most powerful international institutions. Regarding the question of codification, the UN Charter in Article 13 at least assigned the General Assembly to initiate studies and make recommendations 'for the purpose of encouraging the progressive development of international law and its codification'. International lawyers committed to the international rule of law project could hope that codification in central areas of international relations would in the future substitute increasingly disputed norms of nineteenth century European custom and build new judicially controlled institutions.

II. The rule of law project in the post-1990s era

In Walter Benjamin's famous essay on the Philosophy of History, the Angel of History is propelled into the future by a storm with his face turned backwards, facing the past as a catastrophe that keeps piling ruins upon ruins, unable to stay and to awaken the dead. In retrospect, it might be difficult to understand why the post-Cold War period has been regarded by many international lawyers and political scientists as the dawn of cosmopolitism under benevolent and humane Western leadership or even more preposterous as the 'end of history' (Fukuyama). Especially since, in more general terms, the historical events after 1990, which included at least one fully fledged genocide (Rwanda), dozens of bloody civil wars with ever more frequent usage of child soldiers,

---

[41] I take this term from Mohammed Bedjaoui, *Towards a New International Economic Order* (Homes & Meier Publishers 1979) 147.

[42] International Bank for Reconstruction and Development Articles of Agreement (as amended effective 27 June 2012): Art V s 3(a)(ii), Art V 3(b), Sch A; a current critique of Northern dominance in IFIs: Bhupinder S Chimni, 'International Institutions Today: An Imperial Global State in the Making' (2004) 15 European Journal of International Law 1, 20.

the carnage and so-called 'ethnic cleansings' during the break-up of Yugoslavia, a number of illegal military interventions by the two super powers, numerous disastrous famines in Africa and elsewhere, a dramatic acceleration of climate change, the explosion of slum dwellings in the mega cities of the Global South without adequate water, sanitation, and health care, a global HIV epidemic—altogether leading to a combined death toll of more than 20 million human beings, do not in any way seem to justify remembering this era as a bright chapter in the history of mankind. To be fair, the contemporaries in 1990 obviously could not foresee these developments and much of the unremitting enthusiasm within the United States and European intellectual elites before and after the new millennium certainly was induced by the assumed end of the direct nuclear stand-off between the United States and the Soviet Union. In November 1989, eight days after the fall of the Berlin Wall, the UNGA, 'convinced of the need to strengthen the rule of law in international relations' launched the 'United Nations Decade of International Law'.[43] Interestingly and in a way telling was, however, that the decade was initiated by the Non Aligned Movement (NAM) and not a Western project.[44] Despite its vague use of the rule of law concept,[45] it focused on the main elements of the classic interwar international rule of law project, including peaceful settlement of disputes, progressive development of international law, and measures to strengthen the ICJ. Western support for this NAM-initiative was mainly symbolic or lukewarm at best. Be that as it may, a number of new sectorial legal and institutional projects were introduced in the 1990s, which made many international lawyers dream of a brighter future. The creation of new specialized international courts and tribunals in particular nourished the hope for a new era of the international rule of law.

1. Compulsory jurisdiction

At least with respect to judicial enforcement, the last twenty-five years were a time of important institutional developments in selected areas of international law. While the realization of a unified international legal order with compulsory jurisdiction remained an unattained dream up until today, the last twenty-five years have brought about the cherished establishment of ever more sophisticated issue-related international regimes that rely on their own mechanisms of adjudication and enforcement.[46] In the fields of international economic law, international criminal law, and the law of the sea, relatively stable institutions have been established by international law together with sectoral systems of compulsory jurisdiction. As I attempt to show, these new institutions from a rule of law perspective suffer from a double asymmetry, which mirrors the hegemonic

---

[43] UN GA A/RES/44/23.

[44] UN GA A/44/191.

[45] On the political wrangling about the 'Decade of international law', Martti Koskenniemi, 'The Politics of International Law—20 Years Later' (1990) 20 European Journal of International Law 7.

[46] Heike Krieger and Georg Nolte in the Introduction point out to yet another challenge for the judicial enforcement of international law, which lies in the reluctance to accept judicial proceedings based on the re-emphasis of sovereignty: Krieger and Nolte (n 2) 14.

constellations in which they were created: firstly, because of their selective island-like realization, and secondly, as to their concrete modes of operation.

Regarding the problem of selective realization, it must be added that the foundation of sectorial adjudication mechanisms since 1990 took place in the absence of a hierarchical system of courts which judicially guarantees the systemic unity of international law as a legal system. Instead of the aspired world state structures regulated by law and controlled by a world court, as a consequence we now face the challenges of issue-related fragmentation in an institutionally decentralized legal order, where individual regimes such as the WTO, the international investment protection regime, regional human rights instruments, and the international criminal law regime have their own independent courts and tribunals. International law thus has brought about compulsory adjudication within individual regimes, but these partial regimes are not tied together into a comprehensive legal system institutionalized through centralized courts. These developments have led to heated debates about conflicts between norms from within and outside specific legal regimes and about the role of judges in protecting or endangering the 'unity' of the international legal system.[47]

Not surprisingly, the most effective tribunals in terms of the number of decisions taken and enforced were those implementing international economic law regimes, such as the WTO dispute settlement body and the ad hoc tribunals created by the explosion of bilateral investment treaties (BITs) in the 1990s. These regimes have helped to enforce the interests of powerful globally operating economic actors by establishing transnational markets and a highly effective global regime of property protection at the cost of domestic and local interests in regulating economic activities. From a rule of law perspective, one of the main problems of these pockets of compulsory jurisdiction is that the new tribunals recruit their judges and arbitrators from a small circle of highly specialized regime experts. Human rights lawyers do not end up in WTO panels. You need to be a recognized international trade lawyer to be appointed for a judicial position in this regime. The same holds true to a greater or lesser extent for any other specialized international legal regime. It follows that the likelihood of judges and arbitrators that have for many years been socialized as experts in one particular regime not having internalized the biases and values propagated by this particular 'epistemic community'[48] is not very high. These circumstances taken together can lead to a certain individual or collective bias in favour of the rules of that regime, which has erected the judicial mechanism; a bias which—in the absence of a higher layer of judicial bodies with cross-sectoral legal expertise—usually cannot be corrected. But why could this be a problem? Judicial decisions in these regimes may have an enormous influence on various other areas of life, hereby colliding with other values, norms, and international

---

[47] Martti Koskenniemi, 'Fragmentation of International Law: Difficulties Arising from the Diversification and Expansion of International Law: Report of the Study Group of the International Law Commission' (13 April 2006) UN Doc A/CN.4/L.682, para 479.

[48] On the notion of 'epistemic communities' coined by Haas and the issue of interpretation in international law: Michael Waibel, 'Interpretive Communities in international law' in Andrea Bianchi, Daniel Peat, and Matthew Windsor (eds), *Interpretation in International Law* (Oxford University Press 2015) 147.

legal rules. All these other potentially colliding societal interests protected by inter-national and domestic legal norms then tend to be sacrificed on the altar of powerful specialized regimes leading to a process of incremental judicial 'colonisation' of legal regimes with weaker enforcement mechanisms.[49] To trust in constraining practical routines of judicial decision-making generally seems much less warranted in a frag-mented judicial landscape than in a centralized and hierarchical court system.[50]

Most international courts and tribunals also operate in the absence of judicial hierarchies, which guarantee that each decision of a tribunal can be appealed and controlled by at least one subordinated judicial body.[51] In international investment ar-bitration, many decisions are not even publicized, let alone controlled by appeal bodies. Moreover, a number of substantive rules agreed upon in the 1990s and enforced by these highly effective sectorial judicial mechanisms have come under severe criticism of representing in a one-sided manner the interests of capital exporting states, which were in a hegemonic economic and political position after the end of the Cold War.[52] Contested regimes from this angle are the intellectual property rights regime (TRIPS), which arguably for years prevented access of millions of HIV patients to affordable life-saving antiretroviral drugs in poor countries, and the regime of—by now over 3,000—BITs.[53]

It is often overlooked that within a fragmented international judicial system par-ticular rule of law pockets can as a result cancel out legal developments in other subareas of international law. Institutional breakthroughs in one area obstruct rule of law aspirations in another area of international law. International human rights lawyers still advocate an international tribunal adjudicating human rights abuses by transnational corporations and enforceable state obligations to regulate foreign in-vestors, while international investment law in the meantime has erected a highly ef-ficient rule of law system in which transnational corporations can directly challenge these state regulations required by human rights law. The assumption that by creating more and more sectoral rule of law pockets there will one day be a universal rule of law may thus be false altogether. And even if all of these sectoral courts and tribunals

---

[49] Discussing this issue: Dirk Pulkowski, *The Law and Politics of International Regime Conflict* (Oxford University Press 2014) 36; on the 'asymmetric' rule of law in international relations: Jochen von Bernstorff, 'Reflections on the Asymmetric Rule of Law in International Relations' in James Crawford and Sarah Nouwen (eds), *Select Proceedings of the European Society of International Law*, vol 3 (Hart Publishing 2012) 381.

[50] Jason Beckett, 'Fragmentation, Openness and Hegemony: Adjudication and the WTO' in Meredith K Lewis and Susy Frankel (eds), *International Economic Law and National Autonomy* (Cambridge University Press 2010) 54–56; somewhat less sceptical: Joost Pauwelyn, *Conflict of Norms in Public International Law: How WTO-Law relates to other Rules of International Law* (Cambridge University Press 2003) 242–43; and Andreas Paulus, 'Subsidiarity, Fragmentation and Democracy: Towards the Demise of General International Law?' in Tomer Broude and Yuval Shany (eds), *The Shifting Allocation of Authority in International Law: Considering Sovereignty, Supremacy and Subsidiarity* (Hart Publishing 2008) 210; also promoting systemic integration but in a slightly more sceptical tone: Armin von Bogdandy and Ingo Venzke, *In wessen Namen?* (Suhrkamp 2014) 258–64; on various and potentially conflicting 'objectives' of international courts in this context Andreas Follesdal, 'Curb, Channel and Coordinate: The Constitutionalism of International Courts and Tribunals' in Geert De Baere and Jan Wouters (eds), *The Contribution of International and Supranational Courts to the Rule of Law* (Elgar Publishing 2015).

[51] For international investment law: Gus van Harten, *Investment Treaty Arbitration and Public Law* (Oxford University Press 2007).

[52] Chimni (n 42) 1.

[53] Holger Hestermeyer, *Human Rights and the WTO* (Oxford University Press 2008).

became 'other-regarding'[54] institutions, taking into account the jurisprudence of other courts, the multiplication of judicial institutions weakens the position of the ICJ and the overall quest for compulsory jurisdiction. Governments generally have particular international interests which they would like to enforce judicially, and others where they tend to avoid judicial proceedings. Whenever the interest in enforcing some interests judicially prevails over the issue of avoiding disputes in other areas, these governments would generally consider recognizing the jurisdiction of the ICJ. If for instance, a state was interested in having all its law of the sea disputes decided by an international court, it would—in the absence of specialized tribunals—in the past have seriously considered recognizing the jurisdiction of the ICJ for all legal disputes. After the creation of the Law of the Sea Tribunal in Hamburg in 1996, this state can now opt for using this specialized tribunal without having to accept the jurisdiction of the ICJ. The enhanced competition as well as the ensuing pick-and-choose options initiated by the foundation of new sectorial courts and tribunals further weaken the project of compulsory jurisdiction in international relations and ultimately significantly reduce the role of the ICJ. In the decade of 1950–59, the ICJ had to decide thirty-five cases (including advisory opinions) compared to thirty-eight cases in the decade of 1990–99, while the number of UN member states almost tripled in the thirty-year period lying between these two decades.[55]

The shadow of hegemony not only plagues courts and tribunals in international economic law, it also haunts the impressive institutional innovations in the field of international criminal responsibility. In 1993, it was the UN Security Council that, on a doubtful legal basis, established an ad hoc International Criminal Tribunal for the Former Yugoslavia (ICTY) and in 1994 an International Criminal Tribunal for Rwanda (ICTR).[56] Both tribunals through their judgments contributed significantly to the development of international humanitarian law and its criminal enforcement in these post-conflict societies, while their role in healing or deepening the wounds of a society after the experience of genocidal violence remains disputed. Both tribunals and their judicial practice as precursors paved the way for the creation of the statute of the International Criminal Court (ICC) in Rome in 1998. More than any other judicial institution created after the Cold War, the foundation of ICC encapsulated the hope for an international legal order based on individual criminal responsibility, which would deter and if necessary punish inhuman acts committed by state agents in times of conflict. Almost twenty years after the adoption of the Rome Statute, the Court only has

---

[54] Eyal Benvenisti, 'Community Interests in International Adjudication' in Eyal Benvenisti and Georg Nolte (eds), *Community Obligations in International Law* (Oxford University Press, 2018), 70; Yuval Shany, 'One Law to Rule Them All: Should International Courts Be Viewed as Guardians of Procedural Order and Legal Uniformity?' in Ole K Fauchald and André Nollkaemper (eds), *The Practice of International and National Courts and the (De-)Fragmentation of International Law* (Hart Publishing 2012) 15.

[55] On the early years of the Court and the distrust among Third World countries created by the South West Africa case in the 1960s and 70s leading to a decrease in support for the Court during this time: Ingo Venzke, 'The ICJ and the South West Africa Cases' in Jochen von Bernstorff and Philipp Dann (eds), *The Battle for International Law in the Decolonization Era* (Cambridge University Press, forthcoming).

[56] UNSC Res 827 (25 May 1993) UN Doc S/RES/827 (establishing the ICTY); UNSC Res 955 (8 November 1994) UN Doc S/RES/955 (establishing the ICTR).

tried and convicted a handful of perpetrators, and violations of international humanitarian law are occurring at record-high levels. Moreover, while three of the five permanent members have not ratified the statute, the Security Council under the Rome
Statute continues to enjoy far-reaching competencies in questions of instigating and
deferring specific criminal prosecutions. This unfortunately also holds true for the
hard fought so-called 'Kampala compromise' from 2011[57] regarding the prosecution
of the crime of aggression under the statute, which allows the great power-dominated
UN Security Council to block investigations into alleged violations of the crime of
aggression.[58]

Continuous criticism that the ICC Statute through the position of the Security
Council privileged great powers over smaller states and the Court's practice of almost exclusively prosecuting African officials and rebels have led to a severe crisis of
the Court, with more and more states contemplating and realizing a withdrawal from
the institution.[59] In its 'Withdrawal Strategy Document' from 2017, the African Union
states that:

> [A] growing number of stakeholders have begun to see these patterns of only pursuing
> African cases being reflective of selectivity and inequality.... Many arguments have
> been made regarding the systemic imbalance in international decision-making pro-
> cesses. The inherent politics of such processes result in unreliable application of the
> rule of law.[60]

Even though international criminal law has advanced enormously over the last twenty
years through the two UN ad hoc tribunals and the Rome Statute, the problem of the
'privilegium odiosum' (Hans Kelsen) created through the asymmetrical application
of the existing rules remains a fundamental one. Reacting to the Nuremberg trials in
the late 1940s both Kelsen and Morgenthau had criticized that the principle of sovereign equality had not been respected in the creation of the tribunal, insisting that

---

[57] Critical of the qualification of the breach of the *ius ad bellum*: Andreas Paulus, 'Second Thoughts on the
Crime of Aggression' (2009) 20 European Journal of International Law 117, 1121.

[58] In general, the 'determination of an act of aggression by an organ outside the Court shall be without prejudice
to the Court's own findings under this Statute', ICC Review Conference, Resolution RC/Res.6, Amendments to the
Rome Statute of the International Criminal Court on the crime of aggression (11 June 2010) Art 15bis (9). Hence,
the Court is not bound by the assessment of the UN Security Council, however, the UN Security Council can always block the investigation, ICC Review Conference, Resolution RC/Res.6, Amendments to the Rome Statute of
the International Criminal Court on the crime of aggression (11 June 2010) Art 15bis (8).

[59] The United States and Israel (both 2002) as well as Sudan (2008) declared that, despite their signature, they
no longer intend to become a party to the Rome Statute; Burundi has notified its withdrawal from the Rome Statute
on 27 October 2016 (see Depositary Notification C.N.805.2016.TREATIES-XVIII.10); Russia on 30 November
2016 declared that it has no intention to become a party after signing the Statute in 2000; South Africa (Depositary
Notification C.N.786.2016.TREATIES-XVIII.10) and The Gambia (Depositary Notification C.N.862.2016.
TREATIES-XVIII.10) both notified a withdrawal declaration, which they declared null and void in late 2016 after
a change of government (The Gambia) and a constitutional court ruling (South Africa), respectively; the African
Union has mandated its Open Ended Ministerial Committee of Foreign Ministers in 2016 to develop a comprehen-
sive strategy on collective withdrawal from the ICC: Assembly/AU/Dec.590 (XXVI) para 10 (iv), adopted in 2017.

[60] The original documents of the African Union decisions are not available at the time of writing. A previously
circulated draft is available at <www.hrw.org/sites/default/files/supporting_resources/icc_withdrawal_strategy_
jan._2017.pdf> accessed 28 April 2017.

the exclusion of Allied war crimes and axis power judges unnecessarily exposed the tribunal to the charge of 'victor's justice'.[61] The problem of inequality—albeit in a less dramatic form—also seems to haunt the ICC. As long as it seems politically unimaginable or even structurally impossible for the ICC to indict leaders of the most powerful nations for waging illegal aggression or breaches of international humanitarian law, the promise of the rule of law in and through international criminal law will remain unfulfilled.[62]

2. Rule-based collective security

Undeniably, the fall of the Iron Curtain did breathe new life into the practice of the UN Security Council. While the legal infrastructure on which the Council operated remained unaltered, the fact that the United States, the USSR (Russian Federation after 1994), and China could agree on a number of resolutions under Chapter VII of the Charter created high expectations among scholarly observers. For almost fifty years, inaction of the Council had been considered a major problem, now the number of resolutions adopted in the Norwegian room in the UN headquarters exploded.[63] Not only did the Security Council mandate the US-led war to liberate Kuwait in 1990 after its annexation by Iraq. The Council also developed a practice of occasionally drastic economic sanctions against states whose governments had acted in ways which had been considered a breach of, or threat to, peace by a majority of the fifteen Security Council members. An ever more complex and non-transparent sanction bureaucracy within the Council was established, entrusted also to impose and administer sanctions against individuals, such as visa bans and asset freezes against individuals (targeted sanctions).[64] The breathtaking surge of—at times disturbing—activities such as the Council's

---

[61] Jochen von Bernstorff, 'Peace and Global Justice through Prosecuting the Crime of Aggression? Kelsen and Morgenthau on the Nuremberg Trials and the International Judicial Function' in D A Jeremy Telman (ed), *Hans Kelsen in America—Selective Affinities and the Mysteries of Academic Influence* (Springer 2016).

[62] The jurisdiction of the Court over the crime of aggression is further limited by the two following provisions of the 'Kampala compromise': ICC Review Conference, Resolution RC/Res.6, Amendments to the Rome Statute of the International Criminal Court on the crime of aggression (11 June 2010) Art 15bis (4):

> The Court may, in accordance with article 12, exercise jurisdiction over a crime of aggression, arising from an act of aggression committed by a State Party, unless that State Party has previously declared that it does not accept such jurisdiction by lodging a declaration with the Registrar. The withdrawal of such a declaration may be effected at any time and shall be considered by the State Party within three years;

ICC Review Conference, Resolution RC/Res.6, Amendments to the Rome Statute of the International Criminal Court on the crime of aggression (11 June 2010) Art 15bis (5):

> In respect of a State that is not a party to this Statute, the Court shall not exercise its jurisdiction over the crime of aggression when committed by that State's nationals or on its territory.

[63] The total number of Security Council Resolutions adopted until 1989 (646 Resolutions) almost doubled in the 1990s alone (1284 Resolutions) and has since then risen up to 2349 Resolutions (as of March 2017).

[64] On targeted/smart sanctions: David Cortright, George A Lopez, and Linda Gerber-Stellingwerf, 'The Sanctions Era: Themes and Trends in UN Security Council Sanctions since 1990' in Vaughan Lowe, Adam Roberts, Jennifer Welsh, and Dominik Zaum (eds), *The United Nations Security Council and War—The Evolution of Thought and Practice since 1945* (Oxford University Press 2008); especially in the light of the *Kadi* judgment: Frederik Stenhammar, 'United Nations Targeted Sanctions, the International Rule of Law and the European Court of Justice's Judgment in *Kadi* and *al-Barakaat*' (2010) 79 Nordic Journal of International Law 113.

post-1991 Iraq economic sanction regime,[65] the merciless application of which was accused of having caused the death of hundreds of thousands of Iraqi civilians,[66] took place in an institutional setting clearly dominated by only five governments and infamous for its lack of public deliberation and accountability, let alone judicial controls. It was not till then that the failure to introduce rule of law standards for Security Council action at Dumbarton Oaks and San Francisco became fully apparent. The Council also started to engage in highly disputed general legislative activities with binding effect under Chapter VII of the Charter.[67] Not surprisingly, the beginning of the new millennium witnessed the first broader scholarly debate since the early 1950s on the need to introduce rule of law standards for the UN Security Council. And somewhat significantly, the European Court of Justice eventually had to remind the Security Council that targeted sanctions against individuals without any fair trial standards contradict fundamental rule of law standards.[68] Various subsequent initiatives of non-permanent members to reform the rules of procedure of the organ and to introduce ombudsman-structures for targeted sanctions[69] met with little or mixed success, at best.

To make things worse, in particular Western states illegally side-lined the Security Council because the organ was unwilling to legitimize their military interventions.[70] Notorious examples are the NATO intervention in Kosovo in 1999 and the US-led Iraq intervention in 2003. More recently in 2013, the Russian Federation did not shy away from the annexation of the Crimean Peninsula in Ukraine while blocking any critical Security Council action with its veto powers. Even when collective military action had been mandated under a Chapter VII resolution, as in the case of the Libyan civil war in 2011, the absence of efficient controls of the correct implementation of the Security Council resolutions became an issue of international concern. During its bombing campaign in Libya, NATO stood accused of acting outside the mandate set out in the respective resolution when unilaterally interpreting the authorization 'to protect civilians' as a right to a fully fledged military regime change.[71] Despite vehement protests from Russia, China, the African Union, and several countries form Latin America, no procedure within the UN existed to stop or to review the limits of an initially mandated military intervention against the will of one of the permanent Security Council members. The

---

[65] Initiating the sanction regime: UNSC Res 661 (6 August 1990) UN Doc S/RES/661 and UNSC Res 687 (3 April 1991) UN Doc S/RES/687 as well as UNSC Res 986 (14 April 1995) UN Doc S/RES/986 establishing the 'Oil-for-Food Programme'.

[66] Concluding that there has been an excess death toll of at least 227,000 children up to 1998 alone: Richard Garfield, *Morbidity and Mortality among Iraqi Children from 1990 through 1998: Assessing the Impact of the Gulf War and Economic Sanctions* (1999) <http://reliefweb.int/sites/reliefweb.int/files/resources/A2E2603E5DC88A4685256825005F211D-garfie17.pdf> accessed 28 April 2017.

[67] On these legislative resolutions in the field of counter-proliferation: Michael Bothe, 'Weapons of Mass Destruction, Counter-Proliferation' MPEPIL (n 38); generally: Stefan Talmon, 'The UN Security Council as World Legislative' (2005) 99 American Journal of International Law 175.

[68] Joined Cases C-402/05 P and C-415/05 P *Kadi et al v Council of the European Union* et al [2008] ECR I-06351.

[69] See especially the 'Office of the Ombudsperson to the ISIL (Daesh) and Al-Qaida Sanctions Committee' originally established by UNSC Res 1904 (17 December 2009) UN Doc S/RES/1904, whose mandate was later extended on different occasions; see also the 'Focal Point for De-Listing' established through UNSC Res 1730 (19 December 2006) UN Doc S/RES/1730.

[70] Also highlighting the problems of unilateral interventions and a 'more liberal, rather permissive attitude' regarding the use of force: Krieger and Nolte (n 2).

[71] UNSC Res 1973 (17 March 2011) UN Doc S/RES/1973.

spectacular inactivity of the Council two years later in the evolving Syrian tragedy was a direct political consequence of the divisive way in which the Libya resolution had been implemented in the absence of a possibility to review and correct a once allotted UN authorization to use military force. All of these problems arise out of the fatal combination of selective veto powers and non-existing judicial controls. It should be mentioned in this context that over the last twenty-five years the *nemo iudex in re sua* principle, which is one of the very few classic rule of law principles, that at least for Chapter VI resolutions had been codified in the UN Charter (Art 27(3)), was constantly violated in Security Council practice.[72] Not only under Chapter VII but also under Chapter VI did permanent members regularly veto resolutions on conflicts in which they were a party.[73]

Another ongoing rule of law-related issue during the last twenty-five years was the question of abusive conduct of UN peacekeeping personnel during UN mandated peacekeeping missions. Ever more frequent cases of sexual exploitation and corruption as well as the creation of a cholera epidemic by UN staff became issues of international concern.[74] Due to immunity rules, such conduct usually can only be tried in domestic courts in exceptional cases. Again, the question of legal responsibility for acts of UN organs and the lack of adequate judicial procedures led to heated reform debates so far without tangible legal results. Hence, what began as a hopeful new era of collective security in the early 1990s turned into a veritable rule of law crisis of the Security Council, which increasingly paralyses the whole UN Charter system of collective security.[75] Through selective veto powers, ill-defined competencies, and implementation procedures as well as lacking administrative and judicial controls, the legal structures of the Security Council, from a rule of law perspective, unfortunately still in many respects resemble those of an oligarchic 'Polizeistaat' run by a cabinet, which is steered by a handful of hard-headed super-ministers and their private enforcement machineries.

3. Sovereign equality and codification

In terms of sovereign equality between small and big states, the United Nations system with its programmes, funds, and specialized agencies at first sight did not undergo significant changes of its underlying legal infrastructure. While the central organs of the International Financial Institutions (IFIs) are still dominated by the big capital exporting

---

[72] Art 27(3) UN Charter reads as follows: 'Decisions of the Security Council on all other matters shall be made by an affirmative vote of nine members including the concurring votes of the permanent members; provided that, in decisions under Chapter VI, and under paragraph 3 of Article 52, a party to a dispute shall abstain from voting'.

[73] With an in-depth analysis of Security Council practice since 1945: Enrico Milano, 'Russia's Veto in the Security Council: Whither the Duty to Abstain under Art. 27(3) UN Charter' (2015) 75 Zeitschrift für ausländisches öffentliches Recht und Völkerrecht 215; on Russia and international law: Wolfgang Graf Vitzthum, 'Russland und das Völkerrecht' (2016) 54 Archiv des Völkerrechts 239.

[74] Jan Klabbers, 'The EJIL Foreword: The Transformation of International Organizations Law' (2015) 26 European Journal of International Law 9.

[75] On the debates to institutionalize procedural and substantive controls of IO-action: Jochen von Bernstorff, 'Procedures of Decision-Making and the Role of Law in International Organizations' in Armin von Bogdandy, Rüdiger Wolfrum, Jochen von Bernstorff, Philipp Dann, and Matthias Goldmann (eds), *The Exercise of Public Authority by International Institutions* (Springer 2010) 777.

nations, those institutions which are more closely integrated in the UN system continue to work with plenary organs based on the one-state-one-vote basis. As became obvious over the last twenty-five years, those organizational settings, in which states from the Global South could mobilize relatively stable majorities have increasingly been side-lined and replaced by new institutions. While the UN General Assembly, Economic and Social Council (ECOSOC), and Conference on Trade and Development (UNCTAD) during the first thirty years after the Second World War had developed into relevant global agenda- and standard setters, they had lost this role by the end of the century. Western states used the post-1990s era not only to bolster the influence of the IFI's but also to create new institutions in line with their policy preferences, such as the WTO with its special agreements. Due to the debt crisis Third World countries became com-pletely dependent on the World Bank and the IMF, which at the same time gave powerful Western states an unprecedented leverage to influence economic and social policies in these countries.[76] Central components of these IFI-administered reforms were dramatic cuts in public spending on social welfare, agriculture, education, and health systems, the transformation of basic public infrastructure into private enterprises, and the opening of domestic markets, including agriculture, for foreign investment.

With the aim to move decision-making away from the UN General Assembly, as a one-state-one-vote plenary organ, the big industrialized nations also empowered exclu-sive informal cooperation mechanisms like the G8/G7, the Organisation for Economic Cooperation and Development (OECD), or the Basel Committee to coordinate economy-related policies between the strongest economies.[77] Scholars in the 1950s and 60s had argued that the international legal order after formal decolonization ultimately had become truly universal through 'democratic' institutions like the UNGA. After 1990, in many ways the international institutional order went back to the nineteenth century European model of cooperation between ministerial experts from the great European powers in order to satisfy the assumed regulatory needs of a globalizing economy. The ini-tial nineteenth century setup and inherent logic of international organizations in terms of their exclusiveness and regulatory functions is often much closer to the Basel Committee or the G8/G7 than Anne-Marie Slaughter seemed to imply when she cherished 'govern-ment networks' as the 'New World Order' at the beginning of the new millennium.[78] Not accidently, Third World populations—like in the heydays of European imperialism—have no or little voice in these institutions, which until today direct the global economy.

Another similarity with nineteenth-century legal structures is the post-1980s return of bilateralism in international treaty-making, as the field of investment protection can exemplify. Apart from some novel forms of multilateral treaty-making in international environmental law and new specific conventions *inter alia* in the field of international humanitarian law, human rights, and disarmament, it is not unfair to say that the last

---

[76] On structural adjustment policies: Phillip Dann, *Entwicklungsverwaltungsrecht* (Mohr Siebeck 2012).

[77] On strategic institutional choices of powerful states when it comes to creating new institutions and leaving old ones: Eyal Benvenisti and George W Downs, 'The Empire's New Clothes: Political Economy and the Fragmentation of International Law' (2007) 60 Stanford Law Review 595.

[78] Anne-Marie Slaughter, *A New World Order* (Princeton University Press 2004).

twenty-five years were a rather dark era for the project of codification. Compared to the major codification projects of the 1960s, 70s, and 80s, including the Vienna Convention on the Law of Treaties,[79] the two principal UN Human Rights Covenants, the Vienna Conventions on Diplomatic and Consular Relations, the UN Convention on the Law of the Sea,[80] and the Additional Protocols to the Geneva Conventions, the post-Cold War era saw a gradual demise of the codification project. Codification came with equal participation of all states, an aspect of formal rule-making not always to the liking of states in a hegemonic political and military position. Despite new and unprecedented opportunities for rule-making after the end of the bloc confrontation, the codification results of this period are meagre, to put it mildly. Significantly, the International Law Commission in the field of state responsibility in 2001 itself shied away from initiating or recommending a formalized codification process for the end product of more than thirty years of deliberations within the Commission.[81]

Little is left of the enthusiasm that once moved the codification project. The widely held interwar and post-Second World War conviction, according to which 'codification' ultimately remains indistinguishable from progressive development, and that codification also has a role to play in areas where states do not fully agree, has obviously vanished.[82] In an interwar discussion within the League of Nations Expert Committee on Codification, a British representative articulated the—by now lost—spirit of the codification movement as follows:

> The Committee would be making a mistake if it were to choose a subject of secondary importance at a moment when the world was calling for the establishment of the Rule of Law in the Place of the Rule of Force. The Committee would expose itself to the criticism of having been superficial, and of having wasted its time, when its chief object should have been to solve certain major problems of international law.[83]

Today, certainly, many issues of major international concern, such as the liability and taxation of transnational enterprises, mass migration, recognition of governments, and non-intervention into civil wars as well as the use of force against non-state actors amongst many others would still benefit from formalized universal rules.[84] Since the 1990s, however, non-binding 'law' in many areas of international concern has replaced

---

[79] On this codification project and the Third World: Anna Krueger, 'Sources' in Bernstorff and Dann (n 55).

[80] On this process and ambitious projects of redistribution, see Surabhi Ranganathan, 'The Battle for the Law of the Sea' in Bernstorff and Dann (n 55).

[81] On the heyday of the ILC in the 1950s and 60s, considering the 1990s as a 'successful' phase because of the completion of the works on the Articles on State Responsibility: Georg Nolte, 'The International Law Commission Facing the Second Decade of the Twenty-First Century' in Ulrich Fastenrath, Rudolf Geiger, Daniel-Erasmus Khan, Andreas Paulus, Sabine von Schorlemer, and Christoph Vedder (eds), *From Bilateralism to Community Interest* (Oxford University Press 2011).

[82] H Lauterpacht managed to cultivate this interwar spirit in the young post-Second World War ILC: Hersch Lauterpacht, 'Survey of International Law in Relation to the Work of the Codification of the International Law Commission' UN Doc A/CN.4/1/Rev. 1 (1949) reprinted in Elihu Lauterpacht (ed), *International Law—Being the Collected Papers of Hersch Lauterpacht*, vol I 'The General Works' (Cambridge University Press 1970) 445.

[83] ibid 461–62.

[84] Less critical of soft law: Christian Tomuschat, 'The International Law Commission—An Outdated Institution?' (2006) 49 German Yearbook of International Law 77; Nolte (n 81) 781.

binding rule-making.[85] Multilateral treaty instruments in general have been seen with growing frequency as too rigid and resistant to change in order to be able to provide adequate guidance to global regulatory developments. Treaties, however, do not only secure formal equality in the creation and application of global rules, they also carry an unlimited potential for experimentation with new forms of participation and transparent politicization as well as for enhanced flexibility without entirely relinquishing the achievement of formal equality.[86] By contrast, informal regimes and custom in practice often favour strong actors who, in looser unions with self-chosen partners, secure and further expand their technological, economic, and scientific lead by creating new standards and re-interpreting existing ones.[87]

Hopefully my account of the accelerated decay of the international rule of law project in international relations over the last twenty-five years will turn out to be premature. This early twentieth century project, which could have become a truly universal project after formal decolonization, had instead been stalled by powerful Western states in an effort to consolidate a hegemonic political and economic position after the fall of the Eastern bloc. As I attempted to demonstrate in this contribution, these years turned out to be a difficult era for the international rule of law project. Almost unrecognizable in its original contours it today lies in ruins before us. Observers thought that the Cold War bloc-confrontation was the main obstacle for the realization of the rule of law project in international relations. In retrospect, however, post-1980s Western hegemony eventually turned out to be equally problematic if not worse for the idea of the rule of law in international relations. The international rule of law project, with its quest for compulsory jurisdiction, rule-based collective security, formal equality in formalized law-making (codification), and institutionalized implementation originated in the interwar period and culminated in far-reaching reform projects in the decolonization era.[88] It was a common endeavour influenced by both the progressive European cosmopolitan avant-garde, as well as by international lawyers from non-European nations that appropriated the language of international law in an effort to reform existing international legal rules and institutions in line with their counter-hegemonic sensibilities. It culminated with the decolonization process in a short universalistic moment in the early 1960s and 70s and died away when the West, as a reaction, abandoned the project for good; of course not without upholding a shallow rule of law rhetoric in order to legitimize the current unequal status quo. Too wide has since then become the entrenched gap between the early twentieth century visionary goals and its current state of implementation. It is the essence of empire to render this gap invisible.

---

[85] For a study on forms of non-binding norms in international environmental law: Alberto Székely, 'Non-Binding Commitments: A Commentary on the Softening of International Law Evidenced in the Environmental Field' in United Nations, *International Law on the Eve of the Twenty-First Century—Views from the International Law Commission* (United Nations Publication 1997) 173.

[86] Sia S Åkermark and Olle Mårsäter, 'Treaties and the Limits of Flexibility' (2005) 74 Nordic Journal of International Law 509; Jan Klabbers, 'Anthony Aust, Modern Treaty Law and Practice' (2002) 71 Nordic Journal of International Law 203; Christian Tietje, 'The Changing Legal Structure of International Treaties as an Aspect of an Emerging Global Governance Architecture' (1999) 42 German Yearbook of International Law 26.

[87] Pointing towards the dangers for the rule of law project arising out of informal forms of cooperation: Krieger and Nolte (n 2).

[88] On this era J. von Bernstorff and P. Dann (eds), *The Battle for International Law in the Decolonization Era* (OUP forthcoming).

3

The Rise and Decline of the International Rule of Law and the Job of Scholars

Anne Peters

I. International law feeds on preconditions which it cannot guarantee itself

'The state feeds on preconditions which it cannot guarantee itself.'[1] This axiom, formulated by the German constitutional scholar Ernst-Wolfgang Böckenförde, is also true for the international legal order which is created mostly by states. That order feeds on preconditions which it cannot guarantee itself. And this means that international scholarship, too, must come to grips with preconditions and side-conditions over which it has no control itself.

These preconditions and side conditions are not only material and economic, but also intellectual and moral.[2] Does this mean that scholarship must 'succumb' to these factual and ideational realities by adapting its methods and findings to any given political, social, and economic climate? I would argue that this should, in principle, not be the case.

The example of 'national socialist international legal scholarship' which adapted to National Socialism,[3] and the example of a 'socialist international legal scholarship', cherished by Soviet scholars,[4] shows that such type of digestion of a given political reality by scholarship cannot be a good thing. An Islamist international scholarship or an anti-Islamist international legal scholarship would not be a good idea either.

The deeper reason why international legal scholars—if they want to remain scholars—must not simply turn with the political tide, is that international law, as

---

[1] 'Der Staat lebt von Voraussetzungen, die er selbst nicht garantieren kann' (my translation): Ernst-Wolfgang Böckenförde, 'Entstehung des Staates als Vorgang der Säkularisation' in E-W Böckenförde, *Säkularisation und Utopie: Erbacher Studien, Ernst Forsthoff zum 65. Geburtstag* (Kohlhammer 1967) 75, 93, reproduced in E-W Böckenförde, *Recht, Staat, Freiheit: Studien zur Rechtsphilosophie, Staatstheorie und Verfassungsgeschichte* (Suhrkamp 1991) 92, English translation forthcoming in Mirjam Künkler and Tine Stein (eds), *Religion, Law, and Democracy: Selected Writings of Ernst-Wolfgang Böckenförde* (Oxford University Press 2019).
[2] The latter sphere is probably what Böckenförde had on his mind.
[3] Detlev F Vagts, 'International Law in the Third Reich' (1990) 84 American Journal of International Law 661; Michael Stolleis, *A History of Public Law in Germany 1914–1945* (Thomas Dunlap tr, Oxford University Press 2014) 408.
[4] Grigorij I Tunkin, *Theory of International Law* (William E Butler ed/tr, Harvard University Press 1974).

every law, consists of norms, and this means pre-scription and not de-scription. Law is by definition counterfactual. I insist that law does not only *describe* how states behave because otherwise it would not be law. This characterization of law has been recently called into question by Ian Hurd, who analysed the malleable international rules on self-defence, which have been constantly expanded so as to cloak military action with the mantle of 'lawfulness' as a 'law that cannot be broken', as an 'infrangible law'.[5] If indeed the 'rules' are so open that they are apt to 'justify' any behaviour, then they are not norms but only a fluctuating *ex post facto* rationalization. Law properly speaking *pre*scribes how states and other international actors should behave. Law is actually a social instrument designed specifically to deal with the situation that the actors subjected to the norms do not always comply with them, but also break them.

Legal scholarship describes these norms, analyses and comments on them, extracts the norms' general principles, points out consistencies and inconsistencies, fills gaps by relying on principles within the system, or criticizes state behaviour as violating the norms, sometimes makes proposals for better norms, or finally contextualizes, historicizes, and problematizes the norms. All these scholarly intellectual operations relate first of all to the world of the 'ought'.

Most varieties of scholarship also deal with the norms' interaction with the 'is'. Scholarly attention to the interaction between the 'ought' and the 'is' seems appropriate, because—I submit—legal scholars should neither confine themselves to an analysis of norms in clinical isolation, as a 'pure theory of international law' would do, nor just describe norms in function of current power relations, but should seek to combine both strategies by employing legal reasoning, which takes into account the realities of politics and of the economy. Put differently, it is exactly the job of international legal scholars to produce ideas; ideas which—depending on the side conditions—potentially have the power to shape attitudes and actions, hence also law-making and legal interpretation, together with political, social, cultural, and other factors.[6]

II. Three examples of scholars: Hersch Lauterpacht, Antonio Cassese, and Josef Kunz

This style of scholarship is well illustrated by the work of three eminent scholars whose career continued through different political eras, in which the power of international law was weaker or stronger, in function of a political climate more or less favourable to the international rule of law.

---

[5] Ian Hurd, *How to Do Things with International Law?* (Princeton University Press 2017) 79.

[6] On the promise of normative analysis as opposed to purely positive analysis in international legal scholarship: Anne Peters, 'International Legal Scholarship Under Challenge' in Jean d'Aspremont, Tarcisio Gazzini, André Nollkaemper, and Wouter Werner (eds), *International Law as a Profession* (Cambridge University Press 2017) 117, 130–34.

The first example is Hersch Lauterpacht (1897–1960).[7] When Lauterpacht published the first book ever on international human rights in 1945,[8] no one would have thought that, twenty-one years later, two binding international human rights covenants would be adopted. When Hersch Lauterpacht gave his seminal course in The Hague on international human rights in the summer of 1947,[9] not many people believed that eighteen months later a universal declaration of human rights would be adopted by the General Assembly of the new world organization, the United Nations. Lauterpacht, moreover, postulated a general principle according to which individuals are the ultimate addressees of all law: '[H]aving regard to the inherent purposes of international law, of which the individual is the ultimate unit, he is in that capacity a subject of international law.'[10] According to Lauterpacht, the international legal personality of the individual has 'a source independent of the will of States', without requiring an explicit or even just implied consent of the states. On this point, state practice is 'essentially declaratory'.[11] Hersch Lauterpacht had smuggled this doctrinal view into the fifth edition of the textbook of his mentor, Lassa Oppenheim, whose previous editions had been strictly statist. Hence, *already in 1937*, Lauterpacht wrote:

While it is of importance to bear in mind that primarily States are subjects of International Law, it is essential to recognise the limitations of that principle ... In particular, when we say that International Law regulates the conduct of States we must not forget that the *conduct actually regulated is the conduct of human beings* acting as the organ of the State.... Also, although States are the normal subjects of International Law *they may treat individuals and other persons as endowed directly with international rights and duties and constitute them to that extent subjects of International Law* ... The doctrine adopted in many municipal systems to the effect that International Law is part of the law of the land is upon analysis yet another factor showing that International Law may operate *per se* upon individuals ....[12]

The necessity of the status of the individual as a subject was justified by Lauterpacht with reference to the prevention of general irresponsibility due to the establishment of a protective screen by the state.[13]

[7] On his work and life: Ian Scobbie, 'Hersch Lauterpacht' in Bardo Fassbender and Anne Peters (eds), *Oxford Handbook of the History of International Law* (Oxford University Press 2012) 1179–83.

[8] Hersch Lauterpacht, *An International Bill of the Rights of Man* (Columbia University Press 1945); this book then became one chapter in his Hague course: H Lauterpacht, 'The International Protection of Human Rights' (1947-I) 70 Recueil des Cours de l'Académie de la Haye 5.

[9] H Lauterpacht, 'The International Protection of Human Rights' (n 8).

[10] Hersch Lauterpacht, 'The Subjects of the Law of Nations' (1947) 63 Law Quarterly Review 428, reproduced in Elihu Lauterpacht (ed), *International Law: Being the Collected Papers of Hersch Lauterpacht*, vol II part I 'The Law of Peace' (Cambridge University Press 1975) 487.

[11] Lauterpacht, *International Law* (n 10) 532–33.

[12] Lassa FL Oppenheim, *International Law: A Treatise*, vol I 'Peace' (Hersch Lauterpacht ed, 5th edn, Longmans, Green and Co 1937) § 13a, 19–21 (emphases added).

[13] See Hersch Lauterpacht, Chapter 5, 'The Subjects of International Law' in Elihu Lauterpacht (ed), *International Law: Being the Collected Papers of Hersch Lauterpacht*, vol I 'The General Works' (Cambridge University Press 1970) 279–80.

Not many realized at the time that exactly this idea formed the core argument of the Nuremberg judgment of 1946 against the major war criminals whose key phrase was:

> That International Law imposes duties and liabilities upon individuals as well as upon States has long been recognized.... Crimes against International Law are committed by men, not by abstract entities, and only by punishing individuals who commit such crimes can the provisions of International Law be enforced.[14]

It took more than fifty years to operationalize this postulated criminal responsibility with help of a permanent institution, the International Criminal Court (ICC), based on the Rome Statute of 1998. Moreover, the legal justification of this criminal liability has been long in dispute, and still does not unequivocally follow Lauterpacht's construction.

My second example is Antonio Cassese (1937–2011).[15] Cassese studied law and began publishing during the era of the Cold War, an era in which the power of international law was limited and the Security Council blocked. After 1990, in his capacity as the first President of the Yugoslavia tribunal,[16] Cassese ran the Tadić proceedings against a major war criminal. The jurisdictional decision of the Appeals Chamber of 1995 basically created new law, which was immediately accepted. First of all, the decision established the principle that the Security Council has the power to establish a criminal tribunal, but is nevertheless bound by the principles of the Charter.[17] This passage has become a seminal text on the constitutionalization of international organizations. Second, Cassese, together with his colleagues on the bench, found that certain breaches of the rules of the non-international armed conflict are prohibited, and even saddled with criminal responsibility, in the same way as comparable acts in international armed conflict: 'What is inhumane, and consequently proscribed, in international wars, cannot but be inhumane and inadmissible in civil strife.'[18] This part of the decision was a decisive building block of the ongoing approximation of the law of international and non-international armed conflict.

Both the Nuremberg trial and the Tadić proceedings have been called 'Grotian moments' in the formation of international customary law.[19] A Grotian moment is a moment of change in which new rules are more or less instantaneously accepted by the international community. For sure, the changes of the law occurred in a new political context, and depended on this context: The Nuremberg tribunal was 'a political solution to a practical problem' and 'individual responsibility under international law was

---

[14] 'International Military Tribunal, judgment of 1 October 1946' in *The Trial of German Major War Criminals, Proceedings of the International Military Tribunal sitting at Nuremberg, Germany, Part 22 (22nd August 1946 to 1st October 1946)* 446–47.

[15] Introducing a special issue on Cassese: Urmila Dé and Salvatore Zappalà, 'Editorial' (2012) 10 Journal of International Criminal Justice 1025; Joseph HH Weiler, 'Antonio Cassese: Head in the Clouds, Feet on the Ground' (2012) 23 European Journal of International Law 1031.

[16] Cassese was President from 1993 to 1997, and continued to sit as a tribunal judge until 2000.

[17] *Prosecutor v Duško Tadić, Decision on the Defence Motion for Interlocutory Appeal on Jurisdiction* ICTY, Case No IT-94-1-AR72, Appeals Chamber of 2 October 1995, paras 26–48.

[18] ibid, para 119; see for the entire argument: paras 128–36.

[19] Michael Scharf, *Customary International Law in Times of Fundamental Change: Recognizing Grotian Moments* (Cambridge University Press 2013) 67–68 (on Nuremberg) and 148–53 (on Tadić).

[only] a by-product of that solution'.[20] The International Criminal Tribunal for the former Yugoslavia (ICTY) was created in 1993 in reaction to the Yugoslav secession war in whose course atrocious war crimes and genocide had been committed, which screamed for a response. Due to the overall political constellation, the permanent members of the Security Council agreed to establish a war crimes tribunal, and so it was done.

These Grotian moments were surely facilitated by the influence which Lauterpacht and Cassese (respectively) had as legal *practitioners*. Lauterpacht was, *inter alia*, a counsellor to the British prosecution team at Nuremberg, and Cassese was the President of the ICTY at the time of Tadić. But a modified political context and the practitioners' work cannot function as a catalyst of legal change if there is no legal substance to draw on. This substance was the scholarly work of our two protagonists. In their scholarship, they had formulated principles, thought them through and explained their consequences, and fitted them into an intellectual system.[21] Importantly, this ground work was in both cases performed in a political climate which was hostile to international law but could nevertheless unfold its potential once the climate changed.

My third example is Josef Laurenz Kunz (1890–1970), the probably most influential disciple of Hans Kelsen.[22] Kunz's career in some sense followed the opposite trajectory from that of Lauterpacht and Cassese. The latter two had begun to exercise their profession during political periods in which the power of international law was weak, but then lived on to witness a change of the political climate, which was more favourable to the international rule of law, and which they could then exploit. In contrast, Kunz, who earned his degree of Dr rer pol in 1920, started out in the post-Versailles era, in which an international law optimism, the 'Geneva spirit', reigned. Kunz shared Kelsen's cosmopolitan convictions, reinforced by his experience of the First World War.

Kunz then witnessed, as he himself put it, a 'swing of the pendulum', 'from overestimation to underestimation of international law'.[23] He noted, in an article published after the Second World War (in 1950), that a spirit of underestimation of international law had already begun in the 1930s. Kunz also insisted that '[i]nternational lawyers

---

[20]   Kate Parlett, *The Individual in the International Legal System* (Cambridge University Press 2011) 352.

[21]   For Lauterpacht: (nn 8–13); Antonio Cassese had extensively published on problems of non-international armed conflict although he did not (to my best knowledge) exactly discuss the convergence of rules in both types of armed conflict, and the criminal responsibility: Antonio Cassese, 'Current Trends in the Development of the Law of Armed Conflict' (1974) 24 Rivista trimestrale di diritto pubblico 1407, reproduced in Antonio Cassese, Paola Gaeta, and Salvatore Zappalà (eds), *The Human Dimension of International Law: Selected Papers of Antonio Cassese* (Oxford University Press 2008) 3, especially at 33–37; Antonio Cassese 'The Spanish Civil War and the Development of Customary Law Concerning Internal Armed Conflicts' in Antonio Cassese, *Current Problems of International Law: Essays on UN Law and on the Law of Armed Conflict* (A Giuffrè 1975) 287, reproduced in Antonio Cassese, Paola Gaeta, and Salvatore Zappalà (eds), *The Human Dimension of International Law: Selected Papers of Antonio Cassese* (Oxford University Press 2008) 128; Antonio Cassese, 'The Status of Rebels under the 1977 Geneva Protocol in Non-International Armed Conflict' (1981) 30 International and Comparative Law Quarterly 416.

[22]   On Kunz's career: Jochen von Bernstorff, *The Public International Law Theory of Hans Kelsen: Believing in Universal Law* (Cambridge University Press 2010) 283–85.

[23]   Josef L Kunz, 'Swing of the Pendulum: From Overestimation to Underestimation of International Law' (1950) 44 American Journal of International Law 135.

must not forget that international law does not operate in a vacuum, that even proposals de lege ferenda have sense only within the boundaries of political possibilities of
being realised at a particular juncture of history.'[24] Put differently, scholarly writing on
international law, which floats up in the air out of touch with reality, will hardly be 'successful' in the sense of contributing to better law and more global justice.

At the same time, the essence of scholarship is its distance to the object of study.[25]
Without this distance, scholars would be swalled by practice and would lose their capacity
to criticize the law and the practice.[26] It is of course not possible to measure and define
the distance that would be exactly right for all purposes, but rather a matter of judgment.
How far scholarly writing should transcend or keep at bay from practice, from the law as it
stands, from the political climate, and from concerns of feasibility depends on the research
questions. In short, it might always be open to doubts and discussion how 'counterfactual'
scholarly normative reflection should be.

Josef Kunz's reminder of the limits placed on legal scholarship by politics is saturated
with his own academic experience. Kunz had, inspired by the international practice of territorial re-arrangement after the First World War, written an *opus magnum* in two volumes
on the law of option, that is the rules governing the choice of nationality after territorial
changes, published in the 1920s.[27] Josef Kunz here asserted a customary right of option.
In hindsight, we realize that this was too early. Kunz's thesis was—at the time of writing—
wishful thinking. Options of nationality after the First World War were based on specific
treaty provisions and did not give rise to any independent customary obligation. In state
practice after 1989, when the Soviet Union and Yugoslavia broke up, only around half of
the new states allowed for a choice of nationality by the inhabitants of territories which
came under a different jurisdiction. The policy decision of many republics not to grant
such an option was nowhere criticized as running against international law. These events
illustrate that no customary right of option existed in 1990, nor has one come into being in
the course of those events.

However, it nowadays seems fair to say that procedural rules on options of nationality exist. *If* an option is granted, either by treaty or by domestic law, time limits for the
exercise of this right must be reasonable.[28] This rule of reasonableness is apt to deploy
some normative power. To give one example, the inhabitants of Crimea had only one
month after the annexation of the peninsula by Russia in March 2014 to opt for upholding their Ukrainian nationality, and they had to declare this in specific Russian
administrative centres, which were not easily accessible, otherwise they automatically

---

[24] ibid 140.
[25] For a nuanced reflection on this theme: Jochen von Bernstorff, 'International Legal Scholarship as a Cooling
Medium in International Law and Politics' (2014) 25 European Journal of International Law 977.
[26] Peters (n 6) 150.
[27] Josef L Kunz, *Die völkerrechtliche Option* (F Hirt 1925–1928).
[28] cf Art 11 (5) of the *ILC Draft Articles on Nationality of Natural Persons in relation to the Succession of States
with commentaries*, vol II part two, UN Doc A/54/10, ILC YB 1999, 23; Ronen highlights that *the manner* in which
an option of nationality is granted may be subject to international customary limitations: Yael Ronen 'Option of
Nationality' in *Max Planck Encyclopedia of Public International Law* (Online Edition <www.mpepil.com> last update April 2007) para 12. In state practice, the shortest time limits granted before 2009 for the exercise of the right
of option had been three months (ibid para 22).

became Russian nationals.[29] This scheme appears unreasonable. Therefore, the purported Russian nationality of the inhabitants of Crimea is inopposable against third states unless they specifically choose to recognize it, for example for humanitarian reasons.[30]

So Kunz's grand design to some extent bore fruit, and his intellectual groundwork may have contributed to rationalizing subsequent practice. He did not live to see this but—quite to the contrary—suffered career setbacks: His *Habilitation* proceeding at the university of Vienna was opposed by a nationalist colleague at the faculty of Vienna who disliked his cosmopolitan outlooks, and Kunz's promotion was therefore delayed.[31] So Kunz personally had been penalized for his 'progressive' scholarly opinions.

III. Idealist scholarship and international political crises

Let me tie these examples back to the assumption that international law has now entered into a new phase, which may have begun with the illegal Iraq war by the United States in 2003, or maybe with the Russian unlawful annexation of Crimea in 2014. The question is what international legal scholars in this new phase of international law might learn from the historical fate of previous international law scholarship. The subtext of this question might be that the 'idealist' scholarship of the 1990s was naive and utopian in the bad sense.

Does this require scholars who had claimed that a process of juridification, legalization, proliferation, or even constitutionalization of international law has been taking place (I include myself) now meekly admit that this was built on false assumptions which have now shattered? Entire juridical libraries might have been transformed into scrap paper, not by a stroke of the pen of the legislator, as the Prussian prosecutor Julius Hermann von Kirchmann had said in his famous lecture of 1847 with regard to national law,[32] but transformed into scrap paper by totalitarian and xenophobic politics,

---

[29] Art 5 of the Agreement on the Accession of the Republic of Crimea to the Russian Federation of 18 March 2014:

> As of the day of the admission of the Republic of Crimea into Russia and the formation of new federative entities within the Russian Federation, Ukrainian citizens and stateless citizens permanently residing in the Republic of Crimea and in the city with federal status Sebastopol are recognized as Russian citizens apart from those people who within one month from this day express their wish to retain their current citizenship for themselves and their underage children or to remain persons without citizenship.

Unofficial translation <www.academia.edu/6481091/A_treaty_on_accession_of_the_Republic_of_Crimea_and_Sebastopol_to_the_Russian_Federation._Unofficial_English_translation_with_little_commentary)> accessed 26 May 2018.

[30] The inopposability of the new Russian nationality of the inhabitants of Crimea does not only flow from the violation of the procedural rules on options, but mainly from the illegality of the territorial change. A great number of states does not recognize the incorporation of Crimea into the Russian Federation, but explicitly or implicitly qualified the territorial change as unlawful. This also implies that these states do not, as a matter of principle, recognize the new Russian nationality of the inhabitants except if this entails humanitarian hardships.

[31] See Bernstorff (n 22) 285.

[32] In his lecture on the 'Worthlessness of Jurisprudence as a Science' in Berlin, Kirchmann had identified the transitoriness of the subject matter of law 'as the fundamental ill from which the science suffered'. 'By making the accidental its object, it becomes random itself; three corrective words of the legislator, and entire law

by the power of global financial actors, by the rise of new fundamentalist anti-liberal and anti-secular ideologies, and by unbridled military and criminal violence exercised in the Middle East and in the middle of Europe?

It may well be that some highly optimistic scholarship of the 1990s had strayed far off reality. Does this have pernicious consequences for international relations? Can a piece of idealist scholarship, if it comes at the wrong time, or at a time which is not ripe, actually be politically dangerous? It surely cannot be as dangerous as the moves of the politicians of the 1910s, who 'sleepwalked' into the First World War.[33] Also, nobody would claim that Hitler would not have invaded Poland and other countries, had the realist voices in international legal scholarship of the 1920s been louder.

Nevertheless, idealist scholarship could be politically dangerous for different reasons. First, overly idealist scholarship might create a false security about the state of the law.[34] An example would be the scholarly assertion that international law clearly prohibits self-defence against non-state actors. Although some authors espouse that view, many others have criticized it, and overall the current state of the law on this point seems uncertain and in flux. The example shows that in a global academic community, with its diverse and critical voices (and a weakening academic hegemony of the West) the uniformity of writing, which is needed to create false security, will hardly ever come about. It is therefore highly unlikely that naive and illusionary scholarship will disinform other actors about the law as it stands and misdirect their action.

Secondly, naive and illusionary scholarship might constitute an indirect danger through a mechanism at which Josef Kunz hinted in his paper of 1950. Kunz implied that the post-First World War 'Geneva spirit' indirectly caused a problem, because it led to the intellectual backlash of underestimation of international law already in the 1930s, which then in turn facilitated power politics in disregard of international law. However, this view needs some temperance. It would be self-contradictory to insist on the all-importance of the realities of power for the course of international relations, and at the same time to assert that scholarly work (in this case 'realist' writings) is apt to promote realist politics.

Thirdly, idealistic scholarship could commit the crime of omission. By wasting energy for illusionary projects, scholars omit to work on nitty gritty, pragmatic, feasible legal constructs. However, I submit that any work of modest refinement and improvement of the law benefits from exposure to other scholars' grand designs, and be it only in order to stimulate more exacting analysis.

---

libraries become scrap paper.' (my translation): Julius H von Kirchmann, 'Die Wertlosigkeit der Jurisprudenz als Wissenschaft' in Heinrich H Meyer-Tscheppe (ed), *Die Wertlosigkeit der Jurisprudenz als Wissenschaft* (Manutius 1988) 15, 29.

[33] Christopher Clark, *The Sleepwalkers: How Europe Went to War in 1914* (Allan Lane 2012).

[34] One example of overly confident inter-war scholarship is the Hague lecture given in 1931 by James W Garner, 'Le développement et les tendances récentes du droit international' (1931) 35 I Recueil des Cours de l'Académie de la Haye 605. Garner celebrated the new international law, which had been brought about by the sacrifices and the suffering of the Great War and diagnosed 'le progrès le plus remarquable que le droit international ait jamais reconnu', 612. Garner also called for the further development of a law to prevent war as opposed to the so-far prevailing sophistication of rules on proper conduct in war, 610–12, 625.

Overall, despite these three drawbacks, I submit that idealist scholarship cannot cause or contribute to any political crisis. First of all, as Josef Kunz pointed out in the middle of a period of disillusionment with international law, 'in order to establish the new attitude, very likely a distorted picture of the former one will be given'.[35] Writing in 1950, he meant to say that the previous pro-internationalist scholarship was not digested faithfully but rather caricatured. We need to keep this in mind and avoid distorting the scholarship of the 1990s.

Further and more importantly, the assumption of any causal link between overly idealist scholarship and international crisis would overrate the importance of international law, of international legal scholarship, and international legal scholars. Such overestimation is precisely what 'realist' observers seek to avoid. So any naive and illusionary utopianism—as opposed to an adequate *realist utopianism*—to use John Rawls'[36] and Antonio Cassese's term,[37] is what it is: bad scholarship.

IV. Conclusion

It remains a crucial task of scholarship to debunk pseudo-justifications, which states advance for cloaking their actions with the mantle of lawfulness and to reveal that these are not sustainable and not *lege artis*. For example, it was the job of scholars to point out the unlawfulness of the US American Iraq war of 2003, as it was the job of scholars to point out the unlawfulness of the Russian annexation of Crimea in 2014.

Because scholars have no law-making and no law-destroying authority themselves, all depends on their epistemic authority, that is the persuasiveness of their arguments, whether these will be taken up by the political actors, or not. For example, scholars could show that the annexation of Crimea was not justified by the principle of self-determination and that the situation was in legal terms distinct from the situation of Kosovo.[38] This legal finding was then translated into political action: In a United Nations General Assembly vote, 100 United Nations (UN) members explicitly undersigned the statement that Russia violated the territorial integrity of Ukraine and that

---

[35] Kunz (n 23) 135.
[36] John Rawls used the term 'realistic utopia' as a qualifier of his blueprint for a 'law of the peoples' which are his 'reflections on how reasonable citizens and peoples might live together peacefully in a just world': John Rawls, *The Law of Peoples* (Harvard University Press 1999) 7 and preface vi. Rawls continued: 'I contend that this scenario is *realistic*—it could and may exist. I say it is *also utopian* and highly desirable because it joins reasonableness and justice with conditions enabling citizens to realize their fundamental interests.' (7, emphasis added).
[37] Antonio Cassese described his approach as aiming 'to avoid the extremes of both blind acquiesence to present conditions and the illusion of being able to revolutionize the fundamentals': Antonio Cassese, *Realizing Utopia* (Oxford University Press 2012) xvii; see also xxi.
[38] See Anne Peters, Christian Marxsen, and Matthias Hartwig, 'Symposium: "The Incorporation of Crimea by the Russian Federation in the Light of International Law"' (2015) 75 Zeitschrift für ausländisches öffentliches Recht und Völkerrecht/Heidelberg Journal of International Law 1.

UN members were obliged not to recognize the territorial change.[39] However, opinions can then again diverge about the political value of this General Assembly resolution. One might optimistically find that the 100 states which denounced the annexation of Crimea are in fact more than half of the UN members. But one might inversely and pessimistically highlight that 100 is only *a little* more than half of the extant states of the world, and that this is not too much considering that we are here dealing with a violation of a core principle of the international order, the prohibition on the use of force.

However we evaluate the political use or non-use of a scholarly analysis, we can safely say so much: International legal scholars could and can do no more than produce legal ideas which are by definition not merely a description of politics. But scholars should not do less, either.

---

[39] UNGA, 'Territorial Integrity of Ukraine' UNGA RES 263 (4 April 2014) UN Doc A/RES/68/263: the General Assembly '[a]ffirms its commitment to the ... territorial integrity of Ukraine within its internationally recognized borders' (para 1); underscores that the referendum in Crimea had 'no validity' (para 5); and calls upon all states, international organizations, and specialized agencies 'not to recognize any alteration of the status' of Crimea (para 6). The resolution was adopted with 100 votes in favour, 11 against, 58 abstentions. (UN Meetings Coverage GA/11493, 27 March 2014: <www.un.org/press/en/2014/ga11493.doc.htm> accessed 26 May 2018).

4

Coercion, Internalization, Decolonization

A Contextual Reading of the Rise of European International Law Since the Seventeenth Century

Felix Lange

What is the role of international law in today's global politics? Do increasing technical and communicative entanglements promote the rising relevance of international law in international relations, because more and more institutions at the international level base their decisions on international law and more and more disputes are solved by judgments of international courts? Or are there, in contrast, signs of a backlash to the juridicalization of global politics, because new tensions chill the relations between East and West and rising powers start to rearrange the global division of power? What do today's challenges mean for the structures, values, and institutions of international law in the twenty-first century? These questions lie at the heart of the KFG research project on the 'International Rule of Law—Rise or Decline?'. This book engages with the methodological framing of the research theme. What are pertinent methods and indicators for assessing the state and direction of international law? How can we measure a rise or decline of the international rule of law? What do we turn to in our assessment?[1]

One potential methodological approach is historical. By looking at the past, we might be informed about longer trends of international legal development. By comparing the rise and decline in the past with today's world, we might understand contemporary developments in a better way. Hence, the editors of the book have asked to address the 'relevance of historical analogies and prior experiences' as one methodological path for the research project.[2] This contribution engages with the historical approach. It starts by discussing the problems and the potential of historical analogies (Section I) and then depicts different competing narratives of 'rise' and 'decline' of international law in the historical writings of international lawyers and historians (Section II). Subsequently, it propagates a contextual approach to the history of international law, which takes the terminology of the actors of the past seriously, but also leaves room for an assessment of functional equivalents (Section III). The main part of this contribution then applies the contextual approach to the story of international law's universalization (Section IV).

---

[1] Heike Krieger and Georg Nolte, 'The International Rule of Law—Rise or Decline?—Approaching Current Foundational Challenges' in this book, VI, VII.

[2] See Krieger and Nolte, in this volume, 23.

The author concludes with some short tentative thoughts about lessons of this history for the rise or decline of today's international law (Section V).

I. On the problems and the potential of historical lessons

Can history provide lessons for our contemporary debate? Three arguments urge us to be rather cautious with direct 'lessons of history': instrumentalism (1), new challenges (2), and contingency (3). First, historical analogies are often drawn in an over-simplistic manner. For instance, George W Bush based the American justification for intervening in Iraq in 2003 on 'the Munich 1938-metaphor'. Because Saddam Hussein's actions would be similar to Adolf Hitler's aggressive foreign policy of the 1930s, one should intervene militarily instead of continuing with pointless appeasement policies. After not convincing the Security Council with his historical narrative, Bush chose to act with a coalition of the willing.[3] The criticism directed at the shallow legal justification of the American Iraq invasion[4] shows that most international lawyers would have preferred if the US President had taken note of the valid international law instead of advancing superficial historical analogies.[5] Another example of an instrumentalized history is the Russian justification for the annexation of Crimea. Vladimir Putin relied on Kosovo's secession from Serbia, which had been backed by the United States and some European states, for justifying Crimea's secession from Ukraine.[6] Even though the Kosovo case might indeed have set an 'unfortunate precedent' in some regards,[7] some observers questioned that the scale of human rights violations in Kosovo and Crimea had reached a similar level.[8] Second, because social structures develop over time, past events might not be helpful in providing full-fledged solutions for the changing global order of the twenty-first century. As the German Philosopher Georg Friedrich Hegel famously expressed in his Lectures on the Philosophy of History in 1822–23: 'Rulers, Statesmen, Nations, are wont to be emphatically commended to the teaching which experience offers in history. But what experience and history teach is this—that peoples and governments never have learned anything from history or acted on principles deduced from it. Each period is involved in such peculiar circumstances,

---

[3] On the speech of President Bush before the UN: Peter Conolly-Smith, ' "Connecting the Dots": Munich, Iraq and the Lessons of History' (2009) 42 The History Teacher 31, 38–45; also James J Sheehan, 'How Do We Learn From History?' (2005) American Historical Society <www.historians.org/publications-and-directories/perspectives-on-history/january-2005/how-do-we-learn-from-history> accessed 14 July 2018.

[4] For the debate in the American academy: (2003) 97 American Journal of International Law 553.

[5] On the use of analogies in American foreign policy: Yuen Foong Khong, Analogies at War: Korea, Munich, Dien Bien Phu, and the Vietnam Decisions of 1965 (Princeton University Press 1992).

[6] 'Putin: Crimea Similar to Kosovo, West is Rewriting its Own Rule Book' (Russia Today, 18 March 2014) <www.rt.com/news/putin-address-parliament-crimea-562/> accessed 14 July 2018.

[7] Stefan Oeter, 'The Kosovo Case—An Unfortunate Precedent' (2015) 75 Zeitschrift für ausländisches öffentliches Recht und Völkerrecht 51.

[8] Daniel W Drezner, 'Putin's Excuse for a Referendum is Wrong: Crimea Isn't Kosovo—at All' (The Guardian, 17 March 2014) <www.theguardian.com/commentisfree/2014/mar/17/putin-referendum-crimea-kosovo> accessed 14 July 2018; Ilya Somin, 'Why the Kosovo "Precedent" Does not Justify Russia's Annexation of Crimea' (Washington Post, 24 March 2014) <www.washingtonpost.com/news/volokh-conspiracy/wp/2014/03/24/crimea-kosovo-and-false-moral-equivalency/> accessed 14 July 2018.

exhibits a condition of things so strictly idiosyncratic, that its conduct must be regulated by considerations connected with itself, and itself alone.'[9] Even if Hegel might have overemphasized the novelty of some phenomena, it seems true that each politician has to react to the changed 'condition of things' of his or her time. For instance, as Susan Pedersen has stressed, in the inter-war period politicians struggled with the relatively new phenomenon of broad public mobilization for international policy issues in the League of Nations context.[10] Third, contingency as one of the driving forces of historical evolution might thwart learning from the past. If some events are shaped rather by chance than by planning, how can we deduce orientation from these contingent events for our contemporary world?[11]

Nonetheless, if one abstains from transferring past events mechanistically to the present, history seems to be relevant for understanding and explaining today's world. As the British Historian Lewis B Namier has stated in the beginning of the 1950s: 'Can men learn from [history]? That depends on the quality and accuracy of the historian's perceptions and conclusions, and on the critical faculties of the reader—on the "argument", and on the "intellects" to comprehend it.'[12] This means that one not only has to be careful about which historical narrative one embraces but also about how one utilizes the historical argument. In this sense, a deep comparison of different historical instances might prevent superficial instrumental analogies. A cautious adaptation of past experiences to changed contemporary circumstances might help to take the novelty of some challenges into account. Furthermore, awareness for the role of contingency in historical developments might allow for a more conscious treatment of chance as a historical factor. It seems that on the basis of this rather reserved approach to analogies a cautiously interpreted history can provide some orientation and understanding for today.

II. Competing narratives in the history of international law

But what historical narrative are we supposed to learn from? In the course of the twentieth century, the history of international law has been told in many different ways. Especially the question of international law's origin and the reasons for its universal dissemination have caused some controversy. Four competing narratives have been particularly influential. One emphasizes that European international law universalized as a matter of progress (1), a second one retold the story of European universalization as a matter of great power interests (2), a third one highlighted the contributions of

---

[9] Georg W F Hegel, *The Philosophy of History* (Dover 1956, reprinted 2004) 6.

[10] Susan Pedersen, 'Back to the League of Nations' (2007) 112 The American Historical Review 1091, 1094–99.

[11] On contingency eg: Robert Livingston Schuyler, 'Contingency in History' (1959) 74 Political Science Quarterly 321.

[12] On this: Lewis B Namier, 'History' in Fritz Stern (ed), *The Varieties of History* (Meridian Books 1957) 372, 378.

non-European regions to international law (3), and a fourth one pointed to the colonial origins of European international law (4).[13]

(1) At the beginning of the twentieth century, leading Western international lawyers argued that international law originated in modern Europe and reached other regions and states only after they had attained a certain civilizational standard. Already in 1893, the first professional historian of international law, the Belgian Ernest Nys, had located the origins of international law in the Europe of the Renaissance period. According to him, the ideas of progress, freedom, and humanity had spurred the historical evolution of the law of nations.[14] During the inter-war period, Lassa Oppenheim and Franz von Liszt then stressed in their popular textbooks that international law originated in the Christian Europe of the sixteenth and seventeenth centuries. Only in the nineteenth century, some civilized and half-civilized non-Western societies started to adopt the European international legal norms.[15] Historical debates of the time turned on the question whether Hugo Grotius or Francisco de Vitoria was the 'father of international law'.[16] Dutch or Spanish, international law had a European background. After 1945, this historical reading continued to dominate the discussion. Even though the language of civilization was often dropped, the idea of European universalization as a progress story was inherent in many accounts. In his *Concise History of the Law of Nations*, Arthur Nussbaum described the 'tremendous progress' as international law's 'dominant trait'.[17] Similarly, according to the standard account in the Heidelberg *Wörterbuch des Völkerrechts* of 1962, the Peace of Westphalia signalled the starting of a period of European international law which widened in the nineteenth and universalized in the twentieth century.[18] Furthermore, the Dutch scholar Jan HW Verzijl in his voluminous treatise of *International Law in Historical Perspective* emphasized that international law was a 'product of the conscious activity of the European mind' with no essential contributions by an 'extra-European nation'.[19] Also, scholars from the non-Western world, like the Chinese lawyer Wang Tieya, held that it is 'an undeniable fact that modern international law has its origin in Europe and it is the product of Christian civilization' from which it 'expanded to cover all States of the world.'[20]

---

[13]   For a similar, but also somewhat different historical recollection of the narratives in international law: Arnulf Becker Lorca, 'Eurocentrism in the History of International Law' in Bardo Fassbender and Anne Peters (eds), *The Oxford Handbook of the History of International Law* (Oxford University Press 2012) 1034.

[14]   Ernest Nys, *Les origines du droit international* (Fontemoing 1894) 10–12, 164, 404–05; further on this: Martti Koskenniemi, 'A History of International Law Histories' in Fassbender and Peters (n 13) 943; Martti Koskenniemi, 'Histories of International Law: Dealing with Eurocentrism' (2011) 19 Rechtsgeschichte 152.

[15]   Lassa Oppenheim, *International Law. A Treatise* (Longman, Green and Co 1908) 3–4, 44–75, 147–56; Franz von Liszt, *Völkerrecht. Systematisch dargestellt* (O Haering 1898) 2–4, 9–18.

[16]   James Brown Scott, *The Spanish Origin of International Law. Francisco de Vitoria and his Law of Nations* (Clarendon Press 1934).

[17]   Arthur Nussbaum, *A Concise History of the Law of Nations* (first published 1947, Macmillan 1954) ix.

[18]   Hans U Scupin, 'Völkerrechtsgeschichte. III. Erweiterung des Europäischen Völkerrechts' in Hans-Jürgen Schlochauer (ed), *Wörterbuch des Völkerrechts*, vol 3 (De Gruyter 1962) 721; Ulrich Scheuner, 'Neueste Entwicklung (Seit 1914)' in Schlochauer (n 18) 744.

[19]   Jan H W Verzijl, *International Law in Historical Perspective*, vol 1 (A.W. Sijthoff-Leyden 1968) 435–36, 446.

[20]   Wang Tieya, 'International Law in China: Historical and Contemporary Perspective' (1990-II) 221 Recueil des Cours 195, 355.

(2) A second historical narrative also emphasized the European origin of international law but regarded its development not as a story of progress but as a realization of great power interests. In his *Nomos of the Earth*, Carl Schmitt criticized that with the universalization of international law the 'Euro-centric ordering of international law perishes'.[21] According to him, between the sixteenth and the end of the nineteenth century an internal European international law, the *ius publicum Europaeum*, had represented the 'space order' of the world. This order, which had worked on the principle of *mare librum* and the division of territory between state territory, colonies, protectorates, exotic countries, and *terra nullis*, started to dissolve in 1890 with the rise of the United States. In Schmitt's view, thereby an 'empty normativism' replaced the 'concrete order' of recognized countries.[22] One of his disciples, Wilhelm Grewe, some years later provided the most well-known realist account of the history of international law. For the German diplomat and international lawyer, who had conceptualized his work in the early 1940s, the *Epochs of International Law* began with the Middle Ages in Europe. Grewe argued that since the fifteenth century eras of Spanish, French, British, Anglo-American, and Anglo-Soviet domination had brought forth international legal rules, which were structured in line with the interests of the leading hegemons.[23] In Grewe's reading, the development of international law was not necessarily a story of progress, but rather a story of competing great powers framing their interests in the language of international law.

(3) As a critique of the idealistic and realist 'European origin' accounts, authors from non-Western countries developed a third historical narrative by highlighting the contribution of non-European regions to the development of a universal international law. According to the Nigerian scholar Taslim O Elias, the contribution of Carthage and other African indigenous people to the development of international law should not be underestimated (1972).[24] The Indian Ram P Anand argued that rules of inter-state conduct can 'be traced to some of the most ancient civilisations like China, India, Egypt and Assyria'. It would be wrong to assume that 'Christian civilization had enjoyed a monopoly in regard to prescription of rules to govern inter-state conduct', because international law existed longer than 400 years.[25] The Indian Muslim Muhammad Hamidulla even claimed that 'international law owes its origin to Arab Muslims of the Umayad period, who divorced it from political science and law general'.[26] Others pointed to the exchange between European states and non-European entities. The

[21] Carl Schmitt, *Der Nomos der Erde im Völkerrecht des Jus Publicum Europaeum* (first published 1950, 4th edn, Duncker & Humblot 1997) 6.
[22] ibid 111–86, 200–12.
[23] Wilhelm G Grewe, *Epochen der Völkerrechtsgeschichte* (Nomos 1984); Wilhelm G Grewe, *The Epochs of International Law* (De Gruyter 2000).
[24] Taslim O Elias, *Africa and the Development of International Law* (A W Sijthoff 1972) 3–15; also A Kodwo Mensah-Brown (ed), *African International Legal History* (United Nations Institute for Training and Research 1975).
[25] Ram P Anand, 'The Influence of History on the Literature of International Law' in Ronald St J Mac Donald and Douglas M Johnston (eds), *The Structure and Process of International Law: Essays in Legal Philosophy, Doctrine and Theory* (United Nations Institute for Training and Research 1983) 341, 342.
[26] Muhammad Hamidulla, *Muslim Conduct of State* (M Ashraf 1945) XIII; also pointing to the need of paying attention to the Islamic tradition of international law: Majid Khadduri, *The Islamic Law of Nations of Shaybani's Siyar* (John Hopkins 1966) xi–xiii.

Polish scholar Charles H Alexandrowicz underlined that the interactions between East Indian and European sovereigns in the sixteenth and eighteenth centuries had been based on treaty relations and the principle of equality. European powers in some cases even adopted the legal traditions in the East, when they were unsuccessful in imposing their own. For Alexandrowicz, it was only during the nineteenth century that the universal international law had been 'narrowed to a regional (purely European) legal system' caused by a 'doctrinal change, particularly by the abandonment of the natural law doctrine and adherence to positivism of the European brand'.[27] More recently, Arnulf Becker Lorca has claimed that even in the nineteenth century the 'periphery' appropriated the European international law according to its own political ideals. Thereby, international law became a 'Mestizo international law'.[28] According to these scholars, the development of international law had to be credited to different cultures.

(4) Since the 1980s, a fourth strand of historical studies has focused on exposing the dark sides of international law by stressing its colonial past. The German historian Jörg Fisch portrayed in 1984 how the European powers had used international law since the fifteenth century to expand their rule over the world. Fisch depicted how European powers concluded treaties among themselves about the control of African territories by Europeans, the most famous being the Congo Act of 1884–85. Furthermore, he described how the legal status of the overseas territory was conceptualized in the practice of the European states and the writings of European legal scholars.[29] In 2004, Antony Anghie connected the history of imperialism to the making of international law. For him, international law had colonial origins since the time of Francisco de Vitoria. The colonial character of international law came to be particularly obvious when it was applied to the 'peripheries' in the nineteenth century. Anghie claimed that the colonial ideas continued to inform the international governance structures of the twentieth century and the war on terror by the United States.[30] Similarly, the historians Mark Mazower, Lauren Benton, and Lisa Ford have stressed the colonial origins of international law. According to Mazower, the South African colonialist Jan Smuts strongly influenced the founding of the United Nations (UN) hoping to uphold the old imperial order.[31] Benton and Ford claim that international law originated in the British

---

[27] Charles H Alexandrowicz, *An Introduction to the History of the Law of Nations in the East Indies (16th, 17th and 18th Centuries)* (Clarendon Press 1967) 2, 235; for a critique of Alexandrowicz and his thinking, and with further references: Jörg Axel Kämmerer and Paulina Starski, 'Imperial Colonialism in the Genesis of International Law—Anomaly or Time of Transition?' (2016) 12 MPIL Research Paper Series <https://papers.ssrn.com/sol3/papers.cfm?abstract_id=2789595> accessed 16 July 2018.

[28] Arnulf Becker Lorca, 'Universal International Law: Nineteenth-Century Histories of Imposition and Appropriation' (2010) 51 Harvard International Law Journal 475; Arnulf Becker Lorca, *Mestizo International Law. A Global Intellectual History 1842–1933* (Cambridge University Press 2014).

[29] Jörg Fisch, *Die europäische Expansion und das Völkerrecht. Die Auseinandersetzungen um den Status der überseeischen Gebiete vom 15. Jahrhundert bis zur Gegenwart* (Steiner 1984). Fisch also addressed the 'international legal relations' between European and non-European entities and thus might also be regarded as a contributionist; for another important work: Gerrit Gong, *The Standard of 'Civilization' in International Society* (Oxford University Press 1984).

[30] Anthony Anghie, *Imperialism, Sovereignty and the Making of International Law* (Cambridge University Press 2004).

[31] Mark Mazower, *No Enchanted Palace: The End of Empire and the Ideological Origins of the United Nations* (Princeton University Press 2010).

administrative struggles with their colonies in the beginning of the nineteenth century.[32] Hence, while these works often come as critiques of international law's progress narrative, they often embrace the idea that international law was shaped by European actors or practices.

So, what to make out of these competing accounts if we are interested in the rise and decline of international law? For the purpose of the analysis, I adopt a quantitative understanding of rise and decline,[33] which presupposes that an increase in the number of actors taking part in an international system structured by legal rules signals a rise of international law. In the light of this definition, most accounts—despite their contrasting normative undertones[34]—tell such a story of rise. Only the contributionist narrative challenges the idea that international law spread as a European invention to the rest of the world arguing that international law had its roots in other regions. Where the idealist, the realist, and the critical account of European universalization differ is in its causes. The idealists highlight progress, the realists emphasize great power interests, and the critics colonial domination as main factors for the law's expansion. Which narrative should one follow?

III. Methodological quarrels and the contextual approach

The diverging narratives of the history of international law are caused to a certain degree by diverging definitional approaches. If we look back into the past, what are we supposed to describe as international law? Is it the international law we know today as stemming from the sources doctrine of Article 38 of the International Court of Justice Statute? Do we have to follow the depictions of contemporaries of each period and ask what they understood as international law? Or should we be broader and include all legal relations between different highest territorial entities?[35] The definitional question is strongly related to a hotly debated topic of the theory of history: the issue of anachronism. According to this concept, every historian should avoid the importation of terminology of the present into the past. Instead, one should pay close attention to the language and understandings of the contemporaries. The rejection of anachronism has been widespread in Western historiography after the Second World War. In France, Lucien Febvre, the famous co-founder of the *Annales*-School, attacked anachronism as the 'worst of all sins, the sin that cannot be forgiven'. It would be the task of the historian to try to understand what certain texts meant in the time of the

---

[32] Lauren Benton and Lisa Ford, *Rage for Order: The British Empire and the Origins of International law 1800–1850* (Harvard University Press 2016).

[33] For different standards and criteria of 'rise and decline': Krieger and Nolte (n 1) VI.2.

[34] Normatively, the progress explanation embraces the universalization, while Grewe's realist account remains rather neutral and the critical narrative is sceptical of the spread of international law.

[35] On the definitional question: Yasakuni Onuma, 'When Was the Law of the International Society Born?' (2000) 2 Journal on the History of International Law 1, 2–5; Heinhard Steiger, 'Völkerrecht' in Heinhard Steiger (ed), *Von der Staatengesellschaft zur Weltrepublik? Aufsätze zur Geschichte des Völkerrechts aus vierzig Jahren* (Nomos 2009) 3–4.

contemporaries.[36] Similarly, in the Anglo-American world, Quentin Skinner warned before 'sheer anachronism' and advocated to carefully assess the context of historical ideas. The historian should try to reveal what certain philosophical theories and intellectual concepts were supposed to mean in the given time and how they were supposed to be understood in the historical context.[37] In Germany, Reinhard Koselleck, known as the founder of *Begriffsgeschichte* (conceptual history), lauded efforts which tried to understand the past by analysing how certain terms were semantically used in a certain period by the contemporaries.[38] Even though some historians have warned against a too strict understanding of this rule of historical scholarship,[39] to avoid anachronisms is often regarded as an important cornerstone of historical methodology.[40]

In relation to the historical writing about international law, the issue of anachronism has received new attention. Some historians criticized that critical historical scholarship by international lawyers did not engage deeply enough with the standards and debates of the past. Ian Hunter argued that a lot of the critical legal writing on natural law and the law of nations of the early modern period had been 'dogged by debilitating anachronism and presentism'. For him, the writings of Samuel Pufendorf and Emer de Vattel were part of an 'intra-European' debate, thus it would make no sense to presume that 'the law of nature and nations spread a false universalism as a stalking-horse for European imperialism', because a 'true universalism or cosmopolitanism' was not available to these writers.[41] Georg Cavaller criticized Anghie and others for 'the construction of false continuities' which ignore the 'complexity and pluralism of the discourses from various (and often very divergent) centuries'.[42] Others stressed that some of the 'anachronistic interpretations of historical phenomena' by international lawyers give 'no information about the historical contexts of the phenomena one claims to recognize'.[43]

Recently, critical legal scholars have reacted to this theme of criticism. Even though Martti Koskenniemi at first had been sceptical of the 'sin of anachronism',[44] he later pointed to the 'limits of contextualism' and suggested to 'move beyond context'.

---

[36] Lucien Febvre, *The Problem of Unbelief in the Sixteenth Century: The Religion of Rabelais* (Harvard University Press 1982) 5.

[37] Quentin Skinner, 'Meaning and Understanding in the History of Ideas' (1969) 8 History and Theory 3, 7–16, 48–50; on the influence of the so-called 'Cambridge School': Mark Bevir, 'The Role of Contexts in Understanding and Explanation' in Hans Erich Bödecker (ed), *Begriffsgeschichte, Diskursgeschichte, Metapherngeschichte* (Wallstein 2002) 159.

[38] Reinhart Koselleck, 'Begriffsgeschichtliche Probleme der Verfassungsgeschichtsschreibung' in Reinhart Koselleck (ed), *Begriffsgeschichten. Studien zur Semantik und Pragmatik der politischen und sozialen Sprache* (Suhrkamp 2006) 365, 372.

[39] Distinguishing between vicious and legitimate anachronisms: Nick Jardine, 'Uses and Abuses of Anachronism in the History of the Sciences' (2000) 38 History of Science 251; pointing to the potential of anachronism: Achim Landwehr, *Die anwesende Abwesenheit der Geschichte. Essay zur Geschichtstheorie* (Fischer 2016) 239–41.

[40] Nick Jardine stressed that at the turn of the century at least in the history of the sciences 'the fight against anachronism' seemed to have been won: Jardine (n 39) 251.

[41] Ian Hunter, 'The Figure of Man and the Territorialisation of Justice in "Enlightenment" Natural Law: Pufendorf and Vattel' (2013) 23 Intellectual History Review 239.

[42] Georg Cavaller, 'Vitoria, Grotius, Pufendorf, Wolff and Vattel: Accomplices of European Colonialism and Exploitation or True Cosmopolitans?' (2008) 10 Journal of the History of International Law 181, 207–09.

[43] Randall Lesaffer, 'International Law and its History. The Story of an Unrequited Love' in Matthew Craven, Malgosia Fitzmaurice, and Maria Vogiatzi (eds), *Time, History and International Law* (Martinus Nijhoff 2007) 27, 34.

[44] Koskenniemi, 'Eurocentrism' (n 14) 166.

Contextual works would often believe in 'a "positivist" separation between the past and the present that encourages historical relativism, indeed an outright uncritical attitude that may end up suppressing efforts to find patterns in history that might account for today's experiences of domination and injustice'.[45] Similarly, Ann Orford praised the 'legitimate role of anachronism in international legal method'[46] and warned that a too 'historical method' might have a 'constraining effect on critical approaches to the field of international law'. International legal scholars should try 'to undertake a study of how legal concepts, ideas, or principles are transformed in relation to changes in the social world over time, and thus to grasp the present function of legal concepts adequately'.[47] International legal scholarship would be 'necessarily anachronistic' because it would be interested in the 'movement of meaning' and not as much in the historical meaning of a given time.[48]

So which methodological take should one follow? Is it convincing to strictly focus only on the meaning of certain concepts in the contexts of the past? Or should one rather cast off the shackles of the anachronism-allegation? I argue for a contextual reading of the history of international law, which takes the language and contexts of the past seriously. At the same time, my proposed contextual approach embraces analytical tools of the present which are needed to open our view for potential alternative routes to international law's historical development.

On the one hand, it makes sense to carefully assess the terms and language of the sources in order to understand the historical causes of social or intellectual change of the given time. In relation to international law, this means paying close attention to how the contemporaries used the language of 'international law' and what they meant by it. By calling the relations between the Greek poleis or African tribes in the seventeenth century 'international law' in our contemporary sense, one imposes our present understanding on a different time or region.

On the other hand, present categories are often necessary analytical tools to define the research outlook. As Koselleck has stressed, without some categorical concepts of the present, one cannot organize the story of the sources in a meaningful way.[49] In my view, writings on the history of international law should embrace a categorical understanding of international law, which is interested in foreign relations between highest entities in general. Thus, these relations should be integrated in the historical recollection, even if the contemporaries did not employ the language of international law. As Bardo Fassbender and Anne Peters have stressed, particularly 'the roads less travelled by' are the ones which promise to enrich our contemporary understanding of

[45]   Martti Koskenniemi, 'Histories of International Law: Significance and Problems for a Critical View' (2013) 27 Temple International and Comparative Law Journal 215, 229; Martti Koskenniemi, 'Vitoria and Us' (2014) 22 Rechtsgeschichte 119, 128.
[46]   Anne Orford, 'On International Legal Method' (2013) 1 London Review of International Law 166, 175.
[47]   Anne Orford, 'International Law and the Limits of History' in Wouter Werner, Marieke de Hoon, and Alexis Galán (eds), The Law of International Lawyers: Reading Martti Koskenniemi (Cambridge University Press 2017) 1, 7.
[48]   Orford (n 46) 175; embracing Orford's approach: Rose Parfitt, 'The Spectre of Sources' (2014) 25 European Journal of International Law 297.
[49]   Koselleck (n 38) 373.

international normative orders.[50] Hence, even though my contextual approach pays close attention to the terminology of the actors, it includes alternative paths into the narrative of international law.

IV. The regional scope of the history of international law from a contextual perspective

This section tries to exemplify how a contextual approach to the history of international law, which takes functional equivalents of international law seriously, might look. In a cursory overview, it analyses how the system of international law changed its regional scope from the seventeenth/eighteenth centuries (1), over the nineteenth century (2) to the twentieth century (3). While doing so, it draws from the idealistic, realistic, contributionist, and critical accounts of the history of international law. Furthermore, it pays close attention to the contemporary descriptions of the normative rules governing foreign relations in the given time and region. By starting with the seventeenth/eighteenth centuries, my narrative comes close to a traditional (European) historical periodization of the origin of international law.[51] This Eurocentric narrative has recently been a popular subject of critique.[52] However, for the purpose of a tentative and broad sketch, this starting point seems to be helpful not only as a 'convenience'.[53] Since different normative systems of world order existed in different regions during the seventeenth century, the period seems to be a stimulating opening for the discussion.

1. The Chinese investiture system, the Islamic siyar system, and the European law of nations (seventeenth and eighteenth centuries)

In the seventeenth and eighteenth centuries, the world was divided between different empires and regions which framed and shaped their respective normative systems according to their political ideals. The Chinese dynasties, the gunpowder empires of the Islamic world, and the European states developed particularistic normative orders in their respective regions. The principles of the Sinocentric investiture system, the Islamocentric siyar system, and the European law of nations were only applicable in certain territories.[54] Inside the different regions, the rules governing the relations among the different actors followed diverging conceptions.

---

[50] Bardo Fassbender and Anne Peters, 'Introduction: Towards a Global History of International Law' in Fassbender and Peters (n 13) 1.

[51] Often the periods of international law are divided between 1648–1815, 1815–1919, 1919–45 and 1945–90, see for instance the articles on the history of international law in the *Max Planck Encyclopedia of Public International Law* (Online Edition <www.mpepil.com> last update April 2013) and the chapters on Europe in Fassbender and Peters, *The Oxford Handbook of the History of International Law* (n 13).

[52] See n 67.

[53] John M Roberts and Odd A Westad, *The History of the World* (6th edn, Oxford University Press 2016) 533; on periodization of international law in general: Oliver Diggelmann, 'The Periodization of the History of International law' in Fassbender and Peters (n 13) 553.

[54] Onuma (n 35) 1.

The foreign relations of the Chinese dynasties with neighbouring countries were based on a system of homage and investiture. Because China had economic and military advantages over other entities in East Asia, the Qing dynasty shaped foreign relations in that region with its customs, rules, and rituals.[55] The emperor, who was regarded as ruling universally by virtue (dezhi), established vassal relationships with heads of regions surrounding the Chinese empire (cefong). For paying tribute to the dynasty, one could receive the title of king. Usually this meant that the Chinese emperor did not interfere in the domestic affairs of places like Tibet, Mongolia, and Xianjiang as long as they subordinated to the rituals.[56] However, the Sinocentric conception of world order was much more flexible than the depiction as a 'tributary system' signals. If an entity did not send a tributary mission to the emperor, the 'savage' was at times simply left alone outside of the virtue-based system.[57] In any case, the relations were clearly not founded on some idea of formal equality between different actors but were oriented towards the emperor.[58]

The normative orders in the Islamic world proceeded from the views developed by Moslem jurists like Muhammad Al-Shaybani from the eighth to twelfth centuries. According to the siyar system, which is derived from the Qur'an, the Prophet's practices, and relevant practices of the earliest Muslim Caliphs, the world was divided into the territory of Islam (dar al islam) and the territory of war (dar al harab).[59] During Abbasid expansion from the eighth to thirteenth centuries, the goal was to convert the dar al harab to Islam by peaceful and military means.[60] Furthermore, the Islamic jurisprudence propagated that the whole Islamic world should be governed by one Imam.[61] Nonetheless, in practice some normative relationships developed between different Muslim states. For instance, the powerful Ottoman Empire established vassal relationships with North African entities in Algier and Tunis, which became more and more independent over time.[62] Furthermore, the Ottoman Empire already in the sixteenth century negotiated with the Safavid in Persia about the question how the Muslim dynasties could establish stable relations in order to end the many wars.[63]

In Europe, since the Peace of Westphalia, territorial states started to stabilize their political relations through legal rules. The hierarchy model, which during the Middle Ages had centred around the Pope and the Emperor of the Holy Roman Empire,

[55]   ibid 12.
[56]   Shin Kawashima, 'China' in Fassbender and Peters (n 13) 451, 451–56; Rune Svarverud, *International Law as World Order in Late Imperial China. Translation, Reception and Discourse, 1847–1911* (Brill 2007) 8–16.
[57]   Onuma (n 35) 16–17.
[58]   Svarverud (n 56) 8–12; Shotaro Hamamoto, 'International Law. Regional Developments: East Asia' in *Max Planck Encyclopedia of Public International Law* (n 51).
[59]   Mohammad Fadel, 'International Law. Regional Developments: Islam' in *Max Planck Encyclopedia of Public International Law* (n 51); Majid Khadduri, 'Islam and the Modern Law of Nations' (1956) 50 American Journal of International Law 358.
[60]   Onuma (n 35) 18–19.
[61]   Hans Kruse, *Islamische Völkerrechtslehre* (2nd edn, Brockmeyer 1979) 4.
[62]   Fathia Sahli and Abelmalek el Ouazzani, 'Africa North of the Sahara and Arab Countries' in Fassbender and Peters (n 13) 386, 389.
[63]   Colin P Mitchell, 'Am I my Brother's Keeper? Negotiating Corporate Sovereignty and Divine Absolutism in Sixteenth-Century Turco-Iranian Politics' in Colin P Mitchell (ed), *New Perspectives on Safavid Iran: Empire and Society* (Routledge 2011) 33–58.

gradually lost its normative force.[64] A European 'law of nations' emerged, which was based on the conception of a relative equal status of great powers. The normative system was regarded as a Christian order, as the 'respublica christiana' governing relations between Christian European states.[65] Of course, the so called 'myth of Westphalia' has rightfully been criticized for overstating that the Westphalian peace introduced a stable,[66] European-wide 'Westphalian system' overnight, in which the legal principles of sovereign equality and non-intervention were fully developed.[67] However, as historians have argued, the peace treaty was the most important legal document of that time, referred to in many peace treaties to come until the end of the eighteenth century.[68] Two legal developments are regarded as particularly relevant. Firstly, the inter-state character of international law became stronger. Even though non-state actors like the Holy See continued to take part in international legal relations after the treaty, the Catalans, the merchant city combination Hanse, and (some years later after the Congress of Nijmegen) the princes of the Holy Roman Empire were excluded from inter-state affairs.[69] Secondly, the idea of the balance of power among the great powers started to receive a semi-legal relevance. The Treaty of Utrecht, which settled the Spanish war of succession in 1713, explicitly referred to the balance of power. In the minds of the political leaders of the time, the idea had a legal significance.[70]

But how did the diverging normative systems interlink when they came into contact with each other? Even though the relations between the systems were based on different religious and political conceptions, some legal relations emerged. For instance, the

[64] However, pointing to the role that international law played during the Middle Ages: Wilhelm Janssen, 'Die Anfänge des modernen Völkerrechts und der neuzeitlichen Diplomatie. Ein Forschungsbericht (Schluß)' (1964) 38 Vierteljahrsschrift für Literaturwissenschaft und Geistesgeschichte 591.

[65] In comparison to the sixteenth century religion had lost some of its importance: Heinz Duchhardt, 'Peace Treaties from Westphalia to the Revolutionary Era' in Randall Lesaffer (ed), *Peace Treaties and International Law in European History* (Cambridge University Press 2004) 45–58.

[66] The time from 1648 until 1815 was a time of many wars like the Franco-Spanish War (1635–59), the Spanish and Austrian Wars of Succession (1701–14; 1740–48), the Great Northern War (1700–21), the Seven Years' War (1756–63), and the French Revolutionary Wars (1792–02).

[67] The myth of the 'Westphalian System' has been invented by Leo Gross in 1948: Leo Gross, 'The Peace of Westphalia, 1648—1948' (1948) 42 American Journal of International Law 20; for critiques: Andreas Osiander, 'Sovereignty, International Relations, and the Westphalian Myth' (2001) 55 International Organizations 251; Heinhard Steiger, 'Der Westfälische Friede—Grundgesetz für Europa?' in Heinz Duchhardt (ed), *Der Westfälische Friede. Diplomatie—politische Zäsur—kulturelles Umfeld—Rezeptionsgeschichte* (Oldenbourg 1998) 33–80; Heinz Duchhardt, '"Westphalian System". Zur Problematik einer Denkfigur' (1999) 269 Historische Zeitschrift 305; Randall Lesaffer, 'The Westphalia Peace Treaties and the Development of the Tradition of Great European Peace Settlements prior to 1648' (1997) 18 Grotiana 71; Rainer Grote, 'Westphalian System' in *Max Planck Encyclopedia of Public International Law* (n 51).

[68] Heinz Duchhardt, 'From the Peace of Westphalia to the Congress of Vienna' in Fassbender and Peters (n 13) 628, 629.

[69] Even though the German princes of the Holy Roman Empire had successfully claimed the right to conduct foreign affairs (so-called 'Bündnisrecht') at the Peace of Westphalia, at the Congress of Nijmegen (1678–79) they permanently lost the right to participate in multilateral peace congresses as independent parties: Duchhardt (n 68) 633–34.

[70] On this: Heinrich Duchhardt, 'Friedenswahrung im 18. Jahrhundert' (1985) 240 Historische Zeitschrift 265, 266–67; Frederik Dhondt, *Balance of Power and Norm Hierarchy. Franco-British Diplomacy after the Peace of Utrecht* (Brill 2015); on the principle of the balance of power and international law: Alfred Vagts and Detlev Vagts, 'The Balance of Power in International Law: A History of an Idea' (1979) 73 American Journal of International Law 555; on the role of the balance of power in the international legal scholarship of the eighteenth century: Milos Vec, 'De-Juridifying "Balance of Power"—A Principle in 19th Century International Legal Doctrine' (2011) European Society of International Law Conferences Paper Series 5/2011 <https://papers.ssrn.com/sol3/papers.cfm?abstract_id=1968667> accessed 16 July 2018, 10.

Chinese concluded the Treaty of Nerchinsk with Russia as early as 1689, even though the Chinese emperor in general continued to hold the view that the Chinese empire had a superior status to other entities.[71] When later the relations between the West and East intensified, the different conceptions of normative world order caused tensions. Urged by Dutch and British commercial activities, the Qing dynasty had established the so-called 'Canton System' in 1757, which allowed for trade with Western countries in Guangzhou. By the end of the century, the rituals of subordination at the emperor's seat became a problem for the confident Western trade negotiators who did not want to bow to a foreign dynasty.[72]

Similarly, between European powers and the Muslim world normative relations existed. In the seventeenth century, the Ottoman Empire concluded treaties with France (1673), England (1680), and the Netherlands (1680), which were based on the so-called system of *ahadnames* (capitulations). According to this system, the Sultan granted trade concessions as imperial decrees to non-Muslim rulers. Because both the Christian states as well as the Muslim leader claimed superiority, these treaties were often not based on an understanding of equality.[73] However, the parties were willing to make compromises. For instance, in the Treaty of Karlowitz of 1699 between the Ottoman Empire and Poland, the Sultan granted privileges to Poland using the language of an imperial degree, but at the same time waived Polish tributary obligations.[74] In practice, some quasi-equal relations emerged.

How were these international practices conceptualized by the contemporaries? For the Muslim and Chinese world this question is hard to answer. Not many anglophone studies exist, which examine the legal or theological scholarship on international relations by Muslim and Chinese writers during the seventeenth and eighteenth centuries in depth.[75] But there are some indications. While in relation to the Ottoman Empire most of the scholarship on international legal history has focused on the nineteenth century,[76] scholars stress that until the eighteenth century Ottoman scholars rarely engaged with international law which was regarded as a Western practice. Only in the late nineteenth century Ottoman jurists appropriated the Western international legal discourse.[77] In the seventeenth century the Islamic/Ottoman ideals of an 'ever-expanding frontier' and an 'ever victorious army' still dominated the thinking of many Ottoman

---

[71] Chi-Tua Tang, 'China–Europe' in Fassbender and Peters (n 13) 701, 704.

[72] Onuma (n 35) 7; on the Canton System: Kawashima (n 56) 456–57.

[73] Karl-Heinz Ziegler, 'The peace treaties of the Ottoman Empire with European Christian powers' in Lesaffer, *Peace Treaties and International Law* (n 65) 338, 347–50; Umut Özsu, 'Ottoman Empire' in Fassbender and Peters (n 13) 429, 430–37; Becker Lorca, 'Universal International Law' (n 28) 506–11.

[74] Darius Kolodziejczyk, 'Between the Splendor of Barocco and Political Pragmatism: The Form and Contents of the Polish-Ottoman Treaty Documents of 1699' (2003) 83 Oriento Moderno 671.

[75] This partly has to do with a certain research focus on European thinking in current academia; eg of the twenty-one 'people in portrait' in the *Oxford Handbook of the History of International Law* (n 13) only one writer (Al-Shaybani) stems from a non-Western background.

[76] E.g. Umut Özsu and Thomas Skouteris, 'International Legal Histories of the Ottoman Empire: An Introduction to the Symposium' (2016) 18 Journal of the History of International Law 1–4; Cemil Aydın, *The Politics of Anti-Westernism in Asia: Visions of World Order in Pan-Islamic and Pan-Asian Thought* (Columbia University Press 2007).

[77] Berdal Aral, 'The Ottoman "School" of International Law as Featured in Textbooks' (2016) 18 Journal of the History of International Law 70–97.

intellectuals on foreign affairs, even though the Ottoman thinkers gradually gave up the idea of a constant war with the infidels.[78] In relation to China, John Fairbank's depiction of the Chinese world order before the arrival of the Western international law as a hierarchical 'tributary system' has been very influential.[79] While some scholars embrace this idea,[80] there also has been criticism of this terminology recently. Some scholars argue that China was less arrogant than portrayed in Fairbank's account,[81] while others in contrast point to the violent character of Chinese expansion to Central Asia.[82] At least the discussants agree that no Chinese word for tributary system existed and that the system was much more flexible than the depiction of a Sinocentric tributary system signals.[83] In any case, it seems that the Chinese scholar-officials in the seventeenth century imagined their rule as relationships with vassals dominated by a morally pure emperor[84] and did not use the terminology of law for describing their world order.[85]

We know most about Europe, where theologists, philosophers, and lawyers started to translate the Latin expression *ius gentium* into the European languages. Since the sixteenth century, Francisco de Vitoria, Francisco Suàrez, and Hugo Grotius had gradually emancipated the *ius gentium* from its religious, scholastical background and redescribed it as a universally applicable law rooted in a natural law tradition.[86] In 1661, Samuel Pufendorf became the first chair holder of 'The Law of Nature and of Nations' at Heidelberg University.[87] As the discipline professionalized, the evolving legal rules were translated and described as 'Völkerrecht' (Samuel Pufendorf, 1711; Christian Wolff, 1754),[88] 'droit de gens' (Emer de Vattel, 1758),[89] 'law of nations' (Edmund Burke, in the 1770s),[90] and 'international law' (Jeremy Bentham,

---

[78] Virginia H Aksan, 'Ottoman Political Writing, 1768–1808' (1993) 25 International Journal of Middle Eastern Studies 53, 54, 64.

[79] John K Fairbank (ed), *The Chinese World Order. Traditional China's Foreign Relations* (Harvard University Press 1968).

[80] eg Wang Tieya (n 20) 219–25; Marc Andre Matten, *Imagining a Postnational World: Hegemony and Space in Modern China* (Brill 2016) 41–44.

[81] On this: Tang (n 71) 702–04.

[82] Odd A Westad, *Restless Empire: China and the World since 1750* (Basic Books 2012) 9–10; arguing that it should be described as colonialism: Peter C Perdue, 'The Tenacious Tributary System Journal of Contemporary China' (2015) 24 Journal of Contemporary China 1002, 1010–11; on the debate also: Suisheng Zhao, 'Rethinking the Chinese World Order: The Imperial Cycle and the Rise of China' (2015) 24 Journal of Contemporary China 961, 966–70.

[83] On tributary system as 'a Western invention for descriptive purposes' already: Mark Mancall, 'The Ch'ing Tribute System: An Interpretive Essay' in John Fairbank (ed), *The Chinese World Order. Traditional China's Foreign Relations* (Harvard University Press 1968) 63–89; on the flexibility of the system: Westad, *Restless Empire* (n 82) 10; Rana Mitter, 'An Uneasy Engagement: Chinese Ideas of Global Order and Justice in Historical Perspective' in Rosemary Foot, John Gaddis, and Andrew Hurrell (eds), *Order and Justice in International Relations* (Oxford University Press 2003) 207.

[84] Matten (n 80) 37–41.

[85] Sarah C Paine, *Imperial Rivals: China, Russia, and their Disputed Frontier* (Sharpe 1996) 81–82.

[86] On the history of the term: Steiger, 'Völkerrecht' (n 35) 1–49; Heinhard Steiger, *Universalität und Partikularität des Völkerrechts in geschichtlicher Perspektive. Aufsätze zur Völkerrechtsgeschichte 2008-2015* (Nomos 2015) X.

[87] Janne E Nijman, *The Concept of International Legal Personality. An Inquiry into the History and Theory of International Law* (Cambridge University Press 2004) 30.

[88] Samuel Pufendorf, *Acht Bücher vom Natur- und Völckerrecht* (Knochen 1711); Christian Wolff, *Grundsätze des Natur- und Völkerrechts* (Rengerische Buchhandlung 1754).

[89] Emeric de Vattel, *Le droit de gens ou principes de la loi naturelle* (public issue, London 1758).

[90] On Edmund Burke's frequent references: Peter James Stanlis, *Edmund Burke and his Natural Law* (University of Michigan Press 1965) 85–102.

1789).[91] These doctrinal works often used a universalist language referring to 'all nations', but did not address much practice of non-European countries. As Jennifer Pitts has argued, two strands of thinking started to compete with each other: while some writers wanted to apply the law of nations to all nations, others stressed that it was the law of the European club.[92] For the second strand the 'Droit public de l'Europe' (Gabriele Bonnot de Mably, 1748)[93] or the 'positive Europäische Völkerrecht' (Georg Friedrich von Martens, 1786) was in its essence a law of European states.[94]

2. European colonization and internalization of the European international law (the long nineteenth century)

The industrial revolution in the nineteenth century established the basis for a stronger European role in international politics. Through policies of free trade and imperialism, European states influenced and—at times—dominated political developments in other parts of the world. As the historian Jürgen Osterhammel has put it, in no other century did European initiatives have a comparable impact on other regions.[95] The extraordinary power and role model effect of Europe had repercussions for the competing normative systems in the rest of the world. The European law of nations started to expand.

It first reached the Americas. During the sixteenth and seventeenth centuries, the Spanish, Portuguese, French, and British colonialists had displaced the native populations on the American continent. Despite concluding some treaties with local chiefs, most of the time the colonizers did not recognize the indigenous tribes as subjects with legal rights.[96] Only after the descendants of the colonizers had become strong enough to smash the shackles of European domination, the European international law tradition disseminated. Shortly after US-American independence in 1776, France and the Netherlands supported the young country against the British and recognized the United States as a sovereign state. Moreover, after the conclusion of a provisional peace treaty between Britain and the United States in 1782, other European states established diplomatic relations with the former colony. Soon, the English version of Emeric de Vattel's *Le Droit de gens* gained great popularity in the United States and informed the

[91] For a discussion of Jeremy Bentham's *Introduction to the Principles of Morals and Legislation* (1789): Mark Janis, 'Jeremy Bentham and the Fashioning of "International law"' (1984) 78 American Journal of International Law 405.

[92] Jennifer Pitts, 'Empire and Legal Universalisms in the Eighteenth Century' (2012) 92 The American Historical Review 100–03, 117; focusing on the universalistic tendencies in the writing: Charles H Alexandrowicz, 'Doctrinal Aspects of the Universality of the law of Nations' 37 (1961) British Yearbook of International Law 506.

[93] Gabriele Bonnot de Mably, *Le droit public de l'europe fondé sur les traités* (public issue, Geneva 1748); on his writing: Armin von Bogdandy and Stephan Hinghofer-Szalkay, 'Begriffsgeschichtliche Analysen im Spannungsfeld von europäischem Rechtsraum, droit public de l'europe und Carl Schmitt' (2013) 73 Zeitschrift für ausländisches öffentliches Recht und Völkerrecht 209, 222–29.

[94] Georg Friedrich von Martens, *Einleitung in das positive Europäische Völkerrecht auf Verträge und Herkommen gegründet* (Dieterich 1796) 6, 22–32; also Johann Jacob Moser, *Grundsätze des europäischen Völkerrechts in Friedenszeiten* (Raspe 1750).

[95] Jürgen Osterhammel, *Die Verwandlung der Welt. Eine Geschichte des 19. Jahrhunderts* (C.H. Beck 2009) 20.

[96] Fisch, *Die europäische Expansion* (n 29) 39–42, 104–05.

diplomatic and judicial practices of the US governments and courts.[97] In the logic of the time, after Christian settlers in the United States had ousted the Indians and had successfully built up functioning settler colonies, the European law of nations expanded.[98]

Furthermore, in their struggle for independence in the first half of the nineteenth century, Latin American countries turned to Britain and the United States for admission to the international political and legal system. During the Napoleonic Wars in Europe (1808–14), Napoleon had installed his brother on the Spanish throne. As a reaction liberal *juntas* were built in Ecuador, Bolivia, Columbia, Argentina, Chile, and other states. After years of civil wars between the liberals and factions loyal to the Spanish monarch Ferdinand VII, twelve new countries were born between 1810 and 1830 as democratic republics. British and US-American recognition became a crucial factor for a successful consolidation of the young countries. The US government recognized countries which had effectively established their independence, and called for a non-intervention principle on the American continent (Monroe Doctrine of 1823).[99] The British government also subscribed to the non-intervention principle and started to negotiate treaties with Mexico, Columbia, and Buenos Aires, thereby rejecting the conception of the 'Holy Alliance' (Prussia, Austria, and Russia) to crush revolutionary movements based on the idea of Christian European dynastic solidarity.[100] Soon, Latin American countries applied international legal rules and appropriated them according to their own understanding. The Congress of Panama of 1826 led to the 'Treaty of Union, League, and Perpetual Confederation' between Latin American countries applying the language of the European law with certain regional specificities. Even though the treaty was only ratified by Columbia, it can be seen as a symbol for ideas about an anti-colonial international law.[101]

In Asia, China, and Japan came under pressure to adopt the legal language of the European powers. In the mid-nineteenth century, Western politicians threatened Asian states by military force into 'unequal treaties', in order to 'open the door' to Asian markets.[102] In China, the defeat in the Opium War of 1839 led to the Treaty of Nanjing (1842) between Britain and China. According to this model treaty, European powers received rights of unilateral extraterritoriality, consular jurisdiction, agreement tariffs, and a most-favoured nation status. Even though the Chinese emperor tried to avoid the introduction of the language of equality into these treaties, a double standard between the vassal relationships of the Chinese dynasty and the treaty-based commercial relationships with Western powers emerged.[103] At the same time, China adapted

---

[97] Vincent Chetail, 'Vattel and the American Dream: An Inquiry into the Reception of the Law of Nations in the United States' in Pierre-Marie Dupuy and Vincent Chetail (eds), *The Roots of International Law. Liber Amicorum Peter Haggenmacher* (Martinus Nijhoff 2014) 251.

[98] On the recognition of the United States: Mikulas Fabry, *Recognizing States. International Society and the Establishment of New States Since 1776* (Oxford University Press 2010) 26–36; Grewe, *Epochs of International Law* (n 23) 343–48.

[99] Fabry (n 98) 49–58.

[100] ibid 51–54, 58–63; Grewe, *Epochs of International Law* (n 23) 488–89.

[101] Alejandro Alvarez, 'Latin America and International Law' (1909) 3 American Journal of International Law 269; Jorge L Esquirol, 'Latin America' in Fassbender and Peters (n 13) 553, 560–61.

[102] Anne Peters, 'Treaties, Unequal' in *Max Planck Encyclopedia of Public International Law* (n 51).

[103] Kawashima (n 56) 459, 467–68.

to the challenge and internalized some of the Western rules. Because the Chinese dynasty intended to become accustomed with the European tradition, Western international law textbooks were translated into Chinese.[104] Soon, the 'Western' concept of sovereignty contributed to a changed understanding of world order and informed the state-building process in China.[105] At the end of the century, the Qing dynasty not only took part in the peace conferences at The Hague in 1899 and 1907, it also incorporated the principle of consular jurisdiction in its tributary relationships with Korea.[106] Only China's rival Japan was even faster to adjust to the Western norms. After Japan had been forced into unequal treaties by the gun boat diplomacy of the US-American Commodore Matthew Perry, the Meiji government embraced an agenda of Western modernization. Soon Japan used arguments of European international law to challenge China's traditional Sinocentric system. At the end of the century, Japan had achieved the abolition of Western consular jurisdiction and utilized the mechanism of unequal treaties in its relations with Korea and Thailand.[107] Thus, gun boat diplomacy and norm internalization provided for the slow universalization of the European international law in Asia.

Also, the traditional understanding of the Islamic siyar system was challenged by European expansion. The Treaty of Paris (1856), which ended the Crimean War between Russia and a French–British–Ottoman alliance, declared that the Ottoman Empire had become a member of the European club. While politically the treaty was intended to limit the Russian influence in the Balkans, neutralize the Black Sea, and establish the Western states as protector of Christians in Turkey, it also stipulated that the Ottoman Empire was admitted to 'participate in the advantages of public law and the European concert'. Nonetheless, the Ottoman demands of a formal abolition of the capitulation system were ignored, an indication that the relations between European states and the Empire remained problematic and abnormal.[108] In any case, also the Ottoman Empire started to embrace Western models of diplomacy. The government founded a foreign ministry with French as its key working language and established new embassies all around Europe.[109] At the end of the century, Ottoman jurists wrote the first Ottoman international law books embracing the Western international law discourse.[110]

In Africa, European traders and African chiefs had established some treaty relations during the seventeenth and eighteenth centuries. After this 'pre-confrontation' period,[111] during the nineteenth century, European great powers increasingly started

---

[104] ibid 458, 460–67; Tang (n 71) 704–05; Svarverud (n 56) 75–87.

[105] Stephen R Halsey, *Quest for Power. European Imperialisms and the Making of Chinese Statecraft* (Harvard University Press 2015) 6–7.

[106] Kawashima (n 56) 468.

[107] Masaharu Yanagihara, 'Japan' in Fassbender and Peters (n 13) 475, 485–88, 493–97; Kinjin Akashi, 'Japan-Europe' in Fassbender and Peters (n 13) 724–43.

[108] Özsu (n 73) 437–39.

[109] ibid 437–39.

[110] On this: Berdal Aral, 'The Ottoman "School" of International Law as Featured in Textbooks' (2016) 18 Journal of the History of International Law 70–97.

[111] Charles H Alexandrowicz, 'The Role of Treaties in the European-African Confrontation in the Nineteenth Century' in Mensah-Brown (n 24) 27, 28–37.

to set up colonies and colonial protectorates often on the basis of treaties with local rulers.[112] When at the end of the nineteenth century, Germany's colonial ambitions threatened the balance of power on the African continent, the Berlin Congo Conference (1885) established the principle of effectiveness. This meant that only effective control over the colony justified recognition as a colonizer by other European states. Even though the Congo Act included a duty of well-treatment of the African inhabitants, it was not legally owed directly to the indigenous people but to the other non-African treaty parties.[113] Hence, the European legal rules were not regarded as being applicable to the relations with the local population. This became particularly evident through the fact that the humanitarian rules, which developed in the European context of the late nineteenth century, were not held to be applicable, when rebellions by African groups were suppressed.[114]

How did the contemporaries conceptualize the expansion of European international law? In Europe and the United States, where international law came to be an established scientific discipline,[115] the leading international lawyers understood their field of study as European. In the first half of the century, the US-American international lawyer Henry Wheaton stressed that international law was particularly suited for Christian European people or people of European origin.[116] Similarly, the German international lawyer August von Heffter emphasized that international law had always been applicable only to parts of the world. Therefore, it would make sense 'to have given it the name European'.[117] In the latter half of the century, another German, Franz von Holtzendorff, pointed to the superiority of the European culture and underlined that the 'European Law of Nations is ... at present simply the Law of Nations, the common world law of the civilised nations, the legal order of intercourse of the nations living in an historically developed cultural community'.[118] Because an idea of technical and intellectual supremacy of Europe dominated the common perception of the world,[119] a new 'standard of civilisation', which had slowly replaced the reference to 'Christianity', came to play a vital role in the discipline. If a nation was regarded as a 'civilised nation', it could become a member of the European club.[120] At the turn to the twentieth century, European scholars vividly debated whether Japan, China, and Turkey could be recognized as full-fledged subjects of the European law of nations.[121] It is interesting to see that also

---

[112] Fisch (n 29) 42–44.

[113] ibid 87–91; Martti Koskenniemi, *The Gentle Civilizer of Nations* (Cambridge University Press 2002) 121–27; Matthew Craven, 'Between Law and History: the Berlin Conference of 1884–1885 and the Logic of Free Trade' (2015) 3 London Review of International Law 31.

[114] Osterhammel (n 95) 698–701.

[115] Luigi Nuzzo and Milos Vec, 'The Birth of International Law as a Legal Discipline in the 19th Century' in Luigi Nuzzo and Milos Vec (eds), *Constructing International Law. The Birth of a Discipline* (Klostermann 2012) IX.

[116] Henry Wheaton, *Elements of International Law* (Carey, Lea & Blanchard 1836) 44–45.

[117] August Wilhelm Heffter, *Das europäische Völkerrecht der Gegenwart* (Schroeder 1844) 2.

[118] Franz von Holtzendorff, *Handbuch des Völkerrechts auf Grundlage europäischer Staatspraxis* (C Habel 1885) 12–13.

[119] On this: Osterhammel (n 95) 1172–88.

[120] On this: Anghie (n 30) 52–65; Koskenniemi (n 113) 98–178.

[121] For James Lorimer, Turkey, Persia, China, Japan, and Siam had 'partly' received political recognition: James Lorimer, *The Institutes for the Law of Nations*, vol 1 (Blackwood and Sons 1883) 101–02; John Westlake described these states as 'being civilised, though with other civilisations than ours': John Westlake, *Chapters in the Principles of International Law* (Cambridge University Press 1894) 102; Franz von Liszt claimed that Japan became

authors from non-European regions embraced the standard. Scholars like the Japanese Kentaro Kaneko and the Argentinian Carlos Calvo stressed that their respective countries or regions had lived up to the standard.[122] From the Russian periphery, Feodoer Martens underlined that international law would be only applicable to 'those people, which recognise the elementary principles of European cultures and therefore are worthy to be called "civilized nations".'[123] The non-European lawyers from the periphery tried to demonstrate the civilized status of their respective countries in order to become part of the centre.[124]

The system of European international law had not only spread to other regions, but also became more sophisticated during the nineteenth century. The multilateral treaties concluded at the Vienna Congress of 1815 introduced regular meetings of the European major powers (seven congresses and twenty ambassador conferences between Vienna (1815) and Berlin (1878))[125] and professionalized European diplomacy.[126] After the upheavals of the French revolution, the 'Concert of Europe' (Britain, Austria, Prussia, Russia, and France) stabilized European relations according to the political idea of the balance of power.[127] Even though there existed tensions between the parliamentary monarchy Britain and the monarchical 'Holy Alliance' of Prussia, Austria, and Russia, the Concert system guaranteed peace in Europe with relative success. Except for the Crimean War and the German and Italian Unifications Wars between 1853 and 1878, longer periods of peace came to be an emblem of the nineteenth century Europe.[128] The stability of the European order was guaranteed by the great powers. For instance, when Belgium claimed independence against the Netherlands in 1830, Britain and France convinced the Holy Alliance not to intervene. Soon the European powers recognized the small country in a concentrated effort at a Conference in London as an equal member of the European family of nations.[129] De facto, of course, Belgium had to leave major political issues to the great powers.[130] Furthermore, the Congress of

---

a full member of the international community by abolishing consular jurisdiction: Franz von Liszt, *Völkerrecht. Systematisch dargestellt* (3rd edn, O Haering 1904) 4–5.

[122] Kentaro Kaneko, 'Les institutions judiciaires du Japon' (1893) 25 Revue de droit international et de législation comparée 338, 338-339; Carlos Calvo, *Le droit international. Théorique et Pratique* (first published 1887) 155–56; on this: Becker Lorca and Mestizo (n 28) 65–72.

[123] Feodor von Martens, *Völkerrecht. Das international Recht der civilisirten Nationen*, vol 2 (Weidmann 1883-1886) para 41, 181.

[124] Becker Lorca and Mestizo (n 28) 65–72.

[125] George-Henri Soutou, 'Was there a European Order in the Twentieth Century? From the Concert of Europe to the End of the Cold War' (2000) 9 Contemporary European History 329, 330.

[126] The right of precedence, which had led to difficulties at the meetings of the monarchs, was abolished. Diplomacy was instead based on equality between the great powers: Duchhardt (n 68) 650–51; Matthias Schulz, 'Macht, internationale Politik und Normwandel im Staatensystem des 19. Jahrhunderts' in Ulrich Lappenküper and Reiner Marcowitz (eds), *Macht und Recht. Völkerrecht in den internationalen Beziehungen* (Schöningh 2010) 113, 115–16.

[127] In contrast to the eighteenth century, international lawyers now underlined that the balance of power was a political, but not legal principle: Vec (n 70) 11–12.

[128] Osterhammel (n 95) 674–78; Paul W Schroeder, 'The Vienna System and Its Stability: The Problem of Stabilizing a State System in Transformation' in Peter Krüger (ed), *Das europäische Staatensystem im Wandel* (De Gruyter 1996) 107–22.

[129] Fabry (n 98) 80–85.

[130] Schulz (n 127) 116-117; see the emphasis on great powers in: Mark Jarrett, *The Congress of Vienna and Its Legacy. War and Great Power Diplomacy After Napoleon* (Tauris 2014).

Berlin (1878) illustrates how the great powers dominated international politics in the European region. After various uprisings against the Ottoman Empire in the Balkans, Russia had successfully intervened on behalf of the Christian population. However, the Concert did not regard the Russo–Turkish Treaty of San Stefano as a prudent attempt to stabilize the Balkans after the Russo–Turkish War. Especially, they criticized that Russia had acted on its own and not in line with the idea of a balance of power. Thus, in a joint diplomatic effort, the European great powers agreed in Berlin to replace San Stefano with a new treaty which recognized the independence of Romania, Serbia, and Montenegro as *de jure* and Bulgaria as *de facto* sovereigns. Thereby, they produced new subjects of international law on the basis of a common understanding.[131] However, in the late nineteenth century, the Concert was no longer successful in stabilizing the continent. In the wake of high industrialization, major powers combined rapid armament policies with an increasingly militant nationalism. Especially Germany as the new rising economic power demanded its 'place at the sun'. In this context, the partly successful efforts of the peace movement to push for humanitarian rules and an international judiciary at the Hague Peace Conferences of 1899 and 1907 could not prevent the outbreak of the First World War.[132]

3. Institutionalization, decolonization, and the universalization of international law

The First World War ended the European-dominated nineteenth century. The United States entered the world stage as one of the new leading powers. In his Fourteen Points, the American President Woodrow Wilson propagated to apply ideas of democracy, self-determination, and international law to international relations. The newly established League of Nations was supposed to prevent war, lead to disarmament.[133] and introduce an efficient peaceful dispute settlement in form of the Permanent Court of International Justice.[134] At the same time, the liberal system of world order started to be challenged by the Bolshevik Revolution (1917) and its ideas of socialist internationalism. Furthermore, in the 1920s and 1930s, fascism in Italy and National Socialism in Germany emerged as alternatives of world governance based on ethnic and racial categories. The struggle between liberalism, communism, and National Socialism shaped the course of the twentieth century.[135]

---

[131] Fabry (n 98) 99–106.

[132] On the historical debate on the causes of the First World War, on the one side stressing the collective failure of the Great Powers: Christopher Clark, *The Sleepwalkers. How Europe Went to War in 1914* (Allen Lane 2012); on the other side stressing the German main responsibility: Gerd Krumreich, *Juli 1914. Eine Bilanz* (Schöningh 2014); Fritz Fischer, *Der Griff nach der Weltmacht* (Droste 1962).

[133] According to Art 8 Covenant of the League, the member states had the task to reduce armaments to the lowest point consistent with national safety.

[134] On the work of the Permanent Court: Shabtai Rosenne, 'Permanent Court of Justice' in *Max Planck Encyclopedia of Public International Law* (n 51); Peter Krüger, 'Völkerrecht und internationale Politik. Internationale Neuordnung nach dem Ersten Weltkrieg' in Lappenküper and Marcowitz (n 126) 206, 215–18.

[135] Eric Hobsbawn, *The Age of Extremes. A History of the World, 1914–1991* (Pantheon 1994).

Nonetheless, despite these competing ideological actors, on the global level international law expanded. After the end of the First World War, the formerly European system of international law continued to include more and more actors from different regions. The founding of the League of Nations as a system of collective security was not only regarded as a big moment for cooperation and the rule of law at the European level, but also at the international level. Of the around sixty to seventy recognized states of that time, sixty-three at some point became members of the League.[136] Still the majority was European (almost thirty) and therefore the League has been rightly called a 'Eurocentric institution'.[137] But at least a substantial number of Latin American States (twenty), some Asian (seven), and a few African states (three) were also regarded as full members. Even some of the states which remained outside the League took part in international treaty-making as legal subjects. The United States, which due to the isolationist US Senate did never join the League, supported initiatives of multilateral treaty-making like the Kellogg–Briand Pact with its condemnation of war. This Pact also symbolized some growing non-European influence on international law. Japan had not only been founding member of the League but also one of the early drafters of the Kellogg–Briand Pact. States like China, Chile, and Peru later acceded to the Pact.[138]

The system of the League, however, by no means introduced full-fledged sovereign equality of all international actors. The distinction between civilized and uncivilized entities continued to inform political practices. Imperial states like Britain and France retained their African and South East Asian colonies. Furthermore, the League of Nations introduced the Mandates System, which entrusted the former German and Ottoman colonies to the administration of the victorious powers. According to Article 22 Covenant of the League, the mandatory powers had to support the development of the people 'not yet able to stand under the strenuous conditions of the modern world' whose 'well-being and development' would 'form a sacred trust of civilization'. The 'tutelage of such peoples should be entrusted to advanced nations who by reason of their resources, their experiences or their geographical position can best undertake this responsibility'. Ultimately, some 'civilized' countries oversaw the development of more 'primitive' groups and often the practices in the mandated territories could hardly be distinguished from the practices in the colonies.[139]

It would last until after 1945, until the European-dominated colonial system was dissolved. The Second World War had led to immense power transformations. The two new superpowers, the United States and the Soviet Union, were not located in the heart of Europe. As self-proclaimed guardians of a Western and Eastern bloc, the two

---

[136] Including the separate seats for six members of the British Empire: The United Kingdom, Australia, Canada, India, New Zealand, and South Africa. In 1934–35, fifty-eight states were members at the same time.

[137] Zara Steiner, *The Lights that Failed. European International History 1919–1933* (Oxford University Press 2005) 350.

[138] Sixty-three states became members of the pact: Randall Lesaffer, 'Kellogg-Briand Pact (1928)' in *Max Planck Encyclopedia of Public International Law* (n 51).

[139] The territories were categorized into A, B, and C territories depending on their alleged level of development (Art 22 IV, V, VI). In mandates, the Council of the League spelled out the duties of the mandatory powers towards the indigenous population. On the mandate system: Anghie (n 30) 119–23; Susan Pedersen, *The Guardians. The League of Nations and the Crisis of Empire* (Oxford University Press 2015).

superpowers intervened in their hemispheres at their own will (Hungary, Dominican Republic) and led proxy wars in various African, Asian, and Latin American countries.[140] Furthermore, formally European colonial domination started to end. The British and French did no longer possess the political power to retain their colonies. As the Suez Crisis in 1956 symbolized, without the backing of the United States they could not shape international politics on their own initiative.[141] Consequently, independence movements in Asia, Africa, and the Pacific liberated a large number of the former colonies. Furthermore, countries like China, India, and Libya looked for opportunities to develop global politics independent of the Western or Eastern schemes and founded the Non-Aligned Movement (NAM). The newly established United Nations grew from 51 members in 1945, to 115 in mid-1960s and 159 by the end of the Cold War. Soon states from the Global South had a majority in the General Assembly. This non-aligned front initiated declarations on colonial independence (1960)[142] and on friendly relations (1970)[143] stressing the importance of self-determination, non-intervention, and state sovereignty for international politics. As Jörg Fisch has emphasized, it was 'European weakness' rather than European superiority, which provided the final impetus to the universalization of international law.[144] Even though Western powers continued to dominate the Global South via international institutions or via informal mechanisms,[145] formally the principles of the European international law were applicable in (almost) all countries in the world.

How did the contemporaries conceptualize these developments? Of course, scholars noticed the declining dominance of Europe on the world order conception. At the beginning of the century, some authors from non-European regions started to question the universality of international law and developed separatist accounts. The Chilean Alejandro Alvarez famously propagated the idea of a solidarity-based, more progressive 'American International Law' independent from the European tradition, which so strongly relied on the balance of power and intervention.[146] Furthermore, after the 1917 Bolshevik Revolution in Russia, the Soviet academic Yevgeni Korovin claimed that separate systems of European great power law, American international law, and Soviet international law existed and that a global, universal international law was a myth.[147] Dissatisfied with the European international law, these academics tried to create their own accounts of a regional international law. However, the proposals hardly influenced

---

[140] Odd A Westad, *The Global Cold War. Third World Interventions and the Making of Our Times* (Cambridge University Press 2006).

[141] John Roberts and Odd Arne Westad, *The Penguin History of the World* (Penguin Books 2014) 1064–65.

[142] Declaration on the Granting of Independence to Colonial Countries and Peoples (A/RES/1514 of 12 December 1960).

[143] Declaration on the Principles of International law concerning Friendly Relations and Co-operation among States in accordance with the Charter of the United Nations (A/RES/2625 of 24 October 1970).

[144] Jörg Fisch, 'Power or Weakness? On the Causes of the Worldwide Expansion of European International Law' (2004) 6 Journal of the History of International Law 21–26.

[145] Anghie (n 30) 245–72.

[146] Alvarez (n 101) 269; on this: Becker Lorca and Mestizo (n 28) 329; Esquirol (n 101) 562–66.

[147] Yevgeni Korowin, *Das Völkerrecht der Übergangszeit. Grundlagen der völkerrechtlichen Beziehungen der Union der Sowjetrepubliken* (Rothschild 1929) 7–8; on this: Lauri Mälksoo, *Russian Approaches to International Law* (Oxford University Press 2015).

the European mainstream, which celebrated the slow 'universalization' of international law. As stated above, during the inter-war period, Lassa Oppenheim and Franz von Liszt observed a gradual adoption of European international legal norms by some civilized and half-civilized non-Western societies.[148] After the Second World War, with the end of the Mandate System and the start of decolonization, the international legal order then finally seemed to have become universal. In the seventh edition of Oppenheim's *International Law*, Hersch Lauterpacht celebrated the world-wide role of international law and stressed that 'religion and the controversial test of degree of civilization have ceased to be, as such, a condition of recognition of the membership of the "family of nations"'.[149] His American colleague Philipp Jessup emphasized that the times of international society as 'a selective community with a provincial outlook' into which 'the Islamic, much less the Hindu and Buddhist, worlds were not admitted' were over. Instead the international community today would have 'a global membership'.[150] Also, in other parts of the world, one started to embrace the universal international law. In the Islamic world, reformist Muslim jurists declared the category of *dar al harab* to be obsolete. Jurists from Egypt and Syria argued that Jihad was only allowed against the hostile non-Muslim world because under the auspices of the UN peace had become the rule not the exception.[151] The Indian Ram P Anand remarked that through decolonization with 'the emergence and participation of Asian-African countries, international society has become a true world society'.[152] In the Soviet Union under Nikita Khrushchev, Gregory Tunkin argued to turn to an international law based on the principle of peaceful coexistence.[153] Also in China, after a period of isolation under Mao Tse-tung, scholars in the late 1970s highlighted the need to embrace the universally applicable international law.[154] A common understanding of a universal international law was widely shared among international lawyers until the end of the Cold War.

V. Conclusion

On the basis of a contextual approach this contribution has depicted the history of international law since the seventeenth century as a migration of the European international law to the Americas and later to Asia and Africa. It argues that during the seventeenth and eighteenth centuries different normative systems like the Sinocentric investiture system, the Islamocentric siyar system, and the 'European law of nations' existed. During the long nineteenth century, the independence of the North American

---

[148]   Oppenheim (n 15) 3–4, 44–75, 147–56; von Liszt (n 15) 2–4, 9–18.

[149]   Lassa Oppenheim and Hersch Lauterpacht, *International Law. A Treatise*, vol 1 (7th edn, Longmans, Green and Co 1948) 47.

[150]   Philip C Jessup, *The Use of International Law* (University of Michigan Law School 1959) 20–22.

[151]   Fadel (n 59).

[152]   Ram P Anand, 'Role of the "New" Asian-African Countries in the Present International Legal Order' (1962) 56 American Journal of International Law 383, 384.

[153]   Grigory Tunkin, *Das Völkerrecht der Gegenwart. Theorie und Praxis* (Staatsverlag der DDR 1963).

[154]   Hungdah Chiu, 'Chinese Attitudes toward International Law in the Post-Mao Era, 1978–1987' (1987) 21 International Lawyer 1127.

and South American colonies, gunboat diplomacy in Asia, and colonial expansion to Africa led to the spread of the European international order through processes of adoption and imposition. However, it lasted until after the Second World War until the formal inequalities were gradually lifted during the anti-colonial struggles of independence in the Global South. By the end of the Cold War more than 150 states were regarded and regarded themselves as subjects of the international legal order.

In relation to the competing narratives on international legal history, this contribution thus rejects those parts of the contributionist reading which claim that international law had its origin in non-European regions. As explained, if one takes the terminology of the contemporaries seriously, the European normative system of international law rose and expanded from Europe to the rest of the world sidelining the Islamocentric siyar and Sinocentric investiture system, which did not use the language of international law to describe their foreign relations. Furthermore, this contribution merges the idealist, realist, critical, and contributionist accounts by stressing that the causes for the expansion of the European international law were a mix of colonial imposition by great powers and voluntary adoption by states which had just or were in the process of liberating themselves from colonial suppression.

So, what can we learn from this narrative for the rise and decline of today's international law? What will come after the universalization of the European law of nations? For now, it seems rather unlikely that the universalization of the European international legal order will be turned back and that we will get back regional systems of world order which largely ignore themselves. Technological developments have made the world a smaller place and it seems that foreign relations will be governed by some universal normative rules also in the future. However, at the same time the success story of an every expanding European normative order today is challenged. After a peak in the relevance of a more value-based universal international law in foreign relations during the 1990s, we might face a period of stronger regional reorientations. As the current debates about the 'return of geopolitics', a 'multi-polar' world, and the revitalization of the Chinese investiture system demonstrate, the contemporary international law which has been strongly influenced by European conceptions has come under pressure. How the international legal system will adapt to these challenges is one of the most pressing issues of today's international politics.

5

International Law within a Global International Society

Comment on Felix Lange

Andrew Hurrell

This book is concerned with the ways in which commonly held assumptions about the development of international law are currently under threat or challenge. The primary focus is on the period since the end of the Cold War. Indeed, the editors provide an explicit justification in their Introduction for viewing 1990 as a critical juncture. In order to frame this analysis, Felix Lange's chapter provides us with a rich and wide-ranging picture of the longer-term development of international law. The history of international law has been one of the most exciting areas of research both within international law and within the history of international political thought, and Lange's chapter engages very effectively with this dauntingly large body of scholarship.

This comment is divided into four sections. In the first, I will identify some of the core claims of the chapter and also examine the methodological assumptions on which it is based. In the second section, I would like to build on the account that Lange has given us but to underscore and develop further three specific themes, all of which are of ongoing relevance: the importance of mutual constitution in the relations between the West and the non-West; the need to look 'beyond membership'; and the agency of the non-Western world. The third section explores the way in which the mid-twentieth-century developments discussed in the latter part of Lange's chapter are related to the end of the Cold War and to how we view the end of the Cold War. From the perspective of the contemporary *global* legal order, the idea of 1990 as a critical juncture raises some important and difficult questions. And finally, in the conclusion I will return to the idea of the international rule of law and the ways in which our understanding of the universalization of international law and the international rule of law may be related and brought together.

I.

There are, broadly, two ways in which a global legal order might come into being. One is via the coming together on more or less equal terms of a series of regionally based systems, whether made up of states, empires, or other political groupings. The other is by the global dominance of what was an originally regional system. And it is this model that stands behind the global order of the twentieth century with expansion of an originally European international society on to a global scale—first, through the globalizing force of capitalism and the immense transformative impact that it has had on the regions and societies which were drawn into a deepening system of exchange and production relations; second, through the emergence of an often highly conflictual international political system which, as Halford Mackinder argued, came to see the entire earth as the single stage for promotion of the interests of the core powers of the system;[1] and, third, through the development of a global international society whose institutional forms (the nation-state, Great Powers, international law, spheres of influence) were globalized from their originally European context in the course of European expansion and the subsequent process of decolonization.

For the first time in human history there is a single political and legal order that encompasses the entire world. The most taken-for-granted feature of both the practice and the study of international relations and of international law is the existence of a world-wide system of states. The forces of globalization are consistently viewed as undermining the sovereignty and autonomy of states, as empowering non-state actors and global civil society, and as shifting the framework for analysis from one of inter-state relations to one of world or global politics. But globalization should not be seen only in contradistinction to the state. In part this follows from the deep connections between the drivers of globalization and patterns of inter-national and inter-imperial politics. In part, and more fundamentally, the most ignored—or taken-for-granted—aspect of globalization has been the globalization of the nation-state. There is therefore now a single global political system with a set of legal and political institutions, diplomatic practices, and accompanying ideologies that developed in Europe and then the wider Western world and which, in the traditional parlance, 'expanded' to form a global international society.[2]

This idea of the universalization of international law is central to the account that Lange provides. His predominant focus is on the expansion, globalization, or, to use the term in his chapter, the universalization of international law. The first part of the chapter provides an overview of competing narratives on the historical development of international legal order. The second part of the chapter shows how the system of international law changed its regional scope from the seventeenth to the twentieth century—both in terms of the ways in which different regional systems interacted with each other and the ways in which a single global legal order eventually emerged.

---

[1] Mackinder stressed the closing of the frontier and the notion of the international system as 'a closed political space': Halford Mackinder, 'The Geographical Pivot of History' (1904) 23 The Geographical Journal 421, especially 422.

[2] Hedley Bull and Adam Watson (eds), *The Expansion of International Society* (Clarendon Press 1984).

Universalization is central to Lange's understanding of 'rise' and 'decline'. As he puts it:

> For the purpose of the analysis, I adopt a qualitative understanding of rise and decline, which presupposes that an increase in the number of actors taking part in an international system structured by legal rules signals a rise of international law.[3]

As he points out, the contrasting narratives that he examines in the chapter differ in their understandings of universalization, but agree that this represents one of the most critical ways in which the international legal order has developed over time. When we move into the twentieth century, the argument is re-stated:

> Nonetheless, despite these competing ideological actors [involving the struggle between liberalism, communism and national socialism], on the global level international law expanded. After the end of the First World War, the formerly European system of international law continued to include more and more actors from different regions.[4]

And, as we move still further on in time, the changes produced by decolonization complete the process:

> Even though Western powers continued to dominate the Global South via international institutions or via informal mechanisms, formally the principals of European international law were applicable in (almost) all countries of the world.[5]

This is undoubtedly an extremely important set of changes. But, as we shall see, the rise or decline of international law may have been affected in other ways than by the geographical expansion of the system: on the one hand, the expansion of membership may have been accompanied by an erosion of consensus and greater contestation over both the substantive and procedural values of the legal order. On the other hand, shifting power towards new regional actors may exacerbate the conflictual dynamics of international relations and undermine the role of international law within the political system.

Methodologically, Lange is cautious about lessons of the past; he is very well aware of the dangers of anachronism and the important role of contingency; and he is deeply conscious of the need to interrogate critically the ways in which historical arguments are used and abused in the contemporary legal and political order. Indeed, one might go still further and view the competing narratives that are examined in the chapter, not as neutral modes of analysis, but rather as central to the global politics of international

---

[3] Felix Lange, 'Coercion, Internalization, Decolonization: A Contextual Reading of the Rise of European International Law Since the Seventeenth Century' in this book, II.
[4] ibid IV.3.
[5] ibid.

law itself. Many of the traditional histories examined in the chapter tell a story of the history of international law in terms of the present—simply taking a contemporary understanding of international law in general or a particular legal concept and tracing it back through history. Indeed, this mode of engaging with history is often a part of how legal argumentation is developed—think of the way in which post-1918 liberal internationalists invented a seamless 'Grotian' tradition or identified particular 'Grotian moments'. Many of the histories of international law examined in this chapter go further still, telling a history of the present in terms of the future: how a progressivist vision of international law has already expanded in density, depth, and geographical reach and will inevitably continue to expand still further.

As against these much criticized accounts, Lange adopts a modified contextualist approach. He deploys this along two dimensions. The first is to suggest that we can legitimately use the past to examine claims about the novelty of the present. He argues that a 'cautious adaptation of past experience to changed contemporary circumstances might help to take the novelty of contemporary challenges into account'.[6] Secondly, he wants to be open to the plurality of legal visions and legal possibilities:

> I argue for a contextual reading of the history of international law, which takes the language and contexts of the past seriously. At the same time, my proposed contextual approach embraces analytical tools of the present which are needed to open our view for potential alternative routes to international law's historical development.[7]

The importance of these 'potential alternative routes' and 'paths not taken' is unquestionable: we need them precisely in order to understand the way in which the meaning of legal ideas and concepts have shifted across time and space; and to appreciate how particular ideas of order which may have appeared as historical dead-ends can have ongoing and enduring political importance—think of claims made about race and civilization or the recurring importance of pan-regional thinking.[8]

Yet Lange deploys this methodological approach mostly in order to understand the past—'present categories are often necessary as analytical tools to define the research outlook'.[9] This is especially the case with the most fundamental difficulty with the writing of the history of international law, namely what is to count as international law. Is it simply a history of the relations between states or entities that look like states, or do the forms and content of 'international law' need to be expanded as we move across space and time? Lange argues for the former view: 'In my view, writings on the history of international law should embrace a categorical understanding

---

[6] ibid I.
[7] ibid III.
[8] eg: Cemil Aylin, *The Idea of the Muslim World. A Global Intellectual History* (Harvard University Press 2017); Cemil Aylin, 'Beyond Civilization: Pan-Islamism, Pan-Asianism and the Revolt against the West' (2006) 4 Journal of Modern European History 204.
[9] Lange (n 3) III.

of international law, which is interested in foreign relations between highest entities in general.'[10]

This is, of course, a legitimate argument. But one still might wish to go further in exploring how the past and present are linked. The difficulty with strongly contextualist and historicist approaches is twofold. In the first place, they may impede the search for broader patterns of historical development, particularly at the systemic or structural level, and the need for theoretical explanation of these patterns. The broader systemic forest is all too often lost in the detailed contextualist reconstruction of particular trees. Secondly, strong contextualism is hard to reconcile with the necessity and inevitability of normative evaluation. In this chapter, Lange quotes Koskenniemi on the 'limits of contextualism' and the need to 'move beyond context'. This is a very important point that needs to be given further weight if we are to understand how the past may most fruitfully be related to the present, in terms of both explanation and evaluation.

II.

It is true that the history of the globalization of international law remains a highly contested domain. Yet, there are some important aspects which have emerged from recent scholarship and which are of great importance in understanding how we have ended up where we now are.

The first of these has to do with the notion of mutual constitution. The past two decades have seen a very great deal of work that has sought to critique euro-centric accounts of the history of international law and the historical 'expansion' of European international society.[11] This critical and post-colonial scholarship has opened up a very different account of the 'rise of the West' and has challenged both the easy dichotomy between the 'West' and the 'non-West' and also the confident and complacent, image of a global international society created via the universalization of essentially European institutions for the maintenance of order and the pursuit of justice. What Europe was, how the West was created as an idea, and how Western practices of international law and relations became global was, therefore, always the product of interaction and mutual constitution. This idea is related to what Lange calls the contributionist narrative that looks at the non-Western roots or origins of international law or its functional equivalent. But it is distinct from it.

There are many ways in which the idea of mutuality, connections, co-constitution has been developed and through different theoretical lenses. Take, for example, the history of Western political thought. We can only understand core ideas of authority,

---

[10] ibid.

[11] For a recent overview, in general: Tim Dunne and Christian Reus-Smit, *The Globalization of International Society* (Oxford University Press 2017); for a range of other perspectives: Sanjay Seth, 'Historical Sociology and Postcolonial Theory: Two Strategies for Challenging Eurocentrism' (2009) 3 International Political Sociology 334; Barry Buzan and George Lawson, *The Global Transformation. History, Modernity and the Making of International Relations* (Cambridge University Press 2015); Robbie Shilliam (ed), *International Relations and Non-Western Thought. Imperialism, Colonialism and Investigations of Global Modernity* (Routledge 2010).

property, and sovereignty by thinking about how they arose in the context of expansion and empire.[12] Moreover, as Edward Keene has argued, from its very inception, the extra-European order was constructed differently from the European order: while the anarchical ordering of the latter was underpinned by the principle of toleration of difference, the former was constructed to promote a particular kind of civilization transmitted through a set of hierarchical institutions maintained by colonial and imperial powers.[13]

A second point has been to look beyond membership. For English School theorists of international society and for many of the nineteenth- and twentieth-century international lawyers discussed in this chapter, the core question is about how non-Western states and societies become members of international society. For some, the achievement of what Jessup calls 'global membership' is precisely the measure of the successful development of international law. And Lange quotes Lauterpacht who celebrates the world-wide role of international law and who argued that 'religion and the controversial test of degree of civilisation have ceased to be, as such, a condition of recognition of the membership of the "family of nations"'.[14] For those on the other side, not only was the manipulation of membership criteria a central element of how Western power was created and sustained in the period of classical European imperialism, but Western international law has continued with analogous practices, making the sovereignty of non-Western states conditional on externally defined criteria (democracy, human rights, support for terrorism, notions of 'state failure').

The more important analytical point, however, is the need to look beyond membership. Membership is certainly one central dimension of how we would describe a social order. But once membership of the order itself has been secured, we might naturally wish to look more directly at patterns of social stratification within that order (by power, by class, or by status) and at patterns of differential membership within the now apparently universal institutions of international law and society.

The third dimension has to do with the agency of the non-Western world. At a general level we can note all of those writers who have stressed just how much of what the West considers its own came, in fact, from elsewhere; and how global historians have come to tell a story 'that brought in the Rest to help explain the West', as Jeremy Adelman succinctly puts it.[15] But more directly in relation to international law and society a great of recent work has come to stress the complexity of the power relations between Europe and the non-European world, the finer gradations of distinctions between insiders and outsiders, and the differential agency on the part of those at the receiving end of Western power. Hence, for example, the need to focus on the very different paths taken

---

[12] Anthony Anghie, *Imperialism, Sovereignty and the Making of International Law* (Cambridge University Press 2005); on the more general shift in the history of political thought: Richard Tuck, *The Rights of War and Peace* (Oxford University Press 1999).

[13] Edward Keene, *Beyond the Anarchical Society: Grotius, Colonialism and Order in World Politics* (Cambridge University Press 2002).

[14] Lassa Oppenheim and Hersch Lauterpacht, *International Law. A Treatise*, vol 1 (7th edn, Longmans, Green and Co 1948) 47; quoted in: Lange (n 3) IV.3.

[15] Jeremy Adelman, 'What is Global History Now?' (*Aeon*, 2 March 2017) <aeon.co/essays/is-global-history-still-possible-or-has-it-had-its-moment> accessed 22 October 2018.

and strategies adopted, say between China and Japan as they engaged with Western power and Western international law.[16] Or the way in which a straightforward narrative of universalization breaks down when we focus on particular parts of the world. Thus, in the nineteenth century, Latin America is in fact in the vanguard of the development of international law rather than simply a passive 'taker' of outside norms and practices.[17] The importance of the Southern sources of global norms has become an important theme in writing on legal and normative change in the twentieth century—from ideas of human rights to notions of economic development to understandings of sustainability.

III.

This, then, leads to my third comment which has to do with the way in which we view the end of the Cold War and the issue of continuity versus change. Lange finishes his chapter with an examination of the period of decolonization. This was a period in which there was certainly a very great deal of contestation on the part of the Third World against many of the core elements of Western international law. This contestation came in different forms: soft revisionist (as with Brazil); hard revisionist (as with India), and revolutionist (as with China). On the one hand, it was a period in which one could argue that an accommodation was taking place on the part of post-colonial states with the now-global international legal order. Each part of the non-European world had to accept that its own world was no longer 'the' world, and that, whatever pre-existing forms of inter-societal organization may have existed, there was now only one global political order. You could challenge it, rail against it, seek to reject it; but you had no alternative but to live within this political structure. But, on the other hand, for all the continued dimensions of inequality, accommodation was accompanied by a series successful challenges to Western dominance and by an ability to contest dominant Western preferences and, at times, to shift legal understandings and practices—in relation, for example, to the use of force and intervention, to racial inequality, to self-determination, and to the regulation of foreign investment.

As is well known, this capacity for contestation and challenge was greatest in the 1970s, and had faded by the end of that decade.[18] By the early 1980s, the apparent cohesion of the Third World coalition that had brought the Western countries to the negotiating table to talk about a New International Economic Order (NIEO) had been undermined. It had been undermined by the increased differentiation across the developing world (especially the rise of the Asian Newly Industrialising Countries); by

---

[16] Shogo Suzuki, *Civilization and Empire: China and Japan's Encounter with European International Society* (Routledge 2009).

[17] Arnulf Becker Lorca, *Mestizo International Law: A Global Intellectual History, 1842–1933* (Cambridge University Press 2015).

[18] I examine this story in greater length in: Andrew Hurrell, 'Récits d'émergence: la fin du Tiers Monde?' (2012) 56 Journal Critique internationale 17; Brazilian version in: (2013) 33 Revista Brasileira de Economia Política 203.

the strains within the coalition itself; by the loss of sympathetic interlocutors within the North open to Southern demands; by the hard-line rejection of any notion of a North/South dialogue on the part of the United States and its major allies; and by the deteriorating economic and political position of much of the developing world that accompanied the devastating financial and economic crises of the 1980s. The reformist rhetoric of the NIEO had been both defeated and deflated. Power-centred accounts of North/South relations stressed the existence of a 'structural conflict' reducible to contending sets of power and interest—however encrusted within the empty rhetoric of justice.[19] The powerful neo-liberal critique of rent-seeking Southern elites cut deep into progressive third-worldism. On the left, post-colonial writers came over more to view the post-colonial state with deep disdain and the progressivist narratives of both capitalism and communism with even greater scepticism. And critical political economists argued that, to the extent that developing countries 'emerged', it would be as the result of structural changes in patterns of capitalist global production and the spread of neo-liberal ideologies.

In so far as it survived, the Global South came to be defined in transnational social terms rather than as a grouping or category of nation-states.[20] Empirical accounts focused more and more on the social movements that were emerging within and across the Global South in response to neo-liberalism. Normative attention was also shifting away from Southern states and towards social movements and civil society groups within the Global South: The World Social Forum (WSF), anti-globalization groups, post-Seattle protest movements. The idea that the WSF represented the 'New Bandung' precisely captured this shift—away from states and towards different forms of social movements in which the idea of the South as both a focus of protest and a transformative project lived on but in a radically different form.[21]

But how far did the end of the Cold War in fact reverse the longer-term diffusion of power and agency and the longer-term idea of a revolt against Western dominance? From today's perspective the decade of the 1970s looks rather different. Here it is important to see just how closely the dynamics of today's global order were directly the products of Western responses to power diffusion and relative power decline during the previous 'crisis of the West' in the 1970s. Commentators at that time pointed to the diffusion of power and the challenge posed by the Third World to Western order; to the way in which North/South cleavages were shaping the politics of new global issues such as the environment, resource scarcity and nuclear non-proliferation; to the tensions within the capitalist core as the Keynsian orthodoxy unravelled in the face of social conflict, low growth and high inflation; and to the debates surrounding the hegemonic decline of the United States.[22]

---

[19] Stephen Krasner, *Structural Conflict: The Third World against Global Liberalism* (University of California Press 1985).

[20] David Slater, *Geopolitics and the Post-Colonial. Rethinking North-South Relations* (Blackwell 2004).

[21] Michael Hardt, 'Today's Bandung?' (2002) 14 New Left Review 112.

[22] Niall Ferguson, Charles S Maier, Erez Manela, and Daniel J Sargent (eds), *The Shock of the Global: The 1970s in Perspective* (Harvard University Press 2010).

After dallying with the possibility of serious negotiations around a North/South dialogue, the dominant response was two-fold. One major response to declining US and Western hegemony was to foster, encourage, and enforce an aggressive phase of liberal globalization, especially of financial globalization. And yet it was precisely the particular character of economic globalization and debt-fuelled growth that helped to create the conditions both for the rise of emerging powers challenging the Western order from outside and for the societal and political backlash politics that are eroding the Western order from within. The other central feature of the US policy in the 1970s was to revive a policy of active and aggressive interventionism in the South as part of the Second Cold War. Again, whilst this may have been a successful element in the victory of the West in the Cold War, it also helped to foster, deepen, or shift the character of many of the conflicts that are proving so intractable to Washington today, especially in relation to the Islamic world. Seen in terms of both these responses, the long 1970s become more important in understanding where we are today; and the end of the Cold War rather less so.

Contemporary challenges to global order reflect these historical changes and re-inforce the view that we live in a far more diverse world, with more participants, and with a far greater range of voices and views. The resurgence of the political right and the contestation within Western countries merely adds one further dimension to the increased diversity of global international society. The international system is therefore increasingly characterized by a diffusion of power, including but not only to emerging and regional powers; by a diffusion of preferences with many more voices demanding to be heard both globally and within states as a result of globalization, of democratization, and of the backlash against globalization; and by a diffusion of ideas and values, with a reopening of the big questions of social, economic, and political organization that were supposedly brought to an end with the end of the Cold War and the liberal ascendancy. The longer-term movement towards a post-Western world was interrupted but not fundamentally dislodged by the brief and fleeting period of US uni-polarity. So, far from being some kind of normal state, it is the period from 1990 to the early 2000s that is the historical anomaly.

IV.

We can think of the international rule of law in two principal ways. On one side, the rule of law refers to the particular quality of a legal order—a set of values, self-understandings, sometimes even a certain sensibility by which one is able to interpret and evaluate a legal order. For some, these core values are procedural. For others, and increasingly dominant in post-Cold War discussions of the international rule of law, they have to do with consensus over a core set of universal values that animate both normative aspiration and the actual practices of the international legal order. And for others again, they have to do with the systemic character of the international legal order. Indeed, it is the idea of the international legal system and of international law as representing a historically created endowment of rules, values, and argumentative practices that lies behind the intuition that drives this project. Recent challenges do not just affect particular aspects of the legal order or particular functional regimes, but rather speak to how we understand the legal order as a whole and the sense that 'something bigger' is currently underway.

On the other side, the rule of law is understood in relation to the broader political order within which it is embedded. All legal orders depend on conditions—material, moral, institutional—that they alone can never guarantee. This is where we think of the role of international law as 'ruling' or 'governing', or, in the often difficult conditions of international political life, 'taming' conflict and anarchy. On this understanding, the international rule of law is about the role of law in establishing or sustaining international order. This is how the international rule of law was understood in many of the classical debates of the twentieth century, both within international law and international relations. The progressivist project behind the 'rise' of international law would be carried forward by the emergence and strengthening of a system of collective security, by the move towards the codification of law, through the strengthening of compulsory jurisdiction of international courts, and in the spread of law and legalization more generally. The most fundamental challenges would come from the extent to which the legal order remained contaminated by the dynamics of power—either during periods of hegemony and power imbalance (as in the post-Cold War period); or from a tight and highly conflictual balance of power (as in the Cold War); or from the strains and uncertainties of shifting power (as with the contemporary situation).

The universalization of international law, discussed so well in Lange's chapter, speaks to both dimensions of the international rule of law. Yes, we can, as Lange does, speak of the rise of international law in terms of the expansion in geographical range and in terms of global membership. But we can also note other features that complicate this story, especially the way in which challenges of shifting power go hand in hand with claims and assertions of cultural, national, or religious difference.

In the first place, there has indeed been a shift in power or better a diffusion of political agency—in other words, the capacity of a far wider range of states, social groups, and societies to lay claim to cultural recognition and to demand changes in the legal and normative structure of international society. In recent years the focus has been on non-Western 'rising powers', on Southern social movements, or on non-Western religious transnationalism. But, as this chapter reminds us and as I have stressed above, the process of change and challenge is historically far more deeply rooted; and, for all the continued role for hierarchy and inequality, the degree of institutional and normative change has been very substantial. The most crucial dimension of 'global' does not, therefore, lie in the nature of the problems (climate change, nuclear proliferation, etc), nor in notions of interdependence and globalization and the degree to which states, societies, and peoples are everywhere affected by global processes. It lies rather in the increased capacity of a far wider range of states and social actors to become active subjects and agents in the politics and practices of international law and society. It is the diffusion of agency and of political consciousness that has been the important feature of the globalization of international society. This means that the historical self-understandings of a much wider and culturally diverse range of players need to be central to the theoretical and practical analysis both of specific notions of international law and broader practices of international ordering.

Second, there are the problematic ways in which shifting power and agency intersects and meshes with cultural diversity. Greater cultural diversity does not mean the inevitability of cultural or civilizational conflict. For those concerned with the evolution of international legal orders, it is particularly important to underscore the importance of historical construction. The salience of culture is not immutable or given by nature; but rather depends on historical processes and practices that create politically the very identities that are then held to embody cultural difference and that then draw cultural boundaries in particular ways. The shifting salience of culture is therefore a product of historical processes and practices that construct meanings and forge boundaries of exclusion and selective inclusion. The dynamics of both capitalism and geopolitics— the heartland of academic international relations—are the two most powerful sets of systemic forces. But it is the boundary-making role of global and international legal institutions that have become central to understanding both the ways in which cultural diversity is regulated and the patterns of cultural inclusion and exclusion. On the one side, historical processes provide access to power for groups to exploit those cultural claims that have powerful resonance; and, on the other, rather than simply reflect or follow a dominant culture, what matters politically is how groups challenge, resist, exploit, adapt to particular sets of cultural norms and practices.

Third, this combination of diversity and shifting power affect in very profound ways how the rise and decline of the international rule of law is understood and by whom. From the perspective of much of the Global South the 'rise' of the international rule of law in the form of a self-described global liberal order looked very different. From this perspective, it was the United States and Western countries that were the great revisionist powers during the post-Cold War years: in the 1990s in terms of pressing for new norms on intervention and for the opening of markets and for the embedding of particular sets of what it saw as liberal values within international institutions; in the early years of this century, in terms of the attempt to recast norms on regime change and on the use of force. This perspective leads as well to a broader set of critiques of both the excessive normative ambition of the global 'liberal' order and the hubris on the part of those who saw the post-Cold War as ushering in a new golden age of law, global governance, and multilateralism: the selectivity and hypocrisy with which international law was used and abused, the failings of so-called democratic interventionism, and the conscious attempts to de-politicize global governance by going down a technical, functional route and stressing the role of experts as part of the machinery and technology of global governance.

Fourth, as we move into the age of the new nationalism and of backlash politics and consider the sets of challenges that have motivated this project and this book, it is tempting to focus on particular sets of national circumstances, whether to do with Trump or Brexit. Yet, Lange's focus on the universalization of the international legal order is important; precisely, it presses us to think about the global and systemic factors that lie behind many individual challenges and because of the way in which the form that this universalization has occurred shapes the politicization and contestation of international law. On the part of the previously dominant, and especially of an historically strongly exceptionalist United States, it is the perceived challenges to its economic and geopolitical primacy, the powerfully felt sense of a loss of status, its inability to control the forces of globalization that it has itself done so much to drive forward, and the equally powerfully felt sense of the unfairness of the constraints of international legal institutions that has animated both milder forms of US ambivalence towards international law as well as the more vehement and strident rejectionism and nationalism of the present period. On the part of the emerging and developing world, far from socializing emerging states into a single logic of responsible global governance relative success has brought with it a natural desire for recognition and for recognition of what is different, distinct, exceptional. Exceptionality is a hallmark of all great and rising powers—and the conflictual distributional logic of the international political system easily translates claims of exceptionality into suspicion and mistrust. It is within this more troubling global political context that claims about the role of international law and the nature of the international rule of law now need to be debated.

PART III
ACTOR-CENTRED PERSPECTIVES

6

The BRICS as 'Rising Powers' and the Development of International Law

Aniruddha Rajput*

Shifting of the relative power of states in international relations is a regular and cyclical phenomenon. Powers have risen and fallen over the course of history. Correspondingly, their influence over international law has changed with the rise and decline of their power. In the recent past, after the end of the Cold War, the United States emerged as the sole hegemonic power. It was able to—directly and indirectly—influence the creation of international institutions and legal norms. The influence of the United States in the international processes declined rather unexpectedly and rapidly since the global crises of 2008. Over the years, in the background, some other states, in particular Brazil, Russia, India, China, and South Africa (BRICS countries), have been progressing economically and strengthening their network of political influence. They have been described as 'rising powers'. These states have increased their participation in the processes of norm creation and international institutions. International law is in a phase where the former driving engine is—wilfully and otherwise—stuttering and new participants are emerging. This is indeed an uncertain situation and an opportune moment to pose the question: Is international law and international rule of law, in particular, in a state of rise or decline?

This chapter aims at analysing two aspects. First, whether the BRICS countries, as a set of rising powers, can contribute to the development of international law. Second, what would their influence entail for the conceptualization and development of international law in the future. This analysis is followed through the following sections. The first section elaborates on the concept of rising powers. The second section discusses why a focus on these powers appears to provide an appropriate index for the current development of international law. The third section focuses on the participation and influence of BRICS in the shaping of legal norms and institutions, thereby throwing light on their conceptualization of international law and the future of international law. The discussion is summed up in the conclusions.

* I thank Jashaswi Ghosh, Vaishali Movva, Somabha Bandopadhay, Eva Ritte, and Lars Schlenkhoff for their research assistance. The responsibility of the views expressed and errors is entirely mine.

I. The BRICS as rising powers

There is no legal definition of 'rising powers' in international law. The term only represents shifts in international relations. It can therefore be best described as a concept. The literature in international relations has attempted to define it. The criteria identified therein could serve as a basis for the identification of rising powers.

Several parameters have been developed in the literature to identify 'rising powers'. Some of the prominent features are the scale of population and territory, political stability, economic size, military power, economic growth, increasing integration into the global economy, growing international financial power, institutional power, claim for a more influential role in governance, and alternative agenda for global governance.[1] The starting point for their recognition as rising powers was economic heft. Economic heft by itself is insufficient. Rising powers enjoy substantial political influence and have the potential to achieve outcomes.

Brazil, Russia, India, and China (BRICs) are usually treated as rising powers since, together, they meet those conditions.[2] Originally, the acronym BRICs (without capital 's'—South Africa was not included then) was used by Goldman Sachs in 2001 to refer to the rapidly rising economies of Brazil, Russia, India, and China.[3] The BRIC countries started meeting annually, since 2009. South Africa joined in 2010 and the forum became 'BRICS'. These states use this forum to discuss issues of mutual interest and often take concerted positions on issues that impact international law norms and institutions.[4]

The BRICS countries are different from the 'middle powers' such as Japan, South Korea, Australia, and other major European countries. The middle powers have been a part of the US-led efforts during the Washington Consensus era and network. The BRICS countries have 'historically espoused conceptions of international order that challenged those of the liberal developed West.'[5] The BRICS countries have largely been on the periphery of formation and shaping of international law and often referred to as the 'Third World' or the 'Global South'. The BRICS countries host the largest share of the world population, which is still largely poor and has been outside the sphere of the benefits of industrialization and development. They were never part of the Organization for Economic Cooperation and Development (OECD). With shifts in the global power structure, the ability of BRICS countries to articulate their positions and influence outcomes has increased individually, which they have multiplied collectively.

---

[1] Andrew Hurrell, 'Hegemony, Liberalism and Global Order: What Space for Would-be Great Powers?' (2006) 82 International Affairs 1; Andrew F Hart and Bruce D Jones, 'How Do Rising Powers Rise?' (2010) 52 Global Politics and Strategy 63; also: Ashley J Tellis, Janice Bially, Christopher Layne, and Melissa McPherson, *Measuring National Power in the Postindustrial Age* (1st edn, RAND Corporation 2000).

[2] Hurrell (n 1).

[3] Jim O'Neill, 'Building Better Global Economic BRICs' (Goldman Sachs, Global Economics Paper No: 66) <www.goldmansachs.com/our-thinking/archive/archive-pdfs/build-better-brics.pdf> accessed 22 October 2017.

[4] BRICS, 'Ninth BRICS Summit Opens Xi Jinping Chairs the Summit and Delivers Important Speech Stressing Stronger BRICS Partnership for a Brighter Future' < https://www.brics2017.org/English/Headlines/201709/t20170906_1996.html> accessed 17 October 2017.

[5] Hurrell (n 1).

The BRICS countries are all members of the Group of Twenty (G20). Other developing states, like Mexico, Egypt, the United Arab Emirates (UAE), Indonesia, Saudi Arabia, and Turkey, are also members of the G20.[6] These states are economically rising and possess political influence. Often the positions of some of them are similar to those of the BRICS countries. However, they do not command the same influence as the BRICS countries, mostly due to lack of collective effort. The BRICS countries take coordinated and pre-organized positions. Since rising powers is only a concept without a rigid definition, it is possible that some countries amongst the BRICS may lose their influence individually and other rising powers may increase their influence. Yet, the BRICS countries collectively continue to be influential. The BRICS countries represent themselves as a certain philosophy and understanding of international law— something very different from the hegemonic powers of the past. Therefore, most of the conclusions drawn based on the behaviour of BRICS countries may be extended to other rising powers. Also, methodologically, it would be easier to track the positions of BRICS countries to draw general conclusions.

II. The BRICS and the current state of international law

The ability to contribute towards the current state of international law depends on influence and the ability to achieve outcomes. The BRICS countries are influential players in international law processes. Their strengths and presence in institutions have increased and they have managed to enhance their overall influence through regional networks. In the General Assembly of the United Nations, the BRICS countries, even before forming as BRICS, have always had influence based on their command of a numerical majority of states. Historically, they have attempted to shape international law norms in the General Assembly. The process of decolonization and self-determination during the 1960s and 1970s was a large success achieved by these states through concerted action. So was the successful conclusion of the negotiations that resulted in the United Nations Convention on the Law of the Sea. They attempted to resist state responsibility for treatment of aliens through the resolutions on Permanent Sovereignty over Natural Resources and the New International Economic Order. The effort to create legal norms failed after the advent of bilateral investment treaties (BITs). The influence of BRICS countries in the General Assembly and efforts to shape international norms would continue in the future.

The BRICS countries often take common positions on different issues in the General Assembly of the United Nations. An analysis of their voting pattern shows that they mostly vote in same way (almost 70 per cent of the time over a period of thirty-four years from 1974 to 2008).[7] In the past, this may not have been an outcome of a coordinated

---

[6] 2015 Turkey G20, 'G20 Members' <http://g20.org.tr/about-g20/g20-members/> accessed 17 October 2017 (All these states are part of the G20, which is a mixture of developed and developing countries).
[7] For a detailed scientific analysis of voting pattern of BRICS countries: Peter Ferdinand, 'Rising Powers at the UN: An Analysis of the Voting Behaviour of BRICS in the General Assembly' (2014) 35 Third World Quarterly 376; also: Bas Hooijmaaijers and Stephan Keukeleire, 'Voting Cohesion of the BRICS Countries in the UN

position. But they would naturally gravitate together on issues which represented their common aspirations and views. In recent times, the consistency in voting pattern of BRICS countries has increased.[8] There is a high degree of convergence between BRICS and a low degree of convergence between the P5 states.[9] There are only two issues on which BRICS countries are divided: nuclear disarmament and human rights.[10] For example, China and India rarely disagree, except on nuclear disarmament.[11] Additionally, other states within their regions, such as India and the South Asian Association for Regional Cooperation (SAARC), and China and the Association of Southeast Asian Nations (ASEAN), vote on same lines as the regional power in the General Assembly.[12]

For several other multilateral negotiations at the United Nations (UN), the BRICS countries take common positions. They have been a part of G77. They successfully led the G77 alliance at the United Nations Law of the Sea Convention.[13] They continue to use the forum for other negotiations, such as the current negotiations for the development of an international legally binding instrument under the United Nations Convention on the Law of the Sea on the Conservation and Sustainable Use of Marine Biological Diversity beyond Areas of National Jurisdiction (BBNJ).[14] The BRICS countries are active participants in other functions of the UN. India is the second largest contributor of troops (7,471 personnel) to UN peacekeeping.[15] Other BRICS countries make much less contribution; nevertheless, taken together, they make a visible contribution towards peacekeeping efforts on the ground.[16] The BRICS countries have been active in global governance[17] through international organizations, such as the World Health Organization (WHO),[18] United Nations

---

General Assembly, 2006–2014: A BRICS Too Far?' (2016) 22 Global Governance: A Review of Multilateralism and International Organizations 389.

[8] Hooijmaaijers and Keukeleire (n 7).

[9] ibid 383.

[10] ibid 384–86.

[11] ibid 387.

[12] Renan Holanda Montenegro and Rafael Mesquita, 'Leaders or Loners? How Do the BRICS Countries and their Regions Vote in the UN General Assembly' (2017) 11(2) Brazilian Political Science Review <www.scielo.br/pdf/bpsr/v11n2/1981-3821-bpsr-1981-3821201700020005.pdf> accessed 25 September 2017.

[13] Maurice Hope-Thompson, 'The Third World and the Law of the Sea: The Attitude of the Group of 77 Toward the Continental Shelf' (1980) 1 Boston College Third World Law Journal 37.

[14] Division for Ocean Affairs and Law of the Sea, 'Preparatory Committee established by General Assembly resolution 69/292: Development of an international legally binding instrument under the United Nations Convention on the Law of the Sea on the conservation and sustainable use of marine biological diversity of areas beyond national jurisdiction' (UNGA meeting, 19 June 2015) <www.unep.org/regionalseas/what-we-do/conservation-biodiversity-areas-beyond-national-jurisdiction-bbn> accessed 21 September 2017.

[15] Centre on International Cooperation, *Annual Review of Global Peace Operations 2009* (Lynne Rienner Publishers 2009).

[16] Providing for Peacekeeping, 'Country Profiles' <www.providingforpeacekeeping.org/profiles> accessed 22 October 2017; see: Chris Perry and Adam Smith, 'Trends in Uniformed Contributions to UN Peacekeeping: A New Dataset, 1991–2012' (Providing for Peacekeeping No 3) <www.ipinst.org/wp-content/uploads/publications/ipi_e_pub_trends_un_peacekeeping.pdf> accessed 22 October 2017.

[17] Niall Duggan, 'BRICS and the Evolution of a New Agenda Within Global Governance' in Marek Rewizorski (ed), *The European Union and the BRICS* (Springer International Publishing 2015).

[18] WHO, 'BRICS and Global Health' <www.who.int/bulletin/volumes/92/6/14-140889/en/> accessed 25 September 2017; WHO, 'BRICS' Contributions to the Global Health Agenda' <www.who.int/bulletin/volumes/92/6/13-127944/en/> accessed 25 September 2017.

Educational, Scientific and Cultural Organization (UNESCO),[19] and United Nations Development Programme (UNDP)[20].

In 2008, the World Bank agreed to a small 1.46 per cent shift in voting power towards developing nations. In spring 2010, members further expanded the influence of the developing economies by another 3.13 per cent, meaning these countries now account for 47.19 per cent of voting power. Taken cumulatively, these changes have allowed China, India, and Russia to become the World Bank's third, seventh, and eighth largest shareholders respectively.[21] In joint statements, BRICS countries have called for reforms in the global financial architecture to allow them greater participation. They have increased their contributions to the World Bank and the International Monetary Fund (IMF).[22]

They are individually using different ways for enhancing their influence in the global order. Economic diplomacy has been an important tool. BRICS countries are not a major contributor to developmental aid within the UN. But outside the UN they are making major contributions.[23] China has invested in African countries, like Libya, Ghana, Mozambique, Congo, Sudan, and Ethiopia.[24] Since the late 1990s, Sino-African trade has grown rapidly, with China now being Africa's largest trade partner. In 2016, China's exports to Africa stood at US$82.9 billion while imports from the continent were valued at US$54.3 billion. China exports a wide variety of consumer and capital goods to Africa but mainly imports commodities such as oil, minerals, and other natural resources.[25] India has invested in Afghanistan, Nepal and Bangladesh, Sri Lanka and Bhutan. In the year 2016–17, India has given a total of US$458.29 million to these countries as a matter of Indian investment and development projects.[26] Trade between Brazil and Africa climbed from around US$4 billion in 2000 to about US$20 billion in 2010, with a steep rise from 2003. With Sub-Saharan Africa, it increased from US$2 billion to US$12 billion over the same period.[27] Further we see that even Russia has steadily increased its investments in African countries.[28] Russia also invests strongly in

[19] UNESCO, 'BRICS Building Education for the Future Priorities for National Development and International Cooperation' <http://unesdoc.unesco.org/images/0022/002290/229054e.pdf> accessed 25 September 2017.

[20] UNDP, 'Youth and Employment among the BRICS 2014' <www.ipc-undp.org/pub/IPCPovertyInFocus28.pdf> accessed 25 September 2017.

[21] Sewell Chan, 'Poorer Nations Get Larger Role in the World Bank' (*New York Times*, 25 April 2010) <www.nytimes.com/2010/04/26/business/26bank.html> accessed 12 June 2018.

[22] BRICS, 'BRICS Summit—Joint Statement' (BRICS Summit, 16 April 2010) <http://brics2016.gov.in/upload/files/document/5763e23d75e512nd.pdf> accessed 22 October 2017.

[23] Silke Weinlicha, 'Emerging Powers at the UN: Ducking for Cover?' (2014) 35 Third World Quarterly 1829.

[24] David Pilling, 'Chinese Investment in Africa: Beijing's Testing Ground' (*Financial Times*, 13 June 2017) <https://www.ft.com/content/0f534aa4-4549-11e7-8519-9f94ee97d996> accessed 8 November 2017.

[25] Ernst and Young, 'EY's Attractiveness Programme Africa, 2017 Connectivity Redefined' <www.ey.com/Publication/vwLUAssets/ey-attractiveness-program-africa-2017-connectivity-redefined/$FILE/ey-attractiveness-program-africa-2017-connectivity-redefined.pdf> accessed 8 November 2017.

[26] Press Trust of India, 'India's Financial Aid to Afghanistan, Bangladesh, Sri Lanka Sees Dip' (*Economic Times*, 5 April 2017) <https://economictimes.indiatimes.com/industry/banking/finance/indias-financial-aid-to-afghanistan-bangladesh-sri-lanka-sees-dip/articleshow/58034123.cms> accessed 8 November 2017.

[27] 'Brazilian Foreign Direct Investment and Trade with Africa' <https://peoplesbrics.files.wordpress.com/2016/12/africa-brazil-bridging-chapter5.pdf> accessed 25 October 2017; also: The African Development Bank Group Chief Economist Complex, 'Brazil's Economic Engagement with Africa' (2011) 2(5) Africa Economic Brief <www.afdb.org/fileadmin/uploads/afdb/Documents/Publications/Brazil%27s_Economic_Engagement_with_Africa_rev.pdf> accessed 25 October 2017.

[28] Vladimir Shubin 'Russia's Policy Towards Africa' <https://www.ispionline.it/sites/default/files/pubblicazioni/analysis_168_2013.pdf > accessed 25 October 2017.

the other BRICS nations.[29] They are cooperating for knowledge-sharing, technology, and expertise in areas of development.[30]

The BRICS countries are building regional coalitions and collaborations. Regional networks are seen as important instruments for enhancing influence. China has led the establishment of the Shanghai Cooperation Organization (SCO) in 2002 that includes Kazakhstan, Kyrgyzstan, Russia, Tajikistan, and Uzbekistan.[31] China is seeking a closer relationship with ASEAN through ASEAN-Plus 3.[32] China has backed the Regional Comprehensive Economic Partnership (RCEP), which includes all ten ASEAN states as well as Australia, China, India, Japan, South Korea, and New Zealand.[33] The objective of launching RCEP negotiations is to achieve a modern, comprehensive, high-quality, and mutually beneficial economic partnership agreement that will cover trade in goods, trade in services, investment, economic and technical cooperation, intellectual property, competition, electronic commerce, dispute settlement, and other issues.[34] The One Belt One Road Initiative is another major project of China.

India is playing an active part in SAARC. To enhance its soft power, India launched a satellite that would provide services to all SAARC countries, called 'South Asia Satellite GSAT-9'. It is a geostationary communication satellite, the primary objective of which is to provide various communication applications with coverage over South Asian countries.[35] The satellite will provide improved communication, mapping of terrain and natural resources, as well as disaster prediction and management for the next twelve years without any cost to the other SAARC countries.[36]

Russia has developed a dense network of bilateral and regional relationships, such as Commonwealth of Independent States, the Collective Security Treaty Organization, the Organization of Central Asian Cooperation, the Eurasian Economic Community, the Common Economic Space, and the Customs Union of Belarus, Russia and Kazakhstan.[37]

---

[29] Rostam J Neuwirth, Alexandr Svetlicinii, and Denis De Castro Halis, *The BRICS-Lawyers' Guide to Global Cooperation* (Cambridge University Press 2017).

[30] Weinlicha (n 23).

[31] 'Charter of the Shanghai Cooperation Organization' (7 June 2002) <eng.sectsco.org/load/203013/> accessed 17 October 2017.

[32] Kuik Cheng-Chwee, 'Multilateralism in China's ASEAN Policy: Its Evolution, Characteristics, and Aspiration' (2005) 27 Contemporary Southeast Asia 102.

[33] Murray Hiebert and Liam Hanlon, 'ASEAN and Partners Launch Regional Comprehensive Economic Partnership' (Centre for Strategic and International Studies, 7 December 2012) <http://csis.org/publication/asean-and-partners-launch-regional-comprehensive-economic-partnership> accessed 23 September 2017.

[34] Australian Government, Department of Foreign Affairs and Trade, 'Regional Comprehensive Economic Partnership' <http://dfat.gov.au/trade/agreements/rcep/Pages/regional-comprehensive-economic-partnership.aspx> accessed 17 October 2017.

[35] ISRO Government of India, 'GSAT-9' <www.isro.gov.in/Spacecraft/gsat-9> accessed 17 October 2017.

[36] HT Correspondent, 'Countdown to India's Saarc Satellite Take-Off on Track: 5 Things to Know about ISRO's Latest Launch' (*Hindustan Times*, 5 May 2017) <www.hindustantimes.com/india-news/countdown-to-india-s-saarc-satellite-take-off-on-track-5-things-to-know-about-isro-s-latest-launch/story-A61lS4oaL1RSMT9mDgjj9J.html> accessed 17 October 2017.

[37] Stephen Aris, 'Russia's Approach to Multilateral Cooperation in the Post-Soviet Space: CSTO EurAsEC and SCO' (76/10 *Russian Analytical Digest*, 2010) <www.css.ethz.ch/publications/pdfs/RAD-76.pdf> accessed 14 October 2017.

A major factor behind the popularity of these networks is that they are not coercive or exclusive for the states. This increases interconnectedness, which acts as one of the factors in reducing tensions.

These developments show the efforts of the BRICS countries towards increasing their power base. This has ameliorated their capacity to influence institutions and norms. With their efforts, this power is likely to increase in the future.

The BRICS countries do not constitute a homogenous group but a coherent group. They are bound by shared historical experiences in international institutions and norm creation processes. They share common aspirations for the future. During the creation of the institutions and norms of the Washington Consensus, they were left out, but they cannot be ignored anymore. Rather, they may take a central role in various areas of international law. They may not agree on every issue between themselves and may even take diverse or contradictory positions against each other. But on a majority of issues, which are critical from the perspective of the global order, they take common positions. In the past, their positions were not necessarily coordinated in a planned manner. But after the creation of BRICS, an organized effort towards common positions is regularly seen. These positions could assist in reflecting upon the future developments of international law, which is done in the following section.

III. The BRICS and the future development of international law

The impact of the BRICS countries on the future development of international law can be analysed on the basis of their participation and positions in existing institutions and participation in norm creation, along with the articulation of their vision of these institutions and norms. The developments in the field of collective security through the Security Council and non-interference in internal affairs, World Trade Organization (WTO), investment, climate change, and human rights are discussed in this section.

1. UN Charter, Security Council, and Responsibility to Protect (R2P)

In the Washington Consensus era, Western states attempted to expand the use of force under the UN Charter by arguing for the possibility of use of force without the authorization of the Security Council.[38] During Kosovo, the doctrine of humanitarian intervention was proposed to circumvent the necessity of a Security Council resolution to use force against a State.[39] The efforts of the United States and its allies to exercise use of

[38] In context of the US invasion of Iraq: UNSC, 'Statements by Russia and China in the Security Council' (4701st meeting SC/7658, 5 February 2003) <www.un.org/press/en/2003/sc7658.doc.htm> accessed 16 October 2017.
[39] FCO, 'FRY/Kosovo: The Way Ahead: UK View on Legal Base for Use of Force' (7 October 1998); the statement of France in the debate in the Security Council: UN Doc S/PV.3988 (24 March 1999) 8–9; and that of the Netherlands: UN Doc S/PV.3989 (26 March 1999) 4; for a summary of statements of Western states: Christopher Greenwood, 'Humanitarian Intervention: the Case of Kosovo' (2002) Finnish Yearbook of International Law 141.

force unilaterally, without authorization from the Security Council, was resisted by the BRICS countries during Kosovo[40] and Iraq.[41]

Formal and informal discussions have taken place in the UN regarding use of force and humanitarian intervention, primarily under the rubric of Responsibility to Protect (R2P). Western states have supported the idea of R2P in the UN from time to time.[42] The issue was extensively discussed at the World Summit Outcome of 2005 and the framework for R2P was ultimately set out consensually. The World Summit Outcome 2005 Document emphasized that the Security Council has the primary responsibility of maintaining international peace and security and the need of 'addressing international challenges and problems by strictly abiding by the Charter.'[43] The primary responsibility of protection would be on the individual State and the international community should assist in these efforts.[44] Collective action, if necessary, could be taken through the Security Council:

> in accordance with the Charter, including Chapter VII, on a case-by-case basis and in cooperation with relevant regional organizations as appropriate, should peaceful

---

[40] In case of Kosovo, we see that Russia and China harshly criticized NATO's military strikes. Russian officials, nevertheless, arguably pushed the NATO powers into independent action. Publicly, Russian officials condemned the NATO campaign, arguing that '[e]nforcement elements have been excluded from the draft resolution, and there are no provisions in it that would directly or indirectly sanction the automatic use of force.': SC 3837th meeting UN Doc S/PV.3937 (24 October 1998); Russia submitted to the Security Council a draft resolution describing NATO actions as a 'flagrant violation of the United Nations Charter' which was defeated by twelve votes to three: UNSC Res 328 (26 March 1999) UN Doc S/1999/328; also: UNSC, 'Security Council Rejects Demand for Cessation of Use of Force Against Federal Republic of Yugoslavia' (26 March 1999) UN Press Release SC/6659; China similarly condemned NATO action, maintaining that '[w]hen the sovereignty of a country is put in jeopardy, its human rights can hardly be protected effectively. Sovereign equality, mutual respect for State sovereignty and non-Interference in the internal affairs of others are the basic principles governing international relations today' UNGA Res PV.8 (22 September 1999) UN Doc A/54/PV.8; further, in context of the Security Council's Rejection of Demand for Cessation of Use of Force against Federal Republic of Yugoslavia: UNSC, 'Statements by China, Russia and India in the Security Council meeting on 26 March 1999' <www.un.org/press/en/1999/19990326.sc6659.html> accessed 24 October 2017; in the context of Implications of International Response to Events in Rwanda, Kosovo: UNGA, 'Statements by Brazil and South Africa in the General Assembly Plenary Meeting on 20 September 1999' <www.un.org/press/en/1999/19990920.ga9595.html> accessed 24 October 2017; Russia, Belarus, and India on 26 March 1999 proposed that the Council adopt a resolution which would have characterized the NATO resort to force as 'a flagrant violation of the United Nations Charter, in particular Articles 2(4), 24 and 53 and determined that the NATO action constituted a threat to international peace and security'. The draft resolution was defeated by twelve votes (Argentina, Bahrain, Brazil, Canada, France, Gabon, Gambia, Malaysia, Netherlands, Slovenia, United Kingdom, and United States of America) to three (China, Russia, and Namibia): UNSC Res 328 (26 March 1999) UN Doc S/1998/328.

[41] In context of the US invasion of Iraq: UNSC, 'Statements by Russia and China in the Security Council' (SC 4701st meeting SC/7658, 5 February 2003) <www.un.org/press/en/2003/sc7658.doc.htm> accessed 16 October 2017; in context of the US invasion of Iraq: UNSC, 'Statements by India, Brazil and South Africa in the Security Council' (4726th meeting SC/7705, 26 March 2003) <www.un.org/press/en/2003/sc7705.doc.htm> accessed 25 October 2017.

[42] Obama White House, 'President Obama's Weekly Address 2011' Daily Compilation of Presidential Documents 203, 1; Harold Hongku Koh, 'Statement Regarding Use of Force in Libya before the American Society of International Law Annual Meeting' <www.state.gov/s/l/releases/remarks/159201.htm> accessed 24 October 2017; also: Prime Minister's Office, 'Guidance: Chemical Weapons Use by Syrian Regime: UK Government Legal Position' <www.gov.uk/government/publications/chemical-weaponuse-by-syrian-regime-uk-government-legal-position/chemical-weapon-use-by-syrian-regime-ukgovernment-legal-position-html-version> accessed 23 October 2017; Jean-Maurice Rupert, 'Statement on the Protection of Civilians' <www.franceonu.org/france-at-theunited-nations/press-room/statements-at-open-meetings/security-council/january-2009-1025/article/14-january-2009-debate-on-the> accessed 24 October 2017.

[43] UNGA, '2005 World Summit Outcome' (24 October 2005) UN Doc A/Res/60/1, 77–80.

[44] ibid 138.

means be inadequate and national authorities are manifestly failing to protect their populations from genocide, war crimes, ethnic cleansing and crimes against humanity.[45]

Brazil and South Africa have insisted that there should be discussions and agreement on the concept and it should not exceed the framework agreed on at the World Summit Outcome 2005.[46] China has time and again rejected R2P as a legal rule. China has prioritized sovereignty and rejected unilateral use of force under R2P.[47] Russia and India have stated that it is primarily the responsibility of the individual State and that the only exception would be through the formula adopted in the World Summit Outcome. This framework for R2P agreed on at the World Summit Outcome 2005 should not be breached.[48] The positions taken by these states during the debate in the General Assembly in 2009 have not changed until now.[49] The Secretary General in his latest report 'Implementing the Responsibility to Protect: Accountability for Prevention' has affirmed the commitment of not exceeding the framework of the World Summit Outcome of 2005.[50]

The intervention in Libya was authorized by the Security Council and was not based on unilateral action of any State. When the resolution was adopted, all BRICS members were part of the Security Council and they all abstained, except South Africa. South Africa voted in favour of the resolution, but subsequently expressed serious reservations about the manner of implementation of the resolution, and took a narrower view of R2P.[51] The Resolution (1973) on Libya notes in the preamble that the primary

---

[45] ibid 139.
[46] UNSC, 'Remarks by H.E. Ambassador Maria Luiza Ribeiro Viotti, Permanent Representative of Brazil to the United Nations, Plenary meeting of the General Assembly on the responsibility to protect, 23 July 2009' <http://www.responsibilitytoprotect.org/Brazil_ENG.pdf> accessed 22 October 2017; UN, H.E. Mr Baso Sangqu Ambassador and Permanent Representative of South Africa (5 July 2016) <www.un.org/press/en/2016/bio4859.doc.htm> accessed 20 October 2017.
[47] Permanent Mission of the People's Republic of China to the UN, 'Statement by Ambassador Liu Zhenmin at the Plenary Session of the General Assembly on the Question of "Responsibility to Protect"' (24 July 2009) <www.china-un.org/eng/hyyfy/t575682.htm> accessed 24 October 2017.
[48] Permanent Mission of India to the UN, 'Ambassador Hardeep Singh Puri Permanent Representative of India to the United Nations at the General Assembly Plenary Meeting on Implementing the Responsibility to Protect, 24 July 2009' <http://www.responsibilitytoprotect.org/India_ENG.pdf>; Permanent Mission of Russian Federation to the UN, 'Russian—Statement at the July 2009 GA Debate on RtoP Mr Margelov, Special Representative of the Russian President on Cooperation with African Countries' <www.responsibilitytoprotect.org/RussianFederation.pdf> accessed 24 October 2017.
[49] Global Centre for Responsibility to Protect, 'Brazil's Statement at the 2016 UN General Assembly Thematic Panel Discussion, From Commitment to Implementation: Ten Years of Responsibility to Protect' (26 February 2016) <www.globalr2p.org/resources/920> accessed 24 October 2017, and 'China's Statement at the 2016 UN General Assembly Thematic Panel Discussion, From Commitment to Implementation: Ten Years of Responsibility to Protect' (26 February 2016) <www.globalr2p.org/resources/923> accessed 9 July 2018; and 'Statement Delivered by the Delegation of India to the United Nations, at the United Nations General Assembly Thematic Panel Discussion "From commitment to implementation: Ten years of the Responsibility to Protect"—convened by the President of the General Assembly' [Unofficial Transcription] (25 February 2016) <www.globalr2p.org/media/files/india-26-feb.pdf> accessed 9 July 2018.
[50] UNGA, 'Report of the Secretary-General on Implementing the Responsibility to Protect: Accountability for Prevention' (10 August 2017) UN Doc A/71/1016 –S/2017/556.
[51] 'Statement by Ambassador Baso Sangqu, Permanent Representative of South Africa to the United Nations at the Informal Meeting Hosted by the Minister of External Relations of Brazil' (21 February 2012) <www.responsibilitytoprotect.org/S%20Africa.pdf>; also: Chris Landsberg, 'Pax South Africana and the Responsibility to Protect' (2010) 2 Global Responsibility to Protect 436; Stanley Foundation, 'Policy

responsibility to protect is of the Libyan authorities and the interference of the Security Council was not based on 'responsibility to protect' as an obligation of the international community. The text of the resolution represents that the Security Council was acting under its powers under Chapter VII, rather than under the legal obligation of responsibility to protect.[52] The resolution was limited to 'all necessary measures ... to protect civilians and civilian populated areas under threat of attack'.[53] During the discussions following the armed intervention, the BRICS states criticized the actions of the United States and the European states as being beyond the authorization of the Security Council. Russia and China deemed US and European efforts for regime change in Libya to exceed the mandate of Resolution 1973.[54] The positions of Brazil[55] and India were similar.[56] They strongly believed that the Security Council has passed a resolution that authorizes far-reaching measures under Chapter VII of the United Nations Charter, with relatively little credible information on the situation on the ground in Libya.[57]

Post 9/11, in response to terrorism, the United States and its allies have argued for a capacious interpretation of the right of self-defence under Article 51 of the UN Charter and customary international law.[58] These announcements have taken place mostly in the form of policy statements by governments and their legal advisors. The BRICS countries have not responded precisely to the debate about the expansion of the right

---

Dialogue Brief: The Roles of South Africa and the United States for the 21st Century International Agenda' <www.stanleyfoundation.org/publications/pdb/RoleUSandSouthAfrica412.pdf> accessed 17 October 2017.

[52] UNSC Res 1973 (17 March 2011) UN Doc S/RES/1973.

[53] ibid 4.

[54] For statements by China and Russia suggesting that NATO action exceeded authorities under Resolution 1973 (quoting Chinese and Russian official condemnations): Ben Smith and Arabella Thorp, 'Interpretation of Security Council Resolution 1973 on Libya' (International Affairs and Defence Section of the UK Foreign Affairs and Commonwealth Office, 6 April 2011) <www.parliament.uk/briefing-papers/sn05916.pdf> accessed 20 October 2017.

[55] UNSC, 'Permanent Rep. of Brazil to the UN, Letter dated 9 November 2011 from the Permanent Representative of Brazil to the United Nations addressed to the Secretary-General' (11 November 2011) UN Doc A/66/551 - S/ 2011/701; Thomas Wright, 'Brazil Hosts Workshop on "Responsibility While Protecting" Foreign Policy' <https://foreignpolicy.com/2012/08/29/brazil-hosts-workshop-on-responsibility-while-protecting> accessed 17 October 2017 (Brazil has effectively infused this interpretation into global debate).

[56] UNSC Res PV.6498 (17 March 2011) UN Doc S/PV.6498, 6: India:

> The Council has today adopted a resolution that authorizes far-reaching measures under Chapter VII of the United Nations Charter, with relatively little credible information on the situation on the ground in Libya. We also do not have clarity about details of enforcement measures, including who will participate and with what assets, and how these measures will exactly be carried out. It is of course very important that there be full respect for the sovereignty, unity and territorial integrity of Libya. The financial measures that are proposed in the resolution could impact directly or through indirect routes the ongoing trade and investment activities of a number of Member States, thereby adversely affecting the economic interests of the Libyan people and others dependent on these trade and economic ties. Moreover, we have to ensure that the measures will mitigate and not exacerbate an already difficult situation for the people of Libya. Clarity in the resolution on any spill-over effects of these measures would have been very important.'

[57] ibid 5–7.

[58] Harold Hongju Koh, 'Annual Meeting of the American Society of International Law Washington, DC' <https://www.state.gov/documents/organization/179305.pdf > accessed 25 October 2017; UK Government, 'Speech of Attorney General of UK at International Institute for Strategic Studies "The Modern Law of Self-Defence" ' <www.gov.uk/government/uploads/system/uploads/attachment_data/file/583171/170111_Imminence_Speech_.pdf> accessed 22 October 2017; also: George Brandis, Attorney General of Australia, 'The Right of Self-Defence Against Imminent Armed Attack' (EJIL Talk, 25 May 2017) <www.ejiltalk.org/the-right-of-self-defence-against-imminent-armed-attack-in-international-law/#more-15255> accessed 22 October 2017.

of self-defence, unlike in the R2P context. Considering their traditional resistance to-wards use of force without the authorization of the Security Council or against the con-sent of the State where actions are undertaken, it may be expected that they would resist expansion of the right of self-defence. It is, however, difficult to make any certain as-sessment because rising powers have also been victims of international terrorism and may be willing to support an expansive interpretation of self-defence against terrorism. BRICS countries have time and again called for a comprehensive convention for tack-ling terrorism.[59] The proposed convention does not address issues of self-defence and use of force in relation to it.

2. WTO

The WTO is an important institution of the Washington Consensus era which was pushed without enthusiastic participation of the rising powers. China and Russia were not part of its creation. India participated, however reluctantly. China and Russia joined the WTO and the BRICS countries have continued to be active participants in the international trading system through the WTO. They have sought to enforce the existing WTO framework through active participation in dispute resolution.[60] These states have continued to participate in the international trading system despite some of their prominent policies having had to be reversed in light of decisions of the Panel and Appellate Body.[61] The United States have been critical of the WTO and of the Appellate Body. In a recent stand-off, the United States has blocked the consensus for the re-election of Appellate Body members by criticizing the outcome of some decisions. Other members of the WTO have objected to this approach, since the appropriate place for raising these issues is the meeting of the Dispute Settlement Body and not appoint-ment of Appellate Body members.[62]

The BRICS countries have expressed their commitment to actively participate in the existing WTO structures created under the Marrakesh Agreement, resisting protec-tionist measures and with complete commitment to the dispute resolution process.[63]

---

[59] MEA, 'Goa Declaration at 8th BRICS Summit' (16 October 2016) <www.mea.gov.in/bilateral-documents.htm?dtl/27491/Goa_Declaration_at_8th_BRICS_Summit> accessed 25 October 2017; Permanent Mission of People's Republic of China to the United Nations Office, 'Press Release of the Meeting of BRICS Ministers of Foreign Affairs/International Relations' (21 September 2017) <www.china-un.ch/eng/zywjyjh/t1500179.htm> accessed 25 October 2017; also: University of Toronto, 'VII BRICS Summit: 2015 Ufa Declaration, 9 July 2015' <www.brics.utoronto.ca/docs/150709-ufa-declaration_en.html> accessed 25 October 2017.

[60] WTO, 'Disputes by Members' <www.wto.org/english/tratop_e/dispu_e/dispu_by_country_e.htm> accessed 25 October 2017 (India (Total: 175 cases), China (Total: 194 cases), Russia (Total: 50 cases), Brazil (Total: 159 cases), and South Africa (Total: 12 cases). China is the largest participant in all the cases decided by the WTO.

[61] China lost the *Audio Visuals* case where its censorship laws were challenged and India lost the *Solar Panels* case, which was an important policy objective of the government.

[62] WTO, 'WTO Members Debate Appointment/Reappointment of Appellate Body Members' <www.wto.org/english/news_e/news16_e/dsb_23may16_e.htm> accessed 22 October 2017; 'WTO Chief Warns of Risks to Trade Peace' (*Financial Times*, 1 October 2017) <www.ft.com/content/3459f930-a532-11e7-9e4f-7f5e6a7c98a2?mhq5j=e5> accessed 22 October 2017.

[63] BRICS 2017 China, '7th Meeting of the BRICS Trade Ministers Statement' (7 August 2017) <www.brics2017.org/English/Documents/Meetings/201708/t20170831_1824.html> accessed 22 October 2017, 11–13.

Sustaining the world trading system under the WTO and resisting protectionist measures is in the interest of BRICS countries. China has essentially been an export-led growth model. India aspires to increase its exports in service as well as goods, and is taking steps to that effect through efforts such as the 'Make in India Campaign'. Russia wishes to move away from the excessive reliance of its economy on energy products and move towards an export-oriented economy. Brazil understands the need for export of agricultural products to boost its economy. The importance of the WTO is evident from the fact that China undertook several structural transformations in its domestic economy to join the WTO in 2001. Russia joined in 2012. BRICS have expressed the desire that other states should also join the world trading system.[64] Thus, despite deadlock and problems with the progress in the Doha Round, rising powers understand the importance of a multilateral trading system and continue to be at the negotiating table. They have expressed their confidence in the current architecture and the need for taking the Doha Development Round forward. In the recently concluded BRICS meeting, the joint statement declares that:

> We recognize the important role played by international trade and foreign direct investments in the world economic recovery. We call upon all parties to work together to improve the international trade and investment environment. We urge the international community to keep the multilateral trading system stable, curb trade protectionism, and push for comprehensive and balanced results of the WTO's Doha Development Agenda.[65]

The BRICS states, through cooperation—unlike before—have managed to achieve greater results through mutual cooperation.[66] Since 2011, the trade ministers of BRICS countries have been meeting regularly and working towards common positions.[67] Agriculture has been an area of common concern for BRICS countries. On agriculture and especially subsidies, the Marrakesh Agreement could not achieve much through the Agreement on Agriculture from the perspective of developing countries— particularly on curtailing subsidies given by developed countries. The Doha mandate has three pillars on agriculture: access to markets with substantial improvement in access, reduction and eventual elimination of export subsidies for agricultural products, and reducing domestic support measures.[68] The BRICS countries (along with

---

[64] The Bricspost, '5 other Nations Invited to Attend BRICS Summit in China' <http://thebricspost.com/5-other-nations-invited-to-attend-brics-summit-in-china/#.WeULY1uCzIU> accessed 17 October 2017; also: The Bricspost, 'More Members to Join BRICS Bank: Russia' <http://thebricspost.com/more-members-to-join-brics-bank-russia/#.WeULEFuCzIU> accessed 17 October 2017; and: China Daily, 'Xi: Emerging Nations Deserve Role' <www.chinadaily.com.cn/china/2017-09/06/content_31617282.htm> accessed 17 October 2017.

[65] BRICS 2017 China, 'Joint Statement of the BRICS leaders' (16 June 2009, published 26 January 2017) <https://brics2017.org/English/Documents/Summit/201701/t20170125_1403.html> accessed 17 October 2017, 5 (This commitment has appeared in all prior joint statements of BRICS leaders.)

[66] Vera Thorstensen and Ivan TM Oliviera, *BRICS in the World Trade Organization: Comparative Trade Policies Brazil, Russia, India, China and South Africa (BRICS) as Players in the World Trade Organization* (IPEA 2014).

[67] BRICS 2017 China, '7th Meeting of the BRICS Trade Ministers' (n 63) 3.

[68] For a detailed description of the history from GATT until recent discussion at the Doha Round on agriculture and the role of the G20 and specifically the leadership of rising powers: Thorstensen and Oliviera (n 66).

active support of other traditional non-Western countries from the G20) have taken a position that agricultural subsidies should be discussed and agreed upon and the developing countries should reduce their subsidies on agriculture.[69] Developing countries have been seeking a reduction in the standard of proof for establishing subsidies—India and Brazil introduced the concept of 'benchmarking' to define subsidies in order to include only public long-term financing and not private financing. In addition to agriculture, BRICS leaders have emphasized the need for negotiations in the service sector at the WTO.[70]

3. Investment

The practice of BRICS countries regarding the protection of foreign investment is inconsistent and the conclusions are limited to the respective State concerned. They do not take coordinated positions on this issue and act individually based on domestic choices.

Brazil has never entered into BITs with a compulsory dispute arbitration clause. South Africa has abandoned the BIT programme in view of its affirmative action measures.[71] China, India, and Russia are active participants in the BIT programme. After the *Yukos* arbitration cases, Russia has attempted to limit access to investment arbitration through narrow provisions on jurisdiction and compulsory compliance with the 'cooling-off' period prior to commencement of arbitration proceedings.[72] India adopted a Model BIT in 2015. This was a major shift from its earlier model which exposed it to large investment claims.[73] The current model provides narrow grounds for jurisdiction and substantive treatment standards. India is still predominantly a capital importing country, but China has transformed itself into a capital exporting country. China has moved towards liberal standards and broad investment protection standards.[74] However, a common trend amongst the BRICS countries is the insistence on regulatory space of the host State. The BRICS ministers of trade have emphasized it in the following words: 'BRICS countries fully preserve the right to regulate, national policy space, policy-making and approaches to investment in other bilateral, plurilateral and multilateral frameworks and processes.'[75]

---

[69] For a list of areas where the rising powers converge and diverge and other states that have been a part of the coalition based on their negotiating positions: Thorstensen and Oliviera (n 66).

[70] BRICS 2017 China, '7th Meeting of the BRICS Trade Ministers' (n 63) 7.

[71] US Department of State, '2015 Investment Climate Statement—South Africa' <www.state.gov/e/eb/rls/othr/ics/2015/241744.htm> accessed 22 October 2017.

[72] Yaroslav Klimov and Andrey Panov, 'Russia's New Guidelines on Future Bilateral Investment Treaties: Foreign Direct Investment after Yukos Shareholders v Russia' (2017) 8 Norton Rose Fulbright International Arbitration Report 30.

[73] Aniruddha Rajput, 'India's Shifting Treaty Practice: A Comparative Analysis of the 2003 and 2015 Model BITs' (2016) 7 Jindal Global Law Review 201.

[74] Stephan Schill, 'Tearing Down the Great Wall—the New Generation Investment Treaties of the People's Republic of China' (2007) 15 Cardozo Journal and International and Comparative Law 73.

[75] BRICS 2017 China, '7th Meeting of the BRICS Trade Ministers' (n 63) 6.

The practice of the BRICS countries on BITs and investment arbitration would continue to be disparate, where China, India, and Russia would continue to engage with international investment law, albeit based on different models and priorities.

4. Climate change

Under the UN Framework Convention for Climate Change (1992), developing countries had succeeded in getting concessions in the form of the principle of 'common but differentiated responsibilities'.[76] In the Paris Agreement, in addition to the common but differential treatment, India initiated the inclusion of 'climate justice' into the preamble.[77] The concept of 'climate justice' is relatively new.[78] Climate justice links human rights and development to achieve a human-centred approach. This would also include vulnerable groups. It is being interpreted by scholars to mean inclusion of concerns of those that have not been contributors towards climate change. These would include the developing countries, which need to be given sufficient technology and financial support to implement their obligations under the Paris Agreement. Additionally, a wide range of people such as indigenous peoples and vulnerable groups would also be included. Their concerns and their expectations of progress should also be taken into account.[79] Unlike previous agreements, the Paris Agreement takes a nuanced approach on several issues, including the common but differential treatment. It does not adopt a single across-the-board categorization based on pre-set categories of states. The absence of annexures and definitions of 'developed' and 'developing' would allow states to increase ambitions rather than waiting to graduate from one category to another.[80]

BRICS states have continued to express their commitment towards climate change negotiations. They focus prominently on cooperation and proliferation of renewable energy—an important instrument for reducing carbon emissions. However, they continue to insist upon 'common but differentiated responsibilities'.[81] The BRICS ministers of environment met separately in 2015 and agreed upon setting up a steering committee to coordinate efforts and sharing technologies and best practices. They explored possibilities of mutual cooperation to tackle issues of water, air and industrial pollution,

---

[76] United Nations Framework Convention on Climate Change (adopted 9 May 1992, entered into force 21 March 1994) GE.05-62220 (UNFCCC) Arts 3.1, 4.1, 4.2(2).

[77] Vidya Venkat, 'India Demands Climate Justice' (*The Hindu*, 17 November 2016); also: Nitin Sethi, 'Is Modi's Pitch for 'Climate Justice' more than Rhetoric?' (*Business Standard*, 10 November 2015) <www.business-standard.com/article/current-affairs/is-modi-s-pitch-for-climate-justice-more-than-rhetoric-115101401369_1.html> accessed 25 September 2017.

[78] International Bar Association, *Achieving Justice and Human Rights in an Era of Climate Disruption International Bar Association Climate Change Justice and Human Rights Task Force Report* (1st edn, International Bar Association 2014); Edward Cameron, Tara Shine, and Wendi Bevins, 'Climate Justice: Equity and Justice Informing a New Climate Change Agreement' <www.wri.org/sites/default/files/climate_justice_equity_and_justice_informing_a_new_climate_agreement.pdf> accessed 21 September 2017.

[79] Mary Robinson, 'Climate Justice: Challenge and Opportunity' (2011) 22 Irish Studies in International Affairs 67.

[80] Christina Voigt and Felipe Ferreira, '"Dynamic Differentiation": The Principles of CBDR-RC, Progression and Highest Possible Ambition in the Paris Agreement' (2016) 5 Transnational Environmental Law 285.

[81] BRICS 2017 China, 'Joint Statement of the BRICS leaders' (n 65).

waste management, and sewerage treatment. The BRICS Bank, with a US$100 billion corpus, could play a constructive role investing in the promotion of green technology and providing financial aid to help reduce air pollution.[82]

At the climate change negotiations, Russia has distanced itself from the other BRICS countries. The others develop common positions and negotiate as 'BASIC'. The environment ministers of these countries meet regularly.[83] The BASIC and the G77 have a major role to play in these negotiations and they take commonly agreed positions.[84] The BRICS countries are part of G77 and are, therefore, in a position to influence the position that G77 takes at climate change negotiations.[85] BASIC has been discussing and taking common positions on issues based on their discussions and representing the voice of the developing world.[86] The common thread amongst the BASIC countries at climate change negotiations is that, while they are having to comply with their obligations of greenhouse gas (GHG) emissions, they have to simultaneously ensure that they maintain a sufficient level of growth to lift their population from poverty.[87] They take a position that climate change should be dealt with fairly and in a transparent manner and the developed countries have an important responsibility and that these should take the important share of the burden and also provide necessary technological support.[88] BASIC has managed to retain its group identity as well as accommodate individual identity and aspirations.[89]

Individually, BRICS countries have made efforts to reduce their GHG emissions.[90] Brazil and India have been most successful and are expected to achieve their targets through a focus on renewable energy. Russia may be able to achieve its targets since its targets are less ambitious than they appear at face value: it actually lies significantly above current policy projections.[91] China's and South Africa's emissions are increasing and they need to do more to achieve their targets.[92] Alongside efforts at the multilateral level, states are entering into regional arrangements to address the

---

[82] Debidatta Aurobinda Mahapatra, 'BRICS to Push Cooperation on Climate Change, Russia and India Report' <https://www.rbth.com/economics/2015/04/29/brics_to_push_cooperation_on_climate_change_42893>   accessed 17 October 2017.

[83] Anne-Sophie Tabau and Marion Lemoine, 'Willing Power, Fearing Responsibilities: BASIC in the Climate Negotiations' (2012) 3 Carbon and Climate Law Review 197.

[84] Sander Happaerts and Hans Bruyninckx, 'Rising Powers in Global Climate Governance. Negotiating in the New World Order' <https://ghum.kuleuven.be/ggs/publications/working_papers/new_series/wp121-130/wp124-happaerts-bruyninckx-finaal.pdf> accessed 17 October 2017.

[85] Tabau and Lemoine (n 83).

[86] ibid.

[87] ibid 198.

[88] ibid 205–06.

[89] For the role individual and group identity has played at climate change negotiations: Kathryn Hochstetler and Manjana Milkoreit, 'Emerging Powers in the Climate Negotiations: Shifting Identity Conceptions' (2014) 67 Political Research Quarterly 224.

[90] For a country-wise account of efforts taken: William Chandler, Roberto Schaeffer, Zhou Dadi, PR Shukla, Fernando Tudela, Ogunlade Davidson, and Sema Alpan-Atamer, *Climate Change Mitigation in Developing Countries: Brazil, China, India, Mexico, South Africa, and Turkey* (Pew Centre on Global Climate Change 2002).

[91] For an undated performance of states on greenhouse emissions: Climate Action Tracker, 'Russian Federation' <http://climateactiontracker.org/countries/russianfederation.html> accessed 25 September 2017.

[92] Elena Gladun and Dewan Ahsan, 'BRICS Countries' Political and Legal Participation in the Global Climate Change Agenda' (2016) 3 BRICS Law Journal 8, 22; Climate Action Tracker, 'India' <http://climateactiontracker.org/countries/india.html> accessed 25 September 2017.

problem of climate change.[93] India led the creation of the International Solar Alliance, an inter-governmental organization of sun-rich states. The Framework Agreement on International Solar Alliance, which is a treaty, has been signed by several developing as well as developed countries.[94]

5. Human rights

The origin of modern human rights is credited to the West and especially the role of the United States in promoting it through the Universal Declaration of Human Rights. Human rights have been part of the culture, history, and struggle for liberation in India and South Africa. With its participation in the Organization of American States, Brazil has the protection of human rights as a foremost concern. The developments in the field of human rights have taken place during and after the decolonization process with the participation of the non-Western countries. Human rights are universal in nature and one of the central pillars of the UN Charter.[95] The importance of protection and promotion of human rights and the focus on the right to development through the UN Human Rights Council are reflected in the declarations of BRICS leaders. The 2017 Declaration of the BRICS leaders states:

> We reiterate the need for all countries to cooperate in promoting and protecting human rights and fundamental freedoms under the principles of equality and mutual respect. We agree to continue to treat all human rights, including the right to development, in a fair and equal manner, on the same footing and with the same emphasis. We will strengthen cooperation on issues of common interests both within BRICS and in multilateral fora including the United Nations Human Rights Council, taking into account the necessity to promote, protect and fulfill human rights in a non-selective, non-politicized and constructive manner, and without double standards.[96]

Brazil, India, and South Africa are parties to eighteen major treaties for the protection of human rights. Russia and China are party to fewer instruments—eleven and eight respectively.[97] Within their countries, Brazil, India, and South Africa have a strong and independent judiciary that effectively enforces human rights.

---

[93] Robert Falkner, 'A Minilateral Solution for Global Climate Change? On Bargaining Efficiency, Club Benefits, and International Legitimacy' (2015) 222 Centre for Climate Change Economics and Policy, published in (2016) 14 Perspectives on Politics 87; Robyn Eckersley, 'Moving Forward in the Climate Negotiations: Multilateralism or Minilateralism?' (2012) 12 Global Environmental Politics 24.

[94] International Solar Alliance, 'ISA Mission' <http://isolaralliance.org> accessed 17 October 2017.

[95] In addition to several provisions in the UN Charter, the preamble reaffirms the commitment towards protection of human rights: 'to reaffirm faith in fundamental human rights, in the dignity and worth of the human person, in the equal rights of men and women and of nations large and small'.

[96] BRICS 2017 China, 'BRICS Leaders Xiamen Declaration' (4 September 2017, published 8 September 2017) <www.brics2017.org/English/Documents/Summit/201709/t20170908_2021.html> accessed 17 October 2017, 54.

[97] United Nations Human Rights Office of the High Commissioner, 'Ratification of 18 International Human Rights Treaties' <http://indicators.ohchr.org/> accessed 17 October 2017.

In the General Assembly of the UN, the BRICS countries have emphasized the right to development as a human right.[98] This was noted in the resolutions declaring the New International Economic Order and specifically the Declaration on the Right to Development.[99] The BRICS countries have taken steps at the Human Rights Council for gender equality, *inter alia*, with a focus on abuses against women during wartime, eradication of poverty, providing access to education, and physical or sexual violence.[100] The right to food is recognized by all the BRICS countries in their domestic legislations.[101] It is expected that the BRICS Bank may succeed in achieving human rights goals more effectively in view of its objectives and available resources.[102]

There are differences in practices between BRICS countries within their countries and internationally. Although they may represent an overall commitment to human rights, their positions on specific human rights differ vastly. Agreement on some specific rights may be difficult and would take a longer time. But it would not necessarily result in a complete end of human rights.[103]

6. Structural changes: international law and institutions?

The rising powers are increasing cooperation at the regional as well as at the global level. They are negotiating for the creation of new norms through binding obligations at both the levels. The BRICS countries do not appear to be developing conflicting norms at these levels.

BRICS countries have been working through the forum of BRICS mostly for coordinated action on international issues and greater cooperation amongst themselves. BRICS works mostly through declarations and action plans[104] rather than treaties or other binding instruments as such. There is no formal treaty between BRICS countries creating BRICS. Yet, wherever they have deemed it necessary, BRICS states have entered into binding legal instruments from time to time.[105] BRICS have created the BRICS Bank through the Treaty for the Establishment of a BRICS Contingent Reserve Arrangement, 2015.[106] Normally, informalization is used to enhance hegemonic

---

[98] Subrata Roy Chowdhury, Erik M G Denters, and Paul JIM de Waart, *The Right to Development in International Law* (Martinus Nijhoff 1992).

[99] UNGA 'Declaration on the Right to Development' (4 December 1986) UN Doc A/RES/41/128.

[100] For a survey of the efforts of BRICS states: Christian Guillermet Fernandez and David Fernandez Puyana, 'The BRICS Commitment in the Promotion of Equality between Women and Men: Analysis from the Human Rights and Peace Perspective' (2014) 1 BRICS Law Journal 5.

[101] Katharine S E Cresswell Riol, *The Right to Food Guidelines, Democracy and Citizen Participation: Country Case Studies* (1st edn, Routledge 2016) 169.

[102] Jessica Evans, 'The Brics Have a Chance to Succeed Where the World Bank Has Failed' (30 July 2014) <www.hrw.org/news/2014/07/30/brics-have-chance-succeed-where-world-bank-has-failed> accessed 17 October 2017.

[103] Surya Subedi, 'The Universality of Human Rights Agenda: The Impact of the Shift of Power to the East and the Resurgence of the BRICS' (2015) 55 Indian Journal of International Law 177.

[104] BRICS Ministry of External Affairs, 'Leaders Declaration and Action Plan' <http://brics.itamaraty.gov.br/declarations-action-plans-and-communiques/listadecplan> accessed 17 October 2017.

[105] BRICS Ministry of External Affairs, 'Agreements and Memoranda of Understanding' <http://brics.itamaraty.gov.br/agreements> accessed 22 October 2017.

[106] BRICS Ministry of External Affairs, 'Treaty for the Establishment of a BRICS Contingent Reserve Arrangement, 2015' <http://brics.itamaraty.gov.br/media2/press-releases/220-treaty-for-the-establishment-of-a-brics-contingent-reserve-arrangement-fortaleza-july-15> accessed 25 September 2017.

influence and avoid binding obligations.[107] The BRICS countries are using informal arrangements as well as undertaking binding treaty obligations wherever necessary. Moreover, in a multipolar world, the possibilities of enhancing hegemonic influence through informalization would be difficult. With more than one State competing for influence, other states can easily change alliances without the fear of exclusion. Informalization is instead serving as the basis for closer cooperation between the BRICS countries, which is meant to be used for entering into binding obligations at the global and the regional level.

One of the outcomes of the Washington Consensus was a larger presence of private enterprises and businesses. Public sector undertakings have played a major role in the economic structures of some of the BRICS countries. The public sector companies have a global presence and capacity to make a large amount of foreign investments. BRICS countries have emphasized the role of public corporations.[108] The presence of activities of public corporations will not only increase the involvement of states, but also raise several new issues for international law to tackle, from protection of foreign investment to issues of violations of human rights by companies.[109]

IV. Conclusions

The BRICS countries would not simply acquiesce to the original structures and are attempting to shape international law in accordance with their aspirations. These aspirations need not necessarily be seen with scepticism, since they contribute towards strengthening and increasing participation in the existing institutions. The BRICS countries appear to be willing to cooperate with the Western powers, especially through a forum like the G20. BRICS leaders have expressed their commitment to aligning themselves with the priorities of the G20.[110] Thus, the challenge they pose is to hegemony per se rather than to the existing institutions. The BRICS countries continue

---

[107] Heike Krieger and Georg Nolte, 'International Rule of Law—Rise of Decline?—Approaching Current Foundational Challenges' in this book.

[108] BRICS Ministry of External Affairs, 'Sixth BRICS Summit—Fortaleza Declaration' <http://brics.itamaraty.gov.br/media2/press-releases/214-sixth-brics-summit-fortaleza-declaration> accessed 8 November 2017.

[109] Muthucumaraswamy Sornarajah, 'Sovereign Wealth Funds and the Existing Structure of the Regulation of Investments' (2011) 1 Asian Journal of International Law 267.

[110] II BRICS Summit, 'Joint Statement' (16 April 2010) <http://brics2016.gov.in/upload/files/document/5763e23d75e512nd.pdf> accessed 16 October 2017, 3:

> We stress the central role played by the G-20 in combating the crisis through unprecedented levels of coordinated action. We welcome the fact that the G-20 was confirmed as the premier forum for international economic coordination and cooperation of all its member states. Compared to previous arrangements, the G-20 is broader, more inclusive, diverse, representative and effective. We call upon all its member states to undertake further efforts to implement jointly the decisions adopted at the three G-20 Summits.

> We advocate the need for the G-20 to be proactive and formulate a coherent strategy for the post-crisis period. We stand ready to make a joint contribution to this effort.

to participate in the existing structures and shape them as per their priorities. They would actively articulate their choices and preferences in the running of the existing institutions and the creation of new institutions and norms. Creating new institutions and norms is not easy and is time consuming. It is far easier to influence and alter the existing frameworks.[111]

The BRICS countries are coordinating with established Western powers and between themselves through forums, such as the G20 and BRICS respectively, and they are at the same time building their own network of treaties and arrangements. In this situation, the creation of global treaties will become even more difficult to negotiate. The diffusion of power empowers more states, thus requiring greater consensus and greater readiness to give and take. Greater participation of states will enhance legitimacy of pre-existing institutions and future institutions and reduce contestations. This will reduce legitimacy questions and contestations of the institutions and the legal norms so created. During the time of the Washington Consensus, a single hegemonic power had a greater role in the creation of institutions and norms. The other states mostly acquiesced or were simply left aside. With the proliferation of power and increasing role of the BRICS countries, participation and the voice of different states, including smaller and less powerful states, would count. The process for achieving consensus then naturally takes longer. But these treaties have greater acceptability and better compliance. Thus, there will be less treaty-making but effective treaty-making. Multilateral treaty-making will be more difficult but bilateral and regional treaty-making will increase. While treaty-making may become even more tedious and time consuming, increased interactions between states could constitute fertile ground for creation and recognition of new customary law norms.

While the BRICS countries want to shape international law according to their vision, this does not mean it would be something alien to the existing structures—the European origins of international law and the existing instruments of international law remain. The priorities change.

While analysing the interrelationship between the BRICS countries and their concerns on some specific issues, differences remain and they continue to remain. For example, China is not enthusiastic about India's and Brazil's claim for a permanent seat at the Security Council. Understandably so. On issues where mutual interests conflict, there will be divergence. This does not take away the generality of the expectations and aspirations of the group as such. They continue to have common aspirations. They may have differences and tense moments from time to time, but they have managed to resolve their conflicts peacefully. Recently, in 2017, Chinese and Indian armies were at loggerheads over conflicting claims over the so-called Doklam plateau which is of strategic importance for India, Bhutan, and China. Conflicting territorial claims have not been resolved but the military crisis on the border has de-escalated. Indian forces

---

[111] William Burke-White, 'Power Shifts in International Law: Structural Realignment and Substantive Pluralism' (2015) 56 Harvard Journal of International Law 1 (see references thereunder for literature in the field).

withdrew from the region and China abandoned the project of building roads in the region, which was seen as a security threat by India.[112]

Much of the understanding and analysis of the post-Cold War world order was based on the assumption that there would be only one power and that this power would continue to exert influence over international relations. The world order has not remained the same. The absence or failure of a single hegemon, driving multilateral treaties, negotiations, leadership at institutions and the creation of institutions may be seen as a decline of international law. International law is in a state of 'transition', rather than a rise or decline. Transition entails change, and change need not be always bad. The appropriate test would be progress, which may be 'qualitative' or 'quantitative'. Quantitative progress would be an increase in the number of treaties and institutions and qualitative progress would represent greater peaceful interaction between states. The activities of BRICS countries and other rising powers represent qualitative as well as quantitative progress. The regional network of treaties and creation of the BRICS Bank represents a quantitative progress, albeit augmenting the threat of regionalization. The fact that the BRICS countries are willing to engage in institutions and the legal norms shows a qualitative improvement. Krieger and Nolte are correct to note that the 'current developments in the international system may not so much reflect a crisis of the law but may rather signal a need for reconfiguring the role of the state more broadly'.[113] The current state of international law may appear to be in a state of crisis or stagnation, but has potential for rising.

---

[112] Ministry of External Affairs, 'Press Statement on Doklam Disengagement Understanding' (28 August 2017) <http://mea.gov.in/press-releases.htm?dtl/28893/Press_Statement_on_Doklam_disengagement_understanding> accessed 20 October 2017.
[113] Krieger and Nolte (n 107) VI.2.

7

International Law and Its Others

Comment on Aniruddha Rajput

Simon Chesterman

If the rule of law means anything, it is that the law is meant to apply equally to all, regardless of the vacillations of power. This is the founding myth of law at the national level—famously forbidding the rich as well as the poor from sleeping under the bridges of Paris at night. More recently embraced at the international level, the myth was formalized in the United Nations Charter, Article 2(1) of which founds the Organization on the principle of sovereign equality. It is a useful myth, and a popular one—in 2005, every member state reaffirmed their commitment to the purposes and principles of the United Nations (UN) and to an international order based on the rule of law.[1]

Yet, a myth it remains. The history of the rule of law at the domestic and international level is a tale of ongoing struggle to ensure that the powerful as well as the weak are subject to it. That struggle is all the more difficult at the international level, as the absence of a hierarchical structure means that in place of the leviathan's stick there are only the carrots of enlightened self-interest.

For the most part, in times of quiet, the rule of law chugs along, providing stability and predictability in the various interactions of daily life. In such circumstances, it is in the interests of most to comply with the rule of law and accept the security and order that it brings. Yet, when there is a tectonic upheaval, an overturning of the *ancien régime*, bringing those who were powerless into a position to change that order, different priorities may emerge. In particular, for those who operated under an unjust order—colonialism, apartheid—the very legal system itself may be tainted with injustice. The rule of law may remain a political ideal, but politics may require that the rules themselves change.

So it is with the international rule of law today, an order whose very description as 'Westphalian' speaks to its Eurocentric origins. The tectonic shift underway at present is the decline of that West and the rise of its Others—former colonies, the Global South, displaced empires—and the question is what this means for the content and the structure of international law. Will the rise of those marginalized or exploited by the

---

[1] United Nations General Assembly (UNGA), '2005 World Summit Outcome' (24 October 2005) UN Doc A/Res/60/1, 134.

international order lead to a radical overhaul of that order, or an adaptation to the new political reality? Will it be evolution or revolution?

How the international order copes with rising powers is, as Aniruddha Rajput notes in his thoughtful and thought-provoking chapter,[2] more a question of international relations than international law. Yet, it is also true that powerful states generally seek to nudge or push for the normative regime of the day at least to accommodate—and perhaps advance—their interests. Dr Rajput takes as his lens the rise of the 'BRICS' powers in particular—Brazil, Russia, India, China, and South Africa—and considers the possible impact on various areas of law. In this brief response, I will consider the BRICS as a category, before addressing some of the possible changes in the law that he discusses. The conclusion will return to the question of rising powers more generally.

I. BRICS as a category

As Dr Rajput notes, the origins of this subversive category could not be more conventional. Coined by investment bankers at Goldman Sachs almost two decades ago, the acronym was first used in a paper speculating as to which of the emerging economies might plausibly be invited to join the G7 'club'. Tellingly, this was introduced by highlighting the size and trajectory of various economies and the important issues that this raised for 'the transmission of global monetary, fiscal and other economic policies'.[3]

Acronyms are rarely a sound basis for rigorous taxonomy, but since the accession of South Africa in 2010, the grouping has remained relatively stable and now holds an annual summit hosted on a rotating basis among the five countries. Yet, does it make sense as a category?

Dr Rajput appropriately qualifies the claims to unity of the BRICS group, arguing that they may not be 'homogenous' but are nonetheless 'coherent'. He rightly draws a distinction between the BRICS countries and non-Western middle powers such as Japan and South Korea, both of which were brought into the US security umbrella and embraced the Washington Consensus model of economic development. The BRICS remain outside the Organisation for Economic Co-operation and Development, though they have been included in the G20. He goes further to suggest that they share 'a certain philosophy and understanding of international law'.

This seems to be a stretch.

At times, Dr Rajput conflates the BRICS countries with the Non-Aligned Movement or the G77. It is not clear that the BRICS as a grouping could claim 'command of a numerical majority of States'. Normative successes of any such larger grouping might include decolonization, but it would be odd for apartheid South Africa to be given credit for that today. Other initiatives like the New International Economic Order, which he

---

[2] Aniruddha Rajput, 'The BRICS as "Rising Powers" and the Development of International Law' in this book.
[3] Jim O'Neill, 'Building Better Global Economic BRICs' (Goldman Sachs, Global Economics Paper No: 66) <www.goldmansachs.com/our-thinking/archive/archive-pdfs/build-better-brics.pdf> accessed 5 February 2018.

mentions, saw great efforts by India, perhaps, but were limited in lasting impact and not a true priority of the other states.

It is also possible that the BRICS coordination has reached its limit. As Dr Rajput highlights, there was a degree of commonality in their positions adopted up to 2008—measured, for example, by General Assembly votes. That is around the time at which the BRICS states began coordinating more formally. What is striking here is that an analysis of their voting patterns subsequently and up to 2014 shows no greater coordination as a result of that formalization.[4]

As an organization, then, it is possible that the BRICS grouping reflects overlapping interests, rather than a shared set of aspirations. It is telling that the last three BRICS summits were held in parallel with other, more established events—a summit of the Shanghai Cooperation Organisation (SCO) in 2015, the Bay of Bengal Initiative for Multi-Sectoral Technical and Economic Cooperation (BIMSTEC) in 2016, and the Emerging Markets and Developing Countries Dialogue (EMDCD) in 2017.

Lacking a secretariat, BRICS is less an organization than a rotating conference. Though each of the five states is clearly impactful in its own right, it is arguable that as an analytical category today, BRICS as a whole is less than the sum of its parts.

II. Points of tension

None of this takes away from the important points of tension that Dr Rajput highlights in international law.

On their approach to sovereignty and the Responsibility to Protect (R2P), the BRICS states voted with all other members of the UN in favour of R2P in principle. Much as with the unanimous endorsement of the rule of law in the same document, unanimity of support should be seen as an indication of vagueness in the content of what was agreed. Subsequent developments, in particular the expansive interpretation of a Security Council resolution in relation to the conflict in Libya, saw the beginnings of a backlash against R2P on the part of the BRICS states and a great many others.

Yet, is this a true challenge to the existing international order? The defence of sovereignty and principles of non-intervention have echoes in the Five Principles of Peaceful Coexistence,[5] adopted by China and India in 1954. The principles were incorporated into a ten-point 'Declaration on the Promotion of World Peace and Co-operation'[6] at the Bandung Conference the following year, at which Brazil joined as an observer. These in turn formed the normative core of the Non-Aligned Movement,[7] though the

---

[4] Bas Hooijmaaijers and Stephan Keukeleire, 'Voting Cohesion of the BRICS Countries in the UN General Assembly, 2006–2014: A BRICS Too Far?' (2016) 22 Global Governance: A Review of Multilateralism and International Organizations 389.

[5] Five Principles of Peaceful Coexistence in: Agreement Between the Republic of India and the People's Republic of China on Trade and Intercourse Between Tibet Region of China and India (in force 3 June 1954) 299 UNTS 70.

[6] Final Communiqué of the Asian–African Conference (24 April 1955) <http://franke.uchicago.edu/Final_ Communique_Bandung_1955.pdf> accessed 14 June 2018.

[7] Generally: Hans Köchler, The Principles of Non-Alignment (Third World Centre 1982).

absence of Russia and South Africa makes it hard to draw a line to the current normative impact of the BRICS as a grouping.

In any case, the challenge to international law is very different from that posed, say,
by the Soviet Union at the height of the Cold War—or even by the European Union project today. The principles adopted in the 1950s and the resistance to R2P today reflect
not an alternative new vision of international law so much as a conservative defence
of traditional norms of sovereignty and non-intervention. It is not a new 'Eastphalian'
regime; rather, it is an attempt to preserve the original vision of the Westphalian one.

Similarly, in relation to the World Trade Organization, it is the BRICS countries that
are sometimes the staunchest defenders of open trade at a time when certain Western
states are beginning to undermine it. In the first year of the Trump administration,
for example, the annual meeting of the world's elite at Davos under the auspices of the
World Economic Forum saw the unusual spectacle of Chinese President Xi Jinping
giving a robust defence of globalization at a time when President Trump was articulating a protectionist vision of 'America First'.

There is, however, some evidence of BRICS coordination here, with the BRICS trade
ministers establishing, among other initiatives, a new Intellectual Property Rights
Cooperation Mechanism.

Not so in relation to bilateral investment treaties (BITs). As Dr Rajput shows, there
is real division among the BRICS states on BITs: China, India, and Russia actively participate in the practice, while Brazil has long eschewed it and South Africa recently
renounced it. One point of interest here is that the resistance to BITs is transcending
traditional political divides of global North and South, or the West and the rest, as industrialized states like Australia have come to find themselves on the receiving end of
investor claims.

Climate change negotiations have also seen division and the spawning of yet another
acronym—BASIC—coined to reflect the distancing of Russia from the group. As Dr
Rajput points out, BASIC and the G77 coordinate to some degree in this area, though
it is incorrect to suggest that the BRICS countries as a group are 'part of the G77'. Brazil
and India are founding members and South Africa joined subsequently, but Russia remains outside the grouping. China, for its part, is listed by the G77 itself as a member
but does not identify as such. Hence, many positions adopted by the G77 are said to
be adopted by the 'G77 and China'. Brazil, India, and South Africa are also closer on
human rights treaties than Russia and China.

III. Rising powers

Of perhaps greater interest than specific normative regimes that make up the content of
international law are the consequences of the rising powers—the BRICS states among
others—for the structure and the future of international law.

As Dr Rajput notes, the BRICS states cooperate primarily through declarations and
action plans rather than treaties or other binding agreements that might challenge the

normative order. The creation of a BRICS Bank, much like China's leadership of the Asian Infrastructure Investment Bank, could be seen as the establishment of parallel regimes that operate outside existing institutions like the Bretton Woods institutions. Yet, they are modelled precisely on those institutions, albeit with a conservative approach to sovereignty that tends to downplay the importance of linking human rights to development assistance.

In terms of the content of international law, then, one potential impact of the rise of the BRICS states and others is a slowing of the move to universalize human rights and operationalize doctrines such as R2P. It is not clear that a new trajectory is being proposed—states still submit themselves to the Universal Periodic Review, for example, and R2P continues to be invoked—but the velocity appears to be diminishing.

That conservatism explains the first of the structural consequences of new rising powers: the increased difficulty of adopting new regimes. As Dr Rajput presents it, treaty-making may become 'even more tedious and time consuming'. This is an understatement. There are already indications that fewer multilateral agreements are being adopted under the auspices of the UN.[8] If true, this would be the reversal of perhaps the most striking trend in international law from the middle of the twentieth century: the move from bilateralism to multilateralism.

His glass-half-full analysis is that those treaties that are negotiated in this new environment will enjoy 'greater acceptability and better compliance'. One might hope so, but another possible outcome is greater reliance on informal regimes. There is already some evidence of this, as increasing spheres of public life are governed not by traditional domestic or international legal structures but by informal networks of public officials and diverse private actors.

Political power abhors a vacuum. The decline of the West and the rise of its Others brings with it a messier period than the bipolar terror of the Cold War or the irrational exuberance of the brief unipolar moment enjoyed by the United States. Though states remain important actors, the shift to what is perhaps best described as a zero-polar order suggests that the greatest challenge might come not from individual states or groups of states like the BRICS, but to the role of the state as such.

---

[8] Joost Pauwelyn, Ramses A Wessel, and Jan Wouters, 'When Structures Become Shackles: Stagnation and Dynamics in International Lawmaking' (2014) 25 European Journal of International Law 733.

8

Do Non-State Actors Strengthen or Weaken International Law?

The Story of a Liberal Symbiosis

Jean d'Aspremont*

The book in which this chapter is included constitutes an ambitious attempt to evaluate the rise or decline of international law at a time of growing populism, protectionism, unilateralism, and isolationism. It is argued in this chapter that the very terms in which such an inquiry is constructed manifests certain beliefs and sensibilities inherited from liberal legal thought. It is the ambition of this chapter to compare the liberal beliefs and sensibilities informing the question of the rise or decline of international law with the liberalism found in the way in which the concept of non-state actors has been conceptualized, theorized, and used in international legal thought and practice. The question raised by the editors as to whether non-state actors contribute to the strengthening or weakening of international law is thus approached herein by confronting the various distinct sets of liberal discourses which compose the topic ascribed to this chapter. This chapter will show that the question of whether non-state actors strengthen or weaken international law prejudges its very answer and supports an image of international law on the rise. In doing so, the discussion simultaneously shows that liberal discourses are organized around liberal symbioses that are necessary to preserve international lawyers' confidence in the ability of international law to intervene in the problems of the world.

This chapter starts by situating the main line of inquiry of this book and revisits the very question of the rise or decline of international law. In this respect, it makes the claim that this very question epitomises a liberal pattern of legal thought (Section I). The chapter then turns to the concept of non-state actors and argues that such construction similarly expresses liberal thinking (Section II). It thereafter confronts the liberalism permeating the question of the rise or decline of international law with the liberalism carried by the concept of non-state actors. Once all the liberal facets of the question of the rise or decline and those of the concept of non-state actors are

* This chapter draws on enriching exchanges with Georg Nolte and Heike Krieger during a six-month visit at the Humboldt University of Berlin within the framework of the Research Group on the 'Rise or Decline of the International Rule of Law' in 2016–17.

unpacked, it becomes possible to show that the question of whether non-state actors strengthen or weaken international law necessarily supports the idea that international law is on the rise (Section III).

I. The rise or decline of international law as a liberal narrative

It is submitted here that thinking about international law in terms of rise or decline constitutes the manifestation of a very liberal pattern of legal thought directly inherited from the Enlightenment.[1] Unearthing the liberalism of international legal thought— which is sometimes also called liberal legalism[2] or, more simply, legalism[3]—is obviously not new. Liberal patterns of international legal discourses have been extensively scrutinized in the scholarship of the last three decades.[4] It is one of the legacies of critical thought[5] to have made international lawyers more alert to the liberal structure of their legal arguments. Whilst liberalism has long been the object of scholarly attention, it is argued here that the question of the rise or decline of international law can be read as yet another expression thereof, one that has—surprisingly—not drawn much attention. It is the object of this section to unravel the liberal pattern of legal thought at the heart of such an inquiry.

To understand the point made here about the liberal pattern behind the question of the rise or decline of international law, it must be recalled that liberalism does certainly not constitute a monolithic idea. At least two dimensions thereof can be distinguished. On the one hand, the liberal paradigm refers to pluralism, a certain cosmopolitan ethos, the defence of individual liberty as well as some specific configurations of political institutions. According to this first variant of liberalism, international law is meant to be a cosmopolitan project whose institutions can claim some liberal legitimacy as they are supported by (and serve the interest of) individuals. On the other hand, and maybe

---

[1] For a different use of liberalism in international legal thought by reference to a certain configuration of the international society as a collection of liberal democracies: Daniel Joyce, 'Liberal Internationalism' in Anne Orford and Florian Hoffmann (eds), *The Oxford Handbook of the Theory of International Law* (Oxford University Press 2016) 471.

[2] Florian Hoffman, 'International Legalism and International Politics' in Orford and Hoffmann (n 1) 954, 961.

[3] Judith N Shklar, *Legalism: Law, Morals, and Political Trials* (Harvard University Press 1964) viii and 1–28.

[4] See the seminal work of Martti Koskenniemi that revealed the ascending and descending patterns of international legal argumentation which he traced back to the liberal political project: Martti Koskenniemi, *From Apology to Utopia—The Structure of International Legal Argument* (Cambridge University Press 2006); also: Koskenniemi, 'The Politics of International Law' (1990) 1 European Journal of International Law 4; David Kennedy, *International Legal Structures* (Nomos 1987); more recently: Hoffman (n 2); compare with: China Miéville, *Between Equal Rights. A Marxist Theory of International Law* (Pluto Press 2005) especially 314–18.

[5] For a discussion of this legacy and the challenge of liberalism: Andrea Bianchi, *International Law Theories. An Inquiry into Different Ways of Thinking* (Oxford University Press 2016) 135–62. I have argued elsewhere, after the early denial and perplexity of the first encounters with critical thinking, international lawyers came to feel that they had domesticated critical challenges to their liberal modes of argumentation and had completed the extraction of the hidden patterns of their modes of legal reasoning. About this return to the old vocabularies: Jean d'Aspremont, 'Martti Koskenniemi, the Mainstream, and Self-Reflectivity' (2016) 29 Leiden Journal of International Law 641; on the domestication of critique; Pierre Schlag, ' "Le hors de texte, c'est moi": The Politics of Form and the Domestication of Deconstruction' (1989–1990) 11 Cardozo Law Review 1631; Schlag, 'A Brief Survey of Deconstruction' (2005) 27 Cardozo Law Review 741.

more importantly, the liberal paradigm refers to some form of rationalism—what has been called 'the illusion of providing itself with its own foundations'—meant to create the idea of a rational consensus.[6] According to this second variant of liberalism,[7] international law can be reduced to a 'legal-technical instead of ethico-political matter'[8] whereby rules are formally, objectively, and content-independently[9] ascertainable and distinct from a programme of governance or a catalogue of moral values.[10] This reduction of international law to a legal-technical matter alien to a programme of governance is what allows one to uphold the distinction between politics and international law and the idea that the latter has the capacity to tame and contain the former.[11] In other words, this second dimension of liberalism allows international lawyers to think that it is possible to isolate international law from power, morality, antagonism, and the plurality of interests in the international society.[12]

It is well known that the two abovementioned dimensions of the liberal paradigm have, albeit to different degrees, permeated international legal thought and practice. It is submitted here that the question of the rise or decline of international law at the heart of this chapter embodies these two aspects of liberal thinking. Attention is successively paid to the liberal cosmopolitanism (1) and the liberal rationalism (2) at work in the very question of the rise or decline of international law.

1. The rise or decline as liberal cosmopolitanism

It is argued that the question of the rise or decline of international law is informed by an attachment to a cosmopolitan configuration of the international society where representative institutions and multilateral regimes manage the problems of the world in

[6] On this distinction between two dimensions of liberalism: Chantal Mouffe, *The Return of the Political* (Verso 1993) 123–24 (drawing on Hans Blumenberg, *The Legitimacy of the Modern Age*).
[7] On the transposition of the liberal paradigm to international law, see also the remarks of Shklar (n 3) 123–43; for a good illustration: James L Brierly, 'The Basis of Obligations in International Law' reproduced in Hersch Lauterpacht and C Humphrey M Waldock (eds), *The Basis of Obligation in International Law and Other Papers by the Late James Leslie Brierly* (Clarendon 1959) 21.
[8] Koskenniemi, *From Apology to Utopia* (n 4) 82.
[9] It is content-independent because ascertainment is generated in a way that does not hinge on the substance of the institution whose membership to the legal order is tested. On the notion of content-independence: Noam Gur, 'Are Legal Rules Content-Independent Reasons?' (2001) 5 Problema—Anuario de Filosofia y Teoria del Derecho 275; for some classical discussion: Herbert L Hart, *Essays on Bentham* (Clarendon 1982) 243–68 and Joseph Raz, *The Morality of Freedom* (Clarendon Press 1986) 35–37; also: Fabio P Schecaira, *Legal Scholarship as a Source* (Springer 2013) 26–27.
[10] Roberto M Unger, *Knowledge and Politics* (The Free Press 1975) 76–81; Koskenniemi, *From Apology to Utopia* (n 4) 71; Koskenniemi, 'The Politics of International Law' (n 4) 4–5; Timothy O'Hagan, *The End of Law?* (Blackwell 1984) 183; Paul W Kahn, *The Cultural Study of Law. Reconstructing Legal Scholarship* (Chicago University Press 1999) 16–18; Shklar (n 3) 8-9 and 16–23; Olivier Corten, *Le Discours du Droit International. Pour un Positivisme Critique* (Pedone 2009) 45–67.
[11] David Kennedy, 'The Disciplines of International Law and Policy' (1999) 12 Leiden Journal of International Law 9; D Kennedy, 'Tom Franck and the Manhattan School' (2003) 35 NYU Journal of International Law and Politics 397; Koskenniemi, *From Apology to Utopia* (n 4) 158; Koskenniemi, 'The Politics of International Law' (n 4) 5–7; Emmanuelle Jouannet, 'A Critical Introduction' in Koskenniemi, *The Politics of International Law* (Hart 2011) 15; Corten (n 10) 45.
[12] Chantal Mouffe, *The Return of the Political* (Verso 1993) 121, 140.

a way that is congruent with individual freedoms and individual well-being.[13] When guided by such a liberal premise, the rise or decline of international law comes to be measured through the degree of development of such a cosmopolitical institutional architecture and the extent of its (in)ability to promote individual freedom and well-being. For instance, it is liberal to think that that international law is in decline when its value-based character is jeopardized[14] or that international law is on the rise by virtue of a growing participation in international regimes and institutions.[15] The fact that such type of liberalism may have abated in the twentieth century[16] does not prevent it from being resilient and resurface in international lawyers' inquiries into the rise or decline of international law.

2. The rise or decline as liberal rationalism

The question of the rise or decline of international law epitomizes the second aspect of liberalism, namely the idea of a rational consensus on the foundations and modes of operation of international law, thereby allowing international law to meet the growing demand of a domestication of world politics through law.[17] Indeed, the question of the rise or decline of international law comes with the presupposition that there exists some reasonable consensus on the foundations and the content of international law by virtue of which the latter can operate as a technical apparatus that can be—more or less—ascertained and be distinguished from politics and morality. As a result of such liberal presupposition, the rise of international law comes to be associated with the ability of international law and international institutions to displace politics and flatten antagonism and the plurality of interest whilst international law is seen in decline when its institutions and rules appear contested, indeterminate, unable to tame unilateral expressions of powers, or systematically flouted. As a matter of example, it is liberal to think that international law is in decline when it is less complied with[18] or that international law is on the rise when states make use of international organizations.[19]

According to the argument made in this section, the very question of the rise or decline of international law thus reveals two liberal presuppositions, each of them corresponding to one of the two main facets of liberalism in international legal thought

---

[13] This is well illustrated by the work of Wilfried Jenks: Jean d'Aspremont, 'Jenks' Ethic of Responsibility for the Disillusioned International Lawyer' (28 October 2016) Amsterdam Law School Research Paper No 2016-63 <https://ssrn.com/abstract=2860610> accessed 16 June 2018.

[14] See the discussion of this point: Heike Krieger and Georg Nolte, 'The International Rule of Law—Rise or Decline? Points of Departure' KFG Working Paper Series No 1, October 2016, 13.

[15] ibid 14.

[16] According to Martti Koskenniemi, the liberal cosmopolitan ethos may have possibly lapsed in international legal thought, this is the argument defended by Martti Koskenniemi: Koskenniemi, *The Gentle Civilizer of Nations: The Rise and Fall of International Law 1870–1960* (Cambridge University Press 2001).

[17] For Jochen von Bernstorff, the idea of 'more international law is more progress' culminated in the late nineteenth century and beginning of the twentieth century: Jochen von Bernstorff, 'International Legal Scholarship as a Cooling Medium in International Law and Politics' (2014) 25 European Journal of International Law 977, especially 984–86.

[18] See the discussion of this point: Krieger and Nolte (n 14) 10–11.

[19] ibid 18.

as they have been sketched out above. The next section similarly looks into the liberal dimensions of the category of non-state actors, which the editors of this book have put forward as one of the main perspectives from which one should reflect on the question of the rise or decline of international law.

II. Non-state actors as a liberal category of legal thought

Although belligerency[20] and international organizations[21] have been discussed by international lawyers for more than a century, the very notion of non-state actors was sparsely used prior to 1990 in international legal scholarship.[22] Even with the development of the concept of armed conflict of a non-international character after the Second World War,[23] the notion of non-state actors only became a big hit—and the object of a prolific body of international legal literature—in the post-Cold War era. Indeed, a quick inquiry through the search engine of the most comprehensive catalogues of international law suffices to show that, although the term had been occasionally used prior to 1990,[24] it is not until 1990 that one witnessed its dramatic mushrooming in international law works.[25] Although the notion may no longer have the lustre and the appeal it had in the post-Cold War scholarship, it remains a very popular category in international lawyers' common parlance.[26]

It is argued in this section that the very category of non-state actors, as it is designed and deployed by international lawyers, manifests some liberal thinking. It will be more specifically demonstrated here that the liberal character of the notion of non-state actors is twofold and corresponds to the two main dimensions of the liberal paradigm which have been outlined in the previous section. Indeed, on the one hand, the concept of non-state actors feeds into the quest for cosmopolitanism promoted by liberalism. This is what is called here the *inclusiveness* character of the notion of non-state actors whereby actors are made subject to the rules and institutions of international law and contributors to their making and functioning (1). On the other hand, the concept

---

[20] eg the Neuchatel resolution of the Institut de Droit International of 8 September 1900 on the 'Droits et devoirs des Puissances étrangères, au cas de mouvement insurrectionnel, envers les gouvernements établis et reconnus qui sont aux prises avec l'insurrection' <www.idi-iil.org/app/uploads/2017/06/1900_neu_02_fr.pdf> accessed 16 June 2018.

[21] For an interesting study with historical insights on the legal scholarship devoted to the law of international organizations: David J Bederman, 'The Souls of International Organizations: Legal Personality and the Lighthouse at Cape Spartel' (2006) 36 Virginia Journal of International Law 275.

[22] This is not exclusive of the notion being commonly used in other disciplines. This is a point I owe to an exchange with Eyal Benvenisti.

[23] Georges Abi-Saab, 'Cours général de droit international' (1987) 207 Collected Courses 81, 96.

[24] Daniel C Turack, 'Passports Issued on Behalf of Non-State Entities' (1970) 16 New York Law Forum 625; Tiyanjana Maluwa 'The Treaty-Making Capacity of the Holy See in Theory and Practice: A Study of the Jus Tractum of a Non-State Entity' (1987) 20 Comparative and International Law Journal of Southern Africa 155; John Kuhn Bleimaier, 'The Legal Status of the Free City of Danzig 1920-1939: Lessons to be Derived from the Experiences of a Non-State Entity in the International Community' (1989) 2 Hague Yearbook of International Law 69.

[25] The peace palace library engine generates 633 occurrences of the notions of non-state actors and non-state entities.

[26] For a recent set of studies: Math Noortmann, August Reinisch, and Cedric Ryngaert, *Non-State Actors in International Law* (Hart 2015).

of non-state actors expresses the idea of a rational consensus on the foundations and mode of operation of international law by creating an *otherness* and thereby creating an image of international law as a space of peace and order that protects those subdued to its rules from the chaos and conflicts of the outside world (2). These two dimensions of the liberal character of the notion of non-state actors are discussed here.

1. Non-state actors as liberal inclusiveness

To understand the liberal character of the non-state actor category, it is necessary to recall that there was a time when international law was defined mainly through its subjects.[27] Subjects were then the main definitional category to describe international law, its origins, and its goals. It is no coincidence in this respect that the appellation 'international law' directly refers to its main 'fabricants', for, as is well known, it is this reference to nation states as the makers of international law that prodded Bentham's *An Introduction to the Principles of Morals and Legislation* to coin the expression 'international law'.[28] Such construction was made possible by virtue of, among others, an analogy between the state and the individual of the liberal doctrine of politics.[29] This move gave rise to what has been called classical international legal thought.[30] According to this approach, the makers of international law were deemed—originally the sole—subjects of international law in that they enjoy legal personality. There was, thus, a correlation between states as the makers of international law and subjecthood. In this sense, 'International Law [was] conceived of as horizontal law, in which the subjects of the law are also the makers of the law'.[31] The kinship so established between prominence in law-making and subjecthood constituted a conceptual premise that permeated legal scholarship and practice for more than a century. Even with the advent of the modern doctrine of sources as the main definitional mechanism of international law and the shift from a state-based to a source-based definition of international law in the nineteenth century,

---

[27] For a historical account of the concept of subject, see the fascinating work of Janne Nijman: Nijman, *The Concept of International Legal Personality: An Inquiry into the History and Theory of International Law* (Cambridge University Press 2004).

[28] Jeremy Bentham, *An Introduction to the Principles of Morals and Legislation* (first published 1781, Kessinger Publishing Co 2005) 326.

[29] After Hobbes and Spinoza paved the way for a human analogy, Pufendorf ascribed an intellect to the state and created anthropomorphic vocabularies and images about the main institution of international law, ie the state. Such anthropomorphism was later taken over by Vattel—not without adjustment—and subsequently translated itself in the classical positivist doctrine of fundamental rights of states which contributed to the consolidation of modern international law in the nineteenth century. On this point: Michael Nutkiewicz, Samuel Pufendorf, 'Obligation as the Basis of the State' (1983) 21 Journal of the History of Philosophy 15; Fiammetta Palladini, 'Pufendorf Disciple of Hobbes: The Nature of Man and the State of Nature: The Doctrine of Socialitas' (2008) 34 History of European Ideas 26; for a criticism of the analogy: Edwin De Witt Dickinson, 'The Analogy Between Natural Persons and International Persons in the Law of Nations' (1917) 26 Yale Law Journal 564; for the discussion of this analogy: Jean d'Aspremont, 'The Doctrine of Fundamental Rights of States and Anthropomorphic Thinking in International Law' (2015) 4 Cambridge Journal of International and Comparative Law 501; or Anthony Carty, *The Decay of International Law? A Reappraisal of the Limits of Legal Imagination in International Affairs* (Manchester University Press 1986) 44–46.

[30] Koskenniemi, *From Apology to Utopia* (n 4) 106.

[31] Phillip Allott, 'The True Function of Law in the International Community' (1997–98) 5 Global Legal Studies Journal 391, 404.

the correlation between subjecthood and the makers of the international law remained. As a result, an entity not qualifying as a subject could not claim to be participating in law-making and vice-versa. Interestingly, it is this kinship between the prominent law-making role of states and subjecthood that long barred the recognition of an international legal personality to international organizations and other actors.[32] Such kinship was discontinued by the 1949 International Court of Justice *Advisory Opinion on the Reparation for Injuries Suffered in the Service of the United Nations* (hereafter *1949 Advisory Opinion*). This opinion can be understood as constituting a 'constitutionalizing' breaking point whereby law-making and subjecthood came to be severed from one another, for, in the case of international organizations, subjecthood was no longer derived from its law-making role but rather, as is well known, from its functions (the so-called objective school) or the will of its creators (the so-called subjective school).

The severance between centrality in law-making and subjecthood operated in the mid-twentieth century bore two main consequences for international legal thought and the liberal structure of international law. These consequences ought to be sketched out here for the sake of the argument made here. First, as a result of the disconnection of legal personality from law-making, the question of subjecthood came to potentially arise with respect to all kinds of other actors who do not directly or formally participate in law-making. Besides internationally personified international organizations, it became possible to recognize other international legal persons, although this has been less construed as the outcome of a direct conferral of international legal personality upon non-state actors than an indirect consequence stemming from them having rights and duties.[33] The severance between legal personality and law-making thus allowed the recognition of a legal personality to actors deprived of any major law-making powers. The second consequence of the mid-twentieth-century dissociation between law-making and subjecthood pertains to the possibility that a law-making role was recognized for a new range of actors not necessarily endowed with legal personality. In that sense, in the post-*Reparation* era, participation in law-making does not turn the actor concerned into a new legal subject,[34] thereby making it possible to re-think international law-making, state-centrism, participation, and pluralism irrespective of debates on legal personality.

The foregoing should suffice to figure out the extent to which the 1949 severance between law-making and subjecthood promotes a liberal configuration of the international legal order. Indeed, once severed from the question of legal personality, there

---

[32] Bederman (n 21).

[33] Generally: Christian Dominicé, 'La personnalité juridique internationale du CICR' in Christophe Swinarski (ed), *Etudes et essais sur le droit international humanitaire et sur les principes de la Croix-Rouge en l'honneur de Jean Pictet* (Comité International de la Croix-Rouge 1984) 663; in the context of the debate about the responsibility of transnational corporations: Olivier de Schutter, *Transnational Corporations and Human Rights* (Hart Publishing 2006). This has led scholars to deem that the question of international legal personality was described as 'circular', 'sterile', and boiling down to an 'intellectual prison': August Reinisch, 'The Changing International Legal Framework for Dealing with Non-State Actors' in Philip Alston (ed), *Non-State Actors and Human Rights* (Oxford University Press 2005) 37, 69–72; Andrew Clapham, *Human Rights Obligations of Non-State Actors* (Oxford University Press 2006) 60.

[34] On this point: Jean d'Aspremont, 'Cognitive Conflicts and the Making of International Law: From Empirical Concord to Conceptual Discord in Legal Scholarship' (2013) 46 Vanderbilt Journal of Transnational Law 1119.

is room for a more cosmopolitan international legal order whereby other actors are recognized as contributing to law-making. It is noteworthy that the liberal potential of the *1949 Advisory Opinion on Reparations* remained unexploited by international lawyers for several decades. In fact, it is not until the 1990s that international lawyers came to make use of the space created by the severance between law-making and subjecthood in international legal thought. In this respect, it is no coincidence that it is only in the 1990s that the very notion of non-state actors grew central in the discourses of international lawyers. It is submitted here that the emergence of the concept of non-state actors in the 1990s is what materialized the liberal potential of the *1949 Advisory Opinion* as it allowed international lawyers to project a pluralized image of international law and repudiate the state-centric representation(s) of international law that had been dominating legal thought till then. By virtue of the notion of non-state actors, international lawyers have been able to impose the view that, in practice, international law and its making have witnessed a growing pluralization *ratione personae*. The notion, thus, allows the projection of an image where states have ceased to be (perceived as) the only actors in charge of international law. As a result of this image, normative authority is seen as being no longer exercised by a closed circle of high-ranking officials acting on behalf of states, but has instead turned into an aggregation of complex procedures involving non-state actors.[35] Such pluralization has been articulated through notions like 'standard-setters',[36] 'law-takers',[37] or 'participants'.[38] It also manifested itself through the—more contested[39]—recognition of some possible role of non-state actors in the formation of customary international law.[40] It is noteworthy that, to sustain this image of a pluralized international law, an important body of empirical evidences has been produced.[41]

---

[35] This has sometimes been called 'verticalization': Jan Klabbers, 'Setting the Scene' in Jan Klabbers, Anne Peters, and Geir Ulfstein (eds), *The Constitutionalization of International Law* (Oxford University Press 2009) 1, 14.

[36] Anne Peters, Lucy Koechlin, Till Förster, and Gretta Fenner, *Non-State Actors as Standard Setters* (Cambridge University Press 2009).

[37] Math Noortmann and Cedric Ryngaert, *Non-State Actor Dynamics in International Law: From Law-Takers to Law-Makers* (Ashgate 2010).

[38] Jean d'Aspremont, *Participants in the International Legal System* (Routledge 2010).

[39] This view has been contested by the International Law Commission Special Rapporteur in his 2014 Report: Michael Wood, 'Second report on identification of customary international law by Michael Wood, Special Rapporteur' (22 May 2014) UN Doc A/CN.4/672, 32–33.

[40] Jean-Marie Henckaerts and Louise Doswald-Beck, *Customary International Humanitarian Law, Volume I: Rules* (ICRC/Cambridge University Press 2005) xlii. The International Committee of the Red Cross seems to give it significance despite claiming that 'while such practice may contain evidence of the acceptance of certain rules in non-international armed conflicts, its legal significance is unclear'. Juan Pablo Bohoslavsky, Yuefen Li, and Marie Sudreau, 'Emerging Customary International Law in Sovereign Debt Governance?' (2014) 9 Capital Markets Law Journal 55, 63; ILA Committee on the Formation of Customary (General) International Law, *Statement of Principles Applicable to the Formation of General Customary International Law* (2000) 8.

[41] Non-state actors are said to have been expending their say in international law-making processes and that they also wield some influence in the review and amendments procedures of conventional instruments. To buttress that contention, reference is made to how their formal presence and participation in international law-making processes has swollen, as is demonstrated by their (potential) involvement within the framework of the UN Economic and Social Council (ECOSOC), the UN Global Compact, the UN Human Rights Council, the UN Security Council (to a very limited extent), the World Trade Organization (WTO) and within the cooperation policies of the European Community with the Group of African, Caribbean and Pacific Countries (ACP countries). Mention is moreover made of some notorious recent convention-making conferences having also weathered a renewed NGO involvement as is illustrated by the conferences leading to the adoption of the 1997 Convention on the Prohibition of the Use, Stockpiling, Production and Transfer or Anti-Personnel Mines and on their Destruction, the 2008 Convention on Cluster Munitions or the well-known examples of the processes leading to the adoption

It is in this context that it can be contended that the very notion of non-state actors came to function as the very concept through which international lawyers have made use of the cosmopolitan space created by the *1949 Advisory Opinion*.[42] This means that the notion of non-state actors can be considered a liberal inclusive tool feeding the quest for cosmopolitanism promoted by liberalism. This being said, it is important to emphasize that the liberal inclusiveness that came with the 1949 severance between law-making and subjecthood and which was materialized through the notion of non-state actors has another facet. Indeed, inclusiveness that accompanies the notion of non-state actors does not only pertain to the configuration of international of law-making processes, but is simultaneously articulated in terms of bindingness and liability. Said differently, according to this aspect of inclusiveness, the concept of non-state actors has been used in international legal thought and practice, not only to enhance the cosmopolitanism of the international legal order, but also to expand the outreach of international law and subdue new actors and subject them to the rules and institutions of international law. In that sense, inclusiveness is simultaneously managerial as it is about subjecting new actors to the rule(s) of international law and evaluating their behaviour according to the very standards set by international law. Indeed, once one includes them into the realm of international law, one can evaluate their behaviour according to the standards of international law and attach to departures from such standards the consequences prescribed by international law.[43] They actually are included in the regulative space of international law and given the necessary existence that allows them

---

of 1984 Torture Convention, the 1990 Convention on the Rights of the Child, and the 1999 Rome Statute of the International Criminal Court. It is said that, in these situations, it can hardly be denied that non-state actors, through their formal role, have left their imprint in the substance of the rules finally adopted. The same allegedly holds true with respect to the International Law Commission (ILC) which has engaged in regular consultations with NGOs, as is illustrated in its work on the Protection of Persons in the Event of Disaster.

---

[42] The use of the notion of non-state actors to project an image of a pluralised international law, while being dominant, is not exempt from criticisms. Indeed, it could be contended that international law has always been pluralised. For instance, it could be said that NGOs have been involved in international law-making for more than 200 years. It is also often recalled that NGOs have aroused the initiative or have been granted a formal participatory role in various international law-making conferences since as early as the nineteenth century. To name but a few, mention is frequently made of the role of the American Peace Society in the first plan for the Permanent Court of Arbitration; the role of the Geneva Public Welfare Society in the adoption of the 1864 Geneva Convention for the Amelioration of the Condition of the Wounded in Armies in the Field; the role of all the peace societies which sent representatives to the First and Second Hague Peace Conferences; the role of the Inter-Parliamentary Union and the World Court League in the establishment of the Permanent Court of International Justice; and the occasional role of NGOs in the committees and conferences of the League of Nations. A similar role played by the private sector in the same period in the meetings of the International Telegraph Union, the annual conferences of the International Labour Organization, or the Pan American Conferences is also invoked. Generally: Steve Charnovitz, 'Two Centuries of Participation: NGOs and International Governance' (1997) 18 Michigan Journal of International Law 103. It could also be said that the idea of a Westphalian state-centric order has never really existed and has been a straw man created by inter-war international lawyers; further: Richard Collins, 'Classical Positivism in International Law Revisited' in Jörg Kammerhofer and Jean d'Aspremont (eds), *International Legal Positivism in a Post-Modern World* (Cambridge University Press 2014) 23; and d'Aspremont and Kammerhofer, 'Introduction: The Future of International Legal Positivism' in Kammerhofer and d'Aspremont (n 42) 1; further: Andreas Osiander, 'Sovereignty, International Relations, and the Westphalian Myth' (2001) 55 International Organization 251; Pärtel Piirimäe, 'The Westphalian Myth and the Idea of External Sovereignty' in Hent Kalmo and Quentin Skinner (eds), *Sovereignty in Fragments: The Past, Present and Future of a Contested Concept* (Cambridge University Press 2010) 64; Benno Teschke, *The Myth of 1648: Class, Geopolitics, and the Making of Modern International Relations* (Verso 2009).

[43] Frédéric Megret, 'Where does the Critique of International Human Rights Stand. An Exploration in 18 Vignettes' <https://ssrn.com/abstract=1714484> accessed 17 June 2018.

to be subjected to international regulatory frameworks and the standards set by the latter.[44]

It will not come as a surprise that, as far as this managerial aspect of the inclusiveness of the notion of non-state actors is concerned, international humanitarian law and the law of armed conflict have constituted a fertile ground. Whilst reflections about the bindingness of humanitarian law, especially that of provisions like common Article 3 of the Geneva Conventions upon insurgents, predate the post-1990 scholarly frenzy,[45] the pre-1990 debates seemed to have regained momentum. Interestingly, all the stake-holders in this debate ended up agreeing that such non-state actors are bound by some rules of international humanitarian law, but kept disagreeing about what justifies the bindingness of such rules on non-state actors. Said differently, they all came to claim that non-state actors are bound by (certain rules of) international humanitarian law, but stopped inquiring about the foundations thereof. This is why this new post-1990 momentum ended with a consensus on the idea that non-state actors are bound by international law. Yet, this consensus fell short of any common theory of international obligations in relation to non-state actors.[46]

The managerial inclusiveness of the concept of non-state actors did not stop with international humanitarian law. Having agreed on these findings regarding insur-gents, international legal scholars turned their attention to other actors. They raised the same question of bindingness of the rules of international law in relation to non-governmental organizations (NGOs)[47] and multinational companies[48]. In this case, however, no consensus was reached and scholars remained deeply divided.[49] Here too, they suffered from the absence of a theory of international obligations. Yet, this did not preclude international legal scholarship to embark on studies over the conse-quences of the breach of such obligations in terms of responsibility, thereby engaging

---

[44] The same finding as been made regarding colonial entities. See Sundhya Pahuja, 'The Postcoloniality of International Law' (2005) 46 Harvard International Law Journal 459, at 464, 466 (who argues that self-determination entailed the granting of formal legal status to new subjects by rendering them commensurable with currently accepted forms; as a result, the specific form being universalized is already universal, the process securing its occurrence).

[45] On this question in general, see the contributions by Cedric Ryngaert, 'Non-State Actors in International Humanitarian Law' and by Raphaël van Steenberghe, 'Non-State Actors from the Perspective of the International Committee of the Red Cross' in Jean d'Aspremont (ed), *Participants in the International Legal System: Multiple Perspectives on Non-State Actors in International Law* (Routledge 2011); also generally: Michael Bothe, Karl J Partsch, and Waldemar A Solf, *New Rules of Victims of Armed Conflicts: Commentary on the two 1977 Protocols Additional to the Geneva Conventions of 1949* (Martinus Nijhoff 1982); Antonio Cassese, 'The Status of Rebels under the 1977 Geneva Protocol on Non-International Armed Conflicts' (1981) 30 International and Comparative Law Quarterly 416; Clapham (n 33); Cedric Ryngaert, 'Human Rights Obligations of Armed Groups' (2008) 1–2 Revue Belge de droit international 355; Liesbeth Zegveld, *Accountability of Armed Opposition Groups in International Law* (Cambridge University Press 2002); Christian Tomuschat, 'The Applicability of Human Rights to Insurgent Movements' in Horst Fischer (ed), *Crisis Management and Humanitarian Protection: Festschrift für Dieter Fleck* (Berliner Wissenschafts-Verlag 2004) 573.

[46] Zegveld (n 45).

[47] Generally: Pierre-Marie Dupuy and Luisa Vierucci, *NGOs in International Law, Efficiency in Flexibility?* (Edward Elgar Publishing 2008).

[48] On the famous *Texaco v Libya* arbitration (1977): Arghyrios A Fatouros, 'International Law and the Internationalized Contract' (1980) 74 American Journal of International Law 134.

[49] Rainer Hoffmann, *Non-State Actors as New Subjects of International Law: From the Traditional State Order towards the Law of the Global Community* (Duncker & Humboldt 1999).

in ambitious transposition of the Articles on State Responsibility to non-state actors,[50] not always with tangible success.[51] It remains that by allowing more actors to be subdued, this other aspect of the inclusiveness of non-state actors has reinforced the pluralism and cosmopolitanism of international law while also conveying the image that international law subjects actors to its rule in order to serve the interest of individuals.

The foregoing shows that, despite the theoretical paucity of scholarly debates, the notion of non-state actors has continued to perform an inclusive function, filling the space created by the *1949 Advisory Opinion* and allowing new actors to contribute to international law-making processes on the one hand, and subduing new actors to the rule(s) of international law on the other hand. In performing this twofold inclusive function, the concept of non-state actors has allowed international law to be represented as a pluralistic order at the service of a cosmopolitan project.

2. Non-state actors as liberal otherness

It is submitted here that the liberal inclusiveness of the concept of non-state actors, as was described above, has been accompanied by exclusive practices.[52] Indeed, the notion of non-state actors is simultaneously deployed in an exclusionist way, that is a mechanism of 'othering'. Such mechanism of othering,[53] it is argued in this section, corresponds to the other facet of liberalism, namely the construction of international law on the idea of a rational consensus that displaces conflict, chaos, and plurality of interest.

As has been observed elsewhere,[54] the notion of non-state actors, whether deployed in relation to arguments about legal personality, rights and duties, or law-making privileges, has largely been relied on in international legal thought and practice to promote a certain configuration of international law and exclude certain actors from the centre thereof. The notion is about constructing the idea that certain actors are 'the others'.[55]

---

[50] eg the UN Basic Principles and Guidelines on the Right to a Remedy and Reparation for Victims of Gross Violations of International Human Rights Law and Serious Violations of International Humanitarian Law (UNBPG) state that

> ... where a person, a legal person, or other entity is found liable for reparation for a victim, such party should provide reparation to the victim or compensate the State if the State has already provided reparation to the victim (Principle 15).

It is also noteworthy that the ILA Committee on Reparations for Victims of Armed Conflict affirmed that armed opposition groups can be held responsible to provide reparations where they commit violations of international humanitarian law. For an attempt at transposition of the paradigms of the 2001 Articles on State Responsibility to armed groups: Jean d'Aspremont, Andre Nollkaemper, Ilias Plakokefalos, and Cedric Ryngaert, 'Sharing Responsibility Between Non-State Actors and States in International Law: Introduction' (2015) 62 Netherlands International Law Review 49.

[51] See third report prepared by the co-rapporteurs, Cedric Ryngaert and Jean d'Aspremont, available at <http://www.ila-hq.org/>.

[52] On the idea that inclusiveness of human rights comes at the cost of exclusive practices: Megret (n 43) 7.

[53] On the idea of othering in liberal legal thought, see generally Ratna Kapur, *Gender, Alterity, and Human Rights. Freedom in a Fishbowl* (Edward Elgar Publishing, 2018).

[54] This is one of the main ideas of the book by Nijman (n 27) 454ff.

[55] Sébastien Jodoin, 'International Law and Alterity: The State and the Other' (2008) 21 Leiden Journal of International Law 1.

It, thus, puts in place a fundamental narrative of ostracization.[56] Whilst the concept of non-state actors is not alone in functioning as an othering mechanism,[57] it certainly is one of the most powerful constructions of this kind in international legal thought and practice.

Recognizing the ostracization—and more generally the mechanism of othering—that accompany the notion of non-state actors is not groundbreaking. For the sake of the arguments made here, it is of greater relevance to highlight the liberal dimension of the othering effect of the concept. Indeed, the othering performed by the notion of non-state actors comes with a specific vision of what constitutes order and disorder. By othering, the notion of non-state actors comes to constitute order and disorder.[58] In fact, the realm of the state becomes equated with order as it falls under international law. In contrast, disorder is associated with the realm of the non-state (or the 'others'). This is where the liberal dimension of the notion of non-state actors lies. By associating chaos and disorders with the others, the notion of non-state actors displaces chaos, un-settled competition of interests, and disorder outside international law, thereby simul-taneously reinforcing the idea that international law replaces chaos and conflict thanks to the rational consensus that allegedly informs its foundations and mode of operation. Rejecting chaos, plurality of interest, and disorder to the periphery of international law and thus ascribing them to the others, is, according to the understanding of liberalism adopted here, the expression of a liberal pattern of thought.[59]

It will not come as a surprise that the otherness of the notion of non-state actors, like liberal inclusiveness, bears a managerial dimension. Indeed, just like the inclusiveness of the concept of non-state actors allowed the modulation of the ambit of international law and the imposition of rights and duties on other actors than states and international organizations, relegating non-state actors to the realm of the disorder allows inter-national lawyers to pass a judgment on those fringe entities and unruly creatures with a view to legitimizing attempts to regulate their practice.[60] In other words, the disorder constituted by the notion of non-state actors carries an invitation for international law-yers to intervene with a view to ironing out disorders through the subjection of those actors to the rule(s) of international law.[61]

---

[56] It is in this sense that Philip Alston claims that 'these negative euphemistic terms ... have been intentionally adopted in order to reinforce the assumption that the state is not only the central actor, but also the indispensable and pivotal one around which all other entities revolve' in Alston (n 33) 3.

[57] This is a process that has been ascribed to human rights in general: Megret (n 43); also: Makau W Mutua, 'Savages, Victims, and Saviors: The Metaphor of Human Rights' (2001) 42 Harvard International Law Journal 201. On the ostracizing dimension of the idea of civilization in international law, see Liliana Obregon, 'The Civilized and the Uncivilized' in Bardo Fassbender and Anne Peters (eds), The History of International Law (OUP 2012) 917.

[58] On the rage for order of international lawyers: James Crawford, 'International Law as Discipline and Profession' in American Society of International Law, Proceedings of the Annual Meeting, vol 106 (Cambridge University Press 2012) 471, 472.

[59] Susan Marks, 'International Judicial Activism and the Commodity-Form Theory of International Law' (2007) 18 European Journal of International Law 199, 202.

[60] The concept of non-state actors, in this sense, has a ordering and hegemonic function. See Gen Michel Foucault, Les Mots et Les Choses, pp 64–70. In the international law literature, see Anne Orford, 'A Jurisprudence of the Limit', in Anne Orford (ed), International Law and its Others (CUP 2006) 1–33.

[61] Compare with the justification of the intervention of international law(yers) by virtue of narratives of crisis. Generally: Anne Orford, 'The Destiny of International Law' (2004) 17 Leiden Journal of International Law 441; on international lawyers' inclination to seek and find crisis to develop international law, generally: Hilary

III. Liberalism and its symbioses: strengthening or weakening international law?

As is well known, liberal patterns of legal thoughts are full of contradictions.[62] Yet, liberal patterns of legal thoughts are also awash with symbioses, whereby parts of the liberal discourses reinforce one another. It is argued in this section that the question whether non-state actors strengthen or weaken international law prejudges its very answer by virtue of the abovementioned liberal discourses and assumptions it is built in. In other words, from the perspective of the liberal project of international law—both in its cosmopolitan and rational dimensions as they have been described in the previous sections—the question at the heart of this chapter knows only one specific answer, namely that international law is on the *rise*. This one-directional answer to the question whether non-state actors strengthen or weaken international law can be explained as follows.

The previous sections have provided the keys to unpack the question raised by the editors of this book as to whether non-state actors strengthen or weaken international law and especially shed light on the liberal facets of the question of the rise or decline of international law as well as those of the notion of non-state actors. It is submitted in this final section that two specific lessons can be drawn from the combination of the liberal dimensions of the question whether international law is in rise or decline on the one hand with the liberal virtues of the notion of non-state actors on the other hand.

Attention must be drawn to a first specific interplay between the liberal inclusiveness of the notion of non-state actors and the liberal cosmopolitanism of the question of the rise or decline of international law. When these two liberal facets are combined, the notion of non-state actors comes to serve the cosmopolitan project informing the question of the rise or decline of international law. In fact, the liberal inclusiveness of the notion of non-state actors consolidates the very idea of a rise of international law when the latter is measured in terms of liberal cosmopolitanism, for the notion of non-state actors allows international law to be more inclusive, more representative, and more geared towards collective interest. In other words, the notion of non-state actors and especially the possibility of the inclusion of new actors within the ambit of international law, both in terms of law-making and subjection to rules, contribute to an image of international law as a cosmopolitan project, thereby bolstering the narrative of a *rise* of international law.

There is a second—and probably more fundamental—interplay between the liberal dimensions of the question of the rise or decline of international law and the liberal virtues of the notion of non-state actors that ought to be mentioned. It is contended here that the combination of the liberal otherness of the notion of non-state actors and the liberal rationalism of the question of rise or decline similarly makes the notion of

Charlesworth, 'International Law: A Discipline of Crisis' (2002) 65 Modern Law Review 377; for an illustration of such use of crisis narratives: d'Aspremont, 'Jenks' Ethic of Responsibility' (n 13).

[62] Generally: Koskenniemi, 'The Politics of International Law' (n 4).

non-state actors nurture a narrative of *rise* of international law. Indeed, the notion of non-state actors, by virtue of the liberal otherness that accompanies it, helps locate chaos and disorder at the periphery, thereby preserving the order and the rational consensus on which international law is allegedly built. And the more violence is kept and managed outside, the more international law stands out as the vehicle of order and rational consensus. It is in this sense that the liberal otherness of the notion of non-state actors can be said to underpin a narrative of rise. This is also the reason why claims according to which violent non-state actors, like terrorist groups or insurgents, contribute to the decline of international law is not self-evident.[63]

The two abovementioned combinations of the liberal dimensions of the notion of non-state actors and the question of the rise or decline of international law reveal the remarkable symbiosis around which the question whether non-state actors strengthen or weaken international law is articulated. In particular, the foregoing has demonstrated the extent to which the notion of non-state actors turns into a conceptual tool at the service of a narrative vindicating the idea of a rise of international law. Said differently, when it is combined with the liberal facets of the question of the rise or decline, the notion of non-state actors helps project an image of international law on the rise. In that sense, the question of whether non-state actors strengthen or weaken international law, by virtue of its mutually reinforcing liberal dimensions, prejudges its own answer in favour of a narrative of rise of international law, thereby offering assuagement of the current anxieties of international lawyers in time of rising populism, protectionism, unilateralism, and isolationism and providing them with assurances that international law remains capable of displacing disorder, plurality of interests, and more generally 'politics' while simultaneously upholding a cosmopolitan project.

---

[63] Krieger and Nolte (n 14) 20.

9

Liberal or Not?

Comment on Jean d'Aspremont

Michael Zürn

Jean d'Aspremont's contribution suggests that the very question of the rise and decline of international law is an expression of liberal thinking as predominant in international law. Similarly, the conception of non-state actors is seen as dependent on liberal theory leading to a 'self-nourishing' strategy. These are strong and challenging statements put forward in a very elegant way. While there is no doubt that both the question about the rise and decline of international law and the very concept of non-state actors is compatible with liberal theory, I will argue that the connection is much looser than assumed by d'Aspremont. In doing so, I will first discuss different versions of liberal theory and then go on to show that different social theories may have varying notions of the law, but most of them are definitely interested in the question of the rise or decline of law. Similarly, the relationship between the rise of international law and non-state actors is multifaceted and of potential interest for liberal, realist, and critical theory. I identify three sub-themes of the relationship between international law and non-state actors to support this proposition.

I.

Jean d'Aspremont distinguishes two variants of liberal theory. In the liberal cosmopolitan 'configuration of the international society ..., representative institutions and multilateral regimes manage the problems of the world in a way that is congruent with individual freedoms and individual well-being'.[1] In this perspective, individual rights and autonomy in a global perspective are central in liberal thinking. In a globalized world with societal transaction transcending national borders, international law is seen as a mechanism to protect human rights and to maintain the capacity of societies to govern themselves. D'Aspremont identifies a second version of liberalism that he labels as 'liberal rationalism'. In this version, international law 'meets the growing demand of

---

[1] Jean d'Aspremont, 'Non-State Actors and the Social Practice of International Law' in Math Noortmann, August Reinisch, and Cedric Ryngaert (eds), *Non-state Actors in International Law* (Hart Publishing 2015) 4.

a domestication of world politics through law'.[2] In this view, law provides, in contrast to the cosmopolitan version, a realm detached from politics that is necessary to allow for civilized interactions in an internationalized world. Yet, both versions of liberalism view the rise of international law as progressive and normatively desirable.

Both these versions of thinking about international law are relevant, and the distinction between the two is in fact important. However, two queries come to mind: First, not all liberal thinking that emphasizes individual rights is based on cosmopolitan ideas. There is a version of liberalism that puts individual rights in context and sees it as being dependent upon the presence of communities that are co-constitutive with rights and justice.[3] In this view, it is (mostly national) communities and their political institutions (mostly nation states) that are necessary to protect human rights and justice. From this perspective, the strengthening of international law is seen to be much more critical than from the cosmopolitan perspective. It seems important to acknowledge these differences within liberalism since different versions may evaluate the rise of international law quite differently in normative terms. Many liberals challenge globalization and governance beyond the nation state because it is feared that the undermining of the nation state leads to a weakening of political and social rights, of democracy, and of the welfare state on the national level.[4] Liberalism may be less homogeneous in perceiving international law to be progressive, as d'Aspremont suggests.

Second, it may be questioned whether the liberal rationalist version invoked by d'Aspremont is really liberal. Undoubtedly, there is a strong strand of thinking that considers national as well as international law as being a necessary component of the Western script, which is based on instrumental reasoning and rationalism. The 'Stanford School' on World Society Theory,[5] for example, argues that the Western script consists of dominant cultural systems and practices of organizing a society that have produced a world culture. The law as a depoliticized and relatively neutral set of rules to reduce transaction costs in and between national societies is certainly part of this script. Yet, the Stanford School calls this the Western and not the liberal script for good reason. The Western script knows a form of collectivist modernization that can hardly be labelled as 'liberal'. Authoritarian regimes in the West, as well as contemporary China, can be considered good examples. China uses almost all the components of the Western script today—markets, states, rationalism, growth, progress, nationalism— but it can hardly be described as being liberal in the sense of taking the individual autonomy and self-determination as a starting point for justification of the social order.

Taken together, these two objections against the two strands of thinking introduced and labelled as 'liberal' by d'Aspremont raise the question of whether the commonality between the two really is liberalism. In contrast, the commonality between the

---

[2] ibid 5.

[3] eg John Rawls, *The Law of Peoples* (Harvard University Press 1999); Thomas Nagel, 'The Problem of Global Justice' (2005) 33 Philosophy & Public Affairs 113.

[4] eg Robert A Dahl, *On Democracy* (Yale University Press 1998); Fritz W Scharpf, *Das Ende der Sozialdemokratie* (Campus Verlag 1987).

[5] John W Meyer, John Boli, George M Thomas, and Francisco O Ramirez, 'World Society and the Nation-State' (1997) 103 American Journal of Sociology 144.

two versions described by d'Aspremont can be read as a positive appreciation of international law. If this second reading applies, the critique presented by d'Aspremont is not a critique of liberalism, but a critique of an unquestioned welcoming of international law as it exists—to some extent—within different social theories. The affirmation of international law, as identified by d'Aspremont, then is not necessarily inscribed into liberal reasoning, but it is due to the fact that he identified two major variants of reasoning about international law that view international law as normatively positive.

II.

But what are social theories, and which attitudes towards international law are associated with them? Social theories point to broad streams of thinking about social relationships in general, consisting of assumptions about the *conditio humana*, beliefs about causal relationships, and normative propositions. Social theories are encompassing in the sense that they usually include both long-standing traditions of thinking about social relations and competing interpretations of it. Liberalism is a vastly encompassing social theory based on the idea of self-determination. Always accompanied by recurring counter-movements, it has expanded in the real world in a wave-like fashion since the early days of enlightenment.[6] Kant and Locke are probably the two most important early proponents. Individuals and nation states are the constituent actors in politics and society, which bear rights and obligations, while social organizations serve as intermediaries. States are the public institutions that exercise the authority to limit individual activities that have undesirable effects (eg environmental degradation or excessive distributional inequality). At the same time, states must be limited and controlled by the constitution, a legal system, and the public sphere. Key objectives are enlightenment (freeing humanity from the shackles of ignorance), progress, and growth. This liberal reasoning can come in a cosmopolitan or a community-based version. Other encompassing social theories abound. Two important competitors in the context of our debate are certainly realism and critical theory. The former sees states as the constitutive actors that—in an anarchic world—need to have a particularistic outlook and that, from time to time, need to put collective goals above individual rights. Critical theory aims at uncovering the ideological components of both realism and liberalism. It essentially considers liberalism and realism to be theories that at the same time justify and hide relationships of super- and subordination.

Wrapped into different social theories are different conceptions of law and international law. Whereas liberalism certainly considers law as a necessary part of a good social order, it is aware of internal divisions, especially regarding the appropriate relationship between national and international law. Although law is considered to be necessary, liberalism is not indeterminate regarding the content of law. It needs to serve

---

[6] Christian Reus-Smit, *Individual Rights and the Making of the International System* (Cambridge University Press 2013).

self-determination and must be based on public deliberations.[7] In a globalized world society, international law must—according to the cosmopolitan version of liberalism—go behind the national borders, go beyond the consent principle, and thus be intrusive into national societies. Realists see law as instrumental and, to a significant extent, reflective of underlying power relations. In any case, law requires enforcement to be law (Austin 1873).[8] While most realists acknowledge some space for international law as a simple means to help diplomats to manage conflicts,[9] international law is special since it must be limited to the international realm and should not intervene in domestic affairs, especially not using means of enforcement. If it goes beyond this technical realm, it is hegemonic law written by the leading power of the international system. Its existence thus depends on a hegemonic constellation. Critical theory finally regards law as a hidden form of domination, either of liberal–capitalist forces or of hegemonic states. Law is the key mechanism of governmentality,[10] most often based on internalized epistemic orders.

These admittedly short and incomplete sketches of three major social theories serve to make a point that runs counter to the core challenge Jean d'Aspremont submits against the study of the rise or decline of international law. In his view, the 'very question epitomises a liberal pattern of thought'.[11] To the contrary, I want to suggest that the question can be asked from the perspective of very different social theories and thus helps to create interaction between them. Undeniably, different social theories contain different conceptions of law. Independent of these different conceptions of law, the question of whether international law rises or declines is of utmost importance for all of them. The question about the rise or decline of international law can be asked by liberals, realists, and critical theorists—there is no direct association between the very question and liberalism. What is distinct in all the theories is the meaning and the normative evaluation of international law, and hence the question of whether the rise of international law is good or bad.

III.

Different conceptions of national and international law in different social theories clearly incorporate differences in the designated role of non-state actors. Jean d'Aspremont points effectively to this relationship. While I share this argument fully, I doubt whether the very concept of non-state actors makes sense only in terms of liberal thinking. To the contrary, I wish to argue that the distinction between states

---

[7] Jürgen Habermas, *Between Facts and Norms: Contributions to a Discourse Theory of Law and Democracy* (William Rehg tr, Massachusetts Institute of Technology Press 1996).

[8] John Austin, *Lectures on Jurisprudence, or The Philosophy of Positive Law*, two vols (first published John Murray 1873; Robert Campbell ed, 4th edn, rev, Thoemmes Press reprint 2002).

[9] eg Hans J Morgenthau, *Politics Among Nations the Struggle for Power and Peace* (Knopf 1964).

[10] Michael Foucault, *Security, Territory, Population: Lectures at the Collège de France 1977–78* (Arnold I Davidson ed, Graham Burchell tr, Palgrave Macmillan 2009).

[11] D'Aspremont (n 1) 1.

and non-state actors is common to all major social theories. The concept of non-state actors is based on an assumption that is shared by most social theories: that the state, either based on a Jellinekian or Weberian definition, is the key actor in the international realm. Non-state actors are all other actors that have not been created by states. Non-state actors consist of different types. Different social theories vary in the categorization of these different types of non-state actors. The labels 'firms' and 'civil society actors', for example, have a liberal association. Yet, the general relationship between state and non-state actors is a theme for all social theories, even if they come to substantively different conclusions.

At least three sub-themes are relevant for all the three social theories mentioned. The first sub-theme refers to the role of non-state actors such as lawyers, law firms, and multinational enterprises in a seemingly technical and depoliticized version of international law. In all the three social theories, there are strands that question the merely technical character of international law, while other strands may defend it. Arguably, realists and critical theorists are especially worried about the neutrality claim of international law. Realists have always pointed to a close relationship between law and power hierarchies,[12] and critical theorists argue that there is no rule—or law in general—that does not discipline some social groups and serve the interests of others.[13] Yet, there are also liberals who argue that any version of international law contains a social purpose. From this perspective, the idea of legal rationalism is criticized for aiming to prevent legitimate demands of participation in international law. While I do not deny that such a version of liberalism may be a minority within international law, liberals like John Ruggie[14] in international relations were always eager to point to the social purpose of legal rationalism.

The second sub-theme challenges the notion of international cooperation on empirical grounds as a purely executive, legal, or technical matter. International institutions are, in this view, increasingly seen—not only by social theorists, but also by non-state actors—as political institutions exercising public authority that require legitimation. For as long as the intergovernmental level was restricted by the requirement that each member state gave consent, there was contestation only by societal actors. As decisions taken at a level beyond that of the constituent members were legitimated through the legitimacy of their representatives, delegitimation by societal actors was difficult. With the rise of inter- and transnational authorities undermining the consent principle,[15] this has changed. International institutions are now evaluated against normative standards, and they need to be justified by reference to common norms. Furthermore, societal actors are no longer the only actors contesting inter- and transnational authorities; states and even international organizations now employ strategies of contestation

---

[12] Edward H Carr, *The Twenty Years' Crisis: 1919–1939* (Harper & Row 1964).

[13] Robert W Cox, *Production, Power, and World Order: Social Forces in the Making of History* (Columbia University Press 1987).

[14] John G Ruggie, 'International Regimes, Transactions, and Change: Embedded Liberalism in the Postwar Economic Order' in Stephan D Krasner (ed), *International Regimes* (Cornell University Press 1983).

[15] eg Nico Krisch, 'The Decay of Consent: International Law in an Age of Global Public Goods' (2014) 108 American Journal of International Law 1.

and delegitimation. As a consequence, inter- and transnational authorities are often subject to significant legitimation struggles that are systematically produced by the new features of international law. Against this background, two broad claims are put forward: The more political authority international institutions exercise, the more attention they attract, the more actors participate in debates, and the more polarization in opinions takes place. In other words, international institutions and law become increasingly politicized by non-state actors—be it by transnational protest movements, such as 'Occupy', or by right-wing populists within many Western democracies. In some cases, these movements seized power within states and thus became state actors.

This empirical relationship is increasingly studied from different theoretical perspectives. The initial authority–politicization hypothesis may be associated with liberal reasoning.[16] Yet, students of international relations with a critical ambition also study resistance against international rule,[17] and realists question the effectiveness of international law.[18] If we turn the issue to its normative side, different theoretical perspectives yet again differ. In a liberal perspective, politicization leads to a broadening of legitimation efforts beyond technocratic justifications including participatory and fairness-based narratives. At the same time, politicization may also lead to a significant legitimacy gap that can undermine the authorities as such. Critical theorists consider the rise of resistance against international law as an emancipatory movement, while realists emphasize the dangers for a smoothly working international diplomacy.

In making these remarks, I obviously do not want to neglect the differences in perspective by different social theories. I only would like to emphasize that the relationship between international law and non-state actors is studied and reflected upon from different theoretical perspectives. Again, the very focus on this relationship or on the term 'non-state actors' seems not to be the exclusive interest of liberalism. To the contrary, it is one of those issues that are studied and discussed from different perspectives. The rise or decline of international law is of interest to most or even all theories of international law and international institutions. This makes it an especially interesting field of study.

---

[16] Michael Zürn, Martin Binder, and Matthias Ecker-Ehrhardt, 'International Authority and its Politicization' (2012) 4 International Theory 69.

[17] eg Christopher Daase and Nicole Deitelhoff, 'Jenseits der Anarchie. Widerstand und Herrschaft im internationalen System' (2015) 56 Politische Vierteljahresschrift 299.

[18] Daniel W Drezner, *Theories of International Politics and Zombies* (rev, Princeton University Press 2015).

10

From High Hopes to Scepticism? Human Rights Protection and Rule of Law in Europe in an Ever More Hostile Environment

Angelika Nußberger*

I. Paradise or crisis—the status quo of human rights protection and rule of law in Europe

Hopes were dressed up in nice words. In the 1940s pathos was not alien to political speeches; pathos was not even suspicious.

> … right is pre-eminent over might and the purpose of the State … is not its own greatness, power or riches but the individual self-fulfilment of everybody subject to its rule with due respect for his or her dignity and freedom.[1]

'Right is pre-eminent over might'—that is the core formula of what the rule of law means. 'The purpose of the State is the individual self-fulfilment of everybody'—here we find a synopsis of the simple truth: human rights matter.

The quotation is the statement of the former French Minister of Justice Pierre-Henri Teitgen made in the process of elaborating the European Convention on Human Rights (ECHR). Human rights and rule of law, that is not one and the same, but intrinsically linked. He—as well as the other idealists negotiating the draft of the ECHR—wanted to bring about a change in state philosophy and to give a new definition to the responsibility of the state towards the individual. The two 'catchwords' of this new philosophy are human rights and rule of law.

The experiment of living up to this new philosophy—and we have to call it an experiment—started with ten signatures of statesmen who accepted international human rights obligations based on a binding treaty in the early 1950s.[2] It was a little

---

* The chapter reflects exclusively the personal opinion of the author and does not bind the Court in any way. I want to thank Mr Simon Blätgen and Ms Sophie Schuberth for their valuable assistance with the footnotes to the text. All online sources have been last accessed on 6 April 2018, unless indicated otherwise.

[1] Pierre-Henri Teitgen, 'Introduction to the ECHR' in Ronald S J Macdonald, Franz Matscher, and Herbert Petzold (eds), *The European System for the Protection of Human Rights* (Martinus Nijhoff 1993) 3, 4.

[2] Ratifications: United Kingdom (UK) on 8 March 1951, Norway on 15 January 1952, Sweden in 4 February 1952, Saar on 14 January 1953 (from 1947 to 1956 the Saarland was a French-occupied territory—the 'Saar

---

light in an ideologically divided world where human rights were part of ideology on both sides: the West against the East, civil rights against workers' rights, freedom against equality, rule of law against subordinating everything under the aim of reaching communism.

Almost seven decades later, forty-seven European states both in Eastern and Western Europe have ratified the treaty. Europe is no longer divided into two hostile blocks. A comprehensive case law touching upon virtually every aspect of life has been developed. The Court dares to speak of a 'European public order' ('ordre public Européen').[3] In other continents of the world, in Asia, Africa, and South America, the Convention system is seen as a great inspiration. Have we reached paradise? Have we reached what Teitgen and the co-founders of the ECHR had been dreaming of?

It is obvious that the present time can be described very differently. It can be said that there is a risk of the Convention system developing into something that is 'theoretical and illusory' and not 'practical and effective', to use the Court's own often repeated formula. European states with a long history of human rights protection like Switzerland, Denmark, and the United Kingdom voice concerns about undue interference in their sovereign rights and openly complain about the Court's broad—or even seemingly limitless—interpretation of the Convention.[4] These states start questioning their treaty obligations or threaten to leave the system.[5] Some member states—while upholding the label of human rights protection—are seen by many observers to turn

---

Protectorate'—separate from the rest of Germany; between 1950 and 1956, it was a member of the Council of Europe), Ireland on 25 February 1953, Greece on 28 March 1953, Denmark on 13 April 1953, Iceland on 29 June 1953, Luxembourg on 3 September 1953; further details here: Convention for the Protection of Human Rights and Fundamental Freedoms (adopted 4 November 1950, entered into force 3 September 1953) 213 UNTS 221 (ECHR).

[3] eg: *Loizidou v Turkey* (Preliminary Objections) ECtHR App no 15318/89 (1995) 75; *Bosphorus Hava Yollari Turizm v Ireland* ECtHR App no 45036/98 (2005) 156; also: *Al-Skeini and Others v UK* [GC] ECtHR App no 55721/07 (2011) 141.

[4] For Switzerland: Michael von Ledebuhr, 'Mutmaßliche Sozialhilfebetrüger sollen wieder observiert werden dürfen' (*Neue Züricher Zeitung*, 27 February 2018) <www.nzz.ch/zuerich/sozialinspektoren-sollen-wieder-taetig-werden-koennen-ld.1360860>; Daniel Foppa, 'Eiterbeule? Das leistet der Gerichtshof für Menschenrechte' (*Tagesanzeiger*, 5 July 2017) <www.tagesanzeiger.ch/schweiz/standard/Ein-Gericht-in-der-Kritik/story/14782105>; Tilmann Altwicker, 'Switzerland: The Substitute Constitution in Times of Popular Dissent' in Patricia Popelier, Sarah Lambrecht, and Koen Lemmens (eds), *Criticism of the European Court of Human Rights* (Intersentia 2016) 385; for Denmark: Jacques Hartmann, 'A Danish Crusade for the Reform of the European Court of Human Rights' (*EJIL:Talk!*, 14 November 2017) <www.ejiltalk.org/a-danish-crusade-for-the-reform-of-the-european-court-of-human-rights/>; for the United Kingdom: Christopher Hope, 'Britain to be Bound by European Human Rights Laws for at Least another Five Years even if Tories Win Election' <www.telegraph.co.uk/news/2017/05/18/britain-bound-european-human-rights-laws-least-another-five/>; Jon Stone, 'Brexit: Britain Must Stay in European Court of Human Rights if it Wants a Trade Deal, Brussels to Insist' (*The Independent*, 7 December 2017) <www.independent.co.uk/news/uk/politics/brexit-human-rights-european-court-echr-leave-after-theresa-may-tories-european-parliament-eu-a8096546.html>.

[5] The conservative right 'Swiss Peoples Party' handed in a sufficient number of signatures for their people's initiative 'Swiss Law Instead of Foreign Judges' in August 2016: Sibilla Bondolfi, 'An Attack on Human Rights or Strengthening Democracy?' (*Swiss-info*, 12 August 2016) <www.swissinfo.ch/eng/self-determination-initiative_an-attack-on-human-rights-or-strengthening-democracy/42369642>; in a referendum on 25 November 2018, roughly two-thirds of the voters rejected the proposal. In 2016, British PM Theresa May announced she would bring the exit from the Convention on the agenda in the 2020 elections: Will Worley, 'Theresa May "Will Campaign to Leave the European Convention on Human Rights in 2020 Election" ' (*The Independent*, 29 December 2016) <www.independent.co.uk/news/uk/politics/theresa-may-campaign-leave-european-convention-on-human-rights-2020-general-election-brexit-a7499951.html>; in Denmark, the Minister of Justice in a speech in 2017 referred to a controversial opinion poll showing limited public support for continued membership of the ECHR—unless it is reformed: Hartmann (n 4) with further references.

into authoritarian systems[6] and either develop mechanisms for not implementing the Court's judgments[7] or delay implementation for a long period of time.[8] Binding treaty obligations are openly neglected or qualified and seen—for various reasons—as not binding any more.[9] In some member states the national judiciaries, which are meant to implement human rights and rule of law and to closely cooperate with the Court in Strasbourg, are exposed to criticism from all sides—for lack of independence and impartiality as well as for inefficiency.[10]

The Court as the centrepiece of the human rights protection system is also in the focus of criticism: Too little, too much, never the right yardstick used, and in any way futile.[11] The functioning of the whole system is in danger.

Neither the paradise scenario, nor the crisis scenario is really accurate, both are exaggerated. But it seems as if—at least for some—high hopes have turned into scepticism. It cannot be overlooked that human rights protection and rule of law are faced with an ever more hostile environment.

There are many explanations for these developments. Most of them are to be found in the political sphere: disenchantment in view of long-held societal ideals, acceptance of taboo-breaking, populist movements using crisis scenarios for their ends, prioritization of state interests, admiration for an authoritarian style of governance, and rediscovery of nationalism and 'my-country-first approaches', and general scepticism towards whatever form of inter-state cooperation.

At the same time there might also be 'legal' explanations for more critical approaches towards progressive human rights jurisprudence pointing out that human rights are no longer what they used to be and create frictions with other overarching values.

---

[6]   Sergey Rumyantsev, 'Behind Azerbaijan's Facades' (*Open Democracy*, 21 March 2017) <www.opendemocracy.net/od-russia/sergey-rumyantsev/behind-azerbaijan-s-facades>; Steven A Cook, 'How Erdogan Made Turkey Authoritarian Again' (*The Atlantic*, 21 July 2016) <www.theatlantic.com/international/archive/2016/07/how-erdogan-made-turkey-authoritarian-again/492374/>; Larry Diamond, 'Russia and the Threat to Liberal Democracy' (*The Atlantic*, 9 December 2016) <www.theatlantic.com/international/archive/2016/12/russia-liberal-democracy/510011/>.

[7]   See the Russian Law Amending the Law on the Russian Constitutional Court: Federal Constitutional Law N 7 FKZ (14 December 2015) institutionalizing the possibility of declaring judgments of the ECtHR contrary to the Russian Constitution: Rachel M Fleig-Goldstein, 'The Russian Constitutional Court versus the European Court of Human Rights: How the Strasbourg Court Should Respond to Russia's Refusal to Execute ECtHR Judgments' (2017) 56 Columbia Journal of Transnational Law 172.

[8]   eg: Council of Europe, 'Supervision of the Execution of Judgments and Decisions of the European Court of Human Rights—10th Annual Report of the Committee of Ministers 2016' (March 2017) <https://rm.coe.int/prems-021117-gbr-2001-10e-rapport-annuel-2016-web-16x24/168072800b> 91, 106.

[9]   See the statement of the Turkish Foreign Minister Ahmet Davutoglu in reaction to the Court's judgment in *Cyprus v Turkey* ECtHR App no 25781/94 (2014), stating 'we don't see [the ruling] as at all binding, in terms of payment': Tulay Karadeniz and Ece Toksabay, 'Turkey to Ignore Court Order to Pay Compensation to Cyprus' (*Reuters*, 13 May 2014) <www.reuters.com/article/us-turkey-cyprus-davutoglu/turkey-to-ignore-court-order-to-pay-compensation-to-cyprus-idUSBREA4C0AX20140513>; ahead of the ruling, Davutoglu had stated that the Turkish government would see the judgment as 'neither binding nor of any value': Lizzie Dearden, 'Turkey Ordered to Pay Cyprus €90m for 1974 Invasion' (*The Independent*, 12 May 2014) <www.independent.co.uk/news/world/europe/turkey-ordered-to-pay-cyprus-90m-for-1974-invasion-9358319.html>.

[10]   Anja Seibert-Fohr, 'Introduction: The Challenge of Transition' in Anja Seibert-Fohr (ed), *Judicial Independence in Transition* (Springer 2012) 1.

[11]   For critical articles: Heinrich Wefing, 'Doppeltes Unrecht—Warum kneift Europas Justiz, wenn es um die Verletzung von Menschenrechten in der Türkei geht?' (*Zeit online*, 14 February 2018) <www.zeit.de/2018/08/deniz-yuezel-menschenrechte-europa-tuerkei>; Brigitte Pfiffner and Susanne Bollinger, 'Ausufernde Interpretation der Menschenrechte' (*Neue Züricher Zeitung*, 2 February 2012) <www.nzz.ch/ausufernde_interpretation_der_menschenrechte-1.14748269>.

Against this background it is interesting to observe the debate on the 'Copenhagen Declaration', an important step in the reform process of the Convention system.[12] It started out with a text that paid lip service to strengthening the existing strong European human rights protection system, but at the same time included clear attacks on the Court's jurisprudence and seemed to advocate more respect for 'constitutional traditions' and 'national circumstances' than for common values for all.[13] This first draft reunited the criticism of those against a strong human rights protection system for political reasons and those sceptical for 'legal' reasons. Not only the Court[14] and the NGO community,[15] but also the great majority of state delegations strongly reacted to the first draft. As a follow-up it was not only rewritten, but transformed into a completely different document emphasizing continuity and advocating small reform steps.[16] The main change between the first and the last draft concerns the conception of subsidiarity. While the first draft understood subsidiarity almost as a sort of national laissez-faire in the field of human rights in as far as controversial policy areas were concerned, the last draft readjusted its meaning to the one elaborated by the Court in its jurisprudence.

It thus cannot be ignored that the European human rights protection system as it stands is open to criticism. But it is necessary to distinguish between 'good faith criticism' and 'bad faith criticism'. Both have to be taken seriously, but different answers are needed. While the latter is mainly an issue for politics, the former has to be analysed in depth. In so far as it uncovers deficiencies in the system, they have to be adequately addressed, and, if possible, corrected.[17]

It is in this context that I want to ask an intriguing question. Is it really true that human rights and rule of law always go hand in hand? Or do we sometimes have to sacrifice one in order to achieve the other? 'More human rights—less rule of law?' 'Less human rights—more rule of law?'—Is it sometimes necessary to accept compromises? Is it possible that, even if human rights and rule of law are intrinsically interwoven, under specific circumstances conflicts might arise? Might this be one of the reasons for the uneasiness with the present development of the human rights system?

[12] More or less immediately after the creation of the permanent Court in 1998 it became clear that reforms were necessary in order to cope with the backlog of cases. The first important step in this process was the Interlaken conference leading to the elaboration of the 15th and 16th Protocol. Further reform conferences in Brighton and Brussels followed. The Copenhagen Conference and the adoption of the Copenhagen declaration are to be seen in this line.

[13] Draft Copenhagen Declaration on the European Convention on Human Rights (5 February 2018) <https://menneskeret.dk/sites/menneskeret.dk/files/media/dokumenter/nyheder/draft_copenhagen_declaration_05.02.18.pdf>.

[14] European Court of Human Rights, Opinion on the Copenhagen Declaration (19 February 2018) <www.echr.coe.int/Documents/Opinion_draft_Declaration_Copenhague%20ENG.pdf>.

[15] See Joint NGO Response to the Draft Copenhagen Declaration (13 February 2018) <www.omct.org/statements/2018/02/d24721/>.

[16] Draft Copenhagen Declaration on the European Convention on Human Rights, third draft (20 March 2018) restricted document.

[17] For an example of 'good faith criticism': contributions in Popelier, Lambrecht, and Lemmens (n 4); see also the conference on 'Principled Resistance against ECtHR Judgments—a New Paradigm?' in Konstanz (Germany) in June 2017. The proceedings will be published as Marten Breuer (ed), 'Principled Resistance against ECtHR Judgments—a New Paradigm?', forthcoming.

In my chapter I argue that the dynamics inherent in the Convention system can pose a problem to legal certainty. The first pillar of the analysis is the double link between the Strasbourg system of human rights protection and rule of law. On the one hand the Court contributes to developing the concept of rule of law by elaborating standards on the basis of concrete cases. On the other hand the Court is a major player in the international legal system and has to abide itself by the principles it develops (II). The second pillar of the analysis is what may be called 'high hopes' linked to the human rights protection system. Two periods for 'high hopes' are of special importance: the 1950s and the 1990s (III). Looking at these—seemingly well-founded—'high hopes' and later developments, the question arises why some member states have changed their attitude and look at European human rights protection with a critical attitude. Tensions between human rights and rule of law seem to be a relevant aspect in this respect (IV). The current threats and dilemmas the Convention system is faced with have to be seen against this background (V). Finally, we have to ask about lessons learnt. Where to find the solution—correct mistakes or just continue? (VI)

II. The interaction between human rights and rule of law

1. Rule of law as an interpretative principle of the Convention

Rule of law is to be found in the preamble to the Convention.[18] The enumeration of the rights follows in the main text. It was only in 1975, more than two decades after the beginning of the working of the system, that rule of law was invoked in a case before the Court. It was in the famous judgment *Golder v United Kingdom*:

> It may also be accepted ..., that the Preamble does not include the rule of law in the object and purpose of the Convention, but points to it as being one of the features of the common spiritual heritage of the member States of the Council of Europe. The Court however considers ... that it would be a mistake to see in this reference a merely 'more or less rhetorical reference', devoid of relevance for those interpreting the Convention. One reason why the signatory Governments decided to 'take the first steps for the collective enforcement of certain of the Rights stated in the Universal Declaration' was their profound belief in the rule of law.[19]

The case *Golder v UK* was about access to court. A convicted prisoner wanted to come into contact with a solicitor in order to launch an action against a prison guard

---

[18]   Preamble of the European Convention on Human Rights, para 6:

Being resolved, as the governments of European countries which are like-minded and have a common heritage of political traditions, ideals, freedom and the rule of law, to take the first steps for the collective enforcement of certain of the rights stated in the Universal Declaration ...

[19]   *Golder v UK* ECtHR App no 4451/70 (1975) 34.

who had wrongfully accused him of taking part in a prison riot. His demand was refused so that he could not pursue his complaint. As access to court is not explicitly granted in the Convention, it was necessary for the Court to decide if this was a lacuna to be filled. With reference to rule of law as an interpretative principle the Court said 'yes'. Even if access to court is not one of the rights explicitly granted, it has to be seen as part of 'fair trial', which has to be interpreted in the light of the rule of law principle. To quote the wording of the judgment: 'And in civil matters one can scarcely conceive of the rule of law without there being a possibility of having access to the courts.'[20]

Not all the judges of the Court accepted the idea of using 'rule of law' as an interpretative principle, as a tool for deciding cases. It is interesting to note that the British judge Sir Gerald Fitzmaurice found it necessary to dissent on this point: 'The importance attributed to the factor of the "rule of law" in paragraph 34 of the Court's Judgment is much exaggerated.'[21]

But he was all alone with this approach.

2. Case law of the ECtHR as an inventory of the different aspects of rule of law

What started with a cautious reference in the case of *Golder v UK* was later on transformed into a bold statement: '... the rule of law, a concept inherent in all the Articles of the Convention.'[22]

That is what the Court started saying in the 1990s, interpreting all articles in the light of the rule of law principle. What does it mean? Lord Bingham enumerated in his famous book *Rule of Law* the eight 'ingredients' of rule of law.[23] They coincide to a large extent with what the European Court of Human Rights has elaborated in its jurisprudence over the last decades and what the Venice Commission has summarized in a Rule of Law Checklist.[24] The starting point can be a negative one: Rule of law is the opposite of arbitrariness. It comprises elements such as independence of the judiciary, legal certainty, procedural guarantees, *nulla poena sine lege*, *ne bis in idem*, etc. Traces of all these elements can be found in the Court's case law; all that is well known and it is not necessary to further elaborate on it.[25]

---

[20] ibid.
[21] *Golder* (n 19), Separate Opinion of Judge Sir Gerald Fitzmaurice (21 February 1975) 29, 44.
[22] *Amuur v France* ECtHR App no 19776/92 (1996) 24.
[23] Tom H Bingham, *The Rule of Law* (Penguin 2010) 37–39.
[24] European Commission for Democracy through Law (Venice Commission) 'Rule of Law Checklist' (18 March 2016) <www.venice.coe.int/webforms/documents/default.aspx?pdffile=CDL-AD(2016)007-e> accessed 30 June 2018; also: Andrew Drzemczewski, 'The Council of Europe and the Rule of Law. Introductory Remarks Regarding the Rule of Law Checklist Established by the Venice Commission' (2017) 37 Human Rights Law Journal 179.
[25] Geranne Lautenbach, *The Concept of the Rule of Law and the European Court of Human Rights* (Oxford University Press 2013); Tom H Bingham, 'The Rule of Law' (2007) 66 The Cambridge Law Journal 67; Angelika Nußberger, 'The European Court of Human Rights and Rule of Law—A Tale of Hopes and Disillusions' in Marek

3. The exemplary function of the ECtHR system

The Court requires standards of rule of law to be upheld on the national level. Rule of law does, however, not only apply on the national, but also on the international level. To quote once more Lord Bingham:

> For although international law comprises a distinct and recognizable body of law with its own rules and institutions it is a body of law complementary to the national laws of individual states, and in no way antagonistic to then; it is not a thing apart; it rests on similar principles and pursues similar ends; and observance of the rule of law is quite as important on the international plane as on the national, perhaps even more so.[26]

Thus, the rule of law also applies to the Convention institutions, the Court, the Committee of Ministers, the Parliamentary Assembly, as well as the member states in fulfilling their treaty obligations. We may say, the rule of law does not only apply, but applies in an exemplary way. Demanding high standards means accepting being judged by these high standards.

This is the basis for the story to be told: from high hopes to scepticism. Let us start with high hopes. But it is high hopes with a slow start.

III. A European human rights court as a symbol for progress in international law

1. High hopes and a slow start

The drafting process of the ECHR began before the adoption of the Universal Declaration of Human Rights (UDHR) and lasted from May 1948 until November 1950, for about two and a half years—a historical breathing space in Europe with the Nazi atrocities having been overcome, but still vividly present, and the Cold War 'ante portas'.

The focus of the first draft (known as the 'European Movement Convention'[27]) was exclusively on political rights. It designed a strong control mechanism composed of a Court and Commission, even stronger than it is nowadays. Not only was the right to individual petition foreseen, the Court should even be allowed 'to prescribe measures of reparation',[28]

Zubik (ed), *Human Rights in Contemporary World. Essays in Honour of Professor Leszek Garlicki* (Wydawnictwo Sejmowe Warzawa 2017) 162.

---

[26] Bingham (n 23) 110.

[27] The European Movement was a private organization founded on 25 October 1948 with the aim of coordinating the activities of various existing international organizations and representing them in their relations with governments. It submitted a draft convention to the Council of Europe in August 1949.

[28] See Art 13 (b) of the 'European Movement Convention'; see Ed Bates, *The Evolution of the European Convention on Human Rights. From its Inception to the Creation of a Permanent Court of Human Rights* (Oxford University Press 2010) 51ff.

a competence never included in the text of the ECHR,[29] nowadays claimed by the Court 'under very exceptional circumstances'.[30]

The topics discussed in this very early phase of the drafting process are basically the same as those discussed nowadays. Then and now they are prone to controversy—the danger of an (undemocratically) intense encroachment on state sovereignty, the danger of judicial activism, and the danger of overburdening the control institutions with un-meritorious complaints. While some of those participating in the debate in the 1940s and 1950s wanted to see a European Court as a first step towards a federal European state, a true 'European Union', others were interested only in an 'alarm-bell' warning against totalitarian tendencies within member states. The debate was, however, based on the assumption that democratic states did not have to fear to be accused before the new Court as only truly abusive human rights restrictions would be sanctioned.[31]

At that stage, the debate was a theoretical one. Nobody had yet assumed obligations, the question was how to frame obligations. Concluding a treaty is a 'free political game', all negotiating partners are free to include or exclude whatever they want. Rule of law does not come into play. It might, however, foreshadow the consequences to be drawn from the treaty obligations and thus command sincere negotiations.

From this first project it was a long way to go until the adoption of the final text and the opening of the treaty for signature on 4 November 1950.

The reworking of the original draft by the governments was meant to pull out the teeth of a project that was considered to be a dangerous attack on unfettered state sovereignty. The control machinery was reduced to a shadow of the original proposal, with an optional clause for individual complaints, an optional clause for accepting the jurisdiction of the Court, and the Committee of Ministers, a political body, between the Commission and the Court.[32]

Nevertheless, there were high hopes. In the words of the British lawyer Lauterpacht:

Touching, as [the international protection of the fundamental rights of man] does, intimately upon the relations of the State and individual ... it implies a more drastic interference with the sovereignty of the State than the renunciation of war and the acceptance of the principle of compulsory judicial settlement.[33]

States were reluctant to accept such far-reaching commitments. So it was a slow start. Eventually a catalogue of human rights was drawn up and, as already mentioned, rule of law was inserted in the preamble.

---

[29] See Art 41 ECHR (just satisfaction); Art 46 (binding force of judgments).

[30] For one of the most far-reaching examples: *Volkov v Ukraine* ECtHR App no 21722/11 (2013) 208, where Ukraine as the respondent state was required 'to secure the applicant's reinstatement to the post of judge of the Supreme Court at the earliest possible date'; also: *Assanidze v Georgia* ECtHR App no 71503/01 (2004) where the Court demanded the applicant's release at the earliest possible date.

[31] For a detailed description of the background: Bates (n 28) 44–76.

[32] ibid 103ff.

[33] Hersch Lauterpacht, *An International Bill of the Rights of Man* (first published 1945, Oxford University Press 2013) preface XXVII–XXIII.

2. Success as surprise

Against this background of doubts, hesitations, and half-heartedness,[34] it can be seen as a miracle that what was meant not to be effective or at least not to be too effective turned out to be very effective. Progress came as a sort of surprise. Different steps were made in different decades. It is worth giving just a short sketch highlighting some interesting elements jumping from the 1950s to the 1970s and then to the 1990s.

(a) The great leap forward with groundbreaking cases in the 1970s

It was only in the 1970s that the ECtHR adopted groundbreaking judgments and elaborated new doctrinal approaches, above all in *Tyrer v the United Kingdom*,[35] *Marckx v Belgium*,[36] and *Airey v Ireland*[37]. All of a sudden the ECtHR had its own 'trumps' such as the doctrine of the 'living instrument', the doctrine of 'autonomous interpretation', and the doctrine of the 'effectiveness' of human rights protection according to which human rights must not be 'theoretical and illusory, but practical and effective'.

It is not exaggerated to say that the Court had an impact on modernizing society in this period. It took up issues such as discrimination or violent methods of education and helped the vulnerable to make their rights heard.

(b) Europe coming together—reuniting East and West

Success also came as a surprise in so far as the growth of the system was concerned. As noted above, it started out with ten states only from Western Europe and arrived at forty-seven states including all European states with the exception of Belarus and the Vatican State. Why was there such a human rights drive in the 1990s when most of the new member states acceded to the Council of Europe? For central European countries such as Poland, Hungary, Czechoslovakia, it was a first—and necessary—step to become members of the European Union. So they joined with real enthusiasm, perhaps to signal to the whole world that they had changed sides. The same is true for the Baltic states. For the other Eastern European states as well as for the former constituent states of the Soviet Union the question is more difficult to answer. For sure, Gorbachev's idea of the common 'European House' was an inspiration; Gorbachev was the first to talk about membership of the Council of Europe during his first trip to Strasbourg in the late 1980s.[38] Yeltsin followed up on this line. Russia's application was, however, met

---

[34] The forerunners of human rights protection, the United Kingdom and France, were reluctant to accept being bound by the control mechanism of the Convention themselves. It was the United Kingdom who took the lead in 1952 by ratifying the Convention, but neither accepting the right to individual petition to the Convention (Art 25) nor the jurisdiction of the Court (Art 46). France had been a fervent supporter of an effective human rights control mechanism and supported even the setting-up of a Court with a mandatory jurisdiction, but ratified the Convention only more than twenty years after its entry into force, in 1974. And even then it did not accept the right to individual petition.

[35] *Tyrer v UK* ECtHR App no 5856/72 (1978).
[36] *Marckx v Belgium* ECtHR App no 6833/74 (1979).
[37] *Airey v Ireland* ECtHR App no 6289/73 (1979).
[38] Angelika Nußberger, 'Russland und der Europarat. Von der ersten Rede Michail Gorbatschows vor der Parlamentarischen Versammlung bis zu Russlands Vorsitz im Ministerrat' in Reiner Braun and Günther Handke (eds), *Herausforderungen. Michail S. Gorbatschows Leben und Wirken* (Neu Isenburg 2007) 91.

with scepticism. An expert group argued that the country was not 'ripe', it would not be able to fulfil the treaty obligations.[39] Nevertheless, there was a strong political will to see them 'in' and not 'out'. The countries of the Caucasus were also accepted as new members despite their difficult legacy of unresolved military conflicts in Nagorno-Karabakh, South Ossetia, and Abkhazia. The successor states to Yugoslavia followed after the end of the hostilities.

When the new Court was founded in 1998, the right of individual petition was made compulsory.[40] At that moment it was clear even for sceptics that international human rights protection had turned out to be a real success story. But too much success might create too much—even illusionary—hope. A Court can decide cases, but it cannot perform miracles. Some wanted it to change society, others wanted it to guarantee stability. It is, however, difficult to bring about change and stability at the same time. The Court was caught in the dilemma of living up to very different expectations.

IV. The turnaround—crisis and criticism

1. Dilemma between change and stability

In many cases the Court had to opt either for a 'conservative' approach in line with traditional concepts of international law or for an 'innovative' approach developing international human rights law as a sort of *'lex specialis'*.

(a) Enlargement of the Court's competences with respect to the scope of treaty obligations

Belilos v Switzerland, a case dating back to 1988,[41] was the very first case in which a court assumed the competence to decide on the validity of a state's reservation to an international treaty, to declare it invalid and—the most innovative step—to conclude that the state was fully bound by the treaty, that is without the restrictions the reservation had foreseen.

The case was about a student who had taken part in a demonstration without the necessary permission of the police and was therefore fined. She complained under Article 6 ECHR that she did not have a fair trial in this respect. But was Article 6 applicable to her case? In its reservation Switzerland had explicitly stated:

> The Swiss Federal Council considers that the guarantee of fair trial in Article 6, paragraph 1 (art. 6-1) of the Convention, in the determination of civil rights

---

[39] See Council of Europe, Parliamentary Assembly, 'Report on the Conformity of the Legal Order of the Russian Federation with Council of Europe Standards' prepared by Rudolf Bernhardt, Stephan Trechsel, Albert Weitzel, and Felix Ermacora (7 October 1994) Doc AS/Bur/Russia (1994) 7; Parliamentary Assembly, 'Application by Russia for the Membership of the Council of Europe' Opinion 193 (1996) <http://assembly.coe.int/nw/xml/XRef/Xref-XML2HTML-EN.asp?fileid=13932&lang=en>.

[40] Protocol No 11 to the Convention for the Protection of Human Rights and Fundamental Freedoms, restructuring the control machinery established thereby (entered into force 1 November 1998) European Treaty Series No 155 (1994).

[41] *Belilos v Switzerland* ECtHR App no 10328/83 (1988).

and obligations or any criminal charge against the person in question is intended solely to ensure ultimate control by the judiciary over the acts or decisions of the public authorities relating to such rights or obligations or the determination of such a charge.

The Court reasoned that the reservation was invalid as 'a brief statement of the law concerned' was missing despite the respective requirement in the Convention.[42] It concluded as follows:

> In short, the declaration in question does not satisfy two of the requirements of Article 64 (art. 64) of the Convention, with the result that it must be held to be invalid. At the same time, it is beyond doubt that Switzerland is, and regards itself as, bound by the Convention irrespective of the validity of the declaration.[43]

Such an approach had been unheard of. It was a major step out of the framework of traditional international law. According to the regime of reservations in the Vienna Convention on the Law of Treaties, controversial parts of treaties—where the parties object to reservations—would have to be deducted, not added to the treaty. It is true, however, that this regime had been designed for bilateral treaties with reciprocal obligations where no central control instance was foreseen. Thus, Article 21 para 3 of the Vienna Convention reads:

> When a State objecting to a reservation has not opposed the entry into force of the treaty between itself and the reserving State, the *provisions* to which the reservation relates *do not apply* as between the two States to the extent of the reservation. (Emphasis added)

In the model of the Vienna Convention, consent is considered as central. '*Pacta sunt servanda*', but only on the basis of consent. In order to guarantee an efficient human rights protection the Court interpreted the consent given in the most far-reaching way. If Switzerland ratifying the Convention with reservations had given an inch, the Court has taken an ell deleting the reservations and assuming that it could not be otherwise as human rights were at stake. Thus, it created a *lex specialis* interpretation for human rights treaties, contrary to the approach in general international law. There it is the idea of always choosing the 'least-intrusive-to-sovereignty' interpretation which is dominating. Switzerland criticized, but accepted, the Court's judgment in the

---

[42] See Art 57 (former Art 64) of the Convention:

'(1.) Any State may, when signing this Convention or when depositing its instrument of ratification, make a reservation in respect of any particular provision of the Convention to the extent that any law then in force in its territory is not in conformity with the provision. Reservations of a general character shall not be permitted under this Article.

(2.) Any reservation made under this Article shall contain a brief statement of the law concerned.'

[43] *Belilos* (n 41) 60.

Belilos case. The only alternative would have been to withdraw from the Convention altogether.[44]

The Court's approach became permanent practice. But even if it is generally accepted, it still stirs up concern, for example for Turkey in the *Loizidou* case,[45] just recently for Italy in the case *Grande Stevens* about '*ne bis in idem*'.[46] It is worth mentioning that on the international level states objected to a similar approach of the Human Rights Committee.[47] The International Law Commission refused to follow the '*Belilos*-model' in defining the consequences of reservations to which treaty partners object.[48] On the other hand, the Inter-American Court of Human Rights accepted this innovative approach[49] and the International Court of Justice took inspiration from it.[50]

By not accepting the limits of the states' consent to be bound, the Court nevertheless ventured into a dangerous field. What about rule of law? What about legal certainty?

Before responding to these questions, it is worth adding another, 'less historical' example: the case *Di Trizio v Switzerland* of 2016.[51] It is a case about the allegedly discriminatory method of calculating invalidity pensions for women where the Court has found a violation of Article 8 together with Article 14 of the Convention. From the point of view of the Swiss authorities this case also marks a 'transgression' of the Court. Switzerland had consciously and explicitly not ratified the First Protocol to the Convention (P 1). Nevertheless, Article 8 was interpreted in such a broad way as to encompass all claims that would otherwise have to be taken under Article 1 P 1. In the words of the dissenters: 'The approach taken by the majority extends the scope of Article 8 considerably, making Article 1 of Protocol No. 1 to some extent superfluous.'[52]

In the case *Di Trizio*, Switzerland felt again bound beyond its consent or even against its consent. It asked for a review of the case by the Grand Chamber, but was rejected. Despite its irritation, Switzerland has not delayed the implementation of the Court's

---

[44] The judgment led to heated debates in the Swiss Federal Parliament. It was proposed to denounce the Convention and to re-ratify it with a new reservation. This proposal was dismissed by a close vote of sixteen to fifteen (Amtl Bull 1988, StR, 554); also: Daniela Thurnherr, 'The Reception Process in Austria and Switzerland' in Helen Keller and Alec Stone Sweet, *A Europe of Rights. The Impact of the ECHR on National Legal Systems* (Oxford University Press 2008) 320.

[45] *Loizidou* (n 3).

[46] *Grande Stevens and Others v Italy* ECtHR App nos 18640/10, 18647/10, 18663/10, 18668/10. and 18698/10 (2014).

[47] UN Human Rights Committee, General Comment 24, 'Issues relating to reservations made upon ratification or accession to the Covenant or the optional Protocols thereto, or in relation to declarations under article 41 of the Covenant' (Fifty-second session 1994) UN Doc CCPR/C21/Rev.1/Add.6 (1994); for Observations by the Governments of the United States and the United Kingdom on General Comment No 24 (52) Relating to Reservations: (1995) 16 Human Rights Law Journal 422; further Observations by France on General Comment No 24 (52) Relating to Reservations to the ICCPR: (1997) 4 International Human Rights Reports 6.

[48] For a summary of the work of the International Law Commission on the issue of reservations to treaties: <http://legal.un.org/ilc/summaries/1_8.shtml>; for the respective reports and documents: <http://legal.un.org/ilc/guide/1_8.shtml>.

[49] The Effect of Reservations on the Entry into Force of the American Convention on Human Rights (Arts 74 and 75): Inter-American Court of Human Rights, Advisory Opinion OC-2/82 (24 September 1982) IACHR Ser A No 2; Restrictions to the Death Penalty (Arts 4(2) and 4(4) American Convention on Human Rights): IACHR, Advisory Opinion OC-3/83 (8 September 1983) IACHR Ser) No 3.

[50] Rosalyn Higgins, 'Human Rights in the International Court of Justice' (2007) 20 Leiden Journal of International Law 745, 746.

[51] *Di Trizio v Switzerland* ECtHR App no 7186/09 (2016).

[52] ibid Joint dissenting opinion of Judges Keller, Spano, and Kjolbro (2 February 2016) 12.

judgment.[53] It is well known that before ratifying the Convention in 1974 Switzerland had meticulously scrutinized the compatibility of the Swiss legal system with the Convention obligations. The ratification had been tailor-made in order to exclude any potential violations. The Court's subsequent practice could, in the view of the Court's critics, not be foreseen and led to unexpected results.

Pacta sunt servanda. That is a fundamental part of rule of law. But—what are the '*pacta*'? It is true that the Vienna Convention on the Law of the Treaties (Article 31 para 3 b) allows for a change of treaty obligations based on 'subsequent practice'.[54] It can be argued that Switzerland—as well as all the other member states—has accepted the *Belilos* jurisprudence. But did they have a viable alternative? They were confronted with an all-or-nothing-solution. The choice was between 'in' and 'out'.[55] In order to insist on a narrow understanding of what the '*pacta*' were, Switzerland would have had to leave the system, even if an option of ratifying it again under changed conditions might have existed. Can it be denied that there is a certain tension between an effective system of human rights—wished and welcomed—and the principle of foreseeability, an integral part of rule of law?[56]

It was an audacious step the Court had taken. It took it for human rights' sake; it was a step towards progress. Despite some grumbling, it might be said that all's well that ends well, at least in as far as this part of the story is concerned.

(b) Expansion of the Court's jurisdiction

The second well-known example for what is seen as the Court's 'activist' approach going beyond states' consent concerns extraterritorial jurisdiction. Article 1 of the Convention clearly states that states shall secure to everyone 'within their jurisdiction' the rights and freedoms defined in the Convention. How come that Russia is deemed to be responsible for what happens in Transnistria, the United Kingdom for what happens in Iraq, Turkey for what happens in Cyprus? The Court's interpretation of jurisdiction has expanded, step by step, always based on solid and good arguments.[57] But applying the Court's own yardstick, 'foreseeability' as part of 'law', it is probably correct to argue that for those ratifying the Convention before 2000 it was not foreseeable how 'jurisdiction' would be understood in cases such as *Al Skeini v UK*[58] and

---

[53]   ibid Final Resolution RES (2017) 128.

[54]   On this point: Conclusion 8 (3) point 14 of the Draft Conclusions on subsequent agreements and subsequent practice in relation to the interpretation of treaties adopted by the International Law Commission <http://legal.un.org/docs/?path=../ilc/reports/2016/english/chp6.pdf&lang=EFSRAC>.

[55]   In this context also the example of the case *Loizidou v Turkey* where the Court spoke about a 'uniform and consistent practice' of member states although two states had not accepted the prohibition of territorial or substantive restrictions under Arts 25 and 46 of the Convention: *Loizidou* (n 3) 79–82.

[56]   Susan Marks, 'Reservations Unhinged: The Belilos Case Before the European Court of Human Rights' (1990) 39 International and Comparative Law Quarterly 300; Ryan Goodman, 'Human Rights Treaties, Invalid Reservations, and State Consent' (2002) 96 American Journal of International Law 531; Louis Henkin, 'Human Rights and State Sovereignty' (1995) 25 Georgia Journal of International and Comparative Law 31.

[57]   Angelika Nußberger 'The Concept of "Jurisdiction" in the Jurisprudence of the European Court of Human Rights' (2012) 65 Current Legal Problems 241.

[58]   *Al Skeini v UK* ECtHR App no 55721/07 (2011).

Hassan v UK,[59] this all the more so after the restrictive approach in *Banković v NATO states*.[60]

In the context of the present chapter, it is not necessary to evaluate the jurisprudence; the rules developed in the cases after *Banković* have by now been applied consistently for many years, and have undoubtedly contributed to a more effective human rights protection in armed conflicts. Nevertheless, it cannot be overlooked that the uneasiness with the Court's jurisprudence was not just occasional. The Court was not just criticized for a wrong result, but for its approach per se. It is worth quoting the dissenting opinion of Judge Kovler on the interpretation of the 'jurisdiction' in the case *Ilascu v Moldova and Russia*:

> I firmly believe that the Court should follow the traditions of the 'case-law of concepts', in other words start from the idea that the essential concepts of contemporary positive law have been established by generations of jurists and should not be called into question except in exceptional cases.[61]

He started his dissenting opinion with the following quotation: 'The frontier between the judicial and the political is not what it was. Nor are the foundations of legitimacy, still less normativeness, which is becoming plural and increasingly diffuse.'[62] Statements like this one—by judges of the Court—are clear signs of estrangement.

Not taking the states' consent seriously (enough?) might be seen as a first harbinger of crisis and criticism. At the same time, what can be—once again—called an 'audacious approach' considerably advanced human rights protection in situations of military conflict.

(c) The Court's jurisprudence and parliamentary sovereignty

A further problem—and here the protest was even louder—was what was seen as an attack on parliamentary sovereignty. The most famous cases are the prisoners' voting cases where the Court deduced from Article 3 of the First Protocol to the Convention rules about who should or should not be allowed to vote in democratic elections.[63] An absolute ban on prisoners' voting was deemed to be incompatible with the Convention, and this despite the warning bell rung by the dissenters in the case:

> The finding of the majority will create legislative problems not only for States with a general ban such as exists in the United Kingdom...., the judgment in the present

---

[59]   *Hassan v UK* ECtHR App no 29750/09 (2014).
[60]   *Banković and Others v Belgium and 16 other contracting States* (Decision as to the admissibility) [GC] ECtHR App no 52207/99 (2001).
[61]   *Ilascu and Others v Moldova and Russia* ECtHR App no 48787/99, Dissenting Opinion Judge Kovler (8 July 2004) 143, 150.
[62]   ibid 143.
[63]   The text of Article 3 of the First Protocol to the Convention is:

The High Contracting Parties undertake to hold free elections at reasonable intervals by secret ballot, under conditions which will ensure the free expression of the opinion of the people in the choice of the legislature.

case implies that all States with such restrictions will face difficult assessments as to whether their legislation complies with the requirements of the Convention.[64]

The controversy over prisoners' voting rights has led to open defiance and opposition against the Court's judgments. The *Hirst* judgment was adopted in 2005 and has only partially been implemented twelve years later.[65] What is worse, it has inspired others not to take seriously obligations stemming from Article 46, the duty to implement the Court's judgments faithfully. Russia has followed suit, but in an even more categorical manner than the United Kingdom. It has adopted a law prescribing a selective mechanism on the basis of a 'pick-and-choose' principle.[66] The non-implementation of a judgment is allowed when it contradicts the Russian Constitution. It thus reverses the basic rule of international law fixed in Article 27 of the Vienna Convention of the Law of Treaties: 'A party may not invoke the provisions of its internal law as justification for its failure to perform a treaty.'

(d) Questioning of traditional concepts

A good example for explaining the growing scepticism is the perception of the Court's jurisprudence on Article 8 of the Convention and the rights of sexual minorities. Especially in Eastern European countries, above all the Russian Federation, the case law on homosexuals' rights is not accepted as it is seen to contradict traditional values deeply rooted in society. The controversy about the Russian Law on Homosexual Propaganda[67] shows the divergent views clearly. The Russian judge's dissenting opinion appended to the judgment has been met with hostility.[68] The case *Orlandi and Others v Italy*[69] about refusal to register same-sex marriages contracted abroad is comparable; here again two judges from Eastern Europe, the Czech Republic and Poland, dissent and argue that the majority's approach is methodologically not tenable. More generally, they are against the mainstream interpretation of the Convention as a living instrument:

> While the Court must interpret and clarify the provisions of the Convention in the context of the new cases brought before it, it is not mandated to change the scope of the

---

[64] *Hirst v UK* (No 2) ECtHR App no 74025/01, Joint Dissenting Opinion of Judges Wildhaber, Costa, Lorenzen, Kovler and Jebens (6 October 2005) 28, 31.

[65] For an overview: Ed Bates, 'The Continued Failure to Implement Hirst v UK' (*EJIL:Talk!*, 15 December 2015) <www.ejiltalk.org/the-continued-failure-to-implement-hirst-v-uk/>; also: Council of Europe documents CM/ResDH(2009)160, CM/Del/Dec(2015)1236/25, CM/ResDH(2015)251; Council of Europe, 'Supervision of the Execution of Judgments and Decisions of the European Court of Human Rights—9th Annual Report of the Committee of Ministers 2015' 154. The implementation measures proposed were accepted by the Committee of Ministers in December 2017 (DH-DD(2017)1229); nevertheless, it is clear that according to the re-interpreted rules only about 100 prisoners will get the right to vote: <www.gov.uk/government/speeches/secretary-of-states-oral-statement-on-sentencing>.

[66] Russian Federal Constitutional Law (n 7); Goldstein (n 7).

[67] Federal Law No 436-F3 of 29 December 2010 'On the Protection of Children from Information that is Harmful to their Health and Development'.

[68] Laurens Lavryson, 'Bayev and Others v. Russia: On Judge Dedov's Outrageously Homophobic Dissent' <https://strasbourgobservers.com/2017/07/13/bayev-and-others-v-russia-on-judge-dedovs-outrageously-homophobic-dissent/>.

[69] *Orlandi and Others v Italy* ECtHR App nos 26431/12, 26742/12, 44057/12, and 60088/12 (2018).

engagements undertaken by the High Contracting Parties and in particular to adapt the Convention to societal changes.[70]

It is true that the case law has been developing at a breathtaking pace. What was okay yesterday seems no longer to be okay today.[71] The criticism voiced by some of the judges shows more than just uneasiness. It evinces cultural differences in the understanding of what the Convention is and what the Convention should be.

(e) Changes of jurisprudence

In this context one last example might be worth mentioning: the changes of the Court's jurisprudence. Turnarounds in the case law may also cause problems on the basis of rule of law. There were many famous changes in the Court's jurisprudence—*Christine Goodwin v United Kingdom* about the absence of legal recognition of the change of sex,[72] *Bayatyan v Armenia* about conviction of a conscientious objector for refusing to perform military service,[73] *Zolotukhin v Russia* about *ne bis in idem*.[74] The last example is very illustrative. The new standard about how to understand the principle of '*ne bis in idem*' was developed by the Court in 2009. It was applied in subsequent judgments on facts that had happened before 2009, that is at a time when the states could not know that they had to apply a different standard. Retroactivity of law is a problem of rule of law. While it is excluded in criminal law, it can be allowed under exceptional circumstances in other fields of law. The Court assumes that such a retroactive application of newly developed human rights standards is necessary for an effective human rights protection. It is also a question of equal treatment as the first case in which the new standards are applied also comes without a warning. It is generally accepted that the Convention is and has to be a living instrument, otherwise the human rights standards were quickly seen to be outdated and meaningless. But changes of long-standing jurisprudence necessarily create tensions with legal certainty. A very strict application of rule of law principles would require a more conservative interpretation and perhaps a slower path in developing new and far-reaching standards by the Court,

---

[70] ibid Dissenting Opinion of Judges Pejchal and Wojtyczek (14 December 2017) 2.
[71] *Orlandi* (n 69) 24:

> As to legal recognition of same-sex couples, the Court notes the movement that has continued to develop rapidly in Europe since the Court's judgment in *Schalk and Kopf* and continues to do so. Indeed at the time of the *Oliari and Others* judgment, there was already a thin majority of CoE states (twenty-four out of forty-seven) that had already legislated in favour of such recognition and the relevant protection. The same rapid development had been identified globally ...

The dissenters do not accept the relevance of those changes, Dissenting Opinion of Judges Pejchal and Wojtyczek (n 70):

> In our view, even identical societal developments in all States Parties to the Convention cannot alter the scope of their engagements under the Convention. This applied *a forteriori* to societal changes which occur in only some European States. Changes which occur in some States can never affect the scope of the other States' engagements.

[72] *Christine Goodwin v UK* ECtHR App no 8957/95 (2002).
[73] *Bayatyan v Armenia* ECtHR App no 23459/03 (2009).
[74] *Sergey Zolotukhin v Russia* ECtHR App no 14939/03 (2007).

for example by leaving transitional periods. This dilemma is clearly acknowledged by the Court:

> While it is in the interests of legal certainty, foreseeability and equality before the law that the Court should not depart, without good reason, from precedents laid down in previous cases, a failure by the Court to maintain a dynamic and evolutive approach would risk rendering it a bar to reform or improvement (see Vilho Eskelinen and Others v. Finland [GC], App no. 63235/00, § 56, ECHR 2007-II, and Micallef v. Malta [GC], App no. 17056/06, § 81, ECHR 2009). It is of crucial importance that the Convention is interpreted and applied in a manner which renders its rights practical and effective, not theoretical and illusory (see Stafford v. the United Kingdom [GC], App no. 46295/99, § 68, ECHR 2002-IV, and Christine Goodwin v. the United Kingdom [GC], App no. 28957/95, § 74, ECHR 2002-VI).[75]

The dilemma between progress and substantive justice on the one hand and legal certainty on the other hand has manifested itself most visibly in two recent judgments: in *Harkins v United Kingdom*[76] and in *Ireland v United Kingdom*.[77] Both cases concern the Court's duty to revisit binding judgments in the light of new jurisprudential developments. In 2012, the Court had decided in the cases *Harkins and Edwards v United Kingdom*[78] that the extradition to the United States where the applicants faced trial on charges carrying whole life sentences without parole did not violate the Convention. This jurisprudence was modified in the case *Trabelsi v Belgium*.[79] Nevertheless, the Court declined Harkins' second application based on the change in the jurisprudence as inadmissible and found:

> The Court's case-law is constantly evolving and if these jurisprudential developments were to permit unsuccessful applicants to reintroduce their complaints, final judgments would continually be called into question by the lodging of fresh applications. This would have the consequence of undermining ... credibility and authority of those judgments. Moreover, the principle of legal certainty would not apply equally to both parties, as only an applicant, on the basis of subsequent jurisprudential developments, would effectively be permitted to 'reopen' previously examined cases, provided that he or she were in a position to lodge a fresh application within the six-month time-limit.[80]

The finding in the case *Ireland v United Kingdom* was similar; the Court relied heavily on its judgments in the case *Harkins*. In dismissing the request for revision the Court once again put emphasis on legal certainty. The existence of a dilemma cannot be denied in such cases.

---

[75] *Bayatyan v Armenia* ECtHR App no 23459/03 (2009) 98.
[76] *Harkins v UK* ECtHR App no 71537/14 (2017).
[77] *Ireland v UK* (Request for revision) ECtHR App no 5310/71 (2018).
[78] *Harkins and Edwards v UK* ECtHR App no 9146/07 (2012).
[79] *Trabelsi v Belgium* App no ECtHR 140/10 (2014).
[80] *Harkins* (n 76) 56.

2. Malfunctioning of the Court because of its caseload

As is well known, the Court has practical problems in fulfilling the standards it defines for others. To a certain extent it does not and it cannot abide by some of its own standards of fair trial as set down in Article 6 of the Convention.

The most intractable problem is 'length of procedure'. Cases, especially when they are not qualified as 'priority' and come from the so-called high-count countries, are sometimes pending for more than ten years. One example out of many is the case *Feldman and Slovyanskyy Bank v Ukraine*,[81] brought to the Court in 2005 and decided in 2017. Twelve years—it cannot be denied that this is a violation of fair trial. There are a lot of explanations for this malfunctioning: too many applications,[82] not enough financial support for the Court,[83] no possibility to enlarge the system. How should forty-seven judges deal with applications coming from 800 million people, and this in times when human rights violations are widespread all over Europe? All that is true; it is not the Court's 'fault'. But the fact remains that the system does not function in such an exemplary way as it should.

The same applies to legal reasoning. Single judge decisions between 2010 and 2017 were published without reasoning. For sure, that was only an emergency measure. Starting from summer 2017 single judge decisions are reasoned, even if only in a short and succinct manner that might not be really satisfactory. Once again, the Court had to respond to outside needs, but was not (and could not be) exemplary.

The overall perception of the Court's work is still very positive. On the basis of what was explained above, it is, however, understandable that states ask for reforms.[84]

3. The Council of Europe—an agglomeration of false friends?

While the Court is in the centre of the system, it is not the only actor. The other very important actors are the member states. They are expected to be 'like-minded and to have a common heritage of political traditions, ideals, freedom and the rule of law'. Such are the solemn words in the preamble to the Convention.[85] It may be asked, however, if this is wishful thinking or matches reality. Is it true that the member states

---

[81] *Feldman and Slovyanskyy Bank v Ukraine* ECtHR App no 42758/05 (2017).

[82] After setting up the permanent Court in 1998 the number of applications on the Court's docket grew from 7,800 to a peak of 160,000 in 2011 and went down again to 56,200 in the end of 2017; see the analysis of the Court's statistics on the Court's website: <www.echr.coe.int/Documents/Stats_analysis_2017_ENG.pdf>.

[83] Since 2014 the budget of the Council of Europe has been subject to a policy of zero nominal growth and thus to a reduction in real terms. This has led to a loss of roughly twenty posts from the Court's budget.

[84] As explained above, this is mirrored in the discussion about the Copenhagen Declaration, on this issue: Roisin Pillay, 'The European Convention on Human Rights: The Draft Copenhagen Declaration and the Threat to the European Court' (2 March 2018) <http://opiniojuris.org/2018/03/02/33469/>; Antoine Buyse, 'The Draft Copenhagen Declaration—What about Civil Society?' (1 March 2018) <https://strasbourgobservers.com/2018/03/01/the-draft-copenhagen-declaration-what-about-civil-society/>; Mikael R Madsen and Jonas Christoffersen, 'The European Court of Human Rights' View of the Draft Copenhagen Declaration' (23 February 2018) <www.ejiltalk.org/the-european-court-of-human-rights-view-of-the-draft-copenhagen-declaration/>.

[85] Preamble of the ECHR, para 6.

are 'like-minded' when some of them are in conflict with one another—Georgia and Russia, Ukraine and Russia, Armenia and Azerbaijan, to mention just the most obvious and visible disputes? The Court accepts potential violations of Article 3 of the Convention—the prohibition of torture and inhuman treatment—when people are expelled or extradited not only to far-away non-European states, but also between member states to the Convention.[86] Is that a sign of 'common ideals'? Some of the member states openly refuse to fulfil their treaty obligations. One famous example is Russia, which does not accept to pay an outstanding debt of 21 million Euros for 2017 with the argument that the Russian delegates are denied their credentials in the Parliamentary Assembly—a measure that was taken in the aftermath of the Crimea crisis.[87] And, last but not least: What about the growing number of findings of violations of Article 18 of the Convention—is this to be interpreted as a sign of a lack of trust in the authorities of the member states?

It was already in 2014 that the Court had found that Mammadov was put in prison for what is called 'ulterior motives'. The Court considered that Mr Mammadov, who had a history of criticizing the government, had been arrested and detained without any evidence to reasonably suspect him of having committed the offence with which he was charged, namely that of having organized actions leading to public disorder. Further the Court concluded that the actual purpose of his detention had been to silence or punish Mr Mammadov for criticizing the government and publishing information it was trying to hide.[88]

At the end of 2017, the Committee of Ministers initiated for the first time the procedure under Article 46 para 4 of the Convention, a procedure newly introduced in Protocol No 14. The case is pending before the Grand Chamber of the Court.

Concerning Turkish cases, the Court is criticized for being too slow in dealing with the complaints and leaving too much room for subsidiarity.[89] Many observers raise doubts as to the effective functioning of the Court's control machinery—journalists, parliamentarians, and a constitutional court judge are incarcerated for months without any answer of the Court. But Rule 39 of the Rules of the Court, the mechanism for interlocutory decisions, is only applicable in cases of immediate threat to life and health. The Court is working on the complaints, but can decide only after communicating them and hearing the observations of both parties involved, and only after final decisions on the national level. This takes time and prompts discontent. In March 2018, however, the first judgments were handed down in cases concerning human rights violations

---

[86]   This is true eg for the expulsion and extradition of Chechens to Russia, eg *Shamayev and 12 Others v Georgia and Russia* ECtHR App no 36378/02 (2005).

[87]   See the Resolutions by the Parliamentary Assembly nos 1990 (2014), 2034 (2015), 2063 (2015) as well as the decision to suspend the voting rights of the Russian delegation, Doc no 13459 corr (24 March 2014); Lize R Glas, 'The Assembly's Row with Russia and its Repercussions for the Convention system' (30 October 2017) <https://strasbourgobservers.com/2017/10/30/the-assemblys-row-with-russia-and-its-repercussions-for-the-convention-system/>; Sonja Margolina, 'Im Reich des selbstbewussten Autoritarismus' (*Neu Züricher Zeitung*, 22 March 2018) <www.nzz.ch/meinung/im-reich-des-selbstbewussten-autoritarismus-ld.1365093>.

[88]   *Ilgar Mammadov v Azerbaijan* ECtHR App no 15172/13 (2014).

[89]   The criticism is mainly directed against a series of inadmissibility decisions: *Çatal v Turkey* ECtHR App no 2873/17 (2017); *Zihni v Turkey* ECtHR App no 59061/16 (2016); *Mercan v Turkey* ECtHR App no 56511/16 (2016); *Köksal v Turkey* ECtHR App no 70478/16 (2017), further: Wefing (n 11).

in Turkey after the putsch in 2016 with a very clear message: even in a state of emergency, every effort should be made to safeguard the values of a democratic society, such as pluralism, tolerance, and broadmindedness. Criticism of governments cannot be considered as assisting a terrorist organization. Turkey was thus found in violation of Articles 5 para 1 and 10 of the Convention.[90]

V. The Court in difficulties—a threat to rule of law in Europe?

While it is necessary to be aware of deficiencies, they have to be seen in context. The Court manages to decide about 70,000 cases a year and helps to uncover and to counteract injustice in countless cases; not least the Turkish cases decided in 2018 are a good example. There can be no doubt that the Convention system is functioning very well, even if it is not functioning as it would function in an ideal world.

Yet, not only human rights, but also the rule of law is at stake. A system that promises too much but is unable to keep all the promises might be even more problematic than a system that does not raise high hopes. Success obliges. For the Strasbourg system there is the danger of falling from a high pedestal.

Against this background it is necessary to ask if there might be a systemic problem. Perhaps the high hopes in the system were not only exaggerated, but false from the outset?

The clear answer to the question is: No. The high hopes were very well justified. What has been achieved over the decades, starting out from zero human rights protection in a devastated continent, is more than impressive. Nevertheless, some self-reflection, some self-criticism is necessary. It is like reaching adulthood—you need not lose your enthusiasm, but you might see clearer what is feasible and what is not.

First, multilateral human rights treaties based on mutual obligations have deficiencies in so far as the implementation of obligations is concerned. It is true that the Convention's execution system based on the Committee of Ministers' supervision is more effective than any other execution system of human rights treaties. Nevertheless, sanctions for non-implementation of binding judgments are rather lenient;[91] patience is needed.[92]

Furthermore, sanctions within the system of the Council of Europe may hit the wrong ones. One example might be seen in the present situation of the Court. As Russian deputies are denied their credentials and are excluded from the work in the Parliamentary

---

[90] *Sahin Alpay v Turkey* App no 16538/17 (2018); *Mehmet Hasan Altan v Turkey* ECtHR App no 13237/17 (2018).

[91] The execution procedure is mainly based on diplomatic sanctions such as the (repeated) adoption of resolutions by the Committee of Ministers or the initiation of the procedure under Art 46 para 4 ECHR. At the end of the process, there is, however, a real sanction, ie the suspension of the rights to representation and the request to withdraw from the Council of Europe (Art 8 Statute of the Council of Europe).

[92] The non-execution of some judgments is notorious; famous examples are *Hirst* (n 64); concerning Art 41: *Cyprus v Turkey* (n 9); *Ilgar Mammadov* (n 88); see above on the procedure under Art 46 para 4 of the Convention.

Assembly,[93] Russia reacts by no longer paying the contributions. There are thus important budgetary constraints for the Court. The contracts of lawyers working at the Court on a temporary basis might not be prolonged. Those who have to suffer from the consequences are the applicants whose cases are no longer dealt with speedily.

The last and most radical sanction against a member state would be exclusion from the Council of Europe.[94] As a consequence, those seeking human rights protection in Europe would suffer most as they would have nowhere to complain about human rights violations.

That is not to question the adequacy of an international treaty as a framework for a human rights protection system. Nevertheless, we are not dispensed from being aware of its inherent deficiencies.

Second, rule of law and human rights are intertwined, but sometimes it is necessary to sacrifice human rights in order to uphold the rule of law (especially legal certainty) or vice versa. As could be seen from the explanations given above the Court has expanded human rights protection beyond the explicit 'historical' consent given by the states—in its interpretation of the concept of jurisdiction as well as in its interpretation of substantive human rights guarantees. While accepting the concept of a 'living instrument' and thus the foreseeability of an ever larger interpretation of what was meant to be minimum standards, it is difficult to argue that radical changes in the case law or innovative approaches would not upset legal certainty.

Another conflict between rule of law and human rights is unavoidable in so far as the reaction to the non-fulfilment of treaty obligations is concerned. Law must be taken seriously. If the gap between what is laid down in law and what is implemented gets too big, credibility is lost. Thus, the rule of law would require restricting the membership in the 'human rights club' to those who are willing to implement the rights guaranteed. For the sake of an effective human rights protection it is, however, desirable to remain patient even with those not always living up to their treaty obligations.

Third, the Court has to be aware of the fact that it exerts control over the member states' implementation of the Convention, but is hardly controllable and controlled from outside. While two corrective mechanisms, the referral of cases to the Grand Chamber and the reversal of the jurisprudence, can be triggered from outside, the effectiveness of these mechanisms depends on the Court's responsiveness and self-criticism in respect of the states' arguments. The 'dialogue of judges' and the openness for divergent positions are therefore necessary and helpful. Theoretically, it would also be possible to

---

[93] Resolutions nos 1990 (2014), 2034 (2015), 2063 (2015) and Doc no 13459 corr (24 March 2014) (n 87); further: Glas (n 87); Margolina (n 87).

[94] Art 8 of the Statute of the Council of Europe:

> Any member of the Council of Europe which has seriously violated Article 3 may be suspended from its rights of representation and requested by the Committee of Ministers to withdraw under Article 7. If such member does not comply with this request, the Committee may decide that it has ceased to be a member of the Council as from such date as the Committee may determine.

With Art 58 para 3 ECHR:

> Any High Contracting Party which shall cease to be a member of the Council of Europe shall cease to be a Party to this Convention under the same conditions.

change the text of the Convention and the Protocols. That is, however, unlike changes to a Constitution, in practice not a promising mechanism. Currently, member states under the Danish chairmanship are trying out another path and reflecting on some sort of feedback—negative or positive—of the states towards the Court.[95] It is clear, however, that the executive cannot control the Court, nor can political debates exert direct influence on judicial work.

VI. Solving the potential dilemma between human rights and rule of law

What is demanded is a sort of 'realpolitik' in human rights law. The Court can be proud of its achievements in human rights protection. But it cannot ignore that this progress came at a certain price; legal certainty could not always rank first, but sometimes ranked second. As long as everybody wholeheartedly welcomes progress in human rights protection—as was the case in the 1990s—those who have to pay the price, the states, would not complain. In an environment that is more and more critical towards human rights, they do complain. Governments complain in the political arena, national courts decide not to follow the Court, the media pick out and attack judgments they dislike. The Court has to listen carefully to criticism, which is not per se hostile to human rights, but puts the finger on shortcomings. A human rights protection system can only function with the support of those concerned. The Court is not *l'art pour l'art*, but it has obligations towards individuals and towards states.

To paraphrase Churchill who famously held that 'democracy is the worst form of government, except for all the others' we may say: A human rights treaty with a Court as a supervisory organ is the worst form of human rights protection, except for all the others. Churchill's dry British humour may help us to give adequate answers to present threats: With the 'worst system'—'except for all the others'—a lot of good things have been achieved and will—hopefully—be achieved in the future.

---

[95] Thus, the first draft of the Copenhagen Declaration contained the following idea in para 41:

... encourages States Parties to discuss the general development of areas of the Court's case law of particular interest to them and, if appropriate, adopt texts expressing their general views. Such discussions, as well as possible texts adopted, may be useful for the Court as means of better understanding the views and positions of States Parties. Such discussions should respect the independence of the Court.

11

How Should the European Court of Human Rights Respond to Criticism?

Comment on Angelika Nußberger

Geir Ulfstein*

The number and importance of international courts have increased. The rise of the international judiciary gives hope for a world progressively governed by law. However, the international judicialization has recently become the subject of criticism. States complain that international courts represent too much internationalization and legalization, at the expense of national sovereign freedoms. The international courts face the dilemma whether they should resist the criticism or adapt their practices.

Angelika Nußberger, a vice-president of the European Court of Human Rights (ECtHR, or the Court), should be commended for sharing her knowledge, as an insider of the Court, about the developments of the ECtHR and the criticism facing the Court. She also presents ideas how it should address such critique.

Judge Nußberger recounts the grand ideas of the founders of the Court, but also the restrictive attitudes of the member states towards the adoption of the European Convention on Human Rights (ECHR, or the Convention). It is interesting to note that through its practice—including some groundbreaking cases in the 1970s—the Court has fulfilled the visions of its founders to a great extent.

However, the ECtHR has encountered resistance from populist movements as well as from increasingly authoritarian regimes in Central and East Europe and in Turkey. What is more, the Court is also criticized by some of the governments that traditionally have been among its supporters. For example, the Danish government urged member states to reign in the Court by proposing a dramatic extension of the 'margin of appreciation' and by more control through political 'dialogue'. These proposals were rejected in the Copenhagen Declaration, adopted by the Committee of Ministers' High-Level Conference on 13 April 2018.[1]

* This contribution was also supported by the Research Council of Norway through its Centres of Excellence Funding Scheme, project number 223274 PluriCourts—the Legitimacy of the International Judiciary.

[1] 'Copenhagen Declaration' (Committee of Ministers' High-Level Conference, Copenhagen, April 2018) <https://rm.coe.int/copenhagen-declaration/16807b915c> accessed 29 August 2018; see Geir Ulfstein and Andreas Follesdal, 'Copenhagen—Much Ado about Little?' (*EJIL: Talk!*, 14 April 2018) <www.ejiltalk.org/copenhagen-much-ado-about-little/> accessed 29 August 2019.

Nußberger advises us to distinguish between good and bad faith criticism. Both forms of critique 'have to be taken seriously, but different answers are needed. While the latter is mainly an issue for politics, the former has to be analysed in depth. In so far as it uncovers deficiencies in the system, they have to be adequately addressed, and, if possible, corrected.' She notices that the Court has been caught in the dilemma of living up to very different expectations: some want it to change society, others want it to guarantee stability.

In this context, she asks: Is it really true that human rights and the rule of law always go hand in hand? Or may extensive protection of human rights occur at the cost of the rule of law? What should be responses by the Court to the critique?

I. Human rights and the rule of law

The ECtHR may both be a provider of and subject to the rule of law. Nußberger points to 'the double link between the Strasbourg system of human rights protection and rule of law. On the one hand the Court contributes to developing the concept of rule of law by elaborating standards on the basis of concrete cases. On the other hand the Court is a major player in the international legal system and has to abide itself by the principles it develops.'[2] Her main concern is how the Court itself should live up to the standards it requires from the member states.

The rule of law is understood by Nußberger as including the elements set out by Lord Bingham in his book *Rule of Law*, as well as the similar elements enumerated by the Venice Commission in a Rule of Law Checklist. She says that '[t]he starting point can be a negative one: Rule of law is the opposite of arbitrariness. It comprises elements such as independence of the judiciary, legal certainty, procedural guarantees, *nulla poena sine lege, ne bis in idem* etc.'[3]

Nußberger does not cover all these elements. She refers to the malfunction of the Court due to its heavy caseload, which has led to lengthy procedures and thus violation of the principle of fair trial. The workload has also resulted in the initial lack of reasoning in judgments by single judges (2010–17), and brief reasoning by these judges from 2017 (section IV.2). She also reiterates selective domestic implementation of judgments, due to the diversity of values between member states, especially between the traditional members and the new members in Central and Eastern Europe and Turkey (section IV.3).

However, her analysis is primarily restricted to the fact that 'the dynamics inherent in the Convention system can pose a problem to legal certainty'.[4] My comments concern the potential tensions between the protection of human rights and securing legal certainty.

---

[2] Angelika Nußberger, 'From High Hopes to Scepticism? Human Rights Protection and Rule of Law in Europe in an Ever More Hostile Environment' in this book, I.

[3] ibid II.2.

[4] ibid IV.1.

II. **Human rights as** *lex specialis*

Nußberger discusses several areas where the Court has been innovative in its interpretation and has encountered criticism, or even resistance. This includes the effects of reservations to the ECHR and the extra-territorial application of the Convention. The Court has also been criticized for intrusion in parliamentarian sovereignty: a well-known example is the judgments on prohibition of prisoners' voting rights. Further, the ECtHR has challenged traditional values in some Eastern European countries, especially the Russian Federation, in its case law on homosexuals' rights. Finally, there are several examples of the Court changing its previous practice, such as the *Zolotukhin* case,[5] where a new standard by the Court on '*ne bis in idem*' was applied to instances before this standard was adopted.

How should these inventive approaches by the Court be assessed in light of the rule of law? Nußberger argues that the Court in many cases 'had to opt either for a "conservative" approach in line with traditional concepts of international law or for an "innovative" approach developing international human rights law as a sort of "lex specialis".[6]

In this context, the reference to *lex specialis* could have two different meanings: it might represent interpretations in violation of general public international law and/or the principles of interpretation set out in the 1969 Vienna Convention on the Law of Treaties (VCLT)—or developing ECHR as a specialized field within the broader field of international law.

Much focus has been on the Court's challenge to well-established opinion regarding the effects of reservations to treaties. However, the *Belilos* [Plenary] case [7] and the Court's subsequent practice on this issue is an example of its influence on general international law.[8] We have also, in recent jurisprudence, seen that the Court attempts to accommodate the need for a practical and effective interpretation of the Convention and respect for general international law. Examples are *Hassan*[9] on the relationship between the ECHR and international humanitarian law, and *Al-Dulimi*[10] on obligations following from UN Security Council resolutions and the rights set out in the ECHR.

The Court has addressed the VCLT rules of interpretation in several cases. For example, in *Demir and Baykara*, the Court stated that it is 'guided mainly by the rules of interpretation provided for in Articles 31 to 33 of the Vienna Convention on the Law of Treaties'. This is followed by the standard formulation that '[s]ince the Convention is first and foremost a system for the protection of human rights, the Court must interpret and apply it in a manner which renders its rights practical and effective, not theoretical and illusory'.[11] However, in recent case law, the Court has seen no contradiction

---

[5] *Sergey Zolotukhin v Russia* ECtHR App no 14939/03 (2009).
[6] Nußberger (n 2) IV.1.
[7] *Belilos v Switzerland* ECtHR App no 10328/83 (1988).
[8] See International Law Commission, 'Guide to Practice on Reservations to Treaties' (2011) Rule 4.5.3. <legal.un.org/ilc/texts/instruments/english/draft_articles/1_8_2011.pdf> accessed 31 August 2018; Edward T Swaine, 'Treaty Reservations' in Duncan B Hollis (ed), *The Oxford Guide to Treaties* (Oxford University Press 2012) 277, 298.
[9] *Hassan v the United Kingdom* [GC] ECtHR App no 29750/09 (2014).
[10] *Al-Dulimi and Montana Management Inc. v Switzerland* [GC] ECtHR App no 5809/08 (2016).
[11] *Demir and Baykara v Turkey* ECtHR App no 34503/97 (2008) paras 65–66.

between a 'practical and effective' interpretation and applying the accepted canons of interpretation. Thus, the Court said in *Cyprus v Turkey* that '[d]espite its specific character as a human rights instrument, the Convention is an international treaty to be interpreted in accordance with the relevant norms and principles of public international law, and, in particular, in the light of the Vienna Convention on the Law of Treaties'.[12]

It is also important that both effective and evolutive ('living instrument') interpretations are acknowledged parts of treaty interpretation. The International Court of Justice (ICJ) has held that the principle of effectiveness is 'one of the fundamental principles of interpretation of treaties'.[13] The ICJ has also accepted that the interpretation of a treaty can change on the basis of the evolutive intention of the states parties at the time of the treaty's adoption.[14] Thus, the Court is not interpreting the ECHR as a form of *lex specialis* in violation of generally accepted principles of interpretation. However, as I will come back to, one can discuss how far the Court should go in its effective and evolutive interpretation.

III. Human rights and legal certainty

While the Court's practice may not violate international law, it is nonetheless interesting to consider to what extent its use of effective and evolutive interpretation challenges ideas of legal certainty as an aspect of the rule of law. Nußberger discusses, with good reason, the difficulties arising from the Court's changes in its jurisprudence, such as the abovementioned new standards on '*ne bis in idem*' represented by the *Zolotukhin* case. It is easy to understand that member states complain of retroactivity when such standards are applied in subsequent judgments to facts that had arisen before this case.

On the other hand, it seems that the states' criticism of effective and evolutive interpretation is not primarily about such issues of alleged retroactivity. Nor is it necessarily about whether the judgments represent changes in earlier case law. The critique may also arise for issues that have not earlier been dealt with by the Court, such as prisoners' voting rights. In such cases, issues about retroactivity and legal certainty as elements of the rule of law do not arise.

However, the member states' prime concern should rather be seen in the context of too much intrusion by the Court in national sovereign freedom. This is hardly a question about the rule of law or legal certainty, but about how far the Court in its *interpretation* stretches the substantive scope of the Convention, and to what extent it reviews domestic *implementation* under its margin of appreciation; as well as the legal reasoning underlying its interpretation and implementation review.

---

[12] *Cyprus v Turkey* ECtHR App no 25781/94 (2014) para 23 (emphasis added).

[13] *Case Concerning the Territorial Dispute* (Libyan Arab Jamahiriya v Chad) ICJ Judgment 3 February 1994, para 6 at 25; on effective interpretation: Richard Gardiner, *Treaty Interpretation* (2nd edn, Oxford University Press 2015) 179–811.

[14] *Case Concerning the Dispute Regarding Navigational and Related Rights* (Costa Rica v Nicaragua) ICJ Judgment 13 July 2009, para 64; Eirik Bjorge, *The Evolutionary Interpretation of Treaties* (Oxford University Press 2014).

IV. A role for 'realpolitik'?

Nußberger's overall conclusion is that the ECtHR system functions well. The high hopes to the Court were not false. Nevertheless, some self-reflection and self-criticism are necessary. She recommends that the Court should listen carefully to criticism which is not per se hostile to human rights but puts its finger on shortcomings.

What she suggests is a sort of realpolitik in human rights law. This could be interpreted as a recommendation that the ECHR should become some form of a policy organ. Yet, this is not the way to interpret Nußberger. On the contrary, she argues for more respect for the rule of law, especially in the form of legal certainty.

However, if we accept that the most important concern of member states is not about respect for legal certainty, but about how far the Court should go in its effective and evolutive interpretation, the following questions arise: How far should the Court go in its interpretation? How should it practice the margin of appreciation? What about the quality of the Court's legal reasoning?

V. Effective and evolutive interpretation

It may be difficult to distinguish between what should be considered effective and what is evolutive interpretation. The examples Nußberger mentions about the effects of reservations, extra-territorial application of the Convention, prisoners' voting rights, and challenges to traditional values in some Eastern European countries, may have elements of both effective and evolutive interpretation.

There is not much disagreement about the need for judgments that are 'practical and effective'—even if they should be met with strong domestic resistance, as in the case of discrimination against homosexuals in the Russian Federation. The Court may even have to stand up against more collective anti-human rights tendencies, for example in counter-terrorism measures. As acknowledged in the Copenhagen Declaration, the ECHR needs also to be interpreted in accordance with 'present-day conditions',[15] that means evolutive interpretation.

However, a couple of caveats should be added. First, the Court should restrict the Convention's scope in issues of a more mundane character. One recent example is the *Cuenca Zarzoso* case.[16] The applicant complained of noise caused by bars, pubs, and discotheques in the vicinity of his home. The Court concluded that Spain had 'failed to discharge its positive obligation to guarantee the applicant's right to respect for his home and his private life, in breach of Article 8 of the Convention'.[17] It may be questioned whether such issues merit protection by an international human rights court, like the ECtHR.

---

[15] Copenhagen Declaration (n 1) para 26.
[16] *Cuenca Zarzoso v Spain* ECtHR App no 23383/12 (2018).
[17] ibid para 51.

Furthermore, the Court should, through its reasoning, demonstrate that it acts as a judicial organ, and not as a legislator in its evolutive interpretation. For instance, the Court has in its case law not been consistent with respect to the required 'European consensus' in applying the ECHR as a 'living instrument'. In *Magyar Helsinki Bizottság* the Court said that it may have regard to developments in domestic legal systems indicating a '*uniform* or *common* approach or a *developing consensus* between the Contracting States in a given area'.[18] The Court also speaks of a '*broad consensus*'.[19] In *Naït-Liman*, the Court stated that it may assess whether there exists a ' "*European consensus*" or at least *a certain trend* among the member States'.[20]

The discretionary freedom is even more outspoken when it comes to the use of international material. In the *Rantsev* case, the Court referred to practice by the International Criminal Tribunal for the former Yugoslavia (ICTY), but also to the Protocol to Prevent, Suppress and Punish Trafficking in Persons, especially Women and Children (the Palermo Protocol) and the European Convention on Action against Trafficking in Human Beings (the Anti-Trafficking Convention) in its interpretation of slavery, servitude, or forced and compulsory labour under Article 4.[21] But it did not explain the importance of these instruments and the judicial practice for the interpretation of the ECHR. Instead, it seems that the Court preferred to keep the influence of such instruments extremely vague and to allow itself absolute discretion. Such discretion has explicitly been confirmed by the *Tănase*, the *Kiyutin*, and, most recently, in the *A.-M.V.* cases. In all three cases, the Courts said: 'It is for the Court to decide which international instruments and reports it considers relevant and how much weight to attribute to them.'[22] The different standards applied by the Court in determining European consensus and its preferred discretionary freedom in using international instruments may make the Court vulnerable to criticism of unjustified activism—besides undermining legal certainty as an aspect of the rule of law.

VI. The margin of appreciation

The Court has two ways of alleviating the concerns of member states about too much intrusion in national sovereignty. As already discussed, it may restrict the substantive scope of the ECHR by limiting the effective and evolutive interpretation of the Convention. Or it may leave discretion to the states on domestic implementation of the ECHR through the margin of interpretation.

National decision-making organs may enjoy a wider margin of appreciation if they are able to convince the ECtHR that they have taken into account relevant principles of

---

[18] *Magyar Helsinki Bizottság v Hungary* [GC] ECtHR App no 18030/1 (2016) para 138 (emphasis added).
[19] ibid para 139 (emphasis added).
[20] *Naït-Liman v Switzerland* [GC] ECtHR App no 51357/07 (2018) para 175 (emphasis added).
[21] *Rantsev v Cyprus and Russia* ECtHR App no 25965/04, paras 278–80 (7 January 2010).
[22] *Tănase v Moldova* [GC] ECtHR App no 7/08 (2010) para 176; *Kiyutin v Russia* ECtHR App no 2700/10 (2011) para 67; *A.-M.V. v Finland* ECtHR App no 53251/13 (2017).

interpretation, such as the principle of proportionality, as applied by the ECtHR. The Court stated for example in the *von Hannover (No 2)* case that '[w]here the balancing exercise has been undertaken by the national authorities in conformity with the criteria laid down in the Court's case-law, the Court would require strong reasons to substitute its view for that of the domestic courts.'[23]

States seem to be satisfied with the *von Hannover* approach. The Copenhagen Declaration applauds the Court for, in judgments dealing with Articles such as 8–11, generally not substituting 'its own assessment for that of domestic courts, unless there are strong reasons for doing so' if a balancing exercise has been undertaken at the national level 'in conformity with the criteria laid down in the Court's jurisprudence.'[24] It is of importance that the Court in its recent case law also has designated instances of bad faith implementation of ECHR standards. In such instances, the relevant states will not benefit from the deference represented by the margin of appreciation.[25]

However, it is essential that the freedom granted to states should not undermine effective protection of ECHR rights. This is reiterated in the Copenhagen Declaration, setting out that 'strengthening the principle of subsidiarity is not intended to limit or weaken human rights protection.'[26] Nor should the Court abdicate from its role in establishing precedents, not least in its interpretation of the Convention as a living instrument. The Court should also ensure that national variations in the implementation of the ECHR does not threaten the consistent interpretation of the Convention, and thereby threatening legal certainty and the rule of law.

VII. Conclusions

The Court will continue to face critique. This is to some extent an inevitable consequence of its mandate in controlling member states' exercise of the legislative, executive, and judicial powers. However, some of the challenges to the Court's practice may have ramifications that are more dramatic, such as selective domestic implementation of the Court's judgments and even defection from the Court.

I agree with Judge Nußberger in the fundamental importance of the Court respecting the rule of law. Yet, the main worry of some states is that the Court intrudes too much in sovereign freedoms. There are two ways to alleviate this concern. The Court could apply a less expansive and dynamic interpretation of the Convention. Or it could leave more discretion to states in their domestic interpretation, through the margin of appreciation. It is also important that judgments are based on sound legal reasoning.

I have argued that the Court, in its effective interpretation, should avoid interfering in issues that are not of such a gravity to merit international supervision. In its

---

[23]   *von Hannover v Germany (No 2)* ECtHR App nos 40660/08 and 60641/08 (2012) para 107.
[24]   Copenhagen Declaration (n 1) para 28 c.
[25]   B Çalı, 'Coping with Crisis: Whither the Variable Geometry in the Jurisprudence the European Court of Human Rights?' (2018) 35 Wisconsin International Law Journal 237, 269.
[26]   Copenhagen Declaration (n 1) para 10.

evolutive interpretation, the Court should also clarify its use of a European consensus and abandon its unfettered discretion in using international legal instruments for this purpose. This could alleviate uneasiness with respect to the ECtHR as an activist Court.

The Copenhagen Declaration commends the Court for its use of the margin of appreciation. The Court must treat states equally with respect to benefitting from the margin. However, it is also essential for the Court to ensure that deference to domestic decision-makers does not undermine effective implementation of the ECHR.

PART IV
SYSTEM-ORIENTED PERSPECTIVES

12

Is Compliance an Indicator for the State of International Law?

Exploring the 'Compliance Trilemma'

Jeffrey L Dunoff*

Is international law on the rise, or has it entered a period of decline? At this moment, to many the answer is clear. As this book goes to press, a US President threatens to terminate important treaties and defund key international institutions, and nationalist parties deeply suspicious of multilateralism are ascendant in Europe, Asia, and elsewhere. Stepping back from recent electoral developments, many take the international community's inability to halt Syria's civil war, reverse Russia's annexation of the Crimea, or resolve the multiple crises that threaten the European Union (EU), to signal that efforts to create an international order based on the rule of law are in retreat. Others cite reversals at existing international institutions, such as the United Kingdom's decision to exit from the European Union and several African states' withdrawals from the International Criminal Court; the breakdown of efforts to forge new multilateral agreements, as at the World Trade Organization (WTO); and a general diffusion of power and influence from 'rule of law' states to those historically suspicious of ambitious international legal norms, and conclude that the legal order that made possible the accomplishments of liberal internationalism is under siege.

A more sanguine view holds that, as a discipline, international law has long lurched from crisis to crisis. Moreover, dramatic changes in the international order often give rise to new, and often stronger, versions of international law. These competing perspectives raise the question of how one could determine whether widespread anxieties at this time regarding international law's future are well founded. To the extent recent developments reveal a pattern, is the pattern better understood as cyclical or linear? In light of the nature of current challenges, are things different this time?

* I am grateful to Eyal Benvenisti, Dan Bodansky, Jutta Brunnée, Sarah Cleveland, Meg deGuzman, Craig Green, Duncan Hollis, Heike Krieger, Georg Nolte, Mark Pollack, Joel Trachtman, and Michael Zürn for comments on earlier drafts. Some arguments in this chapter draw on collaborative research undertaken with Mark Pollack.

This chapter examines the utility of using compliance—understood as behaviour consistent with applicable rules of international law—as an indicator for the state of international law.[1] To do so, it proceeds in three sections. Section I assumes, arguendo, that compliance is an appropriate marker of international law's influence, and outlines practical and theoretical difficulties associated with measuring and comparing compliance rates. Section II examines whether compliance is an appropriate measure of international law's status in international affairs. Specifically, it explores whether compliance fully captures the effects of contemporary international law, and whether higher compliance rates are necessarily associated with a stronger or more vibrant international rule of law.

Questioning the utility of using compliance as a *direct* indicator of international law's vigour is *not* equivalent to claiming that compliance is irrelevant to determining the status of international law. Thus, Section III provides an alternative account of why compliance is relevant to evaluating the status of contemporary international law. In particular, it develops a claim that, across many domains, contemporary international law faces a 'compliance trilemma'. That is, in many instances, the actors who wish to construct an international rule of law often pursue the goals of (1) widespread participation, (2) ambitious legal norms, and (3) high rates of compliance.[2] However, it is often possible to achieve, at most, two of these goals, giving rise to the trilemma. Hence, compliance remains an important subject of study; not because standing alone it is an accurate indicator of the role of international law in contemporary international affairs, but because efforts to construct an international rule of law confront inescapable trade-offs between pursuit of heightened compliance and other desirable outcomes, such as increased participation and increased depth of international legal norms. A brief conclusion follows.

I. Compliance as an indicator: Empirical and methodological challenges

In recent years, the use of indicators has proliferated across diverse areas of law and policy. The ongoing attempts to define one hundred global monitoring indicators for the Sustainable Development Goals, the United Nations High Commissioner for Human Rights' efforts to measure respect for human rights, and the World Bank's

---

[1] I follow the book's introduction in understanding compliance as adherence to law. Heike Krieger and Georg Nolte, 'The International Rule of Law—Rise or Decline?—Approaching Current Foundational Challenges' in this book ('compliance-based understanding of [the international rule of law] focuses on adherence to the law'). For alternative conceptualizations of compliance: Benedict Kingsbury, 'The Concept of Compliance as a Function of Competing Conceptions of International Law' (1998) 19 Michigan Journal of International Law 345.

[2] This is a broad genaralization and, of course, goals vary in different contexts. E.g., a fact pattern involving navigation rights on a river shared by two states requires the participation of those two states, and there is no need to seek any wider participation. Moreover, many international legal regimes are *constitutive* as opposed to *regulative*; the notion of compliance may be less applicable in these contexts. That said, across many international regulatory regimes, and particularly in the dense regulatory regimes that mark modern international law, the generalization holds.

Worldwide Governance Indicators project are just a few of the most visible examples of a broad drive to mainstream standardized and quantifiable measures into political and legal discourse.

Notably, international legal scholars and practitioners have not been at the centre of this 'measurement revolution'. While they sometimes empirically analyse the behavioural impact of certain treaties, or compliance with particular rules, decisions, or tribunals, by and large they have not devoted substantial attention to developing or analysing system-wide measurements or indices.[3] The failure to do so, however, is not without consequences. International lawyers' relative inattention to data can lead to failures to recognize important trends, result in misguided strategies, and reduce their ability to influence public debate. Given these non-trivial costs, should international lawyers use compliance as an indicator of international law's role in the current global order?

Any effort to use compliance as an indicator will confront a series of practical difficulties. *First*, the use of any indicator presupposes accurate and reliable data. It is often difficult, however, to determine whether particular incidents should be considered cases of compliance or non-compliance. Given the decentralized processes of much international law-making, it is not always easy, or sometimes even possible, to identify the applicable rule of law.[4] Even when we can identify a specific rule, these rules are the result of negotiation and compromise, and often drafted to accommodate a range of interpretations, rendering compliance determinations difficult. For example, whether a particular governmental act violates 'fair and equitable treatment', or unlawfully 'discriminates' against an individual, rarely admits of a straightforward answer, and many such questions are never resolved by a tribunal or other authoritative body. Moreover, the very structure of some legal rules—such as the considerable number of important human rights which are to be progressively realized over time—renders it difficult to measure compliance rates. Hence, compliance questions rarely lend themselves to clear, binary determinations, and we therefore lack reliable and accurate data on compliance across many domains of international law. Indeed, even in areas where the use of data and indicators is most advanced, such as human rights,[5] it remains extremely difficult to obtain accurate data about numbers of violations in any particular state in any particular year.

Second, any effort to construct an indicator out of raw data encounters an additional set of challenges. For example, many indices raise questions of social science 'validity', in the sense that the available data do not always measure the legal phenomena they purport to measure. Consider one example from the Cingranelli-Richards (CIRI)

---

[3] For one notable exception see: Kevin Davis, Angelina Fisher, and Sally Engle Merry (eds), *Governance by Indicators: Global Power Through Quantification and Rankings* (Oxford University Press 2012).

[4] James Crawford and Thomas Viles, 'International Law on a Given Day' in James Crawford (ed), *International Law as an Open System: Selected Essays* (Cameron and May 2002) 69, 89 ('we cannot tell what all of international law was on a given day until after that day').

[5] eg Office of the High Commissioner for Human Rights, 'Human Rights Indicators: A Guide to Measurement and Implementation' (2012) UN Doc HR/PUB/12/5.

Human Rights Dataset, a frequently used index that purports to measure and rank state compliance with numerous human rights norms, including torture. The CIRI index defines torture as:

> the purposeful inflicting of extreme pain ... by government officials .... Torture includes the use of physical and other force by police and prison guards that is cruel, inhuman or degrading. This also includes deaths in custody due to negligence by government officials.[6]

The CIRI definition of torture differs in several key respects from that found in the Convention against Torture (CAT),[7] not least of which being that CIRI includes 'cruel, inhuman and degrading' treatment as a form of torture while the CAT distinguishes these into two different categories of unlawful conduct. Hence, while many acts would surely qualify as torture under virtually any definition, there is substantial reason to question whether the CIRI scores are valid, in the sense of accurately measuring compliance with the international legal norms that they purport to measure.

These difficulties multiply when we move from measuring compliance with a particular rule (eg the prohibition on torture) to compliance with the totality of rules that constitute an international legal regime (eg compliance with international human rights), let alone to compliance with international law as such. Specifically, any effort to create an aggregated index of compliance with regime norms runs a substantial risk of eliding significant variation in compliance rates for different norms. For example, the average CIRI physical integrity index score for 162 states from 1981 to 2006 is relatively constant, suggesting little change in state respect for physical integrity rights during this time period. However, if this index is disaggregated into its component parts, a different story emerges. Specifically, the relatively static average masks increases in respect for human rights in some states, and decreases in respect for human rights in others. Moreover, the flat average score masks declines in respect for certain rights, such as the right not to be tortured, and marked improvements in respect for other rights, such as the right not to be imprisoned for one's political beliefs.[8] Aggregating across multiple states and multiple rights has the effect of cancelling out these changes, and creating

---

[6] David L Cingranelli and David L Richards, 'Short Variable Descriptions for Indicators in the Cingranelli-Richards (CIRI) Human Rights Dataset' (CIRI Human Rights Data Project) <www.humanrightsdata.com> accessed 16 July 2018.

[7] The Torture Convention defines torture as:

> 'any act by which severe pain or suffering [...] is intentionally inflicted on a person for such purposes as obtaining from him or a third person information or a confession, punishing him for an act he or a third person has committed or is suspected of having committed, or intimidating or coercing him or a third person, or for any reason based on discrimination of any kind, when such pain or suffering is inflicted by [a public official].'

Convention against Torture and Other Cruel, Inhuman or Degrading Treatment or Punishment, UNGA Res 39/46 (10 December 1984), Annex, 39 UN GAOR Supp No 51, UN Doc A/39/51.

[8] This argument is drawn from David L Cingranelli and David L Richards, 'The Cingranelli and Richards (CIRI) Human Rights Data Project' (2010) 32 Human Rights Quarterly 401.

the misimpression that respect for physical integrity rights has not changed during the relevant time period. Efforts to aggregate at even higher levels of generality, such as levels of compliance with human rights norms in general, or with international law in general, risks exacerbating this effect.

Third, even if one had perfect data and could accurately assess trends in compliance over time, there are often substantial limits to the causal claims that can be drawn. Specifically, researchers would need to determine the extent to which changes in compliance over time are attributable to changes in the international rule of law, as opposed to other factors. It is difficult to answer this question of attribution with any degree of confidence. Consider, by way of example, the empirical research on human rights treaties. Much of this research is *correlational*; many studies look at respect for human rights before and after treaty ratification, or compare practices of states that join a treaty regime with those of comparable states that did not do so. In general, these studies can reveal that one process, such as ratification of a treaty, relates systematically to another process, such as respecting one or another right. But these studies generally do not prove causation, or that one process has produced another.

To be sure, recent years have witnessed a substantial—and welcome—increase in the amount and quality of data relevant to compliance. And the point emphatically is *not* that scholars should abandon efforts to generate data regarding compliance with international law, or that efforts to create indices related to international law are inevitably flawed. But the considerations reviewed above do suggest that scholars should be sceptical of the seeming precision of indices and should use them only with full awareness of their substantial limitations, as well as their more readily apparent strengths.

II. Is compliance an accurate proxy for the status of international law?

The arguments outlined above can be understood as an 'internal' critique—they accept, *arguendo*, that compliance is an important variable to measure and analyse, but detail some of the difficulties associated with these tasks. The arguments that follow, in contrast, challenge the strategy of foregrounding compliance as an indicator for the state of international law. First, compliance may not serve as an accurate or valid proxy for the status of international law insofar as it may not fully capture the various ways that international law works in the contemporary international domain. Hence a focus on compliance is substantially under-inclusive, as it misses much of international law's impact in contemporary global society. A stronger claim is that compliance rates are unrelated to, and therefore *not* a useful proxy for, other and more important dimensions of international law that we should care about, such as international law's effectiveness. Finally, certain forms of non-compliance may serve to strengthen, rather than undermine, the international legal order. Let us briefly consider each claim in turn.

1. Beyond compliance

Using compliance—state behaviour consistent with applicable international legal rules—as a proxy for the status of international law can be misleading if the concept of compliance fails adequately to account for the diverse ways that international law impacts behaviour, and the various actors that international law can affect. Virtually every study of compliance cites Louis Henkin's dictum that 'almost all nations observe almost all principles of international law and almost all of their obligations almost all of the time'.[9] Few, however, note that Henkin also urged international lawyers to 'think beyond the substantive rules of law to the function of law, the nature of its influence, the opportunities it offers, the limitations it imposes'.[10] Adopting this advice, legal scholars have long understood that international law's impact is not fully captured by measuring compliance. In the 1970s, for example, Abram Chayes emphasized that international law importantly serves 'as a basis of justification or legitimation for action'.[11] International relations (IR) scholars likewise emphasize international law's role as a justificatory discourse. For example, Ian Hurd argues that international law 'provides political resources with which states and other actors legitimate and delegitimate contending policies'.[12] Other IR scholars even go so far as to claim that 'such communicative dynamics may tell us far more about how robust a regime is than overt behaviour alone'.[13] From this perspective, 'the preoccupation with the "violation" of norms as the beginning, middle, and end of the compliance story', appears profoundly misguided.[14]

Moreover, much international law has a 'constitutive', rather than a regulatory, character.[15] International legal norms, such as those regarding statehood or sovereign equality, help to define the relevant actors and shape their identities and interests. Constitutive rules shape the broad contours of world politics, without which those politics would make little sense. Constitutive rules thus have a fundamental influence on outcomes without necessarily exerting any direct causal impact on any specific decision.[16]

In a recent paper, Robert Howse and Ruti Teitel enumerated several effects of international law beyond inducing states to conform their behaviour to international rules.[17] These include:

- providing benchmarks for a wide range of private actors, even when the relevant norms are not formally binding on those actors. For example, the Paris Climate

---

[9] Louis Henkin, *How Nations Behave* (2nd edn, Columbia University Press 1979) 47.

[10] ibid 4–5.

[11] Abram Chayes, *The Cuban Missile Crisis: International Crises and the Role of Law* (Oxford University Press 1974)

[12] Ian Hurd, 'The International Rule of Law: Law and the Limit of Politics' (2014) 28 Ethics and International Affairs 39.

[13] Friedrich V Kratochwil and John Ruggie, 'International Organization: A State of the Art on an Art of the State' (1986) 40 International Organization 753.

[14] ibid 768.

[15] eg Ian Hurd, *How to Do Things with International Law* (Princeton University Press 2017)

[16] Friedrich V Kratochwil, 'How Do Norms Matter' in Michael Byers (ed), *The Role of Law in International Politics: Essays in International Relations and International Law* (Oxford University Press 2000) 37.

[17] Robert Howse and Ruti Teitel, 'Beyond Compliance: Rethinking Why International Law Really Matters' (2010) 1 Global Politics 127.

Accord does not directly bind private parties. Yet, the agreement aims to send a message to market actors that their investment and business decisions should take account of the coming shift to a low-carbon economy. Similarly, when the EU adopts regulations for chemicals or food safety, private producers in other jurisdictions may well change production processes so that they can continue to access EU markets, even if the producers' home jurisdiction has not adopted these regulations;[18]

- influencing the interpretation of domestic law. A 2015 US Supreme Court decision concerning the allocation of foreign affairs powers between the executive and legislative branches turned, in large part, on the Court's understanding of the international legal implications of the act of recognition.[19] Moreover, courts in the United States, Europe, and elsewhere endorse the principle that domestic legislation should be interpreted so as not to conflict with international legal obligations.
- influencing the outcomes of bargaining among public and/or private actors. Legal rules change the strategic environment against which actors negotiate disputes, and, as Coase taught, impact both the substantive and distributional consequences of any agreements reached. Thus, international legal rules will affect state behaviour, even if the resulting agreement is not entirely in compliance with applicable legal norms, as the settlements of many WTO disputes highlights. Much the same analysis applies to bargains or transactions including private parties.

The notion that state compliance is an inadequate measure of international law's effects is even more pronounced for the post-1990 international law that is the focus of this book. Given its regulatory ambition, its increasing reach into the domestic domain, and its growing impact on non-state actors, contemporary international law has effects well beyond impacting state behaviour in the international domain. For these reasons, it is doubtful that contemporary international law's impact can be accurately assessed through examining state compliance rates with legal rules; a richer assessment would take account of law's multiple effects on a broader range of actors.

2. Against compliance

The 'beyond compliance' argument suggests that the focus on state compliance with rules is under-inclusive as it elides many of international law's impacts. The 'against compliance' argument makes a stronger claim: that a focus on compliance is not helpful, as compliance is not related to law's *effectiveness*, which is a more relevant measure of law's role in international affairs. Where compliance refers to whether state behaviour

---

[18] Anu Bradford, 'The Brussels Effect' (2012) 107 Northwestern Law Review 1.
[19] *Zivotofsky v Kerry*, 135 S.Ct. 2076 (2015).

Table 12.1 Compliance/Effectiveness 2 × 2 Matrix

	Effectiveness	
Compliance	High compliance/ High effectiveness	High compliance/ Low effectiveness
	Low compliance/ High Effectiveness	Low compliance/ Low effectiveness

is consistent with an applicable legal norm, effectiveness refers to whether state behaviour has changed as a result of the law. We can easily imagine examples where states substantially change their behaviour to come into compliance with applicable norms (high compliance/high effectiveness), or where states effectively ignore an applicable legal norm (low compliance/low effectiveness). However, there is no necessary relationship between these two metrics.[20] That is, states might readily comply with rules that require them to act in ways they would have acted even in the absence of the rule (high compliance/low effectiveness). Alternatively, a state with an egregiously bad human rights record might significantly improve its human rights performance—yet still remain some distance from compliance with applicable human rights norms (low compliance/high effectiveness). While compliance rates and levels of effectiveness can be understood to run along a continuum, for heuristic purposes we can nonetheless schematically represent their relationship in the two by two matrix shown in Table 12.1. To the extent that particular international legal rules, specific international legal regimes, or international law as a whole, are most often located in the top left or bottom right cells, then compliance can more likely serve as a relatively accurate indicator of the state of international law. To the extent that rules or regimes are more often located in the bottom left or top right cells, then compliance rates may provide a misleading picture of international law's status in contemporary global affairs.

Which cell best captures contemporary international law? Some argue that we might expect international law often to occupy the top right cell (high compliance/low effectiveness).[21] The argument is that states will only sign treaties and assume obligations that they are willing to comply with, particularly if those obligations require states to do what they otherwise planned to do.[22] Consider the 1991 US–Canada Air Quality

---

[20] Eg Kal Raustiala, 'Compliance and Effectiveness in International Regulatory Cooperation' (2000) 32 Case Western Reserve Journal of International Law 387; Lisa A Martin, 'Against Compliance' in Jeffrey L Dunoff and Mark A Pollack (eds), *Interdisciplinary Perspectives on International Law and International Relations* (Cambridge University Press 2012); Timothy Meyer, 'How Compliance Understates Effectiveness' (*AJIL Unbound*, 18 June 2014) <www.asil.org/blogs/how-compliance-understates-effectiveness> accessed 16 July 2018.

[21] George W Downs, David M Rocke, and Peter N Barsoom, 'Is the Good News About Compliance Good News About Cooperation?' (1996) 50 International Organization 379.

[22] Stated more formally, whether a given state joins any particular treaty is not random, meaning that the parties to any particular treaty are systematically different from the states that do not join. This 'selection bias' renders it difficult to make claims about the effects of treaty regimes, eg: Jana von Stein, 'Do Treaties Constrain or Screen? Selection Bias and Treaty Compliance' (2000) 99 American Political Science Review 819.

Agreement.[23] Under this treaty, both states agreed to relatively stringent reductions in emissions of certain pollutants. The treaty's emissions cuts, however, essentially mirrored emissions cuts already mandated by domestic legislation in each state. Thus, the existence of the treaty did not require cuts in addition to those the parties were already committed to undertaking. Similarly, for many years, the whaling treaties contained whale-catch quotas that roughly matched the demand of the whaling industry; compliance was 'nearly perfect, but only because the legal standard codified then-current behaviour'.[24] And the overwhelming majority of states do not engage in genocide or slavery, although this fact likely has less to do with international legal norms prohibiting this conduct, than with widespread beliefs that these practices are morally objectionable.

All of these examples point towards a high compliance/low effectiveness dynamic. To the extent this pattern is widespread in contemporary international law, compliance is not a particularly good indicator of international law's impact on international affairs. I suggest in Section III that this argument contains an important insight—*that levels of compliance are endogenous to the depth of the rules that states create*—but that it oversimplifies and therefore provides an incomplete account of the relevance of compliance to international law's role in global affairs.

3. Is non-compliance ever useful?

Finally, the usefulness of compliance as an indicator turns, in part, on the role and function of *non-compliance*. In advanced domestic legal systems which have diverse institutions to effect legal change and address non-conforming behaviour, non-compliance generally has only a negative systemic impact.[25] Widespread, high-profile non-compliance can corrode the integrity and functioning of these legal orders.

Contemporary international law exists in a very different institutional environment. Law-making occurs in a variety of decentralized and uncoordinated fora; adjudicatory bodies have proliferated, but often have subject area specific or geographically limited jurisdiction and are not hierarchically organized; and centralized, coercive enforcement mechanisms are limited in number and reach. In this highly fragmented and decentralized institutional context, certain types of non-compliance can contribute to, rather than undermine, the international legal order.[26]

This paradoxical role of non-compliance is clearest in the case of customary international law (CIL). Like any other body of law, to stay relevant CIL must evolve in light

---

[23] Agreement Between the Government of Canada and the Government of the United States of America on Air Quality (entered into force 13 March 1991) reprinted in (1991) 30 International Legal Materials 676.

[24] Raustiala (n 20) 392.

[25] Cases of 'civil disobedience', which typically are intended in part as a tool of law reform, serve as a potential exception.

[26] eg Jacob Katz Cogan, 'Noncompliance and the International Rule of Law' (2004) 31 Yale Journal of International Law 189; Allen Buchanan, 'From Nuremberg to Kosovo: The Morality of Illegal International Legal Reform' (2001) 111 Ethics 673.

of changing conditions. Unlike most other bodies of law, however, CIL lacks any formal system of amendment. As a result, states can generally seek to change customary law only by undertaking acts that are inconsistent with the very customary norm that they wish to change.[27] To be sure, sometimes states violate custom because they wish to exempt themselves from generally applicable rules of conduct, to stand outside the law. But other times a 'would-be law-maker wishes to perpetuate the rule of law, whilst changing the particular laws within it'.[28] In these instances, a non-compliant act may trigger 'a process of claim and counterclaim, action and reaction, which leads to the rejection of the formally illegal act or, conversely, to its ratification through the revision, clarification, or termination of the previous rule'.[29] Thus, the continued vitality and relevance of customary international law is premised upon non-compliant acts.

A classic example, of course, is the development of CIL regarding the continental shelf. Prior to the 1945 Truman Proclamation, there was little support for assertion of rights by a coastal state over the seabed beyond territorial limits. In an effort to create a new legal rule, the United States asserted rights 'of the continental shelf beneath the high seas but contiguous to the coasts of the United States'.[30] Within five years, some thirty states had made similar declarations of their own,[31] in 1951 the International Law Commission (ILC) adopted draft articles on the continental shelf, and the principle of coastal state rights in the continental shelf were codified in the 1958 Convention on the Continental Shelf. The Truman Proclamation did not purport to be consistent with existing law. Rather, it was 'a novelty without juristic antecedents',[32] and triggered a process of claim and response that resulted, over time, in creation of a new rule.

Similar dynamics can be seen in other contexts as well. Consider, for example, the well-known *Kadi* saga. While many understandably focus on the controversial rationale and result of the Court of Justice of the European Union's (CJEU) decision in this matter,[33] for current purposes subsequent developments are of greater interest. The *Kadi* decision can fairly be read as an act of non-compliance rooted in concerns over a denial of due process rights afforded to individuals suspected of assisting terrorism. In response, the Security Council made a number of changes to its process for listing suspected terrorists. Among other developments, in 2008 the Security Council introduced a narrative summary for every listing, summarizing the primary reasons for adding an individual's name to the sanctions list and, in 2009, created the office of an independent

---

[27] Jonathan I Charney, 'Anticipatory Humanitarian Intervention in Kosovo' (1999) 93 American Journal of International Law 834, 836 ('[G]eneral international law may change through breach of the current law and the development of new state practice and *opinio juris* supporting the change.').

[28] Robert E Goodin, 'Toward an International Rule of Law: Distinguishing International Law-Breakers from Would-Be Law-Makers' (2005) 9 Journal of Ethics 225, 232.

[29] Cogan (n 26) 197.

[30] Proclamation No 2667, Policy of the United States with Respect to the Natural Resources of the Subsoil and Sea Bed of the Continental Shelf (28 September 1945) 59 Stat 884, 10 Fed Reg 12303 (1945).

[31] Laws and Regulations on the Regime of the High Seas, 1 UN Legislative Series 19 (1951) ST/LEG/SER.B/1.

[32] Daniel P O'Connell, *The International Law of the Sea* (Oxford University Press 1982) 467.

[33] Case C–402/05 P and C–415/05, *P Kadi and Al Barakaat International Foundation v Council and Commission* (2008) ECR I–6351; for a sampling of the debate: Grainne De Búrca, 'The European Court of Justice and the International Legal Order After *Kadi*' (2010) 51 Harvard International Law Journal 1; Enzo Cannizzaro, 'Security Council Resolutions and EC Fundamental Rights: Some Remarks on the ECJ Decision in the Kadi Case' (2009) 28 Yearbook of European Law 593.

ombudsman, which over time developed the capacity to recommend delisting an individual. In the aggregate, these and other changes respond to many of the concerns that the CJEU articulated in its *Kadi* judgment. The changes promote transparency, the right to be heard, and individualized assessments of the fact of each case, and, from a rule of law perspective, represents 'a huge improvement on the initial [Security Council] mechanism'.[34]

Generalizing from these examples, we might say that certain forms of non-compliance are a *design feature*, and not a bug, of CIL.[35] They have neither the purpose nor the effect of undermining respect for the system. Rather they are designed to undermine and change a particular rule, while maintaining and supporting the larger rule system.

To be sure, not every effort to alter existing customary rules is successful. During the Bush Administration, the United States attempted to change existing understandings by asserting the right to engage in preemptive self-defence.[36] These efforts triggered 'a process of counterclaims, responses, replies and rejoinders' often critical of the US position.[37] Moreover, the claim that some non-compliance strengthens the system is emphatically not a generalized defence of lawbreaking. If contemporary international law were nothing other than a story of ongoing and widespread non-compliance it would not constitute a functioning law system. At the same time, however, given international law's peculiar institutional features, 'too little [noncompliance] can lead to ossified and costly structures that do more harm than good'.[38]

The presence of desirable forms of non-compliance problematize the use of compliance as an indicator of international law's role. Indicators should have linear relationships, meaning that higher rates of compliance should indicate a stronger role for international law, and increased rates of non-compliance should indicate a weaker role for international law. The presence of desirable forms of non-compliance, which have the effect of strengthening rather than diminishing the system, are difficult to reconcile with efforts to use compliance as an indicator.

III. Why compliance matters: The 'compliance trilemma'

To claim that compliance is a less than ideal indicator for measuring international law's role in global affairs is not to claim that compliance is unimportant or that it is

---

[34] Juliane Kokott and Christoph Sobotta, 'The Kadi Case—Constitutional Core Values and International Law – Finding the Balance?' (2012) 23 European Journal of International Law 1015, 1024.

[35] Monica Hakimi, 'Unfriendly Unilateralism' (2014) 55 Harvard International Law Journal 105.

[36] eg stating that '[b]ecause deterrence may not succeed, and because of the potentially devastating consequences of WMD use against our forces and civilian population, US military forces and appropriate civilian agencies must have the capability to defend against WMD-armed adversaries, including in appropriate cases through preemptive measures': 'National Strategy to Combat Weapons of Mass Destruction' quoted in 'Contemporary Practice of the United States' (2003) 97 American Journal of International Law 203, 204 n 5.

[37] W Michael Reisman, 'Assessing Claims to Revise the Laws of War' (2003) 97 American Journal of International Law 82.

[38] ibid.

irrelevant to the status of the international rule of law project. Rather, compliance is an essential determinant of international law's role—not because higher compliance rates automatically mean more robust international law, but because efforts to construct international legal regimes face trade-offs among attempts to maximize compliance, participation, and ambition. For current purposes, I label this structural feature of international law the 'compliance trilemma'.

Contemporary international law is commonly said to be marked by its level of ambition, by an increasingly dense universe of legal norms and institutions, and by the number and type of actors it regulates. These features are often thought to give rise to tension between international treaties or regimes that are more inclusive ('broader' or 'wider') and those that are more ambitious ('deeper').[39] Drawing on the collective action literature, some IR scholars argue that it is more difficult for organizations to sustain collective action and produce collective goods as they enlarge their members. A complementary line of thought holds that enlargement increases the diversity of member state preferences, rendering agreement more difficult and, at the limit, producing gridlock. Together, these insights have produced a 'conventional wisdom' which holds that

> [international] institutions must choose between widening and deepening .... [T]he two goals are incompatible: the tradeoff between gains from expanded membership and costs from increasing heterogeneity inevitably suggests that an institution with an expansive mandate will be favored by few states whereas an institution with a constrained mandate will attract a large number of states. Thus, we should observe an inverse relationship between widening and deepening in international institutions.[40]

This trade-off was prominent in debates over the Kyoto Protocol. Fully cognizant of the trade-offs involved, the treaty negotiators embraced a 'deep, then broad' strategy. The treaty was 'deep' in that it provided for relatively stringent and relatively rapid reduction targets. However, this ambition came at the cost of broad participation. The size and scope of the reductions led some industrialized states, including the United States, not to join the treaty, and the states that were willing to accept the Protocol's ambitious requirements represented less than 30 per cent of global greenhouse gas emissions. Negotiators had hoped that, over time, it would be possible to broaden participation. When negotiators attempted to extend the treaty to 2020, however, states such as Japan, Canada, and Russia opted out, leaving countries accounting for only about 15 per cent of global emissions within the treaty regime.

---

[39] Michael J Gilligan, 'Is There a Broader-Deeper Trade-off in International Multilateral Agreements?' (2004) 58 International Organization 459. By 'deeper', I refer to the rule's level of ambition, or 'the extent to which (an agreement) requires states to depart from what they would have done in its absence' as stated in: Downs, Rocke, and Barsoom (n 21) 383. Of course, the level of ambition may vary for every party to an agreement, as a provision that requires great changes by one party may require very little from another. For current purposes, I bracket this heterogeneity, and focus on the overall or average depth of an agreement.

[40] Anu Bradford, 'How International Institutions Evolve' (2014) 15 Chicago Journal of International Law 47, 58.

The logic of the broader–deeper trade-off helps to explain why many trading nations seem are more interested in bilateral or regional trade negotiations than multilateral agreements. The Doha Round of multilateral trade negotiations, launched in 2001 and now involving 164 member states, has essentially broken down. In contrast, bilateral and regional groups of states have completed ambitious agreements, routinely including TRIPs-plus intellectual property commitments, environment and labour-related provisions, and investment and competition coverage, all of which have proved to be infeasible in WTO negotiations.[41]

Thus, the global governance literature has explored the tension between seeking 'broader' and seeking 'deeper' international legal obligations. At the same time, as indicated above, the compliance literature has explored the link between compliance rates and the depth of obligations. The analytic road not taken is exploration of whether there is a conceptual link between the 'broader–deeper' trade-off, and the insight that compliance rates are endogenous to the ambition of the underlying rules. In particular, do states and other international actors in fact face potential trade-offs between levels of ambition, number of participants, and levels of compliance? Specifically, as among these three desiderata, do international actors face a trilemma, such that it is possible to maximize any two, but not all three?

The logic of the trilemma suggests that international actors can select from among one of three distinct options. First, they can have high levels of ambition or depth, and large numbers of participants, but at the cost of relatively low levels of compliance. Alternatively, they can achieve high levels of compliance and substantial ambition, but only at the cost of reduced participation. Finally, they can pursue high levels of compliance and a highly inclusive agreement, but at the cost of relatively low substantive ambition.[42] This trilemma can be captured graphically in Figure 12.1.

A few examples will help to illustrate the various possibilities the trilemma affords. Consider, for example, the international human rights regime. Many human rights treaties are relatively ambitious, setting out numerous substantive and procedural rights. Moreover, many of the most important human rights treaties have nearly universal membership. To name just a few, the International Covenant on Civil and Political Rights (ICCPR) has 169 state parties; the International Covenant on

---

[41] From a game theoretic perspective, some suggest that a 'narrow but deep' approach can work well for problems involving 'club goods', meaning that the participating states can enjoy the benefits of the agreement, even with limited membership, and deny non-participants the benefits of the agreement, eg: Daniel Bodansky, *The Art and Craft of International Environmental Law* (Harvard University Press 2010) 184–85. Others suggest that, in a fragmented legal order with multiple, overlapping regimes, it is possible to bridge the broader–deeper problem by entering into, say, a regional treaty regime that has deep substantive commitments and limited membership, and a global regime that has less ambitious substantive commitments and unrestricted membership, eg: Ryan Goodman and Derek Jinks, 'How to Influence States: Socialization and International Human Rights Law' (2004) 54 Duke Law Journal 621, 663 (discussing global and regional human rights systems).

[42] For a similar argument in the international environmental context: see Scott Barrett, *Environment and Statecraft: The Strategy of Environmental Decision-Making* (Oxford University Press 2003); Daniel Bodansky, 'Legally Binding versus Non-Legally Binding Instruments' in Scott Barrett, Carlo Carraro, and Jaime de Melo (eds), *Towards a Workable and Effective Climate Regime* (VoxEU eBooks, 2015) 155 ('the effectiveness of an international regime is a function of three factors: (1) the ambition of its provisions; (2) the level of participation by states; and (3) the degree to which states comply') <voxeu.org/sites/default/files/image/FromMay2014/Climate%20change%20book%20for%20web.pdf> accessed 20 July 2018, 155.

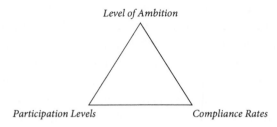

Level of Ambition

Participation Levels   *Compliance Rates*

Figure 12.1 The compliance trilemma—'Pick two, any two'

Economic, Social and Cultural Rights (ICESCR) has 165 parties; the Committee on the Elimination of Racial Discrimination (CERD) has 178 state parties; the Convention Against Torture has 159 parties; the Committee on the Elimination of Discrimination against Woman (CEDAW) has 190 parties; and the Convention on the Rights of the Child has 197 parties.[43] Yet violations of substantive human rights norms remain stubbornly commonplace.[44] Moreover, empirical studies suggest that states with poor human rights practices may continue to violate human rights notwithstanding their membership in treaties prohibiting these practices.[45] Thus, these treaties illustrate the high ambition/high participation/low compliance variant of the trilemma.

The Nuclear Non-Proliferation Treaty (NPT) reveals a similar pattern.[46] With 191 state parties, the NPT enjoys nearly universal membership. Its basic provisions are quite ambitious: states with nuclear weapons will take steps towards nuclear disarmament; states without nuclear weapons will not acquire them; and all states can access peaceful nuclear technology. As the logic of the trilemma suggests, however, ambitious goals and wide membership imply that compliance will be problematic—as it has been in the NPT context. Concerns over the weaknesses in the International Atomic Energy Agency's (IAEA) safeguards system have been acute since the summer of 1991, when international inspectors discovered that Iraq had been operating a clandestine nuclear weapons programme. In a handful of cases, the IAEA Board of Governors has formally determined a state to be in non-compliance with NPT safeguards agreements, including Iraq (1991), Romania (1992), North Korea (1993), Libya (2004), and Iran

---

[43] All figures obtained from the website of the Status of Ratification Interactive Dashboard (Office of the High Commissioner for Human Rights) <indicators.ohchr.org> accessed 16 July 2018.

[44] eg Emilie M Hafner-Burton and Kiyoteru Tsutsui, 'Human Rights in a Globalizing World: The Paradox of Empty Promises' (2005) 110 American Journal of Sociology 1373, 1374 ('the average state has ratified a steadily increasing number of human rights treaties but the percentage of states reportedly repressing human rights has grown over time'). States do not even do a good job of complying with the procedural and reporting obligations associated with human rights treaties; a recent UN report indicated that only about 16 per cent of states parties submit required reports in a timely manner: Navanethem Pillay, 'Strengthening the United Nations Human Rights Treaty Body System' (United Nations High Commissioner for Human Rights, 2012) <www2.ohchr.org/english/bodies/HRTD/docs/HCReportTBStrengthening.pdf> accessed 16 July 2018.

[45] eg Oona A Hathaway, 'The Cost of Commitment' (2003) 55 Stanford Law Review 1821, 1856–58 (finding that non-democratic states with poor human rights ratings are just as likely, and sometimes even more likely, to commit to international human rights treaties than non-democratic states with better human rights ratings).

[46] Treaty on the Non-Proliferation of Nuclear Weapons (1 July 1968) 729 UNTS 169.

(2006). But these formal determinations almost certainly understate the problem of non-compliance, which has prompted the US Department of State and others to complain about 'a crisis of noncompliance' with the NPT,[47] and has triggered a variety of measures outside of the treaty to address proliferation concerns, including condemnation, economic sanctions, travel bans, interdiction of weapons-related material, sabotage, and the unilateral or collective use of force.[48] More generally, the international community is quite a distance from achieving the NPT's core historical purpose of creating a world free of nuclear weapons.[49]

Similar patterns can be found in international humanitarian law (IHL). This body of law seeks to alleviate the effects of armed conflict. All states and other parties to an armed conflict are under an obligation to respect and ensure respect for IHL in all circumstances. This body of law is quite ambitious, identifying a number of rights to be respected in times of armed conflict, and creating dense legal regimes governing land warfare, air warfare, maritime warfare, the law of occupation, the law applicable to peace operations, and the law of neutrality. Participation in the key IHL treaties is universal, or nearly so; for example, 196 states are party to the Geneva Conventions.[50] Compliance, on the other hand, has proven problematic. A series of seminars of the International Committee of the Red Cross (ICRC) with states and other actors revealed 'the unequivocal view of participants was that compliance with IHL was inadequate, and needed to be improved',[51] and at a 2009 conference organized by the Swiss government, states 'identified compliance with IHL as one of the key challenges to the continued relevance of this body of law going forward'.[52] One need not go as far as ICRC President Peter Maurer's recent declaration that '[i]nternational humanitarian law is flouted almost every day, in every conflict around the world' to conclude that non-compliance remains unacceptably high.[53]

---

[47] eg Paula A De Sutter, 'Nuclear Nonproliferation in the 21st Century: Will Multilateral Diplomacy Work?' (Address to the Danish Institute for International Studies, 26 August 2005) <2001-2009.state.gov/t/vci/rls/rm/51864.htm> accessed 16 July 2018.

[48] Including Israel's attack on Iraq's Osirak reactor, air strikes against Syria, and various forms of sabotage against Iran: Dan Bilefsky, 'U.N. Nuclear Watchdog Presses Case Against Syria' (*New York Times*, 9 June 2011) <www.nytimes.com/2011/06/10/world/middleeast/10nations.html> accessed 28 July 2018, A6. More broadly, none of the nuclear powers has forsaken nuclear weapons, and three nuclear states—India, Pakistan, and Israel—are not parties.

[49] Efforts by the Marshall Islands to obtain judgments from the ICJ requiring nuclear powers to comply with the NPT's obligation to undertake 'negotiations in good faith on effective measures relating to cessation of the nuclear arms race at an early date and to nuclear disarmament ...', eg: *Obligations concerning Negotiations relating to Cessation of the Nuclear Arms Race and to Nuclear Disarmament* (*Marshall Islands v United Kingdom*) Judgment (5 October 2016).

[50] Data on states parties to the main IHL treaties is available on the International Committee of the Red Cross (ICRC) website: 'Treaties, States Parties and Commentaries' (ICRC) <www.icrc.org/applic/ihl/ihl.nsf/vwTreaties1949.xsp> accessed 16 July 2018.

[51] ICRC, 'International Humanitarian Law and the Challenges of Contemporary Armed Conflicts' (Twenty-eighth International Conference of the International Red Cross and Red Crescent, December 2003) <www.icrc.org/eng/assets/files/other/ihlcontemp_armedconflicts_final_ang.pdf> accessed 16 July 2018.

[52] ICRC, 'Strengthening Compliance with International Humanitarian Law' 32IC/15/19.2.

[53] ICRC, 'No Agreement by States on Mechanism to Strengthen Compliance with Rules of War' (10 December 2015) <www.icrc.org/en/document/no-agreement-states-mechanism-strengthen-compliance-rules-war> accessed 16 July 2018.

An alternative approach to the trilemma involves low ambition/high participation/ high compliance: International Civil Aviation Organization (ICAO) rules that require flight control centres to have sufficient English-language speakers on duty to communicate with pilots who do not speak the native language of the state whose airspace they are flying through. This rule is relatively non-ambitious (an alternative rule could have provided for the ability to communicate in multiple languages), has very high levels of participation, and enjoys high compliance rates.

The Paris Climate Accord reflects a similar approach to the trilemma. Here, the level of ambition is relatively low, in the sense that states assume only the emission reduction obligations that they unilaterally select for themselves. The number of participants is quite high. The 'trilemma' model suggests that compliance will be relatively high, although since the agreement has not yet entered into effect, only time will tell.

Yet a third variant of the trilemma involves high ambition/low participation/high compliance. Consider, for example, bilateral nuclear arms control treaties, such as the 1972 Anti-Ballistic Missile (ABM) Treaty.[54] This ambitious treaty imposed various limitations on the production and deployment of ABMs, and included rigorous verification measures. Over time, compliance was relatively high; while some allegations of cheating were pressed, no large scale systematic allegations of cheating were proffered, suggesting an overall satisfactory compliance rate, and the treaty was widely seen as successful during its nearly three-decade duration. When there was substantial pressure on the United States to violate the terms of the ABM, President Bush decided to withdraw from the treaty in accordance with its terms.[55]

The structural nature of the trilemma can be seen in Table 12.2 below.
Two qualifications are immediately necessary. First, many treaties and treaty regimes evolve over time, and in these instances the trilemma can have dynamic qualities. Consider, for example, the multilateral trade regime. The roots of the current trade

Table 12.2 Examples of the Compliance Trilemma

	Ambition	Participation	Compliance
Human Rights Treaties	High	High	Low
International Humanitarian Law	High	High	Low
Paris Climate Accord	Low	High	High (predicted)
ICAO English-language requirements	Low	High	High
Bilateral Nuclear Arms Control Treaties (ABM etc.)	High	Low	High

[54] Treaty on the Limitation of Anti-Ballistic Missile Systems (United States–Russia) (entered into force 26 May 1972) 944 UNTS 13.
[55] eg Terence Neilan, 'Bush Pulls Out of ABM Treaty; Putin Calls Move a Mistake' (*New York Times*, 13 December 2001) <www.nytimes.com/2001/12/13/international/bush-pulls-out-of-abm-treaty-putin-calls-move-a-mistake.html> accessed 28 July 2018, A1.

system are found in the General Agreement on Tariffs and Trade (GATT). The GATT, negotiated in 1947, originally consisted of twenty-three Western, market-oriented states. Recalling that only approximately fifty states existed at the time, the size of GATT's membership can be considered relatively robust. The GATT's ambitions, on the other hand, were not overly grand. Although it included many tariff reductions, in fact 'no major government felt that it could promise any important changes in existing practice for the sake of those rules'.[56] Hence, 'for the most part the [GATT's] draftsmen were not trying to legislate the removal of existing trade barriers', and in those few instances where changes were expected, 'exceptions to the rules had to be carved out in almost every such case'.[57] The GATT was highly deferential to state policy choices and trade policies so long as those policies were applied on a non-discriminatory basis. As a result, GATT obligations were not terribly onerous, and by and large state compliance in the early years with GATT obligations was relatively high.

Over time, the number of parties and the volume of international trade grew and, eventually, the GATT evolved into the WTO, which currently has 164 members. The WTO's legal obligations are substantially more ambitious than those of the GATT, including important agreements on intellectual property (TRIPs), services (GATS), and agriculture. As the trilemma would predict, the increased number of participants and greatly expanded reach of legal obligations has led to increased questions regarding compliance. While there is no official index of compliance, each WTO member's trade policies and practices are subject to review under the Trade Policy Review Mechanism (TPRM). As a formal matter, these peer reviews are not intended to evaluate individual member's compliance with specific rules, and they do not contain legally binding findings of compliance or non-compliance. However, they provide feedback to the reviewed state on its performance in the system and, in particular, highlight potentially problematic trade policies or measures. In the diplomatic language of the WTO's secretariat, these reports 'encourage governments to follow more closely the WTO rules and disciplines and to fulfil their commitments'. Even a cursory review of TPRM reports indicates that virtually every trading nation has any number of policies and practices that are not WTO-compliant.[58]

Translating these developments into the language of the trilemma, we might say that the multilateral trading system illustrates how regimes can evidence different approaches to the trilemma over time, in this case shifting from a low ambition/high participation/high compliance system to a high ambition/high participation/low compliance system. See Table 12.3.

It should also be emphasized that the trilemma does not suggest that states will *necessarily* maximize two out of the three desiderata of ambition, participation, and compliance. Rather, it suggests that *at most* states can maximize two out of three. Any

---

[56] Robert E Hudec, 'GATT or GABB? The Future Design of the General Agreement on Tariffs and Trade' (1971) 80 Yale Law Journal 1299, 1311.

[57] ibid 1311, 1312.

[58] To take just one example, it is widely recognized that many of the hundreds of free trade agreements entered into by WTO members would not satisfy the 'substantially all trade' requirement of GATT Art XXIV.

Table 12.3 The Trilemma in Time

	Ambition	Participation	Compliance
GATT (1947–1994)	Low	Medium/High	High
WTO (1995–present)	High	High	Low

Table 12.4 Examples of Treaties that Maximize Fewer than Two Trilemma Features

	Ambition	Participation	Compliance
US–Canada Air Quality Agreement	Low	Low	High
Kyoto Protocol	High	Low	Low

particular treaty can maximize one or none of these desiderata. The 1991 US–Canada Air Quality Agreement, mentioned above, required states to make emissions reductions that were already required under pre-existing domestic law. Thus, this treaty reflects low ambition, low participation, and high compliance. The Kyoto Protocol represents another configuration. This treaty envisioned relatively ambitious emissions reductions. This ambition contributed to the relatively low number of ratifications from states that would have to reduce emissions. Nonetheless, a substantial number of Kyoto Protocol parties had emissions that exceeded its carbon budget.[59] Thus, this treaty reflects a high ambition/low participation/low compliance profile. See Table 12.4.

To be sure, the small number of treaties and regimes discussed here should be understood as illustrative and cannot be taken as conclusive evidence establishing the universality of the compliance trilemma. Nonetheless, this sample does suggest that the trilemma's basic structure can be found across a variety of issue areas (human rights, environment, economics, national security, etc) and across a variety of collective action problems, ranging from coordination to collaboration games. But even the suggestion that states face a trilemma raises numerous questions, including whether the trilemma is inevitable. In this context, it is useful to consider potential counter-examples, which might have the effect of undermining the trilemma, or cabining its scope.

The Montreal Protocol on Substances the Deplete the Ozone Layer[60] mandated dramatic reductions in the production and consumption of chlorofluorocarbons (CFCs) which destroy the stratospheric ozone layer. This treaty has a large number of parties, at present 197. And it is widely considered a resounding success;[61] by 2005, Montreal

---

[59] Corina Haita, 'The State of Compliance in the Kyoto Protocol' (International Center for Climate Governance, December 2012) <www.iccgov.org/en/iccgstudies/the-state-of-compliance-in-the-kyoto-protocol/> accessed 16 July 2018.

[60] Montreal Protocol on Substances that Deplete the Ozone Layer (adopted 16 September 1987, entered into force 1 January 1989) 1522 UNTS 3.

[61] eg Richard Elliot Benedick, *Ozone Diplomacy* (Harvard University Press 1991).

Protocol parties had reduced the production and use of covered substances to 5 per cent of 1987 levels.

Is the Montreal Protocol, then, an example of a high ambition/high participation/high compliance treaty? Perhaps. But one important reason for the treaty's success was its use of differentiated commitments, in particular for developing states. At the time of the negotiations, per capita consumption of ozone depleting chemicals in developing states was very small, but likely to grow significantly over time. As these chemicals had been essential to industrialization in developed states, and as developing states had not caused the ozone problem, developing states showed little interest in joining the ozone treaties. Without their participation, however, the treaties would not succeed.

The treaties addressed this problem in a number of creative ways. First, developing states were given a grace period, originally of ten years, during which they would not have to meet the treaty's substantive obligations. This allowed those states to continue, and even increase, their use of controlled substances. Second, a financial transfer mechanism, the Multilateral Fund, was created, to offset the costs of developing states' transition from ozone depleting substances.[62]

The Montreal Protocol thus illustrates two tools commonly used to address the trilemma. One is the use of differentiated obligations. This strategy, sometimes called variable geometry, helps ameliorate the 'deeper-broader' trade-off, as states that are willing to take on more ambitious obligations are free to do so, but not at the cost of excluding less ambitious states from the treaty regime. Of course, this strategy can be seen as *reinforcing*, rather than repudiating, the basic logic of the trilemma, as the 'cost' of obtaining membership of less ambitious states is a watering down of the treaty's ambitions.

Differentiated obligations are seen in a variety of multilateral contexts. In the EU context, for example, the United Kingdom and Ireland were not willing to take on the obligations of the Schengen Agreement (and subsequent Schengen Convention) regarding the intra-Union movement of non-Union citizens, and chose to remain outside the Schengen Area. Similarly, the European Economic and Monetary Union involved adoption of a common currency and a common monetary policy administered by the European Central Bank; at the time these policies came into effect, only twelve out of the then-fifteen member states opted in.

The Montreal Protocol also illustrates a second strategy for ameliorating the trilemma, the possibility of 'side payments'. These payments can be made in issue areas that are closely related issues addressed by a treaty, as in the Montreal Protocol context, or in issue areas that are unrelated (eg providing favourable tariff treatment to states who join environmental treaties). Side payments can shift the financial costs of treaty ambition to those better able to pay, and thereby help ameliorate the trilemma. As a practical matter, however, redistributional side payments are rarely made in multilateral

---

[62] In addition, the treaty provided that states can only trade in controlled substances with other treaty parties, creating an incentive for states which did not produce ozone-depleting substances but wished to use them to join the treaty.

settings.[63] One concern is that side payments invite moral hazard and other distortions, such as holdout behaviour. Moreover, there is little assurance that they will be effective; a recipient can obtain the payment and later exit the treaty. Hence, direct payments are rarely used. In the Montreal Protocol context, developed states agreed to create a fund to pay for certain measures of environmental protection by developing states, rather than simply agreeing to make an unrestricted side payment.

IV. Conclusion

As conceptualized in this chapter, the compliance trilemma is a general feature of international law, and is not limited to post-1990 international law. Nonetheless, the trilemma has special salience for many of the initiatives that characterized international law over the past few decades. To the extent these efforts seek widespread, if not universal, participation, *and* seek to extend, and deepen, international law's regulatory reach, the trilemma suggests that compliance will be problematic. In these domains, high compliance can only be 'purchased' at a 'cost' to either high participation, or substantive ambition.

Recent political trends suggest that an era marked by efforts to craft ambitious multilateral regulatory regimes may be waning. Many will be tempted to interpret this shift as reflecting an international law more on the 'decline' than on the rise. At the same time, the trilemma suggests that a shift away from ambitious multilateral efforts also presents opportunities. Effective policy responses to a number of pressing international problems may not require universal participation. For example, China, the United States, and the European Union alone account from more than half of global carbon emissions, and the top six emitters account for some 70 per cent of global emissions. As a conceptual matter, a small number of leading states could more quickly craft a more ambitious, and more effective, agreement than could be reached through traditional processes involving all states—without sacrificing high levels of compliance. Much the same is true in the realm of international economic law. The breakdown in WTO negotiating processes is troubling for many reasons. But bilateral and plurilateral agreements continue apace, often achieving levels of ambition that could not be reached in Geneva, and may enjoy compliance rates greater than WTO law.

In short, efforts to construct an international rule of law encounter trade-offs between levels of ambition, number of participants, and rates of compliance. As a result, high levels of compliance, by themselves, tell us little about international law's role in contemporary international affairs. The compliance trilemma does suggest, however,

---

[63] That said, side payments are not unheard of. To conclude the 1911 North Pacific Fur Seal Treaty, the United States made side payments of $100,000 to both Great Britain and Japan: Barrett (n 42) 34. To persuade North Korea to continue in the NPT, the United States provided fuel oil and assistance in the construction of two light water reactors: Alan Riding, 'U.S. and North Korea Sign Pact to End Nuclear Dispute' (*New York Times*, 22 October 1994) <www.nytimes.com/1994/10/22/world/us-and-north-korea-sign-pact-to-end-nuclear-dispute.html> accessed 28 July 2018.

that high rates of compliance are 'purchased' at the 'cost' of other desirable goals, such as high rates of participation or depth of substantive commitments (or both). Thus, compliance by itself is not a useful indicator of the status of international law; it is, however, an important component of any meaningful analysis of international law's strength and vigour.

13

Is There a Compliance Trilemma in International Law?

Comment on Jeffrey L Dunoff

Markus Jachtenfuchs

In his inspiring and thoughtful chapter on whether compliance was an indicator for the state of international law, Jeffrey Dunoff makes three arguments. First, he argues, compliance is difficult to operationalize and measure, conceptually as well as practically. We should not rush towards far-reaching conclusions on the state of international law on the basis of an ill-defined concept and problematic data. Second, compliance is at best a partial indicator for the (international) rule of law. Law is more than behavioural prescriptions, and non-compliance even with behavioural prescriptions is sometimes functional for the law. In other words, even if we had a perfectly valid and reliable measure of compliance, it would at best give us a limited and partial understanding of the international rule of law. Third, although compliance is an imperfect indicator for the international rule of law, it is a key variable for the design of international agreements. Agreements which are both demanding and require a broad membership are likely to have weak compliance. If high compliance is desired, the price to be paid is either small membership or a less demanding agreement.

The first two arguments are closely related and constitute a methodological warning against overestimating the practical usefulness of compliance as an indicator without denying its usefulness in principle. The third argument is substantive and conveys bad news for global governance and international law: Policy problems which require an ambitious agreement with broad membership and high compliance are highly unlikely to be solved.

I. What does compliance mean and how do we measure it?

After reading Dunoff's first two arguments, the reader is in a gloomy mood: Compliance is difficult to measure and many existing indicators measure things that are not the same as compliance. Even if those indicators measure compliance correctly, it is impossible to draw causal inferences from them. In any case, international law is much more than what can be measured by the concept of compliance. As states only sign treaties they actively support or where they have already fulfilled the commitments anyway, compliance is of little use as an indicator of the causal effect of international institutions or international law on state behaviour. And even if compliance could be measured correctly and had value for causal arguments about state behaviour, non-compliance is not always bad but sometimes even functional for a legal system. With all these caveats and reservations, why should anybody ever care about compliance with international law?

This is obviously not the point Jeffrey Dunoff is trying to make in his warning that available measures of compliance have their shortcomings and that a rise or decline of compliance should not be used as a quick shortcut to assess the much broader question of the rise or decline of the international rule of law. But what reads like a discussion of standard methodological problems for the empirically oriented political scientist should not lead to a dismissal of the concept of compliance and of the possibility of measuring social reality in general.

Problems of measurement are inherent in any empirical science. Unfortunately, they are most articulate with the most interesting concepts like power, democracy, equality, freedom, justice, wealth, peace, or the rule of law. Using the gross domestic product as an indicator of wealth has often been criticized as reductionist and materialist; people object that the Freedom House Index does not measure democracy properly or that the number of 1,000 casualties used for distinguishing a war from other types of armed conflicts was arbitrary. The list could go on almost endlessly. All these criticisms often have more of a grain of truth in them.

But there is no way of avoiding these problems of measuring concepts which are not directly observable. We need to discuss these fuzzy concepts even though they are difficult to measure because they are relevant. The bar for replacing a particular way of measuring a concept, into which many years of scholarship have been invested and which has often been used successfully to explain interesting empirical phenomena, is high. Not every available indicator is good, but replacing problematic measurements by common sense assessments or by examples makes matters worse. This problem is particularly acute in the case of concepts that require the collaboration of empirical and normative scholars.[1] In this case, empirical political scientists risk missing the meaning of a concept such as compliance without resorting to legal thinking, and lawyers risk misunderstanding empirical patterns without engaging with the results of political scientists. This is difficult, but this challenge can only be met by a dialogue across disciplines about what is to be measured and how it can be measured. Replacing explicit theory or measurement with implicit theory or measurement is a bad choice. Many problems in empirical compliance research can be solved or at least reduced by careful research design, most notably by careful comparison and operationalization.

Compliance is certainly not the one and only indicator for the international rule of law, which is rather a multidimensional and complex concept. But with all caveats, it is more than a concept that is only interesting for the specialists who study it for its own

---

[1] For an excellent example: Michael Zürn and Christian Joerges (eds), *Law and Governance in Postnational Europe: Compliance beyond the Nation-State* (Cambridge University Press 2005).

sake. By studying compliance, we can say something about the effects of legal norms or international institutions on the behaviour of states (as well as on private organizations and individuals). Even though it is certainly possible that states only sign up to agreements which they find easy to comply with,[2] this discussion should be conducted on the basis of controlled empirical research instead of exemplary evidence or generalizing assumptions. Warning against prematurely concluding that high compliance rates also mean a strong effect of international law on state behaviour is certainly correct and important. One should, however, avoid throwing the baby out with the bathwater. In studies of compliance with European Union (EU) law, we find huge variation across member states and over time.[3] If member states only signed up to legal provisions they find easy to comply with, such a pattern is difficult to explain. The United Kingdom and Denmark, two member states with a long record of vocal opposition against an 'ever closer' European Union and encroachments upon national sovereignty, stand out with high compliance rates. Can we really assume that both states find it systematically easier to comply with new EU legislation and hence have better compliance rates than other member states? And why did member states with a bad compliance record vote for this EU legislation in the first place? Why is the compliance record with specific rules generally improving over time? What this literature reveals is that the cross-national and longitudinal pattern of compliance with international agreements seems to be shaped by a multitude of factors. Also, a study comparing compliance with a functionally equivalent set of rules in national, European, and international law does not find decreasing compliance rates with the weakening of centralized enforcement from national to European and international law.[4]

Not least among the factors influencing compliance is the role of the European Court of Justice and an elaborate procedure for dealing with cases of non-compliance.[5] Another is the distinction between the unwillingness and the inability to comply. Whereas some states are unwilling to comply with a given rule and refuse to do so, others are willing but unable to comply. This distinction is not a minor issue for specialists of compliance studies but of high significance for understanding the functioning of legal rules as well as of high political relevance. In the Eurozone crisis, the European Union was (and is) deeply split over the issue of whether the crisis was caused by member states unable or unwilling to comply with existing rules and whether tightening the supervision of national banks and budgets and sanctioning non-compliance or different rules and assistance were ways out of the crisis. While a certain degree of non-compliance may be functional for international institutions, studying the extent and causes of non-compliance may tell us a lot about the status of international law and

---

[2] An example used in: Lisa L Martin, 'Against Compliance' in Jeffrey L Dunoff and Mark A Pollack (eds), *Interdisciplinary Perspectives on International Law and International Relations* (Cambridge University Press 2012) 591, 605f; also: George W Downs, David M Rocke, and Peter N Barsoom, 'Is the Good News about Compliance Good News about Cooperation?' (1996) 50 International Organization 379.

[3] Tanja A Börzel, Tobias Hofmann, and Diana Panke, 'Caving in or Sitting It out? Longitudinal Patterns of Noncompliance in the European Union' (2012) 19 Journal of European Public Policy 454.

[4] Zürn and Joerges (n 1).

[5] Diana Panke, *The Effectiveness of the European Court of Justice: Why Reluctant States Comply* (Manchester University Press 2010).

may help improve it even if it does not tell us the whole picture. For practical reasons, studying compliance may be preferable to the more interesting but more complex study of problem-solving, that is the degree to which legal rules actually help deal with societal problems.[6]

II. What does the compliance trilemma tell us about global governance?

Jeffrey Dunoff recognizes the importance of compliance as an analytical and theoretical category despite pervasive measurement problems and doubts about the value of compliance as an indicator for the state of the international rule of law. But he goes considerably further: In his statement of the compliance trilemma, he uses compliance as a key concept for assessing global governance. His claim is straightforward: International agreements with high levels of ambition, high participation rates, and high compliance rates are unlikely to exist. In any agreement, states can realistically only have two of the three properties: If they want high levels of ambition and high participation rates, they have to accept low compliance rates; if they aim for high participation and high compliance rates, this is only possible in agreements with a low level of ambition; if high levels of ambition and compliance are the goals, they can only be reached with low levels of participation. In other words, there is a kind of natural limit to what international agreements can achieve. Governance problems which fall under one of the areas which can be dealt with by two of the three factors having high values, can in principle be solved by international agreements.

In this logic, even the economic and monetary problems of the Eurozone can in principle be solved: They require highly ambitious agreements and high compliance rates but luckily only a low number of participating countries. The real problems from the point of view of the compliance trilemma are those that require all three factors—high ambition, high participation, and high compliance. Solving them by international agreements is difficult to impossible. If states conclude highly ambitious agreements with an almost global participation, low compliance is likely to be the consequence. More generally, the compliance trilemma can be read as a warning that international law cannot and should not try to imitate the ideal-typical domestic legal order where highly ambitious laws are addressed to numerous subjects and high compliance is the rule.

Trilemmas, magic quadrangles, and similar constructions have a strong intellectual appeal in showing trade-offs between goals and stimulate research and intellectual debate.[7] The compliance trilemma is intuitively plausible, especially from a point of view which assumes an anarchic international system without the possibility of centralized

---

[6] Pioneered by students of international environmental policy, and in particular Oran Young: Arild Underdal and Oran R Young (eds), *Regime Consequences: Methodological Challenges and Research Strategies* (Kluwer Academic Publishers 2004) as a summary of many years of research.

[7] For a famous example: Dani Rodrik, *The Globalization Paradox: Why Global Markets, States, and Democracy Can't Coexist* (Oxford University Press 2011).

enforcement.[8] However, one could question whether the trilemma is based on the right variables.

This question mainly concerns the 'participation' category. The argument is that *ceteris paribus* compliance becomes more difficult the more parties an agreement has. This is a simple and easily measurable variable. But is it a theoretically meaningful one? The sheer size or numbers of something are often a good proxy for some underlying causal factor which is sometimes easy and sometimes difficult to see. In the compliance trilemma, a causally more interesting factor may be preference heterogeneity, that is the divergence of state preferences towards the agreement in question. An agreement with 200 like-minded states may be easier to achieve and easier to comply with than a peace treaty between two parties hostile to each other and attempting to escape the agreement.

The question is then whether this is a rare exception to the general rule that compliance problems increase with the number of participants to an agreement or whether it puts into question the purported relationship between increasing participation and decreasing compliance (with ambition remaining constant). A number of theoretical arguments reinforces these doubts. Several authors from different fields argue that the type of conflicts between states or the types of issues to be dealt with may be more important than the sheer number of participants. Standard-setting agreements meant to coordinate actor behaviour are one extreme. Technical standards, rules for aviation, or accounting standards are of that type. Once adopted, actors have an incentive to comply in their own interest despite political or economic conflict. Another category of agreements with comparatively low conflict is the regulation of the behaviour of market participants. 'Policy determines politics', Theodore Lowi famously argued half a century ago.[9] In his view, regulating the behaviour of market participants was less conflictual because costs were often diffuse and shifted to firms. The other extreme are cases of redistribution where some participants lose money or power which others gain. Even worse are cases of conflicts over values where fundamental attitudes and identities are at stake. The refugee crisis in the European Union combined the two: It was a redistributional conflict between countries receiving a large number of refugees and those receiving few or none and between net contributors to the EU budget and net receivers. To make matters worse, it was a conflict between different values on national identity, national openness, and the legitimate rights of the European Union to intervene in core state powers. As EU member states clustered into groups, the effective number of parties to the conflict was much lower than the number of EU member states (which is only a tiny subset of all states). But as this was a redistributional conflict with huge financial implications, a strong value element, and huge domestic political costs, compliance—most famously with agreements on the redistribution of refugees among member states—was low.[10]

---

[8]   For a classic statement: Kenneth Waltz, *Theory of International Politics* (McGraw-Hill 1979).

[9]   Theodore J Lowi, 'Four Systems of Policy, Politics, and Choice' (1972) 32 Public Administration Review 298.

[10]   For a concise overview: Philipp Genschel and Markus Jachtenfuchs, 'From Market Integration to Core State Powers: The Eurozone Crisis, the Refugee Crisis and Integration Theory' (2018) 56 Journal of Common Market Studies 178.

One may object that the first type of agreements—international regulatory standards—are cases of low ambition and hence conform to the governance trilemma.[11] Taken together with the second type of agreements, however—highly ambitious agreements among a small number of states on redistributive and/or value issues—one is tempted to draw the conclusion that preference heterogeneity was more relevant for understanding the compliance trilemma than participation numbers. My argument is not that by introducing more and more variables the explanatory model could be made more 'realistic'. The argument is rather that in order to remain parsimonious, it may be better to replace participation with preference heterogeneity in the compliance trilemma.

But even if we accept such a revised compliance trilemma, what implications do we draw from it for the design of international agreements? As I argued earlier, the most disturbing issues the governance trilemma alerts us to are cases of governance problems which require the conclusion of ambitious agreements requiring high compliance among participants with a high preference heterogeneity. In these constellations, the compliance trilemma should not lead us to a fatalist view on the limits of global governance under anarchy but rather to think about institutional design. In many respects, the situation parallels an old argument in EU studies which postulated a dilemma between widening and deepening—the European Union could either admit more members or deepen integration. Several decades later, and after the Eurozone crisis with unprecedented levels of conflict, the European Union has both widened and deepened. Agreements that were difficult to imagine in a smaller Union have been adopted by the larger Union—the European Arrest Warrant, a rapidly growing common border police, and a 500 billion Euro rescue fund (the European Stability Mechanism) are prominent examples. This has been achieved through 'conflict-minimizing integration'[12] that is through mechanisms that reduce the tensions inherent in the governance trilemma.

One might object that what has worked with at least some success in the European Union cannot easily be transferred to the global level because a number of facilitating conditions (such as a strong European Court of Justice which can rely on a strong rule of law commitment) exist to a lesser degree or not at all in the global context. However, my argument was not to argue that highly specific European trajectories could or should serve as a role model for the world. Rather, the EU examples illustrate a number of generalizable theoretical arguments—that preference heterogeneity is more important than the number of participants and, most importantly, that institutional design matters. By choosing the right regulatory strategies, delegating to independent bodies, differentiating responsibilities, making side payments, organizing compliance as a

---

[11] This simple label may hide a huge variety of agreements which also vary in ambition: Tim Büthe and Walter Mattli, *The New Global Rulers: The Privatization of Regulation in the World Economy* (Princeton University Press 2011); Kenneth W Abbott and Duncan Snidal, 'The Governance Triangle: Regulatory Standards Institutions and the Shadow of the State' in Walter Mattli and Ngaire Woods (eds), *The Politics of Global Regulation* (Princeton University Press 2009).

[12] Philipp Genschel and Markus Jachtenfuchs, 'Conflict-Minimizing Integration: How the EU Achieves Massive Integration despite Massive Protest' in Damian Chalmers, Markus Jachtenfuchs, and Christian Joerges (eds), *The End of the Eurocrats' Dream: Adjusting to European Diversity* (Cambridge University Press 2016).

process and a variety of other means, states in the EU, in other regions,[13] and in a global setting are not doomed to choose between two of three important goals. The compliance trilemma is a parsimonious tool for understanding tensions in global governance but not an inescapable structural constraint in an anarchic international system. Its tensions can be mediated or overcome by the clever design of international agreements or institutions.

[13] As witnessed by the huge growth in scope and depth of regional integration beyond the EU: Tanja A Börzel and Thomas Risse (eds), *The Oxford Handbook of Comparative Regionalism* (Oxford University Press 2016).

14

The Rule of International (Environmental) Law and Complex Problems

Jutta Brunnée*

An example of a *complicated* system is an automobile, composed of thousands of parts whose interactions obey precise, simple, known and unchanging cause-and-effect rules....

An ensemble of cars travelling down a highway, by contrast, is a *complex* system. Drivers interact and mutually adjust their behaviours based on diverse factors such as perceptions, expectations, habits, even emotions.... actual traffic flow cannot be predicted with certainty. No one driver is in control and there is no single destination.[1]

I. Introduction

It is perhaps no coincidence that the editors of this book on the 'rise or decline' of the international rule of law asked an international environmental lawyer to assess international law's capacity to tackle complex problems. After all, it may seem obvious that many environmental problems qualify as 'complex', and that an *international* environmental problem is all the more complex, due to the need to involve several, sometimes even all, states in problem-solving and to shift conduct by, as well as address impacts on, a wide range of non-state actors as well. However, understanding complexity, and the distinctive features of complex problems, is more complicated than meets the eye. Indeed, as the opening quote serves to illustrate, there is a difference between a merely *complicated* and a *complex* issue. This difference, in turn, has significant implications for efforts to address complex problems as well as for understanding the role of international law, and the international rule of law, in doing so.

Complexity thinking has its origins in the natural sciences,[2] notably mathematics and physics, where it emerged as a reaction to the dominant Enlightenment paradigms

* I thank Sarah Mason-Case for her helpful comments on a draft version of this chapter.
[1] OECD Global Science Forum, *Applications of Complexity Science for Public Policy: New Tools for Finding Unanticipated Consequences and Unrealized Opportunities* (September 2009) <www.oecd.org/science/sci-tech/43891980.pdf> accessed 11 April 2017, 1–2.
[2] Warren Weaver, 'Science and Complexity' (1948) 36 American Scientist 536.

associated with Newton and Descartes.[3] The common theme in the many strands of complexity (or 'complex systems') theory is that 'the whole is greater than the sum of its parts'.[4] The '[p]arts and the whole co-constitute one another', such that 'complexity neither denies an autonomous existence to the parts composing the system nor seeks to dissolve them into an overarching determining structure'.[5] Hence, while a *complicated* system or problem can be understood through conventional scientific approaches, a *complex* one requires an approach that can accommodate 'non-linear and collective patterns of behaviour'.[6]

In the latter part of the twentieth century, complexity thinking was also taken up in the social sciences. A variety of disciplines, ranging from psychology to urban planning, have sought to identify the traits that render complex, or even 'wicked', problems so resistant to resolution: multiple variables of a problem situation, interconnectedness of the variables, dynamism of the problem situation and variables, incomplete knowledge or understanding of the problem situation, and polycentric nature of the situation.[7] After the end of the Cold War, complexity thinking gained currency in the International Relations (IR) literature,[8] coinciding with the discipline's increased focus on processes of globalization.[9] IR scholars have pursued various lines of inquiry, including into the notions of complex interdependence,[10] cooperation,[11] learning,[12] and socialization.[13] The overarching insight IR scholars have derived from these inquiries is that complexity requires analysts as well as policy-makers to adopt relational and process-focused approaches that are sensitive to 'organizational patterns, networked relationships and historical context' and that privilege 'dynamic flux over stable essences'.[14] Legal scholarship has been considerably slower to engage with complexity theory,[15] and its application to

---

[3] Emilian Kavalski, 'The Fifth Debate and the Emergence of Complex International Relations Theory: Notes on the Application of Complexity Theory to the Study of International Life' (2007) 20 Cambridge Review of International Affairs 435, 437; Antoine Bousquet and Simon Curtis, 'Beyond Models and Metaphors: Complexity Theory, Systems Thinking and International Relations' (2011) 24 Cambridge Review of International Affairs 43, 44.

[4] Femke Reitsma, 'A Response to Simplifying Complexity' (2003) 34 Geoforum 13, 13.

[5] Bousquet and Curtis (n 3) 45.

[6] OECD Global Science Forum (n 1) 2.

[7] Joachim Funke, 'Complex Problem Solving' in Norbert M Seel (ed), *Encyclopedia of the Sciences of Learning*, vol 38 (Springer Verlag 2012) 683; the phrase 'wicked problem' stems from an influential article by two urban planners: Horst WJ Rittel and Melvin M Webber, 'Dilemmas in a General Theory of Planning' (1973) 4 Policy Sciences 155.

[8] John Lewis Gaddis, 'International Relations Theory and the End of the Cold War' (1992/93) 17 International Security 5.

[9] Bousquet and Curtis (n 3) 48; already: John Ruggie, 'Complexity, Planning, and Public Order' in Todd La Porte (ed), *Organized Social Complexity: Challenge to Politics and Policy* (Princeton University Press 1975) 119.

[10] Joseph Nye, *Understanding International Conflict* (Harper Collins 1993) 169.

[11] Robert Axelrod, *The Complexity of Cooperation* (Princeton University Press 1997).

[12] Alexander Wendt, *Social Theory of International Politics* (Cambridge University Press 1999) 170.

[13] Trine Flockhart, 'Complex Socialization' (2006) 12 European Journal of International Relations 89.

[14] Bousquet and Curtis (n 3) 45, 48–49; further: Australian Public Service Commission, 'Tackling Wicked Problems: A Public Policy Perspective' (2007) <www.enablingchange.com.au/wickedproblems.pdf> accessed 12 April 2017.

[15] JB Ruhl, 'Thinking of Environmental Law as a Complex Adaptive System: How to Clean up the Environment by Making a Mess of Environmental Law' (1997) 34 Houston Law Review 933; Julian Webb, 'Law, Ethics, and Complexity: Complexity Theory & the Normative Reconstruction of Law' (2005) 52 Cleveland State Law Review 227.

international law has remained sporadic.[16] Nevertheless, some authors have sought to understand international law itself as 'a complex system that emerges from the actions and interactions of States and other ... actors in their international relations'.[17]

Against this backdrop, I return to my starting proposition. International environmental problems, in particular global climate change, are now widely approached as complex problems.[18] To put it in the terms of the examples in the opening quote: they are increasingly thought of as 'traffic', rather than 'cars'. Indeed, the complexity of tackling climate change far exceeds that of managing 'traffic', seeing as it involves not only the coordination of human conduct, but requires consideration of the problem's environmental, scientific, economic, social, security, and equity dimensions. Accordingly, global climate change has been labelled a 'super-wicked' problem,[19] and complexity thinking is increasingly prominent in the global environmental governance literature. It has been argued, for example, that the United Nations (UN) Framework Convention on Climate Change (FCCC)[20] should be understood 'less as an authority that attempts to govern climate change' and more as interacting with multiple other parts of a complex climate governance system.[21] International environmental law scholarship has only begun to build on these insights. In one recent article, for example, the field as a whole was described as a complex system, composed of a decentralized network of interacting norms, treaties, and institutions that continuously adapt to external change.[22] It is this nascent strand of the literature that I aim to extend in this chapter, focusing on the role of international law in tackling global climate change.

Complexity thinking underscores that, while international law must provide stability to interactions around global climate change, it must also be flexible and highly adaptable.[23] But what are the implications of this functional imperative for the international rule of law? The emergence and evolution of the UN climate regime coincides with the period since the end of the Cold War that the editors of this book have identified for the purposes of assessing whether the international rule of law has been on the 'rise' or in 'decline'. Global climate law, then, lends itself to exploring the trajectory

---

[16] Mark Chinen, 'Complexity Theory and the Horizontal and Vertical Dimensions of State Responsibility' (2014) 25 European Journal of International Law 703; Joost Pauwelyn, 'At the Edge of Chaos? Foreign Investment Law as a Complex Adaptive System, How It Emerged and How It Can Be Reformed' (24 January 2014) <https://ssrn.com/abstract=2271869> accessed 12 April 2017); Steven Wheatley, 'The Emergence of New States in International Law: The Insights from Complexity Theory' (2016) 15 Chinese Journal of International Law 579.

[17] Wheatley (n 16) 581.

[18] OECD Global Science Forum (n 1) 12.

[19] Identifying additional features that render complex problems 'super wicked': time is running out; those seeking to end the problem are also causing it; no central authority; and policies discount the future irrationally: Kelly Levin, Benjamin Cashore, Steven Bernstein, and Graeme Ault, 'Overcoming the Tragedy of Super Wicked Problems: Constraining our Future Selves to Ameliorate Global Climate change' (2012) 45 Policy Science 123, 127–29.

[20] UN Framework Convention on Climate Change (FCCC), reprinted in (1992) 31 International Legal Materials 849.

[21] Michele Betsill, Navroz K Dubash, Matthew Paterson, and Harro van Asselt, 'Building Productive Links between the UNFCCC and the Broader Global Climate Governance Landscape' (2015) 15 Global Environmental Politics 1.

[22] Rakhyun E Kim and Brendan Mackey, 'International Environmental Law as a Complex Adaptive System' (2014) 14 International Environmental Agreements 5.

[23] Also: Harro van Asselt, 'Between the Devil and the Deep Blue Sea: Enhancing Flexibility in International Climate Change Law' (2014) 45 Netherlands Yearbook of International Law 255.

of international law in its encounter with complexity. The 1992 Rio Conference on Environment and Development, during which the FCCC was adopted, has been identified as the high point of international environmental law-making activity,[24] with treaty-making slowing thereafter,[25] or even 'stagnating'.[26] However, for present purposes, the most important shift in the treaty context may not have been the decrease in the adoption of new multilateral environmental agreements (MEAs), but the shift to the adoption of amendments to existing agreements.[27] Furthermore, the perhaps most significant trend in international environmental law-making has been the rise of a spectrum of more or less formal amendment processes, and of various modes of informal standard-setting under the auspices of MEAs, including the FCCC.[28]

Is this rise of 'informality' indicative of a 'decline' of the international rule of law? Even if the yardstick were a decrease in recourse to formally binding rules, the patterns of international environmental law-making activity may not suggest a 'decline', but rather a 'treaty saturation', which in turn accounts for the shift to amendments of and standard-setting under existing treaties.[29] I argue that, in any case, the 'hard' vs 'soft' law distinction is not the most informative metric when it comes to exploring the trajectory of the international rule of law. In offering an alternative framework, I build on the editors' proposition that the international rule of law presupposes a system of distinctly legal norms that 'conforms to a certain standard'.[30] Analytic attention, I suggest, is most fruitfully directed to the distinctive traits of legal norms and practices; traits that transcend traditional conceptions of formality and informality.

I begin by highlighting the main features of climate change as a complex policy challenge. Next, drawing on the interactional account of international law that I have developed elsewhere, I set out what I understand to be the key traits of legality and the rule of law in the international context.[31] I then explore the evolution of customary, 'soft' and treaty-based international environmental law. I focus primarily on how treaty-based

[24]   Between 1990 and 1992, 106 multilateral environmental agreements (MEAs) were concluded. By comparison, between 1970 and 1972, 33 MEAs were concluded, and between 1980 and 1982, 45 MEAs were concluded. In turn, between 2000 and 2002, 88 MEAs were concluded and between 2010 and 2012, 57 MEAs were concluded: Ronald B Mitchell, International Environmental Agreements Database Project (Version 2014.3) (2002–15) <http://iea.uoregon.edu/page.php?query=summarize_by_year&yearstart=1950&yearend=2012&inclusion=MEA> accessed 3 April 2016 (using the notion of MEA to encompass new treaties, protocols to existing treaties, and amendments to existing treaties).

[25]   Stacy Vandeveer, 'Green Fatigue' (2003) 27 Wilson Quarterly 55.

[26]   Generally: Joost Pauwelyn, Ramses A Wessel, and Jan Wouters, 'When Structures Become Shackles: Stagnation and Dynamics in International Law-making' (2015) 25 European Journal of International Law 733.

[27]   Consider these numbers, compiled on the basis of the database maintained by Mitchell (n 24): 1970–72: 33 MEAs (21 new, 3 protocols, 9 amendments); 1980–82: 45 MEAs (19 new, 9 protocols, 17 amendments); 1990–92: 106 MEAs (50 new, 21 protocols, 44 amendments); 2000–02: 88 MEAs (37 new, 15 protocols, 47 amendments); and 2010–12: 57 MEAs (11 new, 10 protocols, 36 amendments).

[28]   Jutta Brunnée, 'COPing with Consent: Law-making under Multilateral Environmental Agreements' (2002) 15 Leiden Journal of International Law 1; Pauwelyn, Wessel, and Wouters (n 26) 740.

[29]   See (n 27).

[30]   Heike Krieger and Georg Nolte, 'The International Rule of Law—Rise or Decline?—Approaching Current Foundational Challenges' in this book, II.

[31]   Jutta Brunnée and Stephen J Toope, Legitimacy and Legality in International Law: An Interactional Account (Cambridge University Press 2010); Jutta Brunnée and Stephen J Toope, 'Interactional Legal Theory, the International Rule of Law and Global Constitutionalism' in Anthony F Lang and Antje Wiener (eds), Handbook of Global Constitutionalism (Edward Elgar Publishing 2017).

law has evolved to grapple with complexity on the one hand, and meeting the demands of the rule of law on the other. The 2015 Paris Agreement,[32] which was adopted under the auspices of the FCCC and employs an unprecedented range of legal 'modes', provides an excellent opportunity to reflect on this question.

II. Climate change as a complex problem

Climate change, with its potential to disrupt natural, economic, and social systems on Earth, represents a grave threat to humanity and demands a determined response. But, as a policy challenge, climate change eludes easy categorization—it is not one problem, but a cluster of interrelated problems.

As an environmental problem, climate change is planetary in scope and, due to its long-term and potentially irreversible consequences, intergenerational in its impacts.[33] It is caused by a wide range of production and consumption processes and its effects are felt around the globe. For this reason alone, climate change is a complex collective action problem. It can be managed only if all states, or at least the major greenhouse gas emitters, cooperate in promoting costly shifts in their economic and energy systems. These challenges are compounded by the fact that far-reaching decisions must be made under conditions of scientific uncertainty and evolving scientific knowledge.[34]

Economic challenges go hand in hand with the environmental ones. The effects of climate change entail potentially significant economic costs, ranging from damage caused by extreme weather events to the need to adapt infrastructure, to effects on coastal cities and other low-lying areas around the world, to shifting vegetation patterns and spread of viruses and species.[35] In turn, mitigation of climate change involves costly shifts in production and consumption processes; and the projected global shift away from fossil fuels already has precipitated concerns over the future of resource-based national economies and carbon-based industrial sectors, including concerns over 'stranded assets'.[36]

Climate change also raises security concerns. For some countries, like small island states, it poses an existential threat.[37] For others, its physical effects might endanger human settlements, supplies of food, water or energy, or economic stability.[38] These

---

[32] FCCC, Decision 1/CP.21 Adoption of the Paris Agreement (29 January 2016) UN Doc FCCC/CP/2015/10/Add.1, Annex (Paris Agreement).

[33] Richard Lazarus, 'Super Wicked Problems and Climate Change: Restraining the Present to Liberate the Future' (2009) 94(5) Cornell Law Review 1153.

[34] On uncertainty in international environmental law: Daniel Bodansky, Jutta Brunnée, and Ellen Hey, 'International Environmental Law: Mapping the Field' in Daniel Bodansky, Jutta Brunnée, and Ellen Hey (eds), *Oxford Handbook of International Environmental Law* (Oxford University Press 2007) 1, 7–8.

[35] Richard SJ Tol, 'The Economic Effects of Climate Change' (2009) 23 Journal of Economic Perspectives 29.

[36] Mark Carney, 'Breaking the Tragedy of the Horizon—Climate Change and Financial Stability' Speech given at Lloyd's of London (29 September 2015) <www.bankofengland.co.uk/publications/Pages/speeches/2015/844.aspx> accessed 27 March 2016.

[37] Ann M Simmons, 'One Looming Consequence of Climate Change: Small Islands Nations Will Cease to Exist' (*Los Angeles Times*, 16 November 2016) <www.latimes.com/world/global-development/la-fg-global-hugh-sealy-qa-snap-20161115-story.html> accessed 13 April 2017.

[38] US Environmental Protection Agency, 'International Climate Impacts' <www.epa.gov/climate-impacts/international-climate-impacts> accessed 13 April 2017.

effects can exacerbate humanitarian crises, promote state failures and border disputes, and produce more conventional threats to national and international security. In 2004, then Chief Scientific Adviser to the Blair government, David King, made headlines by saying that he considered climate change to be 'the most severe problem that we are facing today—more serious even than the threat of terrorism.'[39] Today, roughly 70 per cent of states explicitly consider climate change to be a national security concern, acting as a 'threat multiplier' or an 'accelerant of instability'.[40]

Climate change, furthermore, raises difficult questions of equity and global environmental justice.[41] Historically, emissions of greenhouse gases have been far greater in the industrialized world.[42] But, by 2012, developing countries generated more than half of the world's carbon dioxide (CO_2) emissions, with China and India alone accounting for one-third.[43] Thus, although the CO_2 emissions of most industrialized countries still significantly exceed those of most developing countries, the emissions of large developing countries are projected to continue to rise sharply.[44] In 2005, China surpassed the United States as the world's largest emitter of CO_2;[45] in 2013, its share of global emissions was 29 per cent, compared to the United States' 15 per cent and the European Union's (EU) 11 per cent. In per capita terms, China's emissions (7.4 tonnes) were virtually on par with those of the European Union (7.3 tonnes), but both remained significantly below US per capita emissions (16.6 tonnes).[46] The effects of climate change, in turn, are likely to disproportionately affect developing countries, many of which are especially vulnerable to them.[47] However, industrialized countries have vastly larger economic and technological capacity—not only to mitigate greenhouse gas emissions, but also to adapt to its consequences. Finally, whatever the actual disparities in contributions to and effects of climate change on individual countries, the gulf between radically different perceptions of the problem is not easily bridged. Many developing countries see climate politics as part of a larger pattern of historical and economic injustices and so have demanded that industrialized countries bear the primary

---

[39]   David A King, 'Climate Change Science: Adapt, Mitigate or Ignore?' (2004) 303 Science 176.

[40]   American Security Project, 'Global Security Defense Index on Climate Change' (2014) <www.americansecurityproject.org/climate-energy-and-security/climate-change/gsdicc/> accessed 13 April 2017, 1.

[41]   Stephen M Gardiner, Simon Caney, Dale Jamieson, and Henry Shue, *Climate Ethics: Essential Readings* (Oxford University Press 2010); Henry Shue, *Climate Justice: Vulnerability and Protection* (Oxford University Press 2014).

[42]   FCCC (n 20) preamble: 'the largest share of historical and current emissions has originated in developed countries'.

[43]   Todd Woody, 'Here's Why Developing Countries Will Consume 65% of the World's Energy by 2040' (*The Atlantic*, 3 December 2013) <www.theatlantic.com/technology/archive/2013/12/heres-why-developing-countries-will-consume-65-of-the-worlds-energy-by-2040/282006/> accessed 13 April 2017.

[44]   US Energy Information Administration, 'International Energy Outlook 2011' (2011) <www.eia.gov/pressroom/presentations/howard_09192011.pdf> accessed 13 April 2017, 139.

[45]   World Resources Institute (WRI), 'CAIT Climate Data Explorer' <http://cait.wri.org> accessed 13 April 2017.

[46]   Jos GJ Olivier, Greet Janssens-Maenhout, and Jeroen AHW Peters, *Trends in Global CO2 Emissions—2014 Report* (PBL Netherlands Environmental Assessment Agency 2014) <http://edgar.jrc.ec.europa.eu/news_docs/jrc-2014-trends-in-global-co2-emissions-2014-report-93171.pdf> (accessed 13 April 2017) 24.

[47]   *Climate Change 2014: Impacts, Adaptation and Vulnerability, Working Group II Contribution to the IPCC Fifth Assessment Report* (Cambridge University Press 2014) Summary for Policymakers 30–32.

burden of combating climate change. In turn, many industrialized countries have insisted on developing country participation as a matter of pragmatic problem solving, or even 'fairness'.[48]

And then there are all of us, and how we prioritize and decide as individuals and societies. Here lies an important part of the governance challenge: how to prompt states, political leaders, local communities, and individuals to prioritize and actually tackle the climate challenge? According to some, it is extremely difficult or even impossible to do so. For example, some commentators suggest that human psychology and the challenges inherent in collective action impede effective climate policy,[49] others claim that democracies, in particular, are incapable of dealing with climate change.[50]

Given the multitude of state and non-state actors implicated in the causes and effects of global climate change, any one of the dimensions described above would qualify as complex—as akin to 'traffic'. The amalgam of diverse but interconnected problem dimensions, however, makes the whole of the climate challenge exponentially more complex yet. Competing impulses, non-linear behaviour, and collective action challenges abound as traffic converges, proceeds, and stalls on multiple, criss-crossing levels and across multiple, potentially incompatible, modes of transport. So, how *can* international law contribute to managing this degree of complexity, keeping the 'traffic' going and avoiding a catastrophic 'crash'? I now turn to that question, beginning with reflections on the concept of the international rule of law.

III. The international rule of law

Law is commonly associated with stability and predictability. At the same time, law must be capable of accommodating or even guiding change.[51] These two dimensions are closely intertwined. Indeed, law's resilience is in important parts contingent on its ability to respond to change without compromising the rule of law. This interplay assumes particular importance in the context of the challenges posed by complex problems. In my work with Stephen Toope, I have developed an 'interactional' understanding of international law that I believe is helpful in thinking through these questions.[52] We borrow the concept of 'interactional law' from Lon Fuller. He used the term to highlight the limitations of 'the prevailing conception of law as a one-way projection of authority'[53] and the importance of appreciating law as closely tied to its

---

[48] J Timmons Roberts and Bradley C Parks, *A Climate of Injustice: Global Inequality, North-South Politics, and Climate Policy* (MIT Press 2007) ch 5.

[49] Andreas Glöckner, 'Psychology and Disaster: Why We Do Not See Looming Disasters and How Our Way of Thinking Causes Them' (2016) 7 Global Policy 14; Scott Barrett, 'Collective Action to Avoid Catastrophe: When Countries Succeed, When They Fail, and Why' (2016) 7 Global Policy 40.

[50] Jo Confino, 'It Is Profitable to Let the World Go to Hell' (*The Guardian*, 19 January 2015) <www.theguardian.com/sustainable-business/2015/jan/19/davos-climate-action-democracy-failure-jorgen-randers> accessed 16 March 2016.

[51] Generally: Roscoe Pound, *Interpretations of Legal History* (Macmillan 1923) 1.

[52] Brunnée and Toope, *Legitimacy and Legality* (n 31).

[53] Lon L Fuller, *The Morality of Law* (rev edn, Yale University Press 1969) 221.

social context.[54] The interactional account highlights that, whether particular norms are 'stable' or undergo 'change', international law is inherently dynamic. Like all law, international law is never simply the law 'on the books', but 'lives' through continuous practices (eg implementation, interpretation, justification, contestation) that reinforce existing norms, or develop or even shift them over time.[55]

Our framework posits, first, that legal norms arise in the context of social norms based on shared understandings.[56] Secondly, building on Fuller, we suggest that what distinguishes law from other types of social ordering is adherence to specific criteria of legality, widely associated with 'the rule of law': generality, promulgation, non-retroactivity, clarity, non-contradiction, not asking the impossible, constancy and congruence between rules and official action.[57] When norm-creation meets these criteria and, thirdly, is matched with norm-application that also satisfies them—when there exists what we call a 'practice of legality'—actors are able to organize their interactions through law.[58] This focus on internal traits and practices of legality is useful in the present context. The requirements of legality transcend the 'sources' of international law, disciplining legal interaction on the basis of both formally binding rules and the 'soft' norms that increasingly shape interactions amongst a widening range of international actors.

This conception of the rule of law, meant to ensure that diverse priorities could be freely pursued by autonomous actors under the law,[59] has purchase in the international arena as well.[60] Fuller's canon of legality was concerned with constituting as well as limiting governmental authority. But congruence and reciprocity between citizens and government were at the core of his conception of the rule of law.[61] That is, only when the law and its application meet the requirements of legality will it be able to guide citizens' decision-making, thereby also limiting what governments can do through law. This version of the rule of law holds an important insight for international law: even when a legal order appears to be hierarchical, it is in fact horizontal in important respects. Hence, a horizontal order like international law, even without the features commonly associated with domestic law, can be a legal order. And precisely because states, as the still-dominant international actors, occupy multiple roles at once (subjects, lawmakers, and administrative agencies), transposing the concept of the rule of law to the international level is not only possible but necessary.[62] In this setting, as also highlighted in the framing chapter for this book, its operation is best understood broadly— as enabling and constraining justification and contestation, rather than as concerned only with ensuring compliance or limiting authority.[63]

---

[54] Lon L Fuller, 'Human Interaction and the Law' (1969) 14 American Journal of Jurisprudence 1, reprinted in Kenneth I Winston (ed), *The Principles of Social Order: Selected Essays of Lon L Fuller* (rev edn, Hart 2001) 211.
[55] Also: Krieger and Nolte (n 30) IV.
[56] Brunnée and Toope, *Legitimacy and Legality* (n 31) 56–65.
[57] Fuller, *Morality of Law* (n 53) 39, 46–90.
[58] Brunnée and Toope, *Legitimacy and Legality* (n 31) 7, 27–28, 70–77.
[59] ibid 24.
[60] The following paragraphs draw from Brunnée and Toope, 'Interactional Legal Theory' (n 31).
[61] Fuller, *Morality of Law* (n 53) 19–27.
[62] Jeremy Waldron, 'The Rule of International Law' (2006) 30 Harvard Journal of Law & Public Policy 15.
[63] Krieger and Nolte (n 30) III.

The conception sketched out above has particular strengths when it comes to im-agining a foundation for a rule of law that can operate in today's deeply diverse international society. The requirements of legality that underpin the interactional international law framework are primarily formal in nature:[64] they constrain the ability of all actors, including powerful actors, to proceed in arbitrary or entirely self-serving fashion, but they do not themselves entail thick substantive commitments.[65] Such a substantively thin conception of the rule of law, built around formal requirements of le-gality and upheld by collective practices of legality, is particularly suited to international society's highly variegated political context. Nothing precludes actors from promoting substantive understandings in international law. But a 'thin' international rule of law is possible and, arguably, its requirements are all the more important in the absence of shared substantive values and goals,[66] or as actors work towards shared substance. These features of the international rule of law assume heightened importance when it comes to international law's encounter with complexity. Furthermore, as we have seen, complexity thinking calls for relational, process-oriented, and dynamic approaches. The interactional understanding of legality, focused on the traits of legal norms and emphasizing practices of legality, serves to highlight law's innate capacity to grapple with these postulates. However, as the next section will illustrate, this basic capacity is weaker or stronger, depending on the legal context (custom or treaty-based; formal or informal) in which the relevant practices occur.

IV. The evolution of international environmental law

How do international law-making and legal practice contribute to tackling complex environmental problems and with what implications for the international rule of law? I begin with brief observations about customary law and 'soft' law. I suggest that cus-tomary law, broadly speaking, is less suited to managing complexity than treaty-based law. Hence, the bulk of the discussion is focused on treaty-based regimes, which an-chor international law's most important responses to complexity and can accommo-date formal ('hard') as well as informal ('soft') approaches to standard-setting and accountability.

1. Customary law

How does the customary law framework measure up to the challenges posed by com-plex problems on the one hand, and the demands of the rule of law on the other? Seen

---

[64] Although Fuller referred to the requirements as 'procedural' the term 'formal' arguably better captures their nature and function.
[65] Also: Jan Klabbers, 'Constitutionalism and the Making of International Law: Fuller's Procedural Natural Law' (2008) 5 No Foundations 84.
[66] Martti Koskenniemi, 'The Politics of International Law' (1990) 1 European Journal of International Law 4.

from the latter vantage point, customary law has a number of advantages. The customary law-making process is a subtle combination of unilateral acts—the practices of legality referred to above—and collective action—the requirement that practice must be widespread in order to serve as foundation for custom. Hence, although customary law is inherently dynamic, it is also far more stable than one might assume at first glance. States' practices and legal opinions tend to maintain existing rules, while initiating a shift in the practices and views of a sufficient number of states to generate a new customary norm is relatively difficult. Furthermore, due to these features of the law-making process, customary rules tend to provide broadly textured ground rules for interaction. Customary law, therefore, provides a predictable framework of generally applicable rules that are unlikely to make impossible demands and likely to satisfy the constancy, non-contradiction, and non-retroactivity requirements. However, although the diffuse, fluid nature of the customary law-making process does not negate promulgation and clarity, it does make it harder to identify the precise point at which law arises than do treaty-based processes, with their emphasis on written terms and detailed rules on entry-into-force.[67]

Because it provides open-ended 'meta-principles' rather than highly specific rules, customary law has the capacity to accommodate new or evolving concerns, its relative stability notwithstanding. Thus, the stock of customary international environmental norms has remained remarkably constant over many decades, revolving around the duty to prevent transboundary harm and states' related procedural obligations.[68] Yet, through its due diligence standard, the harm prevention rule also provides a flexible, adaptable yardstick for state conduct. The requirements of due diligence are inherently contextual and may change over time and depending on the risks involved.[69] These features of the harm prevention framework are advantages when it comes to dealing with complex problems, reinforced by the framework's strong emphasis on procedural obligations.[70] Environmental impact assessment, notification, and consultation each address crucial aspects of any effort to grapple with complex issues like climate change.

Alas, for all these strengths, the customary law framework on its own cannot carry the burden of guiding global climate action. While it can help to resolve situations involving transboundary impacts, it would be hard pressed to guide legal interaction between more than 190 states, let alone sub-state or non-state actors. Its conceptual limitations are compounded by the constraints inherent in the general legal framework concerning implementation and dispute settlement. When it comes to harm to the commons or to intergenerational impacts, the harm prevention rule arguably falls

---

[67] Jutta Brunnée, 'The Sources of International Environmental Law: Interactional Law' in Jean d'Aspremont and Samantha Besson (eds), *The Oxford Handbook on the Sources of International Law* (Oxford University Press 2017).

[68] *Island of Palmas Case (Netherlands v USA)* (1928) RIAA II 829; *Trail Smelter Case (USA v Canada)* (1938/1941) RIAA III, 1905, 1965; *Corfu Channel Case (UK v Albania)* (Merits) [1949] ICJ Rep 4; *Case Concerning Pulp Mills on the River Uruguay (Argentina v Uruguay)* [2010] ICJ Rep 4.

[69] *Pulp Mills* (n 68); *Responsibilities and Obligations of States Sponsoring Persons and Entities with Respect to Activities in the Area (Advisory Opinion)* ITLOS Case No 17 (1 February 2011) para 117.

[70] *Pulp Mills* (n 68); *Certain Activities carried out by Nicaragua in the Border Area (Costa Rica v Nicaragua)* <https://www.icj-cij.org/en/case/150> and *Construction of a Road in Costa Rica along the San Juan River (Nicaragua v Costa Rica)* (16 December 2015) <www.icj-cij.org/en/case/152> both accessed 27 August 2018.

short. Although it stands to reason that the harm prevention duty gives rise to an *erga omnes* obligation in relation to areas beyond national jurisdiction, there is little international practice on this point.[71] Similarly, although the law of state responsibility envisages circumstances in which states, other than those directly injured, could invoke another state's responsibility for breaches of obligations owed *erga omnes*,[72] practice is lacking. Furthermore, because collective concern issues are by definition polycentric, they do not easily lend themselves to traditional, bilateral dispute settlement. In any event, the most important role for international law in dealing with complex problems is not that of providing for dispute settlement, but that of guiding proactive and long-term collaboration; a role that has been served primarily by treaty-based regimes, as we will see below.

This all said, leaving aside its inherent limitations in tackling complex environmental problems, it is important to note that customary international environmental law has not 'declined'. While the development of new substantive norms may have stalled, there has been an uptick in states' reliance on the procedural and due diligence requirements that flank the no harm rule, and a corresponding trend towards refinement of those requirements.[73]

2. Soft law

The broad range of norms and standards grouped together under the rubric of 'soft' law has filled some of the conceptual gaps left by customary international environmental law. In one guise, soft law serves as a staging ground of sorts, or a transitional phase on the path towards future custom.[74] For the time being, the various concepts that might better reflect the scope and multidimensional nature of climate change and other complex problems—notably, common concern, common but differentiated responsibilities, precaution, sustainable development—all find themselves in this transitional phase.[75] But even if these concepts never 'harden' into customary law, they can still shape international conduct. Aside from the effects that such concepts nonetheless may have on the legal reasoning of courts, states and other international actors,[76] they can serve as normative underpinnings for treaty-based approaches to environmental problem-solving. In this setting, as guiding principles, they help shape the interpretation and evolution of a given regime. They can also come to be fleshed out in more

---

[71] Daniel Bodansky, Jutta Brunnée, and Lavanya Rajamani, *International Climate Change Law* (Oxford University Press 2017) 49–51.

[72] Jutta Brunnée, 'International Environmental Law and Community Obligations: Procedural Aspects' in Eyal Benvenisti and Georg Nolte (eds), *Community Interests Across International Law* (Oxford University Press 2018).

[73] ibid.

[74] Alan Boyle, 'Soft Law in International Law-Making' in Malcolm D Evans (ed), *International Law* (3rd edn, Oxford University Press 2010) 122, 134–37.

[75] Bodansky, Brunnée, and Rajamani (n 71) 51–55.

[76] Christine Chinkin, 'The Challenge of Soft Law: Development and Change in International Law' (1989) 38 International & Comparative Law Quarterly 850.

concrete and issue-specific ways. As I will show in the next section, in the climate regime, the concepts of common concern and common but differentiated responsibilities, among others, have played these roles.[77]

Soft law has also emerged as a normative response in its own right, with an array of norm and standard-setting processes that do not aim for formally binding effect. In the context of complex problems, informal norm and standard-setting may hold considerable advantages: it is often faster and engenders greater willingness to collaborate and to experiment and adapt; it allows for involvement of, and application to, a wider range of actors than does customary or treaty law; and it may provide for more creative and potentially more effective accountability processes than formally binding law does.[78] Finally, as I also illustrate in the next section, in the context of treaty regimes, soft norms, standards, and processes can be combined in a range of ways with formally binding modes of legality. From an interactional law standpoint, neither the informality of standard-setting and accountability, nor the blending of formality and informality necessarily signal a decline in rule of law terms. What matters most is the extent to which the norms in question meet the requirements of legality and are buttressed by practices of legality.

3. Treaty-based regimes

Treaty-based regimes, in building upon emerging collective interest concepts, such as the ones mentioned in the preceding section, better capture the true scope of complex environmental issues, especially global ones.[79] For example, irrespective of the legal status of the concept, MEAs have designated particular issues as 'common concerns of humankind'. The FCCC preamble elaborates on the proposition that climate change is a common concern by acknowledging that its global nature 'calls for the widest possible cooperation by *all* countries ... in accordance with their common but differentiated responsibilities and respective capabilities'.[80] This framework provides the normative anchor for the climate regime and accounts not only for its universal membership, but also its resilience in the face of the challenges of collective decision-making. The differentiation dimension of the common responsibility frame, too, has been instrumental in shaping the evolution of the climate regime. Since its inception, parties have debated how responsibilities should be differentiated. Over time, the regime's approach shifted from stark South–North differentiation, reflected in the Kyoto Protocol,[81] to the much more nuanced and dynamic differentiation that underpins the 2015 Paris Agreement.[82]

---

[77] FCCC (n 20) preamble and Art 3; further: Brunnée and Toope, *Legitimacy and Legality* (n 31) ch 4.

[78] Pauwelyn, Wessel, and Wouters (n 26).

[79] This section draws upon Jutta Brunnée, 'International Environmental Law and Community Obligations' (n 72).

[80] FCCC (n 20) (emphasis added).

[81] Kyoto Protocol, reprinted in (1998) 37 ILM 22.

[82] For an overview of this evolution: Bodansky, Brunnée, and Rajamani, *International Climate Change Law* (n 71) 26–30.

A key strength of MEAs when it comes to tackling complex environmental problems is that they are not one-off agreements between states, but rather open-ended 'sets of implicit or explicit principles, norms, rules and decision-making procedures around which actors' expectations converge'.[83] The adoption of the underlying treaty, thus, marks not the endpoint of the international legal process but rather its beginning. MEAs typically establish treaty bodies for ongoing exchange and negotiation among parties, supported by treaty secretariats that provide an array of administrative services.[84] They enable the long-term interaction among regime participants that is indispensable in dealing with complex, inherently dynamic, and potentially unresolvable environmental concerns. As the following discussion will illustrate, treaty-based environmental regimes serve to institutionalize collective responses to complexity and provide for extensive procedural elements, including an array of law-making and standard-setting, as well as compliance and dispute settlement, processes. Furthermore, MEAs make room for non-state actor involvement.

(a) Information exchange and scientific assessment processes

Notification, provision of information, assessment, and consultation supply the necessary foundation for any effective effort to address a complex concern, as well as for subsequent efforts to monitor the performance of both the regime and individual parties, with a view to making adjustments where needed. MEAs, therefore, require parties to cooperate in research and scientific assessments and to report on their implementation efforts. Typically, MEAs also enshrine detailed procedural requirements, such as guidelines on how to measure performance, or on what kind of information to report in what manner. One important advantage of such treaty-based requirements is that their scope and content can be specified and nuanced far more than is possible under the general due diligence framework of customary international law.

The FCCC and its Kyoto Protocol, with their elaborate 'monitoring, reporting and verification' (MRV) requirements, provide a good illustration.[85] Unlike the Kyoto Protocol, the 2015 Paris Agreement does not contain legally binding emission reduction obligations.[86] But it nonetheless provides for a 'transparency framework' that is intended to hold states accountable for their emissions performance.[87] Thus, even if the details remain to be developed by the parties,[88] the Paris Agreement subjects all parties to extensive informational requirements pertaining to their greenhouse gas emissions and calls on developed countries to provide information on their financial, technological, and capacity-building support to developing countries. The agreement's transparency framework is complemented by a 'global stock-take' process, which is designed

[83] Steven Krasner, 'Structural Causes and Consequences: Regimes as Intervening Variables' (1982) 36 International Organization 185, 186.

[84] Geir Ulfstein, 'Treaty Bodies' in Bodansky, Brunnée, and Hey, Oxford Handbook (n 34) 875–89.

[85] FCCC (n 20) Arts 7.2, 12, 13; Kyoto Protocol (n 81) Arts 5, 7; further: Bodansky, Brunnée, and Rajamani, International Climate Change Law (n 71) 148–53, 193–94.

[86] See below (n 100–06) and accompanying text.

[87] Paris Agreement (n 32) Art 13; further: Bodansky, Brunnée, and Rajamani, International Climate Change Law (n 71) 249–51.

[88] Paris Agreement (n 32) Art 13.13.

to assess 'collective progress towards achieving the purpose of [the] Agreement and its long-term goals'.[89]

In addition to MRV requirements imposed on treaty parties, many environmental regimes establish or collaborate with international scientific and other expert forums, so as to provide less politicized settings for information exchange and scientific assessment than tend to exist in strictly inter-state contexts. For example, the FCCC established a permanent Subsidiary Body for Scientific and Technological Advice.[90] The regime also draws upon the expertise of the Intergovernmental Panel on Climate Change (IPCC), which operates under the auspices of the World Meteorological Organization and the United Nations Environment Programme.[91] Expert forums such as these are important in building consensus around the scope and urgency of environmental issues and the collective action that is required to address them. Their role in grappling with the complexities of issues like global climate change is an iterative one. Once decisions on the general thrust of collective action are taken, the work of expert bodies turns to supporting the elaboration, refinement, or adjustment of regulatory strategies. This cycle repeats itself, with no definite endpoint. In the climate regime, the IPCC has been instrumental in bringing about acceptance of the need to keep global warming to 'well below 2°C' and to pursue efforts to limit it to '1.5°C above preindustrial levels'.[92] Indicative of the challenges involved is the fact that it took parties more than twenty years to concretize their shared understanding of the FCCC's objective to avert dangerous climate change,[93] by including the temperature goals in the Paris Agreement.

(b) Law-making processes

Law-making processes and the further development of a treaty-based environmental regime are usually in the hands of a plenary body, such as a Conference of the Parties (COP). COPs and their subsidiary bodies provide a stable institutional setting for iterative standard-setting processes and interlocking engagements between technical experts, policy-makers, and lawyers. They have become central venues for international law-making activities around complex environmental problems and their practice reflects the background assumption that decision-making on response action is a collective enterprise.

MEAs also allow for the tailoring of law-making processes with a view to striking a balance between the protection of state sovereignty through consent requirements and the need for timely collective action.[94] Much regime development still occurs through ordinary consent-based processes.[95] For example, when an agreement is amended, or

---

[89]   ibid Art 14; further: Bodansky, Brunnée and Rajamani, *International Climate Change Law* (n 71) 251–53.
[90]   FCCC (n 20) Art 9.
[91]   Bodansky, Brunnée, and Rajamani, *International Climate Change Law* (n 71) 98–99.
[92]   Paris Agreement (n 32) Art 2.1(a).
[93]   FCCC (n 20) Art 2.
[94]   Brunnée, 'COPing with Consent' (n 28).
[95]   See above (nn 27–29); Further on formal treaty development methods in the climate regime: Bodansky, Brunnée, and Rajamani, *International Climate Change Law* (n 71) 85–89.

when an additional treaty, such as a protocol, is adopted, individual states are bound only when they consent to these instruments. But the consent requirements have softened. Under many agreements, especially when technical issues are involved, regulatory approaches can be adjusted with effect for all parties, except those that explicitly opt out.[96] Perhaps more significantly, extensive regulatory detail is adopted through decisions of plenary bodies, without subsequent formal consent by individual states. In most cases, the resulting standards will not be legally binding, although they may well contain mandatory language. For example, under the FCCC and its Kyoto Protocol, provisions on central treaty matters, ranging from inventory and monitoring requirements to the protocol's mechanisms for trading of emission units or reduction credits, were adopted in this way.[97] The Paris Agreement envisages a similar approach for the adoption of standards concerning key matters, such as the communication of and accounting for parties' nationally determined emission reductions and 'common modalities, procedures and guidelines' for monitoring and reviewing parties' commitments.[98]

As the slow evolution of the climate regime illustrates, even formally non-binding standards are subject to difficult negotiations.[99] Nonetheless, on balance, soft regulatory processes allow speedier regime development and adjustment than processes that involve subsequent ratification by individual states. Equally important is that they facilitate agreement upon collective action and adoption of standards applicable to all parties—an important feature for efforts to address complex environmental concerns.

The Paris Agreement highlights the increasing willingness of states to combine a range of legal approaches so as to maximize the potential for and scope of collective and adaptable standard-setting. The Paris 'Outcome' consists of a formal treaty, the Paris Agreement, and a COP decision, which adopts the treaty text and supplements it in many key respects.[100] The Paris Agreement itself contains provisions framed in mandatory terms ('shall') and provisions framed in hortatory or factual terms ('should' or 'will'). The most experimental aspect of the Outcome is that, instead of enshrining binding emission reduction commitments, it relies on non-legally binding, 'nationally determined contributions' (NDCs) by parties. And yet, the Paris Agreement, which entered into force in less than a year, on 4 November 2016,[101] does not simply give parties free reign in determining their NDCs. All parties have binding obligations to 'prepare, communicate and maintain successive' NDCs,[102] and will be subject to extensive procedural requirements, such as the ones related to performance assessment discussed

---

[96] However, in the climate regime, it has proven difficult to use the opt-out approach, due to the sensitive nature of most regime development issues, compounded by the regime's consensus decision-making practice: Bodansky, Brunnée, and Rajamani, *International Climate Change Law* (n 71) 59, 75–77.

[97] Brunnée, 'COPing with Consent' (n 28) 23–31.

[98] eg: Paris Agreement (n 32) Arts 4.8, 4.9, 4.13, 13.13.

[99] Reviewing, *inter alia*, the negotiation of the 'Marrakech Accords,' a package of COP decisions that fleshed out key aspects of the Kyoto Protocol, and of the 'Copenhagen Accord', a political agreement that foreshadowed many aspects of the Paris Agreement: Bodansky, Brunnée, and Rajamani, *International Climate Change Law* (n 71) ch 4.

[100] For a detailed discussion of the different legal modes in the Paris Agreement: Bodansky, Brunnée, and Rajamani, *International Climate Change Law* (n 71) 210–22.

[101] Paris Agreement (n 32) Arts 20, 21; as of 16 April 2017, the agreement had 185 parties: FCCC, 'Paris Agreement—Status of Ratification' <http://unfccc.int/paris_agreement/items/9444.php> accessed 28 May 2019.

[102] Paris Agreement (n 32) Art 4.2.

above.[103] An interesting legal twist in this latter context is that the Paris Agreement stipulates that parties 'shall' communicate their NDCs in accordance with decisions to be adopted by the parties, thereby rendering the content of an otherwise non-binding decision legally binding.[104] The agreement also stipulates that each party's successive NDCs 'will represent a progression' beyond the preceding one.[105] Yet, to emphasize their 'bottom-up' nature, the NDCs themselves are 'housed' outside of the agreement—they are to be communicated to the FCCC secretariat and will be published on the FCCC website.[106]

(c) Non-compliance procedures

Another key feature of multilateral environmental regimes has been their approach to compliance. Formal dispute settlement is rare in MEAs, partly because of states' reluctance to resort to it and partly because it may not satisfactorily address the complex, polycentric concerns underlying the agreement.[107] Quite apart from the diffuse nature of injuries to parties' common interest in compliance with treaty commitments, addressing the underlying environmental concerns requires the greatest possible degree of compliance by the widest possible range of parties. MEAs, therefore, have spawned procedures that assess parties' compliance with their treaty commitments and provide for a range of measures to facilitate or compel compliance.

Facilitation of compliance has been the primary objective of the majority of these compliance procedures. The procedure under the Montreal Protocol on Substances that Deplete the Ozone Layer neatly encapsulates the facilitative approach, aimed, as it is, at 'securing an amicable solution ... on the basis of respect for the provisions of the Protocol'.[108] This cooperative approach recognizes the fact that, in the context of ozone depletion, non-complying parties were most likely to be states with genuine capacity limitations. But the treaty setting also makes it possible to tailor the non-compliance regime to the features of the underlying concern and the needs of the parties involved. For example, under the Kyoto Protocol only developed countries and transition countries had emission reduction commitments.[109] Therefore, capacity building and financial assistance were less appropriate in promoting compliance. Moreover, the Kyoto Protocol regime had certain unique elements, such as its emissions trading mechanisms, which necessitated a tougher approach to compliance. The Kyoto Protocol's compliance procedure, thus, explicitly declared its goals to 'facilitate, promote and *enforce* compliance'

---

[103] See above (nn 87–88, n 98) and accompanying text.
[104] Paris Agreement (n 32) Art 4.8.
[105] ibid Art 4.3.
[106] See Decision 1/CP.21 (n 32) paras 13–14.
[107] Generally: Geir Ulfstein, 'Dispute Settlement, Compliance Control and Enforcement in International Environmental Law' in Geir Ulfstein (ed), *Making Treaties Work: Human Rights, Environment and Arms Control* (Cambridge University Press 2007) 115–34.
[108] UNEP, *Report of the Tenth Meeting of the Parties to the Montreal protocol on Substances that Deplete the Ozone Layer*, Annex II: *Non-Compliance Procedure* (Montreal Protocol NCP), UNEP Dc OzL.Pro10/9 (3 December 1998) para 8.
[109] Kyoto Protocol (n 81) Art 3.1, Annex B.

with the protocol,[110] and provided for automatic triggering of the procedure whenever an expert review revealed questions about a party's implementation of its commitments.[111] In turn, the Paris Agreement, given its reliance on nationally determined, rather than internationally negotiated, emission reduction commitments, returns to a 'mechanism to facilitate implementation ... and promote compliance'.[112] It is to consist of a committee that is 'expert-based and facilitative in nature and function[s] in a manner that is transparent, non-adversarial and non-punitive' and that is to be attentive to 'the respective national capabilities and circumstances of Parties'.[113] The terms of the compliance mechanism, including its triggers and other 'modalities and procedures', are to be developed by decision of the parties.[114]

(d) Involvement of non-state actors

A key facet of environmental concerns' complexity is that they are largely caused by and affect actors other than states. As inter-state agreements, MEAs do not accord direct rights or obligations to non-state actors. The climate regime fits this mould, although the Paris Agreement nonetheless is unusual in acknowledging that the rights of a wide range of non-state stakeholders ought to be considered as states respond to climate change.[115] At a procedural level, however, MEAs have long been accessible to non-state actors, including international organizations, non-governmental organizations (NGOs), or business entities.

An important first dimension of accessibility concerns information about a regime's standard-setting and performance monitoring activities. Although transparency through public availability of documents and data may seem ordinary today, contemporary practice does represent a significant departure from the previously closed, strictly *inter partes*, proceedings.[116] The impact of shifting attitudes has been amplified by technology—treaty websites now enable non-state actors to access not only legal documents and meeting reports, but also web-casts of plenary sessions and scientific and technical information, including that compiled pursuant to parties' procedural obligations under the regime.[117]

In addition to such 'remote' access to information about the practice of the regime and its parties, MEAs generally provide direct access to meetings of the parties. Along with non-party states, inter-governmental organizations and NGOs can obtain observer status at COP meetings, distribute information or policy papers, meet with official

---

[110] *Procedures and Mechanisms Relating to Compliance under the Kyoto Protocol* (Kyoto Protocol NCP), UN Doc FCCC/KP/CMP/2005/8/Add.3 (30 March 2006) para I (emphasis added).

[111] ibid para VI.1.

[112] Paris Agreement (n 32) Art 15.1.

[113] ibid Art 15.2.

[114] ibid Art 15.3. The terms of the compliance mechanisms, along with other aspects of the transparency framework, were adopted in December 2018, in the Katowice Rules. The relevant decisions are accessible at < https://unfccc.int/katowice> accessed 28 May 2019. On the transparency mechanism, see nn 87–89 and accompanying text.

[115] ibid preamble.

[116] Jutta Brunnée and Ellen Hey, 'Transparency and International Environmental Institutions' in Andrea Bianchi and Anne Peters (eds), *Transparency in International Law* (Cambridge University Press 2013) 26.

[117] See eg the website of the FCCC <http://unfccc.int/2860.php> accessed 16 April 2017.

delegations, or report on negotiations.[118] In a formal sense, decision-making remains entirely in the hands of states, and key negotiating sessions will typically be restricted to state delegations. But non-state actors do have opportunities to provide input into law-making processes or even help shape their outcomes.[119] The climate regime has seen extensive involvement of non-state actors throughout its history, with the numbers of non-state participants at times matching those of UN officials and government negotiators.[120] The Paris Outcome, however, harnesses a larger shift in global climate governance to a more transnational, multilevel approach.[121] For example, in cooperation with the FCCC, the Lima–Paris Action Agenda (LPAA) came to catalyse over 10,000 commitments by cities, companies, states, and other non-state actors.[122] In the lead-up to the Paris meeting, FCCC parties also launched the so-called Non-State Actor Zone for Climate Action (NAZCA), an online platform for registering and tracking climate action pledges by companies, cities, subnational, regions, investors, and civil society organizations.[123] The Paris Agreement itself merely acknowledges 'the importance of the engagements of all levels of government and various actors ... in addressing climate change'.[124] But the LPAA and NAZCA were acknowledged and welcomed, respectively, in the COP decision accompanying the Paris Agreement, and the LPAA is to be sustained and scaled up alongside state actions under the Paris Agreement.[125]

Performance and compliance assessment is one area in which MEAs continue to restrict non-state involvement. The Kyoto Protocol's compliance procedure furnishes a typical example. NGOs may submit 'factual and technical information' relevant to the compliance review,[126] have access to meetings of the compliance bodies unless parties object,[127] and have access to the findings of the compliance body.[128] But NGOs cannot trigger the procedure or make formal submissions. In this respect, the Paris Agreement follows suit. None of its three performance assessment processes (transparency framework, global stock-take, compliance mechanism) envisage direct non-state actor involvement.[129] However, outside of the climate regime, NGOs have been increasingly active, compiling rigorous and widely respected performance assessments. While not

---

[118] On the challenges: Brunnée and Hey, 'Transparency and International Environmental Institutions' (n 116) 35–36.

[119] ibid 30–37.

[120] Harro van Asselt, 'The Role of Non-State Actors in Climate Compliance' in Jutta Brunnée, Meinhard Doelle, and Lavanya Rajamani (eds), *Promoting Compliance in an Evolving Climate Regime* (Cambridge University Press 2012) 149, 149.

[121] The UN climate regime is only one of several sites of climate-related governance today, for an overview: Bodansky, Brunnée, and Rajamani, *International Climate Change Law* (n 71) ch 8.

[122] Thomas Hale, '"All Hands on Deck": The Paris Agreement and Non-State Climate Action' (2016) 16 Global Environmental Politics 12, 13.

[123] Currently, there are over 12,500 such pledges: FCCC, 'NAZCA—Tracking Climate Action' <http://climateaction.unfccc.int/> accessed 16 April 2017.

[124] Paris Agreement (n 32) preamble.

[125] Decision 1/CP.21 (n 32) paras 117–24.

[126] Kyoto Protocol NCP (n 110) para VIII.4.

[127] ibid para IX.2.

[128] ibid para VIII.7.

[129] Some opportunities for input could, however, be specified as the details of the mechanisms are elaborated, for an assessment: Harro van Asselt, 'The Role of Non-State Actors in Reviewing Ambition, Implementation, and Compliance under the Paris Agreement' (2016) 6 Climate Law 91, 99–104.

concerned with compliance per se, these assessments did measure states' intended nationally determined contributions in the lead-up to the Paris Agreement against the yardstick of the climate regime's objective and taking into account the principle of common but differentiated responsibilities.[130] In this way, non-state actors have assumed a role that has been politically and, in the absence of formal emissions commitments under the Paris Agreement, legally difficult for the inter-state regime to take on.

(e) The climate regime, complexity, and the rule of law: An initial stock-taking

The demands placed upon a treaty-based approach to climate change are considerable. It must provide a hub for legal interactions around a complex, multipronged, and multilevel problem of global scale, involving all states while also engaging sub-national and non-state actors. The task, furthermore, is to establish a resilient, long-term, but also adaptable regime. By and large, the FCCC has lived up to the postulates of complexity thinking. It provides a stable setting for ongoing interactions between states and other actors, thus reflecting the proposition that complexity is best tackled through 're-lational' approaches, including through avenues for non-state involvement. It provides a framework of procedural rules and guiding principles for collective action, reflecting the insight that complexity demands process-focused approaches embedded in 'organizational patterns'. Finally, the structure of the Paris Agreement indicates that the climate regime has grappled with the need for dynamism. Initially, the climate regime developed quickly, using conventional treaty-making methods. The FCCC and Kyoto Protocol were each negotiated in two years (although the Kyoto Protocol took more than seven years to enter into force).[131] But then the pace of climate negotiations slowed significantly, leaving aside the stream of decisions adopted to flesh out the convention and protocol, and to set the parameters for future negotiations. The Paris Agreement was adopted a full ten years after the entry into force of the Kyoto Protocol.[132] In the intervening time, the treaty-development process was bedevilled by stark political differences and hindered by the regime's consensus-based decision-making.[133] The Paris Agreement's legal architecture seems better suited to subsequent development. The emphasis on standard-setting through COP decisions side-steps the potentially long lag periods between the adoption of a legally binding instrument and its entry into force. The reliance on 'nationally determined contributions', in turn, altogether obviates the need for international emission standard-setting.

The abovementioned features of the Paris Agreement matter not only from the standpoint of complexity, but also from a 'legality' standpoint. The Paris Agreement's approach enhances the climate regime's 'generality', seeing as the vast majority of states now have emission-related commitments,[134] albeit differentiated in type and

---

[130] eg WRI, 'CAIT' (n 45); Climate Action Tracker <http://climateactiontracker.org/> accessed 16 April 2017; further: van Asselt, 'The Role of Non-State Actors' (n 129) 104–07.
[131] Bodansky, Brunnée, and Rajamani, *International Climate Change Law* (n 71) 75.
[132] ibid ch 4 (describing the evolution of the climate regime).
[133] ibid 75–77.
[134] As of 16 April 2016, the Paris Outcome had generated contributions accounting for 98.9 per cent of global carbon emissions: WRI, 'CAIT' (n 45).

stringency. Indeed, the scope for nationally determined differentiation provided by the regime helps ensure that it does 'not ask the impossible' of parties. At the same time, the generality dimension is reinforced by that fact that all parties are subject to the same normative expectations, including the requirement of 'successive' NDCs (published at the FCCC website), the notions of 'highest possible ambition' and 'progression over time' and specific reporting requirements. These elements also speak to the legality requirements of 'promulgation', 'clarity', and 'constancy over time'. Finally, in combination with the regime's transparency framework and compliance mechanism, the detailed reporting requirements will ensure that the 'congruence' of parties' actions with their commitments is systematically assessed.

None of this is to say, of course, that the approach of the Paris Agreement, by definition, is a win for the international rule of law. Indeed, everything will depend on the extent to which parties develop the various elements of the Paris Agreement in keeping with the requirements of legality and the extent to which robust practices of legality evolve in the implementation of the regime. The fact that the Paris Agreement builds upon the well-established practices of its parent regime certainly bodes well. One might even say that, from a 'rule of law' standpoint, the agreement's approach could improve on the 'hard law' approach encapsulated in the Kyoto Protocol. That approach resulted in an emission-reduction regime that applied to only a small number of parties—it was partial rather than general. Some parties' commitments also turned out to be much harder to meet than originally assumed, even if they were not outright 'impossible' to meet. Furthermore, given its five-year commitment period approach,[135] the Kyoto Protocol could not provide for 'constancy over time'. A model that relies on formal amendments to develop an emission regime makes future commitments, let alone timely commitments by all states, less than a certainty. In any event, my point here is simply that the Paris Agreement's turn to a blended formal/informal approach does not necessarily entail a decline in legality.

V. Conclusion

My survey of the evolution of international environmental law in response to 'complex problems' suggests that the rule of law in the field is alive and well. Customary international law provides stable and adaptable ground rules; while there may not have been a major 'rise', there also has been no 'decline'. However, conceptually and in terms of international practice, customary law addresses only a relatively small share of the issues raised by complex problems, especially global problems such as climate change. Soft law can help fill these conceptual and practical gaps and promote norm development. But in the context of a multifaceted, global challenge, a treaty-based regime is needed to facilitate comprehensive, long-term response action and to harness the

---

[135] Kyoto Protocol (n 81) Art 3.2; further: Bodansky, Brunnée, and Rajamani, *International Climate Change Law* (n 71) 176–77.

potential power of legally 'soft' norms and practices. The climate regime, as I hope to have shown, has proven to be adaptable and resourceful in its approach to both complexity and legality. The Paris Outcome builds on the accumulated experience of MEAs with non-binding standard-setting and review processes. But it also reaches beyond that experience, through a move from 'top-down', formally binding, law-making to a 'bottom-up' regime architecture in which states' commitments to emissions-related actions are not internationally negotiated, but nationally determined.

The Paris Outcome may signal a shift in the role of formally binding treaty law in the face of complexity, at least in the climate change context. The role of treaty law appears to be to enshrine the goals, principles, and procedures that serve to underpin and support substantive commitments. In this way, some observers have argued, formally binding law now 'orchestrates' rather than 'regulates' international action, including actions by non-state actors.[136] In and of themselves, these shifts do not signal a decline of international rule of law in the treaty setting. Rather, the evolution of the global climate regime signals the recognition that complex problems may not be amenable to solutions on the basis of fixed substantive commitments. The main weakness of formal standard-setting processes is that they are not conducive to the indispensable wide participation in complex problem solving, and not 'agile' enough to allow repeated cycles of adjustment in light of changes in the myriad factors that make up the climate challenge. But this does not mean that the international rule of law has no role to play. I venture to say that the opposite is true: the requirements of legality that I sketched earlier in this chapter are all the more important in the context of complex problems. In transcending the traditional conceptions of formality and informality, they enable international law to play the perhaps most important role in responding to complexity: to provide a resilient, predictable, but also adaptable, framework for the long-term interaction that is indispensable to enabling reasonably safe 'traffic' flow around issues that are resistant to resolution, or even incapable of final resolution.

---

[136] Matthew Hoffman, 'International Law and Climate Change: Post-Paris Challenges' Remarks (5 April 2016). For a report concerning the event, see <http://www.ccil-ccdi.ca/single-post/2016/03/30/International-Law-and-Climate-Change-PostParis-Challenges> accessed 16 April 2017.

15

Complexity Rules (or: Ruling Complexity)

Comment on Jutta Brunnée

Tomer Broude

I. Three dimensions of complexity and the international rule of law

Jutta Brunnée is probably correct in her opening speculation,[1] that this book's editors purposefully selected a prominent international environmental law scholar to consider the ability of international law to address complex problems within the broader question of the 'rise or decline' of the international rule of law. As Brunnée makes abundantly clear, environmental issues, and in particular climate change, are highly complex problems, to the point of 'wickedness', even 'super-wickedness'.[2] Nevertheless, despite this challenge, by walking through the sources of international law, Brunnée makes a compelling case for cautious and pragmatic optimism about the continuing role of international law in addressing environmental problems. Customary international law is flexible and adjustable. International soft law usefully fills gaps and pushes the substantive envelope. Treaty law is hardly perfect, but it would be good to have more of it in order to truly engage the collective complexity of climate change and other environmental problems, whether global or local. All in all, the system is working, 'resilient, predictable, but also adaptable'.[3] Thus, even from a largely instrumental perspective, international law matters—setting aside cogent arguments for its intrinsic, non-instrumental value.[4]

There is much to be said for this approach. It provides a modestly realistic (as opposed to merely realist) set of hopeful expectations from international law, without at any stage either succumbing to the alarm (as opposed to alarm-ism) that recent deteriorations in international legal frameworks have not unjustifiably generated,[5] *inter alia*

---

[1] Jutta Brunnée, 'The Rule of International (Environmental) Law and Complex Problems' in this book, I.
[2] Richard J Lazarus, 'Super Wicked Problems and Climate Change: Restraining the Present to Liberate the Future' (2009) 94 Cornell Law Review 1153; Kelly Levin, Benjamin Cashore, Steven Bernstein, and Graeme Ault, 'Overcoming the Tragedy of Super Wicked Problems: Constraining our Future Selves to Ameliorate Global Climate Change' (2012) 45 Policy Science 123, 127–29.
[3] Brunnée (n 1) V.
[4] Alon Harel, *Why Law Matters* (Oxford University Press 2016), in particular 149 and 169 with respect to international law.
[5] In the area of human rights: Philip Alston, 'The Populist Challenge to Human Rights' (2017) 9 Journal of Human Rights Practice 1.

in the area of climate change;[6] or to the temptations of supersized promises regarding the prospects of international law, promises which are a legacy of the hegemonic 'liberal internationalism' of the 1990s that needs to be dealt with looking ahead.[7] In so doing, however, this is an approach that seems to duck the 'international rule of law: rise or decline' question. By following the interactional approach to international law, developed by Brunnée in her previous work with Stephen Toope (which also addressed the complex area of climate change),[8] the chapter pursues an unabashedly 'thin' conception of the rule of law,[9] 'built around formal requirements of legality and upheld by collective practices of legality'.[10] The formal requirements of legality build, of course, on those employed by Lon Fuller's magisterial response to positivism.[11] Thus, the focus is ultimately on the qualities of the 'law', and in this respect, the conclusions are foreseeable; where legality is fulfilled—as it is, according to Brunnée's analysis of international environmental law—there is a moral obligation to comply, an obligation whose subjects are expected to respond to, even when the problems addressed are complex. The focus, then, is much less on the 'rule' part—whether international law is actually being taken seriously, more or less, in the behaviour of states under conditions of complexity. This is an empirical question to which the framework adopted does not lend itself easily.

Having said that, is the question—the one left unanswered—the right one? In this comment, I wish to make several focused and somewhat sceptical inquiries and remarks relating to the constitutive elements of the very question asked—about complexity and the international rule of law—rather than to Brunnée's adroit response to it. In so doing, I will largely disengage from the relatively specialized environmental law context, adopting a more generalist lens, looking at the environment of international law, rather than the international law of the environment. My general observations have three dimensions.

First, *ratione materiae*, as it were, I will question whether complexity (within the meaning that Brunnée employs,[12] if in a broader interpretation that more clearly

---

[6] For a very recent survey of domestic and diplomatic steps that the US administration under President Donald Trump has taken, including strong statements aimed at withdrawing from the Paris Climate Accord (FCCC, Decision 1/CP.21 Adoption of the Paris Agreement (29 January 2016) UN Doc FCCC/CP/2015/10/Add 1, Annex (Paris Agreement))—the central accord which Brunnée analyses at length, pointing to its positive contributions to the international rule of law in the sense adopted in the chapter: Michael A Mehling and Antto Vihma, '"Mourning for America": Donald Trump's Climate Change Policy' Finnish Institute of International Affairs (FIIA) Analysis 8 (2017), <https://papers.ssrn.com/sol3/papers.cfm?abstract_id=3051901> accessed 7 June 2018.

[7] For a discussion: Samuel Moyn, 'Beyond Liberal Internationalism' (Winter 2017) Dissent <www.dissentmagazine.org/article/left-foreign-policy-beyond-liberal-internationalism> accessed 30 October 2017; Michael M Mazarr, 'The Once and Future Order: What Comes after Hegemony?' (*Foreign Affairs*, January/ February 2017) <www.foreignaffairs.com/articles/2016-12-12/once-and-future-order> accessed 30 October 2017.

[8] Jutta Brunnée and Stephen J Toope, *Legitimacy and Legality in International Law: An Interactional Account* (Cambridge University Press 2010).

[9] A full discussion of the different possible meanings of the rule of law is beyond the scope of this chapter, an excellent exposition can be found in: Ian Hurd, 'The International Rule of Law: Law and the Limits of Politics' (2014) 28 Ethics and International Affairs 39.

[10] Brunnée (n 1) III.

[11] These are generality, promulgation, non-retroactivity, clarity, non-contradiction, not asking the impossible, constancy, and congruence between rules and official action; see: Lon L Fuller, *The Morality of Law* (rev edn, Yale University Press 1969) 39, 46–90.

[12] Brunnée (n 1) I: '[W]hile a *complicated* system or problem can be understood through conventional scientific approaches, a *complex* one requires an approach that can accommodate "non-linear and collective patterns of behaviour."', in reference to: OECD Global Science Forum, 'Applications of Complexity Science for Public

incorporates political and structural effects) is in fact a special case or rather an all-pervading characteristic of international relations, and by extension, of international law. Secondly, *ratione temporis*, I will query whether—notwithstanding the current angst that international-ist lawyers of many shapes, colours, and sizes may feel and express due to what seems like a tidal-scale assault on international law—the rule-of-law management of complexity is a particularly contemporary issue, or just another iteration of recurrent, resurgent, occasionally even refreshing, frictions that characterize international law. Thirdly, *ratione loci*, I will ask whether the challenges of complexity maintain a special relationship with international law, or whether these are substantially the same as the interactions of these issues with domestic legal systems. Some remarks on complexity and crisis conclude.

II. The fog(s) of international law? Complexity as uncertainty, uncertainty as the rule

In addressing the question of complexity regarding the international rule of law, it is useful to draw an analytical distinction between two terms that are often intermixed, and then to bring them back together again, as far as international law is concerned. The concepts I refer to are 'complex *systems*' on the one hand, and 'complex *problems*', on the other hand. Both of these derive from extra-legal complexity theory, as discussed by Brunnée, and have similar characteristics—non-linear dynamics, 'moving parts' that are greater than their sum (primarily because of their ongoing interaction with each other and mutual reflexivity and dependence), changes over time that are more influential than static elements, and informational gaps.[13] Brunnée aptly refers in illustration to the contrast between a 'car', as a *complicated* system, and 'traffic', as a *complex* one.[14] Taking the analogy one step further, both a car and traffic are *systems*; neither of them is a *problem* as such, unless someone sees them that way. Fixing a broken-down car when one needs transportation, or regulating traffic for public policy purposes—these are both problems that relate to particular and distinct systems. The car is a complicated system (at least for lawyers) and requires special knowledge and expertise to operate. Regulating traffic is complex because of its dynamic and informational aspects, that normally are absent in a car, although this may be a question of degree rather than an absolute distinction.

A complex *problem*, however, has an important additional element—polytely—an abundance of goals, a phenomenon that 'represents goal conflicts on different levels of analysis'.[15] How is a problem defined as a problem, and by/to whom? In other words,

---

Policy: New Tools for Finding Unanticipated Consequences and Unrealized Opportunities' (September 2009) <www.oecd.org/science/sci-tech/43891980.pdf> accessed 30 October 2017 1–2.

[13] For a discussion: Joachim Funke, 'Complex Problem Solving' in Norbert M Seel (ed), *Encyclopedia of the Sciences of Learning* vol 38 (Springer 2012), 682. The complexity literature is vast, and meaningfully engaging with it is well beyond the scope of this comment and the presumption of my own faculties.

[14] Brunnée (n 1) opening citation, referring to OECD (n 12) 1–2.

[15] Dietrich Dörner and Joachim Funke, 'Complex Problem Solving: What It Is and What It Is Not' (2017) 8 Frontiers in Psychology 1153.

how well defined are the goals of the problem-solving exercise? A system, how dynamic and complex it may be, is a descriptive term. A problem, in contrast, has a normative and potentially a prescriptive dimension, whose definition depends on the definition of the goals of addressing the problem (and why it is a problem to begin with). These goals can be clearly and well-defined, or vague and ill-defined. Goals can be ill-defined for a variety of reasons (such as a lack of vision), but with respect to complexity, they are ill-defined primarily because of conflicting goals. To continue still further with the analogy, if one needs to get a car running, the goal seems clear-cut when you are the would-be driver. Regulating traffic is complex, however, not only because of the dynamic attributes of traffic, but because solving the problem of its regulation needs to address a multiplicity of goals: fast and uncongested transportation, minimization of risks and accidents, accessibility, financial costs, environmental sustainability—the list goes on. And, importantly, the hierarchy of these goals may be differently ranked by different people and different stakeholders. In other words, a complex problem, when understood as encompassing polytely, is inherently political. Hold that thought.

What emerges is that a problem becomes a complex one because of a combination of issues that are either endogenous or exogenous to the system, or both. Granted that the environment is an extremely complex system, climate change, for example, is a complex problem first and foremost because of the vast range of non-linear dynamic factors that are involved in generating it and engaging with it, and the scientific uncertainty about effective ways to mitigate or adapt to its effects.[16] These are factors endogenous to the system that underlies the problem. But climate change is a complex problem—for international law, for the sake of the argument—also because of factors exogenous to the issue itself. What are the goals of taking individual or collective steps against climate change? Is the goal the reduction of greenhouse gas emissions? Saving coastal and island communities at whatever cost? How is it to be balanced against goals of economic development and poverty reduction? Attaining gender equality? Promoting indigenous rights? All of these are mentioned in the Paris Climate Accord.[17] These are all questions that derive from the polytelic nature of international environmental law, and again, they are ultimately political, down to the resolution of considering which industrial or agricultural sector will pay the price of climate change policies, or reap benefits, in which polity, and when. Complex problems, not only when related to the international legal context, have two main elements. The first is endogenous uncertainty, the objective difficulty in divining cause and effect in public policy with respect to a particular question. The second is exogenous to the issue, and relates to the uncertainties of the interests and goals, stated and unstated, of the different actors—governmental, non-governmental, strong, weak—that are stakeholders in the issue, and sometimes actors in international law.

---

[16] Merely as an example of this discourse: Alan Ingham, Jie Ma, and Alistair Ulph, 'Climate Change, Mitigation and Adaptation with Uncertainty and Learning' (2007) 35 Energy Policy 5354.

[17] eg the Eighth Preambular Recital of the Paris Accord emphasizes 'the intrinsic relationship that climate change actions, responses and impacts have with equitable access to sustainable development and eradication of poverty': Paris Agreement (n 6).

But are these conditions not actually the norm of international relations and, by extension, of international law? International environmental law in general and climate change make a wonderful case study in this respect, but are these areas significantly more complex than other fields in which public international law dares to tread? Empirical uncertainty prevails in practically all other areas. Does plain packaging of tobacco products reduce smoking?[18] Does increased foreign investment contribute to economic growth?[19] Does international criminal prosecution deter war crimes and crimes against humanity?[20] What about the effects of humanitarian or other military intervention?[21] Genetically modified organisms? Beyond these obvious complexities, however—certainly not just complications—there is the exogenous, political complexity involved. Each of these questions has a political economy, a set of interest groups with hardly shared values.[22] As Anthea Roberts has recently shown, shared values regarding international law are perhaps an aspiration, but are far from reality.[23]

Thus, international law is a complex system, both empirically and politically, and it addresses mostly problems that are complex, in both endogenous and exogenous fogs. However the rule of law is understood, or defined, it faces complexity. Would we truly need it otherwise?

III. Why now? Complexity and the rule of law in inter-temporal perspective

The second point I wish to discuss is whether there is anything special or new in the question of the engagement of the international rule of law with complexity? The editors of this book, in their introduction,[24] have made a bold attempt at periodization, an exercise that is both necessary and inevitably arbitrary.[25] While acknowledging this, they look to the year 1990, as a dividing point between 'classical' international law and the emergence of what they consider to be the international rule of law. The reasons for this appear obvious—the end of the Cold War as we knew it, the resurgent rise of the

---

[18] Research strongly suggests that it does: Colin N Smith, John D Kraemer, Andrea C Johnson, and Darren Mays, 'Plain Packaging of Cigarettes: Do We Have Sufficient Evidence?' (2015) 8 Risk Management Health Policy 21; nevertheless it is a question pertinent to legal findings and at the time of writing, decisions on this matter are still pending at the World Trade Organization (WTO).

[19] It depends, on a variety of factors: Joshua Aizenman, Yothin Jinjarak, and Donghyun Park, 'Capital Flows and Economic Growth in the Era of Financial Integration and Crisis, 1990–2010' (2013) 24 Open Economies Review 371.

[20] For a discussion: Richard Steinberg, *Contemporary Issues Facing the International Criminal Court* (Brill Nijhoff 2016) 184ff.

[21] For an empirical analysis that demonstrates the futility of intervention: Jeffrey Pickering and Emizet F Kisangani, 'Political, Economic, and Social Consequences of Foreign Military Intervention' (2006) 59 Political Research Quarterly 363.

[22] Brunnée asserts that 'legal norms arise in the context of social norms based on shared understandings' in Brunnée (n 1) III, building on Brunnée and Toope (n 8) 56–65.

[23] Anthea Roberts, *Is International Law International?* (Oxford University Press 2017).

[24] Heike Krieger and Georg Nolte, 'The International Rule of Law—Rise or Decline?—Approaching Current Foundational Challenges' in this book.

[25] Jerry H Bentley, 'Cross-Cultural Interaction and Periodization in World History' (1996) 101 American Historical Review 749.

United Nations (UN) Security Council from dormancy, the establishment of numerous international institutions, including (most conspicuously) courts and tribunals, in areas as diverse as international criminal law and international intellectual property.

The reference to the 1990s—merely a quarter of a century later—is in fact very telling, though, for other reasons. The 1990s also saw a conjunction of Western (both complicated and complex) rule of law projects: economic neoliberalism through the 'Washington Consensus', international human rights through the UN system,[26] constitutional transplants in a variety of settings, with the unprecedented empowerment of constitutional and international judicial review.[27] As we now know—and have known for a while—although the constitutions, institutions, and dogmas still exist—their idealized effectiveness has been questionable and they are now very much under fire. Thus, the question 'rise or decline' inevitably reflects a certain nostalgia to a short-lived heyday of something that ostensibly went beyond 'classical' international law. This is indeed debatable, but I will accept this periodization, answering the question regarding complexity: Are international law's challenges more complex now than before 1990, in the sense discussed previously?

The answer is both yes and no. On one hand, we cannot ignore a reality in which international law, since the 1990s and to large extent because of the international liberal euphoria of the time, has been tasked with perhaps overly optimistic missions regarding increasingly complex sets of issue areas. Yet at the same time, we should not underplay the complexity of the issues international law was facing in earlier, post-Second World War days. Let me deal with these in reverse order, first demonstrating the complexity that existed in the international system before the end of the Cold War; and then explaining some of the reasons for subsequently increased engagement of the international rule of law with complexity.

Perhaps the most translucent comparative prism through which to view the prevalence of complexity in international law's ambit over time, is that of conflict. A lively debate has ensued over the last two decades over so-called 'new' wars—conflicts that involve a plethora of non-state actors, are driven by economic interests, ethnic rivalries, or supranational ideologies that cannot easily be identified with the Westphalian state framework.[28] This phenomenon can be contrasted in a caricaturized way with a vision of 'old' wars, which were almost pitched battles between clearly defined state parties with clearly defined goals, a clear beginning and clear ending. These 'new' wars are undoubtedly complex problems, both in the endogenous sense—the existence of such a broad variety of actors exacerbates the uncertainty that is in any case a basic hallmark of all warfare[29]—and in the exogenous sense; polytely is rampant. Consider the

---

[26] On the confluence between neoliberalism and human rights projects: Samuel Moyn, 'A Powerless Companion: Human Rights in the Age of Neoliberalism' (2014) 77 Law & Contemporary Problems 147.

[27] Morton J Horwitz, 'Constitutional Transplants' (2009) 10 Theoretical Inquiries in Law 535; Tomer Broude, 'The Constitutional Function of Contemporary International Tribunals, or Kelsen's Visions Vindicated' (2012) 4 Goettingen Journal of International Law 519.

[28] Mary Kaldor, *New and Old Wars. Organized Violence in a Global Era* (Polity Press 2006); Herfried Münkler, *The New Wars* (Polity Press 2005).

[29] For a discussion of Clausewitz's concepts of uncertainty and friction in warfare as applied to modern wars in Iraq and Afghanistan: Thomas Waldman, ' "Shadows of Uncertainty": Clausewitz's Timeless Analysis of Chance in War' (2010) 10 Defense Studies 336.

chaos in the Middle East in the wake of the so-called 'Arab Spring', even focus only on the Syrian civil war—certainly a 'wicked problem'. What are the goals of international legal involvement in the conflict? Upholding the international law of armed conflict? Preventing and ultimately prosecuting war crimes and crimes against humanity? Restoring political stability regardless of human rights abuses by the incumbent Assad regime? Mitigating the externalities that the influx of refugees from the region has incurred to the European social and political system? Or is it ultimately all about oil? Of course, a conflict of this scale and complex messiness presents a challenge to the international rule of law, and many have emphasized the limited capacity of international humanitarian law to address it properly.[30]

But at the same time, these 'new' wars are clearly not entirely 'new' from an historical perspective. The Second World War, on the global scale, involved numerous non-state actors, militias, and armed groups, not always representing a national interest, even if allied with one.[31] The role of non-state actors in international conflict, or internationalized non-international conflict, has a long history in international law, certainly predating the 1990s, and can very much be understood in the context of Cold War decolonization proxy wars (case in point, the Second Protocol to the Geneva Conventions from 1977).[32] Indeed, were the post-Second World War conflicts in Bangladesh, Vietnam, Nicaragua, Cambodia, Indonesia, Afghanistan (name your Cold War conflict or repressive regime) any less complex, and any less concerning for the international rule of law than today's Sudan, Iraq, Ukraine, or South China Sea? Or is it more a framing issue—that the 1990s raised the internationalist expectations from the international rule of law, an overreach leading now to disappointment? The same (rhetorical) question could be asked in other fields. Is the regulation of nuclear arms significantly more complex today than it was during the Cold War? Is the regulation of international trade significantly more complex than it was in the 1970s? In the *longue durée*—probably not.

In other words, from an inter-temporal perspective one might conclude that the complexity challenge to the international rule of law tells us less about actual 'new' complexities, and much more about the way the latter sees itself, or rather, the way it is seen by utopian internationalists who thought that the 'end of history' signalled a triumph of a particular kind of international legal order. International law has always engaged with complexity, both endogenous and exogenous; polytely, uncertainty, friction—these are all difficult circumstances for the smooth functioning of an international rule of law. But they are not new. Having said that, we must acknowledge that as global society changes, so do the complexities that international law faces. For example, the age of the internet provides citizens unprecedented access to information, but this includes

---

[30] Nicolas Lamp, 'Conceptions of War and Paradigms of Compliance: The "New War" Challenge to International Humanitarian Law' (2011) 16 Journal of Conflict and Security Law 225.

[31] As one example of many, think of the Jewish anti-British organizations in Palestine, which during the war adopted different approaches to cooperating with the British: Yehuda Bauer, 'From Cooperation to Resistance: The Haganah 1938–1946' (1966) 2 Middle Eastern Studies 182.

[32] Protocol Additional to the Geneva Conventions of 12 August 1949, and relating to the Protection of Victims of Non-International Armed Conflicts (Protocol II) 1125 UNTS 609 (8 June 1977).

'fake news' and disinformation. This means that informed opinions on complex problems are both easier to formulate, and more susceptible to manipulation and entrenchment.[33] Global economy is now more technology-driven than ever, making traditional political economy underlying trade and investment agreements out of date. The seeming neatness of the North–South divide has been reversed in many areas, making almost all problems—including climate change—more complex.[34] Civil society, social networks—empowered by technology—are now significant actors in complex arenas. The rise of the regulatory state has floated many complex issues that were once the sole domain of national governments to the level of international law—finance, health, even public morals—all of these governance areas, reflecting complexity, are on the international legal agenda. These may be new forms of complexity, but as such, complexity is not foreign to international law: indeed, complexity rules.

IV. Is international law special? Multilevel complexity and rule of law challenges

Nearing conclusion, we must briefly present a third query: is complexity a special challenge for the *international* rule of law in comparison with domestic rule(s) of law? After all, 'wicked' problems—in their endogenous sense—are not defined solely or even dominantly by their transnational, cross-boundary dimensions. Global warming as a problem and the different ways to mitigate it and adapt to it are no less complex, no less vague, and no less contentious at the levels of private, domestic, localized, urban, municipal, or regional governance than they are on the international level. It is by all measures a multilevel problem, to be addressed through multilevel governance, in which only one part is played by international law.[35] As international lawyers, we sometimes forget that it is not always about us: most complex problems that international law engages with—be it terrorism,[36] migration and refugees,[37] or non-communicable diseases[38]—are indeed such multilevel problems with multilevel solutions. The international rule of law, in its rise or decline, is only one part of a much broader array of human responses to these complex challenges.

---

[33] For one thought-provoking take: John S Brown and Paul Duguid, *The Social Life of Information* (rev edn, Harvard Business Review Press 2017).

[34] Robert B Zoellick, 'The End of the Third World' (Spring 2010) International Economy 40; Ian Bremmer and Nouriel Roubini, 'A G-Zero World' (2011) 90 Foreign Affairs 2.

[35] For a collection of articles: Inger Weibust and James Meadowcroft (eds), *Multilevel Environmental Governance: Managing Water and Climate Change in Europe and North America* (Edward Elgar 2014).

[36] Magdalena Bexell, 'Multi-level Governance and the Rule of International Human Rights Law: The Case of the Voluntary Principles on Security and Human Rights' in Monika Heupel and Theresa Reinold (eds), *The Rule of Law in Global Governance* (Palgrave MacMillan 2016) 181.

[37] Tiziana Caponio and Michael Jones-Correa, 'Theorising Migration Policy in Multilevel States: The Multilevel Governance Perspective' (*Journal of Ethnic and Migration Studies*, 2 August 2017) <www.tandfonline.com/doi/full/10.1080/1369183X.2017.1341705> accessed 7 June 2018.

[38] Roger S Magnusson and David Patterson, 'The Role of Law and Governance Reform in the Global Response to Non-Communicable Diseases' (5 June 2014) 10(44) Globalization and Health <https://globalizationandhealth.biomedcentral.com/articles/10.1186/1744-8603-10-44> accessed 7 June 2018.

Nevertheless, there are several factors that make the international rule of law's involvement with complex problems special in comparison with all other levels. Let me mention three such factors. First, notwithstanding the crucial impact of local and national efforts in the resolution of complex problems, most such problems are collective actions problems, that require sophisticated coordination in the provision of a global public good.[39] This is certainly true of climate change, as Brunnée notes.[40] Thus, international law is necessary, and it needs commitment and 'compliance', which in turn requires an environment that respects commitments—an international rule of law. Second, turning to the political, international law's chief weakness is its frail public legitimation. This is a problem that hardly needs elaboration on the backdrop of the Brexit leave vote and the ongoing redrawing of international law, that is increasingly being referred to as a 'backlash'.[41] If even in what is arguably the most advanced rule of law creation of international law, the European Union, public legitimacy is faltering,[42] what can be said of the universal system? Third, we must ever remind ourselves that international law is almost by definition limited in its effectiveness, whether with respect to complex problems or otherwise. Turning full circle, it is because of these limitations that the international rule of law must be complemented by subsidiary elements of governance at all times and in all cases. Ruling complexity is not a task for international law alone.

V. From complexity to crisis and back again

These have been some structured thoughts on the role of international law in addressing complex problems, such as climate change. If there is an underlying theme in these comments, it is that complexity is a given in a system that claims to provide a semblance of global governance with rule of law elements. Complexity is the norm rather than the exception in international relations. Over time, it has persisted and will continue to do so. And it is a complexity that is not unique to international law, even if international law has some special attributes in this regard.

A final observation is therefore made here, and that relates to the possible conflation of complexity with crisis. As noted, complexity is normal, both old and new. Uncertainty in governance and social regulation is normal and all-pervasive. Having said that, complexity and uncertainty easily trigger anxieties, which can easily lead to a sense of crisis, even to the oxymoronic sense of permanent crisis. Hilary Charlesworth famously referred, somewhat cynically, to international law as a 'discipline of crisis'.[43]

---

[39] For cutting-edge analysis: Anne van Aaken, 'The Behavioral Turn to the International Law of Global Public Goods and Commons' 112 American Journal of International Law 67.

[40] Brunnée (n 1) II.

[41] In a specialized but not unrepresentative context: Karen J Alter, James T Gathii, and Laurence J Helfer, 'Backlash against International Courts in West, East and Southern Africa: Causes and Consequences' (2016) 27 European Journal of International Law 293.

[42] Giandomenico Majone, 'From Regulatory State to a Democratic Default' (2014) 52 Journal of Common Market Studies 1216.

[43] Hilary Charlesworth, 'International Law: A Discipline of Crisis' (2002) 65 Modern Law Review 377.

Climate change lends itself very easily to a rhetoric of such crisis.[44] This rhetoric, however, is false and misleading. As the international rule of law faces a reality check in the 2010s, we should not consider it as being in crisis. Gramsci wrote that 'crisis consists precisely in the fact that the old is dying and the new cannot be born'.[45] We are not in such a condition now; in international law, the new is being born all the time, yet the old is not truly dying. And so, we should not confuse complexity with crisis or be deterred by the continuing challenges faced by international law.

[44] Tomer Broude, 'Warming to Crisis: The Climate Change Law of Unintended Opportunity' (2013) Netherlands Yearbook of International Law 111.

[45] Antonio Gramsci, *Prison Notebooks*, vol II (Joseph Buttigieg ed, Joseph Buttigieg and Antonio Callari trs, Columbia University Press 1992) Notebook 3, s 34, 32–33 (Gramsci was writing on the historical 'crisis of authority'—perhaps conceptually not far removed from the question of the rise or decline of the international rule of law).

16

International Law, Informal Law-Making, and Global Governance in Times of Anti-Globalism and Populism

Jan Wouters

Le droit n'est point fait pour les besoins de l'esprit mais pour les réalités sociales.[1]

I. Introduction

The acceleration and intensification of international exchanges in these times of ongoing globalization are a fact of life. [2] One is often tempted to regard globalization mainly in its economic dimensions and to focus on the enormous increases of cross-border trade in goods and services, and the unprecedented mobility of capital, investments, and ideas across the globe that it generates.[3] This is of course what catches our attention the most, when we are walking through supermarkets, seeing the spread of brands and business firms the world over, reading the latest financial news, and listening to the latest global musical hits. But there is a less visible side to globalization, which has to do with its impacts upon our culture, language and thinking, social behaviour, and ethics.[4] Still less visible but more subtle is the interaction between globalization and the evolution of our domestic, transnational, and international *legal* cultures and systems. Legal scholarship is only slowly picking this up.[5]

---

[1] René Demogue, *Les Notions Fondamentales du Droit Privé. Essai Critique pour servir d'Introduction à l'Etude des Obligations* (Rousseau 1911).
[2] This chapter builds on a number of earlier publications on international law-making, including publications realized as part of the IN-LAW project, in particular Joost Pauwelyn, Ramses A Wessel, and Jan Wouters, *Informal International Lawmaking* (Oxford University Press 2012); Jan Wouters and Linda Hamid, 'Custom and Informal International Lawmaking' in Curtis A Bradley (ed), *Custom's Future. International Law in a Changing World* (Cambridge University Press 2016) 332; and research conducted for Chiara Oldani and Jan Wouters, *The G7 and Global Governance in Times of Anti-Globalization* (Routledge 2018).
[3] A useful tool for measuring the three main dimensions of globalization (economic, social, and political) is the Kof Globalization Index <http://globalization.kof.ethz.ch/> accessed 24 June 2018. In addition to these three indices, an overall index of globalization is available as well as sub-indices.
[4] For this more comprehensive view of globalization, going critically beyond internationalization, liberalization, universalization, and westernization: Jan A Scholte, *Globalization: A Critical Introduction* (2nd edn, Palgrave MacMillan 2005).
[5] Eyal Benvenisti, *The Law of Global Governance* (Nijhoff Publishers 2014); Mireille Delmas-Marty, *Global Law: A Triple Challenge* (Transnational Publishers 2003); Delmas-Marty, 'L'internationalisation du

The present contribution focuses on the impact of globalization on public international law in times of anti-globalism and populism, where globalization itself has increasingly become contested. It will be submitted that traditional public international law has been dangerously unreceptive in capturing new transnational regulatory actors and normative dynamics, which makes it more vulnerable to anti-globalist and populist attacks (Section II). We will also look into the corresponding rise and features of 'informal international law-making' (Section III), and 'global governance' (Section VI), as they may offer some responses to, or at least some defences against, anti-globalist and populist politics. We will also address the current challenges which traditional forms of international law-making, like treaties and customary international law, are currently going through (Sections IV and V). In our concluding remarks (Section VII), we will submit that public international law will have to adapt to both the challenges of globalization and anti-globalism, if it is to remain relevant in regulating international life in the twenty-first century.

II. Public international law

When studying public international law, two of the main mandatory issue areas are the 'sources' and the 'subjects'. Over the past decades, the tensions between these traditional doctrines and the realities of international life have become ever more striking. Jan Klabbers has observed, not without foundation, that 'globalisation seems to have bypassed the discipline of international law completely'.[6] In recent years, anti-globalist and populist politics seem to have added an additional layer of challenges to classical international law.

1. The sources of international law

As is known, in public international law, the term 'sources' can refer either to substantive sources (for instance particular provisions of treaties or norms of customary international law) or to formal sources, that is the methods for establishing norms in the international legal system or, in other words, the processes of international law-making. The most authoritative statement regarding the formal sources of international law, so

---

droit: pathologie ou métamorphose de l'ordre juridique?' in Alceu J Cicco Filho, Ana F Penna Velloso, and Maria E Guimarães Teixeira Rocha (eds), *Direito Internacional na Constituiçao: estudios em homenagem a Francisco Rezek* (Saraiva 2014) 499–501; Jan Klabbers and Mortimer Sellers, *The Internationalization of Law and Legal Education* (Springer 2008); Ralf Michaels, 'Global Legal Pluralism' (2009) 5 Annual Review of Law and Social Science 243; Daniel Mockle, *Mondialisation et état de droit* (Bruylant 2000); Charles-Albert Morand, *Le droit saisi par la mondialisation* (Bruylant 2001); Gaylor Rabu, 'La mondialisation et le droit éléments macrojuridiques de convergence des régimes juridiques' (2008) 22 Revue Internationale de Droit Economique 335.

[6] Jan Klabbers, 'The Idea(s) of International Law' in Sam Muller, Stavros Zouridis, Morly Fishman, and Laura Kistemaker (eds), *The Law of the Future and the Future of Law* (Torkel Opsahl Academic EPublisher 2011) 69, 71.

we teach our students, can still be found in Article 38 of the Statute of the International Court of Justice (ICJ Statute). However, it is well known that this provision is highly imperfect. It dates from the early 1920s, as it also appeared in the Statute of the International Court of Justice's (ICJ) predecessor, the Permanent Court of International Justice (PCIJ).[7] While it still constitutes a useful starting point for teaching the ABC of international law-making processes, Article 38 is nowadays very incomplete and has even some rather troublesome parts. Admittedly, it is still correct to list treaties ('international conventions') and customary international law ('international custom') as the two main sources of public international law, although their pre-eminence is somewhat undermined by recent developments to which we will revert below (Sections IV and V). The reference to general principles of law is more problematic. It refers, in an anachronistic and nowadays politically incorrect manner, to 'civilized nations' and does not spell out whether these principles constitute national or international principles of law.[8] A similar ambiguity rests with 'judicial decisions'. It is highly questionable whether, in the twenty-first century, 'teachings of the most highly qualified publicists of the various nations' should be seen as a—admittedly, only subsidiary—means for the determination of rules of law. In a world of mass academic literature production, who can say which publicists these are, and what their legitimacy is to give normative orientations for today's international community? More importantly still, Article 38 is incomplete. It does not include equity as a source of international law (apart from a limited reference in paragraph 2), nor does it make reference to unilateral legal acts, decisions of international organizations, norms of *jus cogens*, or to soft law. Apart from its outmodedness and incompleteness, there is another issue with Article 38. It does not take into account at all the question of (lack of) democratic legitimacy of the way in which international norms come about. It is written for a largely anarchic international society. Does this still fit the needs and reflect the realities of international law-making in the twenty-first century?

2. Multilateralism, universalism, and the rule of law under threat

This question is crucial in light of current developments in international affairs that appear to increasingly question a global order which is founded upon multilateralism and the rule of law. With the election of President Trump in the United States and the UK's decision to leave the European Union (EU) (Brexit), populist discourses have become increasingly relevant to the future development of international law, as we witness a mounting reluctance to promote the norms and institutions that make up this order. Compared to domestic legislation, international law scores significantly lower in terms

---

[7]   As is known, the PCIJ Statute resulted from the work of an Advisory Committee of Jurists presided by Baron Edouard Eugène François Descamps (1847–1933), professor of international law at the Catholic University of Leuven from 1876 to 1932.

[8]   On these issues: Mads Andenas, Malgosia Fitzmaurice, Attila Tanzi, and Jan Wouters (eds), *General Principles and the Coherence of International Law* (Brill 2019).

of democratic checks and balances, as there are clear limitations in terms of transparency, participation, and democratic accountability of many of its law-making actors, from states to international organizations. This is very relevant as populism tends to apply a strictly dualistic view of the world, between the *pure* People and the *corrupt* elite:[9] international law, which is technical and defined by the establishment, lends itself perfectly to this kind of contestation. For example, one can consider the role of international organizations in turning normative and contested matters from human rights to climate change into technical issues of rule application, which is likely to encourage populist denunciation. In this sense, it could be argued that populists make their own sort of fundamental criticism of *jurocracy* which can be found in some interpretations of international law—that is of a set of norms that is imposed and lacks democratic control and transparency.[10] Here the issue can be seen as relating to the broader contestation that is directed at *loci* of authority situated beyond the nation-state, which tend to be considered illegitimate.[11] The current US President has made no secret of his dismissiveness towards a number of multilateral fora: the United Nations (UN)—threatening in particular to leave the UN Human Rights Council[12]—the World Trade Organization (WTO)[13] and the North-Atlantic Treaty Organization (NATO).[14] One might also argue that, not unlike a number of EU member states in Central and Eastern Europe,[15] a further challenge comes in the form of the pressure placed upon the rule of law.[16] A case in point, the US executive order issued at the start of 2017 restricting travel from a number of mainly Muslim countries—in violation of the 1951 Refugee Convention[17] and the US Constitution—and, more generally, the undeniably harsh rhetoric directed at the US judiciary, has led many scholars to question President

---

[9] Cas Mudde and Cristóbal R Kaltwasser, 'Populism' in Michael Freeden and Marc Stears (eds), *The Oxford Handbook of Political Ideologies* (Oxford University Press 2013) 493.

[10] Note that such accounts tend to ignore the role of the legislature in giving its consent to international treaties, eg: John O McGinnis and Ilya Somin, 'Should International Law Be Part of Our Law?' (2010) 59 Stanford Law Review 1175. This being said, parliamentary consent with treaties gives the latter only a 'thin' form of legitimacy—more generally with regard to 'thin State consent' as being insufficient for legitimizing international cooperation: Joost Pauwelyn, Ramses A Wessel, and Jan Wouters, 'When Structures Become Shackles: Stagnation And Dynamics in International Lawmaking' (2014) 25 European Journal of International Law 733, 734.

[11] David Armstrong, *Civil Society and International Governance: The Role of Non-State Actors in Global and Regional Regulatory Frameworks* (Routledge 2011).

[12] Stephanie Nebehay, 'US Poised to Warn UN Rights Forum of Possible Withdrawal' (*Reuters*, 6 June 2017) <www.reuters.com/article/us-usa-un-rights/u-s-poised-to-warn-u-n-rights-forum-of-possible-withdrawal-idUSKBN18W173> accessed 24 June 2018.

[13] The Economist, 'The WTO Is under Threat from the Trump Administration' (7 December 2017) <www.economist.com/news/leaders/21732108-america-increasingly-resorting-bilateral-trade-measures-wto-under-threat> accessed 24 June 2018.

[14] Thomas Wright, 'Trump Remains a NATO Skeptic' (*The Atlantic*, 27 May 2017) <www.theatlantic.com/international/archive/2017/05/trump-nato-article-five-israel-saudi-arabia/528393/> accessed 24 June 2018.

[15] On democratic backsliding in EU member states: Tanja A Börzel and Frank Schimmelfennig, 'Coming Together or Drifting Apart? The EU's Political Integration Capacity in Eastern Europe' (2017) 24 Journal of European Public Policy 278.

[16] Laurin Liu, '"Protecting the Nation from Foreign Terrorist Entry" and Other Bogeymen: Is Trump's Populism Compatible with the Rule of Law?' (*LSE Human Rights Blog*, 2 February 2017) <http://blogs.lse.ac.uk/humanrights> accessed 24 June 2018.

[17] James Cavallaro and Rebecca Mears, 'Trump's Travel Ban Violates International Treaties: Don't Lose Sight of That Little-Discussed Problem with the Executive Order' (Stanford Law School, 16 March 2017) <https://law.stanford.edu/2017/03/16/trumps-travel-ban-violates-international-treaties-dont-lose-sight-of-that-little-discussed-problem-with-the-executive-order/> accessed 24 June 2018.

Trump's commitment to the rule of law and separation of powers.[18] Despite the still uncertain outcome of the Brexit negotiations, this and the election of an illiberal and populist US President, both signal a rejection of global cooperation and integration which runs counter to the universalism upon which international law is founded. This seems to go hand in hand with a turn in global affairs towards more transactional and utilitarian approaches, which favour unilateral or bilateral interest-focused efforts, as opposed to multilateral cooperation. Multilateralism indeed presupposes the sharing of certain ordering principles, a 'socially constructed indivisibility', and a form of 'diffuse reciprocity' (in the sense of 'a rough equivalence of benefits in the aggregate and over time') between its participants.[19] The extent to which the principles that underpin it are truly under threat is still open to debate. While these matters are beyond the scope of this chapter, the questions and issues raised by these developments should be kept in mind as we consider the future prospects of international law.

3. The subjects of international law

Public international law is only slightly less archaic when it comes to identifying the subjects, that is the actors, of the international legal system. States are still seen as the main subjects of international law. It is states which enjoy the fullest set of international rights and obligations and have the most complete toolkit at their disposal to implement and enforce such entitlements and duties. Originally, other entities were mere 'objects' of international law: they could be the ultimate beneficiaries of certain arrangements agreed to between states, but did not enjoy rights in their own capacity and did not otherwise play a meaningful role in international law.[20]

When there is slightly more openness of public international law in this area, we owe it in the first place to a landmark case of the ICJ: *Reparation for Injuries*. In this Advisory Opinion of 1949, the ICJ affirmed:

> The subjects of law in any legal system are not necessarily identical in their nature or in the extent of their rights, and their nature depends upon the needs of the community. Throughout its history, the development of international law has been influenced by

---

[18] Adam Liptak, 'Donald Trump Could Threaten US Rule of Law, Scholars Say' (*The New York Times*, 3 June 2016) <www.nytimes.com/2016/06/04/us/politics/donald-trump-constitution-power.html> accessed 24 June 2018; *State of Hawaii v Trump*, Civil Rights Litigation Clearinghouse, case 1:17-cv-00050 D Haw (3 February 2017) <www.clearinghouse.net/detail.php?id=15626> accessed 24 June 2018; *Washington State v Trump*, Office of the Attorney General—Washington State, case 2:17-cv-00141 (30 January 2017) <www.atg.wa.gov/executive-order-lawsuit> accessed 24 June 2018.

[19] See, with reference to the writings of Robert Keohane and John K Ruggie: Jan Wouters, Sijbren de Jong, and Philip De Man, 'The EU's Commitment to Effective Multilateralism in the Field of Security: Theory and Practice' (2010) 29 Yearbook of European Law 164, 166–67.

[20] Jan Wouters, Cedric Ryngaert, Tom Ruys, and Geert De Baere, *International Law: A European Perspective* (Hart Publishing 2018) ch 5 on states; for critical reflections: Jean d'Aspremont, 'Subjects and Actors in International Lawmaking: The Paradigmatic Divides in the Cognition of International Norm-Generating Processes' in Catherine Brölmann and Yannick Radi (eds), *Research Handbook on the Theory and Practice of International Lawmaking* (Edward Elgar Publishing 2016) 32.

the requirements of international life, and the progressive increase in the collective activities of States has already given rise to instances of action upon the international plane by certain entities which are not States.[21]

This functional approach was highly innovative in times where it was not even accepted that the UN enjoyed international legal personality. The ICJ broke through the monolithic approach to international legal personality and subjectivity and, thereby, breached the monopoly of states as subjects of international law. It allowed the post-Second World War international legal system to gradually open up to non-state actors: in the first place international organizations, but also a variety of other non-traditional players, such as the Holy See, the International Committee of the Red Cross, and liberation movements. Subsequent dynamics in sub-branches of international law, in particular human rights law and international criminal law,[22] have also brought the individual to the international level, as a subject of rights and obligations—but always under the assumption that the states at hand had, in their sovereign wisdom, ratified the human rights instrument in question and/or had consented to the jurisdiction of the international criminal tribunal involved. A similar development has taken place in international economic law, where numerous bilateral investment treaties make it possible for foreign investors to initiate arbitral proceedings, for instance in case of unlawful expropriation, against the state in which they operate.

Still, even today, states are seen as the 'primary' subjects of international law with original and full international legal personality. All other subjects are regarded as by necessity 'secondary' to states, in that they are only recognized as actors by the mercy of the latter. States continue to protect their pre-eminence in a particularly vigilant manner. How else can one explain that only states enjoy 'plenary powers' and that international organizations only have 'conferred powers'? That only ('peace loving') states can become a member of the UN (Article 4(1) UN Charter) and that most international organizations leave other international actors little more than a modest observer status? And that only states are able to bring claims and be sued before the ICJ (Article 34 ICJ Statute)?

In other words, in today's public international law, entities other than states still only have a limited and 'derived' international legal personality. Here too, we will see that today's international regulatory realities show new dynamics which can hardly be fully understood by reference to the traditional doctrine of the subjects in international law. One might add that this enduring narrowly defined actorness in international law may contribute to its vulnerability in the current wave of contestation towards the liberal order we have touched upon above. In particular, globalization has led to a sensible increase in fragmentation and plurality, when it comes to the number and nature of actors involved, particularly in the form of non-governmental organizations (NGOs)

---

[21] ICJ, *Reparation for injuries suffered in the service of the United Nations*, Advisory Opinion, 11 April 1949, ICJ Rep 1949, 174, 178.

[22] Anne-Laure Vaurs Chaumette, *Les sujets du droit international pénal: vers une nouvelle définition de la personnalité juridique internationale?* (Pedone 2009).

and civil society organizations.[23] Though it has led to an increasing and widely discussed fragmentation of international law, it has not entailed greater transparency or broader participation in law-making processes.[24]

III. The rise of informal international law-making

The ever-changing demands of international society have brought into the limelight new, non-traditional approaches to international law-making. Recent academic literature has shown that international law is not only stagnating in terms of both quantity and quality, but it is also increasingly complemented by 'informal international law-making', a phenomenon involving new outputs, processes, and actors. A fairly rich tapestry of novel forms of international cooperation, ostensibly outside the confines of the traditional frameworks of international law as described above, is booming. The nomenclature used is increasingly diverse and departs from the formal labels of custom, treaty, or international organizations.[25] We have seen the rise of informal international law-making through a great variety of international processes, such as the International *Conference* on Harmonization (in respect of pharmaceuticals), the Kimberly *Scheme* on conflict diamonds, the Proliferation Security *Initiative*, the Copenhagen *Accord* on Climate Change, the International Organization for Standardization's 26000 *Standard* on corporate social responsibility, the Ruggie *Guiding Principles* on Business and Human Rights, the Financial Stability *Board*, the Internet Engineering *Task Force*, or the World Health Organization's Global *Strategy* on Diet.[26]

The concept of 'informal international law-making' was introduced by Joost Pauwelyn, Ramses A Wessel, and the present author in the context of a research project conducted by the Graduate Institute in Geneva, the Leuven Centre for Global Governance Studies, and the University of Twente, with support of the Hague Institute for the Internationalisation of Law. The main objective of this research project was to draw attention to a phenomenon that is omnipresent in global governance, yet largely neglected by international lawyers. We defined 'informal international law-making' as follows:

---

[23] Amitav Acharya, 'The Future of Global Governance: Fragmentation May Be Inevitable and Creative' (2016) 22 Global Governance 453; Fariborz Zelli and Harro van Asselt, 'Introduction: The Institutional Fragmentation of Global Environmental Governance: Causes, Consequences, and Responses' (2013) 13(3) Global Environmental Politics 1.

[24] On fragmentation in international law: Martti Koskenniemi, 'Histories of International Law: Significance and Problems for a Critical View' (2013) 27 Temple International and Comparative Law Journal 215; Gerhard Hafner, 'Pros and Cons Ensuing from Fragmentation of International Law' (2004) 25 Michigan Journal of International Law 16; on the concept of fragmentation in international law and global governance: Timo Pankakoski and Antto Vihma, 'Fragmentation in International Law and Global Governance' (2017) 12 Contributions to the History of Concepts 22.

[25] Joost Pauwelyn, Ramses A Wessel, and Jan Wouters, 'Informal International Lawmaking: An Assessment and Template to Keep it Both Effective and Accountable' in Pauwelyn, Wessel, and Wouters (eds), *Informal International Lawmaking* (n 2) 501.

[26] See the many case studies conducted in Joost Pauwelyn, Ramses A Wessel, Jan Wouters, Ayelet Berman, and Sanderijn Duquet, *Informal International Lawmaking: Case Studies* (Torkel Opsahl Academic EPublisher 2013).

Cross-border cooperation between public authorities, with or without the participation of private actors and/or international organizations, in a forum other than a traditional international organization (process informality), and/or as between actors other than traditional diplomatic actors (such as regulators or agencies) (actor informality), and/or which does not result in a formal treaty or traditional source of international law (output informality).[27]

The term 'informal international law-making' is used in opposition to 'traditional international law-making', as it dispenses with certain formalities traditionally linked to international law. This circumvention of formalities generally occurs in relation to three dimensions: output, process, and actors involved.

First, in terms of output, international cooperation is informal in the sense that it does not normally lead to a formal treaty or any other source of traditional international law, but rather to a guideline, standard, declaration, or even informal policy coordination or exchange. *Second*, in terms of process, international cooperation is considered informal when it takes place in a loosely organized network or forum, rather than traditional, treaty-based international organizations.[28] Forum informality does not, however, prevent the existence of detailed procedural rules, permanent staff, or physical headquarters. Even more importantly, process informality does not exclude informal international law-making in the context or under the broader auspices of a more formal organization.[29] *Third*, in terms of actors involved, international cooperation is seen as informal because it does not engage traditional diplomatic actors (heads of state, foreign ministers, or ambassadors) or traditional subjects of international law, but rather other public authorities, such as ministries, domestic regulators, agencies, sub-federal entities, the legislative and judicial branch, or even private actors alongside public actors or international organizations, all cooperating across national boundaries.

Many of these developments, considered in isolation, are not unprecedented and have accrued, with ups and downs, over time. Alternative forms of output—other than custom and treaty—such as standards, guidelines, and non-binding recommendations of international organizations, are not new. Indeed, debates on international 'soft law' have simmered since the 1970s, when newly independent states sought to utilize, in particular, United Nations General Assembly (UNGA) resolutions.[30]

Ever since Anthony Aust, nearly three decades ago, defined an informal international instrument as 'an instrument which is not a treaty because the parties to it do not intend it to be legally binding,'[31] one cannot help but wonder to what extent

---

[27] Joost Pauwelyn, 'Informal International Lawmaking: Framing the Concept and Research Questions' in Pauwelyn, Wessel, and Wouters (eds), *Informal International Lawmaking* (n 2) 13.
[28] Examples in the area of financial regulation would include eg the Basel Committee on Banking Supervision, or the Financial Action Task Force.
[29] Pointing eg to the OECD as an international organization within which a lot of informal international law-making takes place: Pauwelyn (n 27) 17.
[30] Alan Boyle and Christine Chinkin, *The Making of International Law* (Oxford University Press 2007) 211.
[31] Anthony Aust, 'The Theory and Practice of Informal International Instruments' (1986) 35 International & Comparative Law Quarterly 787.

informal international law-making differs from the concept of 'soft law', which, from a law-making perspective, is similarly defined as 'a convenient description for a variety of non-legally binding instruments used in contemporary international relations'.[32] Soft law, much in the same vein as informal international law-making, is seen by its proponents as an almost ubiquitous phenomenon that comes in an endless variety of forms, such as treaties with imprecise, subjective, or indeterminate language; inter-state conference declarations such as the 1972 Stockholm Declaration on the Human Environment or the 1992 Rio Declaration on Environment and Development; various UNGA resolutions dealing with issues as diverse as disarmament, outer space, or de-colonization; codes of conduct, guidelines, or recommendations of international organizations; and finally, some possibly controversial claimants to soft law status, such as common international standards adopted by transnational networks of national regulatory bodies, NGOs, expert groups, professional and industry associations, or other instruments that do not emanate directly from states.[33] In this last case, it is argued, the use of a non-legally binding form is dictated not by the intent not to be bound, but by their makers' lack of formal law-making capacity.[34] These types of agreements, which some are leery to include in the 'soft law' category,[35] roughly correspond with the phenomenon of informal international law-making.

The rise of informal international law-making goes well beyond soft law. To begin with, as indicated by Joost Pauwelyn, the definition of informal international law-making does not necessarily equate output informality with the lack of legal 'bindingness'.[36] Indeed, while informal international law-making may be informal, that is, take the form of a press communiqué or an agreed statement, rather than a formal treaty, it can still be construed as legally binding under traditional international law.[37] It should also be pointed out that there is nothing 'soft'—that is, vague, aspirational, or deeply contested (as with the effect of UNGA resolutions)—about most informal law-making, such as the standards relating to the internet, medical devices, or financial norms developed in the past few years.[38] What characterizes informal international law-making is not so much that it is non-binding under international law (the hallmark of soft law), but that it generally seems to fall outside traditional public international law altogether. The reason, arguably, lies in the fact that informal international law-making actors, be they governmental agencies, ministries, business associations, or NGOs, lack the legal capacity to make international law. Jean d'Aspremont goes as far

---

[32] Boyle and Chinkin (n 30) 212.
[33] Christine Chinkin, 'Normative Development in the International Legal System' in Dinah Shelton (ed), *Commitment and Compliance: The Role of Non-Binding Norms in the International Legal System* (Oxford University Press 2000) 21, 29.
[34] ibid.
[35] Boyle and Chinkin (n 30) 213.
[36] Pauwelyn (n 27) 15.
[37] 'On the question of form, the Court need only observe that it knows of no rule of international law which might preclude a joint communiqué from constituting an international agreement ...': ICJ, *Aegean Sea Continental Shelf* (Greece v Turkey), Judgment, 19 December 1978, ICJ Rep 1978, 3, 96.
[38] Pauwelyn, Wessel, and Wouters, 'An Assessment and Template to Keep it Both Effective and Accountable' (n 25) 506.

as stating that 'whatever the influence of these non-state actors may be, states and international organizations remain the exclusive international law-makers'.[39]

IV. The slowdown in traditional international law-making and its causes

1. The decline in multilateral treaty-making

In a context of ongoing globalization, public international law is not only challenged by the rise in informal international law-making, but also by the relative decline in the making of traditional international law. Evidence shows that there has been a decline in the generation of new treaties since the early 2000s (see Figure 16.1 below). Since the 1950s, for each decade, the number of new multilateral treaties deposited with the UN Secretary General was around thirty-five. In the ten years between 2000 and 2010, this number declined to twenty, while in the preceding five decades, it had never been below thirty-four. Between 2005 and 2010, only nine new multilateral treaties were deposited, whereas in 2011, 2012, and 2013, not a single one was.[40] The broader UN Treaty Series database confirms this downward trend as of the 2000s, both for bilateral as well as multilateral treaties.[41]

Another indicator that states are increasingly shifting away from traditional international law-making is the follow-up given to draft texts prepared by the International

Figure 16.1 Number of multilateral treaties deposited with the UN Secretary General per year (1945–2014)

[39] Jean d'Aspremont, 'Non-State Actors from the Perspective of Legal Positivism' in d'Aspremont (ed), *Participants in the International Legal System: Multiple Perspectives on Non-State Actors in International Law* (Routledge 2011) 23, 25.

[40] For a more comprehensive review: Pauwelyn, Wessel, and Wouters, 'When Structures Become Shackles: Stagnation And Dynamics' (n 10) 734–37.

[41] See UN Treaty Series <treaties.un.org/Pages/AdvanceSearch.aspx?tab=UNTS&clang=_en> accessed 24 September 2018. Multilateral treaties in this database include closed multilateral treaties, multilateral treaties deposited with the UN Secretary General, multilateral treaties not deposited with the UN Secretary General, and open multilateral treaties.

Law Commission (ILC). Indeed, whereas the ILC's work previously resulted in new multilateral treaties, the most recent time this has happened was more than a decade ago, in 2004.[42]

Some may claim that the picture described above fails to take into consideration various other dynamics of international law, such as the continuing evolution of custom, or the activity of international organizations. Although we agree that intensified international cooperation may lead to a more rapid formation of customary rules in specific instances,[43] today's preference of states for informal cooperation undoubtedly affects customary international law as well, since the essence of its *opinio juris* component relates precisely to the legally binding character of an obligation. Additionally, with fewer multilateral treaties generated, it is becoming increasingly hard to find evidence of *opinio juris* confirmed by sufficiently concordant state practice.[44] As to the output of international organizations: while they continue to function and produce plenty of resolutions, statements, and decisions, many, if not the majority, of normative instruments produced by international organizations are not meant to generate legally binding obligations and may therefore not be conducive to detecting an *opinio juris* either.[45] Moreover, there is a crisis of multilateralism: a great number of international organizations (both at global and regional level) currently face serious challenges, ranging from profound divisions at the UN Security Council, to an almost paralysed WTO, to severe budget cuts and membership dropout, as well as extraordinarily difficult reform processes.

Whether measured by the decline in treaties, or the rise in informal cooperation in many issue areas, informal international law-making is rapidly overtaking—though not replacing—traditional 'hard' forms of international law, that is, custom and treaties. Multiple factors, many issue-specific or country-specific, may explain this trend. We will deal with them below. First of all, the shift from traditional to informal international law-making can partly be explained by the saturation with the existing treaties and changed policy preferences of states. However, at a more fundamental level, the multiple case studies conducted by us within the informal international law-making project[46] converge around deep societal changes that are not unique to international law, but partly result from globalization and affect both international and national legal

---

[42] This was the United Nations Convention on Jurisdictional Immunities of States and their Property, following the ILC's 1991 draft articles on this matter. Until today, the Convention has not yet entered into force due to insufficient ratifications.

[43] With an emphasis on the significance of certain UNGA resolutions during times of fundamental change eg: Michael P Scharf, 'Seizing the "Grotian Moment": Accelerated Formation of Customary International Law in Times of Fundamental Change' (2011) 43 Cornell International Law Journal 439.

[44] Pauwelyn, Wessel, and Wouters, 'An Assessment and Template to Keep it Both Effective and Accountable' (n 25) 736.

[45] Moreover, one must continue to be aware of the distinction between state practice and the practice of an international organization, for these and other related reflections: Jan Wouters and Philip De Man, 'International Organizations as Law-Makers' in Jan Klabbers and Åsa Wallendahl (eds), *Research Handbook on International Organizations Law: Between Functionalism and Constitutionalism* (Edward Elgar Publishing 2011) 190; further on 'institutional' law-making: Ramses A Wessel, 'Institutional Lawmaking: The Emergence of a Global Normative Web' in Brölmann and Radi (n 20) 179, 181–83.

[46] Pauwelyn, Wessel, Wouters, Berman, and Duquet (n 26).

systems, in particular the transition towards a diverse network society and an increasingly complex knowledge society.

2. Saturation and changed policy preferences of states

Some of the slowdown, especially in treaty-making, can be explained by the fact that multilateral treaties now exist on most major subject-matters of international law. A certain saturation, or treaty fatigue, has descended upon states. At first glance, the adoption of the Paris Agreement on Climate Change in December 2015 seems to contradict this, but the enormous flexibility of the agreement, especially regarding mitigation, rather corroborates the thesis that states nowadays prefer to avoid hard legal obligations.[47]

Policy preferences expressed by a number of states also confirm the stagnation hypothesis. The United States and other countries have even formally signalled a growing preference for informal rather than traditional international commitments.[48] In this regard, the 2010 US National Security Strategy refers to the 'shortcomings of international institutions that were developed to deal with the challenges of an earlier time' and calls on US authorities to 'spur and harness a new diversity of instruments, alliances, and institutions'.[49]

The saturation thesis can further be supported by the following findings. To begin with, many multilateral treaties have created their own governance regimes in which non-binding rule-making takes place through Conferences of the Parties (CoPs), Meetings of the Parties (MoPs), or other committees or working groups.[50] Within the area of multilateral environmental agreements in particular, such bodies are very active in developing non-binding rules. To give but a few telling examples, the CoPs of the Biodiversity Convention and the UN Framework Convention on Climate Change (UNFCCC) have literally produced hundreds of decisions and recommendations, and the MoPs of the 1987 Montreal Protocol on Substances that Deplete the Ozone Layer have taken hundreds of decisions on policy, legal, non-compliance, science, technology, and technical issues.[51] The tremendous level of detail and technicality of the norms concerned, as well as the constant need for adjusting, expanding, and updating them, make traditional/formal international law-making a *de facto* less appealing option.[52]

---

[47] Daniel Bodansky 'The Paris Climate Change Agreement: A New Hope?' (2016) 110 American Journal of International Law 288.

[48] With further references to current policy in Germany and Canada: Pauwelyn, Wessel, and Wouters, 'When Structures Become Shackles: Stagnation And Dynamics' (n 10) 739.

[49] US National Security Strategy (27 May 2010) <http://nssarchive.us/NSSR/2010.pdf> accessed 24 June 2018.

[50] Pauwelyn, Wessel, and Wouters, 'When Structures Become Shackles: Stagnation And Dynamics' (n 10) 740.

[51] The decisions and recommendations of these CoPs and MoPs are available at <www.cbd.int/decisions/>, <http://unfccc.int/documentation/documents/items/3595.php>, and <http://ozone.unep.org/new_site/en/index.php> all accessed 24 June 2018.

[52] Jonathan B Wiener, 'Global Environmental Regulation: Instrument Choice in Legal Context' (1999) 108 Yale Law Journal 677.

3. Emergence of a transnational network/knowledge society

The shift from traditional international law to informal international law-making can also be explained by deep societal changes that are not unique to international law, but are partly driven by technological developments and further stimulated by globalization. They affect both national and international legal systems. In essence, it is about the emergence of a transnational network/knowledge society.

We are witnessing a shift from societies of individuals (national level) and a society of territorial states (international level) to a transnational society of networks.[53] These networks both disaggregate and transcend the state, thereby multiplying the types of actors and processes involved in cross-border cooperation. The state remains a pivotal entity of interest, aggregation, legitimation, and control. However, it is supplemented, assisted, corrected, and continuously challenged by a variety of new actors, such as regulators, national and international agencies, transnational corporations, or NGOs. Seemingly outside the traditional framework of international law, these new actors are unable to legally conclude a treaty or join international organizations. Therefore, they are continuously pushing international law-making from the formal to the informal arena.[54]

Besides the new actors and processes driving these interactions, the output or type of cooperation emerging has completely changed and diversified. It used to consist of carefully negotiated treaties consented to by states, or resolutions adopted by international organizations set up by those same states. However, in an increasingly complex society, at levels ranging from the political to the technological (scientific or regulatory), authority flows from other sources too, both public and private[55]—in particular expertise, knowledge, or acceptance by affected stakeholders.[56] In addition, complexity and the resulting uncertainty and rapid change that come with it require more flexible norms or guidelines, grounded in practical experience and expertise, which may be continuously adapted and corrected to take account of new developments and learning.

In sum, the emergence of an increasingly diverse and complex network/knowledge society is transforming the actors, processes, and outputs at work or required to deliver international cooperation. The actors (central state authorities), processes (formal law-making in international organizations), and outputs (rigid treaties or decisions of

[53] Tanja Börzel, 'Networks: Reified Metaphor or Governance Panacea' (2011) 89 Public Administration 49; Mette Eilstrup-Sangiovanni, 'Global Governance Networks' in Jennifer N Victor, Alexander H Montgomery, and Mark Lubell (eds), *The Oxford Handbook of Political Networks* (Oxford University Press 2016) 689; Miles Khaler, *Networked Politics: Agency, Power and Governance* (Cornell University Press 2009); Keith Provan and Patrick Kenis, 'Modes of Network Governance: Structure, Management and Effectiveness' (2007) 18 Journal of Public Administration Research and Theory 229; Anne-Marie Slaughter, *A New World Order* (Princeton University Press 2004); Jacob Torfing, 'Governance Networks' in David Levi-Faur (ed) *The Oxford Handbook of Governance* (Oxford University Press 2012) 99.

[54] Pauwelyn, Wessel, and Wouters, 'When Structures Become Shackles: Stagnation And Dynamics' (n 10) 742.

[55] Axel Marx, Johan Swinnen, Miet Maertens, and Jan Wouters, *Private Standards and Global Governance* (Edward Elgar Publishing 2012); Harm Schepel, *The Constitution of Private Governance: Product Standards in the Regulation of Integrating Markets* (Hart Publishing 2005).

[56] Helmut Willke, *Smart Governance, Governing the Global Knowledge Society* (University of Chicago Press 2007).

international organizations) recognized within the traditional international law framework are not adapted to such developments. This is what explains the rise in informal international law-making. In many cases, these new forms of transnational cooperation arise out of technical necessity, because the actors involved are unable, legally or technically, to conclude a treaty, or because traditional international law-making would simply not be appropriate to the circumstances of a rapidly changing field with a lot of uncertainty, where adaptable, practice-based norms are needed.

4. International law and the anti-globalist/populist backlash

While the link here may not be as straightforward, it seems reasonable to argue that, in the context of global crises—such as the 2008 economic and financial crisis, the 2015–16 migration crisis, international terrorism—public aversion towards globalization, whether in the form of the EU or the International Monetary Fund (IMF), appears to have spilled over into the domain of international law.[57] That is to say that the elite-driven resistance to the rules-based multilateralism discussed above is rooted in discontents among Western public opinion towards international institutions, global cooperation and, by extension, the universalism upon which international law is founded.[58] The (perceived) failure of such organizations to deal with the negative fallout of globalization is, in essence, seen as a failure of international law itself. This has sparked demands for greater democratic control and state-based legitimacy, which goes a long way towards explaining the electoral success of populist leaders who focus on the national interest rather than global ideals. One should be cautious in assuming that international law is to endure simply as a result of its 'moral superiority':[59] a more instrumental view, which correlates acceptance to the perceived benefits it produces might be more useful in ascertaining the challenges faced by international law.[60] When the system that is underpinned by such norms fails to deliver the expected results, those norms are likely to become contested.

An additional dimension to these challenges emerges from non-Western contestation, which has gained momentum over the past decade and is rooted in the universality of international law, that is to say: the assumption that its norms and the underlying values are—and should be—universally shared even if they do, in fact, reflect Western world views. This was combined with a strong consensus on promoting global legalism, as in the reliance on international law for the solution for global collective action problems, thus achieving centralization without the need for global government.[61]

---

[57] For a comprehensive account on these matters: Erik A Posner, 'Liberal Internationalism and the Populist Backlash' (11 January 2017) <https://ssrn.com/abstract=2898357> accessed 25 June 2018.
[58] McGinnis and Somin (n 10).
[59] For such an assessment: Karen J Alter, 'The Future of International Law' in Diana Ayton-Shenker (ed), *A New Global Agenda: Priorities, Practices, and Pathways of the International Community* (Rowman & Littlefield Publishers 2018) 25.
[60] Posner, 'Liberal Internationalism' (n 57) 16.
[61] Erik A Posner, *The Perils of Global Legalism* (University of Chicago Press 2009) 16–27.

The issue is that as power shifts towards emerging countries, and certain basic norms of the global order are put into question and even violated, as with the Russian annexation of Crimea in 2014, such an approach is likely to become more problematic.[62] Crucially, it is in tension with traditional Westphalian sovereignty, which in a globalized world is seen rather as a theoretical construct. By the same token, cosmopolitanism is seen as the ethical alternative to nationalism, shifting the allegiances of citizens to *humanity* as a whole.[63] It is on the basis of this premise that *solidarity* has been referred to as a *potential* structural principle of international law.[64] However, that premise is today very much in doubt: the drivers of the reassertion of national sovereignty, both from Western (*supra*) and non-Western states, though different in their genesis, are similar when it comes to questioning the universality that lies at the heart of international law.

V. Customary international law in an age of informality

Customary international law, while being the historically oldest source of international law, also faces some consequences of the turn to informality by states and public authorities. One could submit that customary international law is marred by both doctrinal and practical limitations that make it ill equipped to address the modern challenges of international cooperation.

1. Custom in crisis?

Almost a decade ago, Andrew Guzman wrote that custom, one of the two main sources of international law, is 'in trouble' and 'under attack from all sides'.[65] This is as valid today as it was then, if not even more so. While some scholars complain that custom is 'wrapped in mystery and illogic',[66] others assert that it has become 'increasingly obsolete',[67] and most, if not all, agree that the traditional doctrine of customary international law is, for lack of a better word, 'a mess'.[68] In line with the ICJ Statute's definition of

---

[62] Edward Newman and Benjamin Zala, 'Rising Powers and Order Contestation: Disaggregating the Normative from the Representational' (2018) 39 Third World Quarterly 871.

[63] Posner, *The Perils of Global Legalism* (n 61) 6.

[64] Rüdiger Wolfrum and Chie Kojima, *Solidarity: A Structural Principle of International Law* (Springer 2010).

[65] Andrew T Guzman, 'Saving Customary International Law' (2005) 27 Michigan Journal of International Law 115, 116; a similar point of view was taken by Bederman, noting that this is 'a time when customary international law is coming under attack by both extreme positivists [who suggest that its processes are illegitimate and non-transparent] and those of a naturalist bent [who regard CIL as merely pandering to State interests]': David J Bederman, 'Acquiescence, Objection and the Death of Customary International Law' (2010) 21 Duke Journal of Comparative & International Law 31, 43.

[66] Anthony D'Amato, *The Concept of Custom in International Law* (Cornell University Press 1971) 4.

[67] Joel P Trachtman, 'The Growing Obsolescence of Customary International Law' in Bradley (n 2) 172; earlier Joel Trachtman wrote about customary international law being under attack 'as behaviorally epiphenomenal and doctrinally incoherent': George Normann and Joel P Trachtman, 'The Customary International Law Game' (2005) 99 American Journal of International Law 541; and about the 'increasing marginalization' of customary international law: Joel P Trachtman, 'Persistent Objectors, Cooperation, and the Utility of Customary International Law' (2010) 21 Duke Journal of Comparative & International Law 221, 232.

[68] James P Kelly, 'The Twilight of Customary International Law' (2000) 40 Virginia Journal of International Law 449, 450.

custom as 'evidence of a general practice accepted as law' (*supra*, Section II), customary international law is said to have two elements: state practice and *opinio juris*. State practice refers to general and consistent practice by states, while *opinio juris* requires that the practice be followed out of a sense of legal obligation.[69] But custom, albeit seemingly simple to define, comes with a laundry list of problems. A brief overview is useful in order to understand why custom finds itself in crisis.

According to Anthony D'Amato, one of the most vexing problems with customary international law is the inherent circularity in the requirement that states must act out of a legal sense of obligation in order to create that obligation.[70] Moreover, in light of the lack of clarity on what constitutes state practice,[71] custom has been characterized as a highly imprecise and vague source of international law.[72] As Louis Henkin famously noted, the state practice that produces customary international law is 'informal, haphazard, not deliberate, even partly unintentional and fortuitous ... unstructured and slow'.[73]

Finally, Trachtman has pointed to the democratic legitimacy deficit of customary international law, as it privileges the role of the executive and is not dependent on parliamentary approval.[74] Moreover, as Steven Wheatley indicates, since customary international law is, by definition, unwritten, the task of identifying, interpreting, and applying customary rules is more often than not left to non-state actors, judges, or even academics.[75]

Notwithstanding the vigorous criticism exposed above, custom has also been widely recognized in the literature as a fundamental source of international law, and defended as having a prominent and indisputable role in international law-making. Sir Michael Wood, in his first report to the ILC, correctly observed:

> It is sometimes suggested that treaties are now a more important source of international law than customary international law. Such generalizations are neither particularly illuminating nor necessarily accurate. Even in fields where there are widely accepted 'codification' conventions, the rules of customary international law continue to govern questions not regulated by the conventions and continue to apply between non-parties. Rules of customary international law may also fill possible lacunae in treaties, and assist in their interpretation. An international court may also decide that it may apply customary international law where a particular treaty cannot be applied because of limits on its jurisdiction.[76]

---

[69] On the definition of custom and its elements: Michael Wood (Special Rapporteur), 'First Report on Formation and Evidence of Customary International Law' (17 May 2013) UN Doc A/CN.4.663.

[70] D'Amato (n 66) 53.

[71] ibid 58; Guzman (n 65) 125.

[72] Karol Wolfke, *Custom in Present International Law* (Springer 1993) xiii.

[73] Louis Henkin, *How Nations Behave: Law and Foreign Policy* (Columbia University Press 1979) 34.

[74] Trachtman, 'The Growing Obsolescence of Customary International Law' (n 67) 187.

[75] Steven Wheatley, *The Democratic Legitimacy of International Law* (Hart Publishing 2010) 150; also observing that customary international law provides excessive discretion to international judges: Trachtman, 'The Growing Obsolescence of Customary International Law' (n 67) 188–89.

[76] Wood (n 69) 35.

2. Contrasting custom and informal international law-making

In spite of the aforementioned shortcomings, customary international law has some features that may be considered attractive. First, it is flexible in content, which may allow it to be more responsive to change. Second, it is formed in a decentralized manner, and therefore unconstrained by procedural requirements and bureaucracy. Third, lack of national parliamentary control might make it attractive to states that, for various reasons, prefer not to engage in lengthy domestic ratification processes. Fourth, since it is formed in ways not entirely consistent with state consent, it may further be useful in solving certain types of international cooperation problems, especially by being binding upon subsequently created states.[77]

Viewed from this perspective, customary international law, it seems, is not that different from informal international law-making. However, as opposed to informal law, the attributes of custom also come with a host of deficiencies. First, even though it is described as flexible, its vagueness and lack of precision reduce custom's ability to shape expectations of future behaviour.[78] Second, despite being formed in a decentralized manner that would arguably allow it to respond quickly to new challenges, customary international law in fact changes too slowly, since it needs consistent, general practice that must further be supplemented by evidence of *opinio juris*.[79] Therefore, customary international law cannot be formed in a coordinated manner in advance. Third, custom does not allow for withdrawal. Therefore, when a state's interests change, it cannot opt out of custom. Fourth, since custom is binding hard law, the costs of violation rise significantly.[80] Consequently, despite their similarities, informal international law-making comes to light as a more attractive alternative in addressing modern challenges.

Although similar in certain respects, customary international law and informal international law-making are also fundamentally different in others. These differences, Helfer and Wuerth argue, are precisely the features that might open the way forward for custom and preserve its relevance in a world of increasing informality.[81] First, custom is universal, in the sense that once formed, it is universally binding upon all states (except, of course, persistent objectors objecting to its formation, and in case of a regional or local custom). On the other hand, informal international law-making, in the same vein as treaties, applies only between the parties that participated to its negotiation. Second, customary international law is normally produced through a non-negotiated process, whereas the manner in which treaties or informal instruments are developed is highly negotiated.[82] Third, custom, as opposed to treaties and informal international

---

[77] Trachtman, 'The Growing Obsolescence of Customary International Law' (n 67) 193–94.
[78] Laurence R Helfer and Ingrid Wuerth, 'Custom in the Age of Soft Law' <www.iilj.org/wp-content/uploads/2016/07/WuerthIILJColloq2014.pdf> accessed 26 June 2018 18.
[79] Harlan G Cohen, 'Finding International Law: Rethinking the Doctrine of Sources' (2007) 93 Iowa Law Review 65, 77.
[80] Helfer and Wuerth (n 78) 17–18.
[81] ibid 4.
[82] Pauwelyn, Wessel, and Wouters, 'An Assessment and Template to Keep it Both Effective and Accountable' (n 25) 506.

law-making, is, by its very nature, an unwritten source of international law.[83] Fourth, custom also differs from treaties and informal law in terms of entrenchment, in the sense that, as indicated above, it does not permit exit.

The foregoing attributes distinguish customary international law from both treaties and informal international law-making. Therefore, they bolster custom's uniqueness and help explain why custom remains a valuable tool for generating international law, at least in areas of state-to-state interaction where distributional or other substantive differences are low, such as *jus in bello*, the interpretation and application of treaties, sovereign and diplomatic immunities, the rules on state responsibility, and the international law of the sea. Moreover, the entrenchment features of custom—that is, it does not permit exit, it often binds states without their consent, some rules have attained the status of *jus cogens* norms—may be useful to states in the same way that constitutions are useful domestically. In this respect, Anthea Roberts argues that customary international law may be understood as framing 'the ground rules for the international system'.[84]

The limited view of custom advanced above indicates that there is a domain for both informal law as well as custom. However, it also remains true that, in an age of increasing informality, custom's domain is quite limited. Nonetheless, it should not be underestimated. Indeed, providing basic rules for state-to-state interaction not only improves stability and predictability, but also opens the way for more extensive cooperation. In a fragmented, multipolar world, these well-established values of custom may continue to play an, albeit limited, but important role.

VI. Global governance

One may wonder what brings international law scholars and practitioners today to global governance. It is interesting to see how the very concept and discipline of 'global governance' itself originated from the social sciences, out of a similar sense of frustration, as Thomas Weiss describes:

> 'Global governance' can be traced to a growing dissatisfaction among students of international relations with the realist and liberal-institutionalist theories that dominated the study of international organization in the 1970s and 1980s. In particular, these failed to capture adequately the vast increase, in both numbers and influence, of non-state actors and the implications of technology in an age of globalization.[85]

---

[83] Wood (n 69) 21.
[84] Anthea Roberts, 'Who Killed Article 38 (1) (b)? A Reply to Bradley and Gulati' (2010) 21 Duke Journal of International and Comparative Law 173.
[85] Thomas G Weiss, 'Governance, Good Governance and Global Governance: Conceptual and Actual Challenges' (2000) 21 Third World Quarterly 295, 796.

In other words, on the side of the social sciences, there was a comparable unease with the traditional approaches to international relations as being too strongly based on the nation state as the basic unit of analysis.[86] Many scholars found that these approaches did not sufficiently reflect the rise of other, non-state actors and the multilevel interactions between various levels of policy-making.

As one can imagine, there is not one standard definition of 'global governance'. Many descriptions and conceptualizations circulate. It is interesting to revisit the oldest known definition of global governance in a seminal article that James Rosenau published in 1995:

> Global governance is conceived to include systems of rule at all levels of human activity—from the family to the international organization—in which the pursuit of goals through the exercise of control has transnational repercussions.[87]

This definition is extremely broad. What strikes the reader is that it expands considerably the conceptual toolkit of the social scientist, in order to better capture and analyse the global transformations of the end of the twentieth century, characterized by the rise and exercise of authority by a great variety of non-state actors.

Thomas Weiss has defined global governance as:

> the sum of laws, norms, policies, and institutions that define, constitute, and mediate trans-border relations between states, cultures, citizens, intergovernmental and nongovernmental organizations, and the market. It embraces the totality of institutions, policies, rules, practices, norms, procedures, and initiatives by which states and their citizens (indeed, humanity as a whole) try to bring more predictability, stability, and order to their responses to transnational challenges – such as climate change and environmental degradation, nuclear proliferation, and terrorism – which go beyond the capacity of a single state to solve.[88]

The attractiveness of this definition, from the viewpoint of an international law scholar, is that it gives a central role to institutions, laws, norms, policies, and rules, and that it recognizes a broad set of actors relevant for cross-border interactions, without confining them to the traditional categories of public international law. Global governance does not only liberate us from the shackles of too rigidly defined sources and subjects of the international legal order. It also opens up our eyes to the many multilevel interactions between global, regional (at macro level), national, subnational, and local levels of rule- and policy-making. It makes it possible to broaden up our legal scholarly

---

[86] Klaus Dingwerth and Philipp Pattberg, 'Global Governance as a Perspective on World Politics' (2006) 12 Global Governance 185, 191, with reference to: Klaus D Wolf and Günther Hellmann, 'Die Zukunft der Internationalen Beziehungen in Deutschland' in Günther Hellmann, Klaus D Wolf, and Michael Zürn (eds), *Die Neuen Internationalen Beziehungen: Forschungsstand und Perspektiven in Deutschland* (Nomos 2003) 588.

[87] James N Rosenau, 'Governance in the Twenty-First Century' (1995) 1 Global Governance 13.

[88] Thomas G Weiss, 'The UN's Role in Global Governance' (UN Intellectual History Project Briefing Note No 15, August 2009) <www.unhistory.org/briefing/15GlobalGov.pdf> accessed 25 June 2018, 1-2.

horizon by studying the interplay between a great variety of norms, not just between different layers of rule-making,[89] but also between public and private law norms,[90] and between formal and informal norms, and institutions.[91] The study of public international law, informal international law-making, and global governance is therefore not to be seen in isolation from each other, but on the contrary, as a continuum where multiple intra- and interdisciplinary perspectives enrich each other.

VII. Conclusion: adjusting international law to globalization and responding to anti-globalism

We have seen that globalization has far-reaching implications, not just in the economic, social, and political spheres, but also in the legal sphere. Still, public international law has not (yet) been able to adjust to these dynamics. Especially its limited responsiveness in terms of the doctrine of the sources and the subjects makes for a huge deficit in capturing the variety of today's cross-border regulatory actors and normative processes. International law has also become more and more criticized in recent anti-globalist and populist discourses. We have contrasted this with the fascinating dynamics of informal international law-making, while also pointing to the challenges which traditional law-making mechanisms like treaty law and customary international law are currently facing.

Informal international law-making can be seen as both an alternative as well as a part in the process of traditional international law-making. In this regard, John Kirton and Michael Trebilcock rightly argue that soft law is not a replacement for hard international law, but '[a]t best, it is a complement'.[92] Traditional/formal international law-making and informal international law-making can interact in a complementary, even harmonious manner. *First*, informal international law-making can lead the way to more

[89] See eg: our book on multilevel regulation: Andreas Follesdal, Ramses A Wessel, and Jan Wouters, *Multilevel Regulation and the EU. The Interplay between Global, European and National Normative Processes* (Martinus Nijhoff Publishers 2008); for a short introduction: Jan Wouters and Ramses A Wessel, 'The Phenomenon of Multilevel Regulation: Interactions between Global, EU and National Regulatory Spheres' (2007) 4 International Organizations Law Review 169.

[90] Jan Wouters and Jed Odermatt, 'International Banking Standards, Private Law, and the European Union' in Marise Cremona and Hans-W Micklitz (eds), *Private Law in the External Relations of the EU* (Oxford University Press 2016) 171; Jan Wouters, 'Private Law, Global Governance and the European Union' in Anne L M Keirse and Marco B M Loos (eds), *Alternative Ways to a New Ius Commune* (Intersentia 2012) 2.

[91] A very important new 'informal' global governance actor is the G20, which constantly interacts with formal institutions: Jan Wouters and Ines Willemyns, 'The Interplay between the G20 and the World Trade Organization: Informal Law-making in Action' in Julien Chaisse and Tsai-yu Lin (eds), *International Economic Law and Governance: Essays in Honour of Mitsoa Mitsushita* (Oxford University Press 2016) 183; Jan Wouters, Sven Van Kerckhoven, and Jed Odermatt, 'The EU at the G20 and the G20's Impact on the EU' in Bart Van Vooren, Steven Blockmans, and Jan Wouters (eds), *The EU's Role in Global Governance: The Legal Dimension* (Oxford University Press 2013) 259; Jan Wouters and Dylan Geraets, 'The G20 and Informal International Lawmaking' in Pauwelyn, Wessel, Wouters, Berman, and Duquet (n 26) 19; Jan Wouters and Thomas Ramopoulos, 'The G20 and Global Economic Governance: Lessons from Multilevel European Governance?' (2012) 15 Journal of International Economic Law 751; Jan Wouters and Sven Van Kerckhoven, 'The OECD and the G20: An Ever Closer Relationship?' (2011) 43 George Washington International Law Review 345.

[92] John J Kirton and Michael J Trebilcock, 'Introduction: Hard Choices and Soft Law in Sustainable Global Governance' in Kirton and Trebilcock (eds), *Hard Choices. Soft Law: Voluntary standards in Global Trade, Environment, and Social Governance* (Routledge 2004) 3.

formal law and law-making. To give but one example, Kenneth Abbott and Duncan Snidal have identified a range of 'pathways to cooperation', some of which explicitly involve the hardening of soft law.[93] They observe, first, how states may sometimes start with a framework convention that over time deepens in the precision of its coverage. They also note that the use of an informal or soft law instrument can subsequently lead to binding legal commitments. Christine Chinkin also contends that soft law can be both elaborative of hard law—by providing guidance in its interpretation—and be subsequently accepted as 'emergent hard law', facilitating the building of custom.[94] In the same vein, David Trubek and others argue that soft law instruments 'can eventually harden into binding rules once uncertainties are reduced and a higher degree of consensus ensues'.[95] *Second*, where a body of hard law already exists, informal law-making processes may provide an avenue to flexibly elaborate and fill in any gaps that form when pre-existing hard law encounters unexpected circumstances. In this respect, traditional/formal and informal international law-making processes serve as complements in dynamic mechanisms of legalization, arguably leading to the progressive development of international law.[96]

Where does all of this lead us to with regard to future options for public international law? There seem to be, broadly speaking, two possibilities.[97] The first is that public international law adapts and gradually incorporates (at least part of) the processes of informal international law-making. As Andrea Bianchi observes:

The huge discrepancy between traditional international law theory and the social practice of [informal international lawmaking] is leading to the marginalization of international law as such. Hence, any effort aimed at reducing the gap might contribute to revive international law and increase its relevance to and practical impact on international relations.[98]

With regard to the more recent challenges international law is facing, as a result of the global shifts flowing from the rise of populism and non-Western contestation, such a scenario could contribute to making it more responsive to these developments. By broadening the range of instruments, actors, and issues, it would constitute a step in the direction of tackling the resistance that appears to flow from the lack of flexibility in international law.

---

[93] Kenneth W Abbott and Duncan Snidal, 'Pathways to Cooperation' in Eyal Benvenisti and Moshe Hirsch (eds), *The Impact of International Law on International Cooperation: Theoretical Perspectives* (Cambridge University Press 2004) 50, 54.

[94] Chinkin (n 33) 30–31.

[95] David M Trubek, M Patrick Cottrell, and Mark Nance, 'Soft Law, Hard Law, and European Integration: Toward a Theory of Hybridity' in Gráinne de Búrca and Joanne Scott (eds), *New Governance and Constitutionalism in Europe and the US* (Hart Publishing 2006) 65, 89.

[96] More generally: Christine Chinkin, 'The Challenge of Soft Law: Development and Change in International Law' (1989) 38 International and Comparative Law Quarterly 850.

[97] See earlier: Pauwelyn, Wessel, and Wouters, 'An Assessment and Template to Keep it Both Effective and Accountable' (n 25) 506–07.

[98] Andrea Bianchi, 'Reflexive Butterfly Catching: Insights from a Situated Catcher' in Pauwelyn, Wessel, and Wouters (eds), *Informal International Lawmaking* (n 2) 209.

The second possibility is that public international law entrenches itself and sticks to its traditional typologies, acknowledging that it is increasingly just one form of international cooperation (mainly for states) within a broader 'legal universe' or 'legal menu' of options from which actors can choose.[99] This entrenchment option does not need to mean the disappearance of public international law. Existing treaties, international organizations, and courts and tribunals will continue to play pivotal roles and new treaties will be created, albeit at a slower pace and especially in traditional areas of international law. The core question here is how exactly public international law will interact with the other parts of the 'legal menu'.

Admittedly, the first possibility sketched above would require a radical transformation of public international law, both procedurally and substantively. Sudden and deliberate change is unlikely. Since the system is largely controlled by states, it is unlikely that these same states will formally agree to end their quasi-monopoly. At the same time, the international legal system has shown in the past—comparing the ICJ's *Reparation for Injuries* Advisory Opinion discussed above (*supra*, Section II)—that it can adapt to organic change in order to reflect new social realities. In terms of actors, although states are currently still the principal subjects and creators of international law, there is no fixed list of subjects of international law that is set in stone. Based on practice and recognition, new subjects and creators of law may and have emerged or disappeared.[100]

In terms of output, we have seen (*supra*, Section II) that Article 38 of the ICJ Statute does not offer an exhaustive list of the sources of international law, but that this has not stood in the way of the emergence and recognition of new sources and law-making processes, such as unilateral acts and decisions of international organizations. Even though it is hard to imagine that Article 38 be formally amended, no such amendment is required for international law to evolve.

Whether or not states like it, or explicitly allow for it, new actors, processes, and outputs are and will continue to play an increasingly important role. The first battleground may become—and has partly already been[101]—cases before international (and domestic) courts and tribunals. It is there that the line and interaction between traditional international law and new forms of cooperation will be tested and contested. Some will undoubtedly close their eyes to new developments, others will engage. Yet, also courts and tribunals will be unable to stop change. After all, whether new modes of cooperation will have an impact or persist will play out not so much at the UN or WTO,

---

[99] For an early realization of this: Michel Virally, 'La distinction entre textes internationaux de portée juridique et textes internationaux dépourvus de portée juridique (à l'exception des textes émanant des organisations internationales)' (1983) 60 Annuaire de l'Institut de Droit International 166.

[100] cf Hersch Lauterpacht, who has pointed out that 'it is important ... to bear in mind that the range of subjects of international law is not rigidly and immutably circumscribed by any definition of the nature of international law but is capable of modification and development in accordance with the will of States and the requirements of international intercourse': Hersch Lauterpacht, 'The Subjects of International Law' in Eliud Lauterpacht (ed), *International Law, The Collected Papers of Hersch Lauterpacht*, vol I: The General Works (Cambridge University Press 1970) 48.

[101] See the examples mentioned by Pauwelyn, Wessel, and Wouters, *Informal International Lawmaking* (n 2) 508.

or before courts or tribunals, but in foreign ministries, national parliaments and regulatory bodies, standard-setting organizations, NGOs, corporate board rooms of multinational enterprises, the media, and individual citizen/consumer decisions.

So, in the end, as the ancient Greeks already acknowledged: πάντα ῥεῖ καὶ οὐδὲν μένει—all flows, and nothing remains the same. If public international law is to remain relevant, it will have to adapt itself continuously to the realities of globalization and international life, and respond to anti-globalist and populist tendencies.

17

International Law in Times of Anti-Globalism and Populism—Challenges Ahead

Comment on Jan Wouters

Andreas Zimmermann and Norman Weiß

I. Introduction

Contrary to widespread assumptions and expectations prevailing during the 1990s,[1] the hope for an ever increasing effectiveness of international law did not then see a universal and lasting breakthrough. Rather, a continuous counter-movement to such concept developed during the last years. Not the least, the institutional set-up of the international legal order, as it has been created in the post-Second World War era, found itself under pressure.[2] The Russian Federation under President Putin returned as a global power, disregarding basic tenets of international law,[3] while China increasingly tries to shape the international legal order.

Additionally, and most importantly, such opposition has been supported, even if it was almost coincidentally, by an increasing part of populations in at least certain Western countries, both from the political right and from the political left.[4] Another striking development challenging the liberal world order is to be seen in the growing de-secularization of politics. While not being restricted to one religion, it calls into question both the secular state, but also the secular global order based on at least a minimum of common values shared by all members of the international society of states.[5]

---

[1] Most prominently: Francis Fukuyama, *The End of History and the Last Man* (The Free Press/Macmillan 1992) 13f, 39f.

[2] Jacob Katz Cogan, 'Representation and Power in International Organization: The Operational Constitution and Its Critiques' (2009) 103 American Journal of International Law 209.

[3] G John Ikenberry, 'The End of Liberal International Order?' (2018) 94 International Affairs 7; Michael Staack (ed), *Der Ukraine-Konflikt, Russland und die europäische Sicherheitsordnung* (Verlag Barbara Budrich 2017).

[4] Noam Chomsky, *Profit Over People: Neoliberalism and Global Order* (Seven Stories Press 1998); James N Breckenridge and Fathali M Modhaddam, 'Globalization as a Conservative Dilemma: Economic Openness and Redistributive Policies' (2012) 68 Journal of Social Issues 559.

[5] Daniel Philpott, 'The Challenge of September 11 to Secularism in International Relations' (2002) 55 World Politics 66.

Most strikingly, several Western governments, out of different motivations, have acted against the liberal world order themselves, and against at least those principles and rules of international law which are intertwined with this concept. To refer to the most prominent examples, the United Kingdom, after a referendum driven by populism, is in the process of leaving the European Union (EU), while at least two more EU member states, Hungary and Poland, increasingly run the risk of violating both EU law and the European Convention on Human Rights, in particular requiring them to uphold an independent judiciary and a free press. At the same time, EU member states disagree about the right way to deal with refugees and migration, largely setting aside considerations of international refugee law, while the United States under President Trump prefer ad hoc political 'deals' over a rule-based international order characterized by the President as being inherently unfair to his country.[6]

It is these detrimental, or at least contradicting, trends that put the normative system of international law under increasing pressure. At the same time, those very developments raise the question how to support, but also eventually readjust, the international legal order for the purpose of maintaining its relevance. It is this challenge that Jan Wouters deals with in his contribution, where he sets out the deficiencies in contemporaneous international law-making. He perceives, and recommends, that 'public international law [ought to] adapt and gradually incorporate (at least part) of the processes of informal international law-making'.[7]

The present contribution takes a short look at the challenges, as presented by Wouters (Section II), and then offers a threefold approach consisting of recommendations for an effective multilateralism, efforts to strengthen the United Nations (UN), and to include multilateralism in the domestic political agenda of Western democracies (Section III). Some considerations with regard to these developments will conclude this chapter (Section IV).

II. Anti-globalism and populism as challenges for 'traditional' international law?

There are currently trends, both in world politics and at the domestic level of at least certain states, that challenge the traditional understanding of international law. That raises the question whether, as Wouters claims, this challenge concerns not only the actual content of rules of international law, that is its substantive rules, or whether these challenges are more far-reaching in that they even challenge the meta-rules of international law on its sources and subjects.

---

[6]   Peter Baker, 'President Trump, Deal Maker? Not So Fast' (*New York Times*, 22 June 2018) <www.nytimes.com/2018/06/22/us/politics/trump-deal-maker.html> accessed 8 October 2018.
[7]   Jan Wouters, 'International Law, Informal Law-Making and Global Governance in Times of Anti-Globalism and Populism' in this book, VII.

1. Diversifying the subjects of international law: back to square one?

In his piece, Wouters claims that the above-described current developments challenge the traditional canon of the subjects of international law. What he fails to mention, however, is that over the last decades the international legal order had to deal
first and foremost with an ever-increasing number of states, first during the historic
process of decolonization, and later and more recently as a result of the breakdown
of the Soviet Union and that of other states. It is submitted that it was this increasing
number of states itself that had already brought about an inherently more complex
system of international law-making, as well as international law enforcement, well
before the current wave of anti-globalism and populist approaches to international
law even started.

Apart from a mere increase in the *quantity* of states, these developments have also
led to an increasing *variety* of states, ranging from wealthy states with a functioning
bureaucracy that are able to influence international law-making across the board to
'failed states' that have almost no influence whatsoever when it comes to either international treaty-making or the development of customary international law. It is this
development which is highly relevant when it comes to the ability of international law
to reflect the interests of the international community at large,[8] well beyond and apart
from other more recent developments. At the same time, it is telling that these factual
developments have however neither altered the more classical understanding of the notion of 'states' in international law, nor the understanding of what rights and duties
states have under international law.

The same holds true, *mutatis mutandis*, when it comes to the normative category
of international organizations. While it is obviously true that there has been a fast and
indeed rapidly growing number of international organizations after 1945, the very concept of such organizations and the fundamental question of how to delineate their respective competences has not changed ever since the International Court of Justice's
(ICJ) ground-breaking 1949 *Reparations for Injuries* advisory opinion.[9] Yet, what has
changed, and what might be perceived as a reason for a populist backlash against the
work of international organizations, is that international organizations have increasingly dealt with areas which have a direct bearing on the daily life of citizens. The World
Trade Organization (WTO) and international investment law are particularly relevant
and recent examples. That stands in contrast to more 'traditional' international organizations such as the UN, which, at least for a long time, were largely concerned with
state-to-state relations only (or at least mostly).[10]

What indeed constitutes a relatively recent trend within the international legal
system is that both individuals and corporations are more or more present as actors

---

[8] Nigel D White, 'Lawmaking' in Jacob Katz Cogan and others (eds), *The Oxford Handbook of International Organizations* (Oxford University Press 2016) 559.
[9] ICJ Reports 1949, 174.
[10] B S Chimni, 'International Organizations, 1945–Present' in Katz Cogan and others (n 8) 113.

at the international level.[11] International instruments on the national as well as international level address civil society; together with non-governmental organizations (NGOs), they are important stakeholders in international cooperation.[12] While there is a strong and ongoing claim for a more inclusive approach,[13] as supported by Wouters,[14] one might wonder whether the process of enlarging the categories of subjects of international law has not already been highly dynamic in the last twenty to thirty years. If that were the case, this would already largely take into account the underlying critique of Wouters. One indeed wonders whether, for example by 1980, one would have expected NGOs as well as corporations to play the role they are currently playing as subjects of international law. If that were indeed the case, one might then wonder how such broadening has not, in and by itself, contributed to the populist backlash that the international legal order is currently facing by granting non-state actors, not legitimized by a popular vote, with an increasing impact on international law-making. It would then have been interesting to analyse whether one ought not to eventually distinguish between NGOs in the true sense representing parts of civil society on the one hand, and (multilateral) corporations lacking any kind of even informal 'democratic support' on the other hand.

It is also worth recalling that, at least traditionallyNGOs, by and large, have a background in northern, industrialized states and thus tend to represent (or at least are perceived as representing) fewer populations living in the southern hemisphere of the earth. This might have contributed to an increased critique even against NGOs[15] and their impact on international law-making.

Interestingly, those governments that came to power due to 'populist' movements tend to rely on traditional notions of international law such as sovereignty, domestic jurisdiction, and the like, all of which in turn presuppose the existence and major role of states within the international legal system. One therefore wonders whether the current wave of anti-globalist and populist movements does not strengthen traditional concepts of what are the 'real' subjects of international law rather than questioning those, while by the same token other non-state subjects of international law somewhat tend to (again) be relegated to the back seat of international law-making.

---

[11] Anne Peters, *Jenseits der Menschenrechte. Die Rechtsstellung des Individuums im Völkerrecht* (Mohr Siebeck 2014); José E Alvarez, 'Are Corporations "Subjects" of International Law?' (2011) 9 Santa Clara Journal of International Law 1 <https://digitalcommons.law.scu.edu/scujil/vol9/iss1/1/> accessed 8 October 2018.

[12] Math Noortmann, August Reinisch, and Cedric Ryngaert (eds), *Non-state Actors in International Law* (Bloomsbury Publishing 2015); Daphné Josselin and William Wallace (eds), *Non-State Actors in World Politics* (Palgrave Macmillan 2001); Norman Weiß, 'Zur Rolle der Zivilgesellschaft für den Schutz der Menschenrechte' in Eckart Klein and Christoph Menke (eds), *Universalität - Schutzmechanismen - Diskriminierungsverbote. 15 Jahre nach der Weltmenschenrechtskonferenz 1993 in Wien* (Berliner Wissenschaftsverlag 2008) 232.

[13] Anne Peters, 'Membership in the Global Constitutional Community' in Jan Klabbers, Anne Peters, and Geir Ulfstein (eds), *The Constitutionalization of International Law* (Oxford University Press 2009) 153.

[14] Wouters (n 7) II.3.

[15] See the contributions in Anton Vedder, *NGO Involvement in International Governance and Policy. Sources of Legitimacy* (Martinus Nijhoff Publishers 2008).

2. Populist movement and the sources of international law

Traditionally, international law-making was reserved to states, be it as actors negotiating and eventually concluding international treaties, or be it in performing acts of state practice and articulating *opinio juris,* and thereby bringing about the creation of new norms of customary law. For quite some time however, international law-making has no longer been monopolized by states. International organizations have created their own law-making processes. International bureaucracies, NGOs, and civil society have increasingly taken part in initiating, drafting, and amending various forms of legal instruments. Nevertheless, their contribution has remained indirect by influencing the behaviour of states vis-à-vis the adoption of new rules of international law. Still, the nature of the international community of states has consistently changed during the last hundred years and can probably best be described as a heterogeneous international society by now.[16]

This brought about, as Wouters rightly points out, a canon of sources of international law beyond the sources formally mentioned in Article 38 of the ICJ Statute which are now recognized as being non-exhaustive in nature and thus enabling those applying international law to take other sources into account.[17] This has also led to the emergence of the issue of 'soft law'[18] traditionally claimed not to abandon the dichotomy of law and non-law by introducing a third category, but rather being understood as a contribution to the progressive development and, possibly, codification of international law.

Yet, it seems that recent populist movements and governments which have been brought to power by such movements, rather than choosing between more traditional ways of regulating state behaviour (that means by entering into treaties, accepting their continued relevance, or arguing that their behaviour is in line with generally accepted rules of customary law) simply tend to disregard any form of legal regulation of their behaviour *tout court.* As a matter of fact, at least the current US administration, as being one of the most prominent examples of a populist-oriented government, either tends to claim that pre-existing legal rules, whatever their nature is, are utterly unfair (and hence should be discarded), or instead does not even engage with international law when it comes to actions which are dear to their constituencies, be it in the field of the use of military force such as in the case of Syria, or be it in the field of migration. Instead, such governments tend to insist on ad hoc solutions regardless of such proposed solutions being compatible with international law, or rather not.

Hence, the diagnosis made by Wouters that the solution might lie in the increased use of informal law-making does not seem to provide a solution to the problem of the current populist movements, unless one were to understand such 'informal law-making'

---

[16] For a very recent discussion: Christian J Tams, 'The "International Community" as a Legal Notion' (2018) Käte Hamburger Kolleg/Global Cooperation Research Papers 21/2018 < https://www.gcr21.org/fileadmin/website/daten/pdf/Publications/Christian-J-Tams_The-International-Community_2198-0411-GCRP-21.pdf > accessed 13 October 2018.

[17] Rüdiger Wolfrum, 'Sources of International Law' in *Max Planck Encyclopedia of Public International Law* (Online Edition <www.mpepil.com> last update April 2013).

[18] Daniel Thürer, 'Soft Law' in MPEPIL (n 17).

as merely being the equivalent of ad hoc 'deal-making'. Yet, the essential stabilizing element and effect of a normative system such as the international legal order lies in the idea that its rules do apply equally to all participants, and that changing them is itself subject to the meta-rules on rule-making, and on the legal consequences in cases of failing to abide by pre-existing rules of international law.

3. Questioning multilateralism and the decline in multilateral treaty-making: does form or content matter?

The second question addressed by Wouters takes a growing discontent with multilateralism into account, which could, sooner or later, change the international legal order as such.[19] There is certainly no doubt that multilateralism has lost active support by leaders who are populists themselves, or act under fear of populist critique.[20] From that perspective, traditional international law in general, and multilateral treaty-making in particular, fits perfectly into the narrative of populist movements and into their worldview. For them, 'obviously' those methods form part of an elitist, anti-people project. In that view, parliamentary consent to international law-making, in particular in the form of the adoption of multilateral treaties, also possesses only a thin and, at best, indirect legitimacy.

Yet, such critique may not provide the sole explanation for the decline of multilateral law-making in recent years.[21] Rather, as Wouters acknowledges, another reason is to be seen in the saturation on certain subject-matters of international law. One wonders, for example, whether the proposed elaboration of additional human rights instruments to address the specific human rights challenges older people face would add much to the already existing guarantees.

On the other hand, we also witness states—especially, but certainly not only the United States—becoming per se more and more reluctant to conclude multilateral treaties, most likely also because such treaties 'increasingly give expression to interests that transcend inter-state relations'.[22] The parallel readiness to deal with multilateral topics in fora such as the G20 also indicates that states, especially major and emerging powers, prefer non-binding and informal 'commitments' over hard legal obligations. Yet, as the result of the latest G20 summit indicates, even such merely political multilateral commitments face more and more criticism, particularly from the current US administration, which makes even such informal instruments increasingly less likely to be able to 'replace' traditional multilateral rule-making.

From the viewpoint of 'populist governments', it is thus not so much the *form* that matters (that means whether a rule is enshrined in a multilateral treaty, which one can then not enter at all, or not abide by, or, if necessary, terminate), but rather the

---

[19] Ikenberry (n 3).
[20] For striking examples: Wouters (n 7) II.2.
[21] ibid IV.1.
[22] Tams (n 16) 18.

content of any given multilateral arrangement. This is confirmed by the recent action taken by the United States vis-à-vis Iran. As far as may be discerned, it seems that the issue of the legal character of the commitments entered into by the 'parties' to the Joint Comprehensive Plan of Action (JCPOA) and the ensuing endorsement thereof by the Security Council has not played any role whatsoever when the United States decided to reinstate its previous sanctions against Iran.

Thus, what is brought out by these considerations is that eventually it is not so much the form that induces 'populist states' to attack multilateral legal regimes (that means whether such rules are enshrined in a formal multilateral treaty, or in a final communiqué of a G7 or G20 summit), but rather their content and, first and foremost, the very idea that the political leeway of individual states is being restricted.

If that were true, and there is certainly much more research to be done on this specific issue, informal law-making (instead of formal treaty-making) would not constitute the magic key to overcome the resistance of populist governments and regimes against any form of international law-making, be it formal or informal.

III. Possible ways ahead

One therefore wonders what options are available to states in order to deal with the situation at hand, provided such states are (still) in favour of multilateralism and a liberal world order if informal law-making is eventually not the solution to the problem. Yet, it ought to be noted at the outset that those considerations depend to a large extent on political considerations and on the political will of those states that continue to believe that a functioning international legal system is not only in their own interest, but, what may be even more important, serves the interest of mankind at large.

1. Doing multilateralism effectively

Following the Melian Dialogue told by Thucydides in his 'History of the Peloponnesian War', states should know about the advantages offered by a rule-based international order.[23] Such an order needs support, trust, and compliance. States should include these elements in their foreign policy and join their efforts to act multilaterally in open fora, a claim already made by US President Wilson in his famous Fourteen Points.[24]

Based on the idea of sovereign equality, states should thus show respect for other countries and ideas, but also convincingly argue for their own ideas, themselves based

---

[23] Christian R Thauer and Christian Wendt (eds), *Thucydides and Political Order. Lessons of Governance and the History of the Peloponnesian War* (Palgrave Macmillan 2016).

[24] Woodrow Wilson, Address to Congress on 8 January 1918 (Fourteen Points): 'I. Open covenants of peace, openly arrived at, after which there shall be no private international understandings of any kind but diplomacy shall proceed always frankly and in the public view.' <http://avalon.law.yale.edu/20th_century/wilson14.asp> accessed 8 October 2018.

on the international rule of law. International organizations can serve as perfect fora for these debates as long as they are used in a constructive manner. They serve as the focal points of public diplomacy and provide transparency to international debates and thus enable a rational decision-making process.

This presupposes that member states support those organizations, both politically and financially (*inter alia* by paying contributions on time), but also by seconding qualified personnel, including as far as the UN are concerned by contributing troops, police and civilians for UN-led or -mandated missions and operations.

At the same time, it seems necessary in order to fight against populist movements to (re-)legitimize the UN, as well other international organizations, by redefining their tasks and eventually reforming their structures and decision-making processes.[25] This would make the respective organization more respectable even vis-à-vis reluctant domestic 'audiences'. It is also important that states do not use double standards in their international relations and in the application of international law. The attempt of the United States under President George W Bush to create a new category of actors under international humanitarian law, that means so-called enemy combatants, to whom the safeguards of international humanitarian law would not apply, is an example of such misguided practice.[26]

2. Strengthening multilateralism in domestic politics

In his chapter, Wouters focuses understandably only on the international perspective of how to react vis-à-vis recent populist and anti-globalist movements. Compliance with international law, however, constitutes a social process that also takes place not the least at the domestic level. It thus seems essential—provided one were to take the populist backlash against the international legal order seriously, rather than considering it to be a mere peripheral and temporary phenomenon—to also consider domestic political strategies that support multilateralism, apart from focusing on possible reactions on the international plane. Among others, it is important to spread knowledge about the underlying issues at stake by actively entering into an open debate as to the advantages and disadvantages of the regulation of certain matters by international law. In that regard, the public debate about the advantages or disadvantages of free trade agreements might at least in the long term constitute a step in the right direction to counter the feeling that institutions created under the aegis of international law are beyond democratic control. This includes paving the way for an open debate as to the pros and cons of the protection of foreign investments by a system of specialized investment tribunals rather than by domestic courts, themselves governed by the rule of law.

---

[25] See the contributions in Dominik Zaum (ed), *Legitimating International Organizations* (Oxford University Press 2013).

[26] Roza Pati, *Due Process and International Terrorism. An International Legal Analysis* (Martinus Nijhoff Publishers 2009).

At the same time, domestic political discourse should nonetheless also include as one point of reference the issue of international responsibility in case of violations of international law.

Accordingly, national institutions, such as government and parliament, ought to include international affairs into the domestic political debate in order to shape an international perspective on a certain question into a politically relevant argument. But at the same time, and vice versa, people and civil society should expect their politicians to bring their legitimate concerns to international fora, and have them openly debated, the recent debate on certain free trade agreements being once again a particularly pertinent example at hand.

If such *do ut des* indeed takes place, it might be reasonable to expect that at least those supporters of populist movements that are still open to rational arguments may eventually be convinced that international law, and the international legal system generally, serves a useful purpose regardless of whether it is more formalistic in nature, or whether instead, as proposed by Wouters, it opts for more informal mechanism, which is a secondary and more technical question

IV. Concluding remarks

In 1986, Antonio Cassese in his famous monograph *International Law in a Divided World*[27] outlined that an 'old' international law designed by the Westphalian system coexists with a 'new' international law that gradually emerged after 1945. He underlined that the 'new' international law did not yet supplant the 'old' one at the time of writing,[28] but he stated his hope that a strengthened modern legal order would serve smaller states, peoples, individuals, and the planet. While much of this vision became reality in the course of the following decades, his warnings against nationalistic and closed societies[29] point at severe problems that, as of today, might more than ever constitute long-standing obstacles for the realization of a true international community.

One wonders whether mere procedural changes such as an 'informalization' of international law are able to counter those developments. Rather, we submit, it is the very substance of international law, and the advantages it creates for states (and their respective populations), that is its output legitimacy, that might eventually then undo the current populist developments.

---

[27] Antonio Cassese, *International Law in a Divided World* (Oxford University Press 1986).
[28] ibid para 225f.
[29] ibid para 230.

PART V
JUSTICE AND LEGITIMACY

18

The International Rule of Law in Light of Legitimacy Claims

Thilo Marauhn

Legitimacy has many meanings. It has been deployed by actors at all levels of the international system, from activists to academics, from politicians to the press, from judges to bureaucrats, each of whom ascribe different meanings to the word. Indeed it is not unusual for any given author to use the word multiple times in the one setting while ascribing different meanings to it every time.[1]

I. 'Rise or decline'—How does legitimacy fit in?

Legitimacy is a complex concept. It is not only hard to define[2] but can also serve a multiplicity of purposes.[3] This chapter neither aims at defining legitimacy nor purports to categorize different uses of legitimacy. It rather looks at legitimacy claims, contrasting them with theories of legitimacy and discussing how such claims may contribute to the 'rise or decline' of the international rule of law.

The editors of this book aim at analysing, and critically assessing, the role of international law in times of a changing global order. This objective rests on several assumptions, two of which necessitate some reflections for the purpose of this chapter. The first of these assumptions is that of a changing global order.[4] A second assumption arises from the editors' introductory thoughts: assessing the role of international law invites commentators to take a look from the outside of international law, rather than from within. These two assumptions give rise to an initial question: how do claims of legitimacy fit into debates about the 'rise or decline' of the international rule of law?

---

[1] Christopher A Thomas, 'The Uses and Abuses of Legitimacy in International Law' (2014) 34 Oxford Journal of Legal Studies 729, 733.

[2] ibid 733–45.

[3] ibid 731–32f.

[4] Heike Krieger and Georg Nolte, 'The International Rule of Law—Rise or Decline?—Approaching Current Foundational Challenges' in this book.

1. A changing global order

The assumption of a changing global order is neither exclusively descriptive nor solely normative. It encapsulates both dimensions. Any international or global order builds on factual elements, primarily international actors, their relative power, their capabilities, and their actions. But an order only emerges if these elements are put into perspective, setting a normative framework beyond the present day, aiming at least at the immediate future. Any notion of 'order' thus entails the ambition to impact future action on the basis of a factual background.[5] 'Order' does not simply reflect on such background but aims at a certain future.[6]

The reference point of this chapter, and the book as a whole, is not a random kind of order but a 'legal' order. Such an order arises from specific rules, procedures, and institutions, qualifying as 'law'. The notion of 'law' has long been accepted at the international level.[7] However, in light of the role of states as authors, addressees, and guardians of international law,[8] international law has always been perceived as horizontal, decentralized, weak, or even fictional.[9] Efforts to enhance the capacity of this particular body of law have been numerous. Among them are efforts to establish an international legal community beyond a conglomerate of individual states.[10]

The editors take matters further: They take note of the unprecedented increase of international legal rules after the Second World War, culminating in the 1990s.[11] I share this assessment but would narrow down its peak to the few years between 1989 and 1995, the end of the Cold War and the Srebrenica massacre.[12] The editors describe the achievements of the first half of the 1990s as a 'rise' of international law, more specifically, they take up the concept of an 'international rule of law', its 'rise' and possible 'decline'.[13] From the perspective of political science, this marks an unprecedented degree of 'legalization' or 'juridification' of international relations.[14]

---

[5] Stephan Kadelbach, Thomas Kleinlein, and David Roth-Isigkeit, 'Introduction' in Stephan Kadelbach, Thomas Kleinlein, and David Roth-Isigkeit (eds), *System, Order, and International Law* (Oxford University Press 2017) 1, 7–9.

[6] For a historical account on the relevance of future: Marie-Christin Stenzel, 'Postponing the Future: Observations on Early 19th Century International Law between Prevention and Positive Creation' in Christoph Kampmann, Angela Marciniak, and Wencke Meteling (eds), *Security Turns its Eye Exclusively to the Future* (Nomos 2018) 207.

[7] Rüdiger Wolfrum, 'International Law' in *Max Planck Encyclopedia of Public International Law* (Online Edition <www.mpepil.com> last update April 2013) paras 15ff.

[8] Ulrich Beyerlin and Thilo Marauhn, *International Environmental Law* (Oxford University Press 2011) 317.

[9] John R Bolton, 'Is There Really "Law" in International Affairs?' (2000) 10 Transnational Law & Contemporary Problems 1.

[10] eg Peter Haas, 'Epistemic Communities' in Daniel Bodansky, Jutta Brunnée, and Ellen Hey (eds), *The Oxford Handbook of International Environmental Law* (Oxford University Press 2008) 791.

[11] Krieger and Nolte (n 4).

[12] Cedric Ryngaert and Nico Schrijver, 'Lessons Learned from the Srebrenica Massacre: From UN Peacekeeping Reform to Legal Responsibility' (2015) 62 Netherlands International Law Review 219.

[13] Krieger and Nolte (n 4).

[14] eg Florian Hoffmann, 'International Legalism and International Politics' in Anne Orford and Florian Hoffmann (eds), *The Oxford Handbook of the Theory of International Law* (Oxford University Press 2016) 954; Phillip-Alexander Hirsch, 'Legalization of International Politics: On the (Im)Possibility of a Constitutionalization of International Law from a Kantian Point of View' (2012) 4 Goettingen Journal of International Law 479.

What then characterizes changes of such a global order? Heike Krieger and Georg Nolte refer to (geo-)political changes, systemic disregard of international law, structural changes in the making of international law, contestations of a value-based international law's existence, and institutional challenges arising, among others, from the proliferation of international organizations and forums.[15] Applying the fact-norm dichotomy[16] results in the distinction between (1) technological, economic, and political changes affecting, among others, the relative power of international actors and (2) ensuing attitudinal changes towards international law by these actors.

I explicitly share the assumption of a changing global order. However, rather than deriving changes from action alone, I will focus on changing attitudes of actors participating in the international system. A changing order is not a totally unprecedented experience, as demonstrated by some of the chapters in this book. Indeed, historically such changes have occurred fairly often—with the Vienna Congress and the Concert of Europe after the Napoleonic wars,[17] with the post-First World War peace treaties,[18] with the establishment of the United Nations (UN),[19] with decolonization,[20] with the breakdown of the Bretton Woods system,[21] and with the end of the Cold War.[22] The question is whether today's changes differ from earlier ones or whether there are significant parallels.[23]

2. Taking a look from outside international law

The second assumption is not quite as straightforward. Assessing the 'rise or decline' of the international rule of law is not easy anyway.[24] Embarking upon this exercise as an international lawyer may at the same time be easier and more difficult than doing the same as an international relations scholar or any other kind of 'external' observer. Martti Koskenniemi has rightly stressed the complications arising from the entanglement of

---

[15] Krieger and Nolte (n 4).

[16] In this context: Sanne Taekema, Bart van Klink, and Wouter de Been (eds), *Facts and Norms in Law: Interdisciplinary Reflections on Legal Method* (Edward Elgar Publishing 2016); Samantha Besson, 'International Legal Theory qua Practice of International Law' in Jean d'Aspremont, Tarcisio Gazzini, André Nollkaemper, and Wouter Werner (eds), *International Law as a Profession* (Cambridge University Press 2017) 268.

[17] Milos Vec, 'From the Congress of Vienna to the Paris Peace Treaties of 1919' in Bardo Fassbender and Anne Peters (eds), *The Oxford Handbook of the History of International Law* (Oxford University Press 2012) 654.

[18] Randall Lesaffer and Marcel van der Linden, 'Peace Treaties after World War I' in Rüdiger Wolfrum (ed), *Max Planck Encyclopedia of Public International Law* (Online Edition <www.mpepil.com> last update 2015, paras 30 paras 30ff.

[19] Thomas G Weiss and Sam Daws, 'World Politics: Continuity and Change since 1945' in Weiss and Daws (eds), *The Oxford Handbook on the United Nations* (Oxford University Press 2008) 3–38.

[20] eg Sundhya Pahuja, 'The Postcoloniality of International Law' (2005) 46 Harvard International Law Journal 459.

[21] Anthony Elson, 'The Breakdown of the Bretton Woods System and First Reform of the International Financial Architecture' in Anthony Elson (ed), *Governing Global Finance: The Evolution and Reform of the International Financial Architecture* (Palgrave Macmillan 2011) 49.

[22] In this context: Alison Pert, 'International Law in a Post-Post-Cold War World—Can It Survive?' (2017) 4 Asia & the Pacific Policy Studies 362; Jeffrey S Morton, 'The End of the Cold War and International Law: An Empirical Analysis' (1999) 13 Global Society 7.

[23] With regard to the evolution of international law: Milena Sterio, 'The Evolution of International Law' (2008) 31 Boston College International & Comparative Law Review 213.

[24] Krieger and Nolte (n 4).

international law scholars with the object of their research.[25] As scholars, who are often involved in practical legal work and consultancy, we cannot simply withdraw to a position of mere observers; we are at least participating observers,[26] if not participants in the first place. If we want to assess 'rise' and 'decline' and if we do not step out of our 'compartment', we may not notice whether the elevator is going up or down. But what are the tools we can apply if we move outside? What are the perspectives we may take? Heike Krieger and Georg Nolte underline that international law may be an object of observation. They even consider it worthwhile to take a look at international law as a whole.[27] Symptoms and causes cannot really be addressed from within. 'Rise or decline' requires a look from the outside.

The role of an observer should not be limited to quantitative assessments. Whether there is 'rise or decline' should not simply be considered in terms of numbers of treaties entering into force, cases decided by international tribunals, or any other counting of legally relevant action. There is a pressing need for a qualitative perspective.[28] This is less due to the inside-outside dichotomy but more to the fact that 'rise or decline' may be perceived differently by different actors, by different observers, and may be hard to determine objectively. Therefore, it is important to establish an understanding of the underlying reasons, opinions, and motivations of certain phenomena which some of us may qualify as 'rise or decline'. Qualitative research from a social science perspective may enlighten international legal scholars in perhaps better understanding the changes we see 'within' international law: debates about the changing role of international legal personality are related to role perceptions of actors towards international law;[29] discussions about customary law remain half-hearted if they limit themselves to the purely internal logic of relating state practice to *opinio iuris*;[30] the political dimension of negotiations cannot be separated from the formalities of treaty-making;[31] and the choice between formal international organizations or informal arrangements may have legal or non-legal reasons.[32]

The second assumption thus links up to the first. Looking at the role of public international law, including at the 'rise or decline' of the international rule of law, from the outside is directly related to analysing the changing attitudes of actors to international

[25] eg Martti Koskenniemi, *From Apology to Utopia: The Structure of International Legal Argument* (Cambridge University Press 2005) 12ff.

[26] eg Gregory Shaffer and Tim Ginsburg, 'The Empirical Turn in International Legal Scholarship' (2012) 106 American Journal of International Law 1.

[27] Krieger and Nolte (n 4).

[28] For the advantages of qualitative work: see Shaffer and Ginsburg (n 26) 1, 4; also: Michael P Scharf, 'International Law in Crisis: A Qualitative Empirical Contribution to the Compliance Debate' (2009) 31 Cardozo Law Review 45.

[29] Roland Portmann, *Legal Personality in International Law* (Cambridge University Press 2010) 10ff.

[30] eg Rudy B Baker, 'Customary International Law in the 21st Century: Old Challenges and New Debates' (2010) 21 European Journal of International Law 173, 176.

[31] John K Gamble, Lauren Kolb, and Casey Graml, 'Choice of Official Text in Multilateral Treaties: The Interplay of Law, Politics, Language, Pragmatism and (Multi)-Nationalism' (2014) 12 Santa Clara Journal of International Law 29, 43ff.

[32] With regard to the distinction between formal and informal: Jan Klabbers, 'Formal Intergovernmental Organizations' in Jacob K Cogan, Ian Hurd, and Ian Johnstone (eds), *The Oxford Handbook of International Organizations* (Oxford University Press 2016) 133, 134; also: Charles Lipson, 'Why Are Some International Agreements Informal?' (1991) 45 International Organization 495.

law. It is on this basis that the question on how the quest for legitimacy fits into debates about the 'rise or decline' of the international rule of law.

3. The quest for legitimacy

In their introductory chapter, the editors point out that the quest for legitimacy in international law 'may be a symptom for a normative crisis, but also for rising expectations and norm development'.[33] They underline the ambivalent effects of references to legitimacy, as either justifying the deepening and broadening of international governance or questioning the very same process. And they note that claims of legitimacy are increasingly used to blur the binary categories of legality and illegality, often in the absence of centralized assessments of international legality.[34]

Daniel Bodansky, looking at legitimacy in international law and international relations,[35] distinguishes between approaches to legitimacy from outside international law and from within. Apart from the legitimacy of international institutions, which international law and international relations scholars are equally interested in, he contrasts approaches focusing 'on the internal qualities of the legal system'[36] with those focusing 'on the political process by which the rules were produced or their substantive outcomes'.[37] Linking the legitimacy discourse to the debate about 'rise or decline' of the international rule of law invites us to move beyond the internal qualities of the legal system and to take a closer look at related political processes and outcomes. In the following, I will analyse, in terms of 'rise or decline', to what extent claims of legitimacy are made either to support or to question existing rules of international law.

Before entering into this analysis, legitimacy must be contrasted to legality. To this end, I build on Jutta Brunnée and Stephen Toope who argue that the 'law's distinctiveness rests in the concept and operation in practice of legal obligations'.[38] Their constructivist approach focuses on 'shared norms' and 'social interaction', arguing that 'shared understandings, criteria of legality and a practice of legality' generate 'distinctive legal legitimacy and a sense of commitment among those to whom law is addressed'.[39] This enables them to demonstrate that law arising from interaction enjoys legitimacy: social legitimacy on the basis of 'widely shared understandings' and legal legitimacy on the basis of criteria and a practice of legality.[40] Their criteria of legality largely build upon

---

[33] Krieger and Nolte (n 4) VII.4.
[34] ibid.
[35] Daniel Bodansky, 'Legitimacy in International Law and International Relations' in Jeffrey L Dunoff and Mark A Pollack (eds), *Interdisciplinary Perspectives on International Law and International Relations: The State of the Art* (Cambridge University Press 2013) 321, 323–24.
[36] ibid 323.
[37] ibid 323–24.
[38] Stephan J Toope, 'Torture: Can International Law Prevent it? A Lecture at Lady Margaret Hall, Oxford University' (8 May 2012) <https://president.ubc.ca/files/2012/05/torturelctr2012may.pdf> accessed 2 July 2018.
[39] Jutta Brunnée and Stephan J Toope, *Legitimacy and Legality in International Law: An Interactional Account* (Cambridge University Press 2010) 7.
[40] ibid 7 and 60.

the eight criteria suggested by Lon Fuller;[41] however, Brunnée and Toope insist that these are not purely about efficacy but include a sense of fidelity, understanding legal obligation 'as an internalized commitment'.[42] In my perspective, the important element of their understanding of legality and legitimacy for the following analysis of 'rise and decline' through the lens of 'legitimacy' arises from the third element of their theoretical approach, that is the practice of legality. International law, in their view, necessitates that 'international legal practices are "congruent" with existing norms'.[43]

This enables us to identify an overarching concept of legitimacy, vested in common values. It allows us to concentrate on actors who have a shared understanding of their actions and are aware of the reasons for such actions. Mere participation in a legitimacy discourse does not necessarily generate such legitimacy. Rather, legitimacy claims reflect attitudes of actors to particular rules of international law (along the lines of the first assumption), taking a look at these rules from the outside (in line with the second assumption), and thereby supporting or contesting the existence of such rules in the presence or absence of a 'practice of legality'.[44]

In the following, I will first distinguish theories of legitimacy from claims of legitimacy (Section II). The main difference between the two—as will be demonstrated—is that theories of legitimacy aim at establishing conceptual underpinnings of governance, whereas claims of legitimacy largely are interest-driven perceptions of individual actors contributing to a discourse without aiming at a broader concept. A theory of legitimacy focuses on the system of international law, its contribution to international or global governance, and largely builds upon legal philosophy and theory. In contrast, a discourse of legitimacy entails competing claims of legitimacy and reflects the attitudes of individual actors or groups of actors, to the object under consideration, in our case, to the international rule of law.

On this basis, I will then discuss certain legitimacy claims in the context of *ius contra bellum* (Section III) and *ius in bello* (Section IV). These will be assessed in a concluding section on the 'rise or decline' of the international rule of law from the perspective of competing legitimacy claims (Section V).

II. Claims vs Theories

Since the end of the Cold War, numerous theories have been developed to enhance legitimacy in international law.[45] Seeing the rise of multilateral treaties already in the 1970s

---

[41] Lon Fuller, 'Positivism and Fidelity to Law—A Reply to Professor Hart' (1958) 71 Harvard Law Review 630.
[42] Brunnée and Toope (n 39) 27.
[43] ibid 96.
[44] ibid 6–7.
[45] eg Mattias Kumm, 'The Legitimacy of International Law: A Constitutionalist Framework of Analysis' (2004) 15 European Journal of International Law 907, 912; Joseph H H Weiler, 'The Geology of International Law—Governance, Democracy and Legitimacy' (2004) 64 Zeitschrift für ausländisches öffentliches Recht und Völkerrecht 547; Jean d'Aspremont and Eric De Brabandere, 'The Complementary Faces of Legitimacy in International Law: The Legitimacy of Origin and the Legitimacy of Exercise' (2011) 34 Fordham International Law Journal 190; Andrea Bianchi, *International Law Theories: An Inquiry into Different Ways of Thinking* (Oxford University Press 2016) 53ff; also: Thomas (n 1) 729.

and in the 1980s, increasingly powerful international organizations, expanding international and global governance, international legal and international relations scholars have perceived a need to look more closely into the political processes underlying these developments, and into their outcomes.[46] As more powers were assigned to the international level, it was argued that 'legality' as such would be an insufficient tool for the multilayered exercise of power at the international level.[47] The drivers of international law-related theories of legitimacy, notwithstanding their diversity, can largely be found in the differences between national political institutions and their decisions, and international institutions and the decisions made within them.[48]

1. Theories of legitimacy

At the national level, theories of political legitimacy have long moved beyond Max Weber's more or less descriptive concept of legitimacy focusing on a 'belief by virtue of which persons exercising authority are lent prestige',[49] and have integrated normative considerations such as the need to justify coercive political power or the right to rule (John Rawls[50]). Jürgen Habermas,[51] it may be argued, overcame the distinction between descriptive and normative concepts of legitimacy.

Beyond the national level, theories of legitimacy have also been discussed with regard to the European Union (EU).[52] Such discourses have been multidimensional:[53] they address procedure and substance, and—in many instances—they address democratic governance (often framed as democratic legitimacy) and the rule of law. Their multidimensional nature serves to bridge heterogeneous and not fully compatible concepts. This is, among others, true for the interface between democratic governance and the rule of law. Constitutionalism has framed this interface by a deliberative circle,[54] linking democratic governance and the rule of law and at the same time filling gaps and overcoming tensions between them. Constitutional literature, pertinent academic debates, and even constitutional courts have referred to such concepts, have refined them and, on occasion, have specified them in great detail.[55] Theories of legitimacy

[46] With regard to international organizations: Tobias Lenz and Lora A Viola, 'Legitimacy and Institutional Change in International Organisations: A Cognitive Approach' (2017) 43 Review of international Studies 939; Jan Klabbers, 'Constitutionalism Lite' (2004) 31 International Organizations Law Review 31.

[47] Jan Klabbers, Anne Peters, and Geir Ulfstein, The Constitutionalization of International Law (Oxford University Press 2009) 37.

[48] Thomas (n 1) 729, 730.

[49] Max Weber, The Theory of Social and Economic Organization (Cambridge University Press 1947) 382.

[50] John Rawls, A Theory of Justice (Cambridge University Press 1999).

[51] Jürgen Habermas, Between Facts and Norms: Contributions to a Discourse Theory of Law and Democracy (Cambridge University Press 1996).

[52] eg Philip Parry, 'The Democratic Deficit of the EU' (2016) 4 North East Law Review 97.

[53] Weiler (n 45) 547.

[54] eg Steven Wheatley, The Democratic Legitimacy of International Law (Oxford University Press 2010) 108; Ian Johnstone, The Power of Deliberation: International Law, Politics and Organizations (Oxford University Press 2011) 7; see the concept of deliberative democracy in Jürgen Habermas, Faktizität und Geltung: Beiträge zur Diskurstheorie des Rechts und des demokratischen Rechtsstaats (Suhrkamp 1998).

[55] eg Martin Krygier, 'Rule of Law' in Michael Rosenfeld and Andras Sajo (eds), The Oxford Handbook of Comparative Constitutional Law (Oxford University Press 2012) 233; Stephen Holmes, 'Constitutions

have served to establish a comprehensive approach to constitutionalism at the national and at the European level.

Theories of legitimacy at the level of international law have largely been developed in response to the growth of international and global governance.[56] Similar to now prevailing theories at the national level, these international law-related theories of legitimacy have largely linked normative and descriptive considerations. They bring together people's beliefs (being descriptive) with the argument for the right to rule (being normative).[57] The focus of pertinent writings, however, seems to have largely been on descriptive legitimacy, without making this necessarily explicit but rather referring to issues of compliance.[58] Thomas Franck asks why powerful nations obey powerless rules.[59] Ian Hurd states that he is 'interested strictly in the subjective feeling by a particular actor'.[60] This notwithstanding, relevant theories seem to have always brought together normative and descriptive legitimacy, at least in practice. This can also be taken from Jutta Brunnée and Stephen Toope, arguing that legal legitimacy depends on shared understandings upheld by legal practice.[61] Similar approaches can be taken from international relations scholars.[62]

Overall, theories on the legitimacy of international law have not only sought to provide a systemic understanding of international or global governance but also of the transfer of power from the national to the international level.[63] They have—and this is important in the context of the 'rise or decline' discussion—largely argued in favour of more international law, and broader global governance, by identifying factors enhancing normative legitimacy: transparency, public participation, deliberation, and increasing respect for human rights.[64] Theories on the legitimacy of international law have hardly ever been critical of an expansion of international law. This has neither been considered to be their object and purpose, nor have they stepped back and taken a sceptical look at the increase of international law and institutions.[65] It is an open question whether this also results from the fact that theories of legitimacy have largely been developed by academics and not by practitioners.

---

and Constitutionalism' in Michael Rosenfeld and Andras Sajo (eds), *The Oxford Handbook of Comparative Constitutional Law* (Oxford University Press 2012) 189, 207.

[56] Kumm (n 45) 907, 912–15.
[57] Daniel Bodansky, 'Legitimacy' in Bodansky, Brunnée, and Hey (n 10) 704, 709.
[58] Andreas Follesdal, 'The Legitimacy Deficit of the Human Rights Judiciary: Elements and Implications of a Normative Theory' (2013) 14 Theoretical Inquiries in Law 339.
[59] Thomas Franck, *The Power of Legitimacy among Nations* (Oxford University Press 1990) 34.
[60] Ian Hurd, *After Anarchy: Legitimacy and Power in the United Nations Security Council* (Princeton University Press 2008) 7.
[61] Brunnée and Toope (n 39) 34.
[62] Michael Zürn, 'Global Governance and Legitimacy Problems' in David Held and Mathias Koenig-Archibugi (eds), *Global Governance and Public Accountability* (Oxford University Press 2005) 260; Jens Steffek, 'The Output Legitimacy of International Organizations and the Global Public Interest' (2015) 7 International Theory 263.
[63] Kumm (n 45) 907.
[64] eg Jean d'Aspremont and Eric De Brabandere, 'The Complementary Faces of Legitimacy in International Law: The Legitimacy of Origin and the Legitimacy of Exercise' (2011) 34 Fordham International Law Journal 190, 223.
[65] eg Kumm (n 45) 907.

2. Claims of legitimacy

In contrast to theories of legitimacy, claims of legitimacy have arisen since the mid-1990s. They do not aim at providing a better understanding of developments initiated and promoted by other drivers. Rather, they serve as drivers themselves, aiming at either promoting or contesting actions and arguments related to the international rule of law. Claims of legitimacy are put forward by bureaucrats and politicians, activists and journalists, governments and academics, and by many others, irrespective of their legal personality under public international law or whether they are directly involved in international law-related processes. These actors are typically motivated to politically push international law in one or another direction by making use of legitimacy claims.

Unfortunately, the literature about the legitimacy of international law has hardly made a distinction between theories and claims of legitimacy. I am convinced, however, that this distinction is indispensable if scholarship wants to maintain the benefits of theories of legitimacy[66] while at the same time understanding and assessing the contribution of claims of legitimacy to political and legal discourse with regard to international law. In the following, I will take up some of the criticism that has been raised towards legitimacy debates[67] in order to explain my understanding and approach to legitimacy claims more comprehensively.

In contrast to theories of legitimacy, claims of legitimacy build on and make use of legitimacy's 'semantic ambiguity'[68] and its 'capacity to be used strategically'.[69] Furthermore, claims to legitimacy make use of the subjectivity of the very notion of legitimacy, privileging 'personal moral intuitions at the expense of the system as a whole'[70]. Indeed, claims of legitimacy are normally used by all kinds of actors 'because they like or do not like [something] and are grasping for an authoritative way to express that emotion'.[71] While I do not think that legitimacy claims are meant 'to supplant legal discourse',[72] I agree with Vesselin Popovsky that 'claiming legitimacy' may serve to challenge 'the existing status of law'.[73]

---

[66] eg Thomas (n 1) 729, 751.

[67] eg David Caron, 'The Legitimacy of the Collective Authority of the Security Council' (1993) 87 American Journal of International Law 552; Martti Koskenniemi, 'Miserable Comforters: International Relations as New Natural Law' (2009) 15 European Journal of International Law 395.

[68] Thomas (n 1) 729, 731.

[69] Referring to Koskenniemi, 'Miserable Comforters' (n 67) 409, claiming that 'fairness' and 'legitimacy' are mediate words, rhetorically successful only so long as they cannot be pinned down either to formal rules or 'moral principles': Thomas (n 1) 729, 731.

[70] Referring to David Caron who argues that 'perceptions that a process is 'illegitimate' are difficult to describe because they reflect subjective conclusions, perhaps based on unarticulated notions about what is fair and just, or perhaps on a conscious utilitarian assessment of what the process means for oneself' in Caron (n 67) 557; Thomas (n 1) 729, 732.

[71] Thomas (n 1) 729, 732.

[72] Taking up James Crawford who describes legitimacy as being 'used as a loose substitute for "legality"' in James Crawford, The Problems of Legitimacy-Speak (2004) 98 American Society of International Law 271: Thomas (n 1) 729, 732; Koskenniemi claims that 'the vocabulary of "legitimacy" itself tends to turn into a politically suspect claim about the existence of a meta-discourse capable of adjudicating the claims unresolved in its object-discourses, and thus, inaugurating legitimacy experts as a kind of world tribunal': Koskenniemi, From Apology to Utopia (n 25) 591, footnote 81.

[73] Vesselin Popovsky, 'Legality and Legitimacy of International Criminal Tribunals' in Richard Falk, Mark Juergensmeyer, and Vesselin Popovsky (eds), Legality and Legitimacy in Global Affairs (Oxford University Press 2012) 388, 407.

Claims to legitimacy are not extraordinary. As pointed out in a different context, they are 'made by virtually every state in the modern era'.[74] They serve to justify particular actions, enhancing cohesion of those claiming legitimacy, marginalizing criticism thereof, and steering perceptions of legitimacy among the audience of such claims[75]— whether this audience is the general public, an expert community, bureaucrats, politicians, or other types of government representatives.

It is noteworthy that such legitimacy claims (in contrast to theories) are predominantly made by looking at international law through the lens of national law, not to say through the lens of one particular national legal system.[76] This does not necessarily constitute a negative impact on international law ('decline') as it is important to ensure that international law remains acceptable to the principal actors in international law which are—notwithstanding the increasing relevance of both international organizations and individuals—still states.[77] Integrating legitimacy claims by states may contribute to ensuring that diverse cultures, diverse traditions, and diverse preferences can exist side by side on a single planet. This in itself seems to be an objective that may be difficult to achieve. But if international law is to be meaningful, then it has to be able to manage diversity.[78] In other words: international law must be able to manage conflicts in order to preserve peace among the members of the international community.

As already indicated, I will now take up the effects of some of the recently made legitimacy claims upon the 'rise or decline' of the international rule of law. I have grouped them as claims 'testing the limits of the law' (Section III), and as claims 'blurring the lines' between established areas of the law (Section IV). To enter into this discussion, I quote Vesselin Popovsky once more. However, I will replace 'legitimacy' by 'legitimacy claims':

Legitimacy [claims] strengthen ... legality when laws meet and reflect public expectations and are largely accepted. [H]owever, when the existing laws are seen as paralyzing the progress, states can undertake legally uncertain actions, while claiming legitimacy and challenging the existing status of law. Such occasional challenges can result in adjustments or developments in law, therefore closing the gaps and reharmonizing legality and legitimacy. Legitimacy [claims] often support ... legality, but can also challenge legality and lead to progressive developments in international law.[79]

---

[74] Bruce Gilley, *The Right to Rule: How States Win and Lose Legitimacy* (Columbia University Press 2009) 10.

[75] Julia Grauvogel and Christian von Soest, 'Claims to Legitimacy Count: Why Sanctions Fail to Instigate Democratization in Authoritarian Regimes' (2014) 53 European Journal of Political Research 635, 63ff.

[76] Thomas (n 1) 729, 730 ('Attempts to transfer notions of democracy and constitutionalism from the national to the international and global levels have raised more problems than they have solved.').

[77] Thilo Marauhn, 'Changing Role of the State' in Bodansky, Brunnée, and Hey (n 10) 727.

[78] Brunnée and Toope (n 39) 80.

[79] Popovsky 'Legality and Legitimacy of International Criminal Tribunals' (n 73) 388, 407.

III. Legitimacy claims testing the limits of the law

The first set of legitimacy claims discussed in the following tests the limits of the law. The examples chosen stem from *ius contra bellum*, the prohibition of the use and threat of force.

1. The prohibition of the use and threat of force

Before addressing such legitimacy claims, it is useful to briefly recall the state of the law as it might be perceived as of the mid-1990s: The UN Charter with its general prohibition on the use of force among states in their international relations brought about a paradigm shift that can best be explained by replacing the concept of *ius ad bellum* by the concept of *ius contra bellum*.[80] This paradigm shift, which could build on the limitations on the use of force laid down in the Covenant of the League of Nations[81] and in the Kellogg–Briand Pact,[82] changed the relationship between rule and exception not by outlawing the use of force per se, but by placing *ius contra bellum* first, and allowing—as a matter of treaty law—for only two exceptions in principle: first, the right to self-defence according to customary international law and Article 51 UN Charter, and secondly, UN Security Council action under Article 42 UN Charter. It may be argued that there are more exceptions that exist as a matter of law: first, as part of the law of the sea, the right to seize pirate ships, the right of boarding, and the right of hot pursuit (Articles 105, 110, and 111 UN Convention on the Law of the Sea) may be read as including exceptions to the prohibition of the use of force;[83] secondly, force may be used for the purpose of rescuing nationals abroad in limited cases under well-defined preconditions;[84] thirdly, interventions by invitation of the government are, as a general rule, permissible—not as an exception but because they do not conflict with the prohibition of the use of force.[85]

Assuming that this was indeed the law as of the mid-1990s, a number of cases can be taken up in which legitimacy claims were made in order to justify military action that could not easily be considered as being covered by one of these exceptions. It

---

[80] Robert Kolb, *Ius Contra Bellum. Le droit international relatif au maintien de la paix internationale* (2nd edn, Helbing & Liechtenhahn 2009).

[81] See Art 12 of the Covenant of the League of Nations (108 LNTS 188) stating that:

[t]he Members of the League agree that, if there should arise between them any dispute likely to lead to a rupture they will submit the matter either to arbitration or judicial settlement or to enquiry by the Council, and they agree in no case to resort to war until three months after the award by the arbitrators or the judicial decision, or the report by the Council. In any case under this Article the award of the arbitrators or the judicial decision shall be made within a reasonable time, and the report of the Council shall be made within six months after the submission of the dispute.

[82] Randell Lesaffer, 'Kellogg-Briand Pact (1928)' in Rüdiger Wolfrum (ed), *Max Planck Encyclopedia of Public International Law* (Online Edition <www.mpepil.com> last update 2010) paras 7ff.

[83] Oliver Dörr, 'Use of Force, Prohibition of' in Rüdiger Wolfrum (ed), *Max Planck Encyclopedia of Public International Law* (Online Edition <www.mpepil.com> last update 2015) para 39 .

[84] Terry Gill and Paul Ducheine, 'Rescue of Nationals' in Terry Gill and Dieter Fleck (eds), *The Handbook of the International Law of Military Operations* (Oxford University Press 2010) 217, 217–19.

[85] Terry Gill, 'Military Intervention at the Invitation of a Government' in Gill and Fleck (n 84) 229, 229–32.

is noteworthy that many of these claims have been based upon human rights or related considerations. Some of them have been discussed so intensely and against such an extensive and long-lasting background of similar arguments that they have even contributed to the development of legal or quasi-legal concepts, such as the idea of 'humanitarian intervention'—which pre-dates the more recent period under consideration[86]—and the discussions about a responsibility to protect.[87]

2. Legitimacy claims to use force

I have chosen to address the following events from the perspective of legitimacy claims in this section: the military interventions in Kosovo (1999), in Iraq (2003), in Libya (2011), the annexation of Crimea in 2014, the action taken against the so-called 'Islamic State' in Iraq and Syria since 2014, in Yemen in 2015, and the military interventions (and non-interventions) in the Syrian civil war since 2015. The events will be briefly sketched, and the arguments for an intervention presented. At the end of this section, the impact of legitimacy claims on legality will be briefly assessed, and tentative conclusions will be drawn in respect of 'rise and decline'.

The 1998–99 Kosovo non-international armed conflict between the Federal Republic of Yugoslavia and the Kosovo Liberation Army was part of the armed conflicts arising from and around the dissolution of Yugoslavia.[88] The military intervention of the North Atlantic Treaty Organization (NATO) between 24 March 1999 and 11 June 1999, *de facto* contributed to ending the conflict. It made Yugoslav and Serb forces withdraw from Kosovo, being replaced by an international presence. The NATO bombing campaign can best be understood against the background of NATO's earlier campaign in Bosnia and Herzegovina, taking place from 30 August 1995 until 20 September 1995, thus after the Srebrenica massacre of July 1995. The 1999 campaign was conducted without the approval of the UN Security Council, even though NATO countries had sought such authorization but had met opposition from Russia and China, indicating that they would veto such a proposal.[89] In light of Article 2(4) UN Charter, in the absence of an armed attack against another state, and in the absence of UN Security Council authorization, it is hardly possibly to justify such operation in legal terms. NATO presented *ex post* and *ex ante* arguments in order to make a claim of legitimacy, speaking of a 'massive humanitarian catastrophe'[90] and referring to the conditions in Kosovo threatening regional stability,[91] the bombing bringing an end to

---

[86]   eg Thomas Franck and Nigel Rodley, 'After Bangladesh: The Law of Humanitarian Intervention by Military Force' (1973) 67 American Journal of International Law 275.

[87]   Andreas Kolb, *The UN Security Council Members' Responsibility to Protect* (Springer 2018) 343–401.

[88]   Independent International Commission on Kosovo, *The Kosovo Report: Conflict, International Response, Lessons Learned* (Oxford University Press 2000) 33–55.

[89]   ibid 142.

[90]   Statement on Kosovo, issued by the Heads of State and Government participating in the meeting of the North Atlantic Council in Washington, DC (23 and 24 April 1999), NATO Press Release S-1(99)62 (23 April 1999) para 8.

[91]   ibid para 8.

the ethnic cleansing of the Albanian population,[92] ending major human rights viola-tions[93] and speeding up the downfall of the Milošević government.[94] In legal terms, none of these arguments can be considered to support the legality of the bombing. Commentators have perceived the arguments by NATO as a legitimacy claim. The International Independent Commission on Kosovo concluded that the NATO military intervention in Kosovo was 'illegal but legitimate'.[95] The legitimacy claim in this case clearly moved beyond the limits of the law but referred to legal arguments, at least as far as the prohibition of genocide and international human rights law are concerned. The claim is not rooted in legal arguments.

The military intervention in Iraq between 20 March and 1 May 2003 had a complex background but generated the clear effect of driving Saddam Hussein out of power.[96] The governments of the United States and the United Kingdom claimed that their ob-jective was 'to disarm Iraq of weapons of mass destruction, to end Saddam Hussein's support for terrorism, and to free the Iraqi people'.[97] The US government believed that Saddam Hussein was not complying with UN Security Council Resolution 1441 of 8 November 2002, and claims of numerous other violations of UN Security Council Resolutions by Iraq were made. As to the legality of the intervention, there was no case-specific explicit authorization by the UN Security Council. It has, however, been ar-gued that the authorization to intervene can be taken as being implied in earlier UN Security Council resolutions, in particular the 1990 resolutions authorizing inter-vention in Iraq in response to the invasion of Kuwait.[98] Many commentators have ex-pressed doubts regarding this argument. Even more determinately, numerous authors have rejected reference to UN Security Council Resolution 1441,[99] among them an in-dependent commission of inquiry set up by the Dutch government.[100] Considering the intervention as unlawful, the legitimacy claims submitted are particularly interesting in this case. There has been no reference to human rights in the first place, nor to re-gime change, but reference to compliance with international law, in particular with binding resolutions adopted by the UN Security Council. The legitimacy claim thus aims at using (potentially or actually unlawful) means to ensure compliance with inter-national law; in other words: violating the law in order to uphold the law. In a way, such a legitimacy claim can be read as a remote reminiscence of the unlawful use of force to

---

[92] ibid para 1.
[93] ibid para 1.
[94] Ralph Steinke, 'A Look Back at NATO's 1999 Kosovo Campaign: A Questionably "Legal" but Justifiable Exception?' (2015) 14 Connections: The Quarterly Journal 43, 48–50.
[95] International Independent Commission on Kosovo (n 88) 4.
[96] Alex Bellamy, 'Ethics and Intervention: The "Humanitarian Exception" and the Problem of Abuse in the Case of Iraq' (2004) 41 Journal of Peace Research 131, 134–38; Rapport Commissie van onderzoek Besluitvorming Irak (Boom 2010) 39–58.
[97] Radio address of President Bush (22 March 2003) <https://georgewbush-whitehouse.archives.gov/news/releases/2003/03/20030322.html> accessed 30 July 2018.
[98] Bellamy (n 96) 134.
[99] eg Elizabeth Henderson, 'Article 2(4) of the United Nations Charter: Whimsical Ideal or Binding Legal Obligation in Relation to Operation Iraqi Freedom' (2004) 10 Canterbury Law Review 105, 115–18.
[100] Rapport Commissie van onderzoek Besluitvorming Irak (n 96) 239–42.

uphold human rights. Any such legitimacy claim disregards the distinct character of international law with its own means of ensuring compliance.

The case of Libya in 2011 seems to be more straightforward. Military action took place on the basis of UN Security Council Resolution 1973 of 17 March 2011,[101] which authorized the use of 'all necessary means' to protect civilians and civilian-populated areas from attack and imposed a no-fly zone alongside a number of targeted sanctions against members of the Gaddafi government.[102] The actual intervention began on 19 March 2011 and lasted until 31 October 2011, formally decided upon by the Security Council when adopting Resolution 2016 on 27 October 2011.[103] There were no debates as to the legality of the intervention as such but on its scope. In particular, questions were raised with regard to the scope of the mandate, with regard to whether the protection of civilians and civilian-populated areas necessitated troops on the ground, and whether eventually the reference to 'protection' could be linked to the 'responsibility to protect'.[104] How do legitimacy claims fit in then? In the case of Libya, they primarily serve to advocate a particular interpretation of Resolution 1973, actually an interpretation supportive of the powers assigned to the intervening governments. It may be argued that the reference to the protection of civilians was used to legitimize a more far-reaching use of force. In contrast to the two previous military interventions, this is much more testing the limits of the law than actually going beyond the law. Given the absence of clear-cut boundaries, claims of legitimacy here serve to develop the law into a particular direction. However, in light of international reactions, this has probably been less successful than assumed. Intervening states, nevertheless, have escaped a clear verdict of illegality in respect of some of their actions. Again, however, legitimacy claims aim at enhancing the means, not at developing human rights or humanitarian standards.

A case that also seems to be fairly clear in terms of the applicable law is the Russian annexation of Crimea.[105] In early 2014, after the 2014 Ukrainian revolution and as part of wider unrest in Southern and Eastern Ukraine, Russia annexed Crimea, which had been part of Ukraine since 1954. The annexation did not occur as a single act but was a sequence of a pro-Russian demonstration, activities of troops without insignia, a declaration of Crimean independence, and eventually a Russian claim on 18 March 2014.[106] While the international community has largely agreed on the process as annexation,[107] the Russian government has made legitimacy claims on the basis of the principle of the self-determination of peoples.[108] Even though it seems pretty clear that

---

[101]   UNSC Res 1973 (17 March 2011) UN Doc S/RES/1973.

[102]   ibid paras 4–23.

[103]   UNSC Res 2016 (27 October 2011) UN Doc S/RES/2016.

[104]   Marie-Eve Loiselle, 'The Normative Status of the Responsibility to Protect after Libya' (2013) 5 Global Responsibility to Protect 317, 336–37.

[105]   Robin Geiß, 'Russia's Annexation of Crimea: The Mills of International Law Grind Slowly but They Do Grind' (2015) 91 International Law Studies 426, 431–47.

[106]   ibid 429–30.

[107]   Thomas Grant, 'Annexation of Crimea' (2015) 109 American Journal of International Law 68, 87–91.

[108]   Address by President Putin of the Russian Federation (18 March 2014) <http://en.kremlin.ru/events/president/news/20603> accessed 30 July 2018.

Russia's arguments are legally not convincing, it is noteworthy that they again promote legitimacy for the use of particular means in light of more or less diffuse objectives. Self-determination, while agreed upon in principle, is a volatile concept both in terms of procedure and in terms of substance. The interesting aspect here is that reference to self-determination, likewise in terms of a legitimacy claim, in the context of the dissolution of Yugoslavia and the former Soviet Union, has in the case of Crimea been used less for purposes of democratic governance but rather for the expansion of territory of the more powerful actor in bilateral relations.

The action taken against the so-called 'Islamic State of Iraq and the Levant' (ISIL) in Iraq and Syria since 2014 is more difficult to assess in legal terms. Interventions by third states largely began as interventions into the Syrian Civil War and the Iraqi Civil War. They were largely driven by the territorial gains of ISIL in early 2014 as well as reported human rights abuses. The US-American-led intervention in Iraq can—at least to the extent to which it was directed against ISIL—be considered as intervention by invitation of the Iraqi government.[109] This argument cannot be maintained in respect of Syria. It can, however, be argued that the acts of terror committed by ISIL against many states qualify as armed attacks. However, ISIL is not a state, and thus it is questionable whether Article 51 UN Charter is really applicable. The question then has to be answered how the violation of Syrian territorial integrity in pursuit of responding to terrorist acts of a non-state actor can be justified. Even though Syria did not effectively control the areas held by ISIL at the time of the attacks, such attacks constitute violations of Syrian territorial integrity.[110] To this end, reference has been made to the 'unable/unwilling doctrine',[111] basically arguing that if a state is unable or unwilling to prevent armed attacks by non-state actors operating on its territory, a military response by other states amounts to self-defence, possibly collective self-defence. These are legal arguments in what may be labelled a grey area of international law. The doctrine is a response to what some states perceive as a gap in international law. Upholding the formal position that military action against ISIL in Syria is unlawful, is perceived to be untenable in light of the security threats arising from such non-state actors by those arguing in favour of the 'unable/unwilling doctrine'. Such a doctrine may be described and categorized as a legitimacy claim, again defending the use of certain means (that is military force) in order to defend something that is protected by international law, among others territorial integrity, freedom from terrorist acts, and others. The legitimacy claim is again made to test the limits of the law, perhaps even to further develop the law. Referring to Popovsky's above-cited statement, the doctrine can be a means to achieve 'adjustments or developments in law, therefore closing the gaps and reharmonizing

---

[109] Karine Bannelier-Christakis, 'Military Interventions against ISIL in Iraq, Syria and Libya, and the Legal Basis of Consent' (2016) 29 Leiden Journal of International Law 743, 750–52.

[110] Christian J Tams, 'The Use of Force against Terrorists' (2009) 20 European Journal of International Law 359, 371–72.

[111] UN Doc S/2014/695 (23 September 2014) Letter dated 23 September 2014 from the Permanent Representative of the United States of America to the United Nations addressed to the Secretary-General, or UN Doc S/2015/563 (24 July 2015) Letter dated 24 July 2015 from the Chargé d'affaires a.i. of the Permanent Mission of Turkey to the United Nations addressed to the President of the Security Council.

legality and legitimacy'.[112] Such legitimacy may serve to enhance the law and to change it at the same time.

Saudi Arabia, in 2015, initiated a military intervention in Yemen as leader of a coalition in order to influence the outcome of the civil war that had begun in 2015.[113] The Saudi Arabian-led intervention supported the acting President of Yemen who had called for the intervention against the Houthi militia, allegedly supported by Iran. Considered as intervention by invitation, there was hardly any international law-based criticism of the fact that Saudi Arabia intervened, but much more criticism of the conduct of operations which, it is argued, have caused a major humanitarian crisis in Yemen—which is not addressed in this section.[114] It is perhaps not surprising in this context that the coalition led by Saudi Arabia largely refrained from making legitimacy claims as to the prohibition of the use of force, simply relying upon more or less formal legality arising from Article 51 UN Charter under the *ius contra bellum*.[115]

Russia has intervened in the Syrian war since September 2015 following an invitation by the Syrian government. While this does not in itself raise questions of legality under Article 2(4) UN Charter, it is interesting that Russia and the Syrian government have both added legitimacy claims to support their position by referring to the need to counter rebel and terrorist activities.[116] What is perhaps even more interesting are the two debates about responding to the use of chemical weapons in Syria and about a human rights-motivated intervention in Syria. On 7 April 2017, the US government struck the Shayrat airbase in Syria, under the control of the Syrian government, in response to a use of chemical weapons in Idlib on 4 April 2017, allegedly by the Syrian government.[117] It is not possible to justify the strike under international law in the absence of a situation of an armed attack or any authorization by the UN Security Council. However, legitimacy claims were made, focusing on responding to the illegal use of chemical weapons by the Syrian government. These claims were widely shared even outside the United States,[118] and again they point towards an ambition by some states to take the law in their hands and ensure enforcement of particularly important rules. Legitimacy claims serve to enhance enforcement in light of undisputed violations of the law. Such claims, however, go beyond the limits of the law by violating core rules included in Article 2(4) UN Charter. Nevertheless, states have refrained from making similar legitimacy claims in favour of intervening in the civil war in support of the

[112] Popovsky (n 73) 388, 407.
[113] Benjamin Nußberger, 'Military Strikes in Yemen in 2015: Intervention by Invitation and Self-Defence in the Course of Yemen's "Model Transitional Process"' (2017) 4 Journal on the Use of Force and International Law 110, 111.
[114] eg Martin Fink, 'Naval Blockade and the Humanitarian Crisis in Yemen' (2017) 64 Netherlands International Law Review 291, 291–95.
[115] Identical letters dated 26 March 2015 from the Permanent Representative of Qatar to the United Nations addressed to the Secretary-General and the President of the Security Council, UN Doc S/2015/217.
[116] Angela Stent, 'Putin's Power Play in Syria: How to Respond to Russia's Intervention' (2016) 95 Foreign Affairs 106, 108–09.
[117] Statement by the US President on Syria Strike (7 April 2017) <www.bbc.com/news/world-us-canada-39524274> accessed 2 July 2018.
[118] eg Joint statement by Federal Chancellor Merkel and President Hollande of France following the air strikes in Syria (7 April 2017) <www.bundesregierung.de/Content/EN/Pressemitteilungen/BPA/2017/2017-04-07-erklaerung-merkel-hollande_en.html> accessed 2 July 2018.

opposition. This may be less due to a different attitude but rather to a factual analysis of the options available in Syria. Therefore, states in this regard seem to focus on ensuring accountability after the end of the war and making use of other—in effect—peaceful mechanisms, such as those of the Human Rights Council.[119]

3. Assessment

Assessing all these legitimacy claims, two aspects should to be underlined: First, legitimacy claims in the context of the prohibition of the use and threat of force mostly refer to values that have become part of positive law, such as self-determination, human rights, and the protection of the civilian population. Secondly, legitimacy claims serve not only to test the limits of the existing *ius contra bellum* but also to push them. Obviously, the structural limitations of international law in respect to compliance and enforcement incite not just states but also many other actors to argue in favour of largely unilateral enforcement. They thereby put one of the most important functions of international law at risk: peace through law. While legitimacy claims thus raise the impression to contribute to the 'rise' of value-based standards, such as human rights, they effectively weaken the more formal rules, such as the prohibition of the use force, which may be perceived as 'decline' of this area of international law. Arguably, collective values unilaterally enforced will not enhance respect for the international rule of law. Legitimacy claims rather weaken than strengthen international law; in the context of *ius contra bellum*, they seem to signal 'decline' rather than 'rise'.

IV. Legitimacy claims blurring the lines

Whereas legitimacy claims in respect of *ius contra bellum* have largely been made by government representatives, it is interesting to note that legitimacy claims related to *ius in bello* have increasingly been put forward by non-state actors, be they academics, activists, or representatives of the Red Cross and Crescent movement.[120] It may be argued that this reflects a more recent success story of this area of the law, attracting the attention of civil society rather than of military experts and military lawyers only. This is not a development that occurs for the first time in history. However, it deserves our attention in so far as it has never before occurred without an effort to push for new law.

---

[119] One example of states focusing on ensuring accountability after the end of the war can be seen in the creation of the International, Impartial and Independent Mechanism to Assist in the Investigation and Prosecution of Those Responsible for the Most Serious Crimes under International Law Committed in the Syrian Arab Republic since March 2011, UNGA Res 71/248, UN Doc A/RES/71/248.

[120] With regard to actors in the law of war: Hans-Peter Gasser, 'International Committee of the Red Cross (ICRC)' in Rüdiger Wolfrum (ed), *Max Planck Encyclopedia of Public International Law* (Online Edition <www.mpepil.com> last update 2016); Mahmoud C Bassiouni, 'The New Wars and the Crisis of Compliance with the Law of Armed Conflict by Non-State Actors' (2008) 98 Journal of Criminal Law and Criminology 711; Anthea Roberts and Sandesh Sivakumaran, 'Lawmaking by Nonstate Actors: Engaging Armed Groups in the Creation of International Humanitarian Law' (2012) 37 Yale Journal of International Law 108.

1. Law of armed conflict

From the mid-nineteenth century until today, there have been four major periods of codification in *ius in bello*. All of them have enjoyed the support of civil society to a lesser or greater extent; and all of them have given rise to political controversies. Even more important in our particular context: all of them have used legitimacy claims in support of law-making.

The first of these periods is linked to Henry Dunant in Europe and Francis Lieber in North America.[121] While their efforts towards a humanization of warfare differ in origin, they both arrived at basically similar outcomes, namely the consideration that the suffering of individuals involved in armed conflict should be limited. Henry Dunant, as can be taken from his account in 'A Memory of Solferino',[122] was deeply moved by witnessing the suffering of thousands of wounded soldiers of the battle of Solferino in 1859, an international armed conflict between the Austrian Empire and the Franco–Sardinian Alliance, and thus was instrumental in the founding of the International Committee of the Red Cross. Francis Lieber, serving US President Abraham Lincoln, contributed to the drafting of instructions on how soldiers should conduct themselves in wartime, adopted by the President in 1863, and having an impact on the final years of the American Civil War.[123]

The second and third periods occurred in the aftermath of the First and Second World Wars, in response to horrible experiences in these conflicts. Notwithstanding the efforts of the peace movement and other humanitarian pressure groups after the First World War, little was achieved in terms of treaties entering into force. An important exception is the 1925 Geneva Gas Protocol,[124] which reaffirmed the prohibition of the use of chemical and biological weapons in international armed conflicts and built upon a legitimacy claim arising from the *Martens Clause*.[125] More successful, given the adoption of the four Geneva Conventions, were the post-Second World War efforts which—building on legitimacy claims aiming at the protection of the civilian population that had suffered so much during the war—have become the cornerstone of modern Geneva law or international humanitarian law.

The fourth period of *ius in bello* law-making on the basis of legitimacy claims is the Diplomatic Conference of Geneva from 1974 to 1977. With a strong input and a convincing legitimacy claim from a non-state actor, the International Committee of the Red Cross, the Geneva Conference effectively negotiated an overhaul and update of international humanitarian law in light of the challenges that had arisen between 1949

---

[121] Amanda Alexander, 'A Short History of International Humanitarian Law' (2015) 26 European Journal of international Law 109; Theodor Meron, 'Francis Lieber's Code and Principles of Humanity' (1997) 36 Columbia Journal of Transnational Law 269; Gasser (n 120).

[122] Henry Dunant, *A Memory of Solferino* (International Committee of the Red Cross 1986).

[123] Burrus M Carnahan, 'The Civil War Origins of the Modern Rules of War' (2012) 39 Northern Kentucky Law Review 661.

[124] Gregory P Noone, 'The History and Evolution of the Law of War Prior to World War II' (2000) 47 Naval Law Review 176, 200–04.

[125] Theodor Meron, 'The Martens Clause, Principles of Humanity, and Dictates of Public Conscience' (2000) 94 American Society of International Law 78.

and the mid-1970s.[126] Notwithstanding the many controversies during the Conference, the outcome can be considered an unprecedented humanitarian and legitimacy-driven process of law-making.

With the exception of some efforts in treaty-making, including the Ottawa and the Oslo Conventions,[127] the more recent efforts to develop in the laws applicable to armed conflict differ from the above processes:

First, recent efforts of civil society and the international community as a whole to take up armed conflict situations do not focus on law-making but primarily on compliance with existing rules. This is true in particular for the many commissions of inquiry that have recently been set up by the UN Security Council, by the UN Human Rights Council, and by other bodies, including regional organizations.[128] Non-compliance is not only simply considered to be unlawful, but it is perceived as signalling a lack of legitimacy.

Second, the object and purpose of these commissions of inquiry is not primarily to prevent further breaches of the law but to ensure accountability for violations of the law.[129] Current interest in international humanitarian law does not so much focus on the dissemination of rules but on holding individuals (not necessarily governments) accountable. This may also be seen in light of the Rome Statute.[130] This treaty has attracted so much attention that the prevention that is part of dissemination has to some extent fallen out of sight.[131] Putting accountability first raises the impression of enormous progress at the international level, which—if it is not met in all circumstances—gives rise to concerns about a 'decline' of international law.

Third, interest in *ius in bello* by the general public and by civil society in particular has been driven by a sense of ownership arising from international human rights law, which has been increasingly applied to situations of armed conflict,[132] without taking into account the different historical origins and the specific functions of each of these two branches of international law. Whereas human rights law is meant to protect individuals against their governments, international humanitarian law aims to ensure the application of minimum humanitarian standards in armed conflict situations by parties to such an armed conflict.[133] From the perspective of civil society, these distinctions are

---

[126] Sylvie S Junod, 'Protocol II' in Yves Sandoz, Christophe Swinarski, and Bruno Zimmermann (eds), *Commentary on the Additional Protocols of 8 June 1977 to the Geneva Conventions of 12 August* (International Committee of the Red Cross 1987) 1325–36.

[127] Convention on the Prohibition of the Use, Stockpiling, Production and Transfer of Anti-Personnel Mines and on Their Destruction (18 September 1997) 2056 UNTS 211; Convention on Cluster Munitions (30 May 2008) 2688 UNTS 39.

[128] Larissa J van den Herik, 'An Inquiry into the Role of Commissions of Inquiry in International Law' (2014) 13 Chinese Journal of International Law 507.

[129] Larissa J van den Herik, 'Accountability Through Fact-Finding' (2015) 62 Netherlands International Law Review 295.

[130] Rome Statute of the International Criminal Court (17 July 1998) 2187 UNTS 3.

[131] Knut Dörmann, 'Dissemination and Monitoring Compliance of International Humanitarian Law' in Wolff Heintschel von Heinegg and Volker Epping (eds), *International Humanitarian Law Facing New Challenges* (Springer 2007) 227.

[132] Cordula Droege, 'Elective Affinities? Human Rights and Humanitarian Law' (2008) 90 International Review of the Red Cross 871, 501.

[133] Thilo Marauhn, 'Sailing Close to the Wind' (2013) 43 California Western International Law Journal 401, 436–37.

less relevant than the objective of a legitimacy claim focusing on the 'human' in human rights law and humanitarian law alike.

It is against this background that I would like to assess more specifically the following three situations that have recently been the object of legitimacy claims in the context of *ius in bello*, and subsequently assess their effects on the 'rise or decline' of the international rule of law: first, the use of chemical weapons in the Syrian civil war; secondly, the use of heavy artillery in Northern Iraq by coalition forces in their fight against ISIL; and thirdly, the debate about unmanned aerial vehicles and their legality. Reference will be made to compliance, accountability, and human rights considerations in respect of all three situations.

2. Legitimacy claims

One of the first uses of chemical weapons in the Syrian Civil War occurred on 21 August 2013, when sarin-filled rockets hit the Ghouta suburbs of Damascus, killing a large number of civilians.[134] The parties to the conflict blamed each other, but none admitted the attack. At the time, Syria was only a party to the 1925 Geneva Protocol, which just applies to international armed conflicts. Given that the Syrian Civil War is a non-international armed conflict, the treaty prohibition of the 1925 Protocol does not apply. Whether the parallel prohibition of chemical warfare in customary international law was and is applicable to non-international armed conflicts is more than doubtful, as it is very difficult to ascertain pertinent state practice.[135] Shortly after the use of chemical weapons on 21 August 2013, Syria became a state party to the Chemical Weapons Convention (CWC), even though, arguably, only as a result of coercive diplomacy.[136] On 14 October 2013, the CWC entered into force for Syria.[137] Under the CWC, Syria has accepted the obligation that it will 'never under any circumstances' use chemical weapons.[138] This not only includes international and non-international armed conflicts, but it goes far beyond these situations, with the use of riot control agents for purposes of domestic law enforcement being the only exception.[139]

Accountability issues were soon raised, and a UN fact-finding mission as well as the Commission of Inquiry on Syria set up by the UN Refugee Agency investigated the

---

[134] Report of the United Nations Mission to Investigate Allegations of the Use of Chemical Weapons in the Syrian Arab Republic on the alleged use of chemical weapons in the Ghouta area of Damascus on 21 August 2013, UN Doc A/67/997–S/2013/553; Thilo Marauhn, 'The Prohibition to Use Chemical Weapons' in Terry Gill, Robin Geiß, Robert Heinsch, Tim McCormack, Christophe Paulussen, and Jessica Dorsey (eds), *Yearbook of International Humanitarian Law 2014* (TMC Asser Press 2016) 25, 27.

[135] ibid 38–39.

[136] Walter Krutzsch, Eric Myjer, and Ralf Trapp, 'Issues Raised by the Accession of Syria to the Chemical Weapons Convention' in Walter Krutzsch, Eric Myjer and Ralf Trapp (eds), *The Chemical Weapons Convention—A Commentary* (Oxford University Press 2009) 689.

[137] See <www.opcw.org/news/article/syrias-accession-to-the-chemical-weapons-convention-enters-into-force/> accessed 30 July 2018.

[138] Art 1 Convention on the Prohibition of the Development, Production, Stockpiling and Use of Chemical Weapons and on their Destruction (3 September 1992) 1974 UNTS 45.

[139] Marauhn, 'The Prohibition to Use Chemical Weapons' (n 134) 25, 31.

attacks,[140] finding the likely use of the nerve agent sarin, among others. Later on, the Organisation for the Prohibition of Chemical Weapons explicitly blamed the Syrian military for using chlorine bombs in 2014 and 2015, and ISIL to have used sulphur mustard in 2015.[141] After further attacks in December 2016 and in April 2017, the US government authorized a missile attack on the airbase of Shayrat.[142] In addition to these developments, there were discussions among academics and civil society representatives on the applicability of the provisions of the Rome Statute.[143] Irrespective of the amendments to Article 8 of the Rome Statute, adopted at Kampala in 2010,[144] the International Criminal Court could only have become active upon referral by the UN Security Council.

It is noteworthy that legitimacy claims voiced by civil society, international organizations, and eventually also governments, focusing on the illegitimacy of the use of chemical weapons in Syria, even beyond the actually applicable law in Syria in 2013, have contributed to improvements in the law, (1) by pushing Syria to become a party to the CWC, (2) by applying general and specific fact-finding procedures, and (3) by strengthening the provisions of the Rome Statute at Kampala. Even though violations of the prohibition of using chemical weapons have continued to occur after these improvements, it can hardly be denied that the effect of pertinent legitimacy claims have been a 'rise' of the international rule of law. Linking this back to the debate about *ius contra bellum*, it is noteworthy that the attacks launched by the US government in 2017 have not necessarily strengthened the international rule of law.[145] They have at least had a dialectic impact on the international rule of law and may perhaps even contribute to its 'decline'. This seems to leave us with an ambivalent outcome of the analysis. However, it may also be argued that the outcome is clearer than expected. The improvement of the applicable law has strengthened the prohibition; only its preventive effects have not yet been achieved. Decentralized efforts to enforce such rules outside the realm of international law, as in the case of the 2017 missile launch of the United States, put the 'rise' that has been achieved by improving the law in question. States must be careful to only make use of permissible means to ensure compliance with the law.

The second situation concerns the use of heavy artillery in Northern Iraq by coalition forces in their fight against ISIL. Media reports of coalition forces using explosive weapons with wide-area effects[146] gave rise to criticism voiced by non-governmental

---

[140] Seventh Report of Commission of Inquiry on Syria—A/HRC/25/65, 128.

[141] Tatsuya Abe, 'Effectiveness of the Institutional Approach to an Alleged Violation of International Law' (2014) 57 Japanese Yearbook of International Law 333.

[142] See, eg, Mika Hayashi, 'The U.S. Airstrike After the Use of Chemical Weapons in Syria: National Interest, Humanitarian Intervention, or Enforcement Against War Crimes?' (*ASIL Insights*, Vol 21 Issue 8) <https://www.asil.org/insights/volume/21/issue/8/us-airstrike-after-use-chemical-weapons-syria-national-interest > accessed 30 October 2018.

[143] Dapo Akande, 'Can the ICC Prosecute for Use of Chemical Weapons in Syria?' (*European Journal of International Law Blog*, 23 August 2013) <www.ejiltalk.org/can-the-icc-prosecute-for-use-of-chemical-weapons-in-syria/> accessed 30 July 2018.

[144] Annex I to ICC Doc RC/Res.5.

[145] Mika Hayashi, 'Reacting to the Use of Chemical Weapons' (2014) 1 Journal on the Use of Force and International Law 80.

[146] eg Susannah George, 'Mosul is a Graveyard: Final IS Battle Kills 9000 Civilians' (*AP News*, 21 December 2017) <www.apnews.com/bbea7094fb954838a2fdc11278d65460> accessed 30 July 2018.

organizations, among others Amnesty International and Human Rights Watch.[147] They referred to the principle of distinction and underlined that 'indiscriminate' and 'disproportionate attacks' are prohibited. They have specified that according to Article 51, para 5, lit b, Additional Protocol I of 1977 and pertinent rules of customary international law, an attack is disproportionate if it may be expected to cause incidental loss of civilian life or damage to civilian objects that would be excessive in relation to the concrete and direct military advantage anticipated from the attack.[148] While they properly restate the law, legitimacy claims come into play when civil society groups suggest that violations of these rules occur without specifically presenting an argument that properly relates specific facts to the law. The military command of the 'Combined Joint Task Force—Operation Inherent Resolve' has continuously stressed that the law of armed conflict is respected, and violations thereof are prosecuted.[149] This requires an assessment by the commander in light of *ex ante* knowledge, not in light of *ex post* knowledge.[150] The challenge of such legitimacy claims by non-governmental organizations is that they create an image of international humanitarian law and suggest a standard that goes beyond the law. In this regard, they blur the lines between the law as it stands and politically motivated claims for higher standards. This is not conducive to the international rule of law. If higher expectations are raised that go beyond the law, and if the impression remains that these standards have not been met, a legitimacy gap[151] is created that—as I would argue—rather weakens than strengthens the law. In contrast to the chemical weapons incidents, such blurring of the lines in light of expectations not being met may be perceived as 'decline' rather than 'rise', even though the actors aimed at a 'rise'.

A similar conclusion may be drawn when addressing the third case mentioned, that is the debate about unmanned aerial vehicles and their legality.[152] This is perhaps one of the more serious examples of blurring the lines between the law of armed conflict and human rights law. Debates about 'drones' have often focused on the legality of

---

[147] Amnesty International and Human Rights Watch, 'Iraq/US-Led Coalition: Weapons Choice Endangers Mosul Civilians' (8 June 2017) <www.amnesty.org/en/latest/news/2017/06/iraq-us-led-coalition-weapons-choice-endangers-mosul-civilians/> and <www.hrw.org/news/2017/06/08/iraq/us-led-coalition-weapons-choice-endangers-mosul-civilians> both accessed 30 July 2018.

[148] ibid.

[149] eg Department of Defense Press Briefing by Colonel Dillon via teleconference from Baghdad, Iraq (23 June 2017) <www.defense.gov/News/Transcripts/Transcript-View/Article/1227963/department-of-defense-press-briefing-by-colonel-dillon-via-teleconference-from/> accessed 30 July 2018.

[150] This, eg, can be taken from: Jean-Marie Henckaerts and Louise Doswald-Beck, *Customary International Humanitarian Law Volume I Rules* (Cambridge University Press 2009) 50.

[151] Tania Voon, 'Closing the Gap Between Legitimacy and Legality of Humanitarian Intervention' (2002) 7 UCLA Journal of International Law and Foreign Affairs 31, 58–61.

[152] Jelena Pejic, 'Extraterritorial Targeting by Means of Armed Drones: Some Legal Implications' (2014) 96 International Review of the Red Cross 67; Stephan Hobe, 'Drones in International Law: The Applicability of Air and Space Law' in Hans-Joachim Heintze and Pierre Thielbörger (eds), *From Cold War to Cyber War: The Evolution of the International Law of Peace and Armed Conflict over the last 25 Years* (Springer 2015) 107; Christof Heyns, Dapo Akande, Lawrence Hill-Cawthorne, and Thompson Chengeta, 'The International Law Framework Regulating the Use of Armed Drones' (2016) 65 International & Comparative Law Quarterly 791; Thilo Marauhn, 'Der Einsatz von Kampfdrohnen aus völkerrechtlicher Perspektive' in Roman Schmidt-Radefeldt and Christine Meissler (eds), *Automatisierung und Digitalisierung des Krieges: Drohnenkrieg und Cyberwar als Herausforderungen für Ethik, Völkerrecht und Sicherheitspolitik* (Nomos 2012) 60.

remote killing rather than on precise legal analysis.[153] This has led to the blurring of several lines between the law of armed conflict and human rights law. First, the applicability of the rules of the law of armed conflict depends on the existence of such conflict. Whether or not such a conflict exists is hardly ever subject to an authoritative ruling of an international body. In most circumstances, the actors themselves—as members of the international community—decide whether there is a situation of an armed conflict.[154] Assessments vary, and different conclusions can be drawn. Secondly, even if the law of armed conflict is applicable, it does not include rules on the prohibition of 'drones' per se. Rather, the law of armed conflict considers unarmed aerial vehicles as platforms, not as weapons.[155] Blurring the distinction between platforms and weapons is not helpful in light of the clear rules that apply to the law of weapons. Thirdly, focusing on the right to life alone in debates about 'drones' misses the distinctions between international human rights law and international humanitarian law (IHL): In contrast to human rights law, IHL neither focuses on the right to life, nor on the protection of physical integrity because the principle of distinction prohibits making the civilian population the object of an attack. This broadens the protection of the civilian population (compared to international human rights law) in the sense that even if neither bodily harm nor death occurs, an attack upon them is unlawful per se.[156] At the same time, the protection is less stringent in that context so collateral damage may occur even if the principle of distinction is respected.[157] It is a misperception to argue that international human rights law and IHL are complementary with respect to the right to life. They are different and pursue a different purpose. It is simply not convincing to generalize and argue that international human rights law and IHL both serve to protect human life. It is even misleading to argue that 'there can be no doubt that the right to life has always provided the background of IHL'.[158] Modern law of armed conflict seeks to protect the civilian population from the effects of fighting, but it does not call into question military necessity as a criterion for balancing.

The balancing is indeed between military necessity and, among others, the protection of the civilian population; it is a misperception to state 'that IHL comes from an epoch when military thinking still largely dominated its architecture',[159] to continue that this 'is susceptible of making a mockery of the entire carefully constructed edifice of IHL',[160] and to then conclude that 'one cannot place full trust in traditional IHL

---

[153] Human Rights Watch, *A Wedding That Became a Funeral: US Drone Attack on Marriage Procession in Yemen* (Human Rights Watch 2014) 21–24.

[154] Katja Schöberl, 'Konfliktpartei und Kriegsgebiet in bewaffneten Auseinandersetzungen' (2012) 25 Humanitäres Völkerrecht 128.

[155] Thilo Marauhn, 'The Notion of Meaningful Human Control in Light of the Law of Armed Conflict' in Wolff Heintschel von Heinegg, Robert Frau, and Tassilo Singer (eds), *Dehumanization of Warfare—Legal Implications of New Weapon Technologies* (Springer 2018) 213.

[156] Junod (n 126) 1449.

[157] Alexander Orakhelashvili, 'The Interaction Between Human Rights and Humanitarian Law: Fragmentation, Conflict, Parallelism, or Convergence?' (2008) 19 European Journal of International Law 161, 169.

[158] Christian Tomuschat, 'Human Rights and International Humanitarian Law' (2010) 21 European Journal of International Law 15, 17.

[159] ibid.

[160] ibid.

without raising some questions'.[161] Distinguishing between the two areas of the law requires precision to ensure optimum protection of not only, but primarily, the civilian population in situations of armed conflict.

3. Assessment

The assessment and analysis of legitimacy claims as presented in the context of *ius in bello* demonstrate an interesting parallel to the analysis of legitimacy claims in respect of *ius contra bellum*. To begin with, they may support 'rise' as well as 'decline'. Legitimacy claims contribute to the 'rise' of the international rule of law in international humanitarian law, when the development of the law and its refinement are at issue. The use of chemical weapons and the (il)legitimacy claims made to counter such use aptly demonstrate this. Again, the weakness of legitimacy claims seems to lie in approaches to unilateral law enforcement or unilateral approaches to ensure compliance with the law. Furthermore, a serious risk for the international rule of law goes along with legitimacy claims raising expectations beyond existing international law. Whenever such expectations are raised—as demonstrated both with regard to the use of heavy artillery in densely populated areas and to unmanned aerial vehicles (drones)—arguments that the law has been complied with (at a lower level)—may be read as formal references to the law in order to escape accountability. This, in my reading, seriously weakens the law even though the actors making such legitimacy claims aim at strengthening it. This leads to the conclusion that a proper assessment of legality serves the international rule of law better than any legitimacy claim can do—in particular in areas where the interpretation and application of the law operates in a decentralized mode, as still is the case with the law of armed conflict.

V. The instrumental character of legitimacy claims

Summarizing the analysis above may provide a plausible basis for assessments of the 'rise or decline' of the international rule of law after the mid-1990s in a perspective of legitimacy.

First, many of the changes in the international order underlying the analysis in this chapter are attitudinal in nature, which means they are vested in actors and reflect their approach to international law. Hence, in this chapter I have not perceived these changes as objective but largely as subjective. This does not mean that the changes do not have a factual basis, arising from technological change, rising or declining economic and political power, alliances entered into, and many other factors. However, such factors do not affect the international rule of law in themselves, but only if actors subsequently change their attitudes towards the law as it stands.

---

[161] ibid.

Secondly, analysing the 'rise or decline' of international law, in my perspective, can hardly be done from within the law. It is necessary to take a look at the law from the outside, at perceptions of the law, at approaches to the law. This easily links to the changing attitudes of actors that are part of the analysis presented here. Looking at the international rule of law from the outside enables any commentator to assess the law in context, to the extent it contributes to the order mentioned above.

Thirdly, legitimacy has increasingly become a matter of concern for international lawyers. It should not be left to international relations scholars but lawyers should act as participating observers in assessing not only the legality of particular situations, but also their legitimacy. In doing so, it is, however, important to distinguish theories of legitimacy from claims of legitimacy. While theories aim at providing a better understanding of the law as such, claims of legitimacy mirror the attitude of particular actors, they are subjective, competing, and may be controversial.

Fourthly, legitimacy claims can contribute to 'rise and decline'. In respect of *ius contra bellum*, the analysis has shown that legitimacy claims may contribute to 'rise' as far as the source is concerned, that is human rights (law), but it may contribute to 'decline' in respect of the means of ensuring compliance, of enforcement—at least if states turn to unilateral enforcement, and in particular to the use of force. As far as *ius in bello* is concerned, similar conclusions may be drawn. In addition, legitimacy claims run the risk not only to blur the lines between distinct branches of the law, but also raise expectations beyond what is feasible. The intentional blurring of the lines and the purposive claim of expectations beyond a clear analysis of legality may be perceived as legitimacy claims that eventually weaken the international rule of law, thus, contributing to 'decline' rather than 'rise'.

Overall, the analysis above has shown that legitimacy considerations will not allow a proper assessment of 'rise or decline' in themselves. Any such assessment must be multidimensional. In the interest of the international rule of law, it is important to first establish a realistic perspective on what international law can achieve at all. In contrast to expectations that have been raised in particular after the end of the Cold War by many scholars, international law has not become a value-based constitutional arrangement of its constitutive entities, whether these are states or individuals. There simply is no global consensus on values. Expecting that international law can actually become the backbone of global values may be philosophically tenable but does not seem to be achievable in practical terms for the time being.

If international legal scholars want to preserve international law as law, and ensure its effectiveness, perhaps even improve its effectiveness, it seems much more plausible to consider public international law as a conflict management system among participating entities, irrespective of whether these are states, international organizations, or individuals. Such a more modest view of public international law will avoid deepening a perceived crisis of international law. Rather, it will serve to strengthen international law.

19

The Relationship between Legality and Legitimacy: A Double-Edged Sword

Comment on Thilo Marauhn

Dana Burchardt

I. A two-dimensional relationship

The question of 'rise or decline'[1] of the international rule of law is multi-dimensional—and so are the answers that an analytical assessment of this question can provide. Thilo Marauhn shows this forcefully in his account of 'legitimacy claims' in the international sphere. He argues that what he calls 'legitimacy claims' put forward by international actors can have a twofold effect on international law: they 'may contribute to "rise", as far as the source is concerned, that is human rights (law), but [they] may contribute to "decline" in respect of the means of ensuring compliance, of enforcement'.[2]

This two-dimensional character of the relationship between legality and legitimacy in international law has been highlighted by others in different terms. Richard Falk, for instance, graphically opposes two questions:

> Does such an approach [that uses legitimacy in international affairs] introduce a needed, yet restricted, flexibility into the operation of international law in a range of circumstances that cannot be adequately anticipated or in relation to which there exists an absence of consensus due to differing political motivations? Or, quite oppositely, does this approach invite geopolitical opportunism, providing powerful states with a generalized excuse for circumventing the carefully crafted constraints of international law?[3]

---

[1] On this notion: Heike Krieger and Georg Nolte, 'The International Rule of Law—Rise or Decline?—Approaching Current Foundational Challenges' in this book.

[2] Thilo Marauhn, 'The International Rule of Law in Light of Legitimacy Claims' in this book.

[3] Richard Falk, 'Introduction: Legality and Legitimacy Necessities and Problematics of Exceptionalism' in Richard Falk, Mark Juergensmeyer, and Vesselin Popovsky (eds), *Legality and Legitimacy in Global Affairs* (Paperback 2012) 3, 18.

The answer that he gives to these questions and that is also reflected in the assessment by Thilo Marauhn is: both. From the perspective of the law, legitimacy is actually a double-edged sword.

Why and to what extent is that so? How does this character of a double-edged sword come about? That is the question addressed in this comment in greater detail. In order to examine the relationship between legality and legitimacy, the observer can take various perspectives. This comment will focus on a norm-related perspective. It will inquire into the reasons for the two-dimensional relationship between legality and legitimacy through the lens of norm theory. It will consider legal norms on the one hand and legitimacy norms on the other hand, interrogating how these different kinds of norms can coexist, interrelate, and influence each other and what functions they can fulfil in the international sphere. By doing so, it will highlight to what extent legal norms and legitimacy norms *compete* and *complement* each other—where the double-edged sword in the relationship between legality and legitimacy can be used for undercutting or rather for defending each other.

II. Legal norms and legitimacy norms

Understanding the relationship between legality and legitimacy as a relationship between norms might not come naturally to lawyers (including international lawyers). While in other disciplines the notion of norms evidently includes both legal and non-legal norms, lawyers might have the tendency to focus more on the norm quality of legal norms and to take less notice of the norm quality of non-legal norms. The discussion about legitimacy in international law is thus rather seldom phrased in these terms. However, when legitimacy is understood in a normative rather than in a descriptive sense, legitimacy considerations as they underlie in the 'legitimacy claims' discussed by Thilo Marauhn can in fact be seen as an expression of norms.[4]

A norm can be defined as a 'standard of appropriate behaviour' for certain actors,[5] as 'prescriptions concerning people's behaviour to each other'.[6] The legitimacy claims that Thilo Marauhn analyses in his chapter fall into this category. These claims relate to standards that can serve, and aim to serve, as a yardstick to assess human behaviour, be it individual or institutionalized. What is more, they can shape, and aim at shaping, the social and political reality. Thilo Marauhn gives various examples of how this has happened in the context of use of force and humanitarian law.[7] For instance, when a legitimacy claim is formulated that states can use force to bring a 'massive humanitarian catastrophe' to an end, this claim can serve as a standard and shape behaviour in

---

[4] Using the term 'legitimacy norms': Andrew Joseph Loomis, 'Legitimacy Norms as Change Agents: Examining the Role of the Public Voice' in Falk, Juergensmeyer, and Popovski (n 3) 72.
[5] Martha Finnemore and Kathryn Sikkink, 'International Norm Dynamics and Political Change' (1998) 52 International Organization 887.
[6] Hans Kelsen, *General Theory of Norms* (Oxford University Press 1991) 1.
[7] Marauhn (n 2).

subsequent similar cases. This indicates that in fact such legitimacy claims can be characterized as norms. Although these norms might be regarded as moral rather than legal in nature, they can have similar effects and functions. Their particularity does not so much concern their effects as norms but rather their content: legitimacy norms relate to a specific kind of behaviour, that is the exercise of political authority and its justification and acceptance.[8]

A key observation by Thilo Marauhn concerns the distinction between legal and non-legal norms. He argues that both in the context of the use of force and of humanitarian law, actors often do not differentiate clearly between legitimacy standards on the one hand and legal standards on the other.[9] This observation can be linked back to a broader development. This 'blurring' between legal and non-legal norms arguably reflects a general tendency in the international sphere. Various dichotomies such as between legal and non-legal norms, between binding and non-binding norms, *lex lata* and *lex ferenda*, between public and private law, have been challenged by practical developments and theoretical approaches alike.[10] This includes, for instance, phenomena such as an informalization of international law and an increased importance of transnational law.[11] In this regard, the fact that the distinction between legal norms and legitimacy norms might have become less clear-cut in the past decades should not be understood as an isolated phenomenon related to legitimacy but linked to a broader transformation of international law and international legal thinking.

This 'blurring of the lines' can have an instrumental dimension: actors might be inclined to use the unclear distinction for their specific purposes. As classifying a norm as legal norm or as a legitimacy norm is not always unambiguous, this classification can be used as a tool in international legal discourse. If an argumentation that aims at making a legal claim is characterized by other actors as 'mere' legitimacy argumentation, this can undermine the persuasiveness of the argumentation—and intends to do so. Legitimacy language can thus be used to devaluate an argument, denying its significance for the strictly speaking legal discourse. The contribution by Thilo Marauhn shows this for instance when he categorizes the discussion about the 'unable or unwilling doctrine' as a legitimacy claim,[12] a characterization that those arguing in favour of this doctrine

---

[8] Daniel Bodansky, 'Legitimacy in International Law and International Relations' in Jeffey Dunoff and Mark Pollack (eds), *Interdisciplinary Perspectives on International Law and International Relations: The State of the Art* (Cambridge University Press 2013) 323, 324.

[9] Marauhn (n 2).

[10] To give but a few examples of the related discussions: critical on the distinction between *lex lata* and *lex ferenda*: Rosalyn Higgins, *Problems and Process: International Law and How We Use it* (Oxford University Press 1994) 10; critical on the concept of 'more or less' binding norms: Jan Klabbers, 'The Redundancy of Soft Law' (1996) 65 Nordic Journal of International Law 167, 181; for a reflection of dichotomies in international legal thinking: Andrea Bianchi, *International Law Theories—An Inquiry into Different Ways of Thinking* (Oxford University Press 2016) 24–25.

[11] eg Joost Pauwelyn, Ramses A Wessel, and Jan Wouters, 'When Structures Become Shackles: Stagnation and Dynamics in International Law Making' (2014) 25 European Journal of International Law 733, 743; Peer Zumbansen, 'Transnational Legal Pluralism' (2010) 1 Transnational Legal Theory 141; Terence C Halliday and Gregory Shaffer, 'Transnational Legal Orders' in Terence C Halliday and Gregory Shaffer (eds), *Transnational Legal Orders* (Cambridge University Press 2015) 3.

[12] Marauhn (n 2).

would probably not share, for it implies that the legal nature of the claim is somewhat downplayed or even denied.

That being said, legal norms and legitimacy norms often are distinguishable for analytical purposes. Under this premise, the remainder of this comment will highlight what the consequences of a coexistence of legal norms and legitimacy norms can be. It will take up the twofold dimensions of this relationship outlined above and discuss to what extend both types of norms can contain competing or complementing standards of behaviour. For the purpose of this contribution, the focus will be exclusively on the relationship between legal norms and legitimacy norms, leaving aside for the moment that both these sets of norms also interact with other kinds of norms, be it moral, religious, or social norms in a narrow sense.

III. Competing and complementing standards

In order to better understand the twofold dimension of the relationship between legal norms and legitimacy norms in the international sphere, it is useful to have a closer look at the different ways in which both kinds of norms can be competing or complementing each other. This analysis will be undertaken here through the lens of some of the various effects that norms can have.[13]

To start with, both kinds of norms, legal and non-legal norms, can have the effect and the potential function to shape social and political reality. Legitimacy norms are no exception to that. By formulating behavioural standards, legitimacy norms create a yardstick for evaluating the behaviour of international actors. Hence, they can ultimately lead to an adjustment of the behaviour to this standard. In particular when there is no legal standard (yet) for providing guidelines in a certain (novel) situation, legitimacy norms can be used as a 'back-up standard' to direct behaviour where law does not. In this context, legitimacy norms can complement law in its function to shape reality based on certain prescriptive standards.

This can be the basis for modifying the corresponding legal standards. In this context, the legitimacy norms can relate to legal norms in two ways. First, they can, although primarily targeting the immediate behaviour of actors, indirectly influence the creation and modification of legal norms. This concerns most importantly the creation and modification of customary international law. If actors behave in a particular way complying with a legitimacy norm—which has, for instance, been claimed in the context of humanitarian interventions—they might create practice that can potentially be the basis for a new legal norm of customary international law. Legitimacy norms can in such situations indirectly contribute to the creation of legal norms, mediated by the behaviour of international actors.

---

[13] On the effects and potential functions of law and especially of international law: Dana Burchardt, 'The Functions of Law and Their Challenges: The Differentiated Functionality of International Law' (forthcoming 2019) German Law Journal.

Second, legitimacy norms can directly address legal norms in view of, or during, the law-making process. Legitimacy norms can be explicitly used as motivation and catalyst for (further) developing legal norms. Used as 'conversation opener',[14] they can be referred to in terms of reasons for amending existing legal norms or creating new legal norms that correspond to the legitimacy norm in question. In this context, the impact of legitimacy norms is framed and limited by the formal requirements and procedures of law-creation. It should be noted that this aspect of the interaction between legal and non-legal norms is neither particular to international law nor to legitimacy norms. When Thilo Marauhn states that 'actors are typically motivated to push international law in one or another direction by making use of legitimacy claims',[15] this rather reflects a phenomenon inherent to the interrelation of different kinds of norms than an issue deserving criticism. It is inherent to legal norm-creation that it is motivated, amongst other things, by considerations termed as non-legal norms, be it legitimacy norms, equality or justice norms, further moral norms, religious norms, or other kinds of norms. Thus, if legitimacy norms play a role during the law-making, this does not challenge the law as such. To take up the example discussed by Thilo Marauhn:[16] when legitimacy claims are put forward as motivations for further developing humanitarian law, this does not undermine the legal norm in their binding and authoritative nature. As new legal norms are created, or existing norms amended, their claim and nature as *legal* remains intact. As a result, this aspect of the relationship between legal norms and legitimacy norms is non-detrimental for the legal norms involved. It might even be perceived as beneficial when the contribution of the legitimacy norm is seen as a constructive element for improving global governance.

Inversely, on the level of the application of existing legal norms, views are more sceptical, focusing on the competing dimension of the interrelation of legitimacy norms and legal norms. Here, legitimacy norms are often perceived as potentially undermining legal norms. This is the case when actors use legal norms and legitimacy norms that have opposing contents to provide guidelines for the same facts. Norm conflicts arise that create a situation in which legitimacy norms and legal norms are competing for compliance. As a result, legitimacy norms can be an obstacle for compliance with legal norms: complying with the legitimacy norms in question is only possible if the behavioural standard set by the respective legal norms is disregarded. What should however be considered is that, in other situations, the enforcement of legal norms and their relationship with legitimacy norms can appear in a more positive light. This concerns cases in which the content both of legitimacy norms and legal norms is congruent. When actors perceive the enforcement of legal norms as being at the same time an enforcement of legitimacy norms, both kinds of norms combine their behaviour-shaping effect. This can result in an enhanced compliance with these norms.[17] The effect of legitimacy norms can thus act as enforcement mechanism for international

---

[14] Friedrich Kratochwil, 'On Legitimacy' (2006) 3 International Relations 302, 304.
[15] Marauhn (n 2) II.
[16] Marauhn (n 2).
[17] eg Thomas Franck, *The Power of Legitimacy among Nations* (Oxford University Press 1990).

law.[18] So from the perspective of compliance, the interrelation between legal and non-legal norms is ambivalent with regard to the beneficial or detrimental effects that it might have for international law.

A further effect of legal and non-legal norms and particularly legitimacy norms that can influence the interaction between these kinds of norms is to stabilize existing expectations and to create and develop new expectations.[19] A prominent case for legal norms which can have these effects can be found in the context of human rights law. Existing or, in some cases, newly shaped expectations regarding political, social, and other guaranties are put into the legal category of rights, giving them a stabilizing framework. For legitimacy norms, similar observations can be made, as the example analysed by Thilo Marauhn shows. Legitimacy claims can be used, for instance, to create high expectations in what humanitarian law can achieve.[20] Taking into account that both legal norms and legitimacy norms can have these expectations-related effects leads to two observations for situations in which both kinds of norms coexist: *First*, when the expectations enshrined in the one kind of norm are higher than the ones reflected by the other kind, a spill-over of the higher expectations to the latter kind of norms is possible. More specifically, when legitimacy norms transport high expectations, for instance with regard to human rights protection, democracy, and accountability, international actors are likely to link the related legal norms to these expectations as well. This can be problematic insofar as it entails the risk that in cases in which reality does not live up to the expectations, actors might connect the subsequent disappointment not only to the legitimacy norm which created or fostered the expectation, but also to the legal norms.[21] *Second*, the two kinds of norms, legal and non-legal, can, although they relate to the same subject matter, have opposing effects with regard to expectations. If the legal norms aim at stabilizing certain established expectations, but the legitimacy norms aim at creating novel expectations different from the former, the effects of these sets of norms might undermine each other. This is the situation that has been described by Thilo Marauhn with regard to the legal norm prohibiting the use of force and the legitimacy norm allowing military intervention in order to end mass atrocities.[22]

The twofold dimension of the relationship between both kinds of norms also lies at the core of one key critique raised against legitimacy claims in the international sphere. As legal norms and legitimacy norms can be competing or complement each other, the inclusion of legitimacy norms into a legal discourse can be used strategically. Actors can actively put emphasis on the latter in order to weaken the effect of the former and ultimately to induce circumvention or non-compliance. This can have different effects for international law, depending on whether only the competing or also

---

[18] On the need to distinguish between legitimacy as reason for compliance and other reasons for compliance: Christopher A Thomas, 'The Uses and Abuses of Legitimacy in International Law' (2014) 34 Oxford Journal of Legal Studies 729, 752.

[19] Christoph Möllers, *Die Möglichkeit Der Normen* (Suhrkamp 2015) 418; *Niklas Luhmann, Law as a Social System* (Oxford University Press 2004) 142–72.

[20] Marauhn (n 2).

[21] On the related issue of trust: Jan Ruzicka and Vincent C Keating, 'Going Global: Trust Research and International Relations' (2015) 5 Journal of Trust Research 8.

[22] Marauhn (n 2).

the complementing dimension of the relationship between legitimacy norms and legal norms plays out in the same situation or not. If there is only one legal norm competing with one legitimacy norm, using this legitimacy norm has an undermining effect for the legal norm concerned. This amounts to a situation of norm contestation: certain actors 'discursively express disapproval'[23] of legal norms on the basis of legitimacy norms.[24] Although actors obtain a greater flexibility by widening the range of possible options based on *either* the legal standard *or* the legitimacy standard, this flexibility is bought at the price of the effects that norm contestation can have for the legal norms concerned and for law in general.

In contrast to this unilateral relationship, the twofold dimension can materialize as follows: invoking a legitimacy norm can compete with one legal norm (for instance the prohibition of the use of force) and complement another (for instance the prohibition of genocide). In such a case, the effect of the legitimacy norm on law is less clear-cut. While potentially undermining one norm, it might endorse the other norm. It is thus not necessarily detrimental to international law in general when actors use legitimacy norms strategically. In fact, in such situations, the question as to what extent the impact of legitimacy norms being referred to in the international sphere is detrimental or beneficial to international law is a normative one. It depends on which weight is normatively attributed to the legal norms concerned. For an observer who considers the legal norm that is complemented by the legitimacy norm to be more important, the benefits would outweigh the detriments for international law. For an observer who attributes a higher weight to the legal norm that the legitimacy norm is competing with, the detriments would prevail.

The strategic use of legitimacy norms can be addressed from an additional perspective, the perspective of the exercise of power. Legitimacy norms and legal norms interrelate on the level of their power-related effects. First, like legal norms, legitimacy norms can have a power-limiting function.[25] Similar to law that provides 'a standard of criticism of behaviour, including the behaviour of officials,'[26] legitimacy norms can offer such a standard as well. In practice, there are often critical assessments of how legitimate the behaviour of certain international actors is.[27] These standards can, as is the case with legal standards, contribute to restraining contingency: the exercise of power becomes more predictable if actors abide by the standard that a legitimacy norm sets. However, although this might be the case if the legitimacy norms in the international sphere operate individually, the opposite effect might occur when legal norms

---

[23] Antje Wiener, *A Theory of Contestation* (Springer 2014) 1

[24] On norm contestation in general: Wiener (n 23); Jonas Wolff and Lisbeth Zimmermann, 'Between Banyans and Battle Scenes: Liberal Norms, Contestation and the Limits of Critique' (2016) 42 Review of International Studies 513; Tiyanjana Maluwa, 'The Contestation of Value-Based Norms: Confirmation or Erosion of International Law?' in this book.

[25] On the power-limiting function of law: Miro Cerar, 'The Relationship between Law and Politics' (2009) 15 Annual Survey of International & Comparative Law 19, 37; Frank Schorkopf, 'Gestaltung mit Recht—Prägekraft und Selbststand des Rechts in einer Rechtsgemeinschaft' (2011) 136 Archiv des Öffentlichen Rechts 323.

[26] Martti Koskenniemi, 'The Mystery of Legal Obligations' (2011) 3 International Theory 319.

[27] For an assessment of the increased interest in legitimacy in international relations: Daniel Bodansky, 'Legitimacy in International Law and International Relations' in Dunoff and Pollack (n 8) 323.

and legitimacy norms are viewed together. If both kinds of norms compete because they differ from each other in terms of standards that they provide, the predictability effect is reduced. When there is a legal standard requiring A and a legitimacy standard requiring B, the behaviour of international actors that might abide with A or with B becomes more contingent—especially when there is no consensus about how to resolve such conflicts of norms.[28] As a result, the coexistence of competing legal norms and legitimacy norms reduces the predictability effect of both kinds of norms. In such cases, both kinds of norms weaken each other with regard to their respective power-limiting effect.

This is closely related to the second—opposing—power-related effect that both legal norms and legitimacy norms can have: they can serve as a tool to exercise power.[29] This is where the 'geopolitical opportunism' mentioned by Richard Falk comes in. Powerful actors can use legitimacy norms as an excuse for circumventing the standards set by legal norms. Legitimacy norms are particularly apt for this kind of use as, unlike legal norms, their content is not formally codified or subjected to certain requirements of norm-creation. Rather, their content is more flexible and less transparent and therefore more easily manipulable by certain (powerful) actors. Although legal norms can also serve as a power-exercising tool, legitimacy norms are even better suited than legal norms to be used for an ad hoc exercise of power through, and with reference to, norms. By way of their power-exercising effect, legitimacy norms thus can affect the power-limiting function of legal norms negatively.

What should be concluded from the above observations? Two remarks seem to be in order. First, no general statement is possible as to whether it would characterize as a 'rise' or rather a 'decline' of the international rule of law when legitimacy norms are referred to in a certain period of time. It depends on the particular case whether a legal norm and a legitimacy norm compete or complement each other. The mere fact that specific actors might invoke legitimacy norms more frequently in some times than in others does not per se allow for a judgement on this matter. Rather, in order to assess the impact of legitimacy norms in a particular situation, all of the abovementioned dimensions of the relationship between legal norms and legitimacy norms should be taken into account. The sum of such qualitative case studies might then permit to carve out certain *particular* tendencies with regard to certain actors, certain fields of law, or other factors. However, a generalization in terms of a 'changing attitude of actors'[30] or a changing character of international law as such can, it should seem, not be based on a stronger or less strong presence of legitimacy considerations alone.

---

[28] This question reflects the debate between absolute positivism, extra-positivism, and the various intermediate approaches. eg it has been suggested to give way to legitimacy norms 'only in exceptional circumstances' in Falk (n 3).

[29] Critical on international law as a tool to exercise power eg: David W Kennedy, 'A New Stream of International Legal Scholarship' (1998) 7 Wisconsin International Law Journal 1; Martii Koskenniemi, 'The Politics of International Law' (1999) 1 European Journal of International Law 4; Bhupinder S Chimni, 'An Outline of a Marxist Course on Public International Law' (2004) 17 Leiden Journal of International Law 1; Antony Anghie, *Imperialism, Sovereignty, and the Making of International Law* (Cambridge University Press 2005).

[30] Marauhn (n 2).

Second, when it comes to the relationship between legal norms and legitimacy norms, should one advocate for absolute positivism, entirely excluding legitimacy norms from the international discourse, in order to protect law from their detrimental impact and to avoid a 'decline' of international law? Considering the two-dimensional relationship between both kinds of norms, such a suggestion should be treated with caution. As legal norms and legitimacy norms both compete and complement each other depending on the specific context, excluding the latter means forgoing the benefits of the interaction with legitimacy norms as much as reducing their disadvantages for international law. What is more, one might doubt how realizable such suggestions would be because non-legal norms are an inherent element of the discourse about behavioural standards in general. Legal norms and legitimacy norms therefore are naturally interconnected so that the approach should not be to avoid this interconnection, but to manage it in a way that strengthens the complementing dimensions and minimizes the competing one. In the end, even a double-edged sword can have one blade that is sharper than the other.

20

The Contestation of Value-Based Norms: Confirmation or Erosion of International Law?

Tiyanjana Maluwa

I. Introduction

International law is the law of the international community. For the international legal scholar, international law is the language through which the discourse of global values is expressed. This claim assumes that there is an international community with an international value system and structures for its enforcement. However, this view is not universally accepted.[1] The period since the middle of the last century, and particularly since the 1990s, has witnessed a growing acceptance in the international legal order of a consolidation of rules and principles primarily aimed at protecting the individual rather than the state. According to Heike Krieger and Georg Nolte, as a result of this shift not only legal theorists but also states have proclaimed, 'a global legal order in which universal values emphasizing the rights of individual persons are reinforced and certain common goods are protected, whereas sovereignty-related discourses had been moved to the background'.[2] Heike Krieger and Georg Nolte argue that if international law is understood as a value-based system, contestation of certain of its rules and principles can be perceived as a symptom of a crisis of the international rule of law; but that, however, the quality or substance of these value-based rules and principles is varied, depending in some cases on 'the eye of the beholder'.[3]

While it is widely agreed that classical individual human rights norms offer the most obvious example of the principal value-based norms of the current international legal order, others that have been identified include norms governing peace and security, duties of solidarity regarding collective goods (such as sustainable development

---

[1] Erika de Wet is a leading proponent of this view: Erika de Wet, 'The International Constitutional Order' (2006) 55 International & Comparative Law Quarterly 51; also generally: Santiago Villalpando, 'The Legal Dimension of the International Community: How Community Interests are Protected in International Law' (2010) 21 European Journal of International Law 387; compare: Dino Kritsiotis, 'Imagining the International Community' (2002) 13 European Journal of International Law 961.

[2] Heike Krieger and Georg Nolte, 'The International Rule of Law—Rise or Decline?—Approaching Current Foundational Challenges' in this book, III.4.

[3] ibid 12–13.

or a healthy environment), and, even most importantly for some, self-determination (national or other). One might also add social progress and development, broadly speaking.[4]

The aim of this chapter is to examine some aspects of the contestation of value-based norms, where they exist and in what form(s). More importantly, the discussion also attempts to identify what such contestation means or entails: whether it is a form of norm-confirmation or norm-creation; and whether it evidences a rise or decline of the international rule of law, or perhaps both, depending on the context and circumstances of the contestation. Indeed, if such contestation represents a rise or decline, one might ask, to paraphrase Heike Krieger and Georg Nolte, whether, as with the quality and substance of the value-based norms themselves, the perceptions of such rise or decline also lie in the 'eye of the beholder' or the normative position and vantage point of the observer?

This discussion is not about the contestation of norms in general. Nor is it about the contestation of all types of fundamental norms in international law. Rather, the focus is on *value-based norms*. And even in this more specific context, I shall mostly limit my discussion to examples drawn from the area of human rights, broadly defined.[5] I also do not offer a detailed discussion of the concept of values as such. Important as this is, a general examination of values in the international legal order—let alone the philosophy of values—would be outside the intended scope of this chapter. Only passing references to the views and opinions of some of the leading scholarly commentators on this are indicated in the section (Section II) that follows below.[6]

Three points should be made at the outset. First, the debates about the international value system remind us that the evolution of value-based norms is a work in progress. It has been observed that the process of evolution of these norms is not unlike that in municipal constitutional orders, where the fundamental value system evolves over a period of time.[7] The constitutionalization of the values in a single document does not necessarily halt their contingent growth in practice, as the scope and content of the norms are moulded by political and historical forces, as well as by judicial inter-pretations, within the community.[8] Second, although, as noted, human rights norms

---

[4] ibid 13; also Otto Spijkers, 'Global Values in the United Nations Charter' (2012) 59 Netherlands International Law Review 361, 363; Otto Spijkers, 'What's Running the World: Global Values, International Law, and the United Nations' (2009-2010) 4 Interdisciplinary Journal of Human Rights Law 67, 79–80; also generally: Otto Spijkers, *The United Nations, the Evolution of Global Values and International Law* (Intersentia 2011) 13–58.

[5] For some of the more general discussions on norms in the recent literature in international law and inter-national relations: Antje Wiener and Uwe Puetter, 'The Quality of Norms is What Actors Make of It' (2009) 5 Journal of International Law and International Relations 1; Antje Wiener, *The Invisible Constitution of Politics, Contested Norms and International Encounters* (Cambridge University Press 2008).

[6] The concept of global values is multifaceted and can be approached from multiple perspectives, such as inter-national law, international relations, politics, and so on, and the copious amount of literature on the subject reflects these multiple perspectives. The work by Otto Spijkers and the vast literature cited therein is indicative of the major writings on the subject from the perspective of international law: Spijkers (n 4); also the writings by Martti Koskenniemi, Pierre-Marie Dupuy, Jean d'Aspremont, Emmanuelle Jouannette, and others cited below.

[7] Christian Tomuschat, 'Obligations Arising for States Without or Against their Will' (1993) 241 Recueil des Cours 195, 217–18.

[8] De Wet, 'International Constitutional Order' (n 1) 63.

provide the most obvious example of value-based norms, the full range of such norms is wider, precisely for the reason that has just been given. Because of their varied nature, the enforcement of the norms of the international value system is shared by multiple actors, including the United Nations (UN), as the principal enforcer, and other actors such as international and regional intergovernmental organizations, international courts and tribunals, states, and even some non-state actors. Thirdly, the sources of the contestation of these norms can also be just as varied: value-based norms have been contested by international organizations and states, acting individually or collectively, and even by individuals. The forms of these contestations have ranged from executive acts by state authorities, to decisions of international organizations, to judicial decisions in national and international courts challenging the legitimacy or applicability of the norms. Given the wide range of issues, this discussion must necessarily be selective in its focus.

I proceed as follows: in Section II, I briefly discuss the concepts of shared values and value-based norms. In Section III, I examine two areas of international law that provide illustrative examples of contestation of value-based norms: the fight against impunity under international criminal law and the countervailing demands for exceptions to immunities; and the debates about the right to intervene and the responsibility to protect. The underlying question in both these cases is: does the contestation of these value-based norms confirm a decline or erosion of international law? Section IV concludes the discussion. The discussion deploys secondary literature to interrogate and interpret primary legal instruments and sources, such as treaties, decisions, and resolutions of various international organizations, in particular the African Union (AU) and the UN.

II. The role of shared global values and value-based norms in international law: a brief survey

It has been suggested that values—sometimes described as the highest moral beliefs of international society—are the purposes for which the international legal system exists and that international law should, therefore, reflect and promote values. Erika de Wet, following Pierre-Marie Dupuy, expresses this view as follows:

> The international value system concerns norms with a strong ethical underpinning, which have been integrated by States into the norms of positive law and have acquired a special hierarchical standing through State practice. Through this combination of superior legal standing and ethical force, these international values constitute a fundamental yardstick for post-national decision-making.[9]

---

[9] De Wet, 'International Constitutional Order' (n 1) 57; also: Pierre-Marie Dupuy, 'Some Reflections on Contemporary International Law and the Appeal to Universal Values: A Response to Martii Koskenniemi' (2005) 16 European Journal of International Law 131.

There has been a fair amount of commentary among international legal scholars in recent times on the role of values in international law. On one side of the debate stand those scholars, mainly but not limited to those of continental European provenance, who have offered value-laden understandings and analyses of international law and the international legal order. These scholars and writers, whom Jean d'Aspremont has categorized as international constitutionalists,[10] have variously advocated the need to underpin the rules and mechanisms of international law with fundamental global values.[11] Other writers include Georges Abi-Saab,[12] Vera Gowland-Debbas,[13] and Robert McCorquodale.[14] But the view that the international legal order must be underpinned by global values is also espoused by adherents of international liberalism, mostly from the other side of the Atlantic. Among these are Thomas Franck,[15] Louis Henkin,[16] Fernando R Tesón,[17] and Anne-Marie Slaughter.[18] All these scholars, as Jean d'Aspremont rightly observes, recognize the role of the collective interest in international law-making and link it to the existence of global *values*.[19] Referring to the proponents of the notion of a new value-based international law, John Dugard, also an advocate for this approach, has written that academic lawyers are understandably excited about the infusion of certain values into mainstream international law and attempt 'to expand and extend them'.[20] But what are these global values?

Thomas Franck famously noted that the progression of international law to the current post-ontological era has enabled international lawyers, freed from the traditional inquiry over whether international law is really law, to focus on other questions, including the most important: is international law fair? Thomas Franck also argued that equally important to the commentator is the normative content of international law and, in particular, whether the content of the legal rules is morally defensible.[21] Writing a decade later, Martti Koskenniemi spoke of the reverence of mainstream international

---

[10] Jean d'Aspremont, 'The Foundations of the International Legal Order' (2009) 18 Finnish Yearbook of International Law 219, 221.

[11] Among these: Bruno Simma, 'From Bilateralism to Community Interest' (1994) 250 Recueil des Cours 217; Christian Tomuschat, 'International Law: Ensuring the Survival of Mankind on the Eve of a New Century: General Course on Public International Law' (1999) 281 Recueil des Cours 9, 237, 306; Erika de Wet, 'The Emergence of International and Regional Value Systems as a Manifestation of the Emerging International Constitutional Order' (2006) 19 Leiden Journal of International Law 611; Nico Schrijver, 'The Future of the United Nations' (2006) 10 Max Planck Yearbook of United Nations Law 1.

[12] Georges Abi-Saab, 'International Law and the International Community: The Long Road to Universality' in Ronald St J McDonald (ed), *Essays in Honour of Wang Tieya* (Martinus Nijhoff 1994) 31–41.

[13] Vera Gowland-Debbas, 'Judicial Insights into Fundamental Values and Interests of the International Community' in A Sam Muller, David Raic, and Hanna J M Thuranszky (eds), *The International Court of Justice: Its Future Role After Fifty Years* (Martinus Nijhoff 1997) 327–66.

[14] Robert McCorquodale, 'An Inclusive International Legal System' (2004) 17 Leiden Journal of International Law 477.

[15] Thomas M Franck, *Fairness in International Law and Institutions* (Oxford University Press 1995).

[16] Louis Henkin, *International Law: Politics and Values* (Martinus Nijhoff 1995).

[17] Fernando R Tesón, 'The Kantian Theory of International Law' (1992) 92 Columbia Law Review 53.

[18] Anne-Marie Slaughter 'A Liberal Theory of International Law' (2000) 94 American Society of International Law Proceedings 240; Anne-Marie Slaughter, 'International Law in a World of Liberal States' (1995) 6 European Journal of International Law 503.

[19] D'Aspremont (n 10) 223 (his emphasis).

[20] John Dugard, 'The Future of International Law: A Human Rights Perspective—With Some Comments from the Leiden School of International Law' (2007) 20 Leiden Journal of International Law 729, 731.

[21] Franck (n 15) 6.

legal scholars for these values, in particular *ius cogens* and *erga omnes* obligations, which he describes as examples of a false universalism or kitsch.[22] In summary, Martti Koskenniemi expressed the scepticism of some earlier commentators that values which are passed off as universal, justifying the claim to international law's universality, are in fact values that are borne of and reflect Western ideology and which are being forced upon non-Western cultures in the name of universality.[23] He thus questions the assumption that Western values, which by definition belong to a particular tradition, can speak in the name of humanity, as universal values. While acknowledging Martti Koskenniemi's critique as skilful and provocative, and presented in the author's characteristically easy, intelligent, and erudite style, Pierre-Marie Dupuy is nevertheless critical of this view. Instead, he offers a more strident advocacy for the infusion and recognition of universal values in international law:

> We should not, therefore, be afraid of demanding the promotion of universal values that have already been integrated into the norms of positive law. They are not (or not only) our (*sic*) part of our European heritage, but the common heritage of mankind, and the automatic suspicion of such norms on principle should be left to those (among whom I will not insult Koskenniemi by including him) nostalgic for Carl Schmidt.[24]

This is as unequivocal a promotion of values in international law as one can expect, which underlies the idea of 'a new value-based international law'. Philippe Sands[25] and Emmanuelle Jouannette[26] are among the more recent scholars to offer insightful commentaries on the evolution of this value-based international law. Philippe Sands traces this movement in modern international law to the adoption of the Atlantic Charter, and identifies some of the values undergirding this evolving international order.[27] Similarly, Emmanuelle Jouannette observes that:

> [International] law has clearly evolved since 1945, with the fundamental stages being the post-World War II period, the 1960s (decolonization), and the 1990s (the end of the Cold War, and the new 'globalization'). [For] their part globalization and the end of the Cold War had, it seemed, enabled the emergence of an inter-subjective consensus on international law and its values, which had simply not existed previously at the global level.[28]

---

[22] Martii Koskenniemi, 'International Law in Europe: Between Tradition and Renewal' (2005) 16 European Journal of International Law 113, 122.

[23] Henry J Steiner, Philip Alston, and Ryan Goodman, *International Human Rights in Context: Law, Politics, Morals: Texts and Materials* (3rd edn, Oxford University Press 2008) 517–21.

[24] Dupuy (n 9) 135.

[25] Philippe Sands, *Lawless World: America and the Making and Breaking of Global Rules* (Viking 2005).

[26] Emmanuelle Jouannette, 'Universalism and Imperialism: The True-False Paradox of International Law' (2007) 18 European Journal of International Law 379.

[27] Sands (n 25) 8ff.

[28] Jouannette (n 26) 385.

But, as I say, this embrace of a convergence of values and international law—or the idea of a value-based international legal order—is not universally shared, and the opposition to this is not limited to the so-called neo-realist international lawyers or sceptical critics like Martti Koskenniemi. Jean d'Aspremont is fairly unequivocal in his rejection of this approach. In his examination of the issue, he first notes the scepticism of some Eastern European legal scholars towards the role of values in the international legal order.[29] He then states the objective of his discussion as follows:

> It aims at laying out an understanding of the international legal order based on (individual and common) interests rather than global values. [This] paper offers an understanding of the international legal order which is stripped of references to global values and exclusively rests on individual and common interests.[30]

Jean d'Aspremont does not deny the existence of global values as such. Rather, he notes that:

> It is acknowledged that the differences between common interests and global values are not always obvious. They can overlap each other; for example, what may constitute a global value can simultaneously serve the interest of all. [Common interests] can always be distinguished from global values, since the former are fundamentally relative, context-dependent and ever-evolving. On the contrary, the concept of global values rests on the idea that there is such a thing as an objective truth independent from its factual context of application.[31]

Jean d'Aspremont's critique of a value-laden international law represents an unabashed reconstruction of a modernized international legal positivism and an attempt at 'deconstructing' the value-oriented accounts of international law-making.[32] He offers a persuasive argument in the context of the stated objective of his discussion, in which he has 'provided a conception of the international legal order based on individual and common interests'.[33] He concludes:

> Interests remain ever-changing and their perception is inescapably subject to the context and position of each individual lawmaker. It has accordingly been argued that we must refrain from conceiving the international legal order in terms of global values or any equivalent makeshift objective standards. We must simply come to terms with the inter-subjective and fickle character of the forces that drive law-making and underlie the international legal order. [It] has been explained why this permanent discussion

---

[29] D'Aspremont (n 10) 224.
[30] ibid 225.
[31] ibid, where he cites Alan Boyle and Christine Chimkin, *The Making of International Law* (Oxford University Press 2006) 17–19.
[32] D'Aspremont (n 10) 256.
[33] ibid.

about the public good should not be feared nor [bemoaned]. While helping modernize international legal positivism in its critique, this ever-growing discussion about what constitutes a common interest offers a greater leverage to promote universality of international law than any table of values open to suspicion of imperialism or hegemony.[34]

As indicated earlier, it is not the aim of this chapter to offer a detailed analysis of the concept of values. Suffice it to make two observations in respect of the foregoing discussion. First, that one underlying question here is that of the objectivity of values in international law, and the critical claim that propositions of international law cannot be both objective and normative. Second, that the concept of values can be examined through the prism of various perspectives. This means that there is not a single, but multiple, definitions of the concept, depending on the context—or 'the eye of the beholder'. Since the present discussion is not about global values in general, but rather value-based norms, it is not pertinent to engage in a detailed definition of these values here. That said, I submit that Otto Spijkers' definition comes closest to an all-embracing definition of global values, and provides a useful marker for the discussion that follows. Otto Spijkers writes:

> Global values are enduring, globally shared, beliefs that a specific state of the world, which is possible, is socially preferable, from the perspective of the life of all human beings, to the opposite state of the world.[35]

This definition suggests at least three things: first, that we conceive of values as *beliefs, as opposed to facts*. Second, that to qualify as global values they must reflect a *global consensus*. Thirdly, they must be *enduring*, not transient, beliefs. To put it differently, fundamental global values are by definition those beliefs that all human beings or communities of states share, with the conviction that their achievement is in everyone's interest. However, this is not to suggest that everything that is characterized as a common interest reflects a shared value.

In order to be binding, values have to be translated into legal norms, institutions, and legal policies. As legal norms, they can be couched in the language and form of rights of either (natural and juristic) persons or communities, within municipal law, or of states and other non-state entities, in international law. Norms may also be expressed in the form of obligations, including limits or restrictions. Today, the language of value-based international law norms suggests that, as Eckart Klein has put it:

> it is not only just norms and principles we are speaking about, rather we undertake to give them the character of values, certainly in order to make them stronger, more

---

[34] ibid.
[35] Otto Spijkers, 'Global Values in the United Nations Charter' (2012) 59 Netherlands International Law Review 361, 363.

convincing, immune against doubts and restrictions, underpinning them with moral authority, in one word: to make them more [absolute].[36]

Most significantly, transformation of values into legal rules (norms) 'does not only serve their respect and application in practice, but also gives them at the same time a legally controlled effect, provided that the law-applying bodies, including and particularly the courts, are able to perform their specific functions'.[37] In other words, only values transformed into legal norms can be applied by the courts, both national and international, although not all such norms need be based on values.

In the period since the end of the Second World War and the adoption of the UN Charter in 1945, value-based norms and principles have been positively incorporated into national law and international law. Thus, for example, the right to human dignity—with its origins in the Kantian idea of the intrinsic value or dignity that characterizes human beings as persons[38]—as a normative principle has found its way into both national constitutions[39] and international treaties.[40] In this respect, the UN is credited with playing a significant role in translating globally shared values into legally binding international commitments, and thus ensuring value-based international norms.[41] To this point, Erika de Wet has argued that:

The international value system is closely linked to the UN Charter, as the latter's connecting role is not only structural but also substantive in nature. In addition to providing a structural linkage of the different communities through universal State membership, the UN Charter also inspires those norms that articulate fundamental values of the international community.[42]

The Charter has not only inspired the articulation of value-based norms, but the incorporation of these norms into the international order has become a fundamental task for the world body. According to former UN Secretary-General Kofi Annan global values are needed because:

[Every] society needs to be bound together by common values, so that its members know what to expect of each other, and have some shared principles by which to

[36] Eckart Klein, 'The Importance and Challenges of Value-Based Legal Orders' (2015) 10 Intercultural Human Rights Law Review 1, 2.

[37] ibid 8.

[38] Immanuel Kant, *Groundwork of the Metaphysic of Morals* (Karl Ameriks and Desmond M Clarke eds, Mary J Gregor tr, Cambridge University Press 1997) 42.

[39] eg Constitution of South Africa (1996) s 10; Basic Law of the Federal Republic of Germany (1949) Art 1(1).

[40] eg Charter of the United Nations (adopted 26 June 1945, entered into force 24 October 1945) 1 UNTS XVI (UN Charter), preamble. Other instruments include the Universal Declaration of Human Rights (adopted 10 December 1948 UNGA Res 217 A(III) (UDHR); International Covenant on Civil and Political Rights (adopted 16 December 1966, entered into force 23 March 1976) 999 UNTS 171 (ICCPR); and International Covenant on the Elimination of All Forms of Racial Discrimination (adopted 21 December 1965, entered into force 4 January 1969) 660 UNTS 195 (ICERD).

[41] Spijkers, 'Global Values in the Charter' (n 35); Otto Spijkers, 'What's Running the World: Global Values, International Law, and the United Nations' (2009-2010) 4 Interdisciplinary Journal of Human Rights Law 67, 80–86.

[42] De Wet, 'International Constitutional Order' (n 1) 57.

manage their differences without resorting to violence. That is true of local communities and national communities. Today, as globalization brings us all closer together, and our lives are affected almost instantly, by things that people say and do on the far side of the world, we also feel the need to live as a global community. And we can only do so if we have global values to bind us together.[43]

Several years after Kofi Annan's statement, Otto Spijkers expressed a similar view in his examination of global values in international law and under the UN Charter, already referred to above. His conclusion bears reproducing here:

In conclusion, we can thus say that the international community is slowly developing certain legal techniques to give a certain prominence to value-based norms, and to ensure that such norms can be defended collectively, by the international community as a whole. Some of the norms that are clearly value-based have been labelled as *jus cogens* norms, or as norms whose compliance is owed *erga omnes*. We might refer to the prohibition of torture as a norm directly based on the value of human dignity. Or we might refer to the prohibition of genocide as a norm protecting the dignity, or the very existence, of peoples. The same can be said of the prohibition of racial discrimination, *apartheid*, and the right to self-determination of peoples. As an example of a norm immediately related to the value of peace and security we might refer to the prohibition of aggression.[44]

Otto Spijkers' conclusion is predicated on two propositions that he articulates in his discussion. First, that most, but not all, value-based norms are non-derogable and thus enjoy the status of *jus cogens*.[45] Second, that compliance with value-based norms is the concern of the international community collectively; thus, we are enjoined '[to] consider all participants in the international legal community as having a legal interest in the compliance with such value-based norms'.[46]

Otto Spijkers, in company with other international constitutionalists, regards the UN Charter as the constitutive document of a legal framework which might be used to guide the international community as a whole in achieving three things: first, defining global values collectively; second, translating those globally shared values into the language of international law; and, thirdly, in collectively defending compliance with these value-based norms of international law.[47] The objective of collective compliance with value-based norms comes under challenge and strain when states, or groups of states, international organizations, or other international actors contest either the content of

---

[43] Kofi A Annan, 'Do We Still have Universal Values?' (Third Global Lecture, delivered at Tübingen University, Germany, 12 December 2003) <un.org/press/en/2003/sgsm9076.doc.htm> accessed 7 August 2018.
[44] Otto Spijkers, 'What's Running the World: Global Values, International Law, and the United Nations' (2009-2010) 4 Interdisciplinary Journal of Human Rights Law 67, 79.
[45] ibid 71–75.
[46] ibid 75–79.
[47] ibid 80.

the value-based norms in question, or the appropriateness of applying them to a particular situation or implementing them in a particular context.

In the context of the overarching question addressed in this book—'The International Rule of Law--Rise or Decline?'—widespread and sustained challenges or contestations of a value-based norm by a significant number of states, perhaps even a majority, would arguably signal the decline or erosion of the norm. But not all challenges or contestations necessarily imply a decline or erosion. For one thing, a supposed decline of a norm may possibly be nothing but a temporary stagnation. In other situations, the decline of a particular norm may be 'off-set' by the rise of a different norm of equal or superior importance for the international community elsewhere. And, in some cases, contestation may also lead to confirmation of the very norm that is apparently being contested. In any case, the issue of non-compliance, which is not dealt with in this chapter, raises other questions, such as: Can we measure values by non-compliance with the norms on which they are based? And does non-compliance with value-based norms have to be justified by the non-complying parties by reference to the content of the values themselves? As regards the contestation of norms in general, Antje Wiener and Uwe Puetter have put forth two propositions, which are relevant, though not central, to this discussion. First, they argue that norms entail an inherently contested quality and therefore acquire meaning in relation to the specific contexts in which they are enacted. Second, they propose that norm contestation is a necessary component in raising the level of acceptance of norms.[48]

The two propositions above can only be tested in specific contexts, for the consequences of contestations of norms will depend on the nature of the norm and form of contestation. Thus, for example, the contestation over the content and meaning of the norm prohibiting aggression enabled states parties to the Rome Statute of the International Criminal Court (Rome Statute) eventually to reach a consensus on the incorporation of the norm in the statute. This is an example of norm contestation that has aided norm-creation or norm-crystallization. On the other hand, the potential contestation of aspects of the Paris Agreement on Climate Change or its rejection by the United States (US) or other states may incline other states towards the option of informal international law-making by agreeing on new international environmental norms without the need for a formal treaty. This is a type of contestation that arguably weakens the formal international law-making processes, but yet produces new norms based on shared values. Perceptions of the rise or decline of the international rule of law in these two examples depend on the observer's vantage point.

III. Contested value-based norms in international human rights law: two case studies

As noted earlier, for many people the recognition and protection of classical individual rights is the principal value of the international legal order today. Human rights are

---

[48] Wiener and Puetter (n 5) 7.

widely recognized as genuine values. Furthermore, there is widespread agreement that some specific human rights norms, for example the prohibition of torture and genocide, have attained the status of *jus cogens*.[49] In his examination of the relationship between *jus cogens* and human rights, Andrea Bianchi has aptly observed that there is almost an intrinsic relationship between peremptory norms and human rights, and that most of the case law in which the concept of *jus cogens* has been invoked is taken up with human rights.[50] He goes on to say:

> The discourse on *jus cogens* and its impact on international law cannot be considered in isolation. The developments that occurred almost at the same time need be recounted only briefly here. In particular, the emergence of the notion of obligations *erga omnes*, that is obligations owed by States to the international community as a whole, and the somewhat ancillary notion of international crimes, namely a system of aggravated responsibility for serious violations of norms of particular importance to the international community, seemed to support a restructuring of the international community on a set of common values and interests, for which *jus cogens* provided, at least potentially, a proper ordering factor by postulating the pre-eminence of certain rules and their underlying values.[51]

By their nature, human rights claim to embody universal values, although that claim remains contested in some contexts and by some societies.[52] Some scholars continue to question the universalism claimed for human rights values and the Western, so-called imperial *mission civilisatrice* of the human rights movement.[53] Despite these discordant views and continuing debates, I subscribe to the view that human rights norms remain the most instructive category of norms in which to explore the phenomenon of contestation of norms and assess the rise or decline of the international rule of law.

There are a number of human rights-related areas in which contestations of value-based norms have arisen in recent years, since the end of the Cold War. Due to considerations of space, only two of these will be recounted here: First, the claims for exceptional immunities against the competence of the International Criminal Court (ICC) to try individuals for serious international crimes; second, the debates relating to the right of humanitarian intervention and, relatedly, the principle of the responsibility to protect. I intend to explore some of the contestations over the values underlying the norms in these areas. I will devote more attention to the first issue, which involves a contestation

[49] Andrea Bianchi, 'Human Rights and the Magic of *Jus Cogens*' (2008) 19 European Journal of International Law 491, 492.

[50] ibid 491.

[51] ibid 493–94.

[52] eg Louis Henkin, *The Age of Season* (Columbia University Press 1990); Chris Brown, 'Universal Human Rights? An Analysis of the "Human Rights Culture" and its Critics' in Robert G Patman (ed), *Universal Human Rights?* (Palgrave Macmillan 2000) 31, 31–32; Eva Brems, *Human Rights and Diversity* (Martinus Nijhoff 2001) 27; Christian Tomuschat, *Human Rights Between Idealism and Realism* (3rd edn, Oxford University Press 2014) 58.

[53] Makau Mutua, *Human Rights: A Political and Cultural Critique* (University of Pennsylvania Press 2002); Samuel Moyn, *The Last Utopia: Human Rights in History* (Belknap Press 2012); Raimon Panikkar, 'Is the Notion of Human Rights a Western Concept?' (1982) 30 Diogenes 75.

of the non-impunity norm and has been at the heart of the dispute between the ICC and the AU that has dragged on for almost a decade, dating back to 2009. The fact that this contestation pits a regional organization of some fifty-four member states against another international organization, of which some of the same AU member states form the largest block, elevates it to a certain level of significance. The contested norm of humanitarian intervention also involves the AU.

The focus on contestations involving the AU or African countries is not accidental. African states, along with other states from the 'Global South', have in the past questioned and resisted, or demonstrated an ambivalence to, some of the rules of international law and the international legal order which they joined upon attaining independence from colonial rule. For some, the objection was that the international law these states inherited at independence represented a system of law that was largely, if not exclusively, of European origin and continued to reflect Western interests and hegemony. Scholarly critiques of the legitimacy of this so-called imperial international law have persisted and grown louder more recently.[54]

Yet, it can no longer be denied that over the last few decades the 'Global South' has participated in and contributed to the development of international law in various ways. This process has in some cases involved both the contestation and confirmation of some of the norms that underpin contemporary international law. In other cases, the contribution has been manifested in the creation of new norms by the previously peripheral actors in the international law-making process. All this has happened in contexts in which the norms in question also reflect globally shared values. African states have played a role in these developments, principally under the aegis of their regional organizations, the Organization of African Unity (OAU) and the AU, in advancing some new human rights norms, for example the right to development, the right to peace, and the right to a healthy environment. These developments involved norm contestations.[55]

1. Impunity through immunity? Norm contestation in the ICC–AU dispute over the Omar Hassan Al-Bashir indictment by the ICC

The story of the deteriorating relationship between the ICC and the AU is by now well known and needs no detailed recounting. At its thirteenth ordinary session held in Sirte, Libya, on 1–3 July 2009 the Assembly of Heads of State and Government of the

---

[54] eg Frederick Snyder and Surakiart Sathirathai (eds), *Third World Attitudes to International Law: An Introduction* (Kluwer Law International 1987); Karin Mickelson, 'Rhetoric and Rage: Third World Voices in International Legal Discourse' (1998) 16 Wisconsin International Law Journal 353. James Gathii, 'International Law and Eurocentricity' (1998) 9 European Journal of International Law 184.

[55] Provided for in the African Charter on Human and Peoples' Rights adopted in 1981. No international human rights treaty had previously provided for these rights. For some detailed examinations of the contribution of African states to international law: Tiyanjana Maluwa, *International Law in Post-Colonial Africa* (Kluwer Law International 1999); and Tiyanjana Maluwa, 'International Law-Making in Post-Colonial Africa: The Role of the Organization of African Unity' (2002) 49 Netherlands International Law Review 81; Adetola Onayemi and Olufemi Elias, 'Aspects of Africa's Contribution to the Development of International Law' in Charles C Jalloh and Olufemi Elias (eds), *Shielding Humanity: Essays in International Law in Honour of Judge Abdul G Koroma* (Brill 2015) 591–613.

AU adopted a decision on the indictment of President Omar Hassan Ahmad Al-Bashir of Sudan by the ICC. The decision announced that '[the] AU Member States shall not cooperate pursuant to the provisions of Article 98 of the Rome Statute of the ICC relating to immunities, for the arrest and surrender of President Omar El-Bashir of The Sudan'.[56] Consequently, African states parties to the Rome Statute had to either follow the AU decision or their obligations under the Rome Statute.[57]

Following the July 2009 decision, a meeting of ministers of justice of the AU, held in November 2009 in anticipation of the ICC Review Conference that was due to be held in Kampala, Uganda, in June 2010, adopted a further decision. At this meeting, African states agreed that '[there] is need for clarity as to whether immunities enjoyed by officials of non-state parties under international law have been removed by the Rome Statute or not'.[58] The decision also called upon African states parties to the Rome Statute to propose amendments to Article 16 of the Rome Statute relating to the powers of the UN Security Council to defer investigations and prosecutions. The proposal was submitted to the eighth session of the Assembly of States Parties to the Rome Statute held at The Hague from 16–26 November 2009. During this session, only two African states (Namibia and Senegal) took the floor to support the proposal, while thirteen non-African states took the floor to oppose it. In addition, the recommendations of the ministerial meeting also related to Article 27 (irrelevance of official capacity) and Article 98 (cooperation with respect to waiver of immunity and consent to surrender) of the Rome Statute, and some procedural issues.[59] The AU subsequently submitted these proposals to the Security Council for its consideration, with the expectation of follow-up consultations between the AU and the Council on the issues raised. The apparent failure by the Security Council to address the AU's concerns despite subsequent efforts by the AU to engage with it has contributed to the souring of relations between the AU and the ICC.[60]

Over the years, since July 2009, there have been concerted efforts by some African countries to secure agreement at subsequent AU summits for a collective withdrawal of African states parties from the ICC, if their requests for preferred reforms remained ignored. One aspect of the AU's preferred reforms that has attracted the most attention and drawn the most criticism—leaving aside the question whether or not the AU, as an international organization, has legal authority to oblige its members to withdraw

---

[56] Decision on the Report of the Commission on the Meeting of African States Parties to the Rome Statute of the International Criminal Tribunal Court (ICC), Assembly/AU/Dec.245(XIII) (3 July 2009) para 10.

[57] At the time of the adoption of the decision, African states already formed the largest block of parties to the Rome Statute. They remain the biggest regional group in the ICC today, with 34 out of the 124 members of the Court.

[58] Recommendations of the Ministerial Meeting on the Rome Statute of the International Criminal Court, Min/ICC/Legal/Rpt (II) (6 November 2009) 1.

[59] Executive Council of the African Union, 'Report of the Commission on the Outcome and Deliberations of the 8th Session of the Assembly of States Parties to the Rome Statute held at The Hague, Netherlands, from 16 to 26 November 2009' EX.CEL/568 (XVI) (29 January 2010).

[60] Here I join company with those commentators who have argued that the AU's position not to cooperate with the ICC imputes to the Court the Council's perceived failure to act upon the AU request, eg: Dire Tladi, 'The African Union and the International Criminal Court: The Battle for the Soul of International Law' (2009) 34 South African Yearbook of International Law 57, 68.

collectively from a treaty or another international organization[61]—relates to the issue of heads of state immunity. While the AU called upon its members to respect the pre-existing (in its view) customary international law norm on heads of state immunity, its critics have argued that this amounts to a contestation of the norm against impunity, which lies at the core of the ICC system and the new international criminal law, and to which the AU has committed itself.[62] The most recent decision was adopted by the twenty-eighth ordinary session of the AU Assembly on 31 January 2017. The adoption of this decision revealed the lingering frustration of African states with both the UN Security Council's and the ICC's apparent unwillingness to take their concerns and proposals relating to Articles 16, 27, and 98 of the Rome Statute seriously, but also how more divisive the issue has become among the AU member states.[63]

As one commentator has pointed out, the 2009 decision (and, I might add, related subsequent AU Assembly decisions on the ICC indictment of Kenyan political leaders[64]) raises a number of critical questions, some of which go to the heart of the debate about the quest for a value-based international law, the protection of human rights, and the global fight against impunity, as well as the political context in which this new value-based international law is expected to operate.[65] As Dire Tladi puts it, perhaps somewhat hyperbolically, these questions and others arising from these debates—for example the accusations of an imperialistic, neo-colonialist, and even racist underpinnings as well as the respective roles of peace and justice in this new vision of international law—represent a battle for the soul of international law itself.[66] To put it in the context of this discussion, these questions again point to the possibility of a contestation of certain value-based international law norms. The story of the AU–ICC standoff over the Al-Bashir indictment can be briefly summarized as follows.

On one side are a set of international law principles articulating what are now regarded as widely shared values: an end to impunity and the promotion of justice and accountability. These principles lie at the core of the international criminal justice system that has evolved especially since the creation of the ad hoc International Criminal

---

[61] eg.. Benedict A Chigara, '"To Be or not to Be?" The African Union and its Member States Parties' Participation as High Contracting States Parties to the Rome Statute of the International Criminal Court (1998)' (2015) 33 Nordic Journal of Human Rights 243; Udombana N Nsongurua, 'Who Blinks First: The International Criminal Court, the African Union and the Problematic of International Criminal Justice' in Tiyanjana Maluwa (ed), *Law, Politics and Rights: Essays in Memory of Kader Asmal* (Martinus Nijhoff 2013) 92, 108–18.

[62] For some of the discussions of the tension and contestation between immunity and impunity in the AU's position on the ICC indictments of African sitting heads of state: Mia Swart and Karin Krisch, 'Irreconcilable Differences? An Analysis of the Standoff between the African Union and the International Criminal Court' (2014) 1 African Journal of International Criminal Justice 38, 51–55; Charles C Jalloh, 'Reflections on the Indictment of Sitting Heads of State and Government' (2014) 7 African Journal of Legal Studies 56; and generally: Leila Sadat and Benjamin Cohen, 'Impunity through Immunity: the Kenya Situation and the International Criminal Court' in Evelyn A Ankumah (ed), *The International Criminal Court and Africa—A Decade On* (Intersentia 2016) 101–24.

[63] See Assembly/AU/Dec.622(XXVIII), Decision on the International Criminal Court (ICC) (31 January 2017) para 8. Rather unusually for AU summit decisions, some sixteen countries entered reservations objecting to the call for African states parties to the Rome Statute to withdraw from the Court, listed in footnote 1 to the Decision.

[64] Sadat and Cohen (n 62); Chandra L Sriram and Stephen Brown, 'Kenya in the Shadow of the ICC: Complementarity, Gravity and Impact' (2012) 12 International Criminal Law Review 219.

[65] Tladi (n 60).

[66] ibid 58.

Tribunal for the former Yugoslavia (ICTY) in 1993 and culminated in the establishment of the ICC. In particular, states parties to the Rome Statute have committed themselves to abide by the obligations entailed in these principles by not only bringing to justice perpetrators of the most serious crimes, but also by cooperating with the ICC to allow it to try such individuals where the states are unable or unwilling to do so in their own national courts.[67] On the other side lies the principle of promoting peace, an antidote to conflict, as a fundamental objective of international law. The maintenance of international peace and security is not only a core function of the UN Security Council but also an obligation incumbent upon all states, both members and non-members of the UN, as a shared global value.[68] The principles of fighting impunity and promoting justice and accountability, on the one hand, and the principles prohibiting the use of force and upholding international peace and security, on the other, are all value-based norms. They are predicated on a belief in globally shared values.

Thus, the thirty-three African countries that are members of the ICC have committed themselves to cooperate with the ICC in bringing to justice individuals suspected of committing acts of genocide, war crimes, and crimes against humanity (and potentially the crime of aggression) under Article 5 of the Rome Statute. At the same time, in terms of Article 4(h) of the AU's Constitutive Act, these countries have, as AU member states, accorded the AU the right to intervene in member states when these same crimes are committed. Article 4(h) provides for:

> [the] right of the Union to intervene in in a Member State pursuant to a decision of the Assembly in respect of grave circumstances, namely: war crimes, genocide and crimes against humanity.

Furthermore, Article 4(o) of the Constitutive Act explicitly condemns and rejects impunity. It articulates the principle of: 'respect for the sanctity of human life, condemnation and rejection of impunity and political assassination, acts of terrorism and subversive activities'. The underlying value connecting the principles enunciated in these provisions is that of *respect for human dignity*, which is said to underpin the new value-based international legal order and has, in some respects, *humanized* international law.[69] There can be no doubt that the fight against impunity and the imperative of bringing perpetrators of grave violations of human rights and international humanitarian law to justice are matters of common interests among states that regard the protection of the sanctity and dignity of human life as a fundamental value and objective of international law. On the face of it, therefore, the AU's decision not to cooperate with the ICC over the indictment and arrest warrant for Al-Bashir would seem to pose a contestation and rejection of this shared value. But does it?

A decade ago, Judge Antônio Trindade, with obvious enthusiasm and optimism, spoke about the advent of a new *jus gentium* which in his view signified a move away

---

[67] Pursuant to the Rome Statute, Arts 5 and 86.
[68] UN Charter, preamble, Arts 1(1), 2(3) and 6.
[69] Theodor Meron, *The Humanization of International Law* (Martinus Nijhoff 2006).

from the traditional model of international law focused on the protection and preservation of the sanctity of the state—the primacy of state sovereignty—to one more concerned with humanity.[70] The idea of an international law comprising of value-oriented
norms aimed primarily at protecting human beings is buttressed by the claim of universality, which Dire Tladi characterizes as perhaps its 'central—and most controversial—
feature'.[71] He cites Bruno Simma's 'third level universality', an approach wherein
Bruno Simma has argued that this concept of universalism implies 'the expansion of
international law beyond the inter-state sphere, [establishing] a hierarchy of norms,
a value-oriented approach, [introducing] international criminal law, by the existence
of institutions and procedures for the enforcement of collective interests at the international [level]'.[72] The reference by Bruno Simma to the introduction of international
criminal law relates to the post-1990 establishment of the various international criminal tribunals, in particular the ICTY, the International Criminal Tribunal for Rwanda,
and the ICC, and points to the idea of a value-laden international law concerned with
protecting humanity and punishing impunity. Article 5 of the Rome Statute and Article
4(h) and (o) of the AU Constitutive Act give expression to this desire and articulate a
value-based norm that moves the focus from the preservation of state sovereignty to
the protection of the individual.

The AU summit decision of 3 July 2009 had, in fact, been preceded by an earlier
decision adopted in February 2009.[73] In the earlier decision, the AU employed a two-
pronged approach. On the one hand, the decision cautioned that, 'in view of the delicate
nature of the peace processes underway in The Sudan, the indictment of Al-Bashir
could undermine the efforts aimed at facilitating the early resolution of the conflict in
Darfur'.[74] On the other hand, it also 'reiterated the AU's unflinching commitment to
combating impunity and promoting democracy, the rule of law and good governance
throughout the entire Continent, in conformity with its Constitutive Act'.[75] The various
summit decisions adopted since then have repeatedly reiterated, with only slight variations in the formulation, these fundamental positions.[76]

So, while on the face of it the AU decision of 3 July 2009 and the position subsequently
adopted by the organization in successive decisions not to cooperate with the ICC suggest a contestation of the universality claimed for the norm of non-impunity, I would
submit that this is not an outright rejection of the norm as such. This is because the AU
member states have not only committed themselves to the non-impunity norm in their
own foundational instrument, but also to another shared global value which underlies

---

[70] Speech presented by Judge Antônio Augusto Cançado Trindade upon receiving the Spring 2008 Wolfgang
Friedmann Award for Outstanding Contributions to the Field of International Law, published as 'The Human
Person and International Justice' (2009) 47 Columbia Journal of Transnational Law 16, 18.

[71] Tladi (n 60) 63.

[72] Bruno Simma, 'Universality of International Law from the Perspective of a Practitioner' (2009) 21 European
Journal of International Law 265, 268.

[73] Assembly/AU/Dec.221(XII), Decision on the Application by the International Criminal Court (ICC)
Prosecutor for the Indictment of the President of the Republic of Sudan (3 February 2009).

[74] ibid para 2.

[75] ibid para 6.

[76] Assembly/AU/Dec.245(XIII), Decision on the Report of the Commission on the Meeting of African States
Parties to the Rome Statute of the International Criminal Tribunal Court (ICC) (3 July 2009) paras 3–4; since 2009,
the AU has adopted fifteen more or less similarly worded decisions on the ICC at its twice-yearly summits.

one of the major principles of the UN Charter, as alluded to above: peace as the basis of international order. The AU Constitutive Act, somewhat following the UN Charter, lays down as one of its fundamental principles '[the] peaceful co-existence of Member States and their right to leave in peace and security'.[77] The value of peace articulated here should be understood at two levels: first, *international* peace (the peaceful coexistence of states) and, second, *internal* peace (the right of states to live in peace). The right to peace as a norm among African states was first articulated in the African Charter on Human and Peoples' Rights,[78] whose Article 18(1) provides that:

> All peoples shall have the right to national and international peace and security. The principles of solidarity and friendly relations implicitly affirmed by the Charter of the United Nations and reaffirmed by that of the Organization of African Unity shall govern relations between States.

So for African states both these values—non-impunity and peace—find their normative expression in the UN Charter and in African regional instruments, which are binding on all the thirty-three African states that are parties to the Rome Statute. Formally, the AU's request to the Security Council to use its powers under Article 16 of the Rome Statute to defer the prosecution of Al-Bashir was premised on the claim that failure to do so would endanger the peace process that was underway in Sudan.[79] By implication, it viewed its peace initiative as more urgent for the resolution of the Darfur conflict than the immediate prosecution of the president by the ICC.

One way of reading the AU's and ICC's positions is that they are part of the endless tensions between universalism and relativism in human rights and the new value-based international legal order. The ICC's position appears to be that justice should not be sacrificed on the altar of peace. The AU insists that while it is committed to combating impunity, upholding the principles of accountability and bringing to justice the perpetrators of gross violations of human rights, the search for justice should be pursued in a way that does not impede efforts aimed at promoting lasting peace and reconciliation between adversaries. But this tension need not be interpreted as a 'clash of civilizations', nor a rejection of one norm against the other. Significantly, the AU did neither in the request to the Security Council nor in any of its subsequent decisions on the ICC state that it objected to the eventual prosecution of the Sudanese president as indicted by the ICC. It is important to bear this in mind, because it confirms the self-declared commitment of the AU member states to fighting impunity and respecting the non-impunity norm.[80]

---

[77] Constitutive Act, Art 4(i).

[78] African Charter on Human and Peoples' Rights (adopted on 27 June 1981, entered into force 21 October 1986) 1520 UNTS 217.

[79] Decision of the Meeting of African States Parties to the Rome Statute of the International Criminal Court, Doc Assembly/AU/13 (XIII) (1–3 July 2009); Charles C Jalloh, Max du Plessis, and Dapo Akande, 'Assessing the African Union's Concerns about Article 16 of the Rome Statute of the International Criminal Court' (2011) 4 African Journal of Legal Studies 5, 8.

[80] For an extended discussion of this question: Djacoba Tchindrazanarivelo, 'The African Union Principle on the Fight Against Impunity and the Arrest Warrant for Omar Hassan El-Bashir' in Marcelo Cohen, Robert Kolb, and Djacoba Tchindrazanarivelo (eds), *Perspectives of International Law in the 21st Century* (Brill 2011) 397–442.

This is not the place to discuss in any detail the debate regarding the respective roles of justice and peace, or the need to balance the fight against impunity with the search for secure peace. I have not addressed the question whether there can be peace without justice or justice without peace. This wider question is very important but falls outside the scope of the present discussion. Suffice it to say that if there is a contestation of these norms, the contestation is on the context in which these competing value-based international law norms should be implemented and on the balancing and sequencing of their implementation. Any contestation, such as it is, does not go to the substantive core and content of the norms themselves. The contestation is perhaps best captured in the now familiar question: *Peace versus justice or peace and justice*? And, if the latter, in a world in which difficult practical choices must be made, *which norm has priority*?[81]

Finally, in addition to the claim that the AU objection represents a rejection of the claim of universality that is made for the norm of non-impunity that underpins the Rome Statute, another charge that has been advanced in some scholarly commentaries is that the ICC is a tool of neo-colonialism and a Western imperial master seeking to exercise power over African subjects and to humiliate African political leaders, and so on.[82] This view is not tenable. The charge that the ICC is a Western neo-colonial tool has been rejected by the great majority of commentators and some African states themselves. These include those commentators who are, nevertheless, critical of the ICC and recognize that the Court bears part of the blame for its troubled relationship with African states, including the perceptions of bias and selectivity of cases.[83] Moreover, the history of the involvement of African states in the process leading to the establishment of the Court belies this claim. Thus, after examining this history extensively in his short but comprehensive monograph, Max du Plessis concludes that:

[the] African support for the ICC described above thus leads to an important conclusion: the court, and the Rome Statute which underpins its substance and processes,

---

[81] The criticism that might be directed at the AU is that its claim that it needed to be allowed time and space to pursue its peace-making efforts has not been borne out with the passage of time, as no progress has been made in resolving the Darfur conflict. Moreover, even the recommendations for resolving the conflict made in 2009 by the African Union High-Level Panel on Darfur (AUHPD), a body appointed by the AU itself to investigate the conflict and make recommendations on how to achieve peace, justice, and reconciliation in Darfur, in particular, and Sudan as a whole, have never been implemented. The counter-argument by the AU would be that no peace initiative can be expected to proceed with any likelihood of success as long as the ICC warrant of arrest continues to hang over President Al-Bashir's head. Whether the AU's peace initiative would have succeeded if its request for the deferral had been granted by the Security Council can only be a matter for conjecture. In any case, the dispute over Al-Bashir's immunity has been rendered moot following his overthrow in a military coup d'état on 11 April 2019.

[82] Among scholarly critiques of the ICC as a modern imperial project targeting Africa under the guise of dispensing international criminal justice: Ugumanim B Obo and Dickson Ekpe, 'Africa and the International Criminal Court: A Case of Imperialism by Another Name' (2014) 3 International Journal of Development and Sustainability 2025; Uchechukwu Ngwaba, 'The ICC, Africa and the Travesty of International Criminal Justice' in Colloque de la Société Africaine pour le Droit International, *L'Afrique et le droit international pénal* (A Pedone 2015) 89.

[83] eg Charles C Jalloh, 'Africa and the International Criminal Court: Collision Course or Cooperation?' (2011–12) 34 North Carolina Central Law Review 203, 209–12.

was regarded by Africa's states parties as being an institution which is *for* Africa. That is, the court has been regarded by the majority of Africa's leaders as supportive of *African ideals and [values]*.[84]

The reference to African ideals and values resonates with the claim of the universality of the norm of non-impunity mentioned earlier. Even if, as some have argued, the value underpinning the non-impunity norm, as with other values espoused by the new international law, has its origin in Western ideology and rationalism, its appropriation as an African value cannot be denied on the assumption that it has been imposed on African societies in the name of a false universalism. It has been observed that 'the human conscience is today revolted by the most heinous crimes—genocide, war crimes, crimes against humanity, various forms of discrimination, [and violations of other rights]'.[85] This human conscience is not bounded by cultural or geographical boundaries, and the values that have emerged from this shared civilizational experience and the substantive norms that have developed on the basis of these values can be claimed universally, in the West as in the Global South, including Africa.

I hold the view that there should be no differentiated geographies of justice under the new international criminal law. The AU's decision not to cooperate with the ICC on the Al-Bashir indictment should not be seen as a rejection of the universality of the norm against impunity, still less of the values that underlie it. In advocating for the withholding of cooperation with the ICC on the indictment and arrest warrant, the AU and the African states that support that position are not contesting the existence of the norm against impunity, but arguing that the competing norm of securing and preserving peace should be given priority in the particular circumstances of the Darfur conflict. In my view, this does not signal or represent a decline or an erosion of the non-impunity norm, merely a temporary stagnation in its application.

2. The right of intervention and the responsibility to protect in the AU Constitutive Act: creating a new norm out of an old value?

As has been shown above, Article 4(h) of the AU Constitutive Act encapsulates not only the norm of non-impunity, but also provides the normative basis for the principle of humanitarian intervention in the African context. This is the first time that a regional organization has incorporated the principle of humanitarian intervention in its foundational legal instrument, even as the status of the principle as a binding norm in international law was being contested. Conventional wisdom suggests that Article 4(h) was inspired by—and was merely following—the emerging principle of the responsibility to protect, which was itself at the time also not yet

---

[84] Max du Plessis, *The International Criminal Court that Africa Wants* (Institute for Security Studies 2010) 25.
[85] Makau Mutua, 'Is the Age of Human Rights Over?' in Sophia McClennen and Alexandra Moore (eds), *The Routledge Companion to Literature and Human Rights* (Routledge 2016) 450, 456.

widely accepted as a binding universal norm in international law. Among other factors, the adoption of the AU Constitutive Act was driven by a desire that all the member states observe certain standards and shared fundamental values. These standards and shared values, including respect for human rights, democratic governance, and the condemnation of unconstitutional changes of government, are articulated in various provisions of Article 4 (setting out the organization's principles). Some of these values have been elaborated in more detail in other legal instruments adopted both prior and subsequent to the adoption of the Constitutive Act, such as the African Charter on Human and Peoples' Rights of 1981 and the African Charter on Democracy, Elections and Governance, adopted in 2007. In their turn these instruments drew upon previous decisions and resolutions of the OAU and the AU as well as legal instruments and resolutions of the UN. Thus, they embody not just African but globally shared values.

The right of intervention—with or without the qualifier 'humanitarian'—has always been a controversial principle in international law, and has been the subject of much political debate and scholarly inquiry. These will not be recounted here, save to observe that it is only in the last three decades, since the 1980s, that the principle has become more settled. The justification for this right is the need to dispense with the old-fashioned theory of state sovereignty, used to fend off criticism of massacres of people perpetrated or permitted by their own governments. This veil of state sovereignty had been used by murderous dictatorial regimes in Africa, notably by Jean-Bedel Bokassa in the Central African Republic, Macias Nguema in Equatorial Guinea, and Idi Amin in Uganda in the 1970s and 1980s, during the era of the OAU. The OAU Charter, like the UN Charter, included among its cardinal principles the principle of non-interference in the domestic affairs of its member states. It was this inglorious history of massacres, gross violations of human rights, and large population displacements resulting from civil conflict within Africa, which the OAU had consistently failed to condemn, and of course the more recent Rwanda genocide, that provided the backdrop to the incorporation of the right of intervention in the Constitutive Act. As I have written elsewhere:

> [In] an era in which post-independent Africa had witnessed the horrors of genocide and ethnic cleansing on its own soil and against its own kind, it would have been absolutely remiss for the Constitutive Act to remain silent on the question of the right to intervene in respect of grave circumstances such as genocide, war crimes and crimes against humanity.[86]

Today, there is wide recognition that the expansion of human rights and humanitarian norms have watered down the concept of state sovereignty and diminished its core claim

---

[86] Tiyanjana Maluwa, 'Reimagining African Unity: Some Preliminary Reflections on the Constitutive Act of the African Union' (2001) 9 African Yearbook of International Law 3, 38. For a brief discussion of the background to and analysis of Art 4(h): Ben Kioko, 'The Right of Intervention under the African Union's Constitutive Act' (2003) 85 International Review of the Red Cross 807.

that the state was free to do as it wished within its own territory, including violating the internationally recognized human rights of its own people, without external interference or criticism. The report of the International Commission on Intervention and State Sovereignty (ICISS), *The Responsibility to Protect*,[87] attempted to reconcile this sovereignty–intervention debate and reconceptualize and redefine the issues involved in intervention of any kind. The establishment of the ICISS by the Canadian government had been in response to UN Secretary-General Kofi Annan's question of when the international community must intervene for humanitarian purposes—a question that he felt compelled to raise in his *Millennium Report* of 2000 following the tragedies of Rwanda and the former Yugoslavia.[88] But it was not until April 2006 that the UN Security Council made the first official reference to the principle of the responsibility to protect in Resolution 1674 on the protection of civilians in armed conflict.[89] The Council referred to that resolution in August 2006 when it adopted Resolution 1706 authorizing the deployment of UN peacekeeping troops to Darfur, Sudan.[90] Repeated references to the principle in subsequent Security Council resolutions since then are thought to have led to the emergence of the still somewhat contentious norm of the principle of the responsibility to protect, which has since been invoked in relation to Security Council-approved intervention in Libya in 2011. The exact limits and contexts circumscribing its application, however, remain a matter for debate, as the inability of the Security Council to authorize similar intervention in the ongoing conflict in Syria amply demonstrates.

Discussions and analyses of the right of intervention encapsulated in Article 4(h) have variously addressed a number of questions, including: how the right is to be implemented; the threshold for invoking it; the practical, legal, and procedural difficulties likely to arise in its implementation; and the role of the UN Security Council, the body with the primary responsibility for the maintenance of international peace and security and the specific right under international law to authorize intervention in terms of Chapter VII of the UN Charter.[91] It is not the objective of the present discussion to examine these questions. The aim, rather, is to demonstrate how the principle enunciated in Article 4(h) has been framed as a principle based on certain shared values not only among African states but globally. Despite lingering contestations about its proper

---

[87] International Commission on Intervention and State Sovereignty, *The Responsibility to Protect* (International Development Research Centre 2001).

[88] UNGA, A/54/2000 (27 March 2000).

[89] UNSC Res 1674 (28 April 2006) UN Doc S/RES/1674, para 4.

[90] UNSC Res 1706 (31 August 2006) UN Doc S/RES/1706, preamble.

[91] eg the discussion of some of the legal and procedural aspects by Kioko (n 86) 815–24; for more extended analyses of Art 4(h): Dan Kuwali, *The Responsibility to Protect: Implementation of Article 4(h) Intervention* (Martinus Nijhoff 2011); Dan Kuwali and Frans Viljoen (eds), *Africa and the Responsibility to Protect: Article 4(h) of the African Union Constitutive Act* (Routledge 2014); Suyash Paliwal, 'The Primacy of Regional Organizations in International Peacekeeping: The African Example' (2011) 51 Virginia Journal of International Law 185; Jeremy Sarkin, 'The Role of the United Nations, the African Union and Africa's Sub-Regional Organizations in Dealing with Africa's Human Rights Problems: Connecting Humanitarian Intervention and the Responsibility to Protect' (2009) 53 Journal of African Law 1; Tim Murithi, 'The Responsibility to Protect, as Enshrined in Article 4 of the Constitutive Act of the African Union' (2007) 16 African Security Review 14.

status as a universally binding norm, it certainly is regarded as a value-based norm within the context of African regional international law.

It may be easier to conclude that the right of intervention has become a value-based norm among African states than to determine how it will be implemented in practice. The ICISS characterized humanitarian intervention as controversial both when it has happened—as in Somalia, Bosnia, and Kosovo—and when it has failed to happen, as in Rwanda. This points to the practical difficulties of implementing the principle. Humanitarian intervention has been applied inconsistently. Since the adoption of the Constitutive Act, there have been at least three situations in which the AU could have invoked Article 4(h) as a ground for intervening: in Burundi, the Central African Republic, and Sudan (over the Darfur conflict). The organization has not been able to do so in Burundi, in part because it could not overcome the objections and threats of the government to resist any such intervention with its own military force. The AU has had a limited presence in Darfur, but only as part of a combined UN–AU peacekeeping operation, the United Nations–African Union Hybrid Mission in Darfur not undertaken as an intervention force under the authority of Article 4(h). Similarly, since 2014, the UN has taken over the peacekeeping operation in the Central African Republic, replacing a largely ineffective AU-led regional peacekeeping force, which was not an Article 4(h) intervention force. These situations show how a combination of political, operational, and financial obstacles, and a lack of political will and serious commitment on the part of the AU member states, will likely always pose an obstacle to the implementation the otherwise well-intentioned principle of the right to intervene. Norm implementation, not norm contestation, is the real problem here.

However, the AU Constitutive Act can still claim credit for being the first international legal instrument to confirm and codify the norm of humanitarian intervention.[92] As with the principle of the responsibility to protect, the right of humanitarian intervention is based on the fundamental value of respect for and protection of human life and people. Yet, when the AU decided to incorporate this norm in its foundational instrument, there was initial concern and criticism from some political and academic commentators.[93] The organization was accused by some of its critics of attempting to usurp the authority of the Security Council. Jean Allain was quite categorical in his view that:

---

[92] Erika de Wet has correctly observed that, in respect of the various interventions and military operations undertaken by the Economic Community of West African states in Cote d'Ivoire, Guinea, Liberia, and Sierra Leone, and that made by the Southern African Development Community in Democratic Republic of the Congo and Lesotho, it seems premature to suggest that the practice of African sub-regional organizations amounts to the emergence of a new customary right to engage in 'first-instance enforcement action'. I agree that all these interventions, which took place prior to the adoption of the Constitutive Act at the behest of the respective sub-regional organizations, cannot be said to have given rise to a new customary norm, as claimed by Paliwal (n 91) 220–21; Erika de Wet, 'The Evolving Role of ECOWAS and the SADC in Peace Operations: A Challenge to the Primacy of the United Nations Security Council in Matters of Peace and Security?' (2014) 27 Leiden Journal of International Law 353, 369.

[93] Jean Allain, 'The True Challenge to the United Nations System of the Use of Force: The Failures of Kosovo and Iraq and the Emergence of the African Union' (2004) 8 Max Planck Yearbook of United Nations Law 237, 264–89.

As a result of the fact that the Protocol, while paying lip-service to the primacy of the UN Security Council, seeks, at every turn, to dissipate its pre-eminence makes clear that intervention as envisioned by the Constitutive Act of the African Union usurps the ultimate control vested in the United Nations System over the use of force.[94]

Nearly two decades later, these fears have not materialized, perhaps in part because, as noted, the AU has not actually invoked Article 4(h) intervention in any situation. Or this may be due to the subsequent realization that, notwithstanding Jean Allain's claims to the contrary, procedurally the authorization of such intervention by the AU would in any case only proceed with appropriate consultation between the AU Peace and Security Council (PSC) and the UN Security Council in terms of the Protocol Relating to the Establishment of the Peace and Security Council of the African Union.[95] According to Article 17(1) of the Protocol, in fulfilment of its mandate in the promotion and maintenance of peace and security in Africa, the PSC shall cooperate and work closely with the Security Council, which the provision explicitly recognizes as having the primary responsibility for the maintenance of international peace and security.

In any case, I argue that the AU has, through Article 4(h), confirmed the evolving principle of humanitarian intervention as a value-based norm of contemporary international law, or at the very least African regional international law. This represents a positive development, not a decline or erosion, of international law in this particular area. In the scheme of norm contestations, I would characterize this as a norm-creating or norm-confirming contestation.

IV. Conclusion

This chapter has examined the contestation of value-based norms in two contexts: contestations over norms relating to the issues of impunity in the case of grave crimes and to heads of state immunity; and the norm of humanitarian intervention and the responsibility to protect. Both these contexts fall within the broad area of international human rights law, which offers most of the widely accepted examples of value-based norms in international law. The case studies selected for examination have limited the discussion to contestations involving the AU, or African states, arising under the provisions of the Constitutive Act of the AU. Quite apart from the constraints of space, the limited focus to contestations by African states is a deliberate and logical choice. For the participation of African states in the modern international legal order, and their collective contribution to the development of international law in the post-colonial era,

---

[94] ibid 287.
[95] Protocol Relating to the Establishment of the Peace and Security Council of the African Union (adopted on 9 July 2002, entered into force 26 December 2003) to establish the operational structure for the effective implementation of the decisions taken by the AU Assembly in accordance with the authority conferred upon it in that regard by Article 5(2) of the Constitutive Act in the areas of conflict prevention, peace-making, peace support, operations and intervention, as well as peace-building and post-conflict reconstruction.

has been characterized by contestations of existing or emerging norms. These contestations have sometimes assumed the form of challenges to both the content and applicability of previously crystallized norms. At other times they have been advanced as part of the process of re-appropriating and expanding existing norms or, in fact, the creation of new norms. One way of approaching the discussion of contestation of norms by African states has been to look at their engagement in international law-making processes under the OAU and AU, principally through the medium of binding multilateral treaties. Elsewhere, I have offered a more extensive discussion of these processes, which have both challenged the legitimacy of some existing norms and led to the creation of new ones.[96] For the most part, these processes took place in the pre-1990 period.

The two areas of norm contestation discussed in this chapter have also been chosen, in part, because they represent developments in international law in the post-1990 era, the period which the contributions to this book have been invited to focus upon. In these particular cases, my overall conclusion is that the contestations at issue do not manifest a decline or erosion of international law. Rather, to the extent that the AU's difference of view with the ICC over the indictment of Omar Al-Bashir is not a rejection of the non-impunity norm, but of the context and sequencing of its application, one cannot speak of norm decline. The African states that are raising discordant voices on the indictment are entitled to be taken in good faith when they protest their sincerity and continuing commitment to the fight against impunity, as encapsulated in the two important provisions in the treaties at the heart of the issue to which they are parties: Article 5 of the Rome Statute and Article 4(h) and (o) of the AU Constitutive Act. As regards the right of intervention, also codified in the Constitutive Act, it has been observed that part of the motivation behind its incorporation was the perception by African states that the UN Security Council had failed to use its powers within the normative framework, structure, and authority of the UN Charter to intervene in the Rwanda genocide. Thus, African states responded to the failure of the Security Council to invoke its existing normative powers by establishing a treaty-based norm of intervention, the first time that a regional international instrument had ever done so. This would seem to be a positive outcome of a creative contestation of norms, which has since found wider acceptance. In this sense, it again does not signal a decline in the international rule of law, but the rise of a norm in this specific area—a new norm based on an old value, the protection of human life and dignity.

---

[96] Maluwa, *International Law in Post-Colonial Africa* (n 55); Maluwa, 'International Law-Making: The Role of the OAU' (n 55).

21

The Eye of the Beholder? The Contestation of Values and International Law

Comment on Tiyanjana Maluwa

Andrea Liese and Nina Reiners

Do you see what I see?
Truth is an offense

…

Doesn't matter what you see?
Or into it what you read
You can do it your own way
If it's done just how I say

(Metallica 1988)[1]

Contemporary international law is widely regarded as a value-based system. Yet, it is contested on which values it is exactly based and what specific values mean at different times and in different social contexts. Does this mean that 'the quality, or substance, of legal rules and principles depend on the eye of the beholder'?[2] And does it mean that the (potential) effects of norm contestation, for example with regard to a rise and decline of values in international law, also lie in the eye of the beholder?[3]

We started our comment with a line from the song 'Eye of the Beholder' by the US-American metal band Metallica. Given that the song appears on the album '… And Justice for All' the above quoted lines can serve as a metaphor for the enforcement of value-based norms. And, the song title matches the metaphor that Tiyanjana Maluwa—albeit without reference to Metallica—used in his analysis. Yet, do the quality and substance of value-based norms lie in the eye of the beholder, that is do they depend on

[1] Eye Of The Beholder Words & Music by James Hetfield, Lars Ulrich & Kirk Hammett © Copyright 1988 Creeping Death Music, USA. Universal Music Publishing Limited. All Rights Reserved. International Copyright Secured. Used by permission of Hal Leonard Europe Limited.
[2] Heike Krieger and Georg Nolte, 'The International Rule of Law—Rise or Decline? Points of Departure' (2016) Berlin-Potsdam Kolleg-Forschungsgruppe (KFG) Working Paper Series No 1, 12f.
[3] Tiyanjana Maluwa, 'The Contestation of Value-Based Norms: Confirmation or Erosion of International Law?' in this book, I

the individual normative position and vantage point of those subject to them, those enforcing them, or those studying them? Or are there—and can we determine—common values that guide the international community and its member states, irrespective of the individual perspective? And, by the same token, does the state of the legal order also lie in the 'eye of the beholder' or can we, as researchers, determine a decline or erosion of international law, for example by analysing whether legal norms change once they have been subject to contestation?

In this comment we seek to challenge both the conceptual assumptions of Maluwa's contribution and the interpretation of the two case studies he presents. We do so as human rights scholars with a background in political science, international relations, and, in particular, norm research. Our aim is twofold: First, and referring to the metaphor of the 'eyes of the beholder' and the song by Metallica with the same title, we answer the question 'Do I see what you see?' Second, we are indeed interested in coming closer to an intersubjective 'truth', that is a shared understanding for determining the alleged erosion of international law or the value-based legal norms of the United Nations (UN) Charter. By focusing on one of the case studies, we illustrate how conceptual choices may predetermine findings. In other words, they guide 'into what you read'. Finally, we argue in favour of being more explicit about these choices to let others 'see what I see' and therefore to be transparent about the type and form of contestation we seek to explain.

I. Do I see what you see? Theoretical and conceptual remarks

Tiyanjana Maluwa asks in his chapter whether the contestation of value-based norms is indicative of a 'confirmation or an erosion of international law' (title) or a 'rise or decline of the international rule of law'.[4] Throughout the first part, he asks whether a rise or decline in values is even objectively assessable, assuming that it might depend on 'the "eye of the beholder" or the normative position and vantage point of the observer'. He also asks if the effect of contestation depends 'on the context and circumstances of the contestation'.[5]

His answer is optimistic: contestation 'does not signal a decline in the international rule of law', it even allows for a rise of 'a new norm based on an old value'.[6] He arrives at this conclusion because he focuses on norm contestation by the African Union (AU) in two cases: impunity for Al-Bashir and the right of intervention and the responsibility to protect in the AU Constitutive Act.

The notion of value-based norms immediately raises the question which, or more precisely whose, values constitute the fundaments of the international legal order. As Maluwa acknowledges, there is no agreement within the international community or among legal scholars as to the substance of value-based norms or with regard to their

---

[4] ibid.
[5] ibid.
[6] ibid IV.

universality. Consequently, the concept of values depends on the context and thus also on the 'eye of the beholder'.[7] Yet, as he argues, it is commonly assumed and accepted that the UN Charter is the source of a value-based international order[8] and that 'classical individual human rights norms offer the most obvious example of the principal [sic!] value-based norms of the current international order'.[9] In the following, we offer five answers from norm research, which restrict the territory on which every beholder has a vantage point.

1. Is the international legal order built on values? Yes!

Maluwa defines values as enduring beliefs that reflect a global consensus.[10] At the same time, he acknowledges that legal values, such as human rights, have been contested and that their universality has been questioned, too. We do not wish to criticize the latter point, as we certainly find many empirical examples to validate this argument. Yet, we wish to hint at the 1993 Vienna consensus on the universality of human rights norms. We also wish to point to the problem that per definition a global consensus can only exist if it is not contested. Of course, the particular meaning of a legal value can be contested, as we will discuss below. We hold that values are part of international norms and hence provide a foundation for collective expectations about the appropriate behaviour of states, irrespective of their universal acceptance. Following newer conceptual work on norms,[11] we apply a definition of international norms as value-based collective expectations for the appropriate behaviour of states (and sometimes other actors) in specific types of situations, which are always formulated with reference to other norms. This means that every norm—legal or non-legal—is composed of three structural elements: problem, value, and behaviour: A norm always includes a value, something 'good' to be enjoyed or something 'bad' to be avoided, for example, a peaceful life, justice, equality, sustainability.

2. Is state commitment to the international legal order, and particularly to human rights norms, a sign that all values are shared by all? No!

The idea that international human rights law is an expression of shared values of the international community, that is all states, is definitely questionable. Why did states conclude human rights treaties and how did customary international law develop? The

---

[7] ibid II.
[8] ibid II.
[9] ibid I.
[10] ibid II.
[11] Carla Winston, 'Norm Structure, Diffusion, and Evolution: A Conceptual Approach' (2018) 24 European Journal of International Relations 638.

following brief summary of international relations theories, which have informed debates on commitment and compliance in international law, comes up with several explanations, none of which assumes that all values are shared by all states all of the time.

A (neo)realist perspective assumes that international law is the outcome of a powerful state's ability and willingness to put norms at the centre of its politics and to institutionalize them beyond their own borders—if this helps to promote and enforce its own interests and values. A prominent example is the slave trade, which was abolished because the then hegemon, Britain, used its power to force recalcitrant states into commitment and compliance with the anti-slavery norm.[12] Consequently, we should not infer from the existence of value-based norms that they are shared by all and that they remain robust once power constellations change. The current debate on rising powers and the related end of the liberal world order—as we know it—is an indication that this realist perspective is still influential. A liberal perspective assumes that international human rights norms stem from the externalization of state interests and values, that are 'locked in'.[13] Especially democratic states are interested in an international system that is based on the same values as their domestic ones. Not only are governments mainly ratifying human rights treaties when they are in line with their preferences, and consequently democratic governments are more likely to commit to civil and political rights than non-democratic states; smaller democracies, newly independent states, and legal activists were also 'the prime movers in codifying most of the provisions of the Universal Declaration of Human Rights (UDHR) in treaty form over the course of the 1950s and 1960s'.[14] The process of their institutionalization is most commonly explained by transnational advocacy coalitions.[15] This perspective is, for example, present and promoted in the quote of Kofi Annan in Maluwa's chapter.[16] Common values also minimize uncertainty and hereby, in line with the democratic peace theorem, facilitate peaceful relationships among states.

What this last perspective includes is what shines through in Maluwa's chapter as 'the eye of the beholder': are value-based norms in fact only a representation of the values of liberal democracies? Closest to Maluwa's own perspective are constructivist perspectives on international human rights norms, which see human rights as 'examples of social constructions: invented social categories that derive their influence from the extent of a *shared* understanding within and across communities'.[17] But even here it is about the extent to which values are shared. In other words, norms can be widely held but this does not mean that they are shared by all. Of course, the norm-centred models and theories in international relations simultaneously rose to fame with the success

---

[12] Stephen D Krasner, 'Sovereignty, Regimes, and Human Rights' in Volker Rittberger and Peter Mayer (eds), *Regime Theory and International Relations* (Clarendon Press 1993) 152.

[13] Andrew Moravcsik, 'The Origins of Human Rights Regimes: Democratic Delegation in Postwar Europe' (2003) 54 International Organization 217.

[14] Beth A Simmons, *Mobilizing for Human Rights: International Law in Domestic Politics* (Cambridge University Press 2009) 108.

[15] Hans Peter Schmitz and Kathryn Sikkink, 'International Human Rights' in Walter Carlsnaes, Thomas Risse, and Beth A Simmons (eds), *Handbook of International Relations* (SAGE Publications 2012) 827, 832–35.

[16] Maluwa (n 3) II.

[17] Schmitz and Sikkink (n 15) 827 (our emphasis).

of the human rights regime since the 1990s: states ratify human rights treaties and are willing to respect, protect, and fulfil their obligations because they *believe* the norms to be indispensable. 'We' need these values for every other form of cooperation in international politics, so that 'we' can trust our trade partners or maintain friendly relationships with other states. 'We' do not need to expect that these friends would engage in any hostile act—because with the commitment to human rights, 'we' share the same values. As has already been described by social constructivist theory, this perspective comes at a price. In order to arrive at a 'we, the friends with the shared values', we need an 'other'—those who question the relevance and validity of the norms and help 'us' to reinforce our community committed to human rights to protect them even more fiercely.

3. Can we assume that all states and societies accept this order without contestation? No!

If norms are widely held but not necessarily shared by all, then contestation should not come as a surprise. And indeed, contestation is nothing new and has been the fate of human rights for a long time. 'Contestation about the validity and meaning of human rights standards is a central concern for scholarship interested in understanding the independent effects of norms. Contestation takes place at international, domestic, and local levels …'[18] Contestation also happens when the norm has been accepted and implemented—namely when it collides with other norms.[19] For Antje Wiener, who Maluwa also quotes, contestation is a 'norm-generative social practice'.[20] Wiener has prominently argued that norms are contested and, therefore, require contestation to work. She has also proposed that different types of norms come with different degrees of contestation.[21] Type 1, which she calls 'fundamental norms', are characterized as formally valid and broadly accepted. Universally accepted human rights norms, such as the prohibition of torture, fall into this category. Yet, Wiener argues that while these are 'highly likely to be agreed in principle', they are 'most likely contested in practice', that is when they are implemented. This conceptualization of norms, as agreed in principle but contested in practice, is indeed helpful when we seek to explain why two seemingly contradictive facts about human rights exist: on the one hand, human rights norms such as the torture prohibition are customary law and the international community declared the universality of human rights in Vienna in 1993. On the other hand, scholars report the contestation of the torture prohibition or other supposedly shared values and non-compliance with their provisions. The conceptualization also alerts us not to mistake a norm contestation (or: non-compliance) for a norm erosion.

---

[18]   ibid 835.
[19]   Andrea Liese, 'Exceptional Necessity—How Liberal Democracies Contest the Prohibition of Torture and Ill-Treatment when Countering Terrorism' (2009) 5 Journal of International Law & International Relations 17
[20]   Antje Wiener, *A Theory of Contestation* (Springer 2014) 1.
[21]   ibid 36.

4. Are contestations necessarily an expression of disagreement with the values that underline the legal order? No, not necessarily!

We argue that it is essential to examine what is contested when we speak of norm contestation. For this purpose, it is helpful to distinguish whether norm contestation addresses the problem definition, the value, or the prescribed behaviour of the very norm in question. Actors could contest that a problem is either less or more important than assumed, for example that climate change is of a different nature than described in a convention. Actors can also contest the prescription of a certain behaviour, for example that reducing greenhouse gases does not help to solve the problem of climate change. Or they can contest the value, for example that sustainability is a value they share. We argue that actors may express disagreement with a legal norm, for example a treaty norm, without contesting the underlying value. It is left to the scholar to determine whether the contestation of interest is actually a contestation of a norm's value or not. We will come back to this point when discussing Maluwa's findings for the observed contestation of the AU with regard to the Al-Bashir case.

5. Will all contestations weaken the legal system or single value-based norms? Again: No!

The questions whether the international rule of law is in danger and whether values are eroding or declining should, in our view, not be answered by studying contestations, but by tracing potential effects of contestation. This can be done quite systematically, given that several hypotheses have already been developed. Thus, it is probably less a question of the 'eye of the beholder' than of forms of contestation, the reaction of norm defenders, the power of the contester, and so forth. We will limit our short discussion of assumptions to these three factors.

On the first one, Deitelhoff and Zimmermann propose to distinguish two types of contestation, namely applicatory and justificatory contestation.[22] While applicatory contestation challenges the application or implementation of a norm, justificatory contestation challenges its validity. They assume that these two different forms of contestation have opposite effects. While applicatory contestation strengthens a norm or at least does not weaken it, justificatory contestations may lead to norm erosion. The underlying logic is that the contestation of the applicability of a norm to a certain situation or the contestation of a certain implementation is based on its general acceptance. Hence, it is not weakening but potentially even bolstering the underlying value as such. In turn, challenges to the underlying foundations of a norm are potentially more damaging when they raise questions concerning the norm's legitimacy.

---

[22] Nicole Deitelhoff and Lisbeth Zimmermann, 'Things We Lost in the Fire: How Different Types of Contestation Affect the Validity of International Norms International Norms' (2013) Hessische Stiftung Friedens- und Konfliktforschung (HSFK) PRIF Working Paper No 18.

Secondly, international norms are not only attacked, but also defended. In fact, this is one reason for providing international institutions with enforcement competencies in the first place. In addition, most norms are embedded in a larger normative structure (eg humanitarian and human rights law) and thus reinforced and sustained by inter-related norms.[23] Furthermore, states and non-state members of the international community may respond to contestations with counter-mobilization.

As a third factor, we are not the first to argue that it matters who contests a norm.[24] But with regard to Maluwa's argument, we would like to emphasize the questions already raised in this regard: How many material and immaterial (eg political and discursive) resources does an actor have? Does the contesting actor command enough international legitimacy to establish a strong counter-discourse? And, the other way around, are the contesters concerned about their international legitimacy or vulnerable to material and social pressure?

II. What do you read into it? How to 'see' the case studies

In his analysis, Maluwa turns to two examples of contestation by African states and members of the AU. In our view, the selection of both cases predetermines the outcome that 'the contestations at issue do not manifest a decline or erosion of international law'.[25] Both cases focus on contestations with regard to the applicability of a norm to a specific situation, that is a form of contestation that is not assumed to weaken international (legal) norms. Furthermore, both cases point to horizontal norm collisions, that is instances in which different international norms prescribe different standards of behaviour. In the first case these are justice versus peace, in the latter these are human rights versus sovereignty. Given that at least the latter belong to the core values of the international community and its legal order, the question of an erosion or decline of the rule of law is not the point. Rather, the question is how the two norms will be balanced. Finally, we lack intersubjective indicators for a decline or an erosion of a certain value in international law. We will briefly illustrate our points regarding the first example. Please note that we do not engage with the presented empirical evidence or narrative.[26] Our comment engages mainly conceptually with the case study.

In the first example, the AU contested the indictment of the former Sudanese President Al-Bashir in front of the International Criminal Court (ICC). Instead, the AU and member states called for non-compliance, reforms of the ICC, and later a withdrawal from the Rome Statute. Maluwa sees this case as one in which the value 'respect for human dignity' and 'the norm of non-impunity' has been contested.

---

[23] Wayne Sandholtz, 'Dynamics of International Norm Change: Rules against Wartime Plunder' (2008) 14 European Journal of International Relations 101.

[24] Thomas Risse, Stephen C Ropp, and Kathryn Sikkink (eds), *The Persistent Power of Human Rights: From Commitment to Compliance* (Cambridge University Press 2013); Harald Muller and Carmen Wunderlich (eds), *Norm Dynamics in Multilateral Arms Control: Interests, Conflicts, and Justice* (University of Georgia Press 2013).

[25] Maluwa (n 3) IV.

[26] For a different reading of the ICC contestation, eg: Kurt Mills, '"Bashir Is Dividing Us": Africa and the International Criminal Court' (2012) 34 Human Rights Quarterly 404.

However, he does not interpret this contestation as 'an outright rejection of the norm'.[27] And, although not explicitly mentioning this term, he refers to a potential norm collision between the value-based norm of non-impunity on the one hand and peace on the other. The AU argued that prosecuting Al-Bashir would undermine the peace process in Sudan, and that the case illustrates 'a world in which difficult choices must be made' with regard to the question 'which norm has priority'.[28] Hence, we question whether this case actually represents an instance in which the underlying values of non-impunity and human dignity were (strongly) contested. Much in the narrative of Maluwa points to an interpretation in which the applicability of the norm to the particular situation of surrendering Al-Bashir was contested. When Maluwa states that 'the contestation is on the context in which these competing value-based international law norms should be implemented',[29] he refers to an applicatory contestation,[30] that is to a form of contestation that is assumed to have no weakening effect on the norm— or its underlying values—as such. Maluwa himself admits that the contestation is not targeting the norm's validity, but its 'application'.[31]

We are concerned that the author offers no indicators for a decline or erosion of international law. Potential indicators could have been ratification status and acceptance of non-impunity norm in diplomatic discourse, compliance with other ICC warrants, increased contestations by other actors than the AU, decreased or lacking third party reactions to non-compliance and contestation, and finally, the adoption of AU claims by other actors. Without these indicators, the interpretation of the findings of the analysis with regard to a rise, a decline, or an erosion do indeed remain in the eye of the beholder. A further point of concern from our perspective as political scientists is that any assessment of rise, decline, or erosion of international law, which focuses only on states, necessarily overlooks other actors that are central to norm dynamics. Norm contestation by states mobilizes counter-movements, both from state and non-state actors, which seek to emphasize the validity of the norm. In other cases, research has been able to show that these movements can successfully socialize states into further commitment and even compliance.[32]

III.   Can we see the same?

We conclude by highlighting the problem which arises if we want to defend common values by invoking the law: at one point, these values have to be identified as such. As

---

[27]   Maluwa (n 3) III.1.
[28]   ibid.
[29]   ibid.
[30]   Deitelhoff and Zimmermann (n 22).
[31]   Maluwa (n 3) III.1: '[T]he AU and the African States that support the position are not contesting the existence of the norms against impunity, but arguing that the competing norm of securing and preserving peace should be given priority in the particular circumstances of the Darfur conflict. In my view, this does not signal or represent a decline or an erosion of the non-impunity norm, merely a temporary stagnation in its application.'
[32]   eg: Margaret E Keck and Kathryn Sikkink, *Activists Beyond Borders: Advocacy Networks in International Politics* (Cornell University Press 1998); Risse, Ropp, and Sikkink (n 24).

Maluwa rightly points to throughout his chapter, perceptions of a rise or decline of the international rule of law depend on the vantage point of the observer—or the eye of the beholder. What follows from this view and what is the starting point of Maluwa's contribution to this book is that contestations are seen as signs of a value change, on the one hand, and as signs of a crisis of international law or the rule of law, on the other. However, any dependence on the eye of the beholder inherits the problematic 'observation that subjective evaluations depend on the evaluator'.[33] The hope is that many eyes see more—but it can also lead to the situation that we all see something different. Who, then, controls the narrative if we have many beholders evaluating the quality of international law? One often used reference in academic debates on international law is the one borrowed from the ancient Indian parable of the blind men and the elephant. Just as each of the blind men touches a different part of the elephant and afterwards claims to know what it looks like, scholars likewise acknowledge that there is no such thing as one truth when looking at the subject of our interest—a rise or decline of the international rule of law. In the end, it seems that the moral of the story is that we all have only limited knowledge and that only the combination of multiple perspectives allows for the big picture—and that something close to truth is unavailable from only one. One thing about the parable is often overlooked though. While universal truth is questioned as the very core of the story, it at the same time reinforces such claims: how could the six blind men arrive at the knowledge that the elephant looked different as a whole than what they thought it did by just judging from the part they touched? Because one person told them they were wrong. Hence, this one person claimed to be able to see the whole truth and was believed by the six men.

We add to this that it is not only the vantage point which is decisive for an evaluation of rise or decline. It also depends on the value system of the observer whether she sees a rise, a decline, or a transformation of the order. Hence, multiple perspectives can be true and several values coexist. Contestation is not inherently indicative of an erosion or a decline of norms, values, or the international rule of law. We have to pay careful attention to the types and forms of contestation, indicators for the state of norms, values or the international rule of law, and we have to study the response to contestations, including by norm-defenders. Only then can we start to move the diagnosis of the state of norms to an inter-subjective research endeavour. If we fail to do so, we will never see the same and the eye of the beholder problem will not be solved.

[33] Tamar Gutner and Alexander Thompson, 'The Politics of IO Performance: A Framework' (2010) 5 The Review of International Organizations 227; Gene A Brewer, 'All Measures of Performance Are Subjective: More Evidence on US Federal Agencies' in George A Boyne, Kenneth J Meier, Laurence J O'Toole Jr, and Richard M Walker (eds), *Public Service Performance: Perspectives on Measurement and Management* (Cambridge University Press 2006) 35.

22

Ensuring Access to Information: International Law's Contribution to Global Justice

Eyal Benvenisti*

I. Introduction

One could understand the theme of this book—'the rise or decline of international law'—as being grounded on the assumption that 'the rise' of international law is intimately linked to global justice, whereas its decline augurs global injustice;[1] that more international law, or stronger adherence to its principles, means a more just world. This chapter partly challenges this assumption, arguing that there is nothing inherently just in more international norms and more international organizations. There is nothing inherently just in a law that is grounded in state consent but in fact represents the interests or values of the few, and the proliferation of state-made norms and institutions may be counterproductive from the perspective of global justice. The association of 'the decline' of international law with global injustice is clearer, although sometimes the rise of national constitutional law, even as a challenge to international law and a check on international organizations, can offer a much needed correction to international institutions and tribunals influenced by the powerful few.[2] The question as to how international law can contribute to global justice therefore requires an assessment of what principles of international law are conducive to global justice, of which we would need more. This chapter seeks to address this question. It also examines contemporary challenges to such principles, challenges that reflect a 'decline' in the commitment to them.

How can international law contribute to global justice? In one sense, international law is *about* global justice—seeking ways and means to reduce inter- and intra-state conflicts and promote human welfare, given existing political, social, and economic constraints. International law has been used to address several specific areas of global

* I wish to thank Hanoch Dagan, Tsilly Dagan, Olga Frishman, Michal S Gal, Sandy Kedar, Doreen Lustig, Faina Melman, and Henning Grosse Ruse-Khan for their helpful comments and Alon Abramovich for excellent research assistance. Research for this essay was supported by the European Research Council Advanced Grant No 323323.

[1] Heike Krieger and Georg Nolte, 'The International Rule of Law—Rise or Decline?—Approaching Current Foundational Challenges' in this book.

[2] Eyal Benvenisti and George W Downs, *Between Fragmentation and Democracy: The Role of National Courts* (Cambridge University Press 2017) 56–65, 149–65.

human concern such as the prohibition on the use of force unless in self-defence,[3] the prevention and repression of crimes against humanity,[4] the promotion of human rights and the granting of asylum to refugees and possibly to some types of migrants,[5] the recognition of a duty to assist countries facing natural disasters,[6] the regulation of labour markets,[7] and the obligations to manage transboundary and global resources equitably and sustainably and to provide development aid.[8] Several systemic approaches have focused on a global rule of law as promoting global justice, and on ensuring the accountability of global decision-makers under the approach of global administrative law.[9] More critical voices have probed international law's use as a tool of global injustice, having served to further the Empire's domination of the New World—criticisms that are designed to discover the law's blind spots and urge reform.[10] Some voices seeking reform have focused on tweaking the concept of 'sovereignty' to insist on solidarity among sovereigns,[11] while others have insisted on certain moral duties for states to mitigate the failures of the state sovereignty system,[12] and to take into account the interests of foreigners.[13]

But how could international law contribute to 'global justice' in the sense that has captured the attention of moral philosophers in recent decades? The 'global justice' literature in moral philosophy focuses on justice among individuals rather than among states, and it often regards international law as part of the problem—not only in the colonial context but also as an inherently unjust order—rather than the key to the solution. Perhaps for the same reasons, international lawyers have by and large ignored the question of global distributive justice as being outside their purview.[14] Questions

---

[3] Charter of the United Nations (adopted 26 June 1945, entered into force 24 October 1945) 1 UNTS XVI (UN Charter) Art 2 (4).

[4] Rome Statute of the International Criminal Court (adopted 17 July 1998, entered into force 1 July 2002) ISBN No 92-9227-227-6 Art 7.

[5] Convention Relating to the Status of Refugees (adopted 28 July 1951, entered into force 22 April 1954) 189 UNTS 137 (Refugee Convention).

[6] On this duty: Kigab Park, 'The Law on Natural Disaster' in Eyal Benvenisti and Georg Nolte (eds), *Community Interests Across International Law* (Oxford University Press 2018).

[7] For a description of how the World Trade Organization shapes national regulation: Gregory Shaffer, 'How the World Trade Organization Shapes Global Governance' (2015) 9 Regulation & Governance 1.

[8] For the development of international law on transboundary ecosystems: Eyal Benvenisti, *Sharing Transboundary Resources* (Cambridge University Press 2002) 156–200.

[9] For a review of community interests in international law: Benvenisti and Nolte (n 6); Bruno Simma, 'From Bilateralism to Community Interests in International Law' (1994) 250 Recueil des cours 217.

[10] eg: Sundhya Pahuja, *Decolonising International Law: Development, Economic Growth and Politics of Universality* (Cambridge University Press 2011); Anthony Anghie, *Imperialism, Sovereignty and the Making of International Law* (Cambridge University Press 2007); Jochen von Bernstorff, 'International Law and Global Justice: On Recent Inquiries into the Dark Side of Economic Globalization' (2015) 26 European Journal of International Law 279; Doreen Lustig, *The International Veil of Corporations: The History of Corporate Regulation in International Law* (forthcoming, Oxford University Press 2019).

[11] Nicolas Politis, 'Le probléme des limitations de la souveraineté et la théorie de l'abus des droits dans les rapports internationaux' (1925) 6 Recueil des cours 1, 5–6; Georges Scelle, *Précis de droit des gens: principes et systématique*, vol 2, 1 (Recueil Sirey 1934); generally: Rüdiger Wolfrum and Chia Kojima, *Solidarity: A Structural Principle of International Law* (Springer 2010).

[12] eg: Ronald Dworkin, 'A New Philosophy for International Law' (2013) 41 Philosophy & Public Affairs 2, 20–22.

[13] eg: Eyal Benvenisti, 'Sovereigns as Trustees of Humanity: On the Accountability of States to Foreign Stakeholders' (2013) 107 American Journal of International Law 295.

[14] For exceptions: Stephen Ratner, *The Thin Justice of International Law: A Moral Reckoning of the Law of Nations* (Oxford University Press 2015); Allen Buchanan, *Justice, Legitimacy, and Self-Determination: Moral Foundations for International Law* (Oxford University Press 2003).

about the nature and scope of obligations that individuals, states, and international organizations in the affluent 'North' have towards the less privileged individuals in the 'South', and in general whether nations should regard the human flourishing of strangers as a matter of concern, are regarded by most lawyers as best left to political deliberation.[15]

In this chapter, I wish to highlight the role of institutions and decision-making procedures in promoting—indirectly—global (and domestic) distributive justice. This focus on institutions and processes at the global level is grounded on the assumption that questions of the just allocation and reallocation of resources are ultimately resolved through processes of public deliberation and contestation (including through the involvement of courts). Therefore, the question is whether law can be instrumental in ensuring the conditions for inclusive and open deliberation and contestation. Focusing on the limited opportunities of politically weaker constituencies to engage effectively in such interactions, I will suggest that the task of the law is to provide these groups and individuals with meaningful voice to more effectively stake their claims for domestic and global justice in the various decision-making fora. In other words, I wish to argue that the key to approaching a more just allocation of resources is not through the direct provision of concrete entitlements like Thomas Pogge's global resources dividend[16] or by providing justifications to those affected (as suggested by Rainer Forst),[17] but by enhancing what Isaiah Berlin called the 'liberty for'[18] of those affected, by addressing the democratic deficits that underlie the skewed distribution (or the lack of redistribution) of assets and opportunities. My claim is that international law can play a role in the political empowerment of weak constituencies (within and between states). In doing so, international law can indirectly shape the distribution and redistribution of resources in a manner that is more dignified and preferable to handing charitable contributions to the poor and vulnerable. Just like the empowerment of labour through freedom of association, rather than by granting employees certain benefits, the enhanced voice for disadvantaged communities will not only increase their bargaining power, but also promote their sense of agency and enhance their dignity.[19]

This chapter claims that international law can and should create the conditions that enable the transformation of the debate about domestic and global distributive justice from the philosophical to the political by the enhancing the voice of the weak and the

---

[15] Claiming that there is no burden of justification between states: Thomas Nagel, 'The Problem of Global Justice' (2005) 33 Philosophy & Public Affairs 113; however, proposing a theory of global justice whose main elements are the protection of basic human rights worldwide: David Miller, 'National Responsibility and Global Justice' (2008) 11 Critical Review of International Social and Political Philosophy 383.

[16] Thomas Pogge, *World Poverty and Human Rights* (Polity Press 2002). It was adopted by the Committee on Economic, Social and Cultural Rights (CESCR), which expects member states to contribute 0.7 per cent of their GNP for development cooperation.

[17] Rainer Forst, *The Right to Justification: Elements of a Constructivist Theory of Justice* (Columbia University Press 2012).

[18] Isaiah Berlin, 'Two Concepts of Liberty' in Isaiah Berlin, *Four Essays on Liberty* (Oxford University Press 1969) 16, 16–34.

[19] Miriam Ronzoni, 'Two Conceptions of State Sovereignty and Their Implications for Global Institutional Design' (2012) 15 Critical Review of International Social and Political Philosophy 573, 580 (claims that '[v]irtually all liberal societies are characterized by a package of institutions and policies aimed at promoting different variations on, and degrees of, a mixed model of freedom').

disregarded.[20] Although international law cannot replace the necessary political debate about what global justice means and how it ought to be implemented, its goal can and should be to contribute to creating inclusive frameworks for deliberation within which a meaningful political debate could take place between competing claims. A meaningful debate requires that all relevant communities can obtain and impart information about the possible outcomes of outstanding policies. Like the freedom of workers to associate, securing voice for the disregarded, while necessary, may also prove sufficient to promoting just outcomes. How can international law contribute to strengthening the voice of the disregarded?

After outlining the claim that the key to global distributive justice is the empowerment of the politically weak, the chapter will describe the underlying connection between international law and the conditions that preclude the political debate about global justice. I will briefly argue that it is the current global political-legal structure that inhibits the political process whereby global justice considerations could be argued, weighed, adopted, and implemented. I will then suggest that international law could be part of the solution for those seeking to promote any version of global justice. The chapter will emphasize the importance of accessing data, information, and knowledge as key to participation and voice and hence necessary for effective political voice.

II. Provide hooks and not fish: the misguided focus on 'justice' as distribution of resources

Pogge's 'Global Resources Dividend'[21] and other schemes for the redistribution of global assets, as well as well-wishing programmes such as the Bill and Melinda Gates Foundation[22] or the Bill Clinton Foundation,[23] have a very strong intuitive appeal. But this appeal is misguided even if it is effective. Its main fault lies in its disregard of agency. It leaves decision-making power in the hands of Northern governments, the Clintons, and the Gates. It leaves the aid recipients in their state of eternal dependency, in the hope that the aid they receive fits their needs and will continue. In other words, the global redistribution of material goods is insufficient because it perpetuates the dependency relationships and denies the agency of the recipients. It ignores the right to individual and collective self-determination of the beneficiaries.

Worse, the assets-redistribution approach is also unnecessary for achieving a more just allocation of resources and opportunities. Arguably, the redistribution of meaningful voice in decision-making venues where decisions are taken about resource management and allocation, about regulation, etc is not only necessary but also sufficient

---

[20] On 'the problem of the disregard': Richard B Stewart, 'Remedying Disregard in Global Regulatory Governance: Accountability, Participation, and Responsiveness' (2014) 108 American Journal of International Law 211.
[21] Pogge (n 16).
[22] Bill & Melinda Gates Foundation, <www.gatesfoundation.org> accessed 8 December 2017.
[23] Clinton Foundation, <www.clintonfoundation.org/> accessed 8 December 2017.

to levelling the political playing field and thereby to levelling opportunities for individuals and communities to influence outcomes and obtain their proper share of global resources. Therefore, the key to approaching a more just allocation of resources is not by devising direct distributive justice tools, but rather by analysing the inherent global democratic deficits that underlie the skewed distribution of assets and opportunities and then seeking to devise means to correct these deficits.

Take, as one seemingly minor illustration of the problem, the European Community's food safety regime.[24] The European Commission's stringent food safety requirements constitute a major barrier to exports entering the European market from developing countries that depend on these exports. The European safety requirements, writes Morten Broberg, have been ranked as one of the foremost factors affecting exports of agricultural and food products from developing countries.[25] Broberg shows the one-sided regulatory process that imposes 'prohibitively strict criteria', shifting all the burdens on the growers in developing countries, burdens that in his view are 'disproportionate' and 'excessive'. As a monopsonic market, Europe can dictate the rules. Shifting to more transparent regulatory processes that provide opportunities for growers to have voice is likely to reduce production costs and increase welfare in developing countries as a matter of right, not charity. From this perspective, the European Union (EU) trumpeting its commitment to assisting these very countries rings hollow.[26]

Among the global justice philosophers, Rainer Forst has come closest to this realization. In his insightful book,[27] he elaborates on the basic right to justification that 'expresses the demand that there be no political or social relations of governance that cannot be adequately justified to those affected by them'.[28] He emphasizes not only the need to provide reasons for those affected by a decision, but also the need to hear them out, thereby having them participate in common decision-making.[29] His emphasis is on persuasion by deliberation, grounded in his faith in 'the forceless force of the better argument or rather the force pushing toward the better argument'.[30]

---

[24] Food Safety: Overview <ec.europa.eu/food/overview_en> accessed 8 December 2017.

[25] Morten Broberg, 'European Food Safety Regulation and the Developing Countries: Regulatory Problems and Possibilities' 3 (Danish Institute for International Studies Working Paper September 2009) <static-curis.ku.dk/portal/files/15584884/PDF> accessed 22 July 2018.

[26] Most probably, the food safety regime violates these commitments: Broberg (n 25) 36–38; also: Consolidated Version of the Treaty on the Functioning of the European Union (9 May 2008) OJ C115/47, Art 208:

 1. Union policy in the field of development cooperation shall be conducted within the framework of the principles and objectives of the Union's external action. The Union's development cooperation policy and that of the Member States complement and reinforce each other. Union development cooperation policy shall have as its primary objective the reduction and, in the long term, the eradication of poverty. The Union shall take account of the objectives of development cooperation in the policies that it implements which are likely to affect developing countries.
 2. The Union and the Member States shall comply with the commitments and take account of the objectives they have approved in the context of the United Nations and other competent international organizations.

[27] Forst, *The Right to Justification* (n 17).

[28] ibid 2.

[29] Rainer Forst, 'The Justification of Human Rights and the Basic Right to Justification: A Reflexive Approach' (2010) 120 Ethics 711, 717–20, 727–28.

[30] Forst, *The Right to Justification* (n 17) 7.

But the assumption that the decision-maker will be convinced by the better argument applies only to decision-makers that are impartial, such as the ideal judge or the expert. Once this assumption is questioned, however, more robust protection of interests is needed. This is why Forst then invokes the concept of consent. But how can consent be facilitated in global decision-making arenas? Suggesting a concept of 'minimal transnational justice' as a middle course between global and international justice, Forst calls for 'minimally fair transnational terms of discourse and of cooperation' where national communities are participants 'of (roughly) equal standing in the global economic and political system', with 'a (qualified) "veto right" of the worst off' in matters of 'basic justice that touch the participatory minimum'.[31] This, of course, calls for definitions of the various components ('the worst off', 'basic justice', 'the participatory minimum'), as well as paying attention to the complex background conditions that could ensure the '(roughly) equal standing' of all those affected by those decisions.

But more importantly, this suggestion leaves the worst off, and any other affected individual, in the reactive position of someone who may have the opportunity to consent, but never the opportunity to initiate, to set the agenda, to upset the existing order because it is unjust. A reactive, even if not entirely passive, right to justification is therefore not enough to ensure voice and usher in globally just policies. Instead, the key to global justice is inclusive participation in decisions—involving all the parties in decisions that affect them. Can international law be instrumental in this endeavour? Before outlining a hesitant positive response, I wish to explore the main structural conditions that impede inclusive political participation in domestic and global decision-making fora, conditions that arguably prevent the just allocation of resources. Understanding these conditions is the first step towards devising institutional remedies that might indirectly contribute to global (and domestic) justice.

III. The negative contribution of international law to global justice

This section explores the systemic democratic failures in contemporary national and international decision-making venues that result in the disenfranchisement of politically weak stakeholders. I will suggest that international law is part of the problem, as it endorses the global arrangement of powers and competences among states, which is

---

[31] ibid 263–65. On 'minimal transnational justice':

> members of societies of multiple domination have a legitimate claim to the resources necessary to establish a (minimally) justified democratic order within their political community and that this community be a participant of (roughly) equal standing in the global economic and political system. And the citizens of the societies benefiting from the present global system do have a collective 'duty of assistance' to use Rawls' terms, to provide these resources (ranging from food, housing and medical care to a basic education, information, the possibility of effective participation, and so on) necessary to attain self-government. . . . minimally fair transnational terms of discourse and of cooperation.

At 265: 'a (qualified) "veto right" of the worst off. Such that no decision can be made that can be reciprocally and generally be rejected by those in the weakest position.'

currently undermining the political agency of many individuals. Understanding this role of international law may offer guidance on its potential role in promoting global (and domestic) justice through its various interlocutors, primarily courts and other reviewing bodies.

To do so, this part identifies four factors that have bearing on the possibility of deliberating on global justice issues (let alone promoting them). These four aspects contribute to the diminishing voice of diffuse voters in public decision-making. Exposing the complicity of international law to the rise of these four factors is key to assessing the ways by which international norms that could offer responses. While international law is part of the failing structure of global governance today, it can be instrumental in providing the necessary response.

As will be outlined below, there are four principal factors that contribute to the diminishing voice of individuals in public decision-making processes. All of them result from structural failures of the current global system of allocating competences to states, a system that faces challenges in our era of global connectedness, interdependency, and the rise of new information and communication technologies. Two of those factors relate—counterintuitively perhaps—not so much to the global sphere but more to the domestic sphere. These are two aspects of the contemporary global legal order that affect the opportunities of citizens within their respective states. The first aspect is the law's shaping of the citizens' possibilities to exit their respective countries and enter other countries. The second aspect is the law's crude way of separating out spheres of decision-making along the political boundaries of states. Together, these aspects limit people's ability to take part in public decisions affecting them, and hinder their ability to demand wealth distribution and redistribution to promote collective welfare. It is not difficult to prove that these two aspects benefit some stakeholders and burden others, and the discrimination that ensues between the competing groups creates global injustice. The third principal way in which international law creates and maintains global inequalities is its fragmented nature, which divides potential actors who demand justice and thereby silences them. The last determinant factor is the growing power of private actors—Facebook, Google, and so forth—whose control of information and communication technologies and of vast amounts of data poses a challenge to state authority and hence diminishes the space for democracy as well as for individual and group agency.

1. International law controls stakeholders' options for 'exit' and 'voice'

The debate about global justice that sets it apart from domestic justice, similarly to the debate about the domestic legal order that often considers it entirely distinct from the international legal order, obscures the contribution of the domestic order to international injustice and vice versa. One cannot speak about the domestic legal and political sphere without taking into account the global context in which it is embedded. The deep insight that Albert Hirschman contributed to our understanding of the dynamics of any human relationship—be it a company, a marriage, or a state—is that it is myopic to ignore the exit options that members have: that in addition to 'voice' within the relationship, people must also have the option to 'exit' the relationship.[32] Relationships within a marriage without the opportunity to divorce are not the same as those where each of the partners can terminate it at will. Having no way out of the relationship seriously undermines the voice of those who are forced to remain inside. For the same reason, the unequal allocation of the right to exit one's state also shapes the parties' relative voice as a citizen. Moreover, someone who has more exit options than others will be less likely to invest in promoting the welfare of the group of which s/he is a member.[33] Since democracy thrives on the collective action of its many members, and in fact is constantly defined by that activity,[34] too much exit could possibly harm the community due to underinvestment in promoting its interests by those who have alternatives (we sometime note this aspect when talking about 'brain drain').[35] For democracy to flourish within states, we can conclude that there has to be an optimal level of exit options—not too few, not too many—and that they should be allocated on an equal basis among voters. For the same reason, there has to be an optimal level of entry options—not overly restricted, not completely closed, and also non-discriminatory. Without opportunities for entry (another state), the right to exit is meaningless, and vice versa.[36]

By necessity, international law regulates the interface of exit/entry as it regulates the movement of individuals. It is international law that recognizes states' wide discretion to allow entry, subject to the recognition (but not enforcement) of the right of exit and the right of entry as individual human rights. To the extent that individuals can rely on their combined exit/entry rights, their voice is secured, as compared to a situation where the ruling regime knows that their options of leaving the country are limited. The availability of these rights shapes the voice that right-holders have (or do not have) in their respective countries.[37]

---

[32] Albert O Hirschman, *Exit, Voice and Loyalty: Responses to Decline in Firms, Organizations, and States* (Harvard University Press 1970); on exit and voice in the context of the EU: Joseph H H Weiler, 'The Transformation of Europe' (1991) 100 Yale Law Journal 2403.

[33] Elinor Ostrom noted that individuals who collectively manage what she terms 'common pool resources' (such as a spring or an aquifer) strengthen their commitment to cooperate with the rest by severely constraining their room for independent action: Elinor Ostrom, *Governing the Commons* (Cambridge University Press 1990) 43–45.

[34] As John Stuart Mill has observed, democracy is the way the community forms itself: John S Mill, *Considerations on Representative Government* (first published 1861, Henry Regnery Company 1962) 168:

> It is by political discussion that the manual labourer, whose employment is a routine, and whose way of life brings him in contact with no variety of impressions, circumstances, or ideas, is taught that remote causes, and events which take place far off, have a most sensible effect even on his personal interests.

[35] On the brain drain phenomenon and its implications: Ayelet Shachar, 'The Race for Talent: Highly Skilled Migrants and Competitive Immigration Regimes' (2006) 81 New York University Law Review 148; Ayelet Shachar, 'Picking Winners: Olympic Citizenship and the Global Race for Talent' (2011) 120 Yale Law Journal 2098.

[36] For a general presumption against states restricting emigration implies limits on the sovereign's right to restrict immigration: Jeremy Waldron, 'Exclusion: Property Analogies in the Immigration Debate' (2017) 18 Theoretical Inquiries in Law 469, 471.

[37] Albert O Hirschman, 'Exit, Voice, and the State' (2011) 31 World Politics 90, 95–96: 'Unfortunately, because of differences in income and wealth, the ability to vote with one's feet is unequally distributed in modern societies.'

Whereas international law limits the exit options of most voters, it enhances the actual and virtual exit opportunities of some voters, such as investors.[38] It is international law that is responsible for the invention of the multinational corporation (MNC) that is on the one hand independent of its foreign parent company, but is simultaneously recognized as owned by a foreign parent company and hence immune from taking by the state of incorporation. This invention—harking back to the so-called Cobden Treaty of 1860 between France and the United Kingdom[39]—is perhaps no less momentous for global business than the very invention of the company,[40] for it is the key to the ability of MNCs to evade political boundaries and circumvent their regulatory regimes. Moreover, if the MNC is operated from a third country, the tax laws of both the host state and the parent company's home state will not apply, and the entire operation could thus benefit from 'tax havens' without contributing to the budgets of either the host or home state, thereby not only pre-empting the political demand for redistribution but also depleting the supply of necessary resources for implementing domestic and global justice policies.[41] As Ronen Palan explains, '[o]nce these legal persons could reside in different locations, there was always the risk that they would go shopping for the best bundles of regulation they could find',[42] picking and choosing from what the different jurisdictions offer them.[43] By increasing the real or virtual exit options of owners (and of their capital or the income thereof), these 'freedoms' of movement and incorporation also increase the owners' voice in all relevant jurisdictions and lower their incentives to contribute to the welfare of the community, while at the same time diminishing the voice of those whose exit options are more limited, as well as their means of promoting community goals.

The result of the skewed exit options—and the virtual immunity of mobile capital from national regulation—is that global justice initiatives (and many domestic justice initiatives) now depend on the discretion of the mobile elements in the global community. And to the extent that these promote global justice initiatives, they do so as a measure of charity rather than as of right. The routinization of private charity intensifies dependency, political disempowerment, and the lack of ownership over one's life opportunities.[44]

---

[38] Eyal Benvenisti, 'Exit and Voice in the Age of Globalization' (1999) 98 Michigan Law Review 167; Benvenisti and Downs (n 2) 52–87.

[39] Peter T Marsh, *Bargaining on Europe: Britain and the First Common Market, 1860–1892* (Yale University Press 1999) 8–27.

[40] Ronen Palan, 'Tax Havens and the Commercialization of State Sovereignty' (2002) 56 International Organisations 151, 168–69.

[41] Tsilly Dagan, 'The Global Market for Tax and Legal Rules' (2017) 21 Florida Tax Review 148, 151:

[T]he ability of individuals and businesses to choose the laws applicable to them or to avoid application of a particular legal regime altogether radically diminishes the effectiveness of redistribution through the tax system,

also available online <papers.ssrn.com/sol3/papers.cfm?abstract_id=2506051> accessed 22 July 2018, 3.

[42] Palan (n 40) 172.

[43] Dagan calls this phenomenon of picking and choosing 'fragmentation': Dagan (n 41) 17–22.

[44] Using the 'Millean' critique of the Good Despot to develop a critique of privatization that focuses on the democratic deficits it creates: Doreen Lustig and Eyal Benvenisti, 'The Multinational Corporation as "the Good Despot": The Democratic Costs of Privatization in Global Settings' (2014) 15 Theoretical Inquiries in Law 125.

2. International law and the fortuitous allocation of spheres of policy-making

Current global interdependencies are responsible for the lack of fit between the group that has the right to vote and the group that is affected by the decisions made by, or on behalf of, the first group. The basic assumption of state democracy—that these two types of stakeholders overlap—was perhaps correct in the world of separate mansions, when territorial boundaries defined not only the persons entitled to vote but also the community affected by those choices. Because of that fit, exclusive state sovereignty was both efficient and democratically just. Today, however, the policies of one government affect foreign stakeholders on a regular basis, without the latter having the right to vote for that government or otherwise being able to influence its decisions. The domestic political process becomes irrelevant as a way to secure community goals.

Moreover, the political boundaries raise the costs for the majorities within a discrete group of states to unite against a common external rival—a powerful foreign state or an even mightier and more ruthless MNC—that practises 'divide and rule' strategies against them, when seeking, for example, concessions for its investment. From this perspective, the spectacular success of the decolonization movement made the numerous new states vulnerable to a new type of exploitation by a handful of powerful states or other global actors. Weaker states that find it difficult to bundle up their disparate preferences submit to the dictates of the few powerful actors and the global institutions that they have created. As a result, the space for discretion that many sovereigns (and hence voters) are left with is severely restricted. The promise of 'sovereignty as freedom' has not materialized for many countries, which experience their traditional or hard-won formal freedom as having erected new types of walls that separate them from each other and from the actual public or private venue of deliberation and decision-making.

3. International law as a fragmented legal space

State authorities have in recent years delegated or surrendered regulatory functions to a fragmented tapestry of various forms of public and private, formal and informal, international and private bodies.[45] The pressure to privatize has further shrunk the space for political deliberation,[46] and all too often the move to such global regulatory bodies has—to varying degrees—eroded the functionality of public participation in politics, traditional constitutional checks and balances found in many democracies, and other domestic oversight and monitoring mechanisms of executive discretion.[47]

---

[45] Benvenisti and Downs (n 2) 14–19, 30–44.

[46] Lustig and Benvenisti (n 44) 139–41.

[47] Discussing strategies to address the evolving gaps in the efficacy of domestic political and legal mechanisms of participation and accountability resulting from shifts of regulatory authority from domestic to global regulatory bodies: Stewart (n 20) 231–68; arguing that by employing international organizations as venues for policy-making, state executives and interest groups manage to reduce the impact of domestic checks and balances: Benvenisti, 'Exit and Voice in the Age of Globalization' (n 38); there may be additional reasons for the concentration of power in the executive and the decline of domestic checks; Bruce Ackerman, *The Decline and Fall of the American*

The multiplicity of single-issue institutions limits the ability of many state executives of medium-sized or small states, and certainly of developing states, to create coalitions that could withstand the domination of the powerful states who are the masters of the treaties. Moreover, with global regulation becoming ubiquitous, heavily influenced by capture by special domestic interest groups that thrive on asymmetric information, the question of voice of individuals in global bodies arises. Also the voice of diffuse voters in domestic bodies diminishes when the states' ability to resist a foreign actor is effectively lost because a discrete group of states finds it impossible to unite against a common external rival—a powerful foreign state or an even mightier and more ruthless MNC—that practices 'divide and rule' strategies against them, when imposing its demands on them.

4. The rise of private power (and data as the new global resource)

In addition to the traditional influence of capital on decision-makers, we are witnessing a revolution in governance as a consequence of the availability of new information and communication technologies. The emergence of giant firms such as Facebook, Google, Twitter, and Amazon—that provide the technologies upon which humanity has come to depend—as well as their accumulation of vast amounts of data poses a challenge to state authority and hence diminishes the space for democracy and individual and group agency. There is growing evidence that these social media companies are able to manipulate public opinion and that they regularly do so, or at least allow others who use their services to do so.[48] Their current status as private actors and their claim to ownership of their algorithms and their vast amounts of data has been met with weak legal responses and no concerted attempt to curtail their freedom.[49]

5. Summary: international law and global injustice

The four contributing factors to the diminishing human agency in the public space converge to pre-empt deliberation on global (and domestic) justice issues that could transform the philosophical debate into a political one. International law is very much a part of the system that is responsible for these four factors. Hence the call for perfecting

---

Republic (Harvard University Press 2010) (discussing what he sees as the domestic factors leading to the rise of an unchecked US presidency).

[48] Demonstrating how Facebook and Google may shape public opinion to serve their own interests: Jonathan L Zittrain, 'Engineering an Election' (2014) 127 Harvard Law Review Forum 335, 335–37; Seth Fiegerman, 'Facebook Is Well Aware that It Can Influence Elections' (*CNN Tech*, 17 November 2016) <money.cnn.com/2016/11/17/technology/facebook-election-influence> accessed 22 July 2018; Trevor Timm, 'You May Hate Donald Trump. But Do You Want Facebook to Rig the Election Against Him?' (*The Guardian*, 19 April 2016) <www.theguardian.com/commentisfree/2016/apr/19/donald-trump-facebook-election-manipulate-behavior> accessed 22 July 2018.
[49] For more on this: Eyal Benvenisti, ' Foreword: Upholding Democracy Amid the Challenges of New Technology: What Role for the Law of Global Governance?' (2018) 29 European Journal of International Law 9.

that system is very much a call upon international law to offer solutions. The question that remains is how international law can develop in ways that respond to these inherent failings of the state system.

IV. The potential positive contribution of international law to global justice

The various misalignments between decision-makers and those affected by their decisions and the rise of private power generate problems of asymmetric information flows between decision-makers and voters. Voters receive less or distorted information about the choices they have and about the motivations of decision-makers, and they also find it difficult to convey their views and preferences to decision-makers and participate in decision-making. Their ability to form opinions on the basis of reliable information and act upon it in the polls is inhibited. Although the information revolution has brought a wealth of data within reach of our fingertips, the ability of individuals to make sense of this data remains limited.[50] Anthony Downs's profound observation about asymmetric information as the key challenge of democracy remains true even in our hyperconnected world. His 1957 prediction, namely that 'a world where perfect knowledge prevails' will never materialize, remains accurate.[51] Therefore, as Downs observed, governments do not assign to 'the preferences of each citizen exactly the same weight as those of every other citizen':[52] quite an understatement that continues to resonate. Recent experience suggests that the communication revolution as such is no panacea.[53] The new communication tools have created new gaps, particularly among groups of voters, empowering those who can easily rally behind specific causes or form almost virtual political parties.[54] It remains beyond voters' capacity to assess and act upon the wealth of data—often deliberately skewed—that is accessible to them, and people tend to rely on proxies in forming their opinions. Individuals unconsciously process the wealth of information in ways that fit their predispositions, a process known in psychology as motivated reasoning.[55]

---

[50] Herbert A Simon, 'A Behavioural Model of Rational Choice' (1955) 69 Quarterly Journal of Economics 99, 101: 'Because of the psychological limits of the organism ... actual human rationality-striving can at best be an extremely crude and simplified approximation to the kind of global rationality that is implied, for example, by game-theoretical models.'

[51] Anthony Downs, 'An Economic Theory of Democracy' (1957) 65 Journal of Political Economy 135, 139.

[52] ibid.

[53] Claiming that the Big Data revolution may lead policy-makers to ignore the preferences of certain stakeholders: Jonas Lerman, 'Big Data and Its Exclusions' (2013) 66 Stanford Law Review Online 55.

[54] eg: Cass Sunstein, #Republic: Divided Democracy in the Age of Social Media (Princeton University Press 2017); Andrew Chadwick, 'Web 2.0: New Challenges for the Study of E-Democracy in an Era of Informational Exuberance' in Stephen Coleman and Peter M Shane (eds), Connecting Democracy: Online Consultation and the Flow of Political Communication (MIT Press 2012) 45, 49–51; Benvenisti, 'Foreword: Upholding Democracy Amid the Challenges of New Technology: What Role for the Law of Global Governance?' (n 49).

[55] Generally: Dan M Kahan, 'Ideology, Motivated Reasoning, and Cognitive Reflection' (2013) 8 Judgment & Decision Making 407; Ulrike Hahn and Adam J L Harris, 'What Does It Mean to Be Biased: Motivated Reasoning and Rationality' (2014) 61 Psychology of Learning and Motivation 41.

1. The discipline of accountability

Domestic public law has sought to respond to the problems of asymmetric information by compelling governments to release information and thereby become transparent and accountable, the assumption being that the release of new information will level the political playing field between stakeholders. Transparency then reduces the power of the 'agents' (the policy-makers) by making more information available to the 'principals' (the public, voters); further citizen participation mechanisms allow the public to take action and ensure that their agents deliver outcomes closer to their preferences.[56] Global administrative law can be seen as an approach to adapting domestic public law tools to global governance bodies.[57] The imposition of accountability obligations on global bodies has not been easy, given the limited incentives of actors at the global level (primarily state executives and special interests) to share decisional authority. The executive or legislative branches of influential state parties to international organizations, for example, are well positioned to assess their behaviour, impose sanctions (eg withhold budgetary allocations), and employ a variety of political and legal mechanisms to exert pressure on them to adopt policies and programmes that are aligned with the priorities and interests of these member states. High-profile international non-governmental organizations (NGOs) may affect international organizations' behaviour by taking advantage of their access to global media outlets or knowledge of international organizations' internal decision-making processes. Special interests, such as the tobacco industry, have learnt to exploit transparency and citizen participation mechanisms to burden or slow adverse regulation.[58] Imposing the discipline of accountability on global bodies has gained some success, but it certainly has not reduced all the information asymmetries and ensured meaningful voice for all and always.

Take, for example, the EU's Impact Assessment Guidelines that require the EU to take into account the effects of EU policies on developing countries,[59] and its evolving practice of commissioning Sustainability Impact Assessments (SIAs) to examine the possible impacts of trade and investment agreements on developing countries.[60] The European Commission has stipulated that in conducting such SIAs during trade

---

[56] Peter Cane, *Administrative Law* (Oxford University Press 2011) 113: '[C]onsultation at an early stage may at least increase levels of compliance later on and reduce the chance that those dissatisfied with any made will seek actively to challenge them.'

[57] Benvenisti, 'Foreword: Upholding Democracy Amid the Challenges of New Technology: What Role for the Law of Global Governance?' (n 49) 24–51.

[58] Georgina Dimopoulos, Andrew D Mitchell, and Tania Voon, 'The Tobacco Industry's Strategic Use of Freedom of Information Laws: A Comparative Analysis' (2016) Oxford University Comparative Law Forum 2; Karen E C Levy, and David M John, 'When Open Data Is a Trojan Horse: The Weaponization of Transparency in Science and Governance' (2016) 3 Big Data & Society 1; Andrew D Mitchell and Tania Voon, 'Someone to Watch Over Me: Use of FOI Requests by the Tobacco Industry' (2014) 22 Australian Journal of Administrative Law 18.

[59] The Evaluation Partnership Limited (TEP), *Evaluation of the Commission's Impact Assessment System—Final Report 17* (Contract Number SG-02/2006, 2007) <ec.europa.eu/governance/impact/key_docs/docs/tep_eias_final_report.pdf> accessed 22 July 2018.

[60] European Commission, 'Trade, Growth and World Affairs: Trade Policy as a Core Component of the EU's 2020 Strategy' COM (2010) 612 <trade.ec.europa.eu/doclib/docs/2010/november/tradoc_146955.pdf> accessed 22 July 2018, 14; also: Lorand Bartels, 'Policy Coherence for Development Under Article 208 of the Treaty on the Functioning of the European Union—Towards a Complaints Mechanism' (2016) University of Cambridge Faculty of Law Research Paper No 18 <ssrn.com/abstract=2754079> accessed 22 July 2018.

negotiations they 'will pay particular attention to wide consultation and involvement of civil society'.[61] By contrast, Lorand Bartels cites problems with the process 'going to the heart of the impact assessment process as it is currently constituted',[62] and recommends 'the involvement of developing countries and civil society, as well as any developing country groups specially affected by the policy at issue'.[63]

The EU guidelines may be too timid a beginning to provide a space for collective deliberations concerning the appropriate global justice aspects of a new global legal order. It is certainly a modest proposal that mitigates some of the failings of the current system but without unravelling it, as a possibly non-controversial lowest global common denominator as regards global justice: the idea that there should be justice in the manner whereby public decisions affect the rights and interests of others.

2. Judicial (and other) review

The availability of national and international courts and other reviewing bodies offers alternative venues for collective decision-making. These bodies also generate information, often appreciated by the public as more reliable than that produced by the executive.[64] The resulting global checks and balances can potentially reduce some of the difficulties of asymmetric information and voice and thereby promote redistributive policies (both domestically and globally).

If we identify the lack of political pressure to maintain the achievements of the welfare state and promote global justice with internal and external democratic failures, perhaps the key to resisting pressures and building countervailing processes lies with 'de-fragmenting' and 'counter-capital' institutions.[65] The natural and traditional candidates for such bodies are domestic courts and (at least some) international courts. To the extent that these courts are independent from captured state executives, they could curb the excessive power of capital and enhance the procedures that offer space for majoritarian voices (indeed, calling courts 'counter-majoritarian' is deeply misleading in a political system controlled by narrow interest groups); a rebalancing of political power is possible. Because judicial bodies need to be coherent to claim legitimacy and are capable of recreating a systemic vision of the domestic and international legal orders (and strengthening the links between the domestic and the international), these bodies have the potential of limiting the possibilities of exiting the law, and of bundling up issues for institutions to decide. Since they require information from various sources to form an independent policy, they tend to lower the requirements with regard to access for

---

[61] Quoting European Commission (n 60) 14; Bartels (n 60) 8.
[62] Bartels (n 60) 10.
[63] ibid 15.
[64] Presenting the informational benefits courts provide to legislatures: Matthew C Stephenson, '"When the Devil Turns . . .": The Political Foundations of Independent Judicial Review' (2003) 32 Journal Legal Studies 59, 62.
[65] Benvenisti and Downs (n 2) 149–65.

petitioners and third parties. Those who are not represented during the negotiations and drafting of the law often have their day in court.

In this context, it is noteworthy that in recent years, and perhaps in response to the globalization of markets and policy-making, national courts have begun to coordinate their jurisprudence along several aspects of public life, from security through gatekeeping and environmental and health-related policies, to controlling international organizations.[66] Being relatively immune to capture by global capital and having the capacity to coordinate their jurisprudence with otherwise competing jurisdictions, courts can 'reclaim democracy' at the domestic level and press for the creation of representative venues within global bodies.[67] The new judicial assertiveness has provided legislators more opportunities to weigh in on global issues and thereby respond to the grassroots demand for voice.

Regional courts have also contributed to this effort, especially by acting on behalf of several states to fend off 'divide and rule' strategies that affected the state's ability to withstand external pressure. The European Court of Human Rights (ECtHR), like other international tribunals, can help resolve the collective action problems of states that are unable to overcome the 'sovereignty trap', and rebuff a powerful state or a multinational company that seeks to force the weaker state to comply with its demands.[68] The Court of Justice of the European Union (CJEU) has been quite successful in this context, imposing European legal standards on sporting associations that sought insulation from public law obligations.[69] Most conspicuously, it led the way in resisting the UN Security Council's counter-terrorism measures.[70] The ECtHR insisted that international organizations cannot hide behind their immunities under international law to evade the employers' duties under national labour laws.[71] Such acts indirectly provide positive spillover effects, as these standards benefit other societies. But courts can also be effective in a more direct manner. For example, most recently, the CJEU insisted that the Council must not ignore the rights of foreign communities when signing treaties with foreign governments.[72]

Moreover, courts can also resolve collective action problems by moving the law forward so that it reflects collective interests.[73] Several decisions of international tribunals have created linkages between trade and the environment, investments and human

---

[66] Discussing how judges and courts also can provide individualized opportunities for multijurisdictional resolution eg: Zachary D Clopton, 'The Global Class Action and its Alternatives' (2018) 19 Theoretical Inquiries in Law 125.

[67] Benvenisti and Downs (n 2) 24–30, 44–49; Eyal Benvenisti, 'Reclaiming Democracy: The Strategic Uses of Foreign and International Law by National Courts' (2008) 102 American Journal of International Law 241.

[68] Benvenisti and Downs (n 2) 149–65.

[69] Case C-519/04 *David Meca-Medina and Igor Majcen v Commission of the European Communities* [2006] ECR I-6991; Case C-415/93 *Union Royale Belge des Sociétés de Football Association ASBL v Jean-Marc Bosman* [1995] ECR I-4921; in these cases, the CJEU was able to resolve the collective action problem created when private sports associations imposed their standards on individual states.

[70] UNSC Res 1267 (15 October 1999) UN Doc S/RES/1267.

[71] *Waite and Kennedy v Germany* App no 26083/94 (ECtHR, 24 February 1999).

[72] Case T-512/12 *Front Polisario v Council of the European Union* [2015] ECR 953, para 228: the Council must 'ensure that the production of products export is not conducted at the expense of the population of the territory in question or imply violations of fundamental rights'.

[73] Benvenisti, 'Sovereigns as Trustees of Humanity' (n 13) 314–18.

rights, showing how treaties can be thickened and the space for politics widened within institutions where initially silenced parties can have voice. These courts can promote policies that take into account the interests and wishes also of those not represented at the negotiation table or the treaty-signing ceremony. Indeed, in their judgments international tribunals have promoted human rights and the sustainable allocation of maritime resources, and redefined global resources as shared, thereby prodding state parties to take each other's interests into account.[74]

As domestic public opinion and legislators become increasingly aware of the growing importance of global capital and the attendant growing pressures on domestic political space, they tend to provide much needed support for increasingly assertive domestic courts. This has been the case not only in developed democracies in Europe, but also in several developing countries. The famous judgment of the Indian Supreme Court in *Novartis v The State of India* (2013),[75] which interpreted India's trade-related obligations narrowly, was both a culmination of case law that ventured to intervene in matters affecting the state's international commitments,[76] as well as a model for other national courts to emulate.

That national courts are a force to be reckoned with can be inferred from the reaction to the budding efforts by powerful states that are seeking to insulate investments from the jurisdiction of national courts. The current effort—in the so-called 'Mega Regional agreements' such as the Trans-Pacific Partnership—is to extend investors-state dispute settlement (ISDS) processes beyond investment to also cover trade-related disputes. It may well be that this recent assertiveness of national courts is the 'problem' that the ISDS hopes to resolve. What seems to policy-makers and their constituencies to be assertiveness—promoting democratic deliberations—is viewed by foreign stakeholders as barriers to trade. No doubt, the *Novartis v India* judgment must have added to the determination of Northern pharmaceutical companies to offer the ISDS as a system that would nullify the *Novartis* precedent and curb its potential ramifications around the developing world.[77]

Indeed, much as international law is responsible for global injustice, so are national and international courts that in the past took part in creating the current system, not only by developing and applying international law but also by developing choice of law norms, including the rules relating to tax liability, that have facilitated the evasive

---

[74] eg: *Gabčíkovo-Nagymaros Project (Hungary v Slovakia)* (Judgment) [1997] ICJ Rep 7; also: Benvenisti, *Sharing Transboundary Resources* (n 8) 209.

[75] *Novartis AG v Union of India* (2013) 13(1) SCR 148 (India); also: *Bayer Corporation and Anr v Union of India and Ors* (2009) LPA 443 (Del.).

[76] In 2003, the Supreme Court of Sri Lanka found that a bill that would have precluded compulsory licensing and parallel importing (regarded as important tools to ensure affordable access to pharmaceutical drugs) required a special majority in parliament because it infringed the principle of equality enshrined in the constitution. SC Special Determination No 14/2003. Courts in Bangladesh, India, and Pakistan prevented the importation of contaminated food and blocked advertising campaigns of foreign tobacco companies: *M Farooque v Bangladesh* (1996) 48 DLR 438 (Ban); *Vincent v Union of India* (1987) AIR 990 (India); *Islam v Bangladesh* (2000) 52 DLR 413 (Ban) (referring to the similar decisions of the Indian court in *Ramakrishna v. State of Kerala* (1968) AIR 1367 (Ker), and *Chest Foundation v Pakistan* (1997) CLC 1379 (Pak)).

[77] Amy Kapczynski, 'Engineered in India—Patent Law 2.0' (2013) 369 New England Journal of Medicine 497.

possibilities available to MNCs and the immunity of capital from national regulation.[78] As part of the problem, they can also become part of the solution.

3. Access to 'private' big data

These 'accountability technologies', however, assume that public bodies have information, which they can and must share. This assumption has been challenged by the rise of new information and communication technologies that allow a handful of companies to amass more data than most state governments will ever have or have the ability to make sense of. These companies govern, in the sense that their algorithms affect our choices, and through their ability to observe and assess our behaviour, they can manipulate our preferences by prioritizing the information that we will be exposed to and by the sophisticated use of behavioural psychology. Both algorithms and data, they claim, are their private property,[79] immune to public interference.

The role of law, including international law, in this context is clear. The right of access of individual stakeholders to an aggregate and anonymized version of data held by public and private global bodies must in principle be free, and free from manipulation and pollution: access to big data holds the potential of reducing the current acute informational problems. Processing the huge amounts of data could provide information about both private and public actions, their motivations and consequences. This knowledge can then empower the various actors to take political action.[80] The data could enlighten us about ourselves, and instruct us on matters like how to improve our health, avoid car accidents, or design more accessible and efficient markets. The data could also suggest areas for attention and perhaps regulation where it is lacking. Big data generated by the public cannot be treated as entirely owned by those who store it. Rather, they are obliged to share the data, even if at cost.

Often, when refusing to share their data, corporations rely on the users' consent to their retention and disclosure policy. Indeed, users who register for the services of big data corporations are usually required to consent to the corporation's policy of collection, use, disclosure, retention, and protection of personal information. But how much weight should be accorded to such consent? Because many of these corporations hold considerable market power, potential users do not have any real alternatives to obtain such services elsewhere, and therefore their consent cannot be viewed as freely given, nor can it justify withholding the data. This consent merely reflects the skewed market relations between the individual user and the mighty service provider. More importantly, corporations with a large market share become the market themselves: much more than a player, the corporation is rather the market maker, architect, and regulator.

---

[78] British courts are responsible for the rule, which spread around the Commonwealth, that foreign control exempts companies from local tax liability: Palan (n 40) 159–63.

[79] eg: Jason Schultz, 'The Internet of Things We Don't Own?' (2016) 59 Communications of the ACM 36.

[80] For a fuller argument: Benvenisti, 'Foreword: Upholding Democracy Amid the Challenges of New Technology: What Role for the Law of Global Governance?' (n 49).

Google, for example, is not merely a player in the search engine market, but rather the manufacturer of people's daily access to knowledge. With this huge influence comes also the responsibility to investigate the implications for the users of the services they provide, and to enlighten the public about them.

Obviously, sharing the information as well as investigating it in-house would entail costs to big corporations. They would have to screen researchers' applications, provide them with resources and training, and risk negative media coverage. Although these costs are not negligible, these are the responsibilities that come with the benefits of being a market maker, and they should be weighed against the potential public good unleashed with the release of the information.

Reducing asymmetric information is a public good. It calls for global efforts to allow access to privately obtained data. It also calls for the prevention of the 'pollution' of information flows by deceit and overload, not unlike the collective efforts needed to protect the environment. The close relationship between asymmetric information and global (and domestic) injustice may be another factor to spur legal responses.

Several governments have recognized the benefits of access to national data, and the rationale applies with equal force in the global context. In an Executive Order issued by President Obama in 2013, he acknowledged that 'making information resources easy to find, accessible, and usable can fuel entrepreneurship, innovation, and scientific discovery that improves Americans' lives and contributes significantly to job creation'. He therefore ordered that 'the default state of new and modernized Government information resources shall be open and machine readable'.[81] The Organisation for Economic Co-operation and Development (OECD) in 2015 and the EU in 2017 have also recognized the collective benefits arising from shared access to data. The EU has embarked on an effort to create a 'Digital Single Market' that is designed 'to fully unleash the data economy benefits'.[82]

This utilitarian perspective is reminiscent of Grotius's justification for opening the high seas to all:

If any person should prevent any other person from taking fire from his fire or light from his torch, I should accuse him of violating the law of human society, because that is the essence of its very nature ... why then, when it can be done without any prejudice to his own interests, will not one person share with another things which are useful to the recipient, and no loss to the giver?[83]

Principles such as good neighbourliness[84] or trusteeship for humanity[85] strengthen this argument. Even the business model of social media providers such as Facebook

[81]   Executive Order No 13642, 78 Federal Register 93, 28111 (9 May 2013) <www.gpo.gov/fdsys/pkg/FR-2013-05-14/pdf/2013-11533.pdf> accessed 22 July 2018.
[82]   European Commission, 'Building a European Data Economy' (9 September 2017) <ec.europa.eu/digital-single-market/en/policies/building-european-data-economy>.
[83]   Hugo Grotius, *The Freedom of the Seas* (first published 1633, Ralph van Deman Magoffin tr, James Brown Scott ed, Oxford University Press 1916) 38.
[84]   Laurence Boisson de Chazournes and Danio Campanelli, 'Neighbour States' in *Max Planck Encyclopedia of International Law* (2006) 1072.
[85]   Benvenisti, 'Sovereigns as Trustees of Humanity (n 13).

and Google, which is based on selling users' data to advertisers, does not limit it being shared for other purposes, such as public uses including the monitoring of government action or academic research.[86]

4. Development aid on the data, information, knowledge axis

To facilitate the voice of the disregarded, it may also be necessary to commit resources to enhancing the capacity of certain disadvantaged groups in society to explore the vast data and make sense of it. This requires the allocation of educational services and other tools. One such example is the Codex Alimentarius Trust Fund (CODEX), designed to help developing countries in transition to increase their participation in the work of CODEX (which establishes food safety and quality standards and fair practices in food trade).[87] Another example is the African Legal Support Facility (ALSF), hosted by the African Development Bank, which has been supporting African governments in the negotiation of complex commercial transactions since 2010. The ALSF is an organization dedicated solely to providing legal advice and technical assistance to African countries.[88] Michal Gal has shown that regional competition law agreements could offer an effective tool for developing countries seeking to improve antitrust enforcement.[89] Here, again, the redistribution of hooks is much more respectful of developing communities than the distribution of fish. Technology transfer such as that envisioned under Article 66(2) of the Agreement on Trade-Related Aspects of Intellectual Property Rights (TRIPS) might prove themselves as potentially empowering and democratizing.[90]

---

[86] Yafit Lev-Aretz, 'Data Philanthropy' manuscript, December 2017 on file with author (providing example of a collaboration of a mobile network organizer and a non-profit organization during the Nepal earthquake crisis in 2015 and states that 'data generated via platforms like telecom operators, satellite companies, and social media networks makes possible a range of insights into economic developments, medical advances, environmental issues, and various other properties of public life that could accelerate the pace and scope of social discovery and development'). For an overview of the various private sector players that have initiated 'data for good' projects: ibid 8–10. Lev-Aretz also suggests a modification of fair information practices that will allow the use of private data for the greater good.

[87] European Commission, 'More Than Codex: FAO, WHO and Wider Partnerships' <ec.europa.eu/digital-single-market/en/policies/building-european-data-economy> accessed 22 July 2018: ('Launched in 2003 by the Directors-General of UN Food and Agriculture Organization and World Health Organization (WHO), the Trust Fund is seeking US$40 million over a twelve-year period to help developing countries and countries in transition to increase their participation in the vital work of the Commission. Increased participation will be achieved by helping regulators and food experts from all areas of the world to participate in international standards-setting work in the framework of Codex; and enhancing their capacity to help establish effective food safety and quality standards and fair practices in the food trade, both in the framework of the Codex Alimentarius and in their own countries. In 2004, its first year of operation, the Trust Fund helped experts from more than ninety developing countries to attend and participate in the Codex standards-setting process. The Trust Fund is based at the headquarters of the WHO'); also: David E Winickof and Douglas M Bushey, 'Science and Power in Global Food Regulation: The Rise of the Codex Alimentarius' (2010) 35 Science, Technology, & Human Values 356.

[88] African Development Bank Group, 'African Legal Support Facility' <www.afdb.org/en/topics-and-sectors/initiatives-partnerships/african-legal-support-facility> accessed 22 July 2018.

[89] Michal S Gal, 'Regional Competition Law Agreements: An Important Step for Antitrust Enforcement' (2010) 60 University of Toronto Law Journal 239, 241–48.

[90] Agreement on Trade-Related Aspects of Intellectual Property Rights (15 December 1993), Marrakesh Agreement Establishing the World Trade Organization, Annex 1C (1869 UNTS 299) reproduced in (1994) 33 International Legal Materials 1197, Art 66 (2):

V. Conclusion

While international law cannot replace the necessary political debate about what global justice means and how it should be implemented, its goal can and should be to contribute to creating inclusive frameworks and venues within which the political debate about the just allocation and reallocation of resources could take place in a meaningful way. The political debate will be meaningful only if communities have access to data, information, and knowledge, and the wherewithal to engage in deliberations on decisions affecting them. Unequal political power may be at least somewhat compensated by judicial and other review bodies. Unfortunately, the new information and communication technologies that make it possible to bridge informational gaps are the same technologies that are being used by various state and non-state actors to limit state authority and diminish the space for democratic deliberation and accountability. As we know from history, however, these recent challenges may well prove momentary and eventually prompt the rise of international law designed to secure the necessary space for inclusive deliberations.

> Developed country Members shall provide incentives to enterprises and institutions in their territories for the purpose of promoting and encouraging technology transfer to least-developed country Members in order to enable them to create a sound and viable technological base.

But see: Suerie Moon, 'Meaningful Technology Transfer to the LDCs: A Proposal for a Monitoring Mechanism for TRIPS Article 66.2' (2011) 12 International Centre for Trade and Sustainable Development <www.ictsd.org/downloads/2011/05/technology-transfer-to-the-ldcs.pdf>:

> This updated analysis of developed country reports has found little evidence that TRIPS Article 66 2 has resulted in significant additional incentives beyond business-as usual for transferring technology to LDC Members. It also concludes that the existing reporting system does not function as an effective monitoring mechanism.

Global Justice, Global Governance, and International Law

Comment on Eyal Benvenisti

Maurice Kamto

Professor Eyal Benvenisti's chapter on 'International Law's Contribution to Global Justice' is undoubtedly a thoughtful piece on international law, which aims at 'seeking ways and means to reducing inter- and intra-state conflicts and promoting human welfare, given existing political, social and economic constraints'. The chapter goes beyond the classical positivist approach of international law based on commentary of treaties' provisions and case law, and assesses 'what principles of international law are conducive to global justice' in an unbalanced international community dominated by a few actors, whether states or 'private power'. It is an accurate picture of the contemporary development of international law that appears to have a negative impact on global justice, but also a potential positive contribution to such justice.

It seems that the perspective of the chapter is more regarding international law than regarding moral philosophy, which would have been the classical approach to global justice by most philosophers and sociologists. In this regard, one could ask whether Kant believes in an evolutionary process towards perpetual peace where global justice considerations could be considered as being achieved—obviously, not. One could have expected the realization of Kant's prophecy after the crumbling of former Soviet Union and the amazing prospects of liberalism with freedom, democracy, rule of law, and well-being for all. That has not happened, meaning that Kant had somehow ignored the very nature of human beings, which determines, in the end, the behaviour of nations. I think that global justice at international level can only be the result of a permanent bargain and a compromise between the multiple and conflicting interests among states.

The approach of the topic depends largely on the definition of global justice.

Justice is assumed to be a fundamental value of every organized or civilized society. At the same time, each society defines for itself its concept of justice, which reflects the state of development, culture, and civilization of that society. The idea of justice is not unknown in international law. But, how does it come into being? If, like in any politically organized society, it is contained in the basic law of the land, is it severable from international politics?

Different views of what justice is have been given in the course of history, in different cultural contexts and disciplines, including in legal theory. Carlo Focarelli, for instance, in his book titled *International Law as Social Construct: The Struggle for Global Justice* after a lengthy consideration of the concept of justice, defines it as 'the protection of the most vulnerable whoever they may be at any time'.[1] This is obviously a very narrow definition of justice, whether at the national level or at the international level.

In my opinion and that of Eyal Benvenisti, the term 'justice' is used in a broad sense, encompassing social, economic, and political justice. Since the rule of law is employed in the pursuit of justice, legal justice is the bedrock of social, economic, and political justice. As a result, various forms of justice must derive their legitimacy from, and rely on, legal justice, which is an instituted and commonly accepted way of achieving justice. In turn, legal justice must reflect the principles of natural or moral justice to save itself from the harshness of positivism. Given the diversity of legal systems, however, there might be other understandings of justice, particularly at the international or transnational level, despite the fact that we are living in a globalized society.

If justice is about values, can we deal with it without a prior answer to the question of whether commonly accepted values exist in the international order? From the legal perspective, the idea of justice presupposes the existence of such common values, as has been said for, it contains 'some legal dos and don'ts with scope for the evolution of new legal oughts'.[2] It requests the presence of fairness, reasonableness, and equity which together work to reflect a sense of justice. The absence of arbitrariness, bias, and prejudice paves the way to the goal of justice, which 'is an ultimate outcome and a recurring feeling of satisfaction for a person who wants his or her legal rights protected, legitimate expectations met, and development aspirations alive'.[3]

Since the understanding of the concept of justice is considerably influenced by culture and civilization as well as domestic law experience and expectations, it is likely that one perceives global justice from one's cultural or national perspective. As a result, cultural relativism and national perspectives accompany the concept of global justice. All the more so because justice is about values, and although it has become a routine to talk of common or shared values of the international community, such values are not that many, or are yet to be established. However, there is at least one thing in common, namely, the role of law. Even this commonality becomes insignificant as soon as a justice-seeker loses hope in the law's effectiveness. In other words, the concept of global justice is based on the assumption that there is an international community with common values and with common interest in the realization of such values.

With regards to the concept of 'global justice', the key questions raised in the chapter are: Can or should international law contribute to global distributive justice? Can and

---

[1] Carlo Focarelli, *International Law as Social Construct: The Struggle for Global Justice* (Oxford University Press 2012) 60.

[2] Yogesh Tyagi 'The Access of Individual to International Justice: Constraints and Corrections' (Report of the English Speaking Section) in Maurice Kamto and Yogesh Tyagi (eds), *The Access of Individual to International Justice* (Centre of Research in International of the Hague Academy of International Law 2015, Brill forthcoming).

[3] ibid.

should international law assist in creating the conditions that would enable the trans-formation of the debate about global distributive justice from the philosophical to the political dimension?

Benvenisti's humanist perspective in answering these questions appears right at the beginning of the chapter. Contrary to most lawyers who regard 'questions about the nature and scope of obligations that individuals, states, and international organizations in the affluent "North" have toward the less privileged individuals in the "South", and in general whether nations should regard the human flourishing of strangers as a matter of concern [for] political deliberation'[4] and not as a matter for international law, Benvenisti wishes 'to highlight the role of institutions and decision-making procedures in promoting—indirectly—global (and domestic) distributive justice'.[5] His essay fo-cuses 'on institutions and processes at the global level' and 'is grounded on the assump-tion that questions of the just allocation and reallocation of resources are ultimately resolved through processes of public deliberation or open contestation (including the involvement of courts). Therefore, the question is whether law can be instrumental in ensuring the conditions for open deliberation and contestation. While focusing on the limited opportunities of politically weaker constituencies to engage effectively in such interactions, I will suggest that the task of the law is to provide them with meaningful voice to more effectively stake their claims for global justice in the various decision-making fora.'[6]

In my view, international law cannot be opposed or even severed from the political debate in this context. It is part of that debate. For instance, the controversy raging in Africa on whether African states should exit from the International Criminal Court is a political debate on an international law issue, which requires international consider-ation for a possible political decision on that issue.

On substance, the chapter exposes the ambivalence of international law vis-à-vis global justice: From the 'negative contribution of international law to global justice'—in so far as 'it contains/nourishes the contributing factors to the diminishing human agency in the public space which converge to pre-empt deliber-ation on global (and domestic) justice issues that could have turned the philosoph-ical debate to a political one',[7] to the 'potential positive contribution of international law to global justice' through discipline of accountability, judicial (and other) review, access to 'private' big data, development aid with respect to the data, information, knowledge axis.[8]

The chapter touches upon so many areas that it would be difficult to make observa-tions on each of them in these brief remarks. Henceforth, I will limit myself to some observations on some key points of substance:

---

  [4] Eyal Benvenisti, 'Ensuring Access to Information: International Law's Contribution to Global Justice' in this book, I.
  [5] ibid.
  [6] ibid.
  [7] ibid III.
  [8] ibid IV.

The essay touches upon the issue of governance, particularly the concept of accountability, which, in my opinion, is one of the main pillars of governance. One would have expected the author to elaborate more specifically on the concept of global governance, which is directly related to global justice, whatever the meaning one might give to this concept. In this regard, consideration could be given, notably, to the following issues:

- international sanctions regimes which appear to be a means of pressure or domination in the hands of the most powerful nations against the others, and which, in some cases, lead to global injustice in so far as it is easy to put a person or a state on the list of sanctions but rather difficult to drop him or her from that list. The mechanism for the settlement of disputes deriving from such situation is yet to be established at international level;
- the management of international sports activities, where both the law and the institutions, on the one hand, and the dispute settlement mechanisms, on the other hand, are 'private', as they have not been set up by states, although the latter are abided to some extent by the laws and decisions of these institutions;
- the cyberspace, especially the internet world, which is still under the domination of some private actors and one or very few governments. The internet law and justice are yet to be established. This is clearly a field of global governance with such unbalanced rules, skills, and technology gaps amongst nations that global justice is looked at as an unaffordable goal. Or, the global governance of our world, which wants to believe that there are some common values shared by all nations and peoples with a common destiny, cannot be abandoned to some individuals and a handful of nations, if not a single one. Global justice commands that a global space, like the cyberspace, be managed in the common interest with the involvement of all the nations;
- lack of international justice for the victims of serious crimes by United Nations officials and global non-governmental organizations on mission and impunity of the perpetrators, *inter alia*, because of lack of convenient fora and immunity.

It seems to me that better governance at the global level involving the sharing of the policy-making and decision-making, accountability, the rule of law, and sanctions, can help improve global justice. Likewise, the development of a global law, conceived as a new legal order in which domestic law is more connected to international law can strengthen global justice, in as much as it would leave no legal vacuum, which usually benefits the powerful governments or nations. In this regard, it is worth reflecting on the relationships of global governance and global justice, and of global law and global justice.

Another expectation was to see how global justice could also be achieved through the access of individuals to international justice, or the international access of individuals to justice.

The global moral perspective of the chapter is rightly concerned by the fate of 'the weak and disregarded'. In the same vein, Eyal Benvenisti's claim 'is that international law can play a role in the political empowerment of weak constituencies (within and between states). In doing so, international law can indirectly shape the distribution and re-distribution of resources, which would be more dignified and preferable to handing them charitable contributions.' There is a good share of moral idealism in such opinion. Indeed, the author 'briefly argues that it is the current global political-legal structure that inhibits the political process by which global justice consider-ations could be argued, weighed, adopted, and implemented'.[9] He 'will then suggest that international law could be part of the solution for those seeking to promote any version of global justice, emphasizing the link between access to data, information, and knowledge as key to participation and voice, necessary for effective political voice'.[10]

One can only agree with the criticism of the author, namely when he focuses on the dependency of the beneficiaries on aid and on other forms of humanitarian assist-ance aimed at introducing some justice in the world, and on the fact that the power of decision-making in this domain remains in the hands of the aid providers. All the same, this world redistribution of assets 'ignores the right to individual and collective self-determination of the beneficiaries'. It is more so because 'the assets-redistribution approach is unnecessary for achieving a more just allocation of resources and opportunities'.[11]

The progressive development of international *normativity* has paved the way for the enrichment of the concept of justice in the international order with the setting up of several new normative standards. For instance, in the field of the environment, the principles of climate justice, common but differentiated responsibilities among states, and intergenerational equity have emerged to take into account not only the inequal-ities of development, but also the need for anticipatory action by present generations vis-à-vis future generations, which also ensure the continuity of human civilization.

Eyal Benvenisti's chapter sometimes revives old debates, and sometimes opens new avenues on topics like power among nations and global justice; complexity of the international order, notably conflicting norms deriving from that complexity and global justice; imbalance of wealth among nations and global justice; information era and global justice. In this regard, it looks like a starting point for a more theoretical reflection on contemporary international law. Two of the most important questions are: Is global justice possible in a complex international community with divergent na-tional interests, imbalance of powers, small number of shared values, and the senti-ment of domination or exclusion by poor nations? Can global justice be conceived and achieved through a single paradigm, encompassing, *inter alia*, international criminal

---

[9] ibid I.
[10] ibid.
[11] ibid II.

justice, international economic justice, international human rights justice, and inter-state justice?

If international law could contribute to the advent of global justice in the main fields of community interests and global governance, including power-sharing in decision-making and allocation of global wealth, in a move from 'Responsibility to protect' to 'Responsibility to develop', it would, no doubt, open a new era for its rise amongst nations and peoples.

Index